WJEC Eduqas
Film Studies
for A Level & AS

Revised Edition

Laura Barbey
Ellen Cheshire
Maxine Crampton
Mark Ramey
Jenny Stewart
Lisa Wardle-Sharp

Consultant Editor: Lisa Wardle-Sharp

Although every effort has been made to ensure that website addresses are correct at time of going to press, Hodder Education cannot be held responsible for the content of any website mentioned in this book. It is sometimes possible to find a relocated web page by typing in the address of the home page for a website in the URL window of your browser.

Hachette UK's policy is to use papers that are natural, renewable and recyclable products and made from wood grown in well-managed forests and other controlled sources. The logging and manufacturing processes are expected to conform to the environmental regulations of the country of origin.

To order, please visit www.hoddereducation.com or contact Customer Service at education@hachette.co.uk / +44 (0)1235 827827.

ISBN: 978 1 3983 7663 2

© Laura Barbey, Ellen Cheshire, Maxine Crampton, Mark Ramey, Jenny Stewart and Lisa Wardle-Sharp 2024

First published in 2018

This edition published in 2024 by
Hodder Education,
An Hachette UK Company
Carmelite House
50 Victoria Embankment
London EC4Y 0DZ

www.hoddereducation.co.uk

The authorised representative in the EEA is Hachette Ireland, 8 Castlecourt Centre, Castleknock Road, Castleknock, Dublin 15, D15 YF6A, Ireland

Impression number   10 9 8 7 6 5 4 3 2 1

Year   2028 2027 2026 2025 2024

All rights reserved. Apart from any use permitted under UK copyright law, no part of this publication may be reproduced or transmitted in any form or by any means, electronic or mechanical, including photocopying and recording, or held within any information storage and retrieval system, without permission in writing from the publisher or under licence from the Copyright Licensing Agency Limited. Further details of such licences (for reprographic reproduction) may be obtained from the Copyright Licensing Agency Limited, www.cla.co.uk

Cover photo © Chan2545 – stock.adobe.com

Illustrations by Integra Software Services

Typeset in India by Integra Software Services

Printed in the UK

A catalogue record for this title is available from the British Library.

Contents

Introduction   2

PART 1 CORE STUDY AREAS   5

Section 1 The key elements of film form   5
   Film form   5

Section 2 Meaning and response   43
   Representation   43
   Aesthetics   57

Section 3 The contexts of film   66
   Social, cultural and political contexts   66
   Production context   72

PART 2 SPECIALIST STUDY AREAS OR 'CASE STUDIES'   80

Section 1 Varieties of film and filmmaking   80
   Hollywood (1930–1990)   80
     1 *Casablanca* & *Bonnie and Clyde*,
Imitation of Life & *Night of the Living Dead*   81
   Contemporary American mainstream film   106
     2 *La La Land* & *Joker*   107
   Contemporary American independent film   124
     3 *Beasts of the Southern Wild* & *Get Out* 125
   British film since 1995   144
     4 *Trainspotting* & *Mogul Mowgli*   145

Section 2 Global filmmaking perspectives   168
   Group A European film   168
     5 *Mustang* & *Portrait of a Lady on Fire*   169

   Group B Film produced outside Europe   188
     6 *Taxi Tehran* & *Parasite*   189
   Documentary film   216
     7 *Stories We Tell* & *For Sama*   217
   Film movements – silent cinema (1)   242
     8 *Sunrise*   243
   Film movements – silent cinema (2)   258
     9 Buster Keaton   259
   Experimental film (1960–2000) (1)   267
     10 *Daisies* & *Saute ma ville*   268
   Experimental film (1960–2000) (2)   280
     11 *Mulholland Drive*   281

PART 3 PRODUCTION   297

Production skills   297
   Glossary of key definitions   317
   References   320
   Index   328
   Acknowledgements   332

Introduction

This book is designed to guide you through the WJEC Eduqas 2017 Film Studies AS and A level courses. These qualifications were designed to encourage you to explore the power and beauty of cinema by examining films from a range of eras and countries, from the mainstream to the experimental, the silent era to the contemporary. This textbook is structured to support the specification and incorporates guidance on the areas of study that can be applied to any of the set films plus in-depth case studies of at least one film for each module.

How to use this book

Part 1 offers a very detailed exploration of the core study areas:

★ film form
★ meaning
★ response and context.

It can be used as an in-depth glossary to help you understand some of the terminology associated with Film Studies and it also includes some case studies from the specification to show you how this new knowledge can be applied. In the examination, knowledge of these core areas could be tested for any film, so a clear understanding of them is crucial.

Part 2 of the book contains the detailed case studies. These case studies take you through the analysis of a film, applying the core areas and the relevant specialist areas outlined by the specification. If the chapter is not on a film you are studying it will still offer relevant theoretical information and context, which can be applied to your chosen film. This part of the book also offers guidance on the production module.

Part 3, the and final part, is a brief overview of study skills and revision techniques to help you get the most out of the qualification and achieve your potential.

The book includes **Independent activities** (IAs) and opportunities for **Stretch & challenge** (S&C). To make the most of this publication you should strive to do as many of these as possible.

Further information

These are the assessment objectives for this specification. Learners must:

AO1 demonstrate knowledge and understanding of elements of film.

To achieve well in AO1 you need to show that you have a secure understanding of the core areas and specialist areas for each module. This includes using subject-specific terminology accurately such as shot types and editing techniques plus demonstrating a clear grasp of the theoretical approaches to film covered on the course such as the auteur approach or spectatorship theory.

AO2 apply knowledge and understanding of elements of film to:

- analyse and compare films, including through the use of critical approaches
- evaluate the significance of critical approaches*
- analyse and evaluate own work in relation to other professionally produced work.

To achieve good marks in AO2 you need to show that you can apply your understanding of the core and specialist modules when analysing films. To do well you should use a range of examples from the films studied to back-up your points and for the Hollywood 1930–1990 module explicitly explore similarities and differences between the films. You should also be able to apply relevant theories or approaches to the analysis of films and reflect on how they improve your understanding. It is important to also be able to reflect on your own creative work and compare it with other films.

AO3 Apply knowledge and understanding of elements of film to the production of a film or screenplay.

High marks here are awarded when your creative work clearly shows that you have a secure understanding of how films are constructed. Your screenplay and storyboard, or film, should use elements of film form in a coherent way and adhere to the required conventions.

---

* These assessment objectives apply for both the AS and A level courses with the exception of the requirement to evaluate the significance of critical approaches, which only applies to the A level qualification.

Introduction

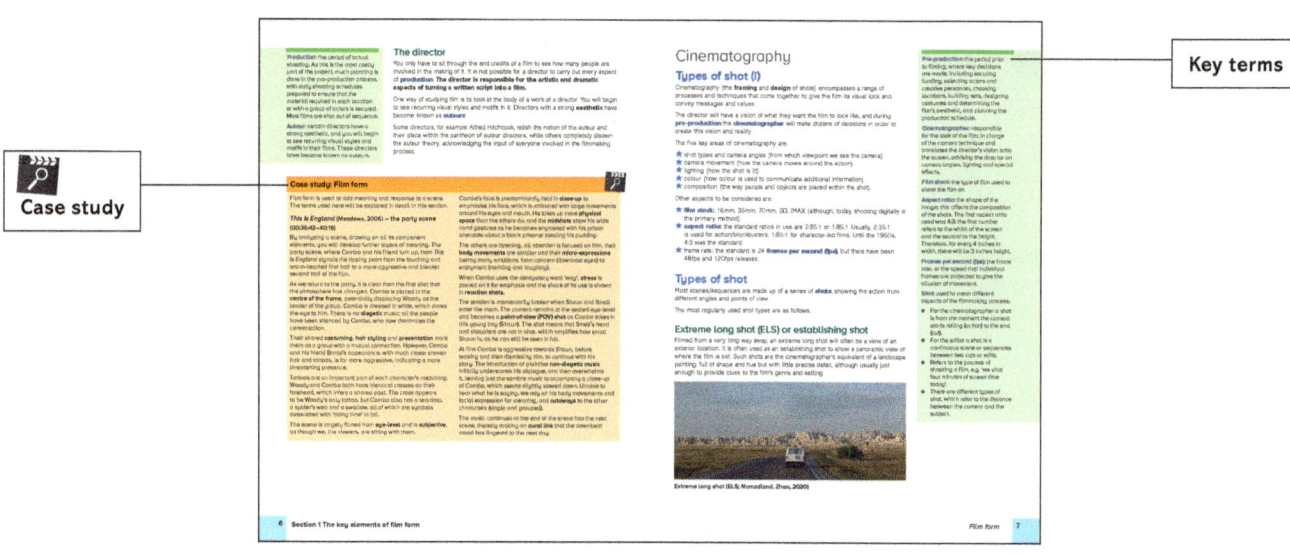

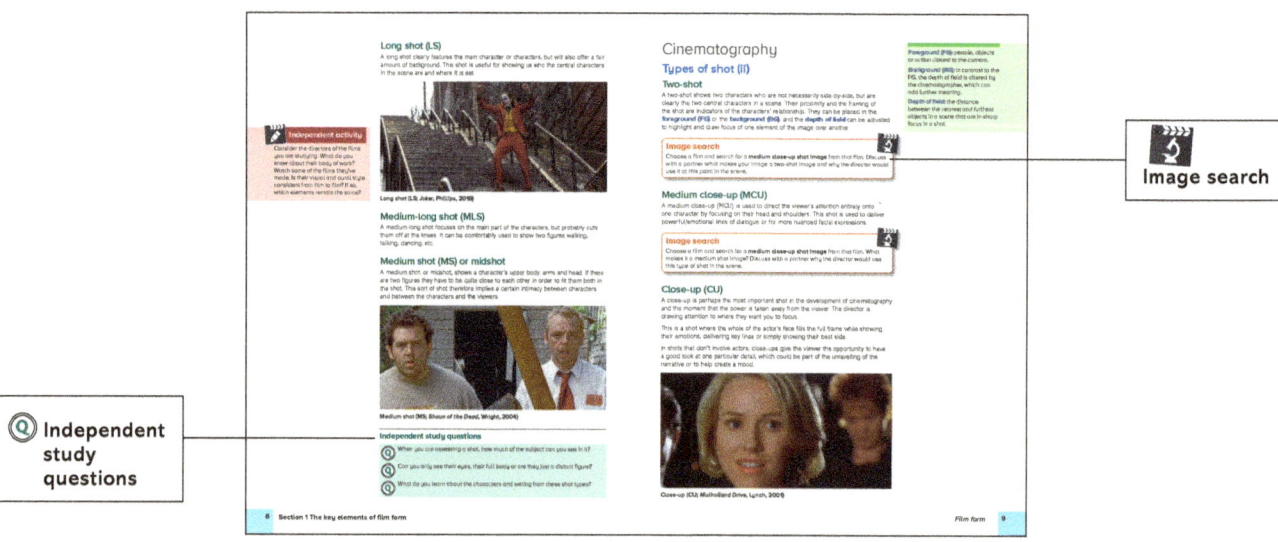

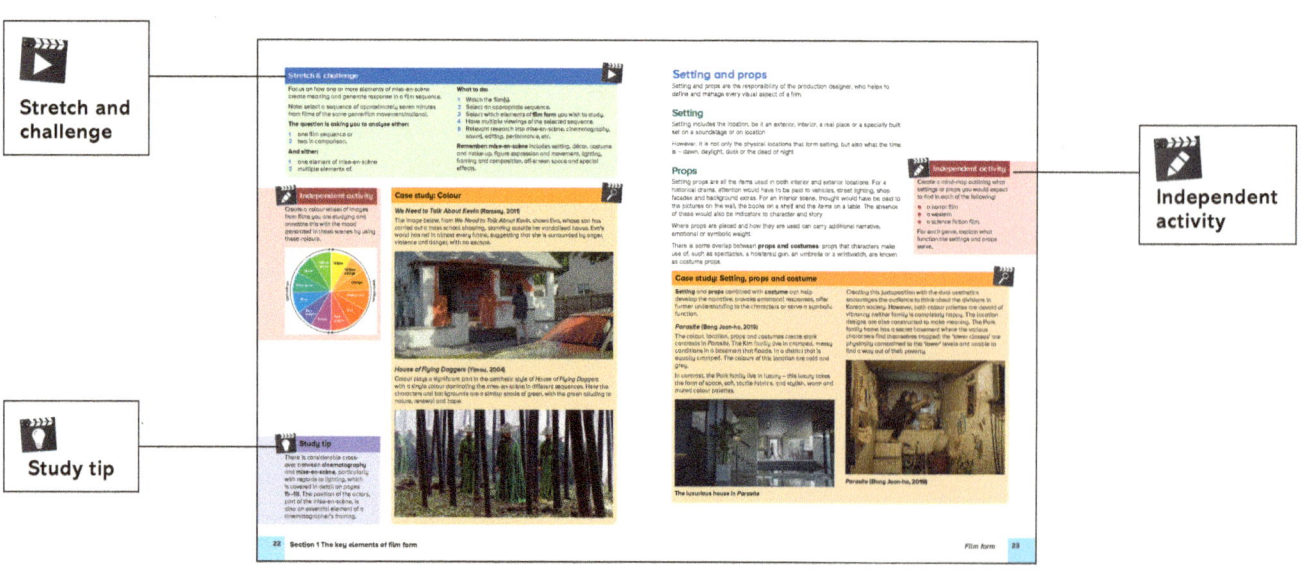

PART 1 CORE STUDY AREAS

Section 1 The key elements of film form

Film form

Film form is everything that filmmakers take into consideration when making a film. It is how the content is expressed, rather than the story itself.

By **studying**, or **reading**, a film, you will see what techniques filmmakers use to:

★ further narrative and character
★ stimulate an emotional response
★ reveal further layers of meaning
★ place the film within a particular genre or style.

Once you have gained an understanding of the fundamentals of film form you will develop your own way of studying a film. Your method may differ from other people's way of studying. You will find that a group studying the same scene will each see and interpret it differently. This is OK.

Why study film form?

A starting point for studying film is to consider all the **essential decisions** the director and key creative personnel use when planning the visual and aural elements of a film.

These elements, known as film form, are:

★ cinematography
★ mise-en-scène
★ editing
★ sound
★ performance.

By examining these in close detail, you will gain further insights into the characters, narrative structure, themes and messages that you may have missed the first time you watched the film.

These elements serve to create a mood and add to the overall **aesthetic** of the film.

Form and meaning

Meaning, in this context, is an interpretation of the narrative based on what we see and hear (**form**). This meaning may be explicit (what the film is about, i.e. the plot) or implicit (what is lying beneath the surface).

As active film viewers, we look for the 'hidden' meanings, and studying **film form** helps us to achieve a deeper understanding of them.

> **Aesthetic:** the style adopted by an artist (in a film's case the filmmaker) or a film movement. For example, despite the different settings of *Trainspotting* (Boyle, 1996) and *Slumdog Millionaire* (Boyle, 2009), both films share a visual look and feel, created by the director's high-energy visual style, by way of his choice of camerawork, editing and music. German Expressionism was an artistic movement that encompassed theatre, dance, architecture, painting, sculpture and film. The aesthetic shared between expressionist films included exaggeration in performance, setting, lighting and disorientating camera angles.

Film form 5

Production: the period of actual shooting. As this is the most costly part of the project, much planning is done in the pre-production process, with daily shooting schedules prepared to ensure that the material required in each location or with a group of actors is secured. Most films are shot out of sequence.

Auteur: certain directors have a strong aesthetic, and you will begin to see recurring visual styles and motifs in their films. These directors have become known as auteurs.

The director

You only have to sit through the end credits of a film to see how many people are involved in the making of it. It is not possible for a director to carry out every aspect of production. **The director is responsible for the artistic and dramatic aspects of turning a written script into a film.**

One way of studying film is to look at the body of a work of a director. You will begin to see recurring visual styles and motifs in it. Directors with a strong **aesthetic** have become known as **auteurs**.

Some directors, for example Alfred Hitchcock, relish the notion of the auteur and their place within the pantheon of auteur directors, while others completely disown the auteur theory, acknowledging the input of everyone involved in the filmmaking process.

Case study: Film form

Film form is used to add meaning and response to a scene. The terms used here will be explored in detail in this section.

This Is England (Meadows, 2006) – the party scene (00:36:42–40:16)

By analysing a scene, drawing on all its component elements, you will develop further layers of meaning. The party scene, where Combo and his friend turn up, from *This Is England* signals the tipping point from the touching and warm-hearted first half to a more aggressive and bleaker second half of the film.

As we return to the party, it is clear from the first shot that the atmosphere has changed. Combo is placed in the **centre of the frame**, potentially displacing Woody as the leader of the group. Combo is dressed in white, which draws the eye to him. There is no **diegetic** music; all the people have been silenced by Combo, who now dominates the conversation.

Their shared **costuming**, **hair styling** and **presentation** mark them as a group with a mutual connection. However, Combo and his friend Banjo's appearance, with much closer shaven hair and tattoos, is far more aggressive, indicating a more threatening presence.

Tattoos are an important part of each character's costuming. Woody and Combo both have identical crosses on their forehead, which infers a shared past. The cross appears to be Woody's only tattoo, but Combo also has a teardrop, a spider's web and a swallow, all of which are symbols associated with 'doing time' in jail.

The scene is largely filmed from **eye-level** and is **subjective**, as though we, the viewers, are sitting with them.

Combo's face is predominantly held in **close-up** to emphasise his face, which is animated with large movements around his eyes and mouth. He takes up more **physical space** than the others do, and the **midshots** show his wide hand gestures as he becomes engrossed with his prison anecdote about a black prisoner stealing his pudding.

The others are listening, all attention is focused on him, their **body movements** are smaller and their **micro-expressions** betray many emotions, from concern (downcast eyes) to enjoyment (nodding and laughing).

When Combo uses the derogatory word 'wog', **stress** is placed on it for emphasis and the shock of its use is shown in **reaction shots**.

The tension is momentarily broken when Shaun and Smell enter the room. The camera remains at the seated eye-level and becomes a **point-of-view (POV) shot** as Combo takes in this young boy (Shaun). The shot means that Smell's head and shoulders are not in shot, which amplifies how small Shaun is, as he can still be seen in full.

At first Combo is aggressive towards Shaun, before teasing and then dismissing him, to continue with his story. The introduction of plaintive **non-diegetic music** initially underscores his dialogue, and then overwhelms it, leaving just the sombre music to accompany a close-up of Combo, which seems slightly slowed down. Unable to hear what he is saying, we rely on his body movements and facial expression for meaning, and **cutaways** to the other characters (single and grouped).

The music continues at the end of the scene into the next scene, thereby making an **aural link** that the downbeat mood has lingered to the next day.

Section 1 The key elements of film form

Cinematography

Types of shot (i)

Cinematography (the **framing** and **design** of shots) encompasses a range of processes and techniques that come together to give the film its visual look and convey messages and values.

The director will have a vision of what they want the film to look like, and during **pre-production** the **cinematographer** will make dozens of decisions in order to create this vision and reality.

The five key areas of cinematography are:

★ shot types and camera angles (from which viewpoint we see the camera)
★ camera movement (how the camera moves around the action)
★ lighting (how the shot is lit)
★ colour (how colour is used to communicate additional information)
★ composition (the way people and objects are placed within the shot).

Other aspects to be considered are:

★ **film stock:** 16mm, 35mm, 70mm, 3D, IMAX (although, today, shooting digitally is the primary method)
★ **aspect ratio:** the standard ratios in use are 2:35:1 or 1:85:1. Usually, 2:35:1 is used for action/blockbusters, 1:85:1 for character-led films. Until the 1950s, 4:3 was the standard
★ frame rate: the standard is 24 **frames per second (fps)**, but there have been 48fps and 120fps releases.

Types of shot

Most scenes/sequences are made up of a series of **shots**, showing the action from different angles and points of view.

The most regularly used shot types are as follows.

Extreme long shot (ELS) or establishing shot

Filmed from a very long way away, an extreme long shot will often be a view of an exterior location. It is often used as an establishing shot to show a panoramic view of where the film is set. Such shots are the cinematographer's equivalent of a landscape painting: full of shape and hue but with little precise detail, although usually just enough to provide clues to the film's genre and setting.

Extreme long shot (ELS; *Nomadland*, **Zhao, 2020)**

Pre-production: the period prior to filming, where key decisions are made, including securing funding, selecting actors and creative personnel, choosing locations, building sets, designing costumes and determining the film's aesthetic, and planning the production schedule.

Cinematographer: responsible for the look of the film; in charge of the camera technique and translates the director's vision onto the screen, advising the director on camera angles, lighting and special effects.

Film stock: the type of film used to shoot the film on.

Aspect ratio: the shape of the image; this affects the composition of the shots. The first aspect ratio used was 4:3: the first number refers to the width of the screen and the second to the height. Therefore, for every 4 inches in width, there will be 3 inches height.

Frames per second (fps): the frame rate, or the speed that individual frames are projected to give the allusion of movement.

Shot: used to mean different aspects of the filmmaking process.

- For the cinematographer a shot is from the moment the camera starts rolling (action) to the end (cut).
- For the editor a shot is a continuous scene or sequences between two cuts or edits.
- Refers to the process of shooting a film, e.g. 'we shot four minutes of screen time today'.
- There are different types of shot, which refer to the distance between the camera and the subject.

Long shot (LS)

A long shot clearly features the main character or characters, but will also offer a fair amount of background. This shot is useful for showing us who the central characters in the scene are and where it is set.

Long shot (LS; *Joker*, Phillips, 2019)

>
> **Independent activity**
>
> Consider the directors of the films you are studying. What do you know about their body of work? Watch some of the films they've made. Is their visual and aural style consistent from film to film? If so, which elements remain the same?

Medium-long shot (MLS)

A medium-long shot focuses on the main part of the characters, but probably cuts them off at the knees. It can be comfortably used to show two figures walking, talking, dancing, etc.

Medium shot (MS) or midshot

A medium shot, or midshot, shows a character's upper body, arms and head. If there are two figures they have to be quite close to each other in order to fit them both in the shot. This sort of shot therefore implies a certain intimacy between characters and between the characters and the viewers.

Medium shot (MS; *Shaun of the Dead*, Wright, 2004)

Independent study questions

- When you are assessing a shot, how much of the subject can you see in it?
- Can you only see their eyes, their full body or are they just a distant figure?
- What do you learn about the characters and setting from these shot types?

Section 1 The key elements of film form

Cinematography

Types of shot (ii)

Two-shot

A two-shot shows two characters who are not necessarily side-by-side, but are clearly the two central characters in a scene. Their proximity and the framing of the shot are indicators of the characters' relationship. They can be placed in the **foreground (FG)** or the **background (BG)**, and the **depth of field** can be adjusted to highlight and draw focus of one element of the image over another.

Foreground (FG): people, objects or action closest to the camera.

Background (BG): in contrast to the FG, the depth of field is altered by the cinematographer, which can add further meaning.

Depth of field: the distance between the nearest and furthest objects in a scene that are in sharp focus in a shot.

> **Image search**
> Choose a film and search for a **medium close-up shot image** from that film. Discuss with a partner what makes your image a two-shot image and why the director would use it at this point in the scene.

Medium close-up (MCU)

A medium close-up (MCU) is used to direct the viewer's attention entirely onto one character by focusing on their head and shoulders. This shot is used to deliver powerful/emotional lines of dialogue or for more nuanced facial expressions.

> **Image search**
> Choose a film and search for a **medium close-up shot image** from that film. What makes it a medium shot image? Discuss with a partner why the director would use this type of shot in the scene.

Close-up (CU)

A close-up is perhaps the most important shot in the development of cinematography and the moment that the power is taken away from the viewer. The director is drawing attention to where they want you to focus.

This is a shot where the whole of the actor's face fills the full frame while showing their emotions, delivering key lines or simply showing their best side.

In shots that don't involve actors, close-ups give the viewer the opportunity to have a good look at one particular detail, which could be part of the unravelling of the narrative or to help create a mood.

Close-up (CU; *Mulholland Drive***, Lynch, 2001)**

> **Further information**
>
> A **deep focus** shot has a great depth of field from front to back, with the foreground, middle ground and background ALL remaining in sharp focus. The placement of objects or actors in the plane of vision allows for the manipulation of size and scale. If an object in the foreground looms larger than anything else in the frame then this is likely to be of greater importance.

> **Image search**
>
> Search for a **deep focus image** from a film you are studying. Discuss with a partner what makes your image deep focus, and what is in the background that requires a deep focus.

The opposite of deep focus is shallow focus, where the small depth field has one plane in focus (i.e. the foreground) and the background out of focus. The eye is drawn to the object or actor in the foreground that is in sharp focus, rather than the blurred image in the background.

***The Worst Person in the World* (Trier, 2021)**

Extreme close-up (ECU)

Extreme close-ups (ECUs) get you almost too close to an actor, allowing the viewer into the character's intimate space to reveal detail or emotions that would otherwise go unnoticed.

Developments in macro-photography have enabled extreme close-ups of individual flecks of colour in an actor's iris or something reflected in them.

> **Image search**
>
> Choose a film and search for an **extreme close-up shot**. What makes your image an extreme close-up? With a partner, discuss why the director would cut to an extreme close-up at this point in the scene. What effect is created?

Cinematography

Camera angles and perspectives

A camera angle is simply the angle from which the camera 'sees' the subject. There are several angles, all of which provide different effects.

Aerial shot

An aerial is often used as an establishing shot or at the opening of a film. It offers a bird's-eye view, swooping over a landscape. An aerial shot is designed to be impressive and is best used at the beginning of a film before the characters and narrative have been established. If used later on, it could remind the audience they are watching a film and break the 'spell'.

Aerial shot (*Alien*, Scott, 1979)

Overhead shot

This shot is literally taken from up high, looking down. Again, it is most frequently used as an establishing shot to set the scene. Although the shot begins as an overhead, it often moves down and inwards towards the characters – drawing the viewer quite literally into the story.

Overhead shot (*Night of the Living Dead*, Romero, 1968)

Eye-level shot

An eye-level shot is taken using the most natural camera angle. The eye-level chosen is usually that of the dominant character. This helps you identify with them, as though you are seeing the world as the character sees it.

Over-the-shoulder shot

Usually used to shoot a conversation, the camera is positioned behind one of the characters, taking in their shoulder, while filming the other. This is often part of a shot/reverse shot (see Editing, page 28).

Over-the-shoulder shot (*Little Women*, Gerwig, 2019)

Camera angles and perspectives

High-angle shot

A high-angle shot is usually taken from just above head-height. Using this shot is a good way of making someone look small and insignificant, simply because we are looking down on them. However, not all high-angle shots serve this purpose.

High-angle shot (*Do the Right Thing*, Lee, 1989)

Low-angle shot

Simply by setting the camera lower than eye-level and looking up at the subject, a low-angle shot can be employed to make a character (or object) dominate the frame, making them more threatening or heroic.

Low-angle shot (*City of God*, Meirelles, 2002)

Objective

With an objective camera angle you are viewing the scene through the eye of an unseen observer. The viewpoint doesn't belong to any of the characters, therefore it can be seen as impersonal.

Subjective

With a subjective camera angle (also known as a **point-of-view (POV) shot**) the viewer is placed in the action either as an active participant or by trading place with a character. This is typically used when the camera replaces the viewpoint of a character looking at someone from afar. In a horror film it could indicate the killer stalking their victim, or it can be used when one character is admiring another.

Independent activity

Watch a scene from any film and note how the camera angles help shape your view of characters or spaces.

Subjective or POV shot (*Portrait of a Lady on Fire*, Sciamma, 2019)

Section 1 The key elements of film form

Cinematography

Camera movements

If the angle of view in the shot is to change without there being an edit, the camera has to move. This can be done in several ways.

Fixed axis

When a camera is attached to a fixed axis it stays rooted to the spot but can turn to follow the action, as when used in:

- ★ a **pan**: when the camera moves from left to right or vice versa. This technique is used to follow a person as they walk across a room or to swing from one part of the frame to another
- ★ a **whip pan**: uses the same movement as a pan but at speed. However, its increased speed often blurs the image
- ★ a **tilt** is when the camera moves its lens up or down. This type of shot may be used to look slowly upwards at a building – thereby emphasising how tall it is.

Shifting axis

When the whole camera moves it is said to have a shifting axis. This type of shot is used when the camera needs to move in a very precise direction. There are different methods for moving the camera:

- ★ **Dolly shot:** the camera is mounted on a wheeled platform called a 'dolly', which is used to move the camera through a space in a relatively straight line. The dolly's wheels have tyres for smooth movement and it can only be used on very flat surfaces.
- ★ **Tracking shot:** the dolly is mounted on a track, which has been laid out in a specific route through the action, and follows a subject from behind, alongside or in front.

Zoom

A zoom isn't an actual camera movement as such, but it does create the illusion of movement by starting off viewing its subject from a distance then zooming in (using a lens with a variable focus length) to look at a small part of it in much greater detail or vice versa. A **crash zoom** is the same movement but quicker.

Track   Zoom   Pan   Tilt
Camera movements

Crane shot

A crane shot is when the camera is mounted on a crane or boom arm and is lowered, raised or swung sideways – like a vertical tracking shot. By using a crane, you can move the camera around the action from one level to another.

Originally, a camera operator would sit at the top of the crane, along with the camera. Today, cameras can be controlled remotely via drones, lightweight/manoeuvrable boom arms and cranes. A camera can now travel up the outside of a wall and pass

Independent activity

Select two films you are studying. Watch the opening sequences multiple times and make notes on the following elements of film form:

- the use of sound
- the use of music
- the camera angles
- the camera movement
- the pace and style of editing.

Then answer the following questions:

1. Do you think this is the work of a director with a strong aesthetic? If so, why?
2. What genre/film movement do you think this film belongs to? Why do you think this?
3. What else struck you about this opening sequence?
4. Who do you think the intended audience for this film would be?

through a half-open window with very little effort, where once that would have required the building of a special wall that could be pulled apart instantly to let the camera and camera operator pass through.

Hand-held

In the early days of filmmaking when films were made on lightweight 16mm film stock, it was easy to pick up a camera and film hand-held.

With the introduction of 35mm and sound, cameras became more difficult to manoeuvre. It wasn't until the 1950s that professional cameras were made small enough to carry and hand-held camerawork could once again be considered.

Initially, documentary filmmakers used hand-held cameras, as this created a sense of reality – it reminds the viewer of home movies that are also usually hand-held – with shaky photography, shifting focus and off-kilter framing. This style became known as **cinéma vérité**.

A camera operator holding a camera can follow the action wherever it goes, creating an immediate 'this is real-life' feel. With hand-held technology, it is possible to film in the most cramped conditions or from the most oblique angles. If you want an incredibly low-level shot, just lie on the floor with your hand-held camera and film from there.

In the late 1950s, fiction filmmakers borrowed this approach to filmmaking, including a group of young French film critics turned directors, who became known as the **French New Wave**. Their influence has had an impact on films' visual styles, particularly for more intimate 'indie' movies, such as *Moonlight* (Jenkins, 2016).

Further information

French New Wave

In the late 1950s a group of French filmmakers emerged, many of whom were writing for French film journals including *Cahiers du Cinema*. Starved of foreign films during and immediately after the Second World War, when film import restrictions were lifted in the early 1950s they absorbed themselves in films of the Hollywood Golden Age. As a consequence, their films are full of artistic references to other films.

Films considered part of the French New Wave were renowned for being shot hand-held, using natural lighting on the streets. The performance style was natural, often improvised, by a youthful cast. They were concerned with how the film was shot and edited, rather than the story itself, and through their experimentations with editing and shooting they reinvented narrative techniques.

The key period of this film movement was 1958–1968, and directors associated with French New Wave are François Truffaut, Jean-Luc Godard, Louis Malle and Agnès Varda. This movement has inspired and influenced many American film directors, including Quentin Tarantino, who named his production company A Band Apart after Godard's film *Bande à part* (1964).

Steadicam

The year 1975 saw the introduction of the Steadicam camera (invented by Garrett Brown). A Steadicam is a type of camera mount that uses weights and counter-balances to keep a camera level, even while hand-held. The Steadicam operator can keep the camera steady for a tracking shot, or can gently move the camera up and down, to create a floating effect, which generates a sense of unease.

Cinematography

Lighting (i)

When watching a film, you are usually attracted to the most brightly illuminated area of the screen. Filmmakers play on this when lighting a shot.

There are two key elements you need to consider when studying how a scene is lit and what further information you can draw from the lighting, as discussed below.

Element 1: Source

Is the cinematographer using natural **available light** or are they filling the frame with deliberately placed **artificial light**?

If they are using artificial light they will usually be employing a **three-point lighting** combination:

★ Point 1: **Key light** – the brightest primary light source; the one that acts like the sun in the sky. The key light throws the dominant shadows, if there are to be any. The intensity of this light leads the film's lighting design.

★ Point 2: **Fill light** – this will be approximately 50–75% of the key light. It is often provided by a reflector bouncing back a softened beam of key light or from a lower angle than the key light. Sometimes the shadows cast by the key light can be too dark and obscure detail – such as expressions on a human face – so the fill light softens the edges of shadows and puts back some of the detail. Using more or less key light can be an aesthetic choice known as **chiaroscuro lighting**, which could be low-key or high-contrast lighting.

★ Point 3: **Back light** – shines from behind (and usually the side) and gives foreground objects an outline, which helps them to stand out from the background.

Most shots are lit using a combination of the above three types of lighting.

An example of chiaroscuro lighting (*Spione*, Lang, 1928)

> **Chiaroscuro lighting:** this term is borrowed from painting, and refers to the bold use of dark and light. It was a favourite for filmmakers whose work falls into film movements or styles that were filming in black and white, particularly German Expressionism (pages 243–253), horror and film noir. It is a kind of painting with light and shadow that makes dramatic moments impactful. It tends to lose its dramatic impact in colour.

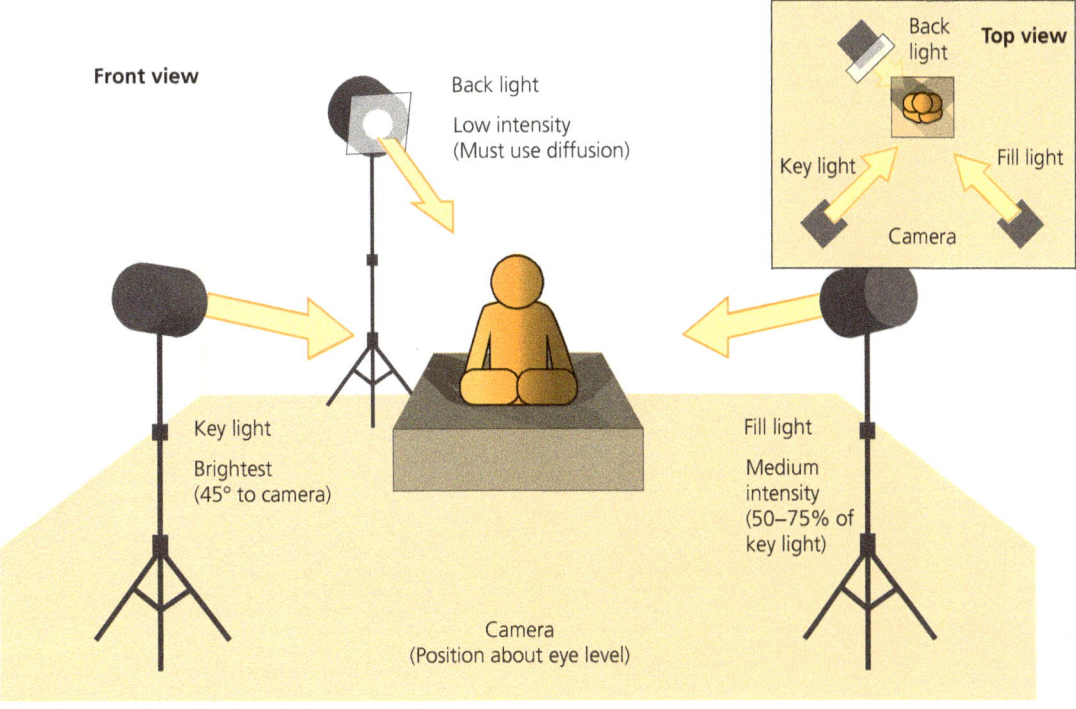

Basic three-point lighting set-up

Lighting (i) 15

> **Further information**
>
> **Film noir**
>
> Film noirs look and feel just like their literal meaning, 'dark films', both in their narrative content and visual style. A film noir world is one of darkness, disillusionment, betrayal, pessimism and moral corruption. The plots often involve murder and the brutality of life.
>
> The use of high contrasting black and whites and obtuse camera angles were prolific and give the films a distorted view of the world. A world of dark streets, lit intermittently by neon signs and car headlights, and the frequent lighting of cigarettes. Made during the decade following the Second World War, these films share strong visual motifs, narrative strands, characters and mood, and mirror concerns in the post-war America over a man's place in society and women's emancipation.

The extremes of both dark and light lighting support or develop:

★ narrative themes of good versus evil
★ characters' situations, e.g. a sense of peril (if well lit) and wrong-doing (if in the shade)
★ a physical allusion to characters' psychological state of mind
★ themes of duplicity, claustrophobia and fatalism.

Independent study questions

 When watching a scene from any film, make notes of what is illuminated and what is in the shadow. How have the filmmakers used lighting to develop the character or mood?

Element 2: Direction

The direction the light travels from source to the object it is illuminating creates different moods. Several different types are used to create distinct effects.

★ **Front lighting:** tends to eliminate shadows and creates a 'flatter' image. This is the kind of lighting that is easiest to work with quickly, so is often found in low-budget or hand-held filmmaking.

Front lighting (*Another Round*, Vinterberg, 2020)

★ **Side lighting:** uses one strong light source on one side, which creates shadows on the opposite side. This creates mystery and intrigue: what is being hidden in the shadow?

Side lighting (*Vertigo*, Hitchcock, 1958)

16 Section 1 The key elements of film form

- ★ **Back lighting:** when the light is behind the object or person being photographed, therefore creating a silhouette. Depending on the strength of light used, this can also create a 'halo' of light around the edge of the silhouetted shape.
- ★ **Under lighting:** when the light (or a reflector) is positioned under the object. This can throw a large shadow behind it and may have a distorting effect on the object or person.

Back lighting (*Belfast*, Branagh, 2021)

Under lighting (*Alien*, Scott, 1979)

- ★ **Top lighting:** rarely used on its own as it just throws a light over a whole scene, with other lights filling in the details. When used in isolation, such as on a human face, the shadows fill the eye-sockets and look very menacing.

Top lighting (*Spione*, Lang, 1928)

Cinematography

Lighting (ii)

Cinematographers also have to consider:

- ★ **Intensity** of the lighting. Is the lighting bright or dim? Consider the difference in lighting in a moody horror such as *Night of the Living Dead* (Romero, 1968) or a sci-fi such as *Alien* (Scott, 1979), with a bright musical such as *La La Land* (Chazelle, 2016).
- ★ **Quality** of the lighting. Is it hard or soft? Does it create harsh shadows or subtle shading? Hard lighting is created from multiple small light sources, whereas soft is created by larger ones.

Element 3: Colour

The cinematographer's use of colour is an important part of the film's aesthetic and is discussed further in the mise-en-scène section on page 21.

Throwing a vivid red light, or a chilly blue, onto a scene can affect the way the viewer responds to what they see. Subtler effects are created by throwing differently coloured lights onto coloured walls or coloured costumes to indicate different times of year. Primary, muted or highly saturated colours are most effective when used to dominate a scene.

This can be done either during production or in **post-production** by **grading**.

> **Post-production:** the work that is required to complete the film, after shooting, including the edit, sound mix, music composition, colour grading and computer-generated imagery (CGI) special effects.
>
> **Grading:** colour film always needed to be graded to make sure that colours remain consistent. Like lighting, grading affects the mood and feel of a film. Documentaries are often 'ungraded' and appear flat and lifeless. By grading, filmmakers draw emphasis to colour themes, such as red in *Shaun of the Dead*, or visually emphasise the mood of a scene by taking out the red, to leave a scene looking blue and chilly. With digital technology it is possible to manipulate the colour palette of a scene or even a whole film.

Case study: Colour in *City of God* (Meirelles, 2002)

Meirelles (director) and Charlone (cinematographer) use two different colour palettes in *City of God* (2002).

The first half of the film, told in flashback, is golden in hue, which indicates the heat of Brazil, as well as the nostalgia of the 'Golden Age' of life in the favelas, when the children had hope, ambition and innocence. The colour reflects their optimism and enthusiasm for life.

The film's second half is narratively darker; the bright lighting has gone and is replaced with darker browns, and greys. These reflect the change in fortune for the young people who are now embedded in the criminal underworld, with little opportunity for escape.

Image search
Darker tones in City of God

Watch the opening scene of *City of God* and note how the colour tones change before and after the flashback. What does this change in colour palette connote about the world and how it has changed?

Black and white

Filming in black and white was the default format in early cinema, although from the outset filmmakers were keen to have colour in the film. Hand-colouring frame by frame or tinting entire sequences a colour to match its mood were early experiments in colour. It wasn't until the 1930s that filming in colour became viable. Colour and black and white were both in use until the early 1970s, when colour dominated.

When shooting in black and white, it is not the hue of the colour that makes an impact but the brightness (how dark or light it is). For instance, to get a deep black a very dark orange colour is most effective, rather than black itself.

Independent activity

Contemporary black and white films hark back to the glamour of the Golden Age of Hollywood or the rebellious French New Wave. But what does releasing a film in black and white mean today? Is it nostalgia? A marker of a film's artiness? An aesthetic consideration? Have a look at some contemporary black and white films then research and read about the directors' intentions.

Casablanca (Curtiz, 1942)

Section 1 The key elements of film form

Cinematography

Composition

Composition is the arrangement of all the visual elements of mise-en-scène in the frame. The choice of camera angle and lighting, combined with the placement of people and objects within the setting, creates the composition of a shot.

As viewing a film is an emotional experience, the way scenes are composed will stimulate an audience's response.

The rule of thirds

The **rule of thirds** is a central premise of composition. If you divide the frame into thirds (using four lines), your main character or object should fall at the intersection of two of these lines. This will draw your eye to the main object, but leave space for further information to be communicated.

The rule of thirds (*Vertigo*, Hitchcock, 1958)

Balance and symmetry

Formal or **symmetrical balanced** composition is used to depict a quiet, restful, static scene. In a two-shot, which uses formal balance, audience interest will naturally shift from one character to the other as each speaks. Having the images displayed evenly within the frame conveys a sense of calm and order.

Formal or symmetrical balance (*Saint Maud*, Glass, 2019)

Informal or **asymmetrical unbalanced** composition is used to challenge or attract attention. You can make a character appear more dominant by positioning them higher or lower in a frame, as well as through lighting and camera angle. Unbalanced compositions are associated with chaos and tension.

Informal or asymmetrical balance (*Saint Maud*, Glass, 2019)

Lines

Compositional lines are the contours of objects, people, props, buildings, trees, vehicles, furniture and so on, and are expressed in straight, curved, vertical, horizontal or diagonal lines.

Lines serve many purposes in visual composition. Combinations of lines may influence each other and convey different meanings. They can divide the composition, direct the viewer's eye, define shapes and lead the viewer to a particular interpretation.

Here are the key types of lines:

★ **Vertical lines** create a strong impression, suggesting power and stability.
★ **Horizontal lines** can also indicate strength but in a more restful way, leaning towards balance and harmony. They can also lead to finality or a sense of ending.

Horizontal lines (*Nomadland*, Zhao, 2020)

★ **Diagonal lines** suggest a sense of action and movement. Opposing diagonal lines suggest conflict and forcefulness.
★ **Organic lines** are lines found in nature. Depending on the way they are used, they can introduce feelings of chaos, complexity or beauty.

The above four types of line are all actual lines. The fifth doesn't visually exist at all, we merely imagine the line:

★ **Implied lines** are created/implied through directional elements such as a hand gesture or the gaze between two people.

Form

Physical forms (such as people and objects) are easy to spot, but filmmakers can also create the illusion of form in the viewer's eye by grouping people or objects together to create **abstract forms**. This link is often made in a triangular movement, allowing the eye to move from one object to another, to create subliminal links.

A triangle pointing upwards suggests strength, stability and solidarity (imagine a mountain). This allows the eye to go from point to point in an upwards movement with ease, reinforcing positive attributes. An inverted triangle lacks stability and suggests weakness and fragility.

Physical forms, inverted triangle (*Trainspotting*, Boyle, 1996)

Mise-en-scène

The term **mise-en-scène** was first used in the theatre, where it refers to all the elements placed on a stage that contribute to the setting or mood the creative team were working towards. In film, it refers to everything on the screen in front of the camera, from the colours and style of the clothes worn by the actors, to the settings and locations, to the feeling created by the lighting (see Cinematography, pages 15–18) and the positioning of the characters in relation to one another.

Everything you see **on screen** (and the six off-screen spaces – for more on these spaces see page 27) has been considered and deliberately chosen to be there. If you can see it, it is there because the filmmaker wants you to see it. How you interpret this information will take time and practice; you can view a film multiple times and find new information on each viewing.

Your response to a film may well be different from others. Your gender, ethnicity, age, life experiences, the books you have read, and the other films, theatre, paintings, photographs and music you have seen/heard or studied all play a part in your interpretation of a film.

Colour

Colour is integral to the cinematographer's repertoire of resources for creating mood and conveying meaning. Colour is an important part of the mise-en-scène to signal a character's mood or also personality, to enhance the narrative arc, to draw attention to something, support a colour motif or to elicit psychological reactions in the viewer. Here, it would be the responsibility of the production and costume designer.

The psychology of colour

★ Red: anger, violence, danger, love, excitement
★ Pink: femininity, sweetness, innocence, playfulness
★ Orange: warmth, happiness, friendly, exoticness
★ Yellow: sickness, madness, idyllic, insecurity
★ Green: nature, renewal, hope, darkness, envy, ominous

★ Blue: cold, calm, melancholy, cerebral
★ Purple: fantasy, mystical, ethereal, ominous
★ Black: fear, grief, sophistication
★ White: sincerity, purity

Stretch & challenge

Focus on how one or more elements of mise-en-scène create meaning and generate response in a film sequence.

Note: select a sequence of approximately seven minutes from films of the same genre/film movement/national.

The question is asking you to analyse either:

1. one film sequence or
2. two in comparison.

And either:

1. one element of mise-en-scène
2. multiple elements of.

What to do:

1. Watch the film(s).
2. Select an appropriate sequence.
3. Select which elements of **film form** you wish to study.
4. Have multiple viewings of the selected sequence.
5. Relevant research into mise-en-scène, cinematography, sound, editing, performance, etc.

Remember: mise-en-scène includes setting, décor, costume and make-up, figure expression and movement, lighting, framing and composition, off-screen space and special effects.

Independent activity

Create a colour wheel of images from films you are studying and annotate this with the mood generated in these scenes by using these colours.

Case study: Colour

We Need to Talk About Kevin (Ramsay, 2011)

The image below, from *We Need to Talk About Kevin*, shows Eva, whose son has carried out a mass school shooting, standing outside her vandalised house. Eva's world has red in almost every frame, suggesting that she is surrounded by anger, violence and danger, with no escape.

House of Flying Daggers (Yimou, 2004)

Colour plays a significant part in the aesthetic style of *House of Flying Daggers* with a single colour dominating the mise-en-scène in different sequences. Here the characters and backgrounds are a similar shade of green, with the green alluding to nature, renewal and hope.

Study tip

There is considerable cross-over between **cinematography** and **mise-en-scène**, particularly with regards to lighting, which is covered in detail on pages 15–18. The position of the actors, part of the mise-en-scène, is also an essential element of a cinematographer's framing.

Setting and props

Setting and props are the responsibility of the production designer, who helps to define and manage every visual aspect of a film.

Setting

Setting includes the location, be it an exterior, interior, a real place or a specially built set on a soundstage or on location.

However, it is not only the physical locations that form setting, but also what the time is – dawn, daylight, dusk or the dead of night.

Props

Setting props are all the items used in both interior and exterior locations. For a historical drama, attention would have to be paid to vehicles, street lighting, shop facades and background extras. For an interior scene, thought would have be paid to the pictures on the wall, the books on a shelf and the items on a table. The absence of these would also be indicators to character and story.

Where props are placed and how they are used can carry additional narrative, emotional or symbolic weight.

There is some overlap between **props and costumes**: props that characters make use of, such as spectacles, a holstered gun, an umbrella or a wristwatch, are known as costume props.

> **Independent activity**
>
> Create a mind-map outlining what settings or props you would expect to find in each of the following:
>
> - a horror film
> - a western
> - a science fiction film.
>
> For each genre, explain what function the settings and props serve.

Case study: Setting, props and costume

Setting and **props** combined with **costume** can help develop the narrative, provoke emotional responses, offer further understanding to the characters or serve a symbolic function.

Parasite (Bong Joon-ho, 2019)

The colour, location, props and costumes create stark contrasts in *Parasite*. The Kim family live in cramped, messy conditions in a basement that floods, in a district that is equally cramped. The colours of this location are cold and grey.

In contrast, the Park family live in luxury – this luxury takes the form of space, soft, tactile fabrics, and stylish, warm and muted colour palettes.

Creating this juxtaposition with the dual aesthetics encourages the audience to think about the divisions in Korean society. However, both colour palettes are devoid of vibrancy; neither family is completely happy. The location designs are also constructed to make meaning. The Park family home has a secret basement where the various characters find themselves trapped; the 'lower classes' are physically constrained to the 'lower' levels and unable to find a way out of their poverty.

The luxurious house in *Parasite*

***Parasite* (Bong Joon-ho, 2019)**

Costume, make-up and hair

The **costume designer** works closely with the other creative departments, particularly the production designer, to ensure that:

★ they are part of the wider aesthetic vision
★ they develop the character
★ designs support or contrast other characters' costumes
★ costumes are suitable for the actor's performance (physical/restrained)
★ costumes appropriate to the setting (both time and location).

The colour of costumes and how they are worn all form part of the character and the story arc. The lighting design and whether the film is being shot in colour or black and white will influence the choice of colours.

As with setting and props, clothes the characters wear provide shortcuts to the film's genre, and historical and social setting. There are certain items of clothing that are genre signifiers, such as Stetson hats in a western.

The clothes worn are not mere accessories, they are key elements in the construction of character and identity. As much care is taken in the choice of clothes in a contemporary rom-com as those set in a historical or futuristic setting.

For the purposes of mise-en-scène, make-up (including special effects make-up) and hair styling also serve as part of the costume.

There are three main uses of make-up:

★ day to day, aka straight make-up or street make-up – this would be used for naturalistic performances, or to enhance an actor's features. Additionally, this make-up may be needed to hide any blemishes, scarring, tattoos, etc.
★ character or transformation make-up would employ specialist make-up alongside facial prosthetics to change a person's appearance. The materials used may include latex or silicone and could be used to make someone look older/younger, fatter or ill
★ special effects (FX) make-up also uses prosthetics made of latex, foam or silicone, but these may be entire body suits and complete head/facial masks as used to create the look of the mythical creature, Pale Man, in *Pan's Labyrinth* (del Toro, 2006). Special effects make-up may also involve some CGI.

Pan's Labyrinth (del Toro, 2006)

An actor may be required to wear contact lenses or false teeth in any of these three make-up uses. Their own hair may be cut, coloured or styled, or they may be required to wear a toupee, extensions or wigs.

Independent activity

Create a collage of images showing the different uses of make-up in one of your focus films. Note how make-up contributes to the construction of character and how a character's make-up alters as the narrative progresses.

Image search
Special effects make-up

Choose a film and search for an image from that film of an actor who has had special effects make-up applied. Discuss with a partner how the make-up develops the character's persona.

Independent study question

Q Select a scene from a film. What are the different functions for the clothes one of the characters wears?

Section 1 The key elements of film form

Case study: Costume, hair and make-up in *Promising Young Woman*
(Fennell, 2020)

Cassie uses her costume, hair and make-up in different ways. Primarily, her natural self is a collection of hyper feminine pastels and pops of candy sweet pink. Her seductress persona has darker costume choices, and her hair and make-up is more adult and sexual (we even see Cassie watching a tutorial on sexy make-up looks). In the final scene, we see a combination of sugary tones in her wig and almost comical 'sexy nurse' costume.

Case study: Costume, hair and make-up in *Vertigo*
(Hitchcock, 1958)

In *Vertigo*, Hitchcock designs his perfect woman – a 'Hitchcock blonde', Madeleine. Edith Head dressed the character in 'classy' grey, black and white outfits; this was to create the effect of Madeleine being a blank canvas for Scottie to project his desires upon. Madeleine is not actually real; she is played by Judy, whose colours are from a much more vibrant and 'alive' colour palette, most notably green, which connotes 'the uncanny'.

Each character has a signature colour in the film, which can be transferred to others when power dynamics lift.

Judy in green

Costume, make-up and hair

Independent activity

Choose two frames from a film you are studying that feature a two-shot. Consider the way in which the position of the actors in relation to one another adds a further layer of meaning. Write 100 words on each frame.

Staging, movement and use of off-screen space

Staging

How characters and objects are positioned in the frame can:

★ add further meaning to their relationship to one another
★ indicate their importance to the narrative
★ draw attention to a particular character/object.

Case study: Staging *Shaun of the Dead* (Wright, 2004)

Consider the two images below from *Shaun of the Dead*. What can we learn about the characters and their relationship to one another from the staging?

Image 1: In the foreground Liz and Shaun are sitting opposite each other, across the fairly wide table. They are placed in the lower half of the screen. In the background is Ed. He is standing, so we see more of his body, and is literally standing between Liz and Shaun, as though his mere presence is pushing them further apart.

Image 2: Here Shaun and Ed are sitting very close together on a sofa, with their arms overlapping. This proximity to one another mirrors their friendship, which seems far closer than that of Shaun and Liz.

Section 1 The key elements of film form

Movement

Rather than camera movement, in this section it is the movement of the actors that is considered. There is naturally some cross-over with the actors' performances and this is discussed in the Performance section on pages 37–41.

Off-screen

When studying film, we tend to focus on what is happening **on screen**, but it is important to remember that there are six **off-screen** spaces:

★ to the left
★ to the right
★ above
★ below
★ behind the set
★ in front of the camera.

The use of the spaces can be subtle, such as walking into frame from the right, across the frame and out of the left; or looking upwards; or for one character to point to action happening off-screen.

A more overt use is when a character **breaks the fourth wall** (see page 34) by addressing the audience, or looking directly into the camera, making the audience complicit in the action.

Renton breaks the fourth wall in *Trainspotting* (Boyle, 1996)

Staging, movement and use of off-screen space

Editing

Editing is the process of arranging all the images in their correct order so that the narrative makes sense, the dialogue flows and you can see what you need to see, when you need to see it. Unlike the other elements of film form, **editing is unique to film**.

In this section you will gain an understanding of the conventions of continuity editing and how filmmakers experiment with editing to develop further layers of meaning.

Continuity editing

Continuity editing, or invisible editing as it is sometimes known, is the dominant editing technique in mainstream cinema. Continuity editing is designed to make the transitions between shots as seamless as possible so as not to draw attention to the film's construction, instead allowing the audience to become immersed in the narrative. The techniques outlined here are commonplace in mainstream films.

Taken altogether, the editing of shots in a scene gives the impression of an entire continuous narrative.

★ An **establishing shot** is usually the point of entry into a scene. It typically begins with a long-shot or establishing shot that establishes a location for the characters, before focusing on one or more of them and their actions.
★ A **shot/reverse shot** editing pattern is used between two people in conversation. Filmed as over-the-shoulder shots, the editor cuts between the two to create the dynamism of the conversation. The camera could be focusing on either the person speaking, or the reaction of the person listening.
★ An **eye-line match** is used in conversations where the two characters have been shot in close-up. To indicate that they are looking at each other, the eye-line has to match the eye height of the other character. If this doesn't match you will spot it.
★ The **180° rule** is used to ensure that we understand where characters/objects are in relation to each other: the angle between any two sequential shots should not exceed 180°. Not following this is called **crossing the line**.
★ The **30° rule** is a general principle that two consecutive shots should have at least a 30° variance between them. Breaking this rule is known as a **jump-cut**.
★ **Cross-cutting** is the parallel editing of two or more events in an alternating pattern, for example the hero coming to the rescue/victim in trouble. Cutting between two scenes heightens interest/suspense, provides conflict and depicts contrast.
★ **Match on action:** most editors prefer to cut between two shots on action, such as the actor reaching for a drink and drinking it. These are two different actions and may be framed differently but the editing makes it seem as though it is a continuous movement.

The final scene of *This Is England* (Meadows, 2006) uses continuity editing

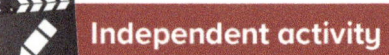

Independent activity

Watch the first five minutes of a crime/thriller made before 1970, and one made after 2000. Note every time you spot an edit. How did the editing affect the pace of the opening?

Shot transitions

Editors need to make creative decisions regarding shot transitions – how you move from one shot to the next. These transitions can manipulate narrative time and space, serve the film's aesthetic style, create mood, develop narrative and character, and generate further meaning.

There are several different ways of achieving these transitions, but most films use the cut, the dissolve and the fade.

Cut

A cut is a straight edit from one image to another with nothing in between. Cuts allow you to travel great distances in time and setting in an instant. Alternatively, they can show you the same action from different angles in a matter of seconds.

Fade
A fade is when the picture emerges out of, or disappears into, black or white. It is most often used at the end of a major scene or act and is the filmic equivalent to the end of a chapter in a book.

Dissolve
A dissolve is when one image overlaps another. As the scene ends you are watching 'image A'; slowly 'image B' emerges from it, until it overwhelms 'image A', which fades away completely. 'Image B' signals the start of a new scene, which could feature different characters or location. This can be particularly effective when creating a feeling of time passing, or to make a connection between two characters or a character and an object or setting.

Other transitions
The following transitions offer a more experimental approach, which can be used to develop further meaning or support a film's aesthetic.

Wipe
A wipe is the most artificial and conspicuous transition. A line travels across the screen from left to right, or vice versa, wiping out the first image and replacing it with a second. *Hulk* (Lee, 2003) uses an array of shot transitions inspired by comic-book panels. There are more subtle uses of a wipe; if something moves across the screen (such as a car) in the same direction as the wipe, at the same speed, then the wipe isn't noticed.

Match-cut
A match-cut is when we cut from one image to something that looks similar or from one action to a similar action. The most cited example of a match-cut is in *2001: A Space Odyssey* (Kubrick, 1968), when the film opens with a prehistoric ape using a bone as a weapon, which he throws into the air, and the shot cuts to a satellite (similar in shape) in space. In one edit we have been transported thousands of years into the future.

Match dissolve
A match dissolve uses the same juxtaposition of images, but dissolves between the two. At the end of the shower scene in *Psycho* (Hitchcock, 1960), we see the victim's blood running into the plughole, dissolving into the black pupil of her dead eye.

Jump-cut
A jump-cut is the result of breaking the 30° rule. This gives a scene an edgy, uneasy feeling, as though we haven't seen everything. Its use startles the viewer, drawing attention to this action. This was a particular technique employed by Jean-Luc Godard, in *Vivre sa vie* (1962), when Nana, hearing a sound outside, gets up and, as the camera pans across the café, there is a series of jump-cuts edited to the sound and rhythm of machine-gun fire outside.

Freeze-frame
This is where a single frame is held on screen for a period of time. It can be used throughout a film as punctuation, for emphasis, or to hold an important image or character's response in the viewer's mind. If the film ends on a freeze-frame this may leave the film open to interpretation. A freeze-frame calls attention to the filmmaking process. Freeze-frames can be seen in the opening sequence of *Trainspotting* (Boyle, 1996).

Time and space

Editing is used in the organisation of time and space, both within individual sequences and throughout the film, in order to create narrative coherence. It can be used in the following ways:

★ **Time** may appear in a **linear form**, where the story starts and progresses forwards until its resolution, which is known as **continuity of narrative**.
★ **Near chronological order** is when the film starts in the present day, and then goes back in time to the beginning of the story and continues forwards in one long flashback until the two points meet, when it can either end or continue on. This is often used to show a character at a moment of peril, joy or anguish, with the flashback used to show how they reached this point.
★ **Discontinuity of narrative** presents the story in a **non-linear manner**, which can be achieved in a number of ways.
 - A film is **reversed** when it starts at the end narrative and works backwards to the beginning. This is complex narrative structure and is rarely used; key examples are *Memento* (Nolan, 2000) and *Irréversible* (Noé, 2002).
 - **Flashbacks** can be used to temporarily disrupt the narrative by inserting a scene from the narrative past in an otherwise linear narrative or as the overarching structure. This structure is usually used to fill in the back-story of the characters.
 - **Flashforwards**, which are also known as prolepsis, move the action from the present to the future. Flashforwards are used less often, and it may not be instantly apparent that we are being shown the future rather than the past. *Arrival* (Villeneuve, 2016) has a good example of the use of a flashforward.
 - **Dreams and fantasies** are inserted in the narrative to offer insights into a character's emotional status or to shed light on the past.

Further information

Cinematic time and space

Films can go anywhere in time and space in a moment. Time may be compressed or expanded: sped up or slowed down; remain in the present or go forwards and backwards. Space may be shortened or stretched; moved nearer or further away; presented in a true or false perspective; or be completely remade into a setting that only exists in film time; space may be eliminated, created or presented in a manner that helps the audience comprehend. It may be real or imagined, enlarged or reduced.

Image search *Time and space*

Search for the key edit in *City of God* where Rocket stands between the gang and the police and the flashback begins (around three minutes from the start of the film). Examine how this pivotal moment is constructed with a combination of editing and other elements of film form.

Near chronological narrative structure

City of God (Meirelles, 2002)

In the opening scene, an edit dissolve between the present and the past is on the two match-cut images of Rocket. Using him as the central point of the flashback indicates that the narrative is being told from his perspective. These two images also reinforce the colour palette of the past and the present. As the film progresses, the colours move from the gold of the past to the blue of the present.

Speed of editing

The length of each **shot**, **scene** and **sequence** sets the tone of what is happening on screen. A shot may last for a few seconds, minutes or the entire film.

A sense of urgency can be manufactured by increasing the frequency of the editing, seeing the action from various shots/angles – perhaps every few frames/seconds in a fight scene, for instance. For a more relaxed mood, scenes can last longer with fewer shot changes, such as in a rom-com. If something is meant to be relaxing, then moving around it slowly, through occasional edits, gives the impression of wandering around in no hurry. Cutting rapidly backwards and forwards between different angles, from close-ups to long shots, all in rapid succession, reminds us of dashing about, with no time to lose, or adds to the chaos of a situation.

Scenes at the beginning of a film, where we are getting to know the characters and the story is unfolding, usually have a slower pace of editing. As the film progresses, this pace may quicken as we cut between storylines and characters.

Shot length

The average number of shots in a classic Hollywood film from the 1940s or 1950s would have been 150 shots. Today, there are about 1,300 individual shots in an average movie. An action movie may have more than twice as many, for instance *Mad Max: Fury Road* (Miller, 2015) has roughly 3,000 shots.

One of the reasons for this change is the move to editing digitally using a **non-linear editing (NLE)** system, making it much easier for shorter shot lengths. Before their widespread use in the 1990s, film editors would literally cut and paste the film negative – not the original shooting negative but a cutting copy.

Historically, each physical frame would have to be examined from the multiple re-takes, angles and shot types. Remember there are 24 frames for each second of screen time. That's a lot of frames.

This is why you will find that, in general, films edited on film would have fewer edits/longer shots. The shot length creates the pace of the film.

> **Scene:** may consist of one shot or a series of shots depicting a continuous event.
>
> **Sequence:** a series of scenes or shots complete in itself. A sequence may occur in a single setting or several settings, i.e. a car chase. Action should match in sequence, where it continues across several consecutive shots with straight cuts – so that it depicts the event in a continuous manner.
>
> **Non-linear editing (NLE):** a digital form of editing and the standard for filmmakers today. Because it is digital, you never lose files, you can edit in any order, you can edit audio and video at the same time, and you can revert to previous versions. This means that you can be more experimental in the editing suite and return to an older version if needed.

Hitchcock edited on film and favoured long take set-ups (*Vertigo*, Hitchcock 1958)

Case study: Speed of editing

Compare these sequences.

We Need to Talk About Kevin (Ramsay, 2011; 01:43:00–01:46:30)

The measured pace of the editing during the emotional conversation between Eva and Kevin is deliberately slow to mirror its importance and the length of time we have waited for this reunion. The scene builds slowly, through a series of **shot/reverse shots** culminating in a fleeting moment of intimacy as the two awkwardly embrace. This embrace is made all the more poignant because of the slow build-up to it. The editing mirrors the stillness of the cinematography, and the sparseness of the setting, costume and make-up that you can see in the image.

City of God **(Meirelles, 2002; 00:00:14–00:04:42)**

The first 2'40" comprises fast edited **cross-cutting** between food being prepared, musicians and an escaped chicken being chased by a gang of youths with guns, led by Lil Ze. There are alternating short bursts of images comprising different **shot types** (ECU, CU, MCU and MS), and **angles** (high, low and eye-level from both humans and chickens) that are cut to the vibrant rhythms of Brazilian music. This creates a heady atmosphere of life in the favelas – a place full of energy and extremes. Out of all this confusion, the pace slows and, in the longest shot in this sequence (15"), we follow Rocket and his friend.

The scene then returns to the fast-paced cross-cutting, now between the chase and the boys, which suggests that danger and violence are just around the corner. As the two stories collide, to illustrate Lil Ze's dominance, he is seen in **slow-motion**, literally taking up more screen time. The pace of the editing slows as the youths gather at one end of the road and the police at the other, with Rocket and the chicken caught in the middle. Rocket's narration begins, the camera circles around Rocket, and we **dissolve** to a **match-cut** image of Rocket as a child.

Image search
Quick cuts Shaun of the Dead (Wright, 2004) 00:04:04–00:04:23

Shaun gets up from the sofa and walks towards the door. A series of six quick-cuts (combined with **frantic-zoom** ECU cinematography) shows him getting ready for work. This 4" sequence is followed by a 10" shot of him adjusting his tie and talking to Pete. Then another sequence of six **quick-cuts** of breakfast preparation. These extreme quick-cuts are used for comic effect and form part of Edgar Wright's **aesthetic**.

Experimental editing techniques

Montage editing and the Kuleshov effect

The **Kuleshov effect** is a film editing process, which has evolved into **montage editing**. The technique was named after the Soviet filmmaker Lev Kuleshov, who made short films in the 1910s and 1920s. He proposed that by putting or juxtaposing two images sequentially, the viewer would gain a greater understanding of the filmmaker's intent than by a single shot.

His research about how viewers process images and make meaning gained from the images presented has been widely studied by psychologists. The research had a profound influence on Soviet film directors Sergei Eisenstein and Dziga Vertov, who, at the time, were moving away from conventional narrative editing towards a new national cinema founded on the principles of **montage editing**. They used montage editing to juxtapose images to create further meaning.

Sergei Eisenstein was at the forefront of a group of **Soviet filmmakers** who took Kuleshov's research on film editing and employed it within a narrative feature film. His most widely studied montage sequence is **'The Odessa Steps'** from *Battleship Potemkin* (Eisenstein, 1925). In this, the continual barrage of images cut quickly together brings about emotions of confusion and helplessness. The images presented sequentially are then paired: high angles with low; close-ups with long shots; small with large. Soon it becomes unclear if we are at the top of the steps or the bottom, as we witness the helplessness and disarray of the people contrasted with the power and uniformity of the army.

Section 1 The key elements of film form

Dziga Vertov was a documentary filmmaker who had been making films since 1919. *Man with a Movie Camera* (Vertov, 1929) has approximately **1,775 separate shots** – a new shot every few seconds. The film can be considered as part of a silent film genre known as **city symphonies**, in which a city is documented and celebrated through the poetic use of images and score.

Unlike continuity editing, montage editing draws attention to the editing process by the frequent cutting between images, which can comprise of different shot types and transitions. The technique of montage (although perhaps not the political ideology) has been incorporated into mainstream cinema and is usually used to demonstrate the passing of time.

> **Image search**
> **'The Odessa Steps' sequence**
> Search for 'Battleship Potemkin Odessa Steps Sequence' online. Watch the scene, then discuss with a partner how the editing makes meaning.

Continuous take

The continuous take is the antitheses of editing, but some filmmakers have deliberately not edited a scene, sequence or even an entire film.

The opening sequence of *Touch of Evil* (Welles, 1958) is an elaborate 330" take. *Rope* (Hitchcock, 1948) was conceived as one long continuous take, but as they were working on celluloid there were limits to the shot length, forcing Hitchcock to film ten shots of lengths varying from 4'37" to 10'06", with the edits cleverly disguised.

With the arrival of digital filming, directors were no longer tied to the limits of a film camera magazine.

Rope **(Hitchcock, 1948)**

Sound

For a visual medium, it is surprising how important sound, particularly music, is to a film. In this section you will gain insights into the ways in which aural elements – speech, music and noise – and the absence of it are used in relation to visuals.

Most films have music comprising an original music score from a **composer (non-diegetic)** and/or existing/new songs (both **diegetic** and **non-diegetic**). Music is used to set the tone, further the character/story and enhance the filmmaker's aesthetic. A **music supervisor** is responsible for bringing the two together. Sound and dialogue are recorded on location by a **sound recordist**, with further sound added during post-production by **Foley** and **additional dialogue recording (ADR) artists**. The **sound designer/sound editor** brings these components together.

Experimental editing techniques

Diegetic and non-diegetic sound

There are two types of soundtrack:

★ **Diegetic sound** is the **vocal and ambient sound** that the characters can hear: the sounds that emanate from within the world of the narrative. This can include sounds such as footsteps when a character is walking or music when a car radio is turned on. The sounds will be those from both the on- and off-screen spaces.

★ **Non-diegetic sound** is the sound that does not come from the actual world of the narrative, including accompanying music (when no one on screen is actually seen playing or listening to music) and voice-overs.

Vocal and ambient sounds (diegetic)

The primary focus for the **sound recordist** on set or location would be to capture the actor's **dialogue** and **performance (vocal sound)**, which would be harder to reproduce later. The **ambient sounds** are recorded on location, but they are often added or enhanced in post-production.

A **Foley artist** focuses on the **ambient sounds** of objects (clinking teacups, etc.), the environment (weather, transport, etc.), human noises (footsteps, drumming fingers, etc.) and special sound effects (bones breaking, stabbing, strangling, etc.).

These sounds are usually pitched at a natural level. When a sound is exaggerated, such as a dripping tap, this is known as a **pleonastic sound**. The sound of the knife being sharpened in the opening sequence of *City of God* is pleonastic.

In an **additional dialogue recording (ADR)** session, actors reproduce missing **vocal sounds** such as the background artistes' chatter, or those that later were deemed unsatisfactory such as a blood-curdling scream. Lead actors may have to carry out ADR work if the original recording is not of good enough quality, or changes in the edit require new lines of dialogue or an alternative delivery of a line.

Narration (non-diegetic)

Although a voice-over narration, such as Renton's in *Trainspotting* (Boyle, 1996), is part of the actor's performance, as it cannot be heard by the characters, this would be considered non-diegetic.

The narrator can be a character within the story, which would indicate that the story is being told from their perspective, or it can be delivered by an omnipresent narrator or storyteller in the 'Once upon a time…' tradition. Narrations can be used to draw the viewer into the world or to provide commentary on the action.

Independent activity

Watch a trailer for four films you are studying from different countries and decades.

- How have they used diegetic and non-diegetic sound?
- Are there voice-overs? If so, how do these match the pace of the visual images used?
- What kind of music is being used, if any?
- What kind of language is used to sell the film to the audience?
- What is the relationship between the editing of the trailer and the sound?

Watch them again with the sound muted.

- What are they key images used?
- What impact did any voice-over or music have?

Consider the following:

- Are these indicative of the genre?
- What are your expectations of these films from the trailers?
- Who is the target audience for these films?

Independent activity

Watch Nerdwriter1's short film on YouTube on how sound design enhances a scene: 'See With Your Ears: Spielberg and Sound Design'. Now watch a short scene from one of the films you are studying and make a list of all the different uses of sound and how they reinforce the action.

Stretch & challenge

Now have a go at storyboarding/writing or editing your own trailer for another film you are studying.

Things to consider:

- A summary of the main elements of the story.
- Who is starring in the film.
- A tag-line for the film.
- Use persuasive language that 'sells' the film; remember that a trailer is an advert for a film.
- The soundtrack and any music that you want to include.

Breaking the fourth wall (non-diegetic)

Breaking the fourth wall is when a character stops interacting with the narrative/other characters, turns to the camera and talks directly to the audience. The dialogue is then non-diegetic – not part of the narrative world.

Section 1 The key elements of film form

Music

Music (diegetic and non-diegetic) helps to create further meaning for audiences. It can do this by:

★ serving as the unseen narrative voice, pushing us towards the appropriate emotive response, whether it be fear, longing or pride
★ highlighting the character's psychological or emotional response to a situation
★ creating a sense of continuity from one scene to the next (sound bridges)
★ building tension and giving a sense of relief/finality.

Music also helps to indicate:

★ the mood or personality of the character/scene
★ period setting
★ location
★ a realistic setting.

There are three types of music:

★ **Background music** (also called a film score, film music, incidental music) is written specifically for a film by one composer and used throughout the film.
★ **Found music** is existing music such as pop songs or classical music/opera.
★ Music and songs **performed** as part of the story.

Background music

A film score can bring all the visual elements together, and can help to add weight, meaning or power to an otherwise flat scene. Try watching a scene with the sound down and you will see how much of an impact music has in creating tension and atmosphere.

Non-diegetic background music is used to:

★ define genres
★ create mood
★ establish setting
★ develop character
★ provide short cuts
★ form part of the aesthetic style
★ further plot
★ enhance action
★ offer in-jokes or knowingness.

Composers themselves disagree as to whether their work should be visible or invisible. You may not even notice that music is playing until it is gone. If it is noticeable, then this too is a form a manipulation.

The music can either enhance or reinforce the action on screen, mirroring the pace of the film created by the cinematography and editing, or it can work against such expectations, which is known as **parallel and contrapuntal sound**.

Background music has to work immediately; there is no time to develop the mood. Some composers use recurring themes to reference the character, location or idea. These are called **leitmotifs**. Probably the most recognisable leitmotif is just the two notes (F and F sharp) used to indicate the approach of the shark in *Jaws* (Spielberg, 1975).

> **Leitmotif:** a reoccurring piece of music that represents characters, actions or themes.

Further information

Silence

Strange as it may seem, the **absence of sound and music** is also a significant part of a soundtrack. A filmmaker may use the lack of sound in the same way as they use the freeze-frame to draw attention to something or signal a change in direction or mood.

Without the music cues to guide emotions, you are left in suspense, which creates a greater tension. Silence is therefore a significant part of the horror filmmaker's use of sound, so much so that it has become a genre trope that a quiet passage will be followed by a loud noise. So, think about silence while you are studying the use of sound.

Independent activity

Read Neil Brand's article on film soundtracks, 'The secret art of the film soundtrack', on the *Guardian* website (September 2013).

- Consider the first and fourth paragraphs as you watch two films from different genres and decades that you are studying.
- Make a note of how music (both diegetic and non-diegetic) is used in two key sequences.
- Consider how the music makes you feel, and what further meaning is generated from the use of the music.

Stretch & challenge

Search for Neil Brand on YouTube and on the BBC Radio 4's *The Film Programme* and you will find a number of films/interviews with Brand analysing film scores. Watching and listening to these will give you a greater understanding of the importance of film music. Brand is also a silent film accompanist of international repute. If you are studying silent film do watch and listen to his work on that, too.

Found music

Even though this is called 'found' music, considerable thought will have gone into the choice of song and how it is used within a scene. If a song is going to be used to underscore a particular piece of action (e.g. walking down a road) or to accompany a fight scene, the rights to use this would have to be cleared before filming, as the performance and the editing would be timed to the music.

A song can be used **diegetically**, such as listening to a vinyl record or by turning on a radio. The whole song may be used or just an important lyrical phrase to either support or work against a character's mood or action. Or it can be used **non-diegetically** – such as the 'Eye of the Tiger' montage training scene from *Rocky III* (Stallone, 1982).

Performed music

There are two types of performed music:

★ Musical numbers that are seen within or as **part of the narrative** (a busker or nightclub act), such as the family singing together in *Captain Fantastic* (Ross, 2016). These are **realist** uses of performed music and can be seen across a number of film genres.
★ Musical numbers that are used to express **heightened emotion**, such as 'Another Day of Sun' in *La La Land* (Chazelle, 2016), are **anti-realist** and are usually only used in musicals.

Parallel and contrapuntal sounds

Filmgoers develop automatic responses to the combination of sounds and images. Filmmakers can either work with these expectations or against them; music is a primary tool in doing this.

Parallel sounds are sounds that go hand in hand with the images on screen: upbeat music for a comedy, sinister music for a thriller. They can also be used to mirror the life of the characters – the music in the opening sequence of *Trainspotting* sounds appropriate for the characters and setting.

A **contrapuntal sound** is one that is in counterpoint to the action: the mood of the sound (often music) you are hearing does not match what you are seeing. For example, if we see children playing, but hear an ominous sound effect or sinister music score, this could be a cue that something bad is going to happen.

Songs offer opportunities to juxtapose sound and image. In *A Clockwork Orange* (Kubrick, 1971) and *Goodfellas* (Scorsese, 1990) scenes of great violence are played out to upbeat energetic music. The music works against what we are seeing. This could be used for humour or to emphasise the characters' gleefulness and/or relaxed attitude to the violence they are perpetrating.

Synchronous and asynchronous sound

Synchronous sound is most commonly used. It simply means that the recorded sounds are exactly aligned to the image on screen, primarily so that the words the actors speak match their mouth movements.

Asynchronous sound is diegetic sound heard before the action that produces it is seen, or sound that continues after that action is no longer on screen. This term can also refer to intentional background sounds not directly related to the image on screen.

Synchronous sounds: contribute to the realism of film as the sounds heard match the actions on screen.

Asynchronous sounds: sound effects that are not matched with a visible source of the sound on screen.

Independent activity

Watch a dialogue-free sequence in any film that relies on music to help convey the emotion. Now watch it again with no music, and then again with a different style of music. Note how this changes the mood and your interpretation of the scene.

Performance

Communication

In this section, you will gain an understanding of how **performance** is used to convey meaning and generate audience response.

Performance includes both individual and ensemble performances, with specific attention being paid to physical expression, vocal delivery, interaction between performers and the specificity of performance for the camera.

A film's visual and aural aesthetic, generated through the cinematography, mise-en-scène, editing and sound, is reflected in the actors' performances. How they are placed within the frame, how they move within it, and how they deliver their dialogue all add to the storytelling and look of a film.

A film's genre, whether it is a Hollywood blockbuster or an independent (indie) film, and the director's vision and working methods all impact on how the film is cast and what style of acting will be used.

Verbal and non-verbal communication

Figure, expression and movement

Film is a visual medium, and you can gain much meaning about what a character is thinking or feeling from these visual elements of performance. **Figure**, **expression** and **movement** all help to build your understanding of a character and their relationship with others. Specifically:

★ **Figure:** If they are sitting still, what pose have they assumed? How do the other characters and ingredients of mise-en-scène relate to them?
★ **Expression:** What thoughts or feelings does the actor's performance project?
★ **Movement:** How do the actors move through the frame? Consider their speed, gracefulness or even their complete lack of coordination.

Their appearance is also relevant: are they neat or dishevelled, young or old, healthy or ill?

These are all **non-verbal communication** elements of performance, which are often more powerful than **verbal communication**, the elements used to deliver dialogue.

Body codes

Actors have a number of techniques at their disposal to help develop their character. These help to generate audience responses. Ten key communication methods (nine non-verbal and one verbal) have been identified in the following table, taken from Argyle, quoted in Fiske, 2010.

		Body codes	
	1	Direct bodily context	Are characters touching each other. If so, how? Combined with the positioning of characters this can reveal much about their relationship.
	2	The proximity of one character to another (or proxemics)	Are the characters close together or far apart? This could reveal how intimate (or not) these characters are and may change over the course of the film.
	3	The orientation of one to another	Are the characters turned towards or away from each other? This could reveal whether they are working together or what they feel about one another.
	4	General appearance	Are they fat, thin, tall, short? Are they well-dressed? How does their appearance compare with those around them?
	5	Head movements	How is the actor using their head to express emotion or suggest meaning? A slow side-to-side shake of the head could indicate sorrow, whereas a fast one disagreement.
	6	Facial expressions	How are these being used to reveal emotions?
	7	Eye movement or contact	Does a character look directly into the eye of another, or do they look down or up? What does this convey? How long is the eye contact held? Does the actor blink frequently or not at all? What are they trying to achieve with the eye contact?
	8	Body posture/body language	Does the way the actor walks or holds themself suggest a particular emotion such as pain or anger? Can you tell whether a character is confident or timid from the way they enter a room or sit? Is their body posture open or closed?

Section 1 The key elements of film form

Body codes		
	9 Gestures (kinesics)	How does the actor use their hands? Are they still or restless? Can you tell how pleased they are to see someone from their wave?
	10 Aspects of speech (paralinguistic codes)	An actor uses a range of techniques (pace, pitch, stress, volume, pause, accents) to deliver lines of dialogue, which develops the character and generates responses.

Stretch & challenge

Watch a scene from any film and consider how the ten body codes shown in the table above are used.

Communication and style

Aspects of speech

Delivering lines of dialogue draws on a range of **verbal communication** techniques such as:

- ★ pitch
- ★ stress
- ★ tone
- ★ volume
- ★ accent
- ★ pausing.

These dramatic aspects of performance help to bring the characters to life and express the required emotion and meaning.

In real life there are certain patterns of speaking that come naturally. People vary their volume and pace, they pause and stumble over words, sentences peter out or are interrupted. If a film is striving for realism in its performance, actors try to emulate this. Highly stylised films might require actors to fully enunciate all words, or deliver them in an exaggerated tone.

The choice of the delivery of speech ensures that a character is well defined, believable and complements the film's overall aesthetic.

Stretch & challenge

Read the screenplay for a particularly dramatic scene from a film you are studying. Then watch the sequence and note how the actors' delivery of the written lines impacts upon how meaning is conveyed.

Pace or tempo

Pace, also known as **tempo**, is a basic principle of dialogue delivery. If what is being said is important, the pace is generally slower so the audience can take it in. This is essential at the beginning of a film as the audience is getting to know the setting, characters and direction of the story. Pace also gives an indication of the character: a **fast-paced delivery** suggests high energy or extremes of emotion. A **slow pace** suggests deep thoughts, indecision or loneliness. An **even pace** suggests control and self-confidence.

Pitch
Pitch is the relative highness or lowness of the tone of a voice; men generally have a lower pitch than women. If a woman has a lower pitch, she could be read as being less feminine.

Stress
Stress is used to place emphasis on key words or phrases; this can be achieved by stretching a word out, pausing or delivering the word/line with a greater force.

Volume
Volume is used for emphasis and as an indication of the emotional energy of a character or their setting.

Pauses
Surprisingly, a key aspect of dialogue delivery is when to stop speaking.

Pauses are used for a number of reasons and each will add weight to the words being spoken. The most significant reasons are:

★ end of a thought
★ searching for the right word
★ to take a breath
★ for emphasis
★ being distracted
★ waiting for a response
★ dawning realisation.

Pauses, combined with gestures or eye movements, develop the character at each stage of the narrative and create further meaning for the audience.

Too many pauses might indicate weakness or confusion. A speech punctuated by pausing can be choppy and hard to follow.

Making pauses too long draws attention to the technique and may make the audience aware they are watching actors deliver lines of dialogue. However, it can be used effectively in an emotionally challenging scene or where there is a power dynamic between the two characters.

Accents
Accents are the most noticeable element of dialogue delivery: the one that is commented upon, celebrated or derided. An accent can be geographically, historically and class appropriate. A British costume drama set in the early 20th century requires actors to speak in a different accent than a contemporary British film. Regional accents evoke different responses, and can be used as a short cut to a character and setting. If an actor is playing a different nationality then there is considerable research needed to ensure the accent is geographically and historically accurate.

However, not all filmmakers want their actors to speak with a geographical or historical accent. This decision is part of the aesthetic of the film.

Performance style

There are three styles of performance and the choice of style supports the aesthetic of the film and/or its genre/setting:

★ **Realism (subtle):** independent; social realist; docu-drama
★ **Classicism (naturalistic):** mainstream; Hollywood
★ **Formalism (overt/stylistic):** art film; expressionistic.

Realist
This performance style should feel authentic; the actors' technique is barely noticed, as they are being 'themselves'. Filmmakers striving for realism seek actors that

are natural on camera and may often employ non-professional actors (actors with no professional training) to achieve this. Our response to this style is to feel the authenticity of the performer and believe that this could be a real, recognisable world.

Improvisation and **method acting** techniques (see the following section) are often used in realist films.

Classical
This is the classic 'Hollywood' style of performance technique, which offers a surface believability. Here, characters are usually played by well-known actors who bring with them a certain set of social and moral values that audiences respond to.

Formalist
Formalist performances may be 'over-the-top', appearing arch or highly stylised. This style is rare, and films in this style would be considered 'art house' films. The rhythm and delivery of lines and/or movement are dictated by the filmmaker's aesthetic.

Improvisation and method acting

The two acting styles that can be used to creative believable characters are **improvisation** and **method acting**.

Improvisation

Improvisation is seen as a tool of the director, and dictates the overriding performance style for all actors. Over a period of weeks, and in some cases even months, actors work with the director to develop their characters. The process allows the actor to inhabit that character and gain insights into what their life was like before the story being told. Doing this, they will learn how the character would respond in a certain situation. This process results in a loose script outline that actors can then develop further when in production. The cinematography for improvisation is often hand-held to allow the camera to follow the action, or a simple fixed shot capturing the scene as it unfolds.

Ad-libbing and **improvising in the moment** is encouraged by some filmmakers to provide a sense of authenticity and momentum.

> ### Stretch & challenge
> Check out Filmmaker IQ's course on 'The Origins of Acting and "The Method"' on YouTube, which traces the origins of acting technique from early Greek theatre to the psychological approaches to performance of the 20th and 21st centuries.

Method acting

Method acting is seen as tool of the actor, although not all actors in the film may employ this method. Method acting developed from an earlier theatrical acting technique – the Stanislavski method – when an actor would explore the emotional inner life of the character to create a verbal and physically realist performance. This technique was brought to Hollywood in the 1950s by the Polish-born American actor and director Lee Strasberg, who developed it further, encouraging actors not to merely play the character but to become the character. The Strasberg method, or method acting as it become known, has been adopted by some of Hollywood's most well-regarded actors including Al Pacino, Robert De Niro, Hilary Swank and Daniel Day-Lewis, and has been the vehicle for many iconic film performances. Today, a method actor would attempt to replicate the experiences of their character as much as they can prior to and during the production. Method actors may also go to extreme lengths of weight gain or weight loss for a role.

> ### Independent activity
> - Select two films you are studying and focus your analysis on one actor from each film.
> - Research the actors' training, career, approach to acting and how/why they were cast in the films.
> - How did you respond to each performance?
> - Consider their performance in light of the various elements outlined in this chapter, particularly verbal and non-verbal communication and performance styles.
> - Compare your own response to the performances with the responses from:
>   – a UK film critic
>   – a US film critic
>   – a blogger
>   – another student
>   – a friend or relative who is not/has not studied film (if possible).
> - Did you respond to the performances in the same way? What responses did you share? How did you differ?

Study tip

Taking notes during screenings is notoriously difficult. Here are some tips.

1. Just write, leaving gaps that you can fill in later.
2. Write in two columns: (A) a rough sequence of events (scenes, places, names, dialogue); (B) things of particular interest (camerawork, lighting, music, where you were moved – you can use emojis for this).

Look over your notes after the screening and check that you can read them. You might want to add to them or rewrite them.

Study tip

Written assignments

1. Do not exceed the recommended length for each piece.
2. Check that you have actually answered the question asked.
3. Double-check how many films and/or elements you are being asked to write about. It's all about the 'and/or'!
4. Make sure you proofread them thoroughly; don't just rely on the spell check.
5. Leave a day or two between completion and submission so you can re-read the assignment with a fresh pair of eyes.
6. Make sure you meet the deadline.

Further information

Casting is a crucial part of the filmmaking process. Consider the impact of the casting decisions made for *La La Land*. The decision to cast Emma Stone and Ryan Gosling over initial choices Emma Watson and Miles Teller had a tremendous impact. Their history of working together provided on-screen chemistry but also played into the characters' desperation, as they were slightly older and yet to achieve their dreams. Actors' physicality, their performance style and their star persona all contribute to creating character, so finding the right fit is central to creating convincing and compelling characters.

Case study: Improvisation and method acting in *One Flew Over the Cuckoo's Nest* (Forman, 1975)

Starring: Jack Nicholson (McMurphy), Will Sampson (Chief Bromden), William Redfield (Harding), Sydney Lassick (Cheswick), Christopher Lloyd (Taber), Brad Dourif (Billy Bibbit), Vincent Schiavelli (Fredrickson), Danny DeVito (Martini) and Louise Fletcher (Nurse Ratched).

For the method actor, having a disability or mental illness is a challenge, which, if done well, results in critical praise. To prepare for their roles, Jack Nicholson and his fellow co-stars spent time in an active psychiatric hospital. They attended group therapy with patients and watched electroconvulsive therapy (ECT) sessions. Many of the cast stayed in character between scenes, which is typical of a method actor. All of the actors who played patients lived in the Oregon State Hospital while in production. The cast also featured non-professional actors, including two central characters: Dr Dean Brooks, the superintendent of Oregon State Hospital, played Dr John Spivey, and Will Sampson, a citizen of the Muscogee Nation (a native North American tribe), made his acting debut as Chief Bromden.

Section 1 The key elements of film form

PART 1 CORE STUDY AREAS
Section 2 Meaning and response

Captain Fantastic **(Ross, 2016)**

Representation
How to approach representation

This aspect of the course asks you to consider how the film you are studying presents society to the audience and what messages about that society are being conveyed.

This section will define representation, explore theoretical approaches and apply them to four films:

★ *Vertigo* (Hitchcock, 1958)
★ *Promising Young Woman* (Fennell, 2020).
★ *Do the Right Thing* (Lee, 1989)
★ *Captain Fantastic* (Ross, 2016)

It is important to remember that representations are shaped, in part, by the society in which the films are produced, so with the case studies in this section it could be expected that the later the film is made the more progressive the representations of social groups will be. The focuses in this section, as stated in the specification, are gender, ethnicity and age, so the case studies presented here explore each of these in turn. Remember, though, that a truly insightful examination of the representation of any of these social groups will include reference to the others. For example, in examining gender, older women are often represented very differently to younger women, black women differently to Asian women, and so on.

> **The specification says**
> Learners study the following in relation to film as a medium of representation:
> - how film creates meaning and generates response through cinematography, mise-en-scène, editing, sound and performance (including staging and direction)
> - how all aspects of film form including narrative contribute to the representations of cultures and societies (gender, ethnicity and age), including the ideological nature of those representations.

Representation

Representation is the way the media, in your case films, represents the world to the audience. The term itself is interesting and can be read as re-presentation, as films, from all genres, are constructed, so reality has gone through a process of mediation before being shown to an audience.

Every filmmaker, or film studio, initially decides on the subject of their film. They choose what story they want to tell, which characters they want to include and from those characters who will be the central protagonist and what events in that character's life will be depicted. Steve Baker breaks this process down as follows:

★ **Selection:** Choosing what to represent.
★ **Organisation:** Structuring that representation.
★ **Focus:** Encouraging the spectator to pay more attention to certain aspects of the representation than others (adapted from Baker, 2011).

These decisions bring into play all aspects of film form and narrative. For example, in terms of selecting narratives, if, as is the case, most films centre on heterosexual, white male protagonists, there are issues about the underrepresentation of minorities and women to be explored.

When it comes to organisation, structuring the narrative, the character with the most screen time is likely to be seen as the most important. The film is telling their story and attributing less importance to the more peripheral characters. With regards to focusing the audience's attention, consider the selection of specific shots; a prevalence of close-ups encourages the spectators to focus their attention on a character's emotions, while consistent use of long shots could be used to display movement and action. Certain traits in characters can be foregrounded through shot choice, thereby emphasising their significance. In mise-en-scène, decisions about staging can come into play, with a dominant, powerful character being higher in the frame than a more submissive, vulnerable one. If the former is a white man and the latter a black man then issues around the representation of racial inequality can be raised.

One way to approach looking at the representations within a film is to ask the following questions:

★ Who is doing the representing?
★ Who is being represented?
★ What social groups are omitted from the representations?
★ What messages about particular social groups are being conveyed?
★ Which characters or social groups have the power in the representations?
★ Do the characters adhere to stereotypes or challenge them?
★ Are the characters typical of characters in films of that genre?
★ What do the representations tell the audience about society at the time the film was made and/or set?
★ How are elements of film form being used to construct the representations?

Independent activity

Choose two female characters of differing ages in any of the films you are studying and compare their representations, focusing on:

- sexuality
- costume
- role in the narrative.

Present your findings in a table.

Stretch & challenge

From one of the films you are studying, choose the lead male and female characters and record how much screen time each one gets in the film.

Representation is important, as seeing your likeness reflected on screen, having role models you can identify with, or feeling like your experiences are an important story to be told, can contribute to increased confidence and feelings of self-worth. It can also have implications on how you are perceived and consequently treated by other social groups.

Stereotyping

Stereotyping of social groups is frequently used in film as a form of shorthand. Peripheral characters in particular can be quite loosely drawn, and using stereotypes quickly and clearly creates a basic understanding of characters for audiences. Although the reasons for using stereotypes can be understood, the practice is loaded with problems as social groups are reduced to a set of typical traits that are reductive and dismissive.

Richard Dyer has written extensively about stereotyping and power (1997, 1998), and agrees that the complexity and variety of a social group is reduced to a few key characteristics through the process of stereotyping. An exaggerated version of these characteristics is then applied to everyone in the group. Stereotypes in film are generally constructed through the character's image and behaviour.

Dyer also argues that those with less power are predominantly stereotyped by those with more, which makes sense when the demographics of those working in senior roles in the film industry are considered. This leads to there being significantly fewer stereotypical representations of white middle-class men in film than of minority groups or women. Dyer argues that the use of stereotypes legitimises inequality, as stereotypes are a 'way to ensure unequal power relations are maintained'. Claude Lévi-Strauss agrees, stating that representations are deliberately placed in **binary opposition** to ensure the dominant culture is maintained and the minorities represented are seen as subordinate and marginalised (see, for example, Lévi-Strauss, 1995).

> **Binary opposition:** when two characters or ideologies are set up against one another. It is an important concept of **structuralism** and can be used to structure representations and help create meaning.
>
> **Structuralism:** the idea that films can best be understood through an examination of their underlying structure, including exploring how meaning is produced through binary oppositions.

Independent activity

Consider the following groups, which are categorised by aspects of gender, ethnicity and age, and list five common stereotypes of each group:

- teenage Japanese girls
- black American young males
- older Jewish women.

Consider what sources you are using to reach these conclusions and think about the power of the media in perpetuating stereotypes.

Independent activity

Think about your family members and friendship groups; are their characteristics easily reduced to a handful of stereotypical traits? Try to list them.

Case study: The representation of gender in *Vertigo* (Hitchcock, 1958)

Hitchcock's masterpiece, *Vertigo*, is widely considered to be his best and most personal film. It was voted the greatest film of all time in *Sight & Sound Magazine*'s prestigious poll in 2012. Perhaps one of the reasons why the film appeals to film critics and audiences alike is that it is a film, in part, about deriving pleasure from watching, something that film fans all understand.

The narrative follows Scottie, a retired police officer, struggling with the acrophobia brought on by the traumatic death of his colleague. Scottie takes on a case that leads to him becoming obsessed with Madeleine, the wife of an old friend, and after her death desperately searching for someone to replace her. On finding a likely candidate, Judy, Scottie attempts to control her and eventually coerces her into becoming 'Madeleine'.

The film should, as all films should, be considered in context. It can perhaps be read as emblematic of men trying to reassert their control over women in post-war America. One of the first things Scottie asks of Judy is that she not go to work but spend time with him instead, saying, 'let me take care of you'. Hitchcock's auteur status, including his level of control over his films and his cinematic preoccupation with blonde women and their ultimate destruction, are also factors that cannot be ignored when considering the representation of women in this film. Madeleine is just one of a number of women punished in Hitchcock's films at the hands of men.

One of the techniques Hitchcock uses to assert Scottie's dominance over 'Madeleine' is the power of the look. It is impossible to look at the gender roles in *Vertigo* without considering how the camera is used to position 'Madeleine' for both Scottie and the audience to enjoy looking at.

Eye-line match-cuts align the spectator with Scottie through most of the film, as a repetitive sequence of shots develops: a shot of Scottie looking off screen, a shot of 'Madeleine' from his point of view, back to Scottie looking and so on. This continues for a lengthy section of the film in which 'Madeleine' appears oblivious to the fact that she is being looked at and also remains silent. She is merely there to be looked at, completely passively.

The notion of women being objectified in cinema is not uncommon and has been discussed by numerous critics and academics.

Representation

In the book *Ways of Seeing* (2008), John Berger summarises the differences between men and women thus: 'men act and women appear'. Laura Mulvey applied this notion of the active male and the passive female to films in her 1999 essay 'Visual Pleasure and Narrative Cinema', which explores the power inherent in Scottie watching 'Madeleine' and how this transfers to the spectator. Mulvey suggests that the dominant view in cinema is masculine and women are presented for men to look at.

In the following images it is evident just how much the purpose of 'Madeleine' is, on the surface, to be looked at. She is framed like a painting in one moment and then pauses in front of Scottie for a stunning back-lit profile image. The shallow depth of field and centring of 'Madeleine' in the composition contribute to a beautiful aesthetic but also make her the focus of the gaze.

Mulvey explores how Hitchcock encourages the spectator to see the world through Scottie's eyes and adopt the 'male gaze'.

However, Mulvey's notion is problematised when the narrative reveals that this is not in fact Madeleine being looked at, but Judy, very knowingly masquerading as Madeleine in order to deceive Scottie. Surely, then, Judy is at this point far from passive but a very active participant in a cruel entrapment. It could be argued though that during this scene the audience is no more aware of this than Scottie, so they simply look at the spectacle of 'Madeleine' with him.

The representation of gender becomes arguably even more interesting after the death of 'Madeleine' when Scottie meets Judy.

Scottie's bullying and subsequent control of Judy, and the makeover he manipulates her into having, has been read as a metaphor for how Hitchcock, and Hollywood in general, treated actresses. The film industry is one in which women in particular are expected to attain impossible levels of physical perfection.

Image search
Introducing 'Madeleine', Vertigo (Hitchcock, 1958) 00:16:11–00:17:46

In this scene of *Vertigo*, both Scottie and the audience see 'Madeleine' for the first time. There is a prevalence of shots from Scottie's point of view to establish his obsession with 'Madeleine'.

In the scene's set-piece, the shot starts as a medium close-up of Scottie and the camera follows his gaze through a zoom-out, pan and zoom-in to finally rest on 'Madeleine'. She is wearing a green dress, which vividly contrasts with its complementary colour, the sensual red of the wall behind her, so the audience's eyes, like Scottie's, are drawn to her.

Compile a collage of 'Madeleine' from Ernie's: how is she made mesmerising in this scene?

Independent activity

Choose any sequence of six shots from the scenes of Scottie following 'Madeleine' before they meet, and screengrab them. Annotate the images, naming the shot types and commenting on the mise-en-scène in each.

Stretch & challenge

Read Mulvey's (1999) essay 'Visual Pleasure and Narrative Cinema' and produce a version of the final section, 'Summary', in your own words.

Stretch & challenge

Consider the representation of Midge, the other significant female character in *Vertigo*. Make notes on her representation as a mother figure to Scottie, her active pursuit of him and her subsequent disappearance from the narrative. Consider, too, the way in which this representation would be altered if the alternative ending, which can be easily found online, had been retained.

Independent activity

Watch Stacy Smith's TED talk 'The Data behind Hollywood's Sexism' to gain a fuller understanding of the issues facing women in the contemporary American film industry.

Case study: The representation of gender in *Promising Young Woman* (Fennell, 2020)

The adjectives in the title of the film refer to the way that men accused of rape are often described by defence lawyers in the courtroom when the jury are being asked to consider the impact of a guilty verdict on them; immediately the idea of the forgotten female victim is highlighted, and this is suggested throughout the film but forms the climax of the narrative. As the film starts, rather than seeing the promising young woman suggested by the title, the pre-credit sequence shows a group of men enjoying a post-work night out. The focus on notions of gender is clear from the outset and the representations of both femininity and masculinity are interesting in the film, although for a female-driven narrative, the film has much to say about masculinity.

Fennell has alluded to the choice of the name Cassandra (shortened to Cassie) for her protagonist in interviews. It refers to a character in Greek mythology who was offered the gift of sight by the god Apollo as he tried to woo her, but when she refused his sexual advances, he cursed her by blighting the gift: she could still see the future but would not be believed. If the viewer has the **cultural capital**, knowledge of this myth establishes the theme of the abuse of power by men in patriarchal societies, and the idea of silencing and making invisible their female victims.

By the time this film was released, Fennell was already associated with the television series *Killing Eve*, as executive producer and head writer of Series 2. This series experimented with gender representations, depicting women as powerful and complex; blending noir, horror, thriller and comedy genres, paving the way for the aesthetic of this film.

Cultural capital: the knowledge of culture, for example literature, films, art and theatre, that a spectator brings to their viewing of a film, which adds extra meaning to that film as a result of associations.

Representation

Masculinity

For a film that deals with the sexual assault of women and associated repercussions, it is surprising that the pre-credit sequence (or cold open) asks the spectator to consider representations of masculinity at the outset, but its function is to establish that patriarchal power is as present as it ever was. The idea of role reversal as a way of rectifying the imbalance of power is immediately dismissed as absurd; the slow-motion close-ups which objectify parts of the male body in badly fitting work clothing are unpleasant viewing, indicating male arrogance and confidence, enhanced by the ironic use of the song 'Boys'. The conversation that follows then dismisses post-feminist notions of equality, as women are still not equal in the workplace, or society, where business deals take place in men-only environments and women are expected to accept it.

The careful **meta** casting of the male characters with actors associated with heartthrob, harmless and nice-guy roles from a television series aimed at young women, in a narrative about assaulting women, creates complex representations of masculinity. The film suggests that the two openly misogynist, predatory men in the opening conversation are less dangerous to women than deceptive men like Jerry, who appears to be a 'nice guy'. This is reinforced by the casting of Adam Brody, whose persona from his previous work is of a harmless romantic interest, who is sympathetic to women. By positioning him as the heroic rescuer of the seemingly drunk Cassie, the spectator is lulled into a passive sense of false security, only to be jolted into active viewing from the moment where he decides to take advantage of the damsel in distress. This is expanded upon by the presence of other actors who have a similar star persona of harmlessness, humour, intelligence and charm: Chris Lowell as the villain, Al, and Bo Burnham as the romantic lead, Ryan. Both characters believe themselves to be respectful of women and the narrative reveals that this is far from the case.

This idea is then further extended by the casting of Christopher Mintz-Plasse as Neil, who is best known for his work in *Superbad* (Mottola, 2007), in which his character has a comic lack of success with women; as Fennell's screenplay indicates: 'this could be the start of any dude-skewed romance'. Neil's behaviour initially creates sympathy – he tidies the flat and he seems nervous, but then, as he ignores Cassie's wishes regarding drugs, rubbing cocaine onto her gums after she has said no, it becomes clear that this film suggests that all men are predatory. The juxtaposition of nervousness and arrogance is emphasised by Mintz-Plasse's comic performance, through which he exaggerates his caring behaviour while also revealing how predatory he is, almost breaking the fourth wall and making the viewer complicit. The clashing of associations brought by actors' charming and comic performances with the actual actions of the characters creates interesting and complex representations, where it becomes clear that it is hard as a spectator not to like these men, despite their behaviour, delivering Fennell's message about the dangerous myth of the 'nice guy'.

At the climax of the narrative, the bachelor party scene, Nina's rapist Al is finally revealed and, again, he appears to be, as he puts it, a 'gentleman'. Cassie's reply in this scene refers to the idea of those who seem to be nice guys posing the most threat to women. The representation of masculinity, then, is fundamentally negative; they are agents of patriarchal power, either overtly or covertly misogynist.

> **Meta:** a deliberate reference to another text and the meaning that brings, often with a sense of irony.

> **Stretch & challenge**
>
> Familiarise yourself with the work of the male actors in *Promising Young Woman* and note the ways in which the personas created by their previous work are used in this film.

Femininity

Equally postmodern, the representation of femininity in *Promising Young Woman* is complex and constantly changing, blending genres and associated female character types in a way that requires active viewing and decoding.

Initially, it deals with a lack of agency in female characters in mainstream genre films: the prominence of the damsel in distress who allows a male protagonist to demonstrate his heroic qualities as a rescuer. At the opening, this idea is inverted, as Cassie uses it to confront men with the reality of who they are, despite what they say about themselves. The knowing use of this familiar trope, as well as the femme fatale archetype, is interesting, as it seems to be less about revenge and more about educating men; and, therefore, it could be argued that this still puts the woman in a secondary role – there seems to be no benefit for Cassie as a character. As with many femme fatale characters, the representation here is complex. While their confidence, intelligence and skill are admirable, there are often misogynistic overtones of insanity or hysteria, the implication being that out-of-control emotions make women dangerous and possibly murderous. There certainly seems to be scope here for the spectator to read the representation as a negative one and lose allegiance with the character.

As well as horror, noirs and female-led revenge thrillers, the film also playfully references female-led rom-coms, where the protagonist is a vulnerable young woman, often a damsel in distress (in a similar way to coming-of-age narrative arcs, the protagonist has suffered in some way, before the film starts) and then is rescued by a nice guy. Here, Fennell shows the part that mainstream genre narratives have to play in misleading the female imagination. An important sequence to analyse is the scene in the pharmacy, which becomes a rom-com romance montage as Cassie and Ryan fall in love. The high-key lighting, lurid colours and overwhelming soundtrack of Paris Hilton's 'Stars Are Blind' create what Fennell has called 'a heightened feminine experience'. This emotional experience is enticing and encourages passive viewing, but maybe not passive *acceptance* through the opening close-up shot, held in a slightly long take, of a kitsch pink kittens card that says 'I Love You', and the exaggerated performance of Bo Burnham as he dances and mimes to the song. These key elements warn the viewer to retain a critical distance and not believe the fairy tale, enjoyable as it is.

Cassie's vulnerability as a damsel in distress is emphasised, highlighted by the mise-en-scene: her long blonde hair, the demure way she dresses in pastel shades and the overly feminine regency furniture of her parents' house; the size of the furniture and wide shots of the rooms and garden. It is this child-like portrayal that positions Cassie as a horror victim, reinforced by a sequence from *The Night of the Hunter* (Laughton, 1955) intercut into the rom-com section of the film as a foreshadowing device, and later through the non-diegetic use of the Bat for Lashes' song 'Pearl's Dream' as Cassie reacts to the revelation of Ryan's involvement in Nina's rape, the climax of the horror narrative where Cassie is shown at the height of her vulnerability before she transforms into her most monstrous self. This suggests that beneath all of the other genres referenced, it is the monster within, a familiar trope from horror, that is key to understanding the representations of both genders.

Representation

Independent activity

Make mind maps for the different character types that apply to Cassie. Find examples to show how they are used in the film.

Stretch & challenge

Watch *Basic Instinct* (Verhoeven, 1992) and consider how Fennell references the femme fatale character played by Sharon Stone, particularly the famous underwear reveal scene.

Stretch & challenge

Read about the #MeToo movement and make notes on why it is an important context for this film.

The film is also concerned with women who collude with patriarchal power, their version of the monster. The film initially satirises this in a sequence where Cassie is watching an online make-up tutorial, featuring Fennell herself in a cameo. Feminist critics have complained that the second act of the film has too much focus on revenge against the women who have colluded with patriarchal power – the extended sequence with Madison and the revenge on Dean Walker, which also involves her teenage daughter, which is disproportionate to the revenge against the rapist Al. In a similar way to the male characters, these women are not prepared to see themselves in a negative way; the only exception to this is the male lawyer who shows genuine remorse. Rather than a message about gender, then, the film reveals the cowardly nature of human beings refusing to take responsibility for wrongdoing.

The film has also been criticised for not featuring the female victim Nina, reinforcing the idea of the invisibility of rape victims. There is an irony here that although the film references the #MeToo movement, through Cassie's desire to carve Nina's name onto Al's body at the climax of the narrative, ultimately her plan would not have led to any real sense of justice for Nina and does seem to suggest that she is irrational, feeding into the hysterical woman trope. The fact that she is easily overpowered and killed by Al shows both her physical weakness and the weakness of her plan; it symbolises the extent of patriarchal power and the inevitable end of any woman who tries to challenge it. The representation of women, then, shows the impact of film and television on the female imagination, and perhaps how this limits the ways in which women see themselves, falling easily into various character types.

Arguably, Hollywood has not really moved on. To a worrying degree women are still in films to be looked at and a lot of a woman's value to filmmakers seems to be in her sexual appeal. The dangerous repercussions of the status of women within the film industry have become all too clear in the recent revelations about the culture of harassment and abuse endured by many. Representations are important and have a real-world impact.

The Bechdel Test

The Bechdel Test is a way of highlighting gender inequality in fiction. It is frequently applied to films, and to pass the test the film simply has to feature at least two named female characters who talk to each other about something other than a man. It has been suggested that only approximately half of all films meet these requirements. The test draws on Mulvey's ideas to a certain extent, as it measures how active the female characters are in film. If *Vertigo* is considered in relation to this test, it fails spectacularly. The only woman Judy nearly has a conversation with is the shop assistant, but Scottie puts a stop to this by taking the active, and controlling, role of deciding what Judy 'wants'.

Stretch & challenge

Apply the Bechdel Test to all the films you are studying on this course and see if the selection surpasses the 50% mark.

Case study: The representation of ethnicity in *Do the Right Thing* (Lee, 1989)

The words of Martin Luther King Jr and Malcolm X appear in the end credits of Spike Lee's *Do the Right Thing*, leaving the audience considering the film's ideological messages. This is a film about racial inequality and police brutality, issues still sadly very pertinent today. The film is dedicated to, among others, Eleanor Bumpurs and Edmund Perry – both black Americans who were killed by police officers. It is a film that shows why the black community needs to fight injustice but perhaps also shows that violence can often just lead to further violence. The decision to quote both Martin Luther King Jr and Malcolm X leaves the film's final message a little more open, as these men had such different approaches in their quests for

Martin Luther King Jr (left) and Malcolm X (right)

Independent activity

Research the ideologies and approaches to tackling racism favoured by Martin Luther King Jr and Malcolm X. Present your findings in a table.

Section 2 Meaning and response

racial equality. Perhaps Spike Lee's intention was not to answer any questions but provoke further debate.

Do the Right Thing is a significant American film, considered the most important film of 1989 by respected film critics Siskel and Ebert (1989). It was nominated for Academy Awards for Best Original Screenplay and Best Supporting Actor, and won numerous awards including Best Picture and Best Director at the Chicago Film Critics Association awards in 1990. The film was part of the New Black Film Wave, marking a major shift in the representation of black Americans in cinema. Roger Ebert argues that Lee's previous film, *She's Gotta Have It* (1986), was the film that started this 'wave'. According to Ebert, black-orientated films prior to this period had either been liberal 'issue-based' films or, in the 1970s, Blaxploitation films with tough, cynical protagonists. These new films were different as they 'considered the black American experience in its own terms, instead of filtering it through implied white values, or tailoring it for white audiences' (Ebert, 1991).

For this section the questions towards the beginning of this chapter will be used as a guide through the analysis of representation.

Who is doing the representing?

Do the Right Thing is clearly a 'Spike Lee Joint', as the posters and DVD cover proclaim. He wrote it, stars in it, directed it and produced it with his company 40 Acres and a Mule Filmworks. His production company's name could point to his agenda in filmmaking as it is a reference to the beliefs held by freed enslaved people that they were to be given land and a mule once released from the bonds of the slave trade. This choice of company name reminds the audience of the historic mistreatment of black people in America and the lies they have been told by the authorities.

This is a significant film by a respected filmmaker but, perhaps most important of all, this is the story of a community told by someone who understands it. Lee was born into a middle-class family in Georgia but grew up in an ethnically diverse part of Brooklyn, so he is, to an extent, writing of what he knows. This is crucial in representation, particularly in the representation of minority groups, as nobody is more qualified to tell a story than someone who has experienced it. This lends authenticity to the representation and prevents the dominant group controlling the depiction of those with less power.

Who is being represented?

Do the Right Thing features a diverse cast of characters of all ages and a range of races and ethnicities, including Koreans and Italian-Americans, but predominantly black Americans. At the core of this film is an exploration of the conflicts between these groups with animosity on all sides but this is balanced by the friendships and sense of community also depicted. There are moments of tenderness and even a begrudging respect at times between characters from different minority ethnic groups. Take Sal's attitude to Mookie's sister Jade as a clear example.

What social groups are omitted from the representations?

Do the Right Thing is dominated by working-class characters and even the relatively successful Sal is shown to have worked hard over a long period of time to build up his business. Characters from the upper/middle classes are almost absent from the representation, with the exception of the yuppie home owner, Clifton.

By only including one relatively wealthy white neighbour, perhaps Lee is making a comment on tokenism. This is the casting of one minority character in a film to create

Independent activity

Look into the cases of Eleanor Bumpurs (below) and Edmund Perry to learn more about the motivations for making this film.

Independent activity

Read Roger Ebert's 1991 article 'It's High Tide for Black New Wave' on rogerebert.com and summarise his key points as a series of bullet points.

Stretch & challenge

Watch *In the Heat of the Night* (Jewison, 1967) and *Super Fly* (Parks, 1972) to broaden your knowledge of the representation of black Americans prior to the New Black Film Wave.

Sal and Jade

Stretch & challenge

Watch Lee's *She's Gotta Have It* (1986) and compare it to *Do the Right Thing*, analysing film form and the overall aesthetic alongside representation issues.

the impression of equality and diversity. The character Token Black in the animated TV series *South Park* is a reference to this practice. It seems more likely, though, that Clifton's purpose in the narrative is revealed in the conversation with Buggin' Out. Clifton is asked why he wants to live in a black neighbourhood and feels the need to defend his right to be there: 'I was born in Brooklyn.' This is an inversion of a scene commonly played out by minority characters in films trying to establish that they are from a country or a place and therefore have a right to be there.

What messages about particular social groups are being conveyed?

This is a complex question with numerous possible answers but one area that could be explored is the linking of young black Americans with aggression, violence and relatively low **socio-economic status**. Despite being produced at a time in American culture when the black middle class was being represented more frequently and there were numerous black role models in the media, this film chooses to focus predominantly on characters with limited hope or aspirations. The film does not really suggest a way out for these characters but perhaps this reflects some harsh truths about society.

Socio-economic status: an individual or group's social position in relation to others, based on education, occupation and income.

Which characters or social groups have the power in the representations?

The film centres on the struggle to establish who has the power, and it changes through the narrative. Sal and his family initially have power within their domain as they celebrate famous Italian-Americans in framed portraits on their walls and have economic power by paying Mookie and Da Mayor for their services. However, by rebelling en masse, the larger black community asserts their power. They ensure their voices are heard and direct their fury about the social injustices they have endured at Sal. But perhaps the group with the most power, ultimately, is the police who, in the film's climactic riot scene, abuse that power with horrific consequences.

Do the characters adhere to stereotypes or challenge them?

This film tackles the issue of stereotypes head on and demonstrates how negative they are with a powerful sequence of shots. Characters of different ethnicities launch a tirade of insults based on ethnic stereotypes directly at the audience by breaking the fourth wall. This is on one hand quite shocking as the language used and emphatic delivery is full of anger and hatred. However, it serves to illustrate just how ridiculous these insults and the views behind them are, as all the groups are directing their anger at someone different. The characters are all both perpetrators of racism and victims of it.

Radio Raheem

The film also includes characters that could be seen as very stereotypical. Da Mayor arguably reflects the common black American stereotype of the 'Magical Negro', Radio Raheem is the archetypal angry young black man, and what could be more stereotypical than Italian-American pizzeria proprietors and Korean shop owners who speak little English? The question then is why Lee chose to populate Bedford-Stuyvesant with stereotypes. It could be that, in some cases, by showing us these characters who initially seem to be broadly drawn stereotypes but then revealing to us their idiosyncrasies he is encouraging the audience to see *beyond* the stereotype. It could also be that he is indeed using a character to represent a sector of society but doing this wilfully to make a point. Maybe, if Radio Raheem represents all angry young black men, then his fate makes a bigger point than just the pointless, tragic death of an individual. The manner of his death, murdered by the police, and the close-up shot of his feet lifted from the ground, evoking lynching, suggest this may well be the case.

Are the characters typical of characters in films of that genre?

To answer this would demand that the film be placed within a genre, which is difficult as it defies simple categorisation. IMDb lists the film as both comedy and drama. It certainly, however, fits within a series of films, the aforementioned New Black Film Wave, and has characters that typify films from this movement. John Singleton's 1991 film *Boyz n the Hood* and the Hughes Brothers' *Menace II Society* of 1993 have parallels with *Do the Right Thing* in that all feature young black men living in a climate of crime, poverty and limited opportunities.

What do the representations tell the audience about society at the time the film was made and/or set?

Through details such as graffiti, the dedications in the end credits to victims of police brutality and quotes from real civil rights activists, Lee is making clear statements about American society in the 1980s. He is drawing the audience's attention to social injustices and by depicting a summer's day getting hotter, moment by moment, conveying just how much the pressure is building up in society.

How are elements of film form being used to construct the representations?

This is a huge question in a film with such a diverse cast of characters, but let's take Radio Raheem as an example. Radio Raheem is possibly the angriest man in the neighbourhood. He is a man of few words but the leitmotif of Public Enemy's 'Fight the Power' blasting from his massive boom box on a loop speaks of his rage at the racial inequality in America and his desire to challenge this. Bill Nunn, who played Raheem, was a tall, well-built actor, and his power and ability to intimidate are accentuated through the use of low-angle shots that emphasise his stature. His body language is very controlled, an imposing stillness that the audience may instinctively read hides a simmering fury. He certainly makes his presence known. With regards to costume, Radio Raheem's T-shirt bears this slogan 'BED-STUY DO OR DIE', which conveys his loyalty to his neighbourhood and community, a loyalty and pride that contribute to his justifiable anger.

Minority ethnic group stereotypes

In 1987, media theorist Manuel Alvarado established four key themes in the representation of minority ethnic groups in the media (Alvarado & Gutch, 1987). These categories can be considered in relation to *Do the Right Thing*, a film made just two years later.

'Exotic'

The colour scheme of the film is dominated by orange and red hues to reflect an African aesthetic, which are bright and cleverly convey the heat of the sun as tensions rise in the community. However, this bright colour scheme also makes the setting seem almost 'exotic' and very different to most filmic depictions of New York. Encouraging audiences to see characters from minority ethnic groups as 'exotic' can be problematic as it highlights their difference and positions them as 'the other'.

Dangerous

Black American characters such as Radio Raheem and Buggin' Out often seem to be on the verge of violence as they make their anger known. However, it is arguably Sal's family and the white police officers that are more dangerous. Consider the use of the baseball bat, wielded by Sal, and Pino's dangerously racist views conveyed by his use of the N-word and describing his black neighbours as animals.

> **Independent activity**
>
> Watch *Boyz n the Hood* (Singleton, 1991) and *Menace II Society* (Hughes Brothers, 1993) and compare the protagonists to characters from *Do the Right Thing*. Draw up a list of similarities and differences.

> **Independent activity**
>
> Research the case of Tawana Brawley and consider the range of responses to the Grand Jury decisions taken.

Spike Lee in a scene from *Do the Right Thing* (1989)

Representation

And, ultimately, it is a white police officer who finally snaps and takes Radio Raheem's life. Alvorado's observations, on this issue at least, are challenged by Lee.

Humorous

There is lots of humour in this film, with notable examples being the Corner Men – Sweet Dick Willie, Coconut Sid and ML – who offer comic relief at regular intervals. This helps the film's climax have more power, as the audience is encouraged to enjoy this community and become invested in their wellbeing. What the film does not do, which has often been a problem in the media, is deride and belittle characters from minority ethnic groups in order to get a cheap laugh. There are moments in the film when there is a danger that the Korean shopkeepers are objects of ridicule but the narrative saves this when Coconut Sid defends them from ML and the angry mob. Feeling threatened after Sal's pizzeria is attacked, the shopkeeper shouts that he is not white, in an attempt to align himself with the black community.

Pitied

Da Mayor certainly appears to be down on his luck, sweeping the sidewalk in front of Sal's shop for a dollar a day to feed his drinking habit. His clothes are dirty and he has the body language of a man beaten by life. His charisma and wisdom combined with his actions of charming Mother Sister and saving Eddie's life from the speeding car make him a likeable character and encourage the audience to pity his lot in life.

Spike Lee

Independent activity

Read the article from *Rolling Stone*: 'Fight the Power: Spike Lee on "*Do the Right Thing*"' (Edwards, 2014) and note what Lee has to say about the power of representations.

Independent activity

Consider the age categories of child, adult and elderly person and create mind maps of how you might expect them to be represented. Condense your mind maps to five key adjectives for each age group.

Case study: The representation of age in *Captain Fantastic* (Ross, 2016)

Captain Fantastic centres on characters living outside of the mainstream, so it might be anticipated that they defy social expectations and challenge stereotypes – and in large sections of the film this is certainly the case. The characters range from small children to elderly grandparents, so the film is an excellent case study for looking at the representation of age.

Children

Children in films are often vulnerable characters who need rescuing and can therefore be employed as a narrative device to evoke a powerful emotional response from some spectators. They can, however, be the characters that motivate the adult protagonists to overcome difficulties and learn life lessons. They can also be the audience's portals into fantastical worlds by being represented as free thinkers with vivid imaginations. Alternatively, they can have wisdom beyond their years or be unruly, mischievous and wild. The range of options is wide but the aforementioned are among the archetypes seen in films from all eras and from all around the world.

Section 2 Meaning and response

The teen rebel is one archetype that has been a staple of cinema certainly since the 1950s, but in *Captain Fantastic* the children are schooled in rebellion from an early age, often quoting the mantra, 'Power to the people, stick it to the man.' This leads to numerous incidents throughout the film of the children defying authorities. Examples include the elaborately choreographed shoplifting of 'Operation: Free the Food' to the mock Christian cult singing to scare off the police officer asking questions about why they are not in school.

This rebellious streak extends to family relationships; as Zaja says, 'Grandpa can't oppress us' when Ben is barred from his wife's funeral. Ultimately, this leads to the child characters having greater responsibility for their own decisions and choices than might usually be depicted in film. In the narrative's resolution it is the children who decide that they will defy both their grandparents and their father, and make their own decisions about how they want to live and, more importantly, who they want to live with. It is also the children who insist on carrying out their mother's wishes in what Zaja terms, 'Mission: Rescue Dad and Mommy.' They are subverting traditional family roles and taking on the role of protecting their parents. This is anchored by Kielyr, and the rest of the children, singing 'Sweet Child O' Mine' for their mother at her cremation. The mother has become the child, cared for by her very driven, determined, decisive children.

An important section of the film to think about when considering the representation of children is the family's visit to Ben's sister, Harper. These scenes juxtapose Ben's children with Justin and Jackson, Harper's children. They have been raised in a far more conventional home by more conformist parents and have been educated in a mainstream school. The representation of Justin and Jackson is much more stereotypical of young teenagers, as they are shown to be motivated by time on games consoles, engaged in consumerism, have limited interest in education and are fairly uncommunicative. Ben's children are so unaccustomed to the typical teen pursuit of playing video games that they, with the exception of Rellian, seem almost traumatised by the violent nature of the game being played.

Adolescent

A central plot thread in this film is Bodevan's journey to manhood and independence, and the film is almost bookended with scenes highlighting this coming-of-age narrative. Indeed, the opening words of the film, spoken by Ben are, 'today the boy is dead and in his place is a man'. This accompanies Bodevan's killing of a deer, eating its heart and having its blood smeared on his face, the first of many **rites of passage** for the character in this film.

Further significant stages for Bodevan include his first, rather enthusiastic, kiss, his standing up to Ben about his college applications, shaving his head and finally his departure to Namibia, which includes another rite, Ben's gifting of the beads and the life advice.

Rite of passage: a ceremony marking an important stage in someone's life.

Stretch & challenge

Read Catherine Driscoll's 'Modernism, Cinema, Adolescence: Another History for Teen Film' (n.d.) to gain a deeper understanding of the way teens have been represented in films historically.

Representation

Stretch & challenge

Research the teen rebel archetype in films by watching:

- *Rebel Without a Cause* (Ray, 1955) (above)
- *The Outsiders* (Coppola, 1983)
- *The Breakfast Club* (Hughes, 1985).

Note the similarities between Jim Stark, Dallas Winston and John Bender.

Independent activity

Look at the top ten films of the year and find out the age of the lead three actors on IMDb. What age group dominates?

Adult

Viggo Mortensen, who plays the father Ben, was 58 at the time of the film's release but in a film that depicts three clear generations he falls into the category adult. Ben is a complex character who at the start of the narrative is very much the head of the family exercising discipline, insisting on schedules and demanding the very best from his children. He sets targets for reading and other tasks and also controls leisure time, for example it is only when Ben gets his guitar that Bo gets his and the family have some fun together. In *Captain Fantastic* we see the burden that being a responsible adult can bring as Ben starts to question if he is doing right by his children in the absence of their mother. His concern about his own influence and power is demonstrated when he states, 'I'll ruin your lives.'

Ben may be a mature, evolved adult but the film shows a man capable of reflecting on his actions and making changes. This can be seen in the scene when he shaves his beard, signalling a new Ben, and is anchored by his increased domesticity at the narrative's climax. The Ben who announces that the 'school bus will be here in 15 minutes' is a different Ben to the rigid, passionate home educator at the start of the film.

Elderly people

Research has found that when older characters do appear on screen, they are often peripheral characters or employed for comic effect. David Cox in the *Guardian* (2012) listed the problematic stereotypes perpetuated by films featuring older people: these included being grumpy, ugly, behind the times, sickly, lonely, rude and depressed.

He also cites Sally Chivers, who, in her publication *The Silvering Screen* (2011), found that narratives featuring elderly people are too often focused on ill health and disability. So, the majority of representations of older characters have generally been somewhat negative. But there is hope that this may be improving as the growing aging population and the associated 'grey pound' is creating a demand for more positive representations within films that centre on older characters rather than marginalise them.

In *Captain Fantastic* elderly people are represented by the characters of Jack and Abigail, Leslie's grieving parents. Jack is played by Frank Langella, who was 78 at the time of the film's release, and Abigail by Ann Dowd, who was 60 (below). Both characters have significant roles to play in the narrative, in particular Jack, who comes into conflict with Ben due to their opposing ideologies. Jack's values are, unsurprisingly, much more traditional than Ben's. He is Christian, adheres to social norms of dress and behaviour, has respect for the authorities and is unarguably the head of his household. Abigail is more open to Ben's views but demonstrates Jack's dominance by stating, 'It's just best to do what he says.'

These traits can be linked to age, as older people are often represented as being more likely to be conventional and fixed in their long-established ways, which can include a more traditional and passive female role.

A tendency in representations of elderly people that is not evident in this film is any signs of frailty or ill health. Both grandparents are portrayed as healthy, vibrant and intelligent. Jack even makes a valiant attempt to keep up with the kid's workout regimen when they move in with him following Vespyr's accident.

Section 2 Meaning and response

The sociologist Lévi-Strauss proposes that all representations are informed by ideology and convey the opinions and values held by the producers of the text. He suggests that decisions are taken to include certain traits and exclude others in order to encourage the audience to focus on the preferred or dominant representation. Consider the films we have looked at here and decide if you agree that there is a clear message the filmmakers are conveying to the audience.

Independent study questions

 What are the common stereotypes associated with the social groups in the films you have studied and does the film challenge or reinforce them?

 Which social groups are absent from the films you have studied and what does this suggest about society at the time the film was made?

Aesthetics

Aesthetics refers to the overall style, feel and 'texture' of a film. To study aesthetics is to study film as an art form and to appreciate a film's beauty and artistic merit. A way to start thinking about the aesthetics of your chosen film is to think of as many adjectives as you can to describe the film's overall style and feel. Then consider how elements of film form, including sound, contribute to the overall style or aesthetic of the film you have just described.

Carol (Haynes, 2015)

> ## The specification says
> *Learners study the following in relation to film as an aesthetic medium:*
> - *the role of mise-en-scène, cinematography including lighting, composition and framing in creating aesthetic effects in specific film sequences*
> - *the role of music and editing in conjunction with the above in creating aesthetic effects*
> - *the significance of the aesthetic dimension in film including the potential conflict between spectacle and the drive towards narrative resolution in film*
> - *the aesthetic qualities of specific films and the concept of film aesthetics*
> - *film aesthetics, approached critically, including the relationship between film aesthetics and the auteur as well as film aesthetics and ideology.*

When considering aesthetics, think about the pleasures gained from watching films. One pleasure is through the narrative. Audiences enjoy how a film answers questions and provides resolution and closure. Another pleasure is an appreciation of the art of film. Certain striking scenes may be rewatched and the overall beauty of particular shots and scenes can be appreciated. These shots and scenes may or may not have a particular narrative function but can be appreciated in their own right as memorable cinematic moments. This is the pleasure of film aesthetics.

 Independent activity

Choose one of the films you are studying. Think of four adjectives to describe the film's aesthetic. Write a short 300-word essay explaining how two key elements of form contribute to the overall aesthetic of your chosen film.

When analysing the aesthetics of your chosen film, consider the artistic choices the filmmakers have made in their creation of the film's overall aesthetic. The director, for instance, may be known for adopting a particular style. Also, consider your film's aesthetic within its wider cultural and institutional contexts. The overall aesthetic of a film may reflect or be part of a particular cultural artistic movement, or typical of its institutional context, such as classical Hollywood cinema.

This section explores film aesthetics through analysis of three visually and aurally striking films:

★ *Under the Skin* (Glazer, 2013)
★ *Moonlight* (Jenkins, 2016)
★ *Carol* (Haynes, 2015).

It focuses on each film's aesthetic style and major artistic influences on their overall aesthetic.

 Independent activity

Choose a film you are studying that you consider to be visually striking. Find three images which exemplify the film's aesthetic. Write a paragraph that explains why these images are particularly striking or memorable.

Case study: *Under the Skin* (Glazer, 2013)

Under the Skin is an artistic science fiction film, which features Scarlett Johansson as an alien in human form. The alien strives to understand what it means to be a human and a woman in today's world, with tragic consequences. Through its art house symbolism and understated narrative, the film explores themes such as immigration, male sexual desire and female experiences of male violence. *Under the Skin*'s aesthetic can be described as 'alien', 'eerie' and 'unsettling'. Director Jonathan Glazer wanted to direct a film that represented an alien view of the world by making the everyday seem otherworldly and strange. *Under the Skin* relies on atmosphere and style, rather than obvious scares or shocks, to create an unsettling viewing experience. Glazer holds on to images, allowing your eyes to wander around the frame and contemplate how the world appears to the alien. Your appreciation of *Under the Skin*'s unique and memorable aesthetics increases the more times you watch it, as repeat viewings uncover its themes and layers.

Under the Skin is notable for its experimental use of sound and music, which adds to the overall unsettling effect of the film. Composer Mica Levy created a score that replicated the alien's alarming and strange experience of the world. It is difficult to distinguish between the sound effects and musical track. Glazer has explained his approach to the film's sound in interviews, saying that he wanted the audience to hear everything in the scene, keeping in sounds such as air-conditioning which might be cut by other filmmakers.

Artistic influences

Under the Skin's aesthetics are influenced by the films of three directors: Nicholas Roeg, Stanley Kubrick and Ken Loach.

Stanley Kubrick's bold, technical and precise visual style was a direct influence on *Under the Skin*'s highly technical visual science fiction sequences. *Under the Skin*'s unique soundtrack compares to the unsettling soundtracks in Kubrick's films *The Shining* (Kubrick, 1980) and *2001: A Space Odyssey* (Kubrick, 1968).

Nicholas Roeg directed a number of artistic and critically acclaimed films of the 1970s. *Under the Skin*'s narrative is reminiscent of Roeg's cult science fiction film *The Man Who Fell to Earth* (Roeg, 1976). Both are British science fiction films about an alien who inhabits human form and both are notable for their surreal imagery. Scarlett Johansson's costume and hairstyle is a homage to Mick Jagger's character Turner in another of Roeg's cult films, *Performance* (Roeg, 1970).

The sequences in *Under the Skin* that were shot on the streets of Glasgow are in the style of British realist auteurs such as Ken Loach. Loach's films often feature working-class characters and are shot in real city locations in a documentary style. Loach uses natural light and characters are shot as though they are being observed. *Sweet Sixteen* (Loach, 2002), for instance, was shot in the working-class areas of Greenock and Port Glasgow in Scotland.

Key sequence analysis: The opening sequences

The first shot in *Under the Skin* is of a white light, evoking birth and creation, as the alien's eye is created. The development of the eye resembles an exploding planet or star. The opening is reminiscent of the 'Star Gate' sequence in Kubrick's *2001: A Space Odyssey*, where mission pilot, Dr Bowman, races across space and encounters strange vortexes of light.

Under the Skin establishes the theme of watching or 'witnessing' at the very start of the film, as we see eyes manufactured for the alien. This theme of voyeurism or 'witnessing' and use of eye imagery is also evident in a memorable image from the film where the alien uses a compact mirror to put on her lipstick.

Independent activity

Watch sequences from the following films:
- *2001: A Space Odyssey* (Kubrick, 1968)
- *Performance* (Roeg, 1970)
- *Sweet Sixteen* (Loach, 2002).

Write a short 300-word essay on how these three films compare to the overall aesthetic style of *Under the Skin*.

Independent activity

Watch the 'Star Gate' sequence from *2001: A Space Odyssey*. Write down three ways in which the opening of *Under the Skin* compares to this sequence.

The strange musical soundscape of an odd buzzing sound merges with sounds of a human voice as the alien learns to form words. The disturbing soundscape continues over shots of the motorcycle being ridden through the rugged Scottish wilderness, making the Scottish environment seem otherworldly. For Glazer, Scotland was the ideal setting due to its sense of wilderness, as it is a less densely populated area of the British Isles. The close-up, eye-level shot of the driver in the centre of the frame as the traffic speeds by him on each side is again reminiscent of the 'Star Gate' sequence in *2001: A Space Odyssey*, where flashes of bright light emanate from the centre of the frame.

Much of the film was shot in the streets of Glasgow. The sequences where the alien wanders through a Glasgow shopping centre (10–11 mins) are shot in a documentary, realist style. The low camera and controlled long tracking shots give the film a realism, yet also a sense of how an alien would encounter this environment where the everyday is made to appear strange.

A montage of shots depicts streets of Glasgow as seen through the window of the alien's white van (11–13 mins). This montage represents the alien's point of view, as she witnesses men walking on the city streets, unaware that they are being watched. The shots are anchored by the unsettling soundtrack, rendering the men unfamiliar and strange. When the alien is stuck in traffic after a football match, the sounds of the crowds are muffled to further distance us from them and enable us to see and hear how the alien encounters these men.

The scenes in *Under the Skin* where the alien drives around Glasgow and interacts with various local men were shot covertly with hidden cameras. Some of the men she encounters were actors and some were real local people, unaware that they were taking part in a scene for a film. Eight cameras were implanted in the van to capture the alien interacting with her potential victims in real time. Some American audiences have commented that the thick Glaswegian accents make the world seem even more alien, as they were unable to understand what the local characters were saying. The spontaneity of the part-improvised, covertly filmed sequences contrasts with the sequences where the alien takes the victims home. In those sequences, controlled tracking shots and elaborate special effects are used.

 Independent activity

Choose two sequences from *Under the Skin*: one where the alien lures a man into the van (13–18 mins) and one where the alien takes the men into her strange environment (19–20 mins). In 100 words, state how the two sequences have different aesthetic styles. State why you think Glazer uses two different styles and what this adds to the overall experience of watching the film.

Aesthetics

Case study: *Moonlight* (Jenkins, 2016)

Moonlight is a coming-of-age story set in Liberty City, Miami, an impoverished black neighbourhood. The film has an almost all black cast; both Jenkins and his co-writer Tarell McCraney, who wrote the unproduced play *In Moonlight Black Boys Look Blue*, are from this area and they have discussed the autobiographical nature of the work in interviews. The story includes the stereotypical issues associated with such an area: poverty, drug addiction, drug dealers and violence. But while this might suggest a social realist aesthetic, *Moonlight* tells a much more personal story of the struggle for identity. While thematically the film is concerned with the intersection between race, class and sexuality, the social issues are very much in the background and the character-driven narrative of black, queer, masculine identity is in the foreground. A visual indicator of this lack of focus on social issues is the use of a poetic realist aesthetic, where the beauty of the environment is heightened in the mise-en-scène and cinematography through the sunlight, blue skies, pastel-coloured houses and the verdant green of the vegetation, often seen as a dreamy, blurry background to the characters in sharp, shallow focus. McCraney has said that Miami is a 'beautiful nightmare'.

The film is divided into three distinct chapters, each one reflecting different parts of the protagonist's life: Little, childhood; Chiron, adolescence; and Black, adulthood. This is a clear indication to the audience that this is a coming-of-age, character-driven narrative.

Another indicator of the avoidance of a social realist aesthetic is the musical score. For the first two chapters, composer Nicholas Britell's score is a classical one, rather than the hip hop that might be expected in a social realist film. While it might be possible to discern the influence of a hip hop bass among the piano, violins and cellos, the classical score is indicative of the universal struggle for a black, queer, masculine identity within such a hypermasculine environment. An interesting example of the use of a classical score in a character-based expressive way, rather than a realist way to create tension, occurs at the start of the second chapter as a non-diegetic score of a slow, sombre piano accompanies some shot/reverse shots between Chiron and the bully Terrell from the gender-divided classroom. The music matches Chiron's sadness and alienation due to the hostility he faces in such a binary situation, which places him with the girls rather than with the hypermasculinity on the other side of the classroom, reflecting the tension between the way that others label him and his struggle to identify himself. The score gives the viewer access to his inner voice. A more mainstream film may have used music that matches the tension and simmering violence of the situation, but *Moonlight* places the viewer firmly with Chiron.

In the final chapter of the film, Chiron has succumbed to the monumental force of societal influences (the suggestion is that very restrictive stereotypes of black masculinity created and maintained by white society have pushed black men into fulfilling them) and become Black, a version of his earlier father figure Juan, an acceptable version of black masculinity with its underlying suggestion of premature death. Diegetic hip hop music replaces the classical score, for example, as Black drives through Atlanta, Georgia at the beginning of the third chapter, he plays 'Cell Therapy' by Goodie Mob. The song, however, is also used in an expressive way as the lyrics deal with the social and political issues present in Atlanta, immersing the viewer in Black's world; it's a new location, ten hours' drive away from Miami, but the overwhelming stereotypes of black masculinity remain the same, as indicated by mise-en-scène: the durag, gold grills and dashboard crown.

In terms of style, there is a deliberate rejection of a mainstream Hollywood aesthetic, what might be considered to be a white and heterosexual orientation of cinema, in the form of realism with, for example, establishing shots and objective camera work. Separating the work into three distinct chapters, one for each stage of Chiron's life, each with a prologue and a distinct visual style, and changing the actor who plays the protagonist for each one, creates a structure which disrupts conventional notions of continuity, although the continuity of character through performance style is maintained through each of the three sections.

Jenkins and his cinematographer James Laxton have both said that they wanted an art house aesthetic, bringing 'art house to the ghetto'. In interviews, Jenkins has named a variety of directors who influenced him, all of whom are outside of the mainstream and only one who is American. Charles Burnett, part of the Black Independent Movement in the late 1960s, is known for authentic representations of black American history, rejecting stereotypes and clichés, and dealing with themes of identity. Jenkins has also said that he was influenced by the French New Wave, and this can be seen predominantly in the numerous fourth wall breaks where characters seem to be inviting the viewer into the narrative. The final shot is also reminiscent of the final shot in *The 400 Blows* (Truffaut, 1959), where Antoine, also reaching the edge of the ocean, peers into the camera with a heartbreaking look of resignation. In *Moonlight*, a young Chiron turns back from looking at the ocean to make eye contact with the viewer, inviting them to ask themselves the central question of the film. Chiron now knows who he is – do we know who we are? It is a final moment of emotional intensity and intimacy. If you are studying *This Is England* (Meadows, 2006), you may have noticed another reference to this closing shot, but used to a very different effect.

An example of the expressionist aesthetic, highlighting the search for a masculine identity through the blue colour palette and the personal significance of the ocean as a place of personal discovery

The film largely uses an expressionist aesthetic, which either allows the viewer to experience the world as the protagonist does or positions us very close to him, creating an intimacy and subjectivity. For example, at the opening the shaky hand-held camera that follows Little reflects his uncertainty about himself; disorientating techniques such as swirling shots, lens flares and blurring at the edges of shots express the inner feelings of the character and the disorientating partial realisation of his sexuality and its consequences in that environment. In interviews, Jenkins and Laxton have said that they wanted to create a dream-like feel that immerses the audience in the protagonist's world. At times the framing of shots can be frustrating, as we see Little/Chiron/Black from behind in many shots. Our frustration mirrors that of the character as we both search for greater understanding of his identity. However, the viewer is given some insight, perhaps more than Little and Chiron, through the use of subjective camerawork. Point-of-view shots focused on male faces and bodies reveal his sexuality, using privileged point of view to create an intimacy and alignment with Little, Chiron and Black, giving us a vicarious experience.

In a way that is very different to mainstream production processes, Laxton has said that he shot 98% of the film himself to ensure that the aim of putting the viewer into the protagonist's world was maintained; as he puts it, 'intense subjectivity'. The film was shot digitally and then the colour palette of each chapter was created in post-production. The first section was made to have the look of Fuji film; it highlights the blues and greens of the colour palette, which helps to reflect the vibrancy of the natural world from a child's perspective in the film. The second chapter was made to look like Agfa film, which has a more muted colour palette, reflecting the more

Independent activity

- Look at the work of Sassen and Hudnall Jr and see if you can identify their influence on particular moments in the film.
- Watch *Chungking Express* (Kar-wai, 1994) and *Beau Travail* (Denis, 1999), and make notes on how they informed the key elements of *Moonlight* to create a distinctive aesthetic.

introspective experience of adolescence. The Kodak look for the third chapter enhances the soft amber colours of the romantic warmth and connection in the diner scene.

Artistic influences

Laxton has cited the photographers Viviane Sassen and Earlie Hudnall, Jr as influences on the cinematography in *Moonlight*; Sassen for the artistic beauty of the way she captures her black subjects and Hudnall for the realistic way that he captures black American lives.

Jenkins has identified his key influences as decidedly art house and in direct opposition to the American mainstream, for example Claire Denis and Wong Kar-wai, after watching Wong Kar-wai's *Chungking Express* (1994), with its dreamy aesthetic, fragmented narrative and symbolic use of colour.

Denis was raised in colonial French Africa and is known for her depiction of colonial and post-colonial themes. Her most famous work, *Beau Travail* (1999), is concerned with masculinity and patriarchal power. Jenkins has said in interviews that he was inspired by her use of metaphors and the connection she created between actors and the audience through the use of powerful performances and cinematography.

Key sequence analysis: Little has dinner at Juan and Teresa's house

As Teresa approaches the car that Little is waiting in, we see a POV shot of her and the camera becomes noticeably hand-held to reflect Little's fear and uncertainty, despite her kind and concerned demeanour. In the following shot, Little is framed from the back of the car. This places the spectator in the backseat, creating intimacy and a vicarious experience, but also deliberately obscuring our view of Little's reaction to her. This also mirrors his uncertainty about this new situation and himself, intensifying the connection between character and viewer. There is a cut to the dining room where smooth panning shots between Juan and Teresa are used rather than cuts to show these confident, self-assured characters and the connection between them; by way of contrast, cuts are used to Little, isolated in the frame. These shots depict his awkwardness, which is difficult viewing as he says very little (his only line in this scene is 'No') and is unable to make eye contact. He is afforded very little screen time, as abrupt cutaways from these shots symbolise his insecurity. This diffident performance is maintained by each actor in the three chapters.

There is a cut to show Little in bed at their house. The non-diegetic score of soft strings signifies peace, and deep focus allows the viewer to see the breeze coming in through the window. The breeze is associated in the film with moonlight and the ocean, all symbolic of Little's search for tranquillity and a feeling of comfort within himself, momentarily depicted in this shot as he has a moment away from the bullies and his crack-addicted mother. This idea is continued in the following shot, which tracks the moving car from behind. We see Little waving his arm in the air through the open window, with the same score repeated – this is a gratifying moment of escape into a carefree childhood. An abrupt cut shows Paula (his mother) emerging into focus as she approaches the camera as if out of a dream or nightmare (her own and Little's). There is a cut to show her in sharp focus, which matches her harsh, angry presence, the reality of Little's childhood, creating feelings of sadness and empathy within the spectator.

Independent activity

Choose three short sequences from *Moonlight*, one from each chapter. Write a short comparison of the different aesthetic of each chapter, considering how it is created through key elements of film form.

Image search
Expressionist aesthetics in *Moonlight*
00:16:43–00:18:51

Watch the swimming lesson scene and compile a series of images that illustrate the expressive aesthetic of the film. Identify the immersive and intimate nature of the shots and the symbolic significance of the sequence as a baptism.

Case study: *Carol* (Haynes, 2015)

Carol is set during the Christmas season of 1952 in New York City. The film is an emotional melodrama about a forbidden love affair between Therese, an aspiring photographer, and Carol, an older woman going through a divorce. Director Todd Haynes' films often deal with issues of identity and sexuality. His films are highly stylised and reinvent and reference cinematic styles. *Carol*'s aesthetic evokes a hazy, dream-like evocation of New York during the 1950s. When developing the film's style, Haynes put together an 'image book' that contained photographs, paintings and images from other films of New York in the 1950s. The setting of New York in the early 1950s is significant, as the city was known for its fashion, hair and beauty trends. America was emerging from wartime austerity and there was a sense of optimism with a recovering economy and growth in consumerism. Movie stars such as Grace Kelly and Audrey Hepburn influenced fashion trends of the period. Indeed, Therese resembles a young Audrey Hepburn, while Carol has the glamour and sophistication of Grace Kelly. However, Haynes noticed that his 'image book' depicted a 'distressed, dirty, sagging city'. This evocation of New York is reflected in the film's colour palette, which consists mainly of light greens, deep pinks, gold and deep reds. Haynes also chose to shoot *Carol* on 16mm film rather than digital, to give the film a grain and further enhance its 'distressed' look.

Independent activity

Create a collage of images of Audrey Hepburn and Grace Kelly alongside images of Therese and Carol in *Carol*. Note any comparisons between the film stars and characters in *Carol*.

Carol's aesthetic develops the psychological depth of the characters. The film has a stillness, reflecting the slow pace of the development of Carol and Therese's relationship. Shots linger as characters gaze at each other through camera lenses and windows. Much direct speech was cut from the script to ensure that dialogue between the two characters was ambiguous, as Carol and Therese are not able to outwardly verbalise their feelings for one another. Instead, gestures and glances become loaded with eroticism. As spectators, we have to be attentive to small gestures and appreciate the nuance of the film's visual style.

Many shots in *Carol* are framed through doorways, obscured surfaces, windows or curtains, reflecting the characters' containment of their sexuality and double lives. In this respect, the film is a comment on the oppressive conservatism of 1950s America, as society disapproved of and criminalised sex outside of heterosexuality. There are several shots where Carol is partially concealed through misty windows, rain, dust and snowfall, reflecting how Therese is captivated by Carol but also distanced from her.

Stretch & challenge

Choose two of the following female photojournalists who influenced the overall aesthetic of *Carol*:

- Ruth Orkin
- Helen Levitt
- Esther Bubley
- Vivian Maier.

Find three photographs taken by each photographer. Write around 200 words comparing their imagery to the look and style of *Carol*.

Stretch & challenge

Watch the documentary *Finding Vivian Maier* (Maloof & Siskel, 2013) about the photojournalist Vivian Maier. Write three examples of how Vivian Maier compares to the character of Therese in *Carol*.

Independent activity

Search online for three Saul Leiter photographs of 1950s New York. Write a couple of sentences underneath each photograph explaining how it influenced the overall aesthetic of *Carol*.

Aesthetics

Artistic influences

Many street photographers of the 1950s who influenced the overall aesthetic of *Carol* were women. Photographers such as Ruth Orkin, Helen Levitt, Esther Bubley and Vivian Maier were photojournalists who captured life in New York during the 1950s. Another key influence on the overall look of *Carol* is the photographer Saul Leiter, who photographed New York in the 1950s. He is known for using reflection and for his impressionistic work. The overall colour palette is muted, with flashes of colour.

Director Douglas Sirk's 1950s Technicolor Hollywood melodramas are another key influence on Todd Haynes' style. Sirk used framing and mise-en-scène symbolically to critique the conformism of American society of the 1950s. He often used garish and contrasting colours, particularly deep reds. Sirk employed framing devices such as doorways and windows for characters. In Sirk's 1955 melodrama, *All That Heaven Allows*, the main character, Carey, is ostracised from middle-class society for dating her working-class gardener. Indeed, Haynes' film *Far from Heaven* (2002) is a homage to All That Heaven Allows. Although the colour palette of Carol is far more understated than Sirk's use of garish bright colours, Sirk's use of mise-en-scène and framing devices continue to influence Haynes in *Carol*, as what is unsaid is instead placed in the mise-en-scène.

> ### Independent activity
>
> Watch sequences from the following melodramas directed by Douglas Sirk:
>
> - *All That Heaven Allows* (1955)
> - *Written on the Wind* (1956)
> - *Imitation of Life* (1959).
>
> List three ways in which *Carol*'s aesthetic is influenced by these melodramas.

***All That Heaven Allows* (Sirk, 1955)**

Key sequence analysis: Therese and Carol first meet in the department store

This sequence analysis considers how the use of colour, framing and symbolic objects contribute to the overall aesthetic of the film.

The colours of the department store consist of pale muted greens and pinks, with splashes of vivid reds in the form of Therese's hat, the characters' lipstick, red bows and Christmas presents. The vivid reds are reminiscent of the 1950s Technicolor melodramas directed by Nicholas Ray and Douglas Sirk, where bright reds would stand out in the frame.

At the start of the scene, when Therese eats alone in the staff canteen, the camera is observational, cutting into people having conversations, reminiscent of documentary-style photojournalism. When Therese is in the store working in the toy department, a slow panning shot reveals glass cabinets of dolls. The dolls are 'trapped' in the department, which reflects Therese and Carol's world.

> ### Image search
> ### Melodrama aesthetic
> 1:47:27–1:49:57
>
> Watch the ending of the film and compile a series of images which show how the aesthetic of Hollywood melodrama is created; identify the emotions evoked by the images you select.

Section 2 Meaning and response

When Therese first sees Carol in the store, the camera views Carol from a distance, and shoppers walk into the foreground of the frame, beginning the recurrent visual motif of Therese's obscured view of Carol, distancing her and simultaneously eroticising her. The scene is all shot in static shots until Carol walks away, after which Haynes employs slow tracking shots into Therese and then Carol walking away. These tracking shots build up the emotional impact of their meeting.

The attraction between the two characters is evoked through subtle glances and gestures, rather than what is said. The slow tracking shots then cut to a close-up of Carol's leather gloves. The gloves function both symbolically to represent Carol's sensuality and sophistication, and as a narrative device, as the gloves provide an excuse for Therese to contact Carol. The camera cuts to a shot of Therese at the end of her shift, the camera seemingly placed inside her locker. This is one of many framing devices, as Therese appears boxed in, confined to societal norms. Again, the camera lingers, allowing us to read Therese's gestures as she appears visibly moved by her subtly erotic attraction to Carol; one she can never outwardly express in 1950s America.

Independent study questions

For each question, refer to one or two key sequences.

Q How does your chosen film's aesthetic helps convey the overall meaning of the film? Discuss.

Q How do mise-en-scène and sound contribute to the overall aesthetic of your chosen film?

Q Who are the key artistic influences on the filmmakers of your chosen film and how do these artistic influences contribute to the overall aesthetic of the film?

Q How are aesthetics created in your chosen film?

PART 1 CORE STUDY AREAS

Section 3 The contexts of film

Social, cultural and political contexts

Studying social contexts

To study films within their social contexts is to examine how films may reflect the dominant attitudes and beliefs of the society in which they are produced. When studying contexts, it is therefore important to consider when a film was made, where it was made and who made it. Some films may engage directly with social issues. Filmmakers may set out to deliberately challenge dominant attitudes and beliefs of the time, through representations, messages and values.

When placing films within their social contexts, consider the following questions:

★ What were the dominant social attitudes towards gender and ethnicity at the time the film was made?
★ How does your chosen film reflect the society in which it was produced?

The specification encourages you to consider the debates films raise about gender and ethnicity, where relevant.

> **The specification says**
>
> Films are shaped by the contexts in which they are produced. They can therefore be understood in more depth by placing them within two important contextual frames.
>
> The first involves considering the broader contexts of a film at the time when it was produced – its social, cultural and political contexts, either current or historical. The second involves a consideration of a film's institutional context, including the important contextual factors affecting production such as finance and available technology.

> **Case study: Studying the social contexts of *Some Like It Hot* (Wilder, 1959)**
>
> *Some Like It Hot* is a Hollywood comedy film about two musicians who disguise themselves as women and join an all-female touring band to escape a group of mobsters. The film raises interesting debates about gender, with its themes of gender identity and cross-dressing. Today, at a time when gender norms and binaries are being increasingly challenged, *Some Like It Hot* can be seen as progressive for its time, as the characters of Joe and Jerry play with gender roles by assuming female identities.

> **Independent activity**
>
> Choose one older film you are studying (e.g. one of the classical Hollywood films produced before 1960). Try to find some reviews of the film at the time it was released. Write one paragraph on each of the following questions:
>
> - How did the critics and audiences respond to the film?
> - Does their response reflect the views of society at that time?
> - How might responses be different if the same film were released today?

To a certain extent, *Some Like It Hot* challenges the gender norms of 1950s America. Film critic David Thomson argues that *Some Like It Hot* was a radical film for the period. The film's famous final line of dialogue, 'Nobody's perfect', challenges heterosexual norms, as Osgood does not care that Daphne is a man – he has fallen in love with the person irrespective of gender. While the line is played for laughs, when watching today, in an era of discussions about trans rights and visibility, the film and its final sequence take on a new resonance.

1950s America and *Some Like It Hot*

Some Like It Hot was produced in 1959 and set in the late 1920s, a period in American history known as the jazz age. The film looks back nostalgically on this period of speakeasies, gangsters, flapper girls and jazz – a period of liberation and fun in comparison to the conservative 1950s. However, by 1959 attitudes in American society were slowly starting to change, with increasing permissiveness.

MGM test screened *Some Like It Hot* to two very different audiences. Their responses reveal changing societal attitudes in late-1950s America. The first screening was to a middle-aged audience in a small American town. They responded with silence and one audience member was reported to have even walked out of the cinema. MGM then screened the film to a younger audience of college students who loved it and laughed throughout.

Young people's responses to *Some Like It Hot* reflect changes in American society during the 1950s, as they had developed their own distinct identity and culture from that of their parents. They began to question the traditional values of their parents' generation. Filmmakers increasingly targeted young people as they had more leisure time and money to spend on movie-going.

Censorship and *Some Like It Hot*

Marilyn Monroe's overt sexuality and suggestive costumes reflect more open attitudes towards sex and sexuality, paving the way for the more explicit films of the 1960s.

Although Marilyn Monroe is still subject to the male gaze, *Some Like It Hot* moves beyond simply representing women as objects of heterosexual male desire. By dressing as women, Joe/Josephine and Jerry/Daphne realise what it is like to be objectified. They question their roles as 'men' and gain a greater sensitivity towards women. This is evident in the sequence where Jerry/Daphne explains to Joe that Osgood has made unwanted sexual advances towards him/her:
'Dirty old man ... I just got pinched in the elevator.'

Some Like It Hot was released at a time when the Production Code, which provided moral guidelines for filmmakers to adhere to, was in force (see Part 2, Section 1, page 97).

Some Like It Hot defies the rules of the code in the following ways:

- unmarried characters in sexual relationships
- hints at homosexuality with male characters flirting with cross-dressing males
- characters seen drinking and gambling at a time of prohibition
- Marilyn Monroe's revealing outfits
- sexual jokes and innuendos.

Director Billy Wilder refused to submit copies of the script for *Some Like It Hot* to the Production Code Administration Office. As a result, *Some Like It Hot* was released without approval from the censors and received a 'condemned' rating. The Catholic

Independent activity

American society in the 1950s was gradually becoming more permissive. A permissive society has more liberal values and increasing sexual freedoms. Write down examples from *Some Like It Hot* that reflect a more permissive American society.

Independent activity

Give more examples from the film of where Joe and Jerry understand what it is like to be a woman. How does their new-found understanding of what it is like to be a woman differ to their attitudes earlier in the film before their transformation?

Social, cultural and political contexts

Independent activity

Research the Hollywood Production Code. Answer the following questions:

1. What was the purpose of the Production Code?
2. What were the key moral guidelines of the code?
3. In which decades was the Production Code most heavily adhered to?

Independent activity

Choose one film you are studying on your Film Studies course. Research the cultural contexts of the film based on the following questions:

1. Does your chosen film belong to a particular artistic movement? If so, discuss how the film reflects the characteristics of that movement.
2. List the key artistic influences on the filmmakers of your chosen film. How are these influences reflected in the film's style and structure?

Juxtaposition: the positioning of two shots, characters or scenes in a sequence to encourage the audience to compare and contrast them.

National Legion of Decency accused the film of being 'outright smut' and 'seriously offensive to Christian and traditional standards of morality and decency'.

The release and popularity of films that defied the code's guidelines, such as *Some Like It Hot* and Alfred Hitchcock's *Psycho* in 1960, demonstrated how the code had become increasingly outdated.

Independent study questions

 How far does your chosen film reflect societal attitudes to gender and/or ethnicity at the time it was made?

 To what extent does your chosen film challenge the dominant attitudes of the society in which it was made?

Studying cultural contexts

To study a film within its cultural context is to explore the relationships between a film and the culture in which it was produced. Placing a film within its broader cultural contexts enables you to understand the significance of the film as a work of art. The film you are studying may be typical of broader artistic modes or styles during the time of the film's production.

You may consider how certain filmmakers developed a particular film style and/or aesthetic. For instance, European filmmakers who came to work for Hollywood studios during the 1920s onwards contributed to the classical Hollywood style. Films from particular cultures outside the USA may have distinct styles that differ from Hollywood cinema. These styles may be in deliberate opposition to Hollywood or develop out of the artistic and cultural norms of that particular culture. Some filmmakers may be influenced by other film cultures outside of their own culture. For instance, Quentin Tarantino adopted the style and structure of European New Wave films in *Pulp Fiction* (1994) through non-linear narratives and long takes.

Case study: Studying the cultural contexts of *Strike* (Eisenstein, 1925)

Strike is a political propaganda film that raises awareness of class struggle and advocates unity, promoting the ideology of the ruling communist party. *Strike* is also the first major Soviet Montage film with a unique cinematic style. The film is based on a series of factory strikes that took place in Russia in 1903, concerning factory workers striking for better wages and treatment. The workers are eventually suppressed by the capitalist factory owners and their spies.

Soviet Montage

Soviet Montage was a key movement in Russian filmmaking from 1924–1930. Russia's leader and founder of the Russian communist party, Vladmir Lenin, considered cinema to be the most important of the arts and a powerful tool in educating the masses. From 1921–1924, Lenin's New Economic Policy allowed for limited private investment to help boost the Russian economy. This helped the growth of the Russian film industry and the flourishing of Soviet Montage.

Soviet Montage was developed by key filmmakers and theorists, including Sergei Eisenstein, Lev Kuleshov, Dziga Vertov and Vsevolod Pudovkin. These filmmakers made revolutionary films that depicted the upheavals leading to the Bolshevik Revolution of 1917. They attempted to make films that would appeal to the masses and constructed a new language of cinema called montage. In montage films, meaning is derived from the juxtaposition of images.

Sergei Eisenstein and 'Collision' Montage

The Soviet Montage directors developed the theory of montage through a series of publications, such as Eisenstein's 'The Montage of Attractions' (1923). As the majority of Russians at the time were illiterate, Russian Montage directors considered the creation of meaning through visual imagery and rapidly edited juxtaposing images to be of prime importance.

All the Soviet Montage directors had a slightly different approach to and interpretation of montage. For Eisenstein, editing could create powerful effects through the juxtaposition or 'collision' of shots. As meanings are created in the minds of the spectator through collision, Eisenstein considered montage to be a powerful propaganda tool and an alternative to the continuity editing that was typical of Hollywood cinema.

Strike as a Soviet Montage film

In Soviet Montage films, characters may appear as stock types who represent particular social classes in Russian society. Characters or 'types' were often performed by non-professional actors. This was known as typage. In *Strike*, workers are depicted as a collective unit, upholding the communist values of people working together for the state. The mass or collective as heroes contrasts with Hollywood cinema, typified by one main hero played by an individual star.

Soviet Montage films contain repeated images or motifs. Animals and the fate of animals is a recurring **motif** in *Strike*. Rural life in Russia is represented as an idyll through happy and free animals such as a kitten and a duckling. All the spies in *Strike* are coded as animals that reflect their characters, such as the Bulldog, the Fox and the Owl. Images of a particular animal cross-fade into the character whose physical attributes resemble the animal.

Strike is most famous for the use of montage in the slaughterhouse sequence. The film cuts between long shots of the suppression of the workers by the army and cattle being slaughtered, followed by a long shot of the defeated workers' lifeless bodies strewn across a field. Through montage, the spectator is invited to make the connection between the civilians and the cow and liken the treatment of cattle to that of the workers.

Strike's cultural influence

Strike was not a commercial success upon its initial release in Russia. The film may have been too ahead of its time and too experimental for popular tastes. However, *Strike* was rediscovered by film buffs in the 1960s and is now considered to be a work of art. Soviet Montage has since influenced filmmakers in Hollywood such as Alfred Hitchcock and Francis Ford Coppola.

Stretch & challenge

Watch a film by Lev Kuleshov, Dziga Vertov or Vsevolod Pudovkin. List five aspects of film style that are similar to Eisenstein's work and five that differ.

Motif: a recurring element that has symbolic significance in a narrative.

Stretch & challenge

Take ten photographs of a place you know that could be used to create a montage. The images should be well selected to reveal something to the audience about this place.

Stretch & challenge

Research where the influence of Soviet Montage can be seen in the films of Alfred Hitchcock. Find screen grabs to illustrate this.

Independent study questions

 What were the key artistic and creative trends at the time of your film's production?

 What are the artistic influences on the filmmakers of your chosen film?

 To what extent is your chosen film typical of the style of films from its country of origin?

Social, cultural and political contexts

Studying political contexts

When placing your chosen film within its political contexts, consider what political movements, issues or events were taking place at the time of the film's production. Some films may engage directly with political issues, while others may hide political messages in a film's subtext. Some filmmakers may set out to make a political point or explore political issues. Other films may use past events to comment on current political issues.

Consider also any political pressures filmmakers may face. Films made within restrictive or repressive regimes may be subject to strict censorship. In these circumstances, filmmakers may use metaphors or allegory as a way to discuss forbidden political issues. For instance, in *Daisies* (Chytilová, 1966) the two female protagonists' playful behaviour and disrespect of rules can be read as a condemnation of communist Czechoslovakia.

As with social and cultural contexts, you should consider when the film was made, where it was made and any possible political motivations of the filmmakers.

Independent activity

Mangrove is based on real events leading up to and including a famous court case.

Research the emergence of the Black Power Movement in Britain and the demonstration which took place on Sunday 9 August 1970 in the Paddington and Notting Hill areas of London.

Answer the following questions:

- How does *Mangrove* offer a more emotional depiction of events? Who do we empathise with and why?
- To what extent does *Mangrove* offer a political representation of events? How are the different sides represented?

Stretch & challenge

Watch the 'Rivers of Blood' speech given by Enoch Powell on 20 April 1968. Read or listen to some responses to it and consider its legacy over 50 years on.

Case study: Studying the political contexts of *Mangrove* (McQueen, 2020)

Mangrove is the first in the five-film anthology series *Small Axe*, broadcast on the BBC and Amazon Prime in November 2020. The series, created, co-written and directed by the artist and filmmaker Steve McQueen, depicts and celebrates life in London's West Indian community between the 1960s and 1980s, key themes being the resilience and joy in the black community. The title *Small Axe* is derived from a Jamaican proverb, which suggests that a small axe could fell a big tree, which is indicative of the collective power of oppressed people against those in power.

As the first film in the series, *Mangrove* brings this idea to life. The first part of the film depicts the Mangrove restaurant as a vibrant hub of unity and cultural identity for the black community, which is seen by the police as a threat in a racially oppressive society. This is suggested by racist graffiti, some of which references the right-wing Conservative MP Enoch Powell (who had just made his 'Rivers of Blood' speech), then PC Pulley, the vindictive antagonist. As the film progresses, the extent of the big tree is revealed: institutional racism within the state, represented by the British police force (many black people had faced police intimidation and wrongful arrest) and the justice system in the late 1960s and early 1970s.

Mangrove, the Black Power Movement and the 1971 Trial of the Mangrove Nine

Mangrove gives a voice to the protagonists of the *Mangrove* case – nine activists who organised a protest against the persistent police targeting of the Mangrove restaurant and were tried for inciting a riot, which is a potent reminder of Britain's overt racism in the recent past.

The film opens amid the black community, celebrating black culture through music and camaraderie. This is followed by scenes involving the protagonist Frank Crichlow, an enterprising Trinidadian man who plans to open a restaurant – the Mangrove – serving West Indian food and drink that will serve as a hub for the local black community. We see him walking through Notting Hill in 1968, and London life is juxtaposed with the Bob Marley soundtrack and enriching Caribbean influences, making the political ideology of the film clear. Malachi Kirby plays Darcus Howe (one of the Mangrove Nine), a member of the British Black Panther Movement who worked at the Mangrove and took part in the demonstrations. A voice-over from Kirby as Darcus Howe, in which he reads the words of C.L.R. James, an important Trinidadian historian and social critic who makes a brief appearance at the restaurant, suggests that the West Indian immigrants have 'perspective' and are 'new types of human beings' who have 'all the traditional values of the English nation'. This view starkly opposes the circulating racist myths about the inferiority/'otherness' of black people, propagated by politicians such as Enoch Powell and those in 'official society'. This sets up the film (and the restaurant) as a political space rather than a piece of nostalgia.

> **Stretch & challenge**
>
> Read about Darcus Howe's work and watch some of his television appearances to gain a greater understanding of his work as a civil rights activist.

The second half of the film is concerned with the trial itself, particularly the passionate and articulate way that British Black Panther leader Altheia Jones-LoCointe and Darcus Howe represent themselves, echoing James' assertion from earlier that immigrants from the West Indies are not 'demoralised or defeated or despairing persons. They are leaders ...', and the inspirational impact of this on left-wing anti-racist politics. Significantly, the Nine did not present themselves as victims, but people who were prepared to challenge the power of the court. They asked for an all-black jury, but were not granted one; after some rejecting of potential jurors, two of the final twelve were black.

> **Independent activity**
>
> Analyse the sequence at the start of the trial (57 minutes into the film, for 20 minutes). How is the racism of the right-wing establishment made clear? How are the protestors and those who represent them portrayed?

McQueen as a filmmaker and Black Lives Matter

The director of *Mangrove*, Steve McQueen, is an award-winning filmmaker and artist. His early films were experimental, often dealing with themes of race, masculinity and violence. His most prominent film thus far is *12 Years A Slave* (2013), which won three Oscars at the 2014 Academy Awards, including Best Picture.

Social, cultural and political contexts

Independent activity

Read this *Guardian* article by Aamna Mohdin (2020): "Racism's Still Around": Notting Hill 50 Years on from *Mangrove*'. Identify the issues that are highlighted in *Mangrove*.

Mangrove and *Small Axe* have received critical acclaim, resonating with the aims of Black Lives Matter, a global protest movement against racism and racially motivated violence that started in the USA in 2013. The murder of George Floyd by US police in May 2020 deeply affected people in the UK and led to a wave of protests as people broke the COVID-19 lockdown to join the anti-racism rallies which took place in 260 towns and cities across the UK. On 29 May 2020, thousands of people in London marched under Black Lives Matter banners, just months before the release of *Mangrove*.

Steve McQueen

Independent study questions

 How far does your chosen film engage with political issues and events?

 What major political movements or events were taking place at the time of your film's production? To what extent have these events shaped the film's text?

Production context

How to approach production context

Along with the other areas, the key elements of film form and meaning and response, production context is a core area that should be studied for each film on the course. The core areas are all interrelated, and knowledge of the production context allows a greater understanding of the other two core areas.

Films made during the Classical Hollywood period 1930–1960 were products of particular studios who retained a tight control over every aspect of the production, see page 82 for more information on the studio system. After this time the production context becomes more complex, and this involves looking at relevant institutional aspects of the key features of a film's production process. These include the type of production companies who financed the production of the film, the budget for production and the key decisions made during the production. For many films, this may involve some tension between the financiers of a film and the creative team; how these tensions are resolved has an impact on the aesthetic and meaning of the finished film. This usually means a consideration of whether the film can be thought of as a Hollywood film or a film independent of Hollywood – an indie.

Another important stage in the life of a film is distribution. This is the type of release a film has, including how many screens it is shown in and the level and type of marketing it receives. It is important to consider whether the distribution company is a Hollywood one or an independent. Independent companies find it difficult to compete with Hollywood companies, so they often aim for critical and/or cultural success rather than the usual commercial success sought by Hollywood. As such, independent distribution usually means a higher degree of creative control for the filmmakers. However, there may be tensions between filmmakers and distributors at this stage if the filmmakers and distribution company have different agendas. Hollywood distribution usually means a much larger budget for marketing and therefore more exposure for the film, but this is usually focused on the presence of stars and an easily recognisable genre; with a low budget independent production, this may prove difficult.

One area where there might be conflict is in the age rating a film receives. Ratings are issued by the British Board of Film Classification (BBFC) in the UK and the Motion Picture Association of America (MPAA) in the US. Hollywood distributors tend to avoid a film receiving an 18 rating, unless it's a horror film, in which case the 18 rating could create a buzz. However, even then, they tend to be cautious, as an 18 rating narrows the audience reach. Therefore, Hollywood distributors tend to consult the classifiers for advice on how to achieve the desired certification. However, independent filmmakers tend to aim for authenticity as a priority over reaching the widest possible audience and/or maximising revenue.

> **Independent activity**
>
> If you are studying any of the films on the course that have received an 18 certificate – *Trainspotting* (Boyle, 1996), *This Is England* (Meadows, 2006) or *For Sama* (Al-Kateab, 2019) – research why that classification is an important production context for those filmmakers in terms of the conflict between profit and authenticity.

Case study: Classical Hollywood
All About Eve (Mankiewicz, 1950)

Key decisions made during production

The production context of *All About Eve* illustrates some of the issues in the Classical Hollywood era, as there was tension between its prestigious writer and director Joseph Mankiewicz (who was at the height of his career during production), and 20th Century Fox, the studio to which he was contracted.

Mankiewicz's career in Hollywood began in 1929, when he was given a contract to write for Paramount. This was followed four years later by a ten-year contract with MGM, where he worked as a writer and producer. His success there led to him receiving an offer from 20th Century Fox, which also included the right to direct.

The year before *All About Eve* was released, Mankiewicz had huge success with the 20th Century Fox film *A Letter to Three Wives* (1949), for which he won two Oscars as writer and director. The film was also nominated for Best Picture. This success and his growing reputation meant that Mankiewicz was given a greater degree of creative control than other directors on studio contracts.

Both films followed the same production process; the studio acquired the rights to two short stories published in *Cosmopolitan* magazine (the use of **existing properties** to create screenplays was, and still is, a common Hollywood production process). In both cases, Mankiewicz wrote the screenplay and directed the film under the supervision of studio head and producer Darryl Zanuck.

> **Existing property:** an existing form of art, such as a film, play, song, book or comic book, that already has a fan base, thus bringing a guaranteed audience to any new film based on the property.

Typical of the Hollywood studio system of the Classical era, the studio head had the final say on creative decisions. Zanuck also worked as producer on *All About Eve*, since it was seen as a prestige picture, and in this era film producers were extremely powerful. They usually selected the writer, director and cast members, and worked with writers on drafts of the screenplay and with directors on revisions to it. It was Zanuck who decided on the title *All About Eve*, which is based on a line from the screenplay (Mankiewicz had originally chosen *Best Performance*, while the Mary Orr-authored short story the film was based on was called *The Wisdom of Eve*).

Mankiewicz's screenplay was an illustration of the fluency and witty dialogue for which he had become famous, and it is considered to be his work more than the work of the studio. Such ideas can be debated when studying auteur directors and the input of key studio collaborators, in this case Zanuck as studio head and producer, Barbara McLean as editor, Alfred Newman as composer and Edith Head as costume designer.

For *All About Eve*, Zanuck and Mankiewicz discussed the casting, using actors who were already on contract to the studio. This was typical of the Classical Hollywood studio system and star system, in which the studio controlled actors' star personas by casting them in particular roles and managing their PR. Both men had different ideas about the casting of *Eve*. Zanuck wanted Jeanne Crain, a Fox star at the height of her career who had starred in *A Letter to Three Wives*. Mankiewicz, however, insisted on Anne Baxter, who had already won an Oscar for Best Supporting Actress and was also on contract to Fox; he felt that she had the skills to play the duplicitous Eve. In the end, Mankiewicz won. Mankiewicz also insisted on another Oscar winner, Celeste Holm, to play Karen. Celeste had left Fox after a dispute with Zanuck over her contract, demonstrating the unusual power the director had in the studio era.

The impact of star personas

Of course, we must also consider the impact of Bette Davis on the success of *All About Eve*. According to AMC's behind-the-scenes documentary series, the film's success is to be attributed to the quality of her performance and the relationship between the character and what the audience knew about her life.

Bette Davis' star quality was indisputable, although she was by that time in her early forties and at the beginning of her freelance career, not on contract to a studio. Zanuck and Mankiewicz were in agreement that she was perfect for the role, despite the differences she'd had with Zanuck in the past. Another surprising aspect of her work on the film was her approval of the script. She had a reputation for objecting to scripts and rewriting them; this was one rare case in which she had no objections. In fact, nervous of her reputation, the filmmakers were pleasantly surprised by her approval of Mankiewicz's screenplay.

A key feature of Hollywood film production is the importance of the Academy Awards, or Oscars. In the Classical Hollywood era, studios nominated talent attached to their output for particular awards. In the case of *Eve*, there was conflict between Bette Davis and Anne Baxter, who both felt that they should be the Fox nomination for Best Actress that year. In the event, Fox put forward both actresses for the award, though neither won. Commentators have suggested that if Fox had managed to persuade Anne Baxter to be nominated for Best Supporting Actress, it would have made it easier for the Academy to give the Best Actress award to Bette Davis. However, the film did end up receiving 14 nominations and winning six Oscars overall. It also revived Davis' career which, in parallel to the narrative of the film, had been in decline due to her age. The film ends with Phoebe posing in the mirror with Eve's award, which is perhaps a warning against becoming too obsessed with them.

Tensions regarding censorship

As the MPAA age-ratings didn't come into operation until 1968, like all Hollywood output, *All About Eve* had to meet the standards of the Motion Picture Production Code (or Hays Code, after censor Will Hays), which was in operation from 1934. The code set out a series of rules designed to ensure that films upheld moral standards and 'correct standards of life'. Film scripts were scrutinised by the Production Code Administration (PCA) office, headed up by Joseph Breen, which had the power to change screenplays that didn't adhere to the code, which was principally concerned

Independent activity

Research the Classical Hollywood studio system and star system, and make notes on how this film showcases 20th Century Fox talent. Which scene from *All About Eve* would you choose to illustrate this?

Independent activity

Research the star persona of Bette Davis and analyse her performance in a particular scene in *All About Eve*. How does her presence as a star and your knowledge of her star persona affect the meaning of that particular scene and your response to it in terms of sympathy and alignment?

with sex, violence and morality. Filmmakers developed clever devices to suggest adult content and subtexts through careful editing and use of innuendo.

Hollywood studios had to carefully construct their films to ensure that they were able to pass through the Hays Office unchanged. The ending of Orr's story had Eve succeed in her plans to seduce and marry the playwright Lloyd, husband of Margo's best friend, and then be cast, as Margo had been, as the lead in Lloyd's plays. However, the Production Code had strict rules against films depicting rewards for immoral actions such as manipulation and deceit, and the ending of the film was changed to comply with the code by suggesting that Eve would receive her punishment at the hands of Phoebe as the cycle started again, and that her success and fame would be short-lived.

Breen's correspondence with the studio shows that the final script seemed acceptable, but that care should be taken in the way that women were dressed and shot; it stipulated that women were fully dressed at all times. Elsewhere, several lines of dialogue received some minor alterations and there was concern from Breen's office that a toilet may be visible in the scenes where Birdie goes in and out of the bathroom from the dressing room; Mankiewicz promised that no toilet would be visible.

However, the most contentious scene was the one in which Addison DeWitt slaps Eve. The censors saw it as implying sadomasochism and asked for the slap to be removed. Eventually it was allowed to remain, and it is possible to read the scene as sadomasochistic, or perhaps that Addison and Eve are two of a kind in other terms rather than sexual; that they are both cold and calculating. Addison's line to Eve where he suggests that they deserve each other certainly suggests this.

It appears that while the censors were focused on the visuals and certain words that were seen as vulgar, the witty dialogue was able to disguise some sexual subtexts. For example, many commentators have found a gay subtext within the film, suggesting that Eve is sexually attracted to Margo, which is perhaps apparent in the dialogue between Margo and her cynical assistant Birdie in the section where they discuss Eve and her obsession with Margo.

This example and others make it seem absurd that all films had to be suitable for all audiences. The themes and content of *All About Eve* are only of interest to adults, so to be concerned with whether the word 'sex' was used, or whether it should be substituted for 'love', treats all viewers as if they are children – a situation that filmmakers became increasingly frustrated by. This eventually led to the gradual relaxing of the code and its eventual termination by the late 1960s, when most people in America could see much more shocking things on television and it became clear that for the Hollywood film industry to survive it needed to cater to specific audiences.

Case study: New Hollywood

Alien (Scott, 1979)

Alien was made right at the end of the era in US film production known as New Hollywood. During this era the studio system disintegrated (see Part 2, Hollywood 1930–1990, page 81) and American filmmakers were no longer on contract to the studios and had far more freedom and creative control, although they often still relied on the Hollywood studios for finance. The studio system had been like a slick factory production line, with everything overseen by the studio. After it came to an end, there was an explosion of creativity and innovation in the industry. However, filmmaking became a much more complex and messy operation, and the production context of *Alien* is an interesting example of this. Although *Alien* is often considered to be an auteur film, many creatives were involved in its production, making the debate around the concept of the auteur a complex one.

Creative and budgetary contexts

Dan O'Bannon and his friend Ronald Shusett, two men known for their work in the science fiction genre, developed the story for the film, originally titled *Starbeast*, with O'Bannon writing the screenplay. It was only when O'Bannon noticed the prevalence of the word 'alien' in the script that he changed the title to *Alien*. Unlike many of the films of the Classical era, which were based on an existing property, this was an original screenplay more typical of the indie sector. However, it had been inspired by existing science fiction stories, particularly those by writer A.E. van Vogt – one of his stories, *Discord in Scarlet*, features a creature based on the life cycle of parasitic wasps, a horrifying idea that is mimicked in the way the alien survives and develops in *Alien*. O'Bannon was also inspired by the work of various artists he'd encountered throughout his career, including Chris Foss, H.R. Giger and Moebius; the latter two also worked on the film's design.

Alien was pitched to various studios and was originally going to be made as a low budget independent production by Roger Corman's company New World Pictures, with O'Bannon as director, but then a friend of O'Bannon's persuaded them to try to get a better deal. This ended up being with Brandywine, a company founded by Gordon Carroll, David Giler and Walter Hill that had ties with 20th Century Fox. Giler and Hill were not happy with the screenplay, and they rewrote sections and made revisions, including adding the android character Ash. Although not a Hollywood film in a straightforward way, the ties with Fox seemed to place the film into a more mainstream way of working, where the screenplay was extensively revised and rewritten to produce a more profitable commodity (in the end, the script was rewritten eight times). However, the original writers were upset that their work had been altered, particularly by people who were not science fiction experts as they were, although Shusett did later admit that Ash had been a good addition. This led to a battle for writing credits involving the Writers Guild of America, which ended up giving O'Bannon sole credit. This illustrates the complexity of a post-Classical Hollywood US film industry, when it was n.o longer the case that the studio mostly took credit for everything.

20th Century Fox was interested in financing the film, as it was looking for a science fiction script that would repeat the success of *Star Wars* (Lucas, 1977), which it had distributed. Fox studio head Alan Ladd Jr ended up having input into the rewrites for *Alien*, changing two of the crew members from men to women. This decision altered the entire meaning of the film, although it was probably mainly motivated by financial considerations of appealing to more women, thus broadening the audience.

The collaboration between Brandywine and Fox gave production a budget of $4.2 million, which was modest compared with the $11 million *Star Wars* received. After considering several other directors, Brandywine offered the project to Ridley Scott, who was keen to repeat the commercial success of *Star Wars* and had impressed them with his method of storyboarding the entire film. Fox was so impressed with Scott's work that it doubled its input into the production budget, bringing the total budget in line with *Star Wars*.

Alien is perhaps more artistic and less solely focused on commercial success than *Star Wars*; it had an extensive creative team for pre-production including involvement from artists and other designers, which Fox had started putting together before appointing Scott. O'Bannon was a visual design consultant, while the counter-cultural cartoonist Ron Cobb was asked to design the interior of the spacecraft *Nostromo*. The artist Moebius designed the spacesuits, and the fantasy artist Geiger designed the big alien, the derelict planet ship and the planetoid's landscape. Through this artistry, the film has more of an 'indie aesthetic', and perhaps seems more typical of an Indiewood film, a film with independent production and Hollywood distribution. It clearly worked: the film won the Oscar for Best Visual Effects and was nominated for Best Art Direction at the 1980 Academy Awards.

The film was made by the British subsidiary of Fox, and it was shot between July and October 1978 at Shepperton Studios in London. Like other films from the New Hollywood era, it was not filmed on the LA Fox studio lot; this distance from the studio head afforded the production team more creative control.

Independent activity

Choose a sequence from *Alien* and analyse how the budget for the film and the creatives involved affect the meaning and aesthetic.

In casting, the team aimed for realism so that the audience could more easily identify with the characters and see them as ordinary people doing a job which just happened to be on a spaceship. For this reason, the cast were a little older than they would have been in an entirely Hollywood-led production. In addition, no major Hollywood stars were cast. John Hurt and Ian Holm were respected British actors, and the other actors came from television, theatre, or were known for supporting roles. The film marked 28-year-old Sigourney Weaver's breakthrough – her character Ripley went on to become one of the most significant female characters in the history of film.

The impact of ratings

Scott has always insisted that *Alien* is a horror film set in space. The visceral nature of the gore was shocking for audiences in 1979; during a test screening, some audience members were sick and reported being terrified. Scott originally conceived of and shot a bleak ending where Ripley was killed by the alien, however this was overruled by the studio, who wanted the alien to die at the end.

Although the Hays Code was long gone by the time *Alien* was in production, Hollywood wasn't prepared to risk an unhappy ending, and so the alien couldn't triumph. Therefore, the film ended up being released in the UK with an X rating (only people over 18 could see it) and in the US it had an R rating (under-17s could see it if accompanied by a parent or adult guardian). Fox had originally pushed for an AA rating (viewers had to be 14 or over) in the UK, but eventually accepted that a higher rating would generate more publicity. At the time, the X rating was associated with horror films, and that meant *Alien* could be successfully marketed as horror. However, the BBFC felt that it was borderline since there are only two X-rated scenes in the film: the chest bursting scene and the decapitation of Ash. Therefore, when the director's cut was released in 2003, the BBFC re-rated the film to a 15 to bring it more in line with ratings of that time, and also with public attitudes towards horror and gore, which had changed. By this time the film was well known, particularly the chest bursting scene, which has since been parodied multiple times, which had lessened its impact.

At first *Alien* was given a limited release, although this was soon followed by a wide release and the film went on to become a commercial success, although the executives at Brandywine sued Fox for withholding profits from them. The case was resolved with the agreement that the two companies would work together on the sequel, and they have continued to collaborate on subsequent films in the franchise, generating enormous profits. This is, therefore, a perfect illustration of the production practices of contemporary Hollywood, which thrives on franchises and universes.

Case study: British film

Belfast (Branagh, 2021)

Production context

Funding and authenticity

Sir Kenneth Branagh was knighted in 2012 for services to drama and the community in Northern Ireland in acting and filmmaking. He has had an extensive and prominent career, and this distinguished him from most other British filmmakers, who often struggle to get their films financed and then distributed. Like many Hollywood actors and directors, Branagh owns his own production company, set up in 1998 as The Shakespeare Film Company and now called TKBC – this gives him creative control over the projects he funds through it.

Belfast was funded by TKBC together with Northern Ireland Screen, one of the screen agencies established by the government to fund the British film industry through the National Lottery. To qualify for screen agency funding, filming must take place in a local location and reflect its culture. As well as a purpose-built set in Hampshire to recreate the street in Belfast the street in Belfast is now derelict there was some footage shot in the city, and a clear focus on Northern Irish life; this ensured that the film qualified for screen agency funding. Screen agency funding, along with the major British television channels, particularly the BBC, is vital in keeping the British film industry alive.

The production budget for the film was a typical indie one; it has not been officially released, but is estimated to be $10–15 million (£8–12 million), which is also the usual production budget of a British film. British films tend to keep budgets low by using real locations, keeping special effects to a minimum and keeping to a tight shooting schedule (*Belfast* was shot in seven weeks). They also tend to avoid employing expensive Hollywood stars; *Belfast* features an array of British actors who often work with Branagh, including Dame Judi Dench, Ciarán Hinds and Jamie Dornan. But, typical of British films, the other cast members are less well known, particularly the lead Jude Hill (this was his first role in a feature film). The choice to use unknown actors in their first film roles is typical of indie films; as well as easing budgetary concerns, it also reinforces the realist aesthetic these types of films often adopt. The casting of Jude Hill, and also Irish actor Caitriona Balfe as his mother, who was then largely known for television roles, gives the film a vital sense of authenticity. There is an interesting debate as to whether the realist aesthetic of many British films is an artistic choice or a financial necessity. The presence of Dame Judi Dench, with her associated high-quality film and theatre acting, lends an intellectual kudos to *Belfast*, something that is also often associated with Branagh, but Dench also has an Irish background, which isn't well known. Ciarán Hinds was also from the same area of Belfast, and Jamie Dornan is a Northern Irish actor, so their presence, in fact, contributed to this sense of authenticity. The inclusion of music from the famous Northern Irish artist Van Morrison also contributed to the authenticity of the film and its celebratory feel.

Another production context for this film is the COVID-19 lockdown of 2020, during which the idea for *Belfast* was conceived. For many people, the pause gave them time to reflect on their lives and identity. Branagh has said in an interview on the IndieWire YouTube channel that he had more time to remember and think about the past. There was an inevitable desire to contemplate his move from Belfast, which changed everything about his life and had a profound effect on his identity.

Belfast is an autobiographical film for Branagh, but it also has universal appeal as a coming-of-age film and explores the theme of pivotal events in people's lives and the impact of the troubles in Northern Ireland.

The film is told through the point of view of a child who doesn't quite understand the world around him, and therefore it fits into a tradition of similar narratives. In the same interview, Branagh was asked whether *Roma* (Cuarón, 2018) had been a possible influence on *Belfast*, but Branagh said that he had not seen it; instead he cited the French film *Au revoir les enfants* (Malle, 1987), which profoundly affected him. Critics have also compared the film to *Hope and Glory* (Boorman, 1987), another British film that is concerned with a child's view of a war, in this case the Second World War. Branagh has talked about the use of black and white giving a greater degree of truth, but it also gives the film an art house aesthetic, which links back to the era of Classical Hollywood and the French New Wave. Branagh has also discussed black and white giving a heightened sense of reality through the association with Classical Hollywood.

Critical and commercial success

The film was first screened at the Telluride Film Festival on 2 September 2021, where it was the most screened film that year and received two standing ovations. Later in the same month it was screened at the Toronto International Film Festival and then at eight other film festivals. Indie films often rely on film festivals to be picked up by distributors; if they are picked up by a Hollywood company, then the film becomes an Indiewood film, as this one is. This is beneficial to a film for several reasons, including that it combines the creative control of independent production with a Hollywood release in cinemas where it is shown on more screens and has a much larger marketing budget. It is not clear at what stage Universal became involved as the distributor, but the film was released in the US by Focus Features, the division of Universal that releases indie films, in November 2021, and by Universal Pictures in the UK and Ireland in January 2022.

Belfast was critically and commercially successful. It was nominated for seven Oscars, including the two most prestigious awards: Best Director and Best Picture. It won Best Original Screenplay, and it also won a Bafta for Best British Film of 2022. However, although it was widely praised for the quality of its acting and direction, it was also criticised by some – including Anthony Lane in his review in the *New Yorker* entitled 'Kenneth Branagh's Airbrushed "Belfast"' – for presenting a sanitised view of The Troubles. However, writing in the *Guardian*, Peter Bradshaw awarded the film five stars, stating that even though the film did not provide a full treatment of The Troubles, there is an emotional truth in their depiction.

The BBFC issued *Belfast* with a 12 certificate for moderate threat, discrimination and infrequent strong language, which meant that it was accessible to a wide audience, thus helping to maximise profits. As with *Alien*, it is an interesting example of a film that is both considered to be a work of art and part of the mainstream.

Independent activity

Read about the advantages of Hollywood distribution. Then find examples of other Indiewood British films and compare them with the success of entirely independent British films, for example *Saint Maud* (Glass, 2019).

Independent study questions

 How has the way in which your film was funded affected its production, and did this lead to a particular aesthetic?

 Has your chosen film been shaped by any historical developments in film production? If so, how?

 To what extent did your film rely on film festivals, awards, reviews and advertising to reach its audience?

Production context

PART 2 Specialist Study Areas or 'Case Studies'

Section 1 AS: American film
A level: Varieties of film and filmmaking

Hollywood (1930–1990)

This chapter will help you to prepare for **Component 1: American film** on the AS course or **Component 1: Varieties of film and filmmaking** on the A level course. You will need to compare two films and apply the core areas with an emphasis on context. Alongside the core areas you will need to apply the specialist study area of auteur for the A level. This chapter will use *Casablanca* (Curtiz, 1942), *Bonnie and Clyde* (Penn, 1967), *Imitation of Life* (Sirk, 1959) and *Night of the Living Dead* (Romero, 1968) as case study films.

For AS

For the comparative study, questions will be based on the core study areas but will foreground a comparison of contexts. Questions will be in two parts. Two questions must be answered: the first part, question (a), will be a shorter answer question, requiring brief discussion of examples. The second part will be a longer answer question, requiring a more detailed exploration of film. There will be a choice of two questions for this part – either (b) or (c). The first question is worth 20 marks and should be allocated 20 minutes, the second 40 marks and 40 minutes.

For A level

One question from a choice of two must be answered on the **Component 1** paper. For this question, you will be expected to compare one film from **Group 1: Classical Hollywood** and one film from **Group 2: New Hollywood**. The full question is worth 40 points and should be allocated 50 minutes.

The specification says

There will be clear points of comparison suggested by the institutional and production contexts of the films: films in the 1940s and 1950s were produced during the Hollywood studio era and its immediate aftermath and effectively established the 'Classical Hollywood style'. The films produced between the later 1960s and later 1980s can all be seen in terms of 'New Hollywood', where a new generation of directors began to show new influences, especially from European cinema.

1 *Casablanca* (Curtiz, 1942) & *Bonnie and Clyde* (Penn, 1967), *Imitation of Life* (Curtiz, 1942) & *Night of the Living Dead* (Penn, 1967)

Casablanca (Curtiz, 1942) is a romantic drama set in the Second World War. The film concerns Rick Blaine, an American expatriate who owns a bar in *Casablanca*, Morocco, a waiting point for refugees fleeing Nazi occupation. Rick must sacrifice his love for Ilsa for the greater war effort. *Casablanca* is the ultimate classical film, exemplifying Classical Hollywood cinema at the peak of the studio era. The film won three Academy Awards, including Best Picture. The film's dialogue, music and imagery are highly memorable and are often cited in popular culture.

Bonnie and Clyde (Penn, 1967) is based on the true story of Bonnie Parker and Clyde Barrow, two outlaws who travelled central USA in the early 1930s, robbing banks and killing people when confronted. The film was a huge success with young audiences, and ushered in a new era of more experimental and graphic Hollywood films. *Bonnie and Clyde* was nominated for ten academy awards and won two Academy Awards for Best Supporting Actress and Best Cinematography.

Casablanca and *Bonnie and Clyde* are important films in American film history. *Casablanca* is one of the most famous and best-loved Classical Hollywood films. *Bonnie and Clyde* is the first 'New Hollywood' film, breaking with Classical Hollywood conventions, incorporating a 1960s European visual style and a graphic depiction of violence. Both films were produced by Warner Brothers and as genre films (*Casablanca* as a romantic drama, *Bonnie and Clyde* as a gangster film) and **star vehicles**.

This chapter will compare film form, representation, aesthetics and contexts in *Casablanca* and *Bonnie and Clyde*. This comparison will help you to understand the changes in Hollywood film from the classical era to the New Hollywood cinema of the late 1960s onwards. It will focus in detail on **contextual comparisons**, exploring the social, cultural, political and institutional contexts of the films. The chapter will then explore the specialist **area of auteur** in relation to the two case study films.

> **Study tip**
>
> This is the only section in the exam in which the two films you have studied must be directly compared in your response. Make sure your notes on the films include detailed observations on ways in which they are similar and ways in which they differ.

> **Star vehicle:** films that are sold on the popularity and persona of the leading star. A role may have been written or produced for this particular star.

Classical Hollywood films

The studio system

From the 1920s to the 1950s, Hollywood was dominated by eight large studios:

★ The Big Five (MGM, Warner, Paramount, RKO and 20th Century Fox) produced and distributed films and owned their own theatre chains.
★ The Little Three (Universal, Columbia and United Artists) produced and distributed films but did not own theatre chains.

These eight major studios controlled the distribution of 95% of films shown in the USA.

Commercial feature films were produced on studio lots, with producers, directors, technicians and stars all working under contract. Each studio developed a particular house style, determined mainly by its chief executive.

Studio production reached its peak in the 1940s, as successful studios efficiently produced mass entertainment films and cinema attendances were at their highest.

After the Second World War, Hollywood studios went into a steady decline. In May 1948, the US Supreme Court ruled that the major Hollywood studios must end 'block booking' – the process of selling multiple films as units to theatres, preventing independent studios getting their own films into cinemas. This resulted in the breakdown of **vertically integrated** studios and the rise of independent studios in the 1950s and 1960s. In the 1950s, cinema attendance also declined due to changes in leisure pursuits, including the growing popularity of television in the home.

> **Vertical integration:** when a company controls the different stages of a product's process or construction. During the studio era, the Big Five Hollywood studios were vertically integrated, as they controlled production, distribution and exhibition.

> **Independent activity**
>
> Research the statistics of cinema attendance in the USA from the 1940s to the 1970s. Present the statistics as a graph.
> - What trends do you notice in cinema attendances?
> - When are there periods of decline and what might account for these?

> **Stretch & challenge**
>
> Read Douglas Gomery's chapter 'Hollywood as Industry', in John Hill and Pamela Gibson (eds), *The Oxford Guide to Film Studies* (1998), for a detailed summary of the Hollywood studio system. Summarise the key points in 200 words.

New Hollywood

The 1950s and early 1960s was a period of decline in Hollywood, marked by expensive flops, such as the Cinemascope film *The Conqueror* (Powell, 1956), and declining audiences. However, a new generation of filmmakers came to prominence in the mid to late 1960s and, freed from the constraints of a studio system, produced fresh new films for younger audiences. These new directors and films revived Hollywood cinema and audience attendance increased.

New Hollywood is a critical term that can refer to the more experimental Hollywood films produced in the late 1960s. There have been various incarnations of New Hollywood, including more experimental films of the late 1980s such as Spike Lee's *Do the Right Thing* (1989) (page 50). This chapter focuses on the first incarnation of New Hollywood films produced in the late 1960s and 1970s.

In New Hollywood films it is the director, rather than the studio, who has the key authorial role. These were cine-literate directors who had a knowledge and interest in European films they saw in arts and independent cinemas, and older Hollywood films they watched in the cinema and on television. Many of these directors learned filmmaking as film obsessives or 'buffs', often with backgrounds in film schools, film criticism and acting. As the studio system was in decline, they were less bound by institutional styles and open to experimentation.

However, the New Hollywood films were not a complete departure from Classical Hollywood films. Many were still produced by major studios. Studios did not reject the star system and instead were keen to exploit the personalities of new film stars such as Warren Beatty, Sidney Poitier, Dustin Hoffman and Robert Redford. In this era, stars were also auteurs, often with a level of creative control in their films.

Applying the core areas of study to *Casablanca* and *Bonnie* and *Clyde*

Film form in Classical Hollywood films

The Classical Hollywood style developed during the later 1910s and 1920s, and was solidified in the 1930s. It is typified by a set of conventions and guidelines which we still see in Hollywood films today. These conventions were flexible, as filmmakers experimented and changes in technology enabled new stylistic innovations.

Overall, Classical Hollywood films follow these unwritten rules or conventions:

- ★ The narratives are 'a chain of events in cause and effect relationship' (Bordwell & Thompson, 2012).
- ★ They were shot in a controlled environment, often on the studio lot, yet are made to appear believable and realistic.
- ★ They have invisible or continuity editing.
- ★ There is one main plot with a limited number of sub-plots.

This formula was incredibly successful.

In *The Classical Hollywood Cinema*, film scholars Bordwell, Staiger and Thompson (1988) describe the typical guidelines for a shooting a sequence in the classical Hollywood style:

- ★ The scene should first establish the time, place and relevant characters.
- ★ Location might be indicated with an exterior shot of the location.
- ★ Characters then take over the narration.
- ★ The scene should reveal character's spatial positions (where they are located within the space and their states of mind).
- ★ The establishing shots should indicate where everyone is located.
- ★ Once location and characters are established, characters then act out their goals.
- ★ The classical scene ends with a step towards the goal and/or a character's reaction to a new piece of information (adapted from Bordwell et al., 1988).

Film form in a scene from *Casablanca*

Let's apply Bordwell, Staiger and Thompson's guidelines to the sequence in *Casablanca* where we are first introduced to Rick. In terms of its formal elements, the sequence is a 'typical' classical Hollywood scene.

> **Image search**
> *Being introduced to Rick* 00:06:00–00:09:00
>
>

Independent activity

Watch one or more of the following New Hollywood films:

- *The Graduate* (Nichols, 1967): a ground-breaking sophisticated comedy about a young graduate, Ben, who is seduced by an older woman, Mrs Robinson. The film deals with themes of alienation and questions the values of American society.
- *Point Blank* (Boorman, 1967): a disorientating, surreal neo-noir crime film about the nature of memory and trauma.
- *The Swimmer* (Perry, 1968): a surreal story about a man who decides to swim home via swimming pools in his upper-class neighbourhood. During this journey he shifts from being an affluent executive to a broken-down outcast.

To what extent do these films differ from Classical Hollywood films in form, representations and ideology? Present these differences in a table and include at least three points for each.

Independent activity

Write a 400-word essay based on the following question:

'To what extent has film form in Hollywood cinema changed since the classical era?'

Refer to the contemporary Hollywood films you have studied to help you answer the question.

1 Casablanca & Bonnie and Clyde, Imitation of Life & Night of the Living Dead

Watch the scene and pause each shot to consider its purpose.

1. Long, establishing, exterior shot. This is a typical way to begin a scene in a classical Hollywood film. The shot establishes place (Rick's Bar, *Casablanca*) and time of day (nighttime).
2. Close-up. This shot draws attention to 'Rick's Café American', further establishing place. As Humphrey Bogart is the star of the film, the audience would assume that Bogart is Rick.
3. Interior long shot. The camera pans around the interior of Rick's bar to establish the space inside it and convey atmosphere. We see conversations between patrons, revealing their spatial positions and giving us an indication of the types of people who frequent Rick's bar. Notice how the filmmakers do not reveal Rick straight away. This builds a sense of anticipation for the audience.
4. Close-up. This shot gives important information establishing the specific date. The cheque is dated 2 December 1941. These are the days leading up to the attack on Pearl Harbor on 7 December 1941, the event that led to the US entering the Second World War.
5. Medium long shot. The shot reveals Rick and key character information. We see his actions (playing chess), his facial expression and some of his surroundings (we know Rick is located in the same bar). This shot gives us an indication of Rick's psychological state. Rick is a loner. He plays chess alone and drinks alone. He looks cynical and weary. The low-key lighting emphasises his cynicism.

6 and 7   Characters are now acting out their goals. These shots illustrate the typical way to shoot two characters having a conversation. Notice the use of shot/reverse shot and the 180° rule. We can easily follow the characters' conversations, their reactions and spatial positioning.

Independent activity

Choose one short sequence that introduces a character from a Classical Hollywood film produced between 1930 and 1960. Pause each shot and note the purpose of each shot. Is your chosen sequence shot in the classical Hollywood style? If so, note which conventions are followed and why.

Film form in *Bonnie* and *Clyde*

Now we shall compare and contrast the opening of *Bonnie and Clyde* with *Casablanca*, to consider the extent to which the film breaks the conventions of classical Hollywood style.

Image search

The opening scene 00:00:00–00:02:00

Watch the scene and pause each shot to consider its purpose.

1. The first shot in *Bonnie and Clyde* after the credits is an extreme close-up of Bonnie's lips. This is in direct contrast to the opening establishing long shots in Classical Hollywood films. Here, the film uses experimental devices from **French New Wave** films, where scenes may begin by deliberately omitting the conventional long establishing shot.
2. The camera pans out to reveal Bonnie's face, followed by a series of medium close-ups of Bonnie naked and restless in her bedroom. The camera is positioned to show that Bonnie is naked, yet does not actually reveal anything. Notice how there is still no full establishing long shot of Bonnie's surroundings, as the focus is on Bonnie's character. Notice also how the bed frame is in the foreground of the shot, suggesting that Bonnie is feeling trapped in her situation.
3. The camera is now placed outside of the bedroom, looking in on Bonnie who is looking outside. The editing so far creates a clear continuity and utilises shot/reverse shot as used in *Casablanca*. Notice how we see Clyde in a high-angle long shot, from Bonnie's point of view.
4. The camera cuts closer to Clyde as he responds to Bonnie's call of 'Hey boy, what you doin' with my mama's car?' Notice the use of shot/reverse shots and medium shots to enable the audience to focus on the characters' interactions and locate characters' spatial positioning and surroundings.

French New Wave: a movement in French cinema of the late 1950s and early 1960s. Directors, such as Jacques Demy, Agnes Varda, Alain Resnais, Claude Chabrol, Jean-Luc Godard and Francois Truffaut, created stylish, energetic and self-conscious films. French New Wave films were typified by on-location shooting, naturalistic acting and ambiguous or unresolved endings. While New Wave directors were inspired by Hollywood auteurs such as Hitchcock, they often broke the rules of Classical Hollywood films. For instance, in *Breathless* (Godard, 1959) the opening scene lacks an establishing shot and a conversation scene breaks the 180° rule.

Analysing this sequence it is evident that *Bonnie and Clyde* breaks some of the conventions of the Classical Hollywood style and narrative, yet is not a complete departure from classical Hollywood. The scene incorporates the style of French New Wave films by lacking establishing shots; however, it still uses conventional devices such as shot/reverse shot.

Section 1 Hollywood (1930–1990)

Stretch & challenge

Watch the French New Wave film *Breathless* (Godard, 1960). Make a list of key moments where the film deliberately breaks the rules of classical Hollywood filmmaking. Then discuss the ways in which *Breathless* influenced the visual style of *Bonnie and Clyde*.

The narrative structure of *Bonnie and Clyde* is conventional, with a chain of events in cause-and-effect relationship and a linear narrative with a clear beginning, middle and end. The film does not end as abruptly as some experimental French New Wave films. There is a sense of closure as Bonnie and Clyde are ultimately punished for their crimes through their violent deaths.

There is a direct relationship between Hollywood films of the classical era, the French New Wave and New Hollywood films. French New Wave director Truffaut adored the classical Hollywood film noir *Gun Crazy* (Lewis, 1950) so he screened it for screenwriters Robert Benton and David Newman when they were developing the story for *Bonnie and Clyde*.

Warner Brothers publicised *Bonnie and Clyde* as a genre film and star vehicle, typical of a Hollywood studio film. The poster for *Bonnie and Clyde* has similarities to the poster for *Gun Crazy*.

Independent activity

Choose one other sequence from *Bonnie and Clyde*. Compare the formal style of the sequence to the Classical Hollywood style of *Casablanca*. Notice where the film departs from the Classical Hollywood style and moments where the film conforms to the classical style. Summarise the differences in less than 100 words.

Independent activity

Compare and contrast two key sequences from *Bonnie and Clyde* and *Gun Crazy*, noting the similarities and differences between the two films.

Cinematography

Casablanca

The lighting in *Casablanca* plays an important role in the overall mood and aesthetic of the film. It conveys characters' psychological states and unspoken emotions, heightening the spectators' emotional response.

Classical Hollywood films conventionally used **three-point lighting**, consisting of a back light, a fill light and a key light. **Low-key lighting**, however, is where the fill light is removed, creating shadows and a mysterious, doom-laden atmosphere. The use of shadows conveys a sense of entrapment, as people who were trying to flee Nazi persecution are stuck in *Casablanca*. A searchlight surveys the area at night, conveying a sense of uncertainty and threat. Notice how the light invades the safety of Rick's bar, casting light and creating shadows as it moves.

1 Casablanca & Bonnie and Clyde, Imitation of Life & Night of the Living Dead

> **Image search**
> ***Where Bonnie is reunited with her family*** 00:01:07–00:01:11
>
> Watch the sequence where Bonnie is reunited with her family. This scene was shot with window cleaner smeared on the lens to give it a dream-like quality. Notice how the lighting and use of a filter make the scene seem like a fantasy, suggesting how different Bonnie's life would be if she had stayed with her family.

Low-key lighting conveys a war-torn world and characters' inner conflicts. When Rick sits in his bar after a chance meeting with Ilsa, the searchlight casts light and shadow, reflecting his despair. The low-key lighting used to convey Rick's turmoil contrasts to Laszlo, who is brightly lit, reflecting his heroic nature and certainty about his commitment to the war.

Female stars were often lit with a soft light to make their eyes sparkle and accentuate their femininity and glamour. Ilsa is often shot in this manner, conveying her tenderness and sadness. When Ilsa visits Rick while he is alone in his bar, she is at first bathed in light, reflecting her innocence, while Rick sits in the shadows, conveying his self-pity.

Bonnie and Clyde

Bonnie and Clyde alternates between realistic cinematography and more expressionistic devices. Director Arthur Penn was inspired by the photography of Walker Evans, an American photographer famous for his Depression-era photographs of farming families living in poverty.

For some scenes, *Bonnie and Clyde* adopts a naturalistic, high-key lighting style. This is evident in the final shootout scene, which makes the violence seem more realistic and vivid. At other times, the film adopts a more hazy, dream-like style.

> **Independent activity**
>
> Research the Depression-era photographs of Walker Evans, Dorothea Lange and Arthur Rothstein. Choose one photo from each artist that most closely resembles a moment from *Bonnie and Clyde*.

The Depression-era photography of Walker Evans

Mise-en-scène

Casablanca

Casablanca takes place in exotic and romantic locations, yet these places become sites of danger and threat. Most of the action is contained in Rick's bar, a place of safety for refugees fleeing the war; yet it also acts as a prison, as characters are often stuck inside. Paris is a city with romantic connotations, and is used here for the flashback sequence when Rick and Ilsa fall in love. However, the romance and safety of Paris are again undercut as the Germans occupy France. Paris now becomes a place of danger.

Although *Casablanca* is set in Morocco, it was filmed on the Warner's studio lot in Hollywood. This is typical of production of the studio era, as elaborate sets could be built and dismantled easily. Lighting and mise-en-scène were also much easier to control in a studio.

Casablanca's final sequence in the airport hangar is an excellent example of how set design and clever use of props create the illusion that the scene is shot in a real location. A cardboard cut-out of the aeroplane was used in the background and the mechanics seen in the distance were very small actors. This use of miniatures in the background with key characters in the foreground creates a forced perspective. The scene also uses fog, a common device in Warner's films to convey atmosphere and disguise the set.

Bonnie and Clyde

In *Bonnie and Clyde*, the use of real Texas locations contrasts with the controlled studio shooting in Classical Hollywood films. The dusty roads and unpredictable weather give the film an energy and realism. This use of exterior locations was inspired by French New Wave films, for which French directors took their cameras out onto the streets of Paris.

In *Bonnie and Clyde*, mise-en-scène evokes the poverty of the Depression era and barrenness of the Texan landscape. The mise-en-scène also subverts some of the conventions of the traditional gangster film. Classical Hollywood gangster films were often set in big cities with nighttime shootouts. *Bonnie and Clyde*, however, is set in rural Texas and the key action sequences take place in daylight.

Objects are used symbolically in *Bonnie and Clyde* to connote *Bonnie and Clyde*'s sexual relationship, as it was still unusual to see explicitly sexual scenes in Hollywood films in 1967. In one sequence, Bonnie handles the barrel of Clyde's gun, suggesting that they are now in a sexual relationship.

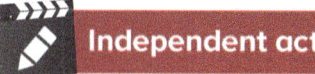

Independent activity

Find images online of the following:
- Publicity stills of Faye Dunaway as Bonnie.
- Female Hollywood stars of the 1930s, including Marlene Dietrich.
- Female characters in French New Wave films, such as *Breathless* (Godard, 1960) and *A Woman Is a Woman* (Godard, 1961).

Create a montage of the images and write 200 words comparing Bonnie's look to 1930s female stars and female characters in French New Wave films.

Bonnie's costumes give her a stylish, cool demeanour, inspired by 1930s Hollywood stars such as Marlene Dietrich. Bonnie's beret is also an homage to the character of Annie in *Gun Crazy* and female characters in French New Wave films. Her costumes inspired fashion trends, as black berets, bobbed hair and midi skirts became all the rage. According to the costume designer for *Bonnie and Clyde*, Theadora Van Runkle, dull colours weren't used in the film because styles had to be palatable by Hollywood standards. The actors were good-looking people who didn't feel the need to look like the real *Bonnie and Clyde*.

Editing

Casablanca

Casablanca is edited in the classical continuity style. The editing disguises transitions from shot to shot, making the film appear as a seamless flow of images. Our attention is not drawn to the edits, thus they appear 'invisible'. In *Casablanca*, the pace of editing is fairly rapid, reflecting the urgency of the situation as the war develops and characters are desperate to gain exit visas.

Casablanca's opening montage is typical of the classical Hollywood use of montage as exposition. A voice-over narration anchors a series of dissolves of ships sailing and people on the move. The opening montage borrows from the documentary genre. It serves to contextualise the story and grounds the film in the realities of war.

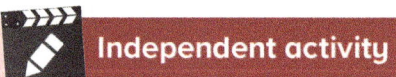

Independent activity

Watch the opening montage sequence in *Casablanca* and the final sequences in *Bonnie and Clyde*. Write 200 words comparing and contrasting the use of editing in these sequences.

Stories are not always edited or conveyed in a linear fashion in Hollywood films, as flashbacks are commonplace. The flashback to Rick's memories in Paris are typical of the Classical Hollywood approach to editing flashbacks, as the camera zooms in slowly on Rick, then dissolves out of focus. The film dissolves into an image of Paris that slowly comes into focus, a conventional device used to signal a flashback in a Hollywood film.

Bonnie and Clyde

The editing in *Bonnie and Clyde* is deliberately stylised and draws attention to itself, a contrast to the 'invisible' editing of classical Hollywood films.

The final sequence of *Bonnie and Clyde* is where the stylish use of editing comes to the fore. The shots leading up to the shootout utilise cross-cutting and fast editing effectively. Quick-cuts juxtaposing the long shot of the birds flying away, to the quick close-ups of *Bonnie and Clyde*'s panicked faces as they realise their fate, was, for film critic Pauline Kael (1967), 'a stunning example of the art of editing'.

Canted angle: when the frame is deliberately slanted to one side. This is often to portray an intoxicated or unbalanced character or to help convey a sense of unease or disorientation.

The final shootout is a montage comprising of 51 shots (around one shot per second). Clyde's death is edited in slow motion, as Penn envisaged Clyde's death to be like a ballet. This contrasts to the sudden death of Bonnie, which evokes shock. Notice how the final shot of the sequence is framed through bullet-shot glass at a **canted angle**, a contrast to the usual long shots that ended Classical Hollywood films. Arthur Penn has described the editing style as 'nervous bursts of energy' (Friedman, 2000). This was to replicate Bonnie's frustration with her life.

Sound

Casablanca

Classical Hollywood films such as *Casablanca* use incidental, non-diegetic music to heighten drama and provoke an emotional response during key dramatic moments. However, in *Bonnie and Clyde* some sequences lack incidental music, which makes the film seem more realistic.

Section 1 Hollywood (1930–1990)

The entire score for *Casablanca* was based on the song 'As Time Goes By', a romantic and nostalgic song that appears in key moments throughout the film to remind the spectator of Rick and Ilsa's love. Composer Max Steiner based the score for *Casablanca* on this popular Broadway song. Different versions of the song can be heard throughout the film, including when Sam plays 'As Time Goes By' on the piano in the bar. Here the sound is diegetic and integral to the narrative, as Rick at first does not allow Sam to play the song because it invokes painful memories of his lost love. However, later on Rick asks Sam to play the song once Ilsa has come back into his life. Also, an orchestral, non-diegetic version of the song is heard over the Paris flashback, evoking Rick and Ilsa's romance.

Casablanca is best known for its quotable dialogue. The witty, snappy dialogue is typical of Warner Brothers' films starring Humphrey Bogart. The dialogue cleverly intertwines the personal and public narrative, as lines such as, 'I stick my neck out for nobody', reflect Rick's isolationist stance and America's attitude to the war before the invasion of Pearl Harbor. However, at the end of the film Rick says, 'it doesn't take much to see that the problems of three little people don't amount to a hill of beans in this crazy world', indicating the wider sacrifices that Americans had to make in the war effort.

Diegetic music in *Casablanca* is also used to reflect particular nations and their role in the war. The scene where the French and Germans sing their anthems is a particularly emotional moment in the film, one that would have resonated with audiences watching at the time. The German soldiers confidently sing their patriotic anthem "*Die Wacht am Rhein*" ("The Guard on the Rhein"), a popular song in Germany that rivalled the national anthem. This represents German power over the refugees in the bar trying to escape Nazi persecution. Victor Laszlo walks over to the band and demands they play the French national anthem *La Marseillaise*, a moment that reflects Laszlo's heroism and defiance. The band look to Rick for approval and his nod of approval is a key turning point for his character, as Rick is now choosing a side in the war effort. The singing of *La Marseillaise* in front of the Germans becomes an act of resistance against Nazi rule. Notice how the entire bar joins in and the sound of voices joining in becomes louder. The camera cuts to a close-up of the French character Yvonne with tears streaking down her face as she sings the anthem, an emotional moment reflecting the sacrifice people made to resist Nazi rule.

Bonnie and Clyde

While music in *Casablanca* parallels action on screen, at times the musical soundtrack in *Bonnie and Clyde* is contradictory to the violence on screen. The bluegrass song 'Foggy Mountain Breakdown' adds a light, comic tone to some crime sequences. The use of bluegrass also evokes the period of the Great Depression and the Deep South locations. Warner Brothers released a soundtrack album for the film in March 1968, as bluegrass music was in fashion as a result of the film's popularity.

Bonnie and Clyde's unique sound is due mainly to the work of the film's editor, Dede Allen, whose background was in sound editing. Her work is notable for the use of sound bridges, beginning the sound from the next scene while the previous scene is playing, which she employs in *Bonnie and Clyde*. Allen was an innovator in the use of sound bridges, which are now commonplace in Hollywood films.

Heightened diegetic sound is used in *Bonnie and Clyde* to shock the spectator. Film scholar Jay Beck explains this heightened use of sound in one sequence (2016). He says that with the escalating violence comes an elevation of soundtrack volume, and quality of gunshots and other acoustic effects. For example, while Clyde is showing Bonnie how to shoot, the loudness of the gunshots undercuts the light atmosphere of the moment they are experiencing.

Independent activity

Watch the opening credit sequence of *Casablanca*. Note how the non-diegetic orchestral score is used to evoke the following:

1. A sense of place – consider how the music evokes the exotic location.
2. Different genres.
3. Dramatic tension.

> **Independent activity**
>
> According to David Smit in *Ingrid Bergman: The Life, Career and Public Image (2012),* the scene in *Casablanca* where Ilsa confronts Rick in his room near the end of the film best exemplifies Bergman's ability to display adoration and devotion. Watch this scene carefully, focusing on Bergman's performance. Write down how Bergman displays adoration and devotion through facial expression and body movement.

> **Stretch & challenge**
>
> Find the screenplay for *Casablanca*. Look at the scene towards the end of the screenplay where Rick and Ilsa sacrifice their love and part company. Now compare the scene in the screenplay with the scene in the film. What do Humphrey Bogart and Ingrid Bergman contribute to the scene through performance that is not stated in the screenplay?

> **Independent activity**
>
> Watch the opening sequence of *Bonnie and Clyde*. Write down examples of how Bonnie's non-verbal communication connotes her boredom and frustration. How do her mannerisms change when Clyde offers her the opportunity of excitement and escape?

Performance

Casablanca

In *Casablanca*, Humphrey Bogart brings a psychological realism to his depiction of Rick. We can infer Rick's troubled state of mind through Bogart's facial expressions. Bogart's acting style was considered to be 'natural' for the period. Other actors on the set of *Casablanca* believed that he brought his own personal unhappiness to his performance. Bogart's performance in *Casablanca* was also a continuation of the world-weary, 'tough guy' persona he had developed in previous Warner Brothers films such as *The Maltese Falcon* (Huston, 1941).

Ingrid Bergman's performance as Ilsa conveys the inner turmoil and conflict Ilsa faces. Like Bogart, Bergman's performance style was 'natural'. Bergman conveys emotion through her eyes, which convey her fear and sadness. Professor David Smit (2012) describes Bergman's distinctive performance skills. One of the things he praises is her emotional range — and her ability to keep that range going through long takes.

Watch Bergman's performance closely in the climactic airport hangar sequences. Notice how her eyes convey her sadness at having to sacrifice her love for Rick and how her performance is heightened by a soft gauze filter and lighting.

Bonnie and Clyde

The performance style of Faye Dunaway and Warren Beatty in *Bonnie and Clyde* is more self-conscious than the performance styles in *Casablanca*, reflecting changes in acting styles in New Hollywood films. Film scholar Jack Shadoian (2003) describes the performance styles of the actors in *Bonnie and Clyde*. He suggests that their awkwardness and the sense that they are alienated from their roles might have been intentional by Penn — to suggest the insecurity, nervousness and non-integrated personalities of his characters.

Warren Beatty plays Clyde with a boyish charm. He often smiles with glee when talking about his past exploits. Beatty evokes the real Clyde Barrow in his performance, as he walks with a limp. Faye Dunaway embodies screenwriters' Benton and Newman's description of Bonnie in their original treatment for the film: as an attractive girl who was both vulnerable and tough, who shot police officers but also wrote poetry, and who loved life but courted death (Goldstein, 1998).

Aesthetics

Casablanca

Casablanca combines the aesthetics of film noir, expressionism, melodrama and documentary. The aesthetics depict a sense of romantic longing, as smoky bars, exotic locations, the foggy runway and wartime costume all contribute to the film's classic look.

The overall aesthetic also stems from Warners' 1940s house style, with low-key lighting, and a combination of a downbeat style found in Warners' detective films and a nostalgic romanticism typical of their melodramas. The film's aesthetic also reflects film scholar Dana Pollen's argument that *Casablanca* is typical of a more modern, tough-minded Hollywood cinema of the 1940s (cited in Geiger & Rutsky, 2013).

Independent activity
Analyse this memorable still from *Casablanca*. How does it reflect the overall aesthetic of the film? Consider the use of lighting, costume and location.

Independent activity
Watch the film *Mildred Pierce* (Curtiz, 1945), another Warner Brothers film also directed by Michael Curtiz. Do you notice any similarities with *Casablanca* in the overall aesthetic of the film?

Bonnie and Clyde

Bonnie and Clyde's overall aesthetic is an amalgamation of French New Wave films and a homage to Classical Hollywood films. The use of iconic music, fast motion, slow motion and extreme close-ups illustrates how *Bonnie and Clyde* merged the aesthetics of New Wave filmmaking with Hollywood cinema. The colours used in *Bonnie and Clyde* reflect the barren farmlands of Texas during the Great Depression, with various shades of yellow, brown, gold and green.

Independent activity
Analyse the overall aesthetic of *Bonnie and Clyde* using the still here left to aid your analysis. Consider the use of colour, costume, setting and camera positioning.

Independent activity
What are the most memorable images from *Casablanca* and *Bonnie and Clyde*? Why do you think they are so memorable and iconic? How do these images reflect the overall aesthetics of the films? Screengrab the images and annotate them.

Consider the extent to which *Casablanca* and *Bonnie and Clyde*'s aesthetics are typical of the time in which they were made. Although *Casablanca* has a unique memorable look, it also reflects the look of Hollywood studio films of the 1940s. Likewise, although *Bonnie and Clyde* is set in the 1930s, the film's hip aesthetic and use of zooms, jump-cuts and extreme close-ups is typical of the late 1960s experimental style of filmmaking.

Representations

Age

Casablanca

In *Casablanca* Rick is an older leading character. Humphrey Bogart was 42 when he played Rick. It is necessary to the narrative that Rick is a middle-aged character. When we are first introduced to Rick, he is world-weary and cynical, a man who has loved and lost. We learn about Rick's past – in 1936 he fought on the side of the loyalists in Spain and lived in Europe for some years. The Rick we see in the flashback sequence is a happier, younger and lighter Rick than the cynical middle-aged Rick. Rick's transformation at the end of the film to a man willing to make personal sacrifices for his country reflects how American people should be willing to undergo change. Ilsa is portrayed as a much younger, more innocent character than Rick. Ingrid Bergman was 27 when she played Ilsa. Her innocence is often conveyed in the film by soft lighting, making her look angelic.

Bonnie and Clyde

In *Bonnie and Clyde* the main characters reflect the growing counter-cultural movement in the USA during the late 1960s. The counter-culture refers to a period when many young people were questioning the old, established order and norms. The feminist movement grew, as women questioned the traditional roles of housewife and mother. Attitudes towards sex loosened, reflected in more explicit sexual context in films. This counter-cultural attitude is reflected in the sequence where Bonnie kisses lawman Frank Hamer in a picture to send to the press. Here Penn wanted to reflect counter-cultural kids who had contempt for authority.

Gender

Casablanca

Casablanca conforms to traditional gender norms of the 1940s. Rick's masculinity, defined by toughness and cynicism, is typical of 'tough guy' characters in Warner's detective films. Ilsa conforms to traditional notions of femininity, as she is represented as being innocent and emotional. She often functions as an object of the male gaze and is lit in a manner that accentuates her beauty. It is Rick who has the most agency in the film. Rick makes the decision to sacrifice his love for the greater good. The narrative is also told through the perspective of the male character, Rick, and we often view Ilsa from Rick's perspective. In one sense, Ilsa functions mainly as a narrative device in Rick's transformation.

Bonnie and Clyde

To a certain extent, *Bonnie and Clyde* subverts traditional gender roles. Clyde contrasts with the traditionally masculine character of Rick in *Casablanca*. Bonnie is an overtly sexual woman in need of excitement and danger, yet the film suggests that Clyde is not a strong enough man for her, and indeed he may not even be sexually attracted to her. Clyde is impotent, as hinted at in the dialogue when he says, 'I ain't much of a loverboy.' Beatty's portrayal of Clyde reflects a new kind of male star that emerged in New Hollywood films, one that was self-doubting and playing against generic expectations. This contrasts with the self-assured, confident personas of male stars in classical Hollywood films.

Classic Hollywood gangster films focus on the male hero, with women in supporting roles as the wife or moll. In *Bonnie and Clyde*, the female character is given an equal role and one of power and agency. This representation of Bonnie as a strong woman reflects the civil rights movement as **second wave feminism** came to the fore.

Independent activity

Watch the trailers for Bogart's earlier Warner Brothers' films *The Maltese Falcon* (Huston, 1941) and *High Sierra* (Walsh, 1941). Consider how *Casablanca* develops Bogart's persona and representation of a traditional, 'tough guy' masculinity.

Second wave feminism: a period of feminist activity that began in the USA in the early 1960s and continued to the early 1980s.

Bonnie is introduced first in the opening sequence and we see Clyde from her point of view, an inversion of the male gaze. However, it is Bonnie whose body is on display in the opening sequences as she conforms to conventional notions of female beauty.

Women in the late 1960s march for equality

Ethnicity

Casablanca

Casablanca has a multicultural cast, mainly from Western nations. Although the film is set in Morocco, Moroccans are relegated to the background. The main characters in *Casablanca* reflect their nation's role in the war: Rick represents America, Laszlo represents French resistance fighters, and Ilsa, a Norwegian, represents European women whose personal lives have been devastated by Nazi occupation and the war. Supporting cast members were made up of immigrant actors. The studio's publicity department boasted that the set was the most cosmopolitan in Southern California because of the number of different nationalities that the cast and crew of the production represented (Isenberg, 2017).

For some critics, the character of Sam was quite progressive for a Hollywood film of the 1940s. Usually, black characters were relegated to the roles of maids and butlers, and were often crude stereotypes. Although Sam has a supporting role and is at the servitude of white characters, he is portrayed with dignity, and is Rick's confidant and friend, as well as an entertainer.

Bonnie and Clyde

In *Bonnie and Clyde*, the leading characters represent poor southern whites hit by the grinding poverty of the Great Depression. Black characters appear in the background and are not given lines of dialogue or any substantial role in the narrative.

Political, social and cultural contexts

Political contexts

Casablanca

For film scholar Thomas Schatz, *Casablanca* is 'an anthem of America's commitment to the war' (1998, page 317). To fully understand *Casablanca*, it is therefore important to have some knowledge of the political events of the time, as they are integral to the film's plot.

> **Independent activity**
>
> Describe the character traits of the main female and male lead characters in *Casablanca* and *Bonnie and Clyde*. Write a list of the similarities and differences between Bonnie and Ilsa, and Clyde and Rick. Argue in one paragraph how far *Bonnie and Clyde* is a departure from traditional gender roles of the classical Hollywood era.

> **Independent activity**
>
> Find images of the following supporting characters who appear in *Casablanca*, then write a description of them:
> - Major Heinrich Strasser (Conrad Veidt)
> - Signor Ferrari (Sydney Greenstreet)
> - Yvonne (Madeleine Lebeau).
>
> For each character, state:
> - their nationality
> - how their ethnicity is represented
> - who they support in the war.

1 Casablanca & Bonnie and Clyde, Imitation of Life & Night of the Living Dead

Casablanca, Morocco, was a French Colony and became a holding place for refugees escaping Nazi rule while attempting to get exit visas to Lisbon, Portugal. As a result, a black market in forged visas sprang up. These refugees were a mixture of political refugees, members of underground movements and escapees from German concentration camps. Jack Warner, president of Warner Brothers, heard about these refugee stories and together with associate producer Hal B. Wallis came up with the idea for *Casablanca*.

Rick is the embodiment of the USA's initial reluctance to enter the war.

Rick's transformation, from a self-serving character who tries to stay neutral, to a character willing to make sacrifices for the greater good, reflects the USA's entry into the Second World War. Here, Rick's personal relationship with Ilsa is intertwined with the political narrative. Rick's willingness to sacrifice his love for Ilsa sends the message to ordinary Americans that sacrifice is necessary as the USA must support the allied war effort to defeat the evils of fascism.

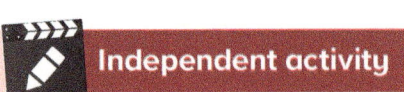

Independent activity

Analyse the final sequences of *Casablanca* and note how the film's political messages are conveyed through formal elements, including dialogue.

At first, Captain Renault represents the Vichy government, in power in France between 1940 and 1944, in French-controlled Morocco. The Vichy government was loyal to the Nazis after surrendering to them, which many French people saw as a betrayal. In the film's final sequences, Renault pours a glass of Vichy water, discards the bottle into the bin, which he then kicks over, symbolising his rejection of the Vichy government and Nazi regime, and willingness to stand side-by-side with Rick.

The character of Victor Laszlo is a symbol of the resistance movement. The resistance was composed of people who, under Nazi oppression, helped the allies at great risk to their own safety. Laszlo is devoted to resisting Nazi rule and willing to sacrifice himself to ensure Ilsa's safe passage out of Casablanca. In this sense, he is the true hero of the film.

The dates when *Casablanca* is set are important for understanding the political context of the film. The plot starts on Tuesday 2 December 1941 and takes place over four days. The film ends with Rick sacrificing his love for Ilsa on Friday 5 December 1941. On Sunday 7 December 1941, the Japanese navy launched a military strike against a US Naval base at Pearl Harbor, Hawaii. The bombing of Pearl Harbor led to US entry into the Second World War.

Bonnie and Clyde

While *Casablanca* was produced at a time when the nation was uniting for the war effort, *Bonnie and Clyde* was produced during a period of discord in the USA. Political events in America in the late 1960s influence *Bonnie and Clyde* indirectly. Rather than uniting the nation, the Vietnam War divided America, as many young people opposed the war. The 1960s was a decade characterised by violent events including: the Vietnam War; the battle for Civil Rights; and the assassinations of Dr Martin Luther King and Robert Kennedy.

The Vietnam War influenced the way Arthur Penn made the film, with images of graphic violence. Penn stated that people needed to view guns as terrifying instruments.

The graphic violence in the film's final sequences is politically significant, reflecting a mood of pessimism after a summer of riots and the rising death toll in the Vietnam War. In the film's final sequence, Clyde has a gunshot to the head, a reference to the 1963 assassination of President John F. Kennedy.

Social contexts

Casablanca

Casablanca was released in the USA on 23 January 1943, and was an instant commercial and critical success. *Casablanca* was released at the same time as the British Prime Minister Winston Churchill and American President Franklin D. Roosevelt were attending a summit in Casablanca. This conference was headline news and as such gave Warner Brothers plenty of free publicity, increasing the film's popularity.

Casablanca was produced for a mass audience at a time when cinema-going was the key leisure activity.

Bonnie and Clyde

While Hal B. Wallis at Warner was intricately involved in all aspects of the production of *Casablanca*, the executives at Warner Brothers did not approve of *Bonnie and Clyde* and initially only gave the film a short release in cinemas. However, the film gained popularity and upon its second release in theatres it became a huge hit.

In contrast to *Casablanca*, *Bonnie and Clyde* was produced during a period of declining profits and fragmented audiences.

Rather than appeal to a mass audience, *Bonnie and Clyde* targeted the baby boomer generation. The boomers referred to young people who were born just after the Second World War. They were known as a more rebellious generation, and many were anti-establishment and questioned the values of their parents' generation. Between 1964 and 1972, this generation developed a counter-cultural movement and campaigned for racial and gender equality, and an end to the Vietnam War. In the late 1960s, these boomers were now teenagers and young adults who were more receptive to more experimental foreign films.

As a result of the release of films such as *Bonnie and Clyde* and *The Graduate*, audience attendance in the USA rose significantly. In the UK, however, *Bonnie and Clyde* garnered a mixed response.

Faye Dunaway and Warren Beatty attend the premiere of *Bonnie and Clyde* in Paris, France

Students protest against the Vietnam War, 1965

Cultural contexts

Casablanca

Casablanca's cultural contexts are intertwined with its social and political contexts, as the Second World War had a profound effect on American society and reignited the war genre. Many Hollywood films were produced to help boost morale, with patriotic films in which ordinary people came together for the common good. In 1942, agencies in the Office of War Information were established to ensure that films contributed to national morale. These agencies reviewed film scripts and produced educational films. Many American filmmakers such as Frank Capra and John Ford were enlisted into the forces and made documentary and propaganda films.

Casablanca inspired numerous homages and parodies, including the Woody Allen film *Play It Again Sam* (1972), whose main character identifies with Rick in *Casablanca*. More recently, *La La Land* (Chazelle, 2016) references *Casablanca* both visually and in its narrative. The final scenes in *La La Land*, where Sebastian encounters Mia in his jazz club, reworks Rick's chance meeting with Ilsa in Rick's bar in *Casablanca*.

Bonnie and Clyde

Bonnie and Clyde's scriptwriters, Robert Benton and David Newton, were both fans of the French New Wave and were inspired by the unconventional relationship between the two characters Patricia and Michel in French New Wave film, *À bout de soufflé* (*Breathless*) (Godard, 1960). Bonnie's poem, in *Bonnie and Clyde*, copies the exchange of letters between the characters of Jim and Catherine in the New Wave film *Jules et Jim* (Truffaut, 1962).

Stretch & challenge

Watch French New Wave film *Jules et Jim* (Truffaut, 1962). Compare the letters exchanged between Jules and Jim and Bonnie's poem in *Bonnie and Clyde*.

Scriptwriters Benton and Newman originally wanted French New Wave director François Truffaut to direct *Bonnie and Clyde*. Although Truffaut liked the script, complications with finances meant he was unable to direct the film. It was star and producer Warren Beatty who said, 'You've already written a French New Wave film. What you need is a good American director' and brought Arthur Penn on board.

Bonnie and Clyde deals with the theme of celebrity, as the film was produced in an age of mass media, where celebrity images were circulated on television and in newspapers and magazines. *Bonnie and Clyde* were both portrayed in the media as self-publicists. Benton and Newman were influenced by the character of Michel in *À bout de soufflé* (*Breathless*), who reads newspaper accounts of his actions.

It was *Time* magazine that, in 1967, heralded in the New Hollywood cinema, putting *Bonnie and Clyde* on the cover with the flash 'The New Cinema: Violence … Sex … Art…'.

Institutional contexts

Casablanca

Casablanca is a hybrid of two popular genres produced at Warner Brothers: the film noir and the melodrama. All the key talent who produced the film were on contract at Warner Brothers, including the director, producer and cinematographer (discussed in detail in the auteur section of this chapter), as well as popular actors in major and minor roles.

Bonnie and Clyde reflects the move away from studio control. One of the reasons the film was shot on location in Texas was that executives at Warner Brothers were unable to interfere with the making of the film. Studio head Jack Warner did not like the film when he saw it, calling it 'the longest two hours and ten minutes I ever spent'. Jack Warner sold his share in Warner Brothers a few weeks later, signalling the end of the studio moguls.

Casablanca contains no explicit references to sex and its use of language may seem tame compared with films today. This was because *Casablanca* was produced at a time when the Production Code was in force. The Production Code was a set of moral guidelines, most rigidly applied from 1934 to 1954, which were voluntarily adopted by Hollywood studios as a way to prevent the government from banning or censoring films. The original code was devised under the leadership of Will Hays, president of the Motion Picture Producers and Distributors of America (MPPDA) from 1922 to 1945, and it is therefore sometimes known as the Hays Code.

The code set out a series of rules designed to ensure that films upheld moral standards and 'correct standards of life'. Film scripts were scrutinised by the Production Code Administration (PCA) office. Filmmakers developed clever devices to suggest adult content through careful editing and use of innuendo.

Bonnie and Clyde

Bonnie and Clyde was produced at a time when the PCA was seen as increasingly stuffy and outdated. The explicit scenes of nudity and violence in the film reflect resistance to the PCA. Indeed, just one year after the film's release in 1968, the PCA was disbanded and replaced with a ratings system that is still in use today.

Independent activity

Research the Production Code in more detail. List the rules Hays put in place.

State how *Casablanca* adheres to the Production Code. Then list the ways in which *Bonnie and Clyde* defies the code.

Specialist study area: auteur

The term auteur is the French word for 'author'. The French New Wave critics and filmmakers of the 1950s were keen to establish film as an art form, therefore it was important to ascribe an 'artist' or author to the work of art. These French critics credited certain Hollywood directors of the studio era as auteurs, including Alfred Hitchcock, Orson Welles, Howard Hawks and John Ford. For French critics, these directors were particularly impressive due to their unusual degree of control over their films while working in a studio system.

In 1962, American film critic Andrew Sarris expanded the idea of the auteur theory for American audiences in his essay 'Notes on the Auteur Theory'. Sarris argued that a director must accomplish a high technical competence with a personal style in terms of a film's overall look, feel or meaning. He proposed that an auteur director should repeat their signature characteristics over a group of films.

Later in the 1960s, critics began to question the focus on the director as auteur, as the theory did not always account for the collaborative nature of commercial filmmaking, and the importance of key figures such as the producer and scriptwriter.

Director Alfred Hitchcock at work

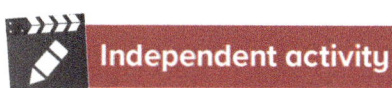

Independent activity

Watch 'The Origins of Auteur Theory' on Filmmaker IQ's YouTube channel for more information about Sarris' expansion of auteur theory.

1 Casablanca & Bonnie and Clyde, Imitation of Life & Night of the Living Dead

Independent activity

Choose one of the following directors who the French New Wave critics considered to be auteurs working in a Hollywood studio system:

- Alfred Hitchcock
- Orson Welles
- John Ford
- Howard Hawks.

Research the director's work (there are plenty of websites available on each director).

Define the director's distinct style in less than 50 words. Which films are considered to be the director's 'masterpieces'?

However, the notion that the director can be an auteur has not been entirely dismissed. Some directors in Hollywood still have a high degree of control over their films and key trademarks can be established over their body of work. Consider, for instance, the films of Quentin Tarantino and Tim Burton. Also consider their regular collaborations with key personnel; the style of Tarantino's films can be partly ascribed to editor Sally Menke, who, until her death in 2010, edited all his key films. Composer Danny Elfman frequently collaborates with Tim Burton and his notable compositions contribute to the overall aesthetic of Burton's films.

Today, the notion of the auteur is used loosely and expands beyond the director to recognise the collaborative nature of filmmaking, including the influence and contribution of key personnel and talents such as the star, cinematographers and editors. Even studios during the studio era can be given auteur status, as each studio developed a distinct house style.

The specification defines auteur as:

> any contributor who has had an impact on the film. This could be director, star, composer, cinematographer or institution for example.

For your chosen film, consider the contributions of key talent on the film and how key talents leave their 'trademark' on the film.

Applying auteur study to Casablanca and Bonnie and Clyde

Casablanca

Casablanca is a good example of collaborative filmmaking within a studio system. The film combines the talents of the producer, director, scriptwriters, stars, composers and cinematographer. Chris Tookey (2009) noted that *Casablanca* was

> proof that great films are often made not by auteurs but by collaboration between craftsmen, at uncomfortable speed, within an authoritarian studio system.

Consider the input and trademarks of some of the following key talent on *Casablanca*:

Executive Producer: Jack Warner

Jack Warner

Jack Warner entered the film business with his three brothers, Harry, Albert and Samuel, in the early 1900s. By 1923, Warner Brothers was a fully incorporated film company. Jack was critical of the Nazi regime and became fully committed to the war effort. Warners made more films about the war than any other studio. Jack Warner was known as a tough and committed executive producer. Along with his brothers, Jack Warner developed the studio's distinct style.

Producer: Hal B. Wallis

Hal B. Wallis

Wallis was responsible for putting together the budgets and recruiting actors, directors and personnel for each film he produced at Warners. It was Wallis who developed the idea for *Casablanca* by buying the film rights for an unproduced play, *Everybody Comes to Ricks*, for $20,000. He then assigned scriptwriters Julius and Philip Epstein to adapt the play for the screen. He closely supervised the production and editing of *Casablanca*, chose the actors and the director, Michael Curtiz, and even wrote the film's famous final line of dialogue, 'Louis, I think this is the beginning of a beautiful friendship.'

Director: Michael Curtiz

Curtiz was an Austrian émigré who was based at Warners for most of his career. He directed over 100 films for them, including some of their biggest hits. Curtiz was a highly regarded, efficient and accomplished commercial director who could turn his hand to different genres.

Here are just three notable films directed by Curtiz at Warners:

★ *The Adventures of Robin Hood* (1938) – an expensive Technicolor swashbuckler.
★ *Angels with Dirty Faces* (1938) – a classic gangster film starring James Cagney.
★ *Mildred Pierce* (1945) – a film noir melodrama starring Joan Crawford.

Curtiz is not usually considered an auteur in the same sense as Hitchcock and Welles.

Notable motifs of his style include:

★ high crane shots
★ unusual cinematography using props to frame characters
★ camera movement
★ subjective POV shots
★ high-contrast lighting and use of shadow.

Cinematographer: Arthur Edeson

Arthur Edeson was an acclaimed Hollywood cinematographer. He was contracted to Warners fairly late in his career, from 1936 to 1947. Edeson was adept at the two dominant aesthetics of film: realism and expressionism. His expressionist style can be seen in the cinematography of the classic films *All Quiet on the Western Front* (Milesone, 1930) and *Frankenstein* (Whale, 1931). Edeson was the cinematographer on an earlier Warner Brothers film starring Humphrey Bogart, *The Maltese Falcon* (1941). It is considered by many film critics to be the first film noir, renowned for its low-key lighting and use of shadows. In *Casablanca*, Edeson utilises the expressionistic low-key noir style.

Composer: Max Steiner

Max Steiner was a Vienna-born composer who created Hollywood film scores for over 300 films from the 1930s to the 1960s. He is often referred to as the Godfather of film music. Steiner was influenced by German and Austrian composers and symphonies, particularly Wagner's use of leitmotifs. Steiner created dramatic, memorable scores that matched the themes and characters on the screen. He was able to perfectly synchronise music to the action on screen (a technique known as 'mickey mousing'). The musical scores Steiner composed for over the credits of films were highly dramatic and set the tone for the whole film.

Bonnie and Clyde

New Hollywood films ushered in a new era of auteurs, as power shifted from major studios to young directors and stars. Many key auteurs emerged in American cinema of the late 1960s and continued in the 1970s. Directors such as Woody Allen, Martin Scorsese, Brian De Palma and Robert Altman all made critically acclaimed films during this period.

Screenwriters: David Newman and Robert Benton

Newman and Benton were frequent collaborators. They were both film fans and wrote *Bonnie and Clyde*, their first ever film script, in the style of a French New Wave film.

Director: Arthur Penn

From the 1950s to the 1970s, Arthur Penn directed some of the key artistic films of American cinema.

Penn favoured on-location shooting with small production teams. Many of his films reveal a fascination with American myths and culture, classic American genres and feature characters who are 'outsiders'.

Michael Curtiz

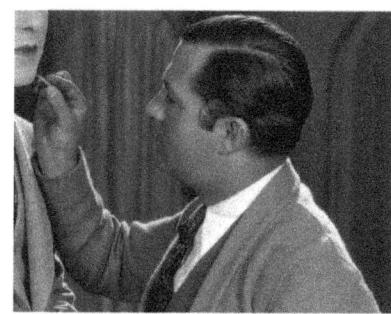
Arthur Edeson

Max Steiner

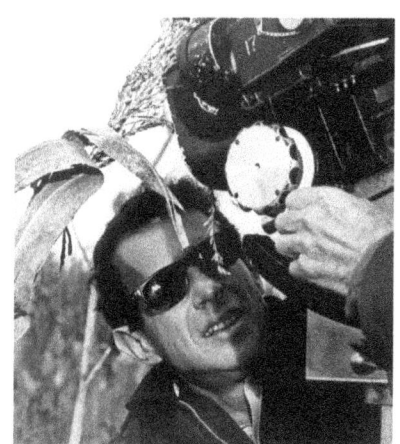
Arthur Penn

1 Casablanca & Bonnie and Clyde, Imitation of Life & Night of the Living Dead

Independent activity

Watch two Arthur Penn films produced between 1958 and 1975. Note any similarities in the films' visual styles, structures and themes to *Bonnie and Clyde*.

The following are three of Penn's most critically acclaimed films:

★ *The Left Handed Gun* (1958) – Penn's directorial debut, re-telling the story of Billy the Kid.
★ *Mickey One* (1965) – a surreal film influenced by the French New Wave.
★ *Night Moves* (1975) – a neo-noir that reflects the cynicism of mid-1970s America.

Editor: Dede Allen

Allen pioneered the use of jump-cuts and audio overlaps in Hollywood cinema. She often worked in New York and was given relative freedom when editing films. Indeed, her style became known as the 'New York School of Editing'. Allen trained a number of editors in her style.

Independent activity

Consider three key talents' input on *Casablanca* and three on *Bonnie and Clyde*. Make a list of where each key talent's trademark is most evident in each film.

Producer and lead actor: Warren Beatty

Beatty was only 29 years old when he produced and acted in *Bonnie and Clyde*. According to Robert Benton, Warren Beatty was a key influence on the film. It was Beatty who hired Newman and Benton, selected most of the cast and oversaw the script development. Beatty's involvement reflects the trend in New Hollywood of star-auteurs. Other key stars of the period, including Robert Redford and Jack Nicholson, directed and produced films.

Independent study questions

Q How do your two Hollywood films reflect their different social, cultural and political contexts?

Q To what extent is the director the auteur of your two Hollywood films?

Q What were the factors that led to a period of experimentation in Hollywood films in the late 1960s?

Q How are your two chosen Hollywood films' visual style shaped by their production and institutional contexts?

Q To what extent do your two chosen Hollywood films reflect attitudes to gender within American society at the time they were made?

Q How far do your two chosen Hollywood films engage directly with political issues or events?

Q To what extent were New Hollywood films a break from Classical Hollywood films?

Contexts: *Imitation of Life & Night of the Living Dead*

Social, political and institutional contexts

Social and political contexts

Imitation of Life (Sirk, 1959) is a melodrama; a glossy and glamorous studio picture that was typical of the studio system in terms of its aesthetic. However, it also explores some of the new dynamics in the evolving family unit in the 1950s.

The character of Lora Meredith was played by Lana Turner, a Hollywood megastar. Her most famous role in *The Postman Always Rings Twice* (Garnett, 1946) embedded her persona as a glamorous femme fatale. Her off-screen persona was aligned with her star persona; *Imitation of Life* was a comeback film for Turner after a scandal that involved her daughter stabbing Turner's gangster boyfriend in 1958. Turner was also married five times by 1958 (twice to Joseph Crane).

Section 1 Hollywood (1930–1990)

In the film, Lora is a struggling actress who rejects the advances of a sleazy agent to maintain her integrity and rejects her dedicated boyfriend's proposal in order to pursue her career.

One of the central debates of the film is her ability to be a 'good mother' if she is not married and is a working actress. A single mother was seen as a threat to the stability of the nuclear family at the time.

The relationship between mothers and daughters is a theme central to the film. In the 1950s, teenagers were a demographic on the rise. During this economic boom, teenagers had more disposable income to spend on fashion, cars and going out; they were freer than generations before who had to go to war. The morals and desires of teens during this time were at odds with those of their parents' generation. Teenagers were becoming rebellious; this was a threat to the status quo of the family unit. Rebellious teens were often labelled 'delinquents'.

Lana Turner

Lana Turner (right) and Sandra Dee (left) in *Imitation of Life*

Sandra Dee

In *Imitation of Life*, there are two sets of strained mother–daughter relationships.

Lora Merideth is the sexy, independent, ambitious actress, played by the scandal-ridden Lana Turner. Susie, her daughter, is played by Sandra Dee, whose star persona is of the 'squeaky clean' teen. But she falls in love with her mother's boyfriend.

Annie Johnson is the wholesome, down-on-her-luck maid, played by Juanita Moore. Her daughter, Sarah Jane, is played by Susan Kohner, who denies her black heritage and wants to 'pass' as white, running away from home and shutting down her relationship with her mother. She screams at her mother: 'I want to be white, white, WHITE.' Sarah Jane is ashamed of her mother and of her blackness. Her character is presented as an ungrateful delinquent teen, whereas her mother is dignified and grateful. The issue of gratitude is poignant here; the younger generations want more from life than the generation before, rejecting the concept that they should be thankful for Lora's benevolence that ultimately keeps Sarah Jane, Annie and, to an extent, Susie and Steve 'in their place'.

Annie says to Lora at one point: 'How do you tell your child that she was born to hurt?' This line frames racism for a white audience through the eyes of an empathetic, non-threatening mother who is the heart, soul and conscience of the film,

Juanita Moore

Susan Kohner

Independent activity

Do some research into the civil rights movement.
- What practices were used to suppress black voters?
- Who were the Little Rock Nine?

Image search
Compare two scenes in Imitation of Life

01:17:00–01:18:00 and

01:19:00–01:21:00

Watch these two scenes: where Sarah Jane meets her boyfriend and the one with the line 'It never occurred to me that you had any friends.'
- What are the contrasts between the two scenes? Consider sound and location in particular.
- What do these two scenes explore about the relationships between the four women? Consider how cinematography, performance and mise-en-scène are significant.

although her acceptance of her role of servitude in Lora's household is seen as old-fashioned by her daughter and problematic to contemporary audiences.

The Annie/Sarah Jane relationship is particularly significant when we consider the context of the era.

In 1954, the US Supreme Court ruled that segregation of schools was unconstitutional, but it took until 1957 for black students to successfully enrol in colleges in the South.

Famously, in 1955, Rosa Parks refused to give up her seat on a bus, prompting both outrage and support across the USA. This brought civil rights into mainstream news and raised white consciousness of the inequalities of the day.

In 1957, President Eisenhower passed the Civil Rights Act; this was the first push for racial equality in a generation. This new law meant that *all* Americans had the legal right to vote, making discriminatory practices (mostly in southern states) illegal. This did not change the systemic racism in society overnight (you could argue that the issue still exists), but it did move the discussion into the news, people's homes and the streets.

Susan Kohner (who played Sara Jane) is of Mexican descent on her mother's side and Czech on her father's. In the 1934 version of the film, directed by John Stahl, the character of Peola, played by Fredi Washington, was a black actress and activist.

Imitation of Life became part of the conversation surrounding racism in 1959; it was primarily aimed at white women, who could have read Lora as a 'white saviour' figure but seen her love life as rather scandalous. To modern audiences the reading switches – we read her love life and career ambitions as ahead of their time; we admire her persistence and integrity in those areas of her life. But her relationship with Annie reveals microaggressions, subtle unconscious biases that are not acceptable today. For example, in a revealing exchange, Lora is surprised to learn that Annie has a life outside of the household and is a pillar of her community.

Juanita Moore's performance as Annie is heart-wrenching, but her character appears to be an amalgam of two stereotypes: 'The Mammy' and 'The Magical Negro'.

The Mammy was an old-fashioned (even for 1959) representation of 'motherly' black women as contented domestics, a representation born in the era of the slave trade. To begin with, Annie is an unpaid servant – at one point in the film Sarah Jane plays a controversial impression of a 'Mammy' as she serves Lora and her guests. In the film this is framed as disrespectful; however, it could be read as Sarah Jane engaging in a form of protest.

'The Magical Negro' was a cinematic trope used to help white protagonists out of trouble or to act as a sympathetic ear, usually offering 'magic' wisdom to the white protagonist to further their journey of self-discovery. This character usually vanishes, often dying in some form of self-sacrifice to help the white protagonist. Annie's role in the film is to comfort Lora and offer advice; her death teaches Lora the importance of her relationship with her daughter.

In 1968, nine years after *Imitation of Life*, *Night of the Living Dead* was released. In the intervening years the USA had gone through a major shift in its identity – it became increasingly liberal and violent.

★ Movements towards a more inclusive and liberal-thinking society based on the equality of its citizens included the John F. Kennedy presidency; the birth of the women's liberation movement; the rise of the civil rights movement, led by Martin Luther King; the 1964 Civil Rights Act; the 1965 Voting Rights Act and the 1967 Summer of Love.

★ Incidents that demonstrated a backlash against new ideas of equality and liberalism included the assassinations of President John F. Kennedy in 1963 and civil rights leaders Martin Luther King (1968) and Malcom X (1965); the Cold War; the Vietnam War; the Cuban Missile Crisis; and the Detroit race riot of 1967.

Debates around the meaning of the film have raged since its release. Even though the matter of race is not discussed in the film, it is impossible to ignore when you consider the social and political contexts of 1968, 'The year that changed America'. *Night of the Living Dead* was released only five months after the assassination of Martin Luther King.

Duane Jones was the first black actor to lead a horror film. As Ben, he embodies all the heroic attributes expected of a hero in this genre. He is handsome, level-headed, capable and resourceful – a leader. Whereas Annie was passive, Ben is active – and angry.

The film initially follows Barbara, but she is quickly established as too hysterical to be the protagonist, as she descends into a catatonic state of fear. Ben's entrance into the farmhouse brings reassurance to the audience that there is a 'hero'. However, the characters in the film treat Ben with an air of mistrust to begin with, and some (Mr Cooper) with outright aggression.

If we consider the farmhouse to be a microcosm of American society, then the characters within it are representative of different factions within society. For example, Mr Cooper, an older white male, represents the generation of men who were seen to consider themselves above women, youth and people of colour, and think that it is 'common sense' that they should be both heard and respected, rights that groups which characters in the film represent are fighting for in the real world.

Ben is shot by the 'ignorant' sheriff's deputy, while the sheriff looks on. They do not recognise him as human; this is representative of the attitudes of some bigoted and racist Americans of the era – the death of Ben the charismatic hero is parallel to the assassination of Martin Luther King. The resolution does not offer the audience comfort; it is a bleak message about the future. The hero dies and the ignorant, mindless sheriff remains.

It is part of the frustration of the film that Ben is not listened to; the cleverest person in the room is ignored. This became part of the horror trope 'final girl' in the slasher genre during the 1970s; for example, in the *Halloween* and, later, *Scream* franchises.

Horror films often break down boundaries that mainstream studio films cannot touch. In *Night of the Living Dead*, Ben slaps Barbara – this act of violence was controversial and shocked viewers.

The zombie genre allows directors to explore violence and gore with gusto. The mindless, bloodthirsty 'ghouls' representing humans' 'desire' for violence are already dead, so the violence is 'fantastical' and therefore slightly more acceptable. The level of violence in *Night of the Living Dead* was shocking in 1968, and still is today. The elevated level of gore can be read as a response to a society that has been exposed to violence through the Vietnam War, with the 'ghouls' representing the 'enemy'.

It can be read that the 'ghouls'/zombies are a representation of the fear of communism. In the Cold War era, the enemy was an idea – the zombie horde is a faceless group with the sole mission of destruction of Americans. Because the enemy was an idea, it was faceless, it could be anyone – even your brother, for example. Johnny turns into one of 'them' and kills Barbara. This fear of others is known as 'the enemy within' and implies that you should be suspicious of those around you, even neighbours or family, because they could harbour communist beliefs and try to indoctrinate you.

Independent activity

Read Google Arts & Culture post on 1968, the year that changed America, to find out more about the social and political context in which the film was made.

Zombie/ghoul make-up design is a blend of the human and the 'fantastical'

Independent activity

Read the following articles:

- *The Hollywood Reporter*, 'The Lingering Horror of "*Night of the Living Dead*"': see *The Hollywood Reporter* website
- Roger Ebert's review of the film from 1969: see the Roger Ebert website. Warning: there is contextual use of the N word.
- Criterion essay: '*Night of the Living Dead*: Mere Anarchy is Loosed': see the Criterion Collection website.
- An essay by Brian Eggert about the film: see the Deep Focus Review website.

Night of the Living Dead **(Romero, 1968)**

> ### Image search
> ### *Zombies attack the farmhouse* 01:20:00–01:29:00
>
> Watch this scene. How and why does the cinematography change?
>
> Observe Karl Hardman's performance as Harry Cooper. How has it altered in this scene?
>
> In the moment when Karen kills her mother (at around 01:25), how is sound used to make meaning? How have the techniques of German Expressionism (page 243) been used to make meaning?

Independent activity

- One of the reasons why *Night of the Living Dead* gained 'cult' status was because it was frequently on television and easily available on home video. This is because there was a mix-up with the copyright. What was it?
- *Night of the Living Dead* is 'a great story of independent cinema: a midnight hit turned box-office smash that became one of the most influential films of all time' (Klawans, 2018). Read the article about how *Night of the Living Dead* became a success: search on the Criterion website for 'Mere Anarchy is Loosed'.

Institutional contexts

Imitation of Life was produced by Universal during the tail end of the old Hollywood studio system, when studios were trying to find new ways to get people back to the cinema as admissions were in decline. The biggest hit of the year was MGM's *Ben Hur*, a 'swords and sandals' epic that was a box office hit and won the Academy Award for Best Picture.

Universal was one of the 'Little Three' and specialised in production; it was and still is synonymous with the 'monster movie'. In the late 1950s, the studio was diversifying its output and focusing on vehicles for its big stars. Douglas Sirk directed Universal's 'A list' glossy melodramas, which were considered 'women's pictures' and therefore not as 'important' as male-driven narratives.

Night of the Living Dead was made in the early years of new Hollywood; it can be seen as an antidote to the 'stuffy' 'cinéma du papa' output of the major studios. This film appealed to and was aimed at young audiences; although it can be described as a 'B movie', it has none of the 'camp' horror appeal of many of the horror films to that date. It was made outside of the studio system and is a true independent film. It is also one of the most profitable indie films of all time, made on a micro budget of $114,000; its 'All Time Worldwide Box Office' (The Numbers (n.d.)) is £30 million. It has been added to the Library of Congress for its cultural significance.

Applying auteur study to *Imitation of Life* and *Night of the Living Dead*

Imitation of Life

Director: Douglas Sirk

Douglas Sirk, like Fritz Lang (Spione), fled Europe and the Nazi regime in the late 1930s. He was already an established filmmaker and obtained a contract with Columbia, where he made a wide range of films; his first was the anti-war *Hitler's Madman* (1943). His output was prolific. In 1951, he made four feature films, for Columbia and Universal, which was not unusual in this era of 'entertainment factories'. In 1954, *Magnificent Obsession* started an era of beautiful, 'lush' melodramas, followed soon after by *All that Heaven Allows* in 1955 and *Written on the Wind* in 1956. However, *Imitation of Life* is considered his greatest success.

Although Sirk made films in a range of genres, his melodramas are 'frightful, emotional warfare lurking beneath the facade of seemingly complacent bourgeois life in the United States in the 1950s' (Barson, n.d.).

Sirk's work explores the visual motifs of the glossy and lush world of the bourgeoisie, but within this visual signature hides a thematic one – the cracks in the facade, the broken heart of American society.

Other influences on the film include his frequent collaborator and producer Ross Hunter, and the forceful persona and performance of Lana Turner.

Night of the Living Dead

Writer/director/producer: George A. Romero

George A. Romero is considered to be one of horror's greatest auteurs. Known as 'the father of the zombie movie', he directed, wrote and edited *Night of the Living Dead*. You can safely say that this film is a demonstration of his 'caméra-stylo' and the singular vision of the director.

The shoestring budget did push the filmmaking into a specific style – the black and white film stock was cheap to buy; the homemade aesthetic was innovative but essential to production.

Romero's catalogue of work remained firmly in the horror genre, and '…of the Dead' became a franchise that tackled a different social issue with each new film:

★ *Night of the Living Dead* and racism
★ *Dawn of the Dead* and commercialism
★ *Day of the Dead* and the military (thecinemaarchives.com).

He returned to the franchise in the 2000s with three more instalments: *Land of…*, *Diary of…* and *Survival of…*. Although these later films are not considered to be particularly special, his contribution to the horror genre is undeniable. Without Romero there would be no *Shaun of the Dead* (2004), *28 Days Later* (2002) or *The Walking Dead* (TV series, 2010–2022). The auteur signature of Romero has not been assimilated into the codes and conventions of the zombie horror genre.

Independent activity

Research Douglas Sirk's legacy. He was underappreciated in his time, with his greatest work being dismissed as 'films for women'. Read these articles to find out what film critics think of him today:

- 'Where to begin with Douglas Sirk' (Cleary, 2021): see the BFI website.
- 'White Melodrama: Douglas Sirk' (Gallagher, 2005): see the Senses of Cinema website.

Section 1 A level: Varieties of film and filmmaking
(Not studied at AS level)

Contemporary American mainstream film

This chapter will help you prepare for **Component 1: Varieties of film and filmmaking** on the A level course. Alongside the core areas of study you will need to apply the specialist study areas of **spectatorship** and **ideology**. This chapter will use *La La Land* (Chazelle, 2016) and *Joker* (Phillips, 2019) as case studies.

For A level
One question from a choice of two must be answered on the **Component 1** paper. For this question you would be expected to write about one film from **Group 1: Mainstream film** and one from **Group 2: Contemporary independent film** with no expectation that the films be compared in your response. The full question is worth 40 points and should be allocated 50 minutes.

The specification says
La La Land is a throwback to an earlier era of Hollywood filmmaking as well as an original, highly stylised take on the musical romance – a love story involving a musician and an aspiring actress.

Joker presents a mentally unstable villainous protagonist which creates a range of complex spectator responses.

2 *La La Land* (Chazelle, 2016) & *Joker* (Phillips, 2019)

La La Land (2016) built on Damien Chazelle's success with *Whiplash* (2014) and like that film has the niche culture of jazz at its core. This film is arguably unusual for a contemporary mainstream American film, as the genre, a musical, harks back to Hollywood's golden age. The film's style boldly incorporates an eclectic mix of homage and expressionistic moments into its more conventional romantic narrative. Still, as a heterosexual romance, the film does in some ways typify contemporary Hollywood output. The film also had a reasonably large budget, two established, attractive, young stars and explored the populist theme of the American Dream – factors that help place it in the mainstream.

Joker (2019) is the origin story of the popular DC villain. It follows Arthur Fleck's evolution from mild-mannered social outcast to anarchist icon. The film was a hit with audiences in 2019 but courted controversy due to its portrayal of mental health, violence and masculinity.

This chapter will explore film form, context, aesthetic and representation in *La La Land*. It will also apply a feminist approach to the film's key ideological messages, and introduce the concept of spectatorship, exploring this feature in both *La La Land* and in regard to the various audience responses to *Joker*.

Contemporary Hollywood

Modern Hollywood is dominated by the 'Big Five' studios, who make and distribute film. According to StudioBinder (Deguzman, 2024), the Big Five are:

★ Warner Bros.
★ Paramount Pictures
★ 20th Century Studios
★ Universal Studios
★ Columbia Pictures.

> **Independent activity**
>
> Read StudioBinder's 'What are the Major Film Studios – Hollywood's Big Five' (2024) for background on each studio, and to find out about the evolution of independent Studios like A24, and the impact of streaming services like Netflix.

La La Land

The biggest success story of 2016, the year *La La Land* was released, was the $200 million production *Rogue One: A Star Wars Story*, which took over $530 million at the US box office alone, according to boxofficemojo.com (2016a). This would have been added to substantially by worldwide sales and merchandising, making a tremendous profit for Disney and the other major production companies and distributors involved.

However, *La La Land* was produced for just $30 million by Summit Entertainment, a subsidiary of Lionsgate, which also acted as the US and UK distributor for the film. Lionsgate had previously distributed very successful franchises such as *Saw* and *The Hunger Games*. The question arises, then, is this inventive musical really a product of mainstream Hollywood at all? It owes nothing to the **conglomerates** that dominate the industry and is instead fundamentally a passion project from a relatively new filmmaker. The story of how the film was produced sheds some light on this.

> **Conglomerate:** a company that owns and controls a diverse range of other businesses.

> Use boxofficemojo.com to find where *La La Land* features in the top 100 highest grossing films of 2016 in the USA. How does it differ from the films in the top ten in terms of genre and style?

Contexts

Institutional context

Matt Mueller at ScreenDaily.com (2016) provides great insight into how *La La Land* came to be produced in the article 'How Damien Chazelle Made "*La La Land*" for just $30m'. He writes of how Chazelle and composer Hurwitz, college roommates from Harvard, wrote the script and the score for this film, before 2014's *Whiplash*. The latter was a phenomenal success for a $3.3 million indie film. Its success was even more astonishing as it featured no major stars and had an unconventional theme – jazz drumming. It took the typical independent film route from short to feature via the festival circuit with the help of smaller companies Bold Films, Blumhouse Productions and Right of Way Films, and went on to be a commercial and critical success. It took over $13 million at the US box office and won three Oscars and the Grand Jury prize at the Sundance Film Festival. Chazelle explains,

> I made *Whiplash* in order to make La La Land, so as soon as the doors opened even an inch, we were charging right in with this script.

(Mueller, 2016)

Whiplash (Chazelle, 2014)

In 2010, Chazelle pitched *La La Land* to New York indie film producers Fred Berger and Jordan Horowitz. They admired the ambition and determination to try and produce a film that was, according to Berger, 'essentially impossible in the mould of Hollywood financing' (Mueller, 2016). This suggests that the film was considered a risky proposition for a mainstream production, as the musical genre does not have a secure and established audience in the present day.

However, the script was optioned in 2011 by Focus Features, a subsidiary of NBC Universal (Comcast), songs were written and pre-production started. Unfortunately, Focus Features pulled out of the project at this stage, clearing the way for Lionsgate to step in following Chazelle's triumph with *Whiplash* in 2014. According to boxofficemojo.com (2016b), in 2016 Lionsgate's revenue of $665 million gave it a 5.8% share of the US box office, so *La La Land* was certainly produced and distributed by a major Hollywood studio. The film was shot in just 42 days on location in Los Angeles, and Lionsgate gave Chazelle and his team the artistic freedom to make the film they wanted. In some ways, this nostalgic genre film had the backing of a big studio not dissimilar to films produced in Hollywood's golden age. In addition, Chazelle had similar levels of autonomy as directors in New Hollywood. He is an auteur, ex-film student director and shot the film on location, both of which were common characteristics of New Hollywood films. *La La Land* was, in effect, afforded the best of both worlds.

Independent activity

Read the film's 'Production Notes' online for detailed insight into the making of the film and insight into the key personnel (Summit Entertainment, 2016).

Social, cultural and political contexts

It has been argued that *La La Land* was released at a time in which America was craving escapism. The musical genre is by nature far removed from reality. Musicals are often vibrantly coloured and include distracting song and dance numbers and themes of romance. Movie musicals reached the height of their popularity in the 1940s, when audiences flocked to the cinemas to escape the all too real tragedies of a world at war. *La La Land* is certainly nostalgic, looking back fondly to the early days of jazz in its score and themes, and to the golden age of Hollywood and 1960s European cinema in its **intertextual** references to classic musicals. This would prove to be very appealing to an America looking to the past with affection.

Intertextual: the practice of one media text paying homage to or referencing another. An example would be Sebastian in *La La Land* swinging around a lamppost like Gene Kelly's character Don in *Singin' in the Rain* (Kelly & Donen, 1952).

Geoff Nelson's (2017) article on pastemagazine.com reported on a poll taken just before Trump's election in 2016. The poll found that 52% of all Americans felt life was better in the 1950s, and 72% of Trump voters believed this was true. Cas Mudde at *Newsweek* (2016) calls this a politics of nostalgia and argues that the UK is similarly affected – 'the emphasis was on a glorious past, sold as the blueprint of a magnificent future'.

Stretch & challenge

Read and summarise Cas Mudde's (2016) *Newsweek* article 'Can We Stop the Politics of Nostalgia that have Dominated 2016?' on Newsweek.com.

An alternative perspective on why the film's release was perfectly timed is that cinemagoers were hoping to escape from the turbulence, fear and instability of Trump's America. The title of John Patterson's (2017) review of the film in the *Guardian* certainly suggests this:

> *La La Land*: Why this Magical Musical Will Transport You From Trump-World.

Either way, in 2016 a lot of potential moviegoers were looking at the past with affection.

It is often reported that *La La Land* pays homage to, or borrows from, numerous classic musicals but it is worth noting that the film's more recent cultural context also points to some contemporary trends and possible inspirations.

Since 2010, a number of Best Picture winners and nominees at the Academy Awards have traits in common with *La La Land*. Consider 2011's winner *The Artist* (Hazanavicius, 2011), which harks back to the era of silent film in its themes and use of black and white cinematography, or 2014's winner *Birdman* (Iñárritu, 2014), which has a soundtrack dominated by jazz drumming. *Birdman* also has stylistic similarities

Stretch & challenge

Watch *The Artist* and consider the parallels the narrative has with *La La Land*.

with *La La Land* in its use of long takes, a trait also shared with Best Picture nominee *Gravity* (Cuarón, 2013). These films are bucking the trend as 'the average shot length of English language films has declined from about 12 seconds in 1930 to about 2.5 seconds today' according to James Cutting, a psychologist at Cornell University, in an interview with Greg Miller (2014).

Although Chazelle conceived of *La La Land* before these films were released, aspects of their style may have had some influence on the final film.

Film form in mainstream cinema and *La La Land*

Just as Classical Hollywood largely adhered to linear narratives and continuity editing and New Hollywood sought to break out of these rigid structures and incorporate art film techniques inspired by European filmmakers, there is a range of techniques and styles favoured by contemporary American mainstream filmmakers. The **tentpole** releases of most of the conglomerates of contemporary Hollywood in recent years have been **high-concept**, fast-paced, large-budget spectacles, often in the fantasy or action genres, with broad family appeal. Contemporary Hollywood invests heavily in production, special effects and marketing to maximise the chance of garnering massive profits. This can lead to an over-reliance on genre films and very few risks being taken.

When considering film form, it could be argued that contemporary Hollywood films can no longer be analysed in isolation from their intertextual references and that the way that audiences consume media – absorbing special features, repeating viewings and the variety of formats available – will impact upon their responses.

> **Tentpole:** a movie with a massive budget deemed by the studio to carry less financial risk. It is marketed heavily and given an extended saturation release. Its revenue is intended to help financially support the other films released by the studio.
>
> **High concept:** films centred on a relatively simple scenario that can be easily pitched with a succinctly stated premise.

Cinematography

The film is shot in widescreen and is presented in the 2:55:1 CinemaScope ratio, a popular form between 1953 and 1967 but rarely used today. This contributes to the nostalgia of the film and is set up from the film's titles, which start with a boxy black and white Summit logo before the screen visibly widens to reveal the famous CinemaScope logo in glorious colour.

Maintaining the nostalgia, Chazelle and the film's cinematographer, Linus Sandgren, filmed the musical numbers in a style that pays tribute to musicals from Hollywood's golden age. The song and dance scenes are designed to look like they are filmed in single takes, as this is how such scenes would have been filmed on the vast soundstages of classical Hollywood. To achieve this on more difficult location shoots, Sandgren utilised numerous ambitious and innovative techniques, but eventually he had to incorporate some cuts. These were cleverly hidden with whip pans to create the illusion of a single shot. The film's opening sequence, 'Another Day of Sun', is a clear example of the complexity of this shoot, as it involved the EZ-Pass ramp, which links two of Los Angeles' major freeways, being closed for an entire busy August weekend. This demonstrates the ambition and scale of a contemporary Hollywood mainstream production, as location shoots of this nature would not be viable for low-budget, independent filmmakers.

The complexity of the camera movements in the film's musical sequences, a variety of panning and tracking shots, take the audience right into the action and make the film more immersive. The audience is invited to be part of the dance. In an interview with IndieWire, Sandgren told Chris O'Falt (2017a) that the music had a huge impact on the film's cinematography. The 'dance' of the cameras on this production, stopping and starting and pushing into the action on the beat, adds a rhythm to the sequences that makes some cuts, often used to give a scene pace and tempo, unnecessary.

Another example of complex cinematography is the 'Someone in the Crowd' musical number, where Mia is persuaded to go to a Hollywood party by her flatmates. The camera follows the women dancing, first separately and then in unison. The shoot was proving to be difficult, so a wall with a double archway was built between rooms allowing Mia to go through one archway and the camera through the other. This is another aspect of creative cinematography made possible through a reasonably large budget.

Outside the immersive long-take musical sequences, the film has more realistic scenes where the narrative follows the fluctuations in Sebastian's and Mia's careers and relationship. These sections are generally filmed in a more conventional way but lighting is frequently used to draw the spectator's attention to a particular character and black out the rest of the scene. Sandgren told IndieWire (O'Falt, 2017a) that to create this intimacy,

> we move in and spot them up, which was also a metaphor for their dreams of being in the spotlight and performing.

Mise-en-scène

The backdrop of Los Angeles is crucial to this film and is one of the allusions of the film's title. *La La Land* is a nickname given to Hollywood that conveys its appeal to dreamers, those aspiring to stardom and immortality. The film includes iconic locations such as the Griffith Observatory, which featured in Nicholas Ray's 1955 film *Rebel Without a Cause*, and the famous 'You Are the Star' mural, featuring numerous instantly recognisable faces from Hollywood's golden age, painted by Thomas Suriya in 1983. These visual references evoke Hollywood's rich and glamorous history and reward spectators' prior knowledge of film culture.

If the images of LA featured in the film are examined closely, an eclectic mix of old and new is seen, offering the city an almost timeless quality that reflects some of the themes of the film. Sebastian is a character looking back fondly to the early days of jazz, and this nostalgia is reflected in the car he drives and the clothes he wears. He drives a 1982 Buick Rivera and he is styled after the character Roland in Jacques Demy's 1961 film *Lola*. Mia, however, has one foot in the past, seen by her huge Ingrid Bergman poster and wardrobe inspired by the costumes of Bergman, Judy Garland and Ginger Rogers, but is moving with the times, driving a Prius, which Sebastian implies is driven by most people in modern LA.

Use of colour in *La La Land* is an aspect of the mise-en-scène that has been written about extensively and, from the film's vibrant opening sequence featuring dancers sporting simple costumes with blocks of bright colour, it is easy to see why it has attracted attention.

Stretch & challenge

Read 'La La Land's Many References to Classic Movies: A Guide' by Aisha Harris (2016) on slate.com; then watch the song and dance numbers from at least two of the films she references. Compare the cinematography of them to the opening scene of *La La Land*.

Independent activity

Read Chris O'Falt's (2017a) 'How La La Land Cinematographer Linus Sandgren Taught His Cameras to Dance' on IndieWire.com for a more detailed analysis of the film's cinematography.

Image search
Mia and Ingrid Bergman 00:09:00–00:12:10

Watch the scene of Mia in her room after the audition. She returns home dejected and flops down on her bed; we see on her wall a huge image of Ingrid Bergman.

Why do you think the image of Bergman is so prominent? What does it suggest about her character at this point in the narrative?

> **Stretch & challenge**
>
> Read Julie Miller's (2017a) article for *Vanity Fair*, 'Emma Stone and Ryan Gosling's *La La Land* Costumes Were Inspired by These Old Hollywood Stars', and create a collage of images of the stars she references and the lead characters in *La La Land* to compare their looks.

> **Independent activity**
>
> Read 'Never Shined So Brightly: The Use of Color in *La La Land*' by Zosha Millman (2017) on filmschoolrejects.com for an interpretation of the use of colour in the film.

> **Independent activity**
>
> Read Chazelle's interview with Chris O'Falt (2017b) on IndieWire: 'Why "*La La Land*" was so much harder to edit than "*Whiplash*"'.
>
> What does he say about musical scenes being the breath of the film?

> **Independent activity**
>
> Choose two 3-minute sequences from the film: one musical number and a more realistic sequence. Compare the editing.

> **Image search**
> ***The dinner scene***
> 01:17:00–01:24:18
>
> Watch the dinner scene. How is the aesthetic of this scene different to the majority of the film, and why? Consider the lighting composition, use of colour and shadow. Consider how the sound and cinematography contribute to the tonal shift in the scene.

Numerous locations in the film were repainted or dramatically lit to create a stimulating, colourful, unreal world. Part of the reason for this was to make the transitions between the colourful musical sequences and scenes of everyday life less jarring. Mary Zophres, the film's costume designer, spoke to the *Los Angeles Times* about the film's expressionistic use of colour (Ordona, 2017). She explained that the colour in the scenes dissipate as the film progresses because it's an expression of the lead characters' romantic emotion. This is why Mia is wearing just black and white at her one-woman show.

Editing

Tom Cross, the film's editor, and Chazelle had a very experimental approach to putting the film together, and the editing process was consequently lengthy and involved. The finished film has two distinct editing styles: dream-like musical sequences consisting of extended takes with limited cuts; and the more realistic everyday life scenes comprising shorter takes with a much faster-paced edit. Striking the balance between these two styles was the greatest challenge for the filmmakers.

Two useful scenes to compare when considering the film's editing are the opening freeway sequence and the dinner scene. The opening demonstrates how spectacular and immersive the long take can be. The sequence works to establish the film as a musical from the outset and as Cross told the *Hollywood Reporter*,

> the final touch was when we put the title of the film on the last downbeat of the musical number, so it kind of separated that number from the rest of the movie in a way that felt like an overture.
>
> (Giardina, 2016)

Overtures, pieces of music used at the beginning of films to set the tone, are a staple of musicals with notable examples being *South Pacific* (Logan, 1958), *West Side Story* (Wise & Robbins, 1961) and *Sweet Charity* (Fosse, 1969). So, as well as establishing a location, introducing our protagonists and setting the film's mood, the overture places the film in a long line of classic films in the musical genre.

The dinner scene, in contrast, illustrates perfectly how faster cuts can help ramp up the tension and convey to the audience the conflict arising in the relationship. The editing technique used was referred to by Chazelle as 'a staccato cutting pattern' (O'Falt, 2017b) that incorporated a series of short take close-ups creating a claustrophobic stilted atmosphere. As the conversation becomes more strained, the camera moves in from over-the-shoulder shots, with them both in the frame, to close-ups isolating them from each other and capturing their escalating emotions. The only cutaway in the scene, the record reaching the end, could be read as symbolic of their relationship declining. The diegetic music from the record stopping, leaving silence, contributes to this heightening of tension.

> **Stretch & challenge**
>
> Listen to the podcast featuring Chazelle and the film's editor Tom Cross discussing their process and make notes about it. The podcast is available on IndieWire (O'Falt, 2017b).

Sound

As stated earlier, Chazelle worked closely with Justin␣urwitz, the score composer, from the film's inception. They previously collaborated on Chazelle's earlier films, jazz musical *Guy and Madeline on a Park Bench* (2009) and *Whiplash*. Their biggest challenge in creating the multifaceted soundtrack for the film was creating music that sounded timeless enough to evoke the classic musical but also captured wide-ranging emotions, as the film is about complex characters experiencing love, heartbreak, joy and disappointment.

The music and lyrics reveal an awful lot about the characters. Sebastian is seen performing a range of different musical styles, from the jazz he loves to banal 1980s pop covers. Ryan Gosling spent three months learning to play piano for the role; his quest for authenticity was not dissimilar to Sebastian's jazz preservationist ideals. The range of music he has to play contributes to the film's love affair with the past as the traditional music is celebrated and commercial pop derided. Consider Mia's dance at the 1980s party and the dancers who take to the stage at The Messengers' concert as evidence of this.

This could be read as a précis of the film's core ideology: those who take risks in pursuit of their dreams should be commended and rewarded.

The music is not the only aspect of sound required to make the film feel like an authentic classic Hollywood musical. Sound editor Ai-Ling Lee explained to *Deadline* (Grobar, 2017) that, in the duet scene, when Mia and Sebastian are dancing, many different kinds of shoes and surfaces were tried to replicate the sound of Fred and Ginger.

Performance

The lead roles in *La La Land* presented an extra challenge for casting as the actors had to be able to sing and dance, and, as Chazelle told *Variety*, 'those worlds don't overlap as much as they used to' (McNary, 2017).

Chazelle also wanted the singing to be conversational, so that it felt like singing but not singing (McNary, 2017).

Achieving this is key to the performances in the film feeling naturalistic and authentic within the highly artificial genre of a musical. Part of the verisimilitude comes from the genuine palpable connection and affection between the lead actors. Emma Stone and Ryan Gosling appear on screen together for a third time in this film, having co-starred in *Crazy, Stupid, Love* (Ficarra & Requa, 2011) and *Gangster Squad* (Fleischer, 2013). Producer Fred Berger told ScreenDaily that Ryan and Emma were 'the beating heart of the movie' (Mueller, 2016).

This on-screen chemistry between stars is an indefinable yet powerful pull to audiences and has been since the heyday of Hollywood when fans would flock to see Bogart and Bacall or Tracy and Hepburn sizzle on screen.

Independent activity

Listen to the film's soundtrack and consider the lyrics of the songs 'City of Stars' and 'Someone in the Crowd'. Note what they bring to your understanding of the characters.

Independent activity

Watch two scenes of Sebastian playing piano or keyboard, one of him playing the jazz he loves and another of him playing commercial pop music. Make notes on body language and facial expression, and how these convey the character's feelings in these scenes.

Independent activity

Read Matt Grobar's (2017) article 'From "Boogie Nights" to "Mean Streets"' to discover more about the process of recording sound for *La La Land*.

Crazy, Stupid, Love (Ficarra & Requa, 2011)

Bogart and Bacall in *To Have and Have Not* (Hawks, 1944)

Stretch & challenge

Watch Mia's first audition sequence and note how the cinematography encourages the audience to focus on aspects of performance. List the techniques used.

Stretch & challenge

Watch and take notes from the *Vanity Fair* video '*La La Land*'s Choreographer Explains the Freeway Dance Scene' available on YouTube.

Independent activity

Read Julie Miller's article for *Vanity Fair*, 'The Clever Tricks that Made *La La Land* Look Technicolor and Timeless' (2017b), to gain insight into the film's production design, a key part of its aesthetic.

Stretch & challenge

Read the complete *New York Times* article 'LA Transcendental: How *La La Land* Chases the Sublime' by Mekado Murphy (2016) and use the films and artists referenced to create a mood board for *La La Land*.

Independent activity

Find three frames from the film that have a similar tone and atmosphere to Hopper's painting *Nighthawks* (below). List the techniques used to create this mood.

Edward Hopper, *Nighthawks* (1942)

Emma Stone won the Academy Award and Screen Actors Guild award for Best Actress for her role in *La La Land*. in both ceremonies the clip used to demonstrate her skill is the sequence in which Sebastian turns up at her family home to persuade her to go back to LA and audition for the film role that launches her career. Analysis of this sequence points to some of her strengths as an actress, as Stone's extraordinarily expressive face and large eyes display emotion clearly. Another useful sequence for exploring this is Mia's first audition scene in the film.

As a musical, the range of performance is more varied than in films from other genres. Alongside acting, time should be spent considering the styles of dance seen and the genres of the music performed and how these impact on delivery.

Aesthetics

As explored earlier, a crucial part of *La La Land*'s aesthetic is its combination of old and new. Chazelle told ScreenDaily that he wanted to combine an MGM musical with a modern landscape and characters, experiencing a life where their dreams didn't always match up to the old films (Mueller, 2016).

One key inspiration was Jacques Demy, whose 1964 film *The Umbrellas of Cherbourg* was described by Chazelle as the 'most perfect in form that I know' (DW, 2017). This was just one of the films screened by Chazelle for the cast and crew to help convey his desired aesthetic; others included Hollywood classics *Top Hat* (Sandrich, 1935) and *Singin' in the Rain* (Kelly & Donen, 1952).

Alongside film, art was an influence on the overall look of *La La Land*. In the *New York Times* article 'LA Transcendental: How *La La Land* Chases the Sublime', Mekado Murphy (2016) comments on the film's lighting, saying of the Griffith Observatory scenes that the way in which Chazelle captured the building and the city called to mind the art of Edward Hopper.

Murphy's observation is extended by Dave Calhoun in *Time Out* (2016), applying it to the film as a whole and incorporating a reference to the director of *The Umbrellas of Cherbourg* (Demy, 1964). He says that the look of Los Angeles 'could be called Demy meets Edward Hopper' because of the use of pastels, soft light, twilight and street lamps.

Chazelle describes the processes used to achieve this aesthetic in the *New York Times* (Murphy, 2016) speaking of the decision to,

> use real LA, do things in-camera without digital effects, but try to find those moments where real life looks as fake as possible.

Billy Stevenson (2017), on the Senses of Cinema website, points to other inspirations, suggesting the shots used in the film,

> resemble the kind of hyper-cinematic stylisation pioneered by artists like Jeff Wall and Gregory Crewdson.

There is a notable section of the film, the epilogue, with a very different expressionistic aesthetic when the spectator is shown what might have occurred if the couple had travelled to Paris together. These sequences evoke films such as *An American in Paris* (Minelli, 1951) and break from the relative realism seen earlier in the film by using imaginative theatrical sets and inventive techniques.

Sound contributes to a film's overall aesthetic and Chazelle had a clear concept of how he wanted the city of LA to sound. He gave the sound editors film references of *Mean Streets* (Scorsese, 1973) and *Boogie Nights* (Anderson, 1997) to inspire them to capture the bustling ambient sounds of a major city.

Representations

Contemporary Hollywood still has a long way to go with regards to the depiction of diverse social groups as explored in the Representation section of this book (pages 44–57). To summarise,

> White, straight, able-bodied men remain the norm on screen in film.
>
> (USC, 2017)

This is particularly pertinent for this module as the films considered in the USC research that provided these findings were from the mainstream. In fact, *La La Land* was one of the films analysed. A lack of diversity among those behind the camera is a contributing factor to this problem, which is still persisting in contemporary Hollywood. In 2014, film producer and writer Stephen Follows discovered that women make up only 23% of crew members on the 2,000 highest grossing films of the past 20 years.

Age

The ages of the two lead characters in *La La Land* are relevant to the narrative in that they are both experiencing something of a crisis with regards to their careers, which could be exacerbated by their ages. Mia, the barista who wants to be a movie star, and Sebastian, the jazz purist who wants to run his own club but can't hold down a steady job, are torn between their dreams and the reality of making a living. Mia confronts this when trying to talk her way out of returning to LA for the audition that launches her career, 'you change your dreams and then you grow up'.

She responds to Sebastian's accusations that she is a baby by saying, 'I'm not a baby, I'm trying to grow up.' This notion of 'growing up' and facing reality is central to the film and can be seen again in their argument over dinner about Sebastian's commitments with The Messengers. He says, 'this is what you wanted from me' and clarifies, 'to be in a band, to have a steady job'. He tries to justify his decision to sacrifice his artistic integrity in favour of a steady income by stating, 'it's time to grow up'.

The ages of the characters and their stages in life changed from the original screenplay and initial casting of Emma Watson and Miles Teller as the leads. Casting slightly older actors contributes a little more urgency to the characters' dreams and ambitions that shapes the film's narrative.

Gender

Critics of the gender representation in this film have suggested that Mia is quite a passive character and that her key decisions and actions are motivated by Sebastian. There is certainly evidence to support this perspective on the film, as it is Sebastian that comes to find Mia at work after their first meeting and he is instrumental in persuading her to put on her one-woman show, and he attends the audition that launches her career. Mia is also shown as an audience member at many of Sebastian's performances, passively watching him actively performing.

The counter-argument to this is that Mia leads this narrative as the audience is placed with her for the first few scenes and it is arguably Mia who achieves the most success by the end. This argument is explored in more depth later in this chapter when a feminist ideological reading of the film is offered (pages 120–122).

Sebastian's sense of masculinity is a key feature of the film and his insecurity about it motivates some of the decisions he makes. It can be seen in the brief standoff he has with Bill, his employer at the restaurant, which sees Sebastian capitulate as he soon realises that he has no power in the negotiation because he needs the job.

Independent activity

Re-watch the epilogue. Consider the looks in this scene in relation to the aesthetic of the rest of the film. What impact do you think the combination of such different styles has on your response to the narrative?

Independent activity

Choose a scene set in a busy city street from *La La Land*, *Mean Streets* and *Boogie Nights*, and compare the sounds used to convey the pace and atmosphere of an urban location.

The scene is echoed later at the party where Sebastian and Mia meet, as he says of the singer in his 1980s cover band, 'he doesn't tell me what to do'. Mia replies, 'he just told you what to do', to which he rather pathetically argues, 'I know I let him.' In these examples Sebastian's sense of emasculation is used largely for comic effect but it has more serious implications in the narrative when it becomes clear that he takes the sell-out job that compromises his artistic integrity, playing keyboard for The Messengers, to satisfy the traditionally masculine breadwinner role that he mistakenly thinks Mia wants him to adopt.

> **Image search**
> ### Sebastian and Bill 00:25:00–00:26:00
> Watch the scene in which Sebastian has a brief standoff with Bill. How does Chazelle use **proxemics** to establish power dynamics?

Proxemics: the positioning of characters in relation to each other, props and location.

Independent activity
Read 'The Politics of Nostalgia' by Samuel Earle (2017) on Jacobinmag.com. How does Earle explore this trend for looking to the past?

Ethnicity

A more problematic aspect of the nostalgic appeal of the film, explored earlier in the political context section (page 109), is, according to some critics, its underrepresentation of characters from minority ethnic groups.

The others, in some criticisms of *La La Land*, are the significant black American and Hispanic populations of Los Angeles that it has been claimed are underrepresented in the film. The film's opening sequence includes a diverse cast and minority characters can be seen throughout the film but these are predominantly peripheral characters who play no real role in the narrative.

The only major role for a black actor is John Legend's role as Keith, the lead singer of The Messengers. His portrayal could also elicit some criticism as he is shown to have sold out the authentic soul of jazz music, undeniably music of black origin, to play commercially successful pop music instead. It is left to the white male lead, Sebastian, to try and save pure jazz.

The jazz club scenes do feature a lot of black performers and black people dancing in the crowd but invariably the camera and the lighting direct the audience's attention to our leads, Sebastian and Mia, thereby marginalising those of other ethnicities.

> **Stretch & challenge**
> Read Billy Stevenson's (2017) article 'From Los Angeles to *La La Land*: Mapping Whiteness in the Wake of Cinema' on the Senses of Cinema website to explore these ideas in more depth.

Independent activity
After watching your focus film all the way through once, uninterrupted, note the memorable moments or scenes and consider which character you identified with the most at those moments. Then re-watch the film, paying particular attention to your memorable scenes, and analyse the techniques the filmmaker used to create an impact on spectators and encourage them to identify with a particular character.

Spectatorship

For both the AS and A level exams, spectatorship is a specialist subject area for contemporary American film. Spectatorship is the study of how individuals view and respond to films, and includes an examination of how the film positions members of the audience – what point of view a spectator is encouraged to assume.

> **Stretch & challenge**
> Summarise the chapter on spectatorship in Jill Nelmes' *Introduction to Film Studies* (2011) in 500 words or less.

Active versus passive spectators

Debates around the issue of spectatorship have historically centred on a relatively simple question. Are film audiences a homogenous mass who all respond identically to the narratives and spectacles provided for them by the film industry or are they made up of individual spectators who play a role in determining their own responses to the texts they choose to consume? Active spectatorship theory suggests each spectator is different, so there are as many different responses to a film as there are viewers.

A useful way to think about spectatorship is to see the interpretation of a film as a dynamic interaction between the text and the audience. The filmmakers use aspects of narrative and film form to construct a story, which is often loaded with meanings they hope to communicate to the person watching. The spectator plays their role by bringing to this interaction their own ideologies formed by their past experiences and their own perspectives shaped in part by demographic factors.

Reasons for uniformity or diversity of responses

Film form

Early models of communication such as the **magic bullet theory** and the **hypodermic needle model** suggested that a largely passive mass audience unquestioningly accepted the content of, among other forms of communication, propaganda films and Hollywood movies (Davis & Baron, 1981). These models explored the capacity of Hollywood films to use escapist narratives to distract the population from social problems such as poverty and inequality. This is an interesting area of thought when the popularity of *La La Land* in a modern world facing numerous conflicts and injustices is considered.

The concept of the mass audience with a unified response has since been challenged but it can still be argued that filmmakers employ all aspects of film form to encourage a particular response from their audience. Soaring orchestral scores are used to try and provoke emotion, close-up shots selected to encourage identification and a rapid edit used to ramp up tension and suspense. All consideration of film form should include close attention to what impact the filmmaker is intending to have on the spectator.

Narrative

Decisions about how to tell the story and how to construct the narrative have a tremendous impact on audience response. Incorporating binary oppositions encourages the spectator to take a side and feel invested, using archetypes can lead the audience to have certain expectations of characters and creating enigma in the film's opening scenes can draw an audience in to seek the answers to their questions.

Also worth consideration is whether the narrative structure and style encourages spectators to become lost in the story or instead reminds them that they are watching a film. In relation to *La La Land*, Anna Leszkiewicz in the *New Statesman* (2017) said that, although the film is immersive, the experience of watching it is too 'referential' and 'self-consciously cinematic' to take the audience to another place.

The film's intertextuality may encourage spectators to become less emotionally involved in the narrative as they instead focus on spotting the references to art and classic films.

> **Stretch & challenge**
>
> Construct a diagram with the film at the centre. On one side list the techniques a filmmaker may use to try and elicit a particular response. On the opposite side list the factors about individual spectators which may impact upon their response.

> **Independent activity**
>
> Select three very different key sequences from the contemporary Hollywood film you are studying, ideally an emotional scene, a scene in which tension is created and an expository scene. For each scene consider how film form is being used to encourage a specific response and focus from the audience.

> **Independent activity**
>
> Consider whether the film you are studying is truly immersive and if not note the narrative techniques that remind the spectators they are watching a film. These may include, among other things, manipulations of time, direct address or generic **tropes**.

Trope: a recurring or significant theme.

> **Stretch & challenge**
>
> Research or revisit at least two of the narrative theories listed below and apply them to your contemporary Hollywood film. How might the film's narrative structure impact upon a spectator's response to the film?
>
> - Syd Field's three-act plot structure (1979)
> - Vladimir Propp's character functions (1928)
> - Tzvetan Todorov's model of narrative (1966)
> - Lévi-Strauss' binary oppositions (1995).

2 La La Land (Chazelle, 2016) & Joker (Phillips, 2019)

Stretch & challenge

Research the following terms and think of a film you have seen that uses the technique. What impact does it have on your response to the narrative?

- Distanciation
- Self-reflexivity
- Focalisation
- Subjectivation

Independent activity

Watch three films from your course in one week in different settings and using different technology, for example one on a laptop with a friend, one on your phone on public transport and, if you are lucky, one on a cinema screen in a quiet, dark room. Consider the impact of your viewing context.

Demographic: sector of the population.

Viewing context

Films are created with the intention that they will be seen on a large screen as part of an audience and indeed this used to be the only way films could be viewed. A spectator's response would be impacted upon by the reactions of fellow audience members, laughing at funny moments or screaming at jump scares. The large image makes the film more spectacular and immersive, and in contemporary cinemas the surround sound places the spectator at the heart of the action. Technology such as 3D and IMAX arguably heighten this immersion further and mainstream US films are often seen in these formats. Perhaps most importantly though, when viewing a film at the cinema that is all the spectator is doing, they have dedicated that time to getting lost in the on-screen world.

Compare this to watching a film on a laptop while chatting with friends on social media. The film may be paused repeatedly, breaking up the narrative, and the spectator may be distracted and miss important plot points or emotional scenes. The context in which a film is viewed will undeniably have an impact on the spectator's response to it.

Demographic factors

Demographic factors that may impact upon spectator response include:

★ gender
★ ethnicity
★ age
★ socio-economic background
★ sexuality.

Established earlier, big-budget productions aimed to appeal to as large a cross-section of the population as possible in order to secure a huge audience and thus maximise profit. To increase the chance of achieving this broad appeal, extensive audience research is conducted, including pre-production surveys and focus groups, and, post-production, test screenings. Feedback from test screenings can lead to scenes being re-edited or in some instances rewritten and reshot. The people invited to test screenings are from diverse social groups to give insight into which demographics the film is likely to be most successful with. This helps the production companies and distributors know where and when to screen the film and who to target their expensive marketing campaigns at. This suggests that demographic factors play a significant role in determining a spectator's response. This could be largely due to identification, as people often find it easier to relate to people more like themselves.

Preferred, negotiated, oppositional readings and *La La Land*

Films are generally produced for mass consumption, particularly mainstream Hollywood films, which tend to have high budgets and therefore require large audiences to generate a substantial revenue to cover costs. As established earlier, however, not every spectator will respond to these films in the same way. This can be considered by applying Stuart Hall's encoding/decoding model (Hall, 1973). This model explains that when creating a media text, in this case a film, the producers encode a range of meanings – place messages within the narrative. Some of this is done deliberately as they have a concept of the morals or ideologies they want the film to convey. Some is less deliberate as filmmakers, like anyone else, have subconscious beliefs and attitudes that seep into their work. These beliefs have often been shaped by the society in which the film is made, which is why the study of context is so crucial. The spectator's role is then to decode the text and decide what the filmmaker is trying to impress upon them.

Hall argued that there are three ways of reading and decoding texts:

★ **Dominant reading:** when spectators take away the meaning from the film that the filmmakers intended and accept what they have been shown relatively passively.
★ **Negotiated meaning:** when viewers negotiate the film's perspectives or ideas, agreeing with some of the film's messages but not all of them.
★ **Oppositional reading:** when the spectator understands the film's messages but rejects them.

Applying Hall's theories is arguably easier when a media text other than a film is analysed: adverts have clear, preferred readings as they want the viewer to buy the product; newspaper columns often use persuasive language to argue a very clear viewpoint on an issue. Films, however, are often more complex, offering multiple interpretations.

Applying Hall's ideas to *La La Land* could, however, work as follows:

★ The **preferred reading** is that the film is a romantic exploration of the transformative power of love and the American Dream, and the spectator leaves the cinema impressed by the film's artistry and is emotionally uplifted.
★ A **negotiated reading** could be that the spectator is moved by the characters achieving their dreams but finds their relationship unconvincing or unbalanced and therefore problematic.
★ An **oppositional reading** could include a spectator finding Sebastian's obsessions with jazz regressive and self-indulgent rather than inspiring and charming.

In general, contemporary Hollywood output, in particular the high-concept blockbusters that dominate the box office, tend to have very clear preferred readings. These films are less likely to use narrative devices such as open endings or characters with ambiguous motivations that encourage the spectator to challenge the message or seek an alternative reading.

Ideology

For the A level exam, ideology is a specialist subject area for contemporary American film. Ideology involves the main messages and values conveyed by a film, which are often revealed through the behaviour or beliefs of the main character.

Mainstream cinema often presents dominant ideologies, whereas alternative or independent films are more likely to challenge the prevailing ideologies.

We might therefore anticipate that, as a mainstream Hollywood film, *La La Land* would present to the audience the dominant ideologies of contemporary American society. The narrative will probably reveal a world dominated by white middle-class men, with women and minority characters playing secondary, supporting roles. Heterosexual love will dominate and a successful life would be one focused on finding fulfilment through gainful employment, happy relationships and the traditional family unit.

An argument could be made that the film does just that. Sebastian's vocation is explored and he achieves his dream of owning his own jazz club. Mia also secures a successful career, ends the narrative in a happy relationship and completes the family unit with a child.

Linked to this is another dominant ideology frequently seen in films: the notion of the American Dream. This is the idea that with hard work anyone in America can secure success and happiness and achieve their goals, even if their aspirations are very ambitious. Central to this ideology is the notion of equality of opportunity. *La La Land* is a film about dreamers and it could be argued that Sebastian and Mia achieve their dreams through perseverance and hard work.

There are of course alternative ways of looking at the film and a specific ideological approach that can be considered in relation to *La La Land* is a feminist one.

> **Stretch & challenge**
>
> Produce an example of a preferred, negotiated and oppositional reading of another film you have studied on this course.

> **Independent activity**
>
> Watch the *Saturday Night Live* sketch '*La La Land* Interrogation' on YouTube and consider what readings the characters are demonstrating.

The exam board's Guidance for Teaching suggests a number of ways in which a feminist ideological approach to film can be taken:

A By looking at an avowedly feminist filmmaker who attempts to make a film that embodies any of the central tenets of feminist thought.

B The approach adopted by feminist scholars in 'recuperating' or 're-validating' the women's picture, the family melodrama or the musical as films enjoyed by female audiences which also reveal important ideas about women's lives and their struggles within patriarchy.

C The approach by feminist scholars in studying genres and films by male directors which have been assumed to be targeting men and to expose the contradictions in their underlying ideologies.

D The approach by some feminist scholars which focused on theory itself and produced specific theoretical insights such as Laura Mulvey's in relation to the 'male gaze'.

E Something as simple as the ideas or subversions that contemporary female filmmakers bring to their films (WJEC, 2017).

A number of these approaches could be useful in taking an alternative look at *La La Land*.

A feminist interpretation of *La La Land*

As expressed in the gender section of this chapter (pages 115–116), some critics of *La La Land* express frustration at the representation of gender in the film, as Sebastian plays a pivotal role in Mia achieving success by helping her overcome her doubts and insecurities. He also fails to attend the performance of her one-woman show, despite the fact that she is seen on numerous occasions in the film supporting him from the audience. These interpretations suggest that the film plays into the problematic concept of men being active and driving the narrative, while women are passive and in need of guidance and motivation.

However, one way of applying a feminist ideological approach to the film is a consideration of the techniques Chazelle employs to place Mia at the centre of this film's narrative rather that Sebastian. This starts from the film's opening few scenes where, after a fleeting glimpse of a grumpy Sebastian caught in traffic on the freeway, the camera and consequently the spectator stay with Mia for the first few scenes. Sebastian does not reappear for 17 minutes, by which time the spectator has discovered a lot about Mia's ambitions and dreams, experienced the failed audition with her, and is therefore encouraged to care about her and feel invested in her wellbeing.

Independent activity

Watch three films made by female directors and consider how they represent women.

Stretch & challenge

Research and summarise at least three of the following challenges to, or developments of, Mulvey's ideas of the male gaze as outlined in *Visual Pleasure and Narrative Cinema* (2009):

- Kaplan and Silverman's argument that both male and female spectators can adopt the gaze.
- de Lauretis' idea that female spectators engage in 'double identification' relating to both the active and passive characters.
- Stacey's argument that spectators don't always adopt the role expected of their gender.
- Neale's consideration of gay spectators and the positions they may take.
- Dyer's exploration of how men are objectified in cinema too.
- Mulvey's own 'Afterthoughts on Visual Pleasure and Narrative Cinema'.

Anna Leszkiewitz (2017) certainly sees Mia as the film's focus and has an interesting perspective on the scenes of Mia watching Sebastian perform. She argues that these scenes don't really focus on Seb; they are important to the audience because Mia is watching, and she can be seen to develop emotionally through the ways in which she reacts to his music.

Aside from the angry glare Sebastian shoots Mia in the road rage of the film's opening moments, the audience is predominantly placed with Mia and look at him through her eyes.

> **Image search**
>
> ***The gaze*** 00:16:00–00:25:00
>
> Watch the first scene of Sebastian playing piano in the restaurant. It is a complex but interesting example of the gaze: a core topic in feminist film theory. It could almost be interpreted as a reversal of the Ernie's scene in *Vertigo* (Hitchcock, 1958) explored in the representation section (pages 45–47), but Chazelle makes a significant change. The audience sees Mia watching the piano player and expects that through an eye-line match we will then see what she is looking at: Sebastian. If at this point the audience was shown Sebastian playing piano it would suggest he is there to be looked at and she is the controller of the gaze, and thus Mulvey's notion of the male gaze would be subverted. What actually happens, though, is a non-linear cut to Sebastian in his car, allowing the spectator to be brought up to date with his side of the story. Only after the spectator has caught up with Sebastian do the two narratives, and characters, finally meet at the restaurant, where we see each of them looking towards the other: there is then an equality to the gaze.

Leszkiewitz (2017) also compellingly argues that, for her, 'this is Mia's film'. The audience sees her writing, auditioning and performing without Seb being there, and the film's opening and closing scenes are filmed through her eyes.

Mia achieves her ambitions and the American Dream, as she becomes a credible actress and star, appears to be in a loving relationship and has a family. Sebastian, however, in always looking backwards, has realised his ideas for a successful jazz club but ends the film looking forlorn and alone as Mia disappears into the night with her new partner.

Independent activity

Re-watch the fantasy sequence at the close of the film and consider Sebastian's role in Mia's ideas of what could have been.

Independent study questions

- What are the main messages and values of the film?
- Does the film reinforce, challenge or reject dominant attitudes within the society it is made in?
- Which characters are the spectators encouraged to align themselves with?
- What is the preferred reading of your focus film?
- What is an oppositional reading of your focus film?

Joker

Spectatorship

Joker (Phillips, 2019) is the controversial story of a man alienated from society. The controversy is derived from the viewers' changing allegiance as we morally evaluate Arthur's violent actions; the concern is that some people in society will have an alignment and allegiance with Arthur's violent desires, as if they are rioters at the climax that holds Joker up as a hero.

The iconic status of Joker is controversial in itself. In 2012 in Aurora, Colorado, a mass shooter killed 12 people and injured 58 at a screening of *The Dark Knight Rises*. At the time it was reported that he told police to call him 'the Joker'.

Independent activity

Read Yohana Desta's article, 'The *Joker* Didn't Inspire the Aurora Shooter, But the Rumor Won't Go Away' (2019) and summarise why, when *Joker* was released, there were 'worries of copycats'.

> **Independent activity**
>
> Read '"The System's Broken" and "Joker" Director Aimed to Explore that On Screen' from npr.org (Gross, 2020).
>
> What does Phillips say about the system and mental health in the article?

At the time of *Joker*'s release there was a debate in the media about the effect the film could have on the spectator. This can be broken down into two ways of reading the film:

★ **Preferred reading:** the audience 'agrees' with the way producers want the audience to interpret or read the film.
★ **Oppositional reading:** the audience 'creates' their own meaning, which is not always in line with the producers' reading.

The preferred reading is that Joker is a loner anti-hero, and the film shines a light upon those people forgotten and unseen by society.

The oppositional reading is that Joker is an 'Andrew Tate' figure, an incel, alt-right representation in a glamourised anti-hero. *Times* film critic Stephanie Zacharek (2019) dismissed the film, stating that Joker 'lionises and glamorises Arthur even as it shakes its head, faux-sorrowfully, over his violent behaviour'.

How these readings are constructed

Spectators read the film differently depending on their cultural selves and individual belief systems. Phillips has constructed a film where the spectator is pushed and pulled between pity for Arthur and fear of Joker.

There are a few key moments where Phillips manipulates form, even though this is a mainstream film. Phillips does not start with the establishing shot of the city to establish the verisimilitude; he uses sound to build the world of the film – the radio tells the audience that Gotham is dangerous and filthy. Phillips pushes into an enigmatic figure at a dressing table (similar to the silhouetted introduction of Heath Ledger in *The Dark Knight*). His back is to us; he is not receptive to the camera's gaze like a traditional star. However, the audience recognises this is the protagonist, as we are allowed subjective access to him; usually in a mainstream film the 'hero' must have an element of likeability or be an 'anti-hero' with whom the audience can align themselves with, often through humour. In *Joker*, Phillips does not use likeability or humour, but pain and pity as a way for the audience to emote and form an alignment. In a tight close-up we see Arthur pulling his face into a painful smile as a tear runs down his cheek. The spectator draws on their own emotional intelligence and personal self to create an empathetic response in the exposition stage. Phillips often uses a track away at the end of scenes to establish Arthur's isolation in an uncaring world.

Our reading of Arthur becomes more complex as his understanding of the world starts to unravel and his coping mechanisms (his medication, his mother, his dream of being a comedian) are removed. Phillips has led the spectator to sympathetically align with a character that has moments of heroism. His first murders are in self-defence, to help a female on the subway; the victims are Wall Street jerks. So far, this character trajectory is not out of the ordinary for a Hollywood anti-hero.

But the murders are a turning point. From this moment, our subjective access becomes uncomfortable. We see him dance in the bathroom as if he is an insect emerging from a chrysalis; he dances up the iconic steps as a metaphor for his journey to his true 'self'. Our observation of these moments is visceral; we are drawn in by the music and motion, but may be repelled by the juxtaposition of our awareness of his violent intent. We are shocked and repulsed at the sudden violence when he kills Murray and Penny, and other disturbing behaviour, such as creating an imaginary girlfriend, Sophie, and his alarming interaction with Bruce.

On the one hand, this film is a mix of cool early 1980s aesthetics inspired by the grime of *Taxi Driver*, big name stars such as Robert DeNiro and Joaquin Phoenix (which appeals to the cultural capital of cinephiles), and it is a sympathetic deep dive into the psyche of a criminal who feels as if the world is against him. On the other hand, does this film's cool, retro look and soundtrack glamourise the actions of Arthur? Phillips builds and then destroys our alignment, leaving the audience to question: When did Arthur go too far? When did I stop feeling sorry for Arthur and start to fear him? When did he become the Joker?

The final scene in the film in the Arkham Asylum is threatening but also played for laughs, with a Benny-Hill-style chase creating blood-stained footprints as the final image. Phillips' final image in the film concludes for us that we should be frightened of Arthur, and we should also laugh with him. He is gleefully acting out the desires of our shadow self. He is the ultimate anti-hero, the antidote to the seriousness of Batman. We are supposed to like and loathe him. He is, after all, the Joker.

Phillips explains that 'Art comforts the disturbed and disturbs the comfortable' (Gross, 2020).

Conclusion

La La Land is an intriguing case study that offers insight into how mainstream Hollywood films tend to reflect the dominant ideologies of the society in which they are produced. The film, however, invites numerous interpretations as some of the narrative devices employed leave aspects of the story open and diverse spectator positions possible. As spectatorship theory demonstrates, everyone watching this film will feel something different.

Joker is an example of a mainstream film that is challenging and subverting the dominant ideologies of the society in which it was produced.

Independent activity

On 6 October 2019, Mark Kermode wrote on Twitter (now X) about film criticism and four different views of *Joker*.

Find this tweet and read the four articles. Create a table to summarise the articles, and compare and contrast the different ways of reading the film.

Stretch & challenge

Read the articles below and then answer this question: Does Joker glorify violence?

- Terry Gross (2020): 'The System's Broken' and '*Joker*' Director Aimed to Explore that On Screen'
- Frederic Dodds (2020): "Joker" Proves the Power of Empathy'
- Ken Severson (2020): 'Is "*Joker*" Dangerous? The *Joker* Movie Controversy Explained

Section 1 AS: American film
A level: Varieties of film and filmmaking

Contemporary American independent film

This chapter will help you prepare for **Component 1: American film** on the AS course or **Component 1: Varieties of film and filmmaking** on the A level course. Alongside the core areas of study you will need to apply the specialist study area of **spectatorship** for the AS and A level and **ideology** for the A level. This chapter will use *Beasts of the Southern Wild* (Zeitlin, 2012) and *Get Out* (Peele, 2017) as case studies.

For AS
Two questions must be answered from a choice of three in section B of the **Component 1** paper. For these questions you would be expected to write about one American independent film. The first compulsory question is worth 10 marks and should be allocated 10 minutes, the second 20-mark question is from a choice of two and you should allow 20 minutes.

For A level
One question from a choice of two must be answered on the **Component 1** paper. For this question you would be expected to write about one film from **Group 1: Mainstream film** and one from **Group 2: Contemporary independent film** with no expectation that the films be compared in your response. The full question is worth 40 points and should be allocated 50 minutes.

The specification says
The independent American films characteristically explore non-mainstream cinema subjects and voices, and tend to adopt stylistic features associated with lower budget production.

Beasts of the Southern Wild features a young female protagonist within a very distinct and marginalised regional community.

Get Out uses the very mainstream genres of Horror and Comedy to deliver conventional spectator pleasures but also develops telling social critique and some challenging ideological questions for the spectator.

3 Beasts of the Southern Wild (Zeitlin, 2012) & Get Out (Peele, 2017)

Beasts of the Southern Wild (Zeitlin, 2012) centres on a young girl named Hushpuppy and her life in the Louisiana bayou before and after a catastrophic flood. Reviews of the film praise Zeitlin for his imaginative vision, and the film's themes and aesthetic are certainly highly original, surely a key aim of any filmmaker working in the contemporary American independent film industry.

However, in many ways the film is also typical of the output of this sphere of film production. The film is low budget, arguably targets a niche audience and was financed outside of the six major Hollywood studios. It was marketed largely through word of mouth, critical acclaim and publicity generated by film festival success and award wins.

Indie film *Get Out* (2017) was Jordan Peele's feature film debut, made for only $4.5 million and shot over 23 days. It was picked up at the Sundance Film Festival and released by Universal Studios. The film's social critique helped it garner word-of-mouth popularity leading it to it becoming one of the most popular films of the year and a 'cult classic'.

This chapter will explore both films' credentials as a way of looking at the contemporary American independent film scene, examining the films' unusual styles and representation of idiosyncratic characters. It will also further investigate the concepts of spectatorship and ideology introduced in the previous chapter.

Independent activity

Read and make note of the key points explored in Franz Lidz's (2012) article on the making of *Beasts of the Southern Wild* in *Smithsonian Magazine*, which can be found online. Write a summary of what motivated Zeitlin to tell this story.

> **Independent activity**
>
> Magic realism is a genre that incorporates magical or fantasy elements into a predominantly realist film. What aspects of this film fall into the genre magic realism? Note at least three examples.

American independent films

Bob Rosen, one of the founding board members of the non-profit organisation that is now called Film Independent, suggested four criteria for what makes a film independent. He suggested that independent films should be 'risk-taking in content and style', express a 'personal vision', be backed by 'non-Hollywood financing' and demonstrate the 'valuation of art over money' (Ortner, 2012).

Beasts of the Southern Wild certainly meets these criteria. The film combines the sub-genre of magic realism with the emotive topic of the fate of the dispossessed poor after a natural disaster. This could be considered to have restricted appeal to mainstream audiences and therefore convey willingness to risk-take on the part of the filmmakers.

This could account for the film initially having a limited release, playing on only four screens across the USA. The film was unquestionably the result of a personal vision and passion project for Zeitlin – the film having started life as a one-act play written by his friend Lucy Alibar.

In terms of financing, *Beasts of the Southern Wild* was produced outside Hollywood by Court 13 for just $1.8 million and funded primarily by the not-for-profit foundation Cinereach. The film went on to take a worldwide gross of over $21 million and was therefore a commercial success. However, profit was not the motivating factor for the production company. The desire to tell this story was what motivated Zeitlin and Court 13, as he stated in an interview "How Benh Zeitlin Made *Beasts of the Southern Wild* in *Smithsonian Magazine*:

> I wanted to celebrate people living on the precipice of destruction, hanging onto and fighting for their homes.
>
> (Lidz, 2012)

Court 13 is an arts collective that was formed far from Hollywood at Wesleyan University in Connecticut, USA. Its mission is shaped around the idea of representing outsiders and embracing the challenges that working outside the system brings.

The term 'outsider art' was created by art critic Roger Cardinal to describe art created outside the boundaries of official culture, so the term works perfectly for this film and the independent film scene in general.

Beasts of the Southern Wild is also a typical 'indie' film, as it challenges mainstream Hollywood conventions by foregrounding an exploration of character over a focus on action and entertainment. It also forgoes the stereotypical Hollywood happy ending which ties up all the loose ends for an open conclusion that, although hopeful, is steeped in sadness and loss.

> **Independent activity**
>
> What indications are there in the film's final moments of what the future holds for Hushpuppy? Write a paragraph summarising the messages of the final scene.

Beasts of the Southern Wild

Contexts

Institutional contexts

The Independent Film & Television Alliance (n.d.) states that independent companies produce at least 500 films per year, constituting more than 70% of film production in the USA. *Beasts of the Southern Wild* was released in 2012, a year in which independent box office takings in the USA amounted to $4.5 billion: 41.7% of the total box office for the year. From 2000 to 2011 the historical average percentage of the US market attributed to 'indie' films is 35%. This statistic is particularly impressive when you consider that America went through a major recession in 2007, so independent filmmakers will have had to fight hard to get their projects funded in a risk-averse financial climate.

Role of film festivals and awards

Film festivals played a significant role both in bringing *Beasts of the Southern Wild* to the screen and in publicising it to a wider audience, typical of numerous contemporary independent films.

Independent filmmakers often launch their careers by directing short films and Benh Zeitlin is no exception. One of his early films, a stop-motion animation entitled *Egg*, won Best Animation Short at the 2005 Slamdance Film Festival in Utah. In 2008 he made his first short live action film, *Glory at Sea*, inspired partly by Hurricane Katrina. It was conceived as a 5-minute film with a month-long shoot and a budget of $5,000 but became a 25-minute film that took 18 months to produce and cost $100,000. The film premiered at the 2008 South by Southwest Festival in Austin and went on to win the Wholphin award there and numerous other awards at festivals that year. With each festival win came publicity and credibility for Zeitlin as a new director to watch out for.

The Sundance Institute and its influential film festival played a significant role in Zeitlin's career as he was selected for the prestigious Sundance Institute Directors Lab Program, which annually supports just eight projects. It is a non-profit organisation founded by Robert Redford.

Having worked on *Beasts of the Southern Wild* in the Sundance Directors Lab, Zeitlin was eligible to apply for financial support from the Sundance Institute, as the organisation provides over $400,000 in financial support to Feature Film Program Alumni each year. The Sundance Institute/NHK Award, which includes a $10,000 cash prize, was awarded to Benh Zeitlin and Lucy Alibar in 2010.

The Sundance Festival's role in securing the film an audience was crucial. The film premiered at the festival to a standing ovation and received predominantly positive press. The film has a rating of 'Universal acclaim' and a metascore of 86 on Metacritic, a website that aggregates reviews from leading critics. In total, *Beasts of the Southern Wild* has won 74 awards including the Grand Jury Prize at the Sundance Film Festival and the Camera d'Or in Cannes. This has generated positive publicity for the film and led to the film getting a much wider release, with it being screened at 318 cinemas at the height of its popularity.

Award nominations, even without the win, have a huge impact on a film's success and *Beasts of the Southern Wild* was nominated for four awards including Best Picture and Best Director at the 85th Academy Awards in 2013.

The Oscar nominees were announced on 10 January 2013 and the impact of this on the box office takings of the film was startling. The weekend of 18 January saw a rise of over 2,000% in takings from the previous weekend and the film was screened on 71 American cinema screens that weekend having only been on four screens the preceding week. The television broadcast of the 2013 awards ceremony had 40.4 million viewers, so acted as great promotion for the film. As Keith Simanton of IMDb points out about the ceremony, the film being lauded by a famous star acts as, 'a super great trailer being played in everyone's home across their TV screens' (Allen, 2015).

Role of major studios in distribution

Marketing films is a costly part of the distribution process, with conservative estimates suggesting that the marketing budget should be 50% of the overall budget and others suggesting that for independent films this should be up to three times the film's production costs. A route commonly used by independent filmmakers is to secure a distribution deal with one of the major US studios which, according to the Independent Film & Television Alliance, 'have gradually become more marketing and distribution specialists in the US marketplace than production entities' (2013). *Beasts of the Southern Wild* was distributed by Fox Searchlight

Independent activity

Read Peter Bradshaw's review in the *Guardian* of *Beasts of the Southern Wild* (2022). Bradshaw describes the film as 'outsider art'. Why?

Stretch & challenge

Watch Zeitlin's short film *Glory at Sea*, which is available online, and make notes under the headings of film form:

- cinematography
- mise-en-scène
- sound
- editing
- performance.

Repeat this process for *Beasts of the Southern Wild*, then use your notes to compare the films.

Stretch & challenge

Research the Directors Lab Program and watch other films it has helped bring to the screen. How do these films compare with *Beasts of the Southern Wild*?

Independent activity

Analyse the poster below. How are the distributors trying to appear to an art house audience?

Pictures, the 'independent' arm of the conglomerate Fox, for its theatrical release in the USA. The benefit of an independent film securing a theatrical release is not only to allow audiences to see the film on the big screen and collect box office revenue, but also to encourage critics to review the film in the press. Fox Searchlight Pictures used a counterprogramming strategy to try and maximise revenue from *Beasts of the Southern Wild*. The film was released in the summer, traditionally the season of major blockbusters, to attract audiences that would find a more alternative film appealing. The benefits of having an established major studio take care of distribution is that it will have years of experience, significant resources and global reach. Fox Searchlight Pictures is part of 20th Century Fox Film, one of the largest producers and distributors of motion pictures, with thousands of staff and offices all around the world. 20th Century Fox Home Entertainment then released the Blu-ray and DVD in the USA, taking over $11 million.

Social, cultural and political contexts

Hurricane Katrina and Black Lives Matter

Beasts of the Southern Wild does not directly reference Hurricane Katrina but it is easy to see why audiences and critics alike often mention the film and the disaster in the same breath. The film does focus on the impact of a natural disaster on a community comprised predominantly of the demographics worst hit by Hurricane Katrina. Zeitlin maintains, however, that he did not intend the film to be a political one. He stated that although he feels strongly about environmental issues, he also wanted people who didn't believe in global warming to see it (Rea, 2012).

Hurricane Katrina struck the Gulf Coast of the USA in August 2005, bringing winds of up to 140 miles per hour. The storm devastated the communities affected and its aftermath was catastrophic as immense flooding occurred due to breaches in the levees – the embankments built to avoid such floods. Hundreds of thousands of people were displaced from their homes and estimates suggest more than $100 billion in damage had been caused. More than 1,800 people across seven states were killed, with the city of New Orleans being particularly affected. Eighty per cent of the city was submerged under 20 feet of water at the height of the hurricane. People of colour, elderly people and poor people were disproportionately affected by the destruction and loss of life.

The government's slow and ineffective response to the disaster provoked much criticism and protest. This response has since been investigated by the Federal

Stretch & challenge

Watch Spike Lee's 2006 documentary on Hurricane Katrina, *When the Levees Broke: A Requiem in Four Acts*, to gain greater insight into the disaster. Collect screengrabs from the documentary footage and compare them to similar shots from *Beasts of the Southern Wild*. Use these to assess the impact televised images of the storm and its aftermath had on the film's overall aesthetic.

Emergency Management Agency's internal watchdog, which concluded that the criticism was largely deserved. Some argue that the government may have responded differently if the demographic of those affected by the storm had been different. As Jamelle Bouie explained on Slate.com (2015), for black Americans this was confirmation of America's 'indifference to black life'.

Rapper Kanye West famously made this point to a large television audience at NBC Universal's 'A Concert for Hurricane Relief' in 2005 when he said that President George Bush didn't care about black people (you can find this clip on YouTube).

There are moments in *Beasts of the Southern Wild* that echo images from news coverage of Hurricane Katrina. Jamelle Bouie (Slate.com, 2015) asserts that,

> Black collective memory of Hurricane Katrina ... informs the present movement against police violence, 'Black Lives Matter'.

The film's messages and values certainly resonate in a world where social inequality continues to be a huge problem and campaigns such as 'Black Lives Matter' are still very much needed.

Film form in independent films and *Beasts of the Southern Wild*

Independent filmmakers often have greater creative freedom than mainstream filmmakers, as the financial risks they are taking are smaller. It is therefore much more difficult to summarise the conventions of independent films than mainstream Hollywood films, as by nature, 'indies' tend to be about doing things differently – defying conventions. They can therefore be more easily defined by what they are not. They are not as likely as mainstream productions to be genre films and they are less likely to follow a traditional narrative structure. *Beasts of the Southern Wild* is definitely a drama but it is also classed in the fantasy and adventure categories by IMDb and incorporates aspects of magic realism as mentioned earlier. In terms of narrative, the film is conventional in that it is predominantly linear but the Elysian Fields scenes could be read as real or figments of Hushpuppy's imagination. This openness to various interpretations is characteristic of independent films, which generally encourages audiences to explore their own responses to the narratives more freely.

Independent films are more likely than mainstream films to break the 'rules' of film form. The filmmaker may choose a shot from an unusual perspective or use mise-en-scène with greater symbolic meaning. They might structure a scene in a less formulaic way by foregoing an establishing shot or making greater use of contrapuntal sound to challenge the spectator.

However, film audiences generally do have a set of expectations of independent film. According to Grant in his book *Film Genres: From Iconography to Ideology* (2007), academic David Bordwell has argued that 'art cinema itself is a genre, with its own distinct conventions' (page 1), and maybe the same can be said of independent films in general. Sherry B. Ortner (2012, page 3), of the University of California, reflects on these typical traits, arguing that,

> One of the striking features of contemporary independent films is a pervasive darkness – of mood, of tone, of look, of story.

This can be explored in relation to *Beasts of the Southern Wild*.

Independent activity

Read and summarise Jamelle Bouie's (2015) article 'Where Black Lives Matter Began' to gain a fuller understanding of the impact the government's response to the storm had on racial politics in the USA. The article can be found online.

Independent activity

Does your understanding of the film's social and political context impact upon your response to Wink and Hushpuppy resisting the intervention of the authorities? Respond to this question in 100 words or less.

Independent activity

Choose three contemporary American independent films and three contemporary mainstream films and analyse the opening scene of each. Write a short essay on how these films use the elements of film form differently.

Cinematography

There is certainly a 'darkness' to some of the key themes of the film: disaster, poverty and loss. The settings, including makeshift, water damaged and mud-stained homes, reflect this. *Beasts of the Southern Wild* was predominantly shot on 16mm film to give the shots a grainy quality that reflects this grittiness of the Bathtub location. Director of photography on the film, Ben Richardson, set the film's cinematography apart from mainstream cinema. He wanted to 'shy away from shiny, sparkly visuals and keep the photography grounded' (ARRI News, 2017).

The film was principally shot using an Easyrig, which, according to Nofilmschool.com in 'Easyrig Mini is a Budget Version of One of the Most Interesting Camera Stabilizers Out There' (Hardy, 2015), falls somewhere between a Steadicam and traditional hand-held footage. It 'produces a type of movement that mirrors the movement of the body when the camera operator is walking around'.

This lends documentary-style realism to a lot of the footage and also places the spectator in the action, creating immersion. One useful example is the firework scene where the camera operator takes the audience running through the location with the characters. Benh Zeitlin explained his approach to cinematography to *Filmmaker Magazine* (Anderson, 2013) thus,

> I would direct the cameraman like an actor. Rather than giving technical directions, he had to perform like a documentary cameraman ... He had to be reacting to the world in the same way that Hushpuppy did.

This use of the camera to echo Hushpuppy's responses and the prevalence of shots either of her or from her perspective helps to keep her at the centre of the narrative and encourages spectators to align themselves with her. The opening scene demonstrates this clearly as the audience, with Hushpuppy, are down with the animals.

Zeitlin also makes great use of close-ups, combined with shallow depth of field, to focus the spectator's attention on one character blurring out any distractions in the shot. These techniques encourage the spectator to consider what a character may be thinking or feeling at a specific moment, thus foregrounding the psychology of a character, as is typical in independent films.

Mise-en-scène

Realism was prioritised when selecting the mise-en-scène for most of the film and is characteristic of a lot of independent cinema. The filming location of Isle de Jean Charles in south Louisiana, USA is severely affected by land loss, so conveys the sense of peril and emergency very authentically. The BP oil spill occurred just as filming commenced, so the filmmakers had additional challenges to overcome, which contributed to the film's theme of communities surviving disasters.

Independent activity

Read '10 Lessons on Filmmaking from *Beasts of the Southern Wild*'s Benh Zeitlin' (Anderson, 2013). What was his approach to cinematography?

Stretch & challenge

Create a storyboard using the first ten shots of the film to help you understand the way the camera is being used. For each shot identify the shot type, camera movement and shot duration, and note the impact that shot may have on the spectator.

Local artists and boatbuilders constructed the homes and other structures in the film to reflect the lifestyles of the inhabitants of the Bathtub.

The aurochs, an extinct species of wild cattle, are a less realistic but key metaphorical aspect of the film's mise-en-scène, and were inspired by cave drawings Zeitlin encountered on a visit to France. As Zeitlin told the French Association of Directors of Photography (AFC) in 'Conversation with Cinematographer Ben Richardson about his Work on "Beasts of the Southern Wild", by Benh Zeitlin' (Most, 2013):

> They were the mark our ancestors made before going extinct. The aurochs were always the building blocks of the film: it is the predator versus their prey, maybe a metaphor about the fearlessness in Louisiana because it tests them.

One of the most profound moments in the film is when Hushpuppy finally encounters the aurochs she has been fearing throughout the narrative and boldly stands up to them. The character directions in the screenplay state, 'Hushpuppy raises her chin in confident defiance' and 'the aurochs lowers her head with respect'. This body language conveys Hushpuppy's strength of character and fearlessness. Her simple line at this point, that 'You're my friend, kind of' suggests that she realises that the fear and challenges she has faced, represented by these extinct creatures, have been instrumental in helping her develop strength of character. The resilience and resolve that she developed in the face of adversity enabled her to cope with Wink's death and look to the future with optimism.

The aurochs certainly depart from visual realism but arguably help the spectator to visualise and engage with Hushpuppy's vivid imagination.

Editing

Hushpuppy was prioritised in the edit by ensuring that the majority of shots included her or were from her point of view.

The film is, for the most part, linear and follows a fairly conventional narrative structure for an independent film. This allows the audience to experience Wink's decline, from his appearance in a hospital gown approximately 14 minutes into the film to his eventual death, alongside Hushpuppy. Her naivety and youth, combined with the narrative clues foreshadowing Wink's death, could even encourages spectators to feel they have a better sense of what is coming than Hushpuppy and feel anxious about the loss she is to face.

Wink's flashback of meeting Hushpuppy's mother is arguably lent greater power by being the only such scene in an otherwise linear film. Throughout the narrative, Wink appears to be a character firmly placed in the present: pragmatic, hedonistic and living hand to mouth. To see him reminisce about meeting Hushpuppy's mother in such a romanticised, surreal flashback reveals a softer, more vulnerable side of his character.

Sound

The music of *Beasts of the Southern Wild* is frequently praised in reviews of the film, and orchestras have performed the score to audiences worldwide including events in London, New York and New Orleans. Benh Zeitlin co-wrote the film's Cajun and folk music score with Dan Romer. Music plays a significant role in conveying the atmosphere and life in the Bathtub. Zeitlin said,

> jazz-funeral culture is a huge part of the celebration sequence at the start of the film that defines the town. A funeral in New Orleans begins with these tragic dirges but then transforms into a celebratory, joyous party.

(Stevens, 2015)

This sequence, and this music, is crucial in conveying the positive aspects of living in a vulnerable place at a challenging time. The sense of fun, community, of appreciating life and the world is palpable.

Independent activity

Read 'Rebel Charm: Benh Zeitlin on *Beasts of the Southern Wild*' (Stevens, 2015) on BFI.org.uk. Zeitlin describes Court 13's process to the BFI and it helps to explain why the sets look so organic and authentic.

Note: you will need to look at this text again in the next activity.

Image search

The Bathtub

Select a range of images of the Bathtub. How is mise-en-scène used to construct meaning? Consider how the set design and character design can make meaning.

Independent activity

Look again at 'Rebel Charm: Benh Zeitlin on *Beasts of the Southern Wild*' (Stevens, 2015) on BFI.org.uk. Re-read the paragraph under the heading 'Was the editing process as complicated as the shoot?' Why was it important to tell the story from Hushpuppy's point of view?

Independent activity

Watch Wink's memories of Hushpuppy's mother approximately 34 minutes into the film and consider all aspects of film form. What is seen and, crucially, what remains unseen? What do these choices suggest about Wink and what do you learn about Hushpuppy's mother? Note down your responses.

Independent activity

Watch the celebration sequence approximately 5 minutes into the film with no sound and then re-watch it with the music on. Note the impact the score has on how you respond to the scene. Try playing a different piece of music over the scene too and see what impact this has on your response.

Dialect: a form of language that is peculiar to a region or social group.

Image search
Hushpuppy's accent and dialect

Watch the opening scene and take note of Hushpuppy's use of language.

Independent activity

Find three examples of the heartbeat in the film and write 50 words on each, exploring how the sound is being used and what meanings are being conveyed by its use.

Independent activity

Choose the two sequences from the film that you feel portray Hushpuppy at her strongest and at her most vulnerable. Make notes on her facial expressions, body language and movements in these scenes and compare them.

Another key aspect of film sound in *Beasts of the Southern Wild* is Hushpuppy's voice-over. From the film's opening moments and throughout, this helps to convey her isolation as well as giving the spectator insight into how she perceives the world. She has nobody else to talk to so is sharing her story with the audience.

Hushpuppy's accent and **dialect** are important factors to consider when analysing the use of sound in this film.

Her use of language may be considered endearing and childlike by some spectators and encourage them to feel protective of her. Others, however, may struggle to fully understand what she is trying to communicate and it could have a distancing effect.

An important feature of the soundtrack of this film is the recurring use of a heartbeat.

The audience hear the heartbeat with Hushpuppy and her response conveys how important and magical she thinks this is. The heartbeat in the film represents life but also Hushpuppy's desire to connect with another. This makes the use of this sound later in the film in relation to Wink profoundly moving.

Performance

The film was cast with non-professional actors who were able to bring their own experiences and stories to the film. Dwight Henry, whose role as Wink was his first acting job, was a local baker who had experienced Hurricane Katrina.

Independent activity

A useful scene to examine for performance is approximately 51 minutes into the film, when Hushpuppy and Wink are in their home after the flood: fighting, drinking, arm-wrestling and at the scene's conclusion falling asleep together. Make notes on how their complex relationship is portrayed in this scene and how aspects of film form are used to convey meaning.

Quvenzhané Wallis was cast as Hushpuppy and Amy Biancolli (2012) writes in '*Beasts of the Southern Wild*' Review: Wet and Wild of her performance:

> it isn't one. It's a fact. Onscreen she simply is, a being as elemental, incontestable and strong as the advancing aurochs.

Wallis is compelling and naturalistic, and arguably this is because she had not been trained to act so is just being Hushpuppy. Zeitlin incorporated aspects of Wallis' personality and world view into Hushpuppy. Her body language in the film balances defiance and power with vulnerability and fear. It is understandable with this range that, at the age of nine, she became the youngest ever nominee for the Academy Award for Best Actress.

Aesthetics in *Beasts of the Southern Wild*

The originality of the film is tied to the film's aesthetic, as the artistic choices made in terms of the look, rhythm and music offer a sensory spectacle. The audience is taken to a world rarely seen on a cinema screen.

Some of the most memorable moments in this film are not tied to the narrative but stand on their own as moments of beauty. The use of twinkling lights and the muted soulful singing in the Elysian Fields scene are not required to propel the narrative forwards but they create a strangely beautiful but disconcerting environment.

Independent activity

How is the movement, positioning and body language of the actors within the space used to convey meaning in the Elysian Fields scene? Note down your response.

Section 1 Contemporary American independent film

> **Stretch & challenge**
>
> Select five frames from the film and annotate them, focusing not on what they convey about the characters or contribute to the narrative but instead highlighting how they use visual elements such as contrast, colour, lines, framing, tone, lighting, negative space, pattern and balance/imbalance.

> **Independent activity**
>
> Do you think the film's strong aesthetic contributes to the meanings being conveyed? Write down at least three examples of the aesthetic anchoring the meaning.

Representations

Independent films tend to be, as mentioned earlier, more focused on character development and exploration than spectacle and action. As such, characters in indies are less likely to be archetypes or stereotypes and more likely to be well-drawn, complex representations of individuals. The inhabitants of the Bathtub are a close community and share ideologies but they are diverse in terms of age and ethnicity.

> **Independent activity**
>
> Look up the definitions of 'stereotype' and 'archetype'. How do the terms differ?

Age

Although there is a range of ages represented in *Beasts of the Southern Wild*, the clearest comparison is between Wink and Hushpuppy. Wink as the elder, the parent, would stereotypically be expected to display the wisdom acquired with age. He certainly has authority and a high status in his community, and is regarded as a leader at times. An example of this is his role in blowing up the levee. He gives instructions to his friends and contributes to the plan's success when others have failed. Interestingly, the young Hushpuppy also plays a pivotal role by following Wink's directions. This is a key dynamic between them, as throughout the narrative Wink prioritises teaching Hushpuppy how to survive, particularly when he realises how unwell he really is. A clear example of this is the fish-catching scene. Hushpuppy's respect for her father's knowledge is demonstrated by her use of 'Daddy says' or 'Daddy always saying' in her voice-over. She is being shaped by his views and ideologies. Miss Bathsheba is another adult whose authority and wisdom help form Hushpuppy's view of the world. It is the aurochs, which the teacher speaks of and shows her tattoos of, that come to dominate Hushpuppy's imagination and represent her fears.

Children, and arguably girls in particular, are typically represented as physically and emotionally vulnerable. Hushpuppy challenges many of these stereotypes, as she is relatively independent, has her own brand of wisdom and copes admirably in traumatic situations.

> **Image search**
> *The final scene*
> 01:26:00–01:28:00
>
> Watch the final scene. How does the voice-over at the film's conclusion demonstrate Hushpuppy's insight into life?

Her ability to be so positive in such harrowing circumstances conveys a resilience and strength of character beyond her years, and as the film ends she is depicted as a leader of her community. The final words of the screenplay confirm this intention.

Gender

The film was made in 2012 and set in the then present, so this and the fact that contemporary independent films often feature progressive gender representations would lead audiences to anticipate a narrative that avoids gender stereotyping. Wink, however, clearly holds the belief that strength and the ability to cope in adverse conditions are masculine characteristics, as Hushpuppy is encouraged to toughen up by being more like a man. This is demonstrated through Wink challenging her to arm wrestle, and through encouraging her by praising her in masculine terms, 'Hushpuppy you the man' and 'You're gonna be the king of the Bathtub' being two clear examples.

Wink also highlights Hushpuppy's gender as a means of criticising her for showing emotion or fear. When she speaks of her anxiety about his health he says, 'That's just a side effect of being a stupid little girl.'

Hushpuppy's androgynous clothing

This could also contribute to why Hushpuppy's clothing through most of the film is primarily practical and fairly androgynous. In the opening scene her clothing is described in the screenplay as, 'boys' underpants and a child-sized wife-beater [vest]'. In the hospital she is washed, dressed and re-styled by the staff in a more stereotypically feminine way and her discomfort is apparent through her more inhibited body language.

Ethnicity

Ben Kenigsberg, writing in *Time Out Chicago* (2012), had some serious concerns about the representations in *Beasts of the Southern Wild*, pointing out that in the Bathtub, the mainly black residents are depicted as 'alcoholics, inattentive parents or fools who accidentally set fire to their homes'.

> **Independent activity**
>
> Read '"Beasts of the Southern Wild", Pros and Cons: Weighing the Arguments around the Most Divisive Movie of the Year' by Matt Singer (2012) in IndieWire. Summarise the arguments.

The film's representations of ethnicity do sometimes edge towards some disturbing stereotypes, with the inhabitants of the Bathtub being shown as poor, dirty and even animalistic at times. These representations are apparent from the opening moments of the film when Hushpuppy plays with dirt before being fed herself alongside the animals, as Wink shouts, 'share with the dogs'.

However, the film arguably represents a community within which ethnicity is irrelevant. The characters face the same challenges and live similar lives regardless of race.

> **Independent activity**
>
> Read bell hooks' (2012) article 'No Love in the Wild' to gain fascinating insight into some of the issues critics of the film's representations of race, gender and class.

> **Independent activity**
>
> Read 'Roger Ebert on the Nature of Film: A Movie is Not a Logical Art Form' (Renee, 2013) on the nofilmschool.com website. What does Ebert state about voyeurism and film as an emotional medium?

Spectatorship

For both the AS and A level exams, spectatorship is a specialist subject area for contemporary independent film. Theories of spectatorship were explored in the previous chapter (pages 116–117) but can be examined in relation to *Beasts of the Southern Wild*.

It has been argued that independent films are more challenging for audiences as they are more open to interpretation and invite a wider range of responses. This supports the notion of the active spectator.

Emotionally engaging the spectator is a key aspect of spectatorship studies and the emotional impact of this film was certainly crucial to Zeitlin. He suggested to *Filmmaker Magazine* that authenticity is central to achieving this: 'You want to shoot a party, you have a party. You want to shoot a flood, you go to a flood' (Anderson, 2013).

Numerous studies have been conducted into the emotional impact of films on the spectator, and theories broadly fall into two categories:

★ The **identification view** allows that spectators may engage with a film to the point that they are able to imagine themselves in the character's situation and truly empathise with that individual. This can be referred to as imaginative identification.

★ The **assimilation view** posits that real identification is rare and spectators instead tend to experience sympathy or antipathy. The spectator is an external observer viewing the characters from the outside.

It has also been argued that spectators feel very different emotions to those experienced by characters and this is referred to as the **asymmetry of emotional response**. Using Wink's death scene as an example, you might argue that the spectator feels grief just like Hushpuppy. It is unlikely, however, that you would feel grief on the same level as her. Zeitlin worked hard to keep Hushpuppy at the film's centre. For many spectators, this may result in their emotional response being dominated by protective concern for Hushpuppy's wellbeing rather than grief for the loss of Wink.

Most theories of the active spectator, as discussed in the previous chapter, share the notion that the spectator plays a role in interpreting a film and people will have diverse responses to any scene. A theory that challenges this, and places the spectator in a passive role, is the idea of **emotional contagion**.

As Coplan (2006) says, this has been defined by psychologists Elaine Hatfield, John Cacioppo and Richard Rapson as,

> the tendency to automatically mimic and synchronize expressions, vocalizations, postures, and movements with those of another person, and, consequently, to converge emotionally.

According to Coplan (2006, page 29), Carl Plantinga argues that filmmakers try to exploit this tendency by constructing 'scenes of empathy' to encourage spectators to 'catch' the emotion the onscreen character is feeling. A scene of empathy typically features shots of long duration, with shallow depth of field, which take the spectator increasingly close to the protagonist's face. To maximise the chances of the spectator experiencing emotional contagion, the narrative will generally slow in pace for these scenes.

Zeitlin certainly utilises these techniques to make Wink's death a scene of empathy. He employs long takes, shallow depths of field and a series of close-ups of both characters.

The use of Hushpuppy's voice-over is also crucial in encouraging identification, as we have privileged insight into her thoughts throughout the film.

It could be argued that the magical realist aspects of the narrative such as the aurochs and the ice caps disrupt the realism of this film and prevent the spectator becoming fully immersed. The incorporation of these aspects of Hushpuppy's imaginary world could conversely take the spectator closer to the protagonist as the spectator sees how Hushpuppy is feeling.

> **Emotional contagion:** the creation of empathy; we tend to align our emotions with those we see on screen.

> **Independent activity**
>
> Consider your own emotional response to this film. Make notes under two headings:
> - 'Techniques used that helped me relate to Hushpuppy' and
> - 'Factors that prevented me from relating to Hushpuppy'.

> **Study tip**
>
> When writing about your own response to the film it is advisable to write about the range of different feelings provoked. It is also useful to broaden your vocabulary of terms for different emotions. Spend some time looking up synonyms of the more common ones and try to incorporate them into your analysis.

Independent activity

Read Amy Coplan's (2006) article 'Catching Characters' Emotions: Emotional Contagion Responses to Narrative Fiction Film' and reduce her argument down to 200 words.

Ideology

For the A level exam, ideology is also a specialist subject area for contemporary American independent film. Ideology was defined in the previous chapter but a specific ideological approach that can be considered in relation to *Beasts of the Southern Wild* is a Marxist one.

The film director, Eisenstein, one of the key proponents of Marxist film theory, argued that,

> American capitalism finds its sharpest and most expressive reflection in the American cinema.
>
> (Hauke, 2013)

However, independent films are intended to challenge the hegemony of Hollywood, so it might be anticipated that this not be the case with *Beasts of the Southern Wild*.

Russian director Sergei Eisenstein

Marxist film theorists assert that Hollywood's traditional narrative structures should be challenged, and filmmakers should avoid dictating the spectator's response and allow them to interpret the film in their own way. Deep focus is advocated to allow spectators to choose what element of the frame to give their attention to. Zeitlin certainly does not adhere to this principle as he favours shallow focus to direct the audience's attention to specific characters in particular moments.

The fact that this character is more often than not Hushpuppy would also not adhere to another Marxist filmmakers' principle: the goal of creating narratives that prioritise the community over the individual. *Beasts of the Southern Wild* unquestionably celebrates the close-knit Bathtub community and suggests some equality through scenes of communal eating, teamwork and close friendships. Wink even goes so far as to suggest one of his drunken friends could step into his parenting role if their plan to blow up the levee goes awry.

However, Hushpuppy's centrality to the narrative means that even though the film ends on a group shot this really is her story and in the closing moments, through her position at the front and centre of the grouping, she is shown as a leader.

Marxist theorists tend to applaud films that contextualise and analyse hierarchical relationships. This film certainly does this. Capitalism, industrialisation, wealth and material possessions are not celebrated. Instead, community, nature and strength of character are praised. *Beasts of the Southern Wild* asserts that this community possesses things lacking in the industrialised world. Social class is a key representation in the film and the Bathtub is portrayed as a community where few work, income is low and living standards are compromised. The division between social classes can also be seen in the film with the inhabitants of the bayou being set up in opposition to the people from the rest of America, on 'the dry side'. Blame for this division is clearly levelled at more privileged Americans. This may resonate particularly strongly in contemporary America and the social divisions exploited by Donald Trump in his presidential campaign.

The film cheers the underdog throughout, as the audience is encouraged to share the joy of these characters surviving in the most challenging of situations. A clear example is the negative portrayal of the heavy-handed authorities trying to evict the vulnerable Wink and the young Hushpuppy very forcefully.

The film explores concepts central to Marxist film theory, but perhaps structurally Zeitlin leads the spectator a little too firmly towards a preferred reading and places too much emphasis on the individual.

The natural environment of the Bathtub

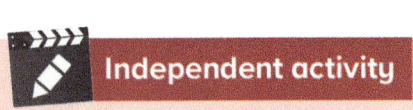

Independent activity

Consider how the US authorities are represented in the film and summarise what this suggests about the film's overall ideology in 200 words or less.

Section 1 Contemporary American independent film

Independent study questions

Q How is film form used to encourage the spectator to relate to Hushpuppy?

Q How does the film challenge or reinforce existing stereotypes of age, gender and ethnicity?

Q How does the film's unique aesthetic engage the spectator?

Q What are the film's key messages and how are they conveyed?

Q What does applying Marxist film theory bring to your understanding of the film?

Get Out

Jordan Peele's film *Get Out* (2017) is a fast-paced, entertaining horror with elements of comedy that taps into the fears of systemic racism embedded in American society.

In an interview with the *Guardian*, Peele explains why horror and comedy codes and conventions fuse together so successfully:

> The reason they work, why they get primal, audible reactions from us is because they allow us to purge our own fears and discomforts in a safe environment. It's like therapy. You deal with deep issues that are uncomfortable with the hope that there is a release. (Anthony, 2017)

The protagonist, Chris, parallels Peele's own fears and experiences in a horrific world where post-racial liberal America is a facade. In *Get Out* we see Chris code-switch to slightly different personas depending on his environment of private (safe) or public (uncomfortable and dangerous) spaces. For example, the party scene is semi-autobiographical for Peele; he wrote a scene set in a white world of 'polite society' that is full of microaggressions. In every conversation the white party guests are keen to discuss race; we initially laugh at their awkward statements but they swiftly result in Chris being fetishised and objectified. Peele is using the comedic discomfort of the scene to start a conversation about race.

Contexts

Get Out was released in 2017, which was a pivotal moment in American history. Barack Obama had served two terms as President of the United States and on January 20, Donald Trump was sworn in as the 45th president.

The era represents a paradigm shift in American ideology. When Trump was sworn in, he issued a series of executive orders, undoing many of Obama's key policies, such as by banning the entry of refugees from seven Muslim-majority countries (Iran, Iraq, Libya, Somalia, Sudan, Syria and Yemen), and famously vowing to 'build a wall' to protect the USA from illegal immigration via Mexico.

In 2017, the USA entered an era of increased political and social division. The #MeToo and Black Lives Matter movements were well established and characterised by massive protests, such as the Women's March. In this era defined by protest, one march is particularly significant. In August of 2017, a 'Unite the Right' rally was held in Charlottesville, Virginia by white supremacists, including neo-Nazis and Klansmen. The marchers clashed violently with peaceful counter-protesters, resulting in a white supremacist deliberately driving his car into the crowd, killing one person and injuring 35. Controversially, Trump made a statement after the attack, but did not condemn violence or white supremacy, instead saying that there were 'very fine people on both sides'. The then mayor of Charlottesville, Nikuyah Walker, stated on CNN that Trump's attitude to race had 'contributed to a hostile climate' in her city and beyond.

Get Out sits in between the liberal Obama years and the divisive Trump administration. Although the film was in production in 2016 when Obama was still in power, the ideological and political divisions of America were starting to be perceived in Trump's rhetoric during his campaign run for the White House. *Get Out* appears to predict in nightmarish fashion what Peele perceives to be a latent systemic racism 'lying in wait' in the American suburbs.

Indie filmmaking and horror: *Get Out*

Horror films like *Get Out* are a staple of indie filmmaking; they are relatively cheap to make with a good return on investment. Horror films also allow indie directors to be visually creative and make social commentary, for example by depicting fear and society as some kind of physical monster on screen.

Get Out had a small budget of only $4.5 million, but its box office return was $255.4 million. Peele was known for his sketch comedy TV series *Key & Peele*, which helped him secure funding for *Get Out*, the film that firmly placed him on the map and earnt him Oscar nominations for Best Picture, Best Director and Best Original Screenplay, and a Best Actor nomination for Daniel Kaluuya. Peele won the Best Original Screenplay Oscar that year and is now considered to be a director of auteur status. He has since directed further horror films, *Us* (2019) and *Nope* (2022), which both had bigger budgets but similar messages and values to *Get Out*.

Get Out was produced by Peele's own production company, Monkeypaw Productions, and by Blumhouse Productions, which has a strong catalogue of horror films such as *Paranormal Activity* (Peli, 2007) and *Insidious* (Wan, 2010). The film was distributed by another company with a strong horror pedigree, Universal.

Peele has cited several indie films as inspiration for *Get Out*, including *Rosemary's Baby* (Polanski, 1968) and *The Stepford Wives* (Forbes, 1975), two films that were produced and released in the New Hollywood era and explored feminist issues set against a backdrop of the second wave of feminism.

Film form

Mise-en-scéne

Peele uses mise-en-scène to introduce us to Chris through his apartment; it is a visual shorthand that informs us about his character. The camera roams around the Brooklyn apartment, allowing the audience to absorb key information. He is a successful photographer, and his camera is a tool that allows him to uncover the truth of the Armitage family. The camera is also a weapon in the fight against racial injustice and violence.

Peele creates a remote and affluent white suburb for the Armitage house. The house design has a plantation aesthetic, with grand white pillars and gardens, while echoes of the slave trade reappear with the use of bingo cards in a scene that has connotations of a slave trade auction. The suburbs are often depicted in horror films, particularly in the slasher genre. They represent middle America, and usually a middle America under threat by something that is represented by the monster or killer. In this film, however, it is the inhabitants of the suburb itself who are the monsters, and therefore a threat to society. Peele has imbued particular props with symbolic power, for example Missy's cup. It is her torture device and tool for hypnosis; it is shown in close-ups to signify its power, which are enhanced by the high-pitched scraping sound that adds a warning cry. The china cup symbolises the fragility of the powerful American middle class. This power is also symbolised in the party guests' white or red costumes; the Armitages and those already enslaved do not wear white or red.

The character design of Rose transforms as her true intentions are revealed. At the start of the film, she is a Brooklyn 'cool girl', similar to the character she portrayed in the TV series *Girls*. Once her true intentions are revealed, however, her costume, hair and make-up all change. She wears only white, her hair is severe and scraped back from her face, she drinks milk and nibbles on Froot Loops. At this point, her look reflects her desire for white supremacy; she is dressed as a hunter in jodhpurs and there are photographs of her victims on the wall behind her.

Cinematography

The film's aesthetic grows darker and more threatening as it develops, transitioning from day to night as the terror grows. Cinematography is particularly important when we are discussing spectatorship issues, as the camera is our eyes.

Peele needs to establish that this environment is threatening to Chris. In order for the audience to emote, we must see the world through his eyes. Therefore, his character receives extended screen time to create emotional connection, consisting of lengthy reaction shots and point-of-view shots.

The close-up pictured below is a key image. It encapsulates Chris' vulnerability, fear and desperation, and the breaking of the fourth wall in this moment is a plea to the audience for help. The intensity is built by slow zooms in of Chris as the scene progresses, drawing in the audience.

Independent activity

Read the article 'Allison Williams Breaks Down the Infamous Froot Loops Scene in "*Get Out*"' in *Business Insider* (Guerrasio, 2017). What does Williams propose this scene does to explore Rose's character?

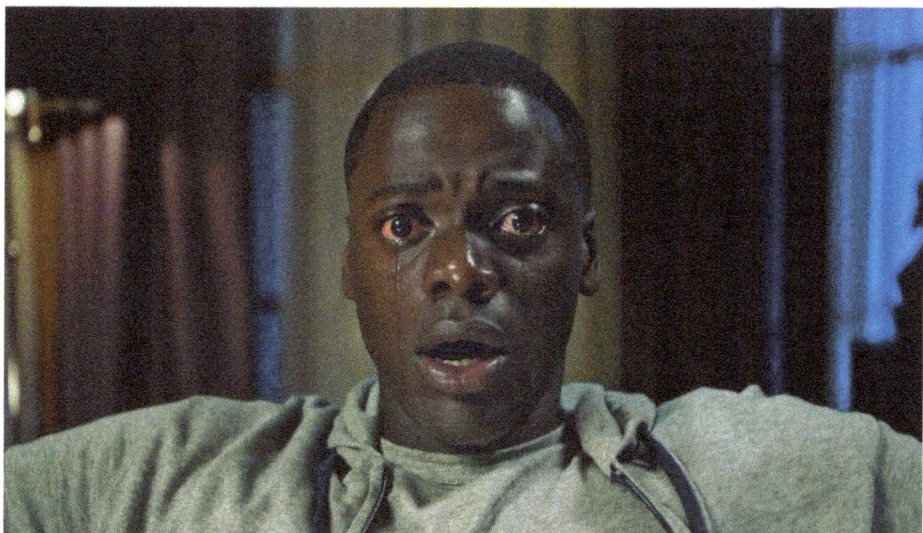

The sunken place delivers some experimental cinematography. In the infinite void in which Chris is prisoner, there is a window into the world that is the shape of a TV screen. This echoes what he did on the night his mother died – he was comforted by the TV. But it also represents his inaction and feelings of powerlessness. The long shots used by Peele in the sunken place create an expanse of negative space that isolate Chris and are juxtaposed to the intense close-up.

Sound

Sound anchors our emotional reaction to a scene, especially in horror where the music guides our sense of terror or safety. A good example of Peele using sound to construct classic horror techniques in *Get Out* is the opening scene (00:00:00–00:03:30) This pre-credits sequence opens with silence and the sound of crickets; this establishes the isolation of Andre who is talking to an off-screen Rose about his discomfort at being lost in a 'creepy ass suburb' feeling like 'a sore thumb out here'. Peele is encouraging the audience to share the discomfort of Andre.

The silence is significant in this scene. It works in combination with the long take to build suspense – we see the car stalk Andre before he does, giving the audience more information than the character. This creates dramatic irony. Peele decided to use an eerie rendition of 'Run, Rabbit, Run' here. It is coming from the car radio and is therefore diegetic. This song has a childlike tune, but it is calling for the rabbit/victim/Andre to run, which is what the audience are calling for too. It can also be read as a kind of eerie taunt from the point of view of the hunter wanting the prey to run, in order to give chase; a bigger thrill for the hunter. Silence is used when the door slams shut to give a full stop to the pre-credits scene.

Over the credits (00:03:30–00:04:00), Michael Abels the composer worked with Peele to combine musical styles. He combined traditional African music with an orchestral score. In the NPR article, 'Michael Abels, Composer of Jordan Peele's "Us", Balances Terror with Empathy' (Greiving, 2019), Abels said that Jordan wanted the score to be 'gospel horror', a distinctly African American voice. He wanted it to feel like something that would be familiar, yet completely terrifying. The credits soundtrack is 'Sikiliza Kwa Wahenga'. The translation from Swahili is 'Listen to your ancestors.' Abels used this to invoke a kind of ancestral warning and sense of dread from the beginning of the film. In the *Billboard* article, '"Get Out" composer Michael Abels on Realizing Jordan Peele's Musical Vision & Bringing Out the Ghosts', Abels states that 'he wanted African-American voices in the score that would represent the African souls lost from slavery, lynchings and other social injustices. They served as Chris' tie to his ancestors, while also warning Chris to danger ahead'.

Another significant use of sound is the teacup as a hypnotic trigger. In the first hypnosis scene (00:31:00–00:36:35), the slow stirring and tapping of the teacup is familiar, soothing and sinister, lulling Chris into the sunken place. This symbolises control and subjugation, an immersive and disorientating experience mirroring Chris's descent into hypnosis. From the DVD commentary, Peele said: 'The sound of the spoon is like a trigger. It's something that's mundane but becomes a tool of control. It's simple, but it gets under your skin'. Sound is used to confirm our alignment with Chris in this scene too. We hear the rain at Missy's suggestion as if the audience is hypnotised too. The minor key music gives the audience a fraction of uneasy understanding prior to the action unfolding, which ignites the audience's fight or flight response. Peele allows the audience to feel the discomfort and desire to run as Chris does in this scene.

The sounds of the sunken place are minimalistic – a lot of low frequency rumbling, high-pitched drones and subtle musical elements – to encourage the audience to feel as trapped and helpless as Chris does. It sounds ghostly, and also has a deep resonating orchestral tone that anchors the audience's emotional response as fearful.

Editing

Making the familiar unfamiliar is a horror and a comedy trope, and this effect can be achieved through editing. The pace and style of editing alters between comedy and horror in several important moments. For example, in the party scene (00:42:16–00:46:23) Peele cuts into the middle of awkward conversations between Chris, Rose and the guests; through the repeated cutting to reaction shots of Chris, the relentless inappropriate behaviours and micro aggressions he feels are communicated to the audience.

Editing controls the pace which controls the tension – slower edits to build tension and faster edits to drive the action. For example, 'the keys' moment at 01:05:15–01:10:30 demonstrates a slow building of pace as shots gradually become shorter to echo Chris's growing sense of panic. Each edit contributes to the film's growing sense of unease. In contrast, the fight scene between Chris and Jeremy at 01:31:20–01:32:20 juxtaposes the suspense by creating a cathartic moment. The editing during the fight is fast, mimicking the panic, confusion and anger of the two men.

Another scene that demonstrates the importance of timing is 'Walter running' (00:28:47–00:30:53). Chris walks through the house at night. The edits are long, creating a slow pace, a sense of quiet and calm, or perhaps an eerie sense of dread to audiences who have an understanding of horror conventions. Spectators with an understanding of horror will be expecting a jump scare in this scene as they will recognise the combination of conventions that lead to a jump scare, in this case the lone protagonist slowly walking through the seemingly quiet house. In the Deadline article, '"Get Out" Editor Gregory Plotkin on Working With Jordan Peele to Refine His Ending' (Grobar, 2017), Gregory explains: 'If the audience expects you to stay on a shot for four seconds, I'm going to stay on it for ten… I think it's easier to cut than to not cut, so I've always taken pride in trying to hold things a little bit longer, make people uncomfortable. They know something's coming. Sometimes you're able to actually defuse it, because if you think it's coming at five seconds, after ten seconds you're like, "All right, nothing's going to happen." And then at second 12: Boom, something comes out.'

Jump scares are created when the slow pace of a scene is suddenly broken with a shocking cut, usually to something jumping out at the protagonist. There are three jump scares in this scene. The first is at 00:29:30 when Georgina suddenly appears in the background. The second is at 00:30:20 when Walter suddenly appears from the darkness running ferociously at Chris. The third is at 00:30:25 when Georgina appears in the window gazing at her reflection. In *Get Out*, these jump scares establish that 'something is off' about the characters of Walter and Georgina; their movements are unnatural as if they are not quite human. The usual response to a jump scare is laughter; it is the cathartic release of tension. In the case of Walter running, there is something comedic about the way he appears from the darkness and runs past Chris; this is from the absurdity of his actions and Chris's (and the audience's) fearful response to them. In this scene it is the classic horror combination of 'jump scare' editing and the high-pitched violin music that guide our emotional response from fear to laughter and back again.

Performance

Chris is an everyman character. He is a rational, stable, non-violent (and somewhat passive) protagonist in the first half of the film; he absorbs many of the microaggressions directed at him, for example from the police officer and the party guests. Walter and Georgina's performances are both multi-layered; they are Armitages with glimpses of their mind-enslaved selves peeping through in pivotal moments, such as Georgina's 'no, no, no, no'. In Walter and Logan's performances, their true selves break through the hypnotic spell with a camera flash; the actors play two characters in one take with different mannerisms and voices. Peele directed the actors playing hypnotically enslaved characters to show that they (as Armitages) have a secret they are desperate to tell.

Representation in *Get Out*

Age

There are two age groups in the film – we have Chris, Rod and Rose representing millennials, and Dean, Missy and the other guests are the older, baby boomer generation. The generation gap is lessened by the Armitage children, who align with their parents' beliefs. The older generation appears to be clinging on to a bigoted and, in their eyes, idealised version of white America that no longer exists, by hiding in their remote suburb, ignoring the changes in the world.

Ethnicity

Ethnicity can be defined by shared cultural beliefs and practices; race can be defined by shared physical traits. In *Get Out*, Peele explores how black and white characters

Independent activity

Editing and sound work together to create jump scares. Watch the 'Walter running' scene from *Get Out* (00:28:47–00:30:53) without sound. Note how the impact is different. Then watch the scene a few more times with different types of music. How can the impact be manipulated by sound?

Now read the whole Deadline article: '"Get Out" Editor Gregory Plotkin on Working With Jordan Peele to Refine His Ending'. What does he explain about how sound and editing work together?

Independent activity

Why do we laugh after a jump scare? Do we react differently when we are in a group in the cinema compared to when we are watching on our own at home?

Independent activity

Read the *Guardian* article 'Jordan Peele on Making a Hit Comedy-Horror Movie Out of America's Racial Tensions' (Anthony, 2017). What does Peele explain about the casting rationale? What were his concerns with casting a British actor?

Note: you will be re-reading part of this article again in the next activity.

appear to have different cultural experiences. Black characters are represented as heroic victims of white characters' desire for dominance and supremacy. Black characters are represented as being awake to the threats of American society. Rod acts as a conscience, screaming at Chris to 'Get out!', as though Rod is verbalising deep-rooted fears that are the result of the black experience in America. Although Rod is a stereotypically comedic 'sidekick' character, his comedic premonitions turn out to be true, and ultimately that suspicion and fear saves Chris. We witness Chris code-switching when talking to either white or black characters, and his confusion when Walter and Logan do not respond appropriately.

There was originally a darker ending to the film in which Chris did not escape, but Peele felt that a more hopeful resolution was what America needed. In the world created by Peele, the worst fears of black Americans are realised; white characters are 'evil' and attempt to return black Americans into a state of enslavement. The last scene is particularly symbolic, because we see the red and blue lights of a police car. It would appear that rescue is at hand, however, this is not a comforting sound or visual; for Chris, the oncoming police car is to be feared. It does not represent safety but a real threat because systemic racism is embedded in systems of power and authority, including the police in the USA. However, when we see that it is Rod in the car, the audience feels a cathartic release of tension.

Gender

Peele begins the film with a suspenseful action sequence involving male characters, establishing men as the active agents. We see the action unfold through a male eye; Chris' persona is that of quiet confidence and humility. He embodies a 'final boy' character trope, undergoing a transformation to defeat the antagonists who embody his deepest fears.

Women in the film are deceitful agents of cultural supremacy. Rose, in particular, is the central antagonist. Her duplicity is the biggest threat to Chris because it is so well hidden. She begins the narrative as the perfect girlfriend and a 'white saviour'; as we see in the scene with the police officer, she protects Chris. Their body language is close and loving, and she is wearing similar colours to him. However, when this is revealed to be an act – she is a femme fatale and has been catfishing Chris – her look is replaced and becomes more severe and heartless; her aesthetic and performance are completely altered. When we see her drinking milk in her room with photographs of her ex-boyfriends hung on the wall, it becomes clear that she, too, is 'evil' and a hunter. The photographs are her trophies, like a hunter would hang a deer's head on a wall. She represents Peele's fear of betrayal by white liberal middle America.

Spectatorship

Horror and comedy have similar structures in terms of audience reaction. The films build towards moments of laughter, or the 'jump' (usually followed by laughter); this is a cathartic release of tension. Peele playfully constructs visceral moments of release throughout the film by blending horror and comedy responses – you jump, then laugh.

Audiences have different reactions depending on where they view a film, whether it be in a cinema or with other people at home. Our reactions are bigger and we laugh out loud when we are with other people. The social element of viewing a film increases pleasure. Often when we are watching horror, a jump-scare is followed by an involuntary release of laughter. For example, when Walter runs towards Chris, we jump and then laugh. This fright and then realisation of safety is one of the pleasures of the horror genre. We get pleasure from feeling frightened. The most graphic piece of 'body horror' in the film involves the operation scene; we are shielded from a large part of the scene by cross-cutting to Chris' escape. Our imaginations fill in the blanks and we construct more terrifying images in our mind than Peele can construct on screen.

In the opening scene, Peele gives us a false hero, Andre, whom we meet again later on. In the party scene, the spectator recognises Andre in a similar way to Chris – that shared experience creates a bond. By that point in the film, we are aligned with Chris and Rose, we are positioned to experience these conversations with them and it creates a feeling of discomfort that we as an audience share. In the party scene, this discomfort turns into a feeling of threat when Logan/Andre attacks Chris. This is where the spectator begins to morally evaluate Chris' actions as the danger is no longer comedic; the spectator forms an allegiance with Chris as he becomes more active from this point.

Another turning point for the spectator is when Rose reveals her true colours. In 'the keys' scene, this moment is significant for the spectator because we have created an alignment with her. Peele has constructed this character to be an ally in Chris' fight, so her duplicity betrays the trust of both Chris and the audience. This betrayal sets the tone for the final third of the film: Chris's fears are realised and the audience is required to be active and asked to question their own beliefs, reactions and morality.

Ideology

Another insightful tool when studying *Get Out* is to examine the ideological critical approach of the American Dream.

The American Dream is the belief that every citizen should have an equal opportunity to work hard and achieve success within the capitalist system. It is a dream founded on the desires of immigrants and echoed in Martin Luther King Jr's famous 'I have a dream' speech. This ideological concept is deeply flawed, however, as not everyone starts from the same place. People of colour in particular have suffered oppression and inequality. The American Dream is, therefore, unattainable for most – it is a myth. Therefore, an analytical approach that recognises the mythical nature of this 'dream' is appropriate to apply to *Get Out*, as the film explores the inequalities of this ideological belief. Peele explains how he was inspired by his post-Obama era concerns to write *Get Out*, to tap into racial tensions in Trump's America.

Chris is a successful black American man, before the Armitage cult target him. The American Dream is real for the Armitages, too; they are privileged, wealthy and powerful. However, the American Dream is shown to be a different experience for black Americans, who are represented as subject to the systemic racism embedded in systems of power and authority in the USA.

Independent activity

Look again at the fourth paragraph of the *Guardian* article, 'Jordan Peele on Making a Hit Comedy-Horror Movie Out of America's Racial Tensions' (Anthony, 2017). What does Peele say is the contextual 'genesis' for the film?

Conclusion

Zeitlin's goal for *Beasts of the Southern Wild* was to:

> take some of the language of artistic, lyrical film, but to have the heart of it be wisdom and big questions and simple ideas and universal themes. I think that is one of the reasons why people see it as not an art film that's trying to push you away, but one that is trying to draw you in. And it's about things everyone goes through. (Anderson, 2013)

By combining an unusual premise, memorable and unique characters, and a distinctive aesthetic, Court 13 has produced a truly original independent film. Its success is testament to the quality of the filmmaking and the fact that spectators can usually relate to some of the characters' experiences.

Get Out is an example of a hugely successful indie film – Jordan Peele became the first black director and writer to have his debut film reach over $100 million at the box office. It is one of the few horror films to be driven by an examination of racism, capturing the spine-chilling racial tensions that exist in America.

Section 1 AS: European film
A level: Varieties of film and filmmaking

British film since 1995

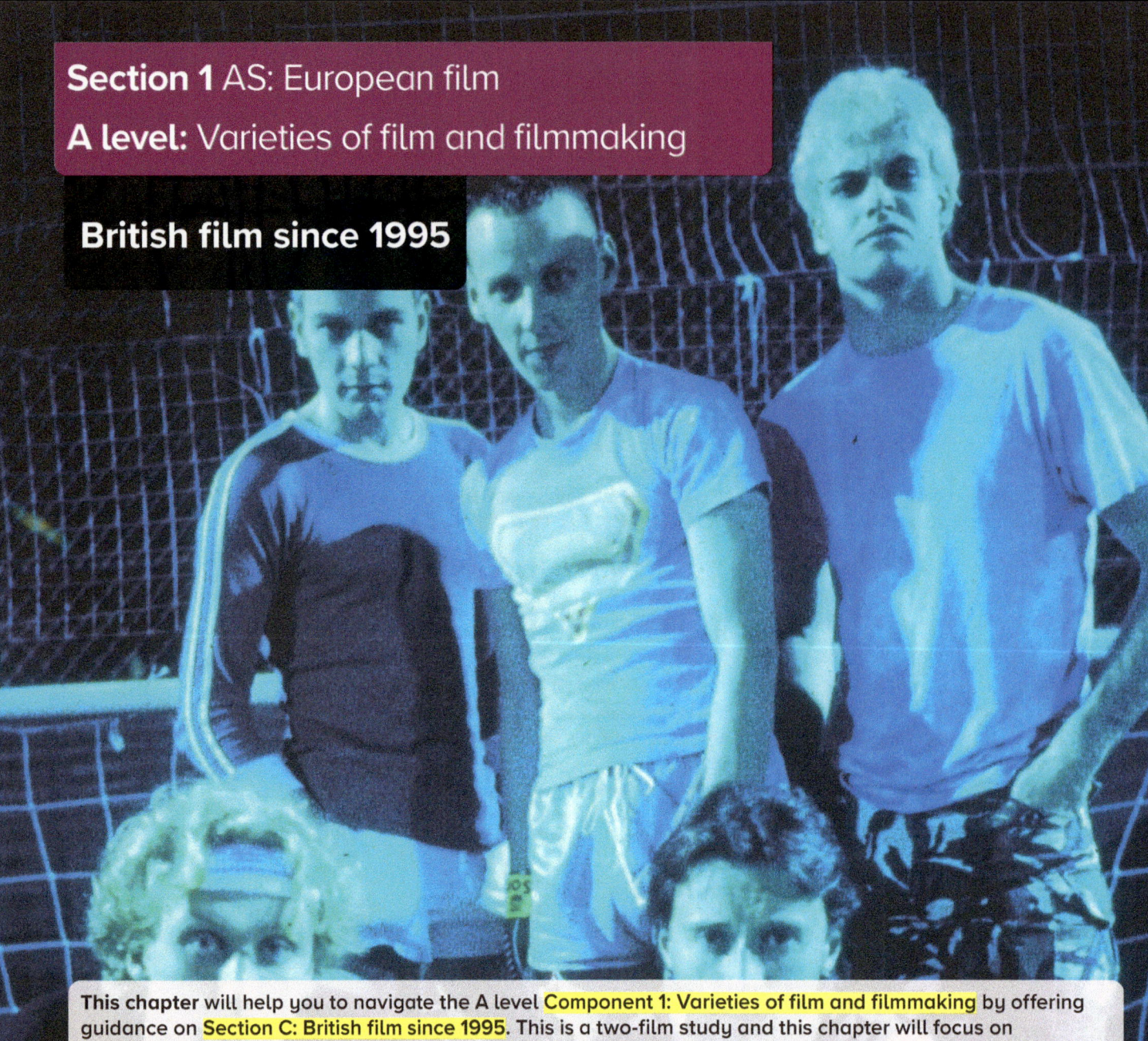

This chapter will help you to navigate the A level **Component 1: Varieties of film and filmmaking** by offering guidance on **Section C: British film since 1995**. This is a two-film study and this chapter will focus on *Trainspotting* (Boyle, 1996) and *Mogul Mowgli* (Tariq, 2020). Aside from the core areas of study, students must also focus on specialist study areas: ideology and narrative for A level, just narrative for AS. This includes critical approaches to narrative for AS and critical approaches to narrative and ideology for A level.

For AS

You answer two questions and must refer to both your chosen films in both answers. The first compulsory question should be allocated 20 minutes. The second question is selected from a choice of two and you should allow 40 minutes. These questions may test an understanding of critical approaches to narrative.

For A level

You answer one question from a choice of two and must refer to both your chosen films. You should spend 50 minutes on your response. These questions may test an understanding of critical approaches to narrative or ideology.

The specification says

Trainspotting ... *raise[s] questions about different kinds of social and national identities.*

... Mogul Mowgli *explores cultural identity and family in a nuanced way of storytelling that has been described in part as an abstract magical realist narrative.*

4 *Trainspotting* (Boyle, 1996) & *Mogul Mowgli* (Tariq, 2020)

Trainspotting is in many ways the defining British film of the 1990s. Many of its energetic cast and crew have now become household names (people such as Danny Boyle and Ewan McGregor); it spawned a sequel, *T2 Trainspotting* in 2017 and a huge variety of youth-oriented merchandising, not least the cult source novel by Scottish writer Irvine Welsh. *Trainspotting* may sound geeky but it is anything but ... it was and still remains 'cool'. Its cinematic charisma earmarked the film for controversy, as its subject matter is, at least on the surface, about heroin addiction in a working-class community in Edinburgh.

Mogul Mowgli is a significant film for showcasing the many talents of its star, music composer, rapper and co-writer Riz Ahmed. Extensive online interviews with Ahmed and director and co-writer Bassam Tariq express the passion they both felt for the semi-autobiographical story, which deals with issues of identity in regard to the legacy of British colonialism, specifically of Partition in India and its effect on future generations. The film had both critical and cultural success, and is considered by some commentators to have played a significant part in constructing a 'brown gaze', an aesthetic where a shared understanding of culture is apparent without the need to explain the references.

This chapter will explore both films' credentials as a way of looking at British films since 1995, including examining contexts, film form, representation, ideology and critical approaches to narrative.

Stretch & challenge

Watch *Shallow Grave* (Boyle, 1994) and note the thematic similarities with *Trainspotting* and compare how the films use aspects of film form.

Independent activity

Read the novel *Trainspotting* (Welsh, 1994), or at least the first page, and contrast it with the opening of the film. What differences do you notice and why do you think those changes were made?

Independent activity

Look at the BFI *Statistical Yearbook* online. It's full of brilliant information and it's free.

British film

Given the dominance of Hollywood in our culture, the UK film industry and its success stories are often overlooked. The BFI *Statistical Yearbook* is a superb online resource, detailing the contemporary state of the industry, recording in the 2022 edition that the top 100 films released in UK cinemas during 2021 earned almost 98% of the box office. The majority of these films were either USA produced or UK produced with USA studio backing. The box office share of such USA products in 2021 was 91.5%.

The top 20 box office earners in 2021 accounted for just over 72% of all takings and the list of their production/distribution companies reads like a Hollywood studio roll-call. Universal released the year's top earning film *No Time to Die* along with *Fast and Furious 9*, *The Addams Family 2*, *The Croods: A New Age* and *House of Gucci*. Walt Disney released six films and Warner Brothers released four films. Sony also released four films and one was released by Paramount.

Hollywood is still king in the UK, as it is in many regions around the world. But that isn't to say that the UK doesn't have a vibrant and historic film industry. It absolutely does but it is largely always overshadowed by the financial power and long reach of the Hollywood majors.

Trainspotting

Contexts

Institutional contexts

The film was made by Channel 4 Films. This company was renamed in 2006 as Film4 Productions and Film4 is the name of the company's TV film channel. Its back-catalogue, stretching back to 1982, is also a catalogue of UK cultural attitudes and interests. Its films' subject matter is often controversial and leftfield although it has been behind relatively mainstream successes too, not least *Trainspotting*, which for a £1.5 million budget generated £48 million worldwide on its release.

Danny Boyle is one of Britain's highest profile filmmakers, a director in television and film as well as a producer. His film work includes the worldwide smash hit *Slumdog Millionaire* (2009) for which he won, as director, one of its eight Oscars. In making his first feature film, *Shallow Grave* (1995), Boyle put together a team of actors and filmmakers some of whom would go on to make *Trainspotting*. The two films share: director, cinematographer, editor, writer, producer, production company, UK distributor and actors Ewan McGregor, Peter Mullan and Keith Allen. The latter appears in both films as the same drug dealer and *Trainspotting* acts as the prequel to his character's eventual death in *Shallow Grave*. Boyle's status as a national arts icon was cemented when he successfully directed the staging of the 2012 Olympic Opening Ceremony.

Social, political and cultural contexts

In the early 1990s the UK faced a divisive time due to a recession and an increasing dislike of the Conservative government that had been in power since 1979. The National Lottery was launched along with Sky and Channel 5, and the Channel Tunnel opened. Two infamous criminal cases led to moral panics. First, in 1995 Leah Betts, a young teenager, died in an incident connected to ecstasy use and news coverage of this tragic death contributed to the moral panic surrounding the new rave culture. Second, in 1993 Jamie Bulger, a toddler, was brutally murdered by two young boys, leading to fears over the malign influence of violence on film. Also during this period a huge Poll Tax riot occurred in London and sporadic rioting continued to flare up in working-class urban areas around the country. By 1996, however, there were signs of a new dawn contributed to by the feel-good success of the English football team at the European Championships and the mainstream arrival of the effervescent Spice Girls. The high-tempo introduction to *Trainspotting* is, then, in some ways a reflection of this period: energised and upbeat. The music of Iggy Pop's 1970s anthemic song 'Lust for Life' erupts on screen as we see Renton and Spud, running from security guards in well-heeled Edinburgh. Renton's narration of Welsh's iconic and nihilistic 'Choose life' monologue also sets the tone for the film's iconoclasm.

At the end of the film Renton leaves Begbie, Spud and Sick Boy, and runs off with the money received from a drug deal. The feeling created by the film's dénouement is optimistic. Renton has quit heroin and is going straight. He's leaving his violent, nihilistic, wastrel friends behind and is moving on – literally crossing a bridge (Waterloo Bridge) to a new life that he's chosen. 'I'm going straight and choosing life …' he happily tells us in a voice-over as the dance music of Underworld ushers in a positive and energised vision of the future.

The generation that was sired by the baby boomers and went on to make punk and then slacker rock, as typified by bands such as Nirvana, was called Generation X. This generation found some purpose in rave culture and lost some of its existential angst but in the mid-1990s there was still plenty of disillusionment with contemporary culture and the diseased capitalist dream. In the USA this feeling of generational malaise was evidenced by the riots at Woodstock 99 and in films such as *Fight Club* (Fincher, 1999). This mood of alienation and disillusionment is also evidenced in *Trainspotting* until its end.

Independent activity

Watch the opening scenes of *Fight Club*. It is a perfect example of Generation X's malaise and self-loathing.

The film heavily features British music culture in the 1990s. It takes the audience on a journey through contemporary musical culture moving from punk to anthemic rave: starting with Iggy Pop's 'Lust for Life', a song from 1977, and ending with 'Born Slippy' by Underworld from 1996. The 1990s saw an explosion of creativity, particularly in the UK, which was labelled by journalists 'Cool Britannia'; the dance scene, Brit-pop bands like Blur and Oasis and even pop creations like the Spice Girls gave Britain, for a time, a musical sense of positivity and energy. This is very much mirrored in the film's closing sequence with its high-powered percussive beat.

The film is the first of a number of Irvine Welsh adaptations. *Trainspotting* is based on his book of the same name, which was published to acclaim in 1994. Other adaptations have been: *Acid House* (McGuigan, 1998); *Filth* (Baird, 2013); and *T2: Trainspotting* (Boyle, 2017). The screenplay effectively captures a number of features from the source novel such as: a focus on Renton; AIDS; drug abuse, in particular heroin; violence; and low-level criminality. Some characters get more novel time than screen time and it is perhaps significant that some of the ones edited out in the adaptation are black or female. That said, the film and novel are arguably largely about the male experience of living in the working-class Edinburgh suburb of Leith and Renton's posse of male friends do form the focal point of the novel, as they do eventually the film.

Reading the book is strongly advised, not least because the unavoidable sheen of glamour that the film possesses is very much missing; in the novel the main characters are all seriously flawed and damaged, yet Begbie and Sick Boy in particular are even more detestable.

Film form

The film largely follows a linear pattern and is very much focused on the viewpoint of Renton, whose voice-over and close-up intro and outro the film. In the intro, however, he is suspended in time, literally in a freeze-frame, staring provocatively at the audience. Later he walks towards the audience but becomes unfocused. A possible reading of these two cinematic devices is that in the former Renton is trapped and in the latter he is free but at a cost to his own identity.

There are a number of jump-cuts and montages in the film, along with dream sequences (Renton's cold turkey) and fantasy sequences (Renton's OD and the toilet-diving escapade) but generally the film progresses in a linear fashion. The passing of time is partly communicated through music, starting with Iggy Pop in the 1970s and ending with mid-1990s dance from Underworld.

Interiors such as bars, pubs, cafés, squalid shooting galleries, flats, bedrooms and so on form the bulk of the film's settings, but when Renton does step out of his Edinburgh suburb of Leith he appears ill at ease. His visit to the Highlands with Tommy, Spud and Sick Boy is the clearest example of this. Renton's escape to London reflects his attempted maturation but he ends up swapping his childish bedroom with train wallpaper for a grotty bed-sit, funded by renting expensive flats to yuppies. Only in the final scene of the film, as he advances towards the audience, does he exude confidence in his environment. Although significantly he is in transit at this point and unfocused, having double-crossed his so-called friends and made it rich with cash made from a drug deal.

Cinematography

The image below shows the recurring aesthetic of very low-level, worm's-eye view framing that communicates a sense of a life with limited perspectives and ambition. Renton is literally 'low life' and his world is just one step up from the gutter.

> **Image search**
> *Worm's-eye view perspective* 00:00:00–00:02:12
>
> Compile and analyse a series of screengrabs which reflect the worm's-eye view perspective from the opening of the film, as the characters run along the streets of Edinburgh and are then introduced. How does this unusual angle influence viewer response and overall meaning?

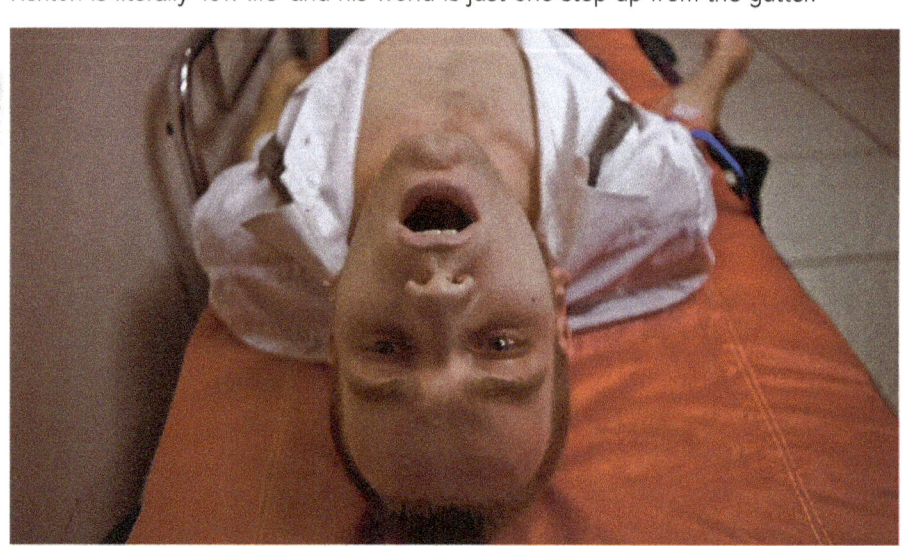

When Renton overdoses, we see him sink, in a surreal shot, into the carpet, which symbolises that he has lost touch with reality. The spectator is given a vicarious view of this experience through a number of POV shots. A doctor revives Renton with adrenalin and the irony of Lou Reed's song 'Perfect Day' underscores this visual nightmare. The combined effect of these POV shots is to situate Renton at his literally lowest point, close to death. The shots both pacify and objectify him as well as placing us in his rapidly dying body.

The film terminates in London, which is depicted as a land of questionable opportunity but undoubted cultural pull. The enduring appeal of London is signalled by a recreation of The Beatles' famous Abbey Road photo as the film's characters cross the road; this creates a tone of comic irony, replacing iconic musicians with addicts and criminals.

Mise-en-scène

The shabby brown tones and drab minimalism of a dilapidated drug den are perfectly communicated through set design, costume and colour palette. However, this is not evidence of social realism but rather hyper-realism or a heightened realism.

Exterior shots of the flats which house the drug den depict the colour-coordinated cubes of working-class life; they serve as symbols of a banal and packaged individualism rather than depictions of a grim social reality. These cells hide their contents from us and their conformist normality reflects something Renton is escaping from.

Editing

The title sequence freeze-frames give the main characters in the film an immediate iconic status. Aside from foregrounding the notion of football as attractive and presenting the protagonists as an embattled team, the sequence also serves to introduce the key symbolic ideas of their characterisations: Renton as a cynical gremlin; Sick Boy, cool and argumentative; Begbie as violent and sadistic; Spud as a fool; and Tommy as the embattled honest straight.

Jump-cutting is an intriguing editing technique used throughout Spud's awkward, hyperactive interview. Here the edit works alongside the sparse mise-en-scène and claustrophobic set to create a comic effect. The juxtaposition of the interviewers' static body language and stern faces plus the absurdity of the space, with its awkward distance between Spud and them, all makes for comedy but is heightened by the abruptness of the jump-cuts and Spud's winning manner.

Sound

Music

The music in the film is chronological in its appearance and often has some narrative importance in terms of commentating on scenes rather than merely accompanying them. Thus 'Lust for Life' introduces Iggy Pop (an idol of Tommy's who is referred to in the film a number of times) as well as augmenting Renton's 'Choose life' monologue. The drug-induced haze of Lou Reed's 'Perfect Day' also acts as a counterpoint to Renton's far-from-perfect OD. 'Born Slippy', the anthem that concludes the film, ushers in mainstream rave culture and energises a nation.

Renton's voice-over

Throughout the film Renton narrates and his acerbic, cynical, foul-mouthed and resigned delivery perfectly captures the 'exhaustion' of Generation X. His escape from a dead-beat life of remorseless drug abuse and empty friendships is suggested

Stretch & challenge

Listen to Iggy Pop's song 'Nightclubbing', which is also heard in the film. How does it convey a sense of drugged inertia and disorientation?

by his sense of epiphany at the end of the film. Here he chooses life even though it is the life he has been previously criticising. Behind his euphoric smile, as he crosses the bridge in London to literally a new life, the spectator can't help but feel that Renton may be still deluding himself.

Performance (A level only)

The delivery of the voice-over has already been discussed but there are other, perhaps more subtle areas of the various performances on offer worth discussing.

Spud and Begbie, left and right

First, it is interesting to see how each of the main characters is defined through both mise-en-scène and through their performance. Renton is a smirking cynic and his final treachery is therefore not unexpected. Indeed, he has already messed up Tommy's life with the infamous 'video swap'. His relationships are paper thin and it is only towards clueless Spud and perhaps Tommy that he exhibits any compassion. With Sick Boy there is a sense of parity; they are after all best friends, but by the same argument their friendship is not deep. They are in some sense copies of each other: cool and rebellious types out for their own ends. Renton's only successful love making is with a teenage schoolgirl and on the whole he exists in a bubble of his own making: a narcotic, solipsistic world not unlike the 'carpet grave' into which he disappears when he ODs. His relationship with his parents is awkward: a sense of failure and disappointment overlaying their disgust at his addiction. But ultimately McGregor plays Renton as a likable, articulate and cheeky bestial gremlin. What prevents the audience from despising Renton is his boyish charm and the fact that we are positioned in the narrative to follow his journey. Thus, Sick Boy, despite his intellectual posturing, entrepreneurial nature and cool pop cultural asides, is somehow more of a despicable character.

Spud is, as we have already noted, aimless and amiable. His character acts as comic relief and incidents involving him are the comic high points of the film. The terrible faeces-covered sheet incident at his girlfriend's parents and his speed-assisted job interview are all played for laughs involving broad physical humour or verbal delivery. Generally, Spud is depicted as the moral core of the group, a happy-go-lucky buffoon but someone who wouldn't hurt a fly. This is achieved through his shambling gait, inarticulate speech and hapless behaviour.

In direct contrast to these three characters we have Begbie, played by Robert Carlyle as a firecracker of a character: incendiary, explosive and indiscriminately aggressive. Carlyle makes Begbie strut like a bantam fighting cock, chest puffed out, short sharp hand movements, fierce verbal delivery full of expletives. The final scene where he is incandescent with rage reflects his defining feature. He is feared and despised. He is a bully and a sociopath, and when we laugh at his antics it is largely out of shock at his brazen nerve. Significantly, Begbie is a heavy drinker, a trait linking him to a stereotypical aspect of Scottish culture, so his scorn for hard drug use is presented as hypocritical.

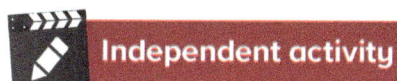

Independent activity

Find evidence of other Scottish stereotypes in film.

Aesthetics

Surrealism and hallucination

The hyper-realism of the set design and cinematography is also enhanced by sequences that are clearly reflective of Renton's deranged mind. They are surreal in that they have a dream-like quality but more accurately they have the taint of nightmare, most obviously in the 'baby on the ceiling' hallucination of an addict enduring 'cold turkey' and the rescue of morphine suppositories from 'the Worst Toilet in Scotland'. Renton is forever disappearing and escaping. The nightmares only really become inescapable when he fights his addiction.

Independent activity

Look at the first and most famous example of surreal short film making, *Un Chien Andalou* (1929) written by Dali and Buñuel (who was also the director), to gain an understanding of surrealism.

Humour

The film is permeated with an ironic tone; this is not a social realist film and that is, of course, why so many people took offence. The characterisations and dialogue are witty, as well as the situations the characters find themselves in, such as the surrealism of 'the worst toilet in Scotland'; the schadenfreude of Renton and Sick Boy shooting a thug's dog in the park; and the social embarrassment of stealing and playing of Tommy's sex tape. Strictly speaking the use of humour is not an obvious link to a film's aesthetics but the use of symbolism and surrealism are aesthetic choices and the fact that they are often used for a humorous rather than an estranging effect gives them credence in this section.

Stretch & challenge

Choose a comic scene from the film and explain how the humour is achieved.

Representations

The following representations are illustrative of the binary categories at work in the film. However, the most controversial representation is that of drug use and drug culture. Even now it is hard not getting charmed by Renton and Sick Boy's smart patter, their cool 'heroin chic', and the trendy music and stylistics of the film itself. For some critics and viewers at least, the film is too soft on drugs: one dead baby and Tommy's death from AIDS being deemed not weighty enough for the catastrophe of heroin addiction in working-class areas of urban Scotland.

Stretch & challenge

Research the AIDS epidemic and how it helped define an era, as well as how it fuelled homophobia.

Age

Age is represented through the nihilism of the Generation X experience, most vividly evidenced through the death of Allison's and Sick Boy's baby: they are unable, it seems, to successfully give life to a new generation. A contrasting generational representation occurs through the schoolgirl, Diane. Here is someone who is more in control of her own destiny and sexuality (unlike Renton).

Renton's parents and Spud's mum are sympathetically presented, somewhat in contrast to the norm of social realist, kitchen-sink dramas where the older generation is often portrayed as out of touch and spirit crushing. Renton is not running from his mum and dad but rather himself. Indeed, they offer a loving vision of humanity, largely devoid from the rest of the film's self-interested and venal characterisations.

Gender

Gender representation is largely male-focused but both Tommy and Spud's girlfriends get screen time as does Sick Boy's girlfriend, Allison (another heroin addict) and Renton's on/off schoolgirl lover, Diane. However, these characters are largely love interests to the main protagonists and the film has little interest in them. Diane is the most empowered but the issue of her being perhaps under the legal age of consent creates numerous problems for the analyst as well as Renton. Renton's monologue in the London club towards the end of the film suggests that gender equality will become the norm: 'One thousand years from now there will be no guys and no girls.' The fact that Begbie discovers this, to his horror, with a transgender lover is a fitting commentary on his ultra-macho sexual redundancy.

Ethnicity

The film is largely filmed from a white male Scottish perspective and most screen time is devoted to 20-something Renton. Interestingly, the source novel does feature a black supporting character. Celtic ethnicity is, however, notably represented and Tommy's trip with Spud, Renton and Sick Boy to the Highlands leaves them all underwhelmed. It is as if even Tommy, the physically most stereotypical Scot, has become severed from his ethnic origins. If the film is about forging an identity and standing on your own two feet without crutches, then, for Tommy, the loss of his girlfriend and his sense of Gaelic identity could in part explain his descent into heroin addiction.

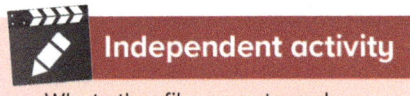

Independent activity

What other films create and challenge notions of Gaelic identity?

Narrative

In terms of narrative the exam board's Guidance for Teaching suggest studying the following:

★ Representation of time
★ Use of narration/voice-over
★ How dialogue propels the narrative
★ Creation of drama or action
★ Character development – heroes and villains, ambiguity
★ Character alignment and identification
★ How narratives present an ideological viewpoint
★ Enigma codes
★ Generic narratives and formulas
★ Binary oppositions

The narrative construction of *Trainspotting* is largely linear and absolutely anchors our focus on the film's main protagonist, Renton. This is achieved through his voice-over starting the film and the first freeze-frame image introducing us to him in close-up.

The plot absolutely follows Renton and there are very few scenes where he isn't present. He starts and ends the film, and it is his journey that the audience is primarily encouraged to follow. The film is, however, also an ensemble film (as evidenced by the marketing) and so we also do find out about main subsidiary characters such as Spud, Begbie and Sick Boy.

Critical approaches to narrative – formalism and structuralism

A formalist conception of narrative distinguishes between plot and story, and certainly *Trainspotting* matches this conception. The plot concerns the structuring of story information, effectively the order of events as presented in screen time; story is the world of the material that extends beyond plot, it is what we infer, rather than what we see.

We enter the story of Renton's life quite a long way into his descent into heroin addiction, and only hints from his parents and friends paint a backdrop of his life that precedes the first plot point: his escape from the security guards.

In terms of structuralist theory, there are clear binary opposites at work in the film. Binary opposites in narrative highlight the principle of conflict giving power and drive to the plotted material. Spud and Begbie are polar opposites. Sick Boy and Renton are evil twins. Drug users and non-drug users seem to exist in uneasy company with each other. Work and leisure do not seem to mix and no one seems able or willing to do conventional work. In the novel, Sick Boy becomes a pimp and Begbie a hardened burglar and thief. There are other binaries at work in terms of class, age, gender, region and nation, all referenced earlier.

Genre is a less obvious tool to use in this case but certainly films that concern drug abuse rarely end in such an upbeat, feel-good manner as *Trainspotting*. Usually, the genre conventions require a sacrifice for the criminality displayed, but in *Trainspotting* only Tommy and the baby die and they are both innocents. Perhaps that is the overarching ideological message behind the film: drugs kill innocence. For just that reason Renton's escape can thus be read as a rebirth.

In terms of specific narrative techniques used in the film, the obvious conceit is that of using a voice-over to familiarise and engage the audience with the film's central protagonist: Renton. Our alignment with Renton makes the subsequent narrative that plays out engaging enough to stick with. Interestingly, the source novel is voiced by many of the characters, not only Renton, so the accumulation of their awful lives makes the novel a far harder read (psychologically not aesthetically) than the film.

In terms of cause and effect there are no enigmas left unsolved other than the exact character arcs of all the main cast: *T2 Trainspotting* was conceived in part to answer those broader questions. The use of a flashback to kick-start the film is an effective means of creating discontinuity in the narrative flow but the audience only realises this has happened later in the film.

From the sections covered above it should be clear that all aspects of film form, such as mise-en-scène, etc., have been used in this film to develop character insights and give sub-textual information to critical plot points.

Trainspotting affords us many opportunities to apply an ideologically critical approach not least from the broad perspectives of politics and feminism. A political approach would involve applying various political ideologies to the text. For example, the anti-materialistic and anti-consumerist stance of Renton in his 'choose life' monologue clearly presents him as a character who does not feel enfranchised by the opportunities given to him in a liberal democracy such as the

Independent activity

Create a checklist of the suggested areas to cover in the study of narrative by the exam board and make notes on each section from each British film you study.

UK. Renton is a disenfranchised nihilist and as such his political views are paper thin and without partisan allegiance. He is angry and disillusioned and pointedly apolitical.

Conversely, a feminist critical approach yields more insights. A feminist perspective would note the literal side-lining of the protagonists' girlfriends in the opening montage of the football match. Here, the young women are acting the thankless task of 'supporters' and that is largely their role throughout the film. As such, the film tends to operate within a fairly traditional patriarchal structure: the main protagonists are all male who activate the plot and women play a largely passive supporting role. However, Diane's character is arguably a female representation that challenges this hegemonic view. Diane is very much in control. She makes decisions and initiates action, not least by sleeping with Renton. That she is still a schoolgirl and deceiving her liberal middle-class parents turns her act of empowerment into something more questionable and troubling; not least from the very illegality of the sex act with Renton, something she cunningly reminds him of. Diane is therefore powerful but, like many of the characters in *Trainspotting*, even she is flawed.

Ideology

Ideology is a complex notion but in essence it is a belief that permeates a social group. Such beliefs can be relatively harmless or deeply pernicious. The following ideologies reflect commonly held beliefs at the time and reflect the tensions that a film can bring into the social discourse.

AIDS

Aside from the Archie Gemmill goal, the one time we see a TV show in the film is when it's a fake game show hosted by Dale Winton about AIDS, which haunts Renton's drug withdrawal hallucinations. The graffiti outside Tommy's flat ('AIDS, Junky, Scum') also references the hostility faced by people with AIDS and the tale told to Renton of Tommy's death by a friend is far from empathetic. Renton tests negative for AIDS. AIDS was clearly a social problem and it still is a pressing problem for addicts who share needles.

Addiction and drugs

Renton is infantilised by his addiction. When he returns to his parental home and the room he had as a child, there is hope that perhaps from this old nest he will be reborn. However, the controversial and graphic detail of heroin use in the first section of the film suggests that it is also a very pleasurable 'high' and in the opening sequence we see Spud high and happy.

Sexuality

Renton suggests that in a thousand years from now, there will be no men and women, and that he's heterosexual by default rather than decision.

Aside from this very contemporary and liberal view on gender difference and sexuality, the film contains some nudity – male as well as female – and some positive representations of empowered and sexually active women. The sexually active schoolgirl, Diane, who Renton meets at a club, is perhaps the most shocking representation.

However, the film is partly about the absence of sexuality, as, aside from Tommy, none of the main characters have regular girlfriends because heroin is their lover. When Tommy loses his girlfriend, he soon becomes an addict too.

Image search
The opening scene and drug use 00:02:12–00:05:16

- Make a collage of screengrabs from this opening scene. How does it establish the rise and fall narrative arc of the film by showing the pleasures of drug use while also suggesting that these are relatively brief compared to the misery which will ensue?
- Identify the hypocrisy suggested of those who are opposed to heroin use. How does this contribute to the ideology of the film and the way that life in Scotland and Britain is represented?

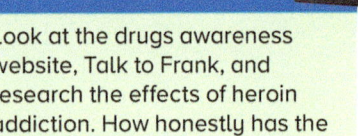

Stretch & challenge

Look at the drugs awareness website, Talk to Frank, and research the effects of heroin addiction. How honestly has the film portrayed these effects?

Scotland and England

Trainspotting explores the differences between Scotland, where most of the film takes place, and England, where later in the film Renton decides 'to find something new'. Leaving heroin and Scotland behind he heads to London, introduced with an upbeat dance track and a highly ironic montage of the tourist stereotype that is our capital with Big Ben, red buses and cockneys.

The mediated reality of Scotland and England is a far cry from the actual truth. In the scene following this cheesy montage of London, we see Renton as a rental agent letting out overpriced city apartments.

Ideology and nihilism

As the narrative is restricted almost entirely to Renton's perspective, an analysis of his ideological position is beneficial for the study of *Trainspotting*. Renton's ideological standpoint can best be described as **nihilism**.

Independent activity

Watch the first couple of minutes of the film, where Boyle asserts Renton's nihilistic beliefs; we have access to Renton's internal 'Choose life' monologue, accompanied by Boyle's bold, fast, immersive editing and 'Lust for Life' by Iggy Pop as the soundtrack.

This monologue reveals Renton's rejection of societal norms and the meaninglessness he associates with a conventional lifestyle. The repetitive use of 'choose' followed by mundane life details emphasises his contempt for the hollow nature of such choices.

Nihilism can be further divided into three areas:

1. Rejection of meaning: Nihilists believe that life has no meaning or purpose. Human existence is insignificant in the grand scheme of things.
2. Scepticism of morality: Nihilists reject the acceptance of established ideological, moral and ethical norms.
3. Individual: Nihilists create individual moral and ideological codes, and sometimes their own 'worlds'.

How does the 'Choose life' monologue explore these ideas? And at what other points in the film does Renton demonstrate these nihilistic qualities?

Image search
The great outdoors
00:30:49–00:32:52

Watch the scene where Tommy is attempting to lead Spud, Sick Boy and Renton on a refreshing walk in the great outdoors: a stereotype of Scottish nature and its rugged outdoor appeal.

Renton rebels and says that it's 'shite' being Scottish. They all get back on the train and return to the city where in the next scene they are all back on the heroin, sadly soon followed by Tommy.

Stretch & challenge

Visit the Scottish tourist board's website, Visit Scotland. How far does its vision of Scotland contrast with that of *Trainspotting*?

Nihilism: a belief that life is without objective meaning, purpose or value. Nihilists often assert that morality is subjective, and that traditional values and beliefs are unfounded and should be rejected. Renton's nihilism is a reaction to an oppressive and deprived socio-economic society, as explored earlier in this chapter, and a coping mechanism for his addiction.

Independent activity

How does Renton's point of view evolve in the film? Try comparing the monologue in the closing scene with the one from the opening. What does it reveal about Renton's ideological beliefs?

Nihilism can be read as both a crisis and an opportunity. In crisis, it can create detachment, despair and disillusionment. Renton succumbs to despair and hits rock bottom after Spud's arrest; we can chart his descent into addiction.

In terms of an opportunity, Renton dismantles cultural beliefs through his rejection of established ideological beliefs; he demonstrates a keen intellect and ability to articulate his complex ideology. He also rejects outdated values and suggests that the collapse of old ideologies gives opportunities for individuals and society to re-evaluate and create more life-affirming ones. Life affirmation includes acknowledging the darkness and despair of the human condition. It is Diane who explains to Renton that he should 'find something new'. The void that addiction and nihilism has left in Renton is filled with new and exciting ideas with his move to London; he embraces capitalism, and ultimately decides to 'choose life'.

Mogul Mowgli

Contexts

Mogul Mowgli tells the story of Zed, a British-Pakistani rapper – played by Ahmed – who is based in New York, but before going on tour returns to England for a tense reunion with his traditional family. While in England, Zed collapses and is diagnosed with an autoimmune disease that threatens to put an end to his dreams.

Bassam Tariq and Riz Ahmed

Institutional and production contexts

Mogul Mowgli (2020) is the first feature film directed by American director Bassam Tariq. He is best known for co-directing the award-winning documentary *These Birds Walk* (2013), about runaway children in his place of birth, Karachi, Pakistan. His family relocated to the USA when he was young and he has said in interviews that 9/11, which happened just before his 15th birthday, had a profound effect on him, leaving him feeling that he had to be an 'apologist' for Muslim culture and leading him to explore what it means to be Muslim in his work – the film is semi-autobiographical. A complex sense of Muslim identity pervades the film, which is also pertinent to the work of Tariq's collaborator, Riz Ahmed, who co-wrote the screenplay, and co-produced and starred in the film. Ahmed's parents had moved from Karachi to the UK before his birth. After Ahmed saw *These Birds Walk*, he and Tariq became friends and he asked Tariq to direct the music video for his Riz MC track 'Mogambo' in 2018, for which Tariq was also the cinematographer.

Independent activity

Watch the music video for 'Mogambo' alongside Riz Ahmed's discussion of the lyrics and meaning. Identify the similarities in terms of themes and style between it and *Mogul Mowgli*.

Mogul Mowgli is an independent production involving nine production companies. It was mostly financed by Pulse Films, a UK company in which the US/Canadian company Vice has a controlling stake, and Left Handed Films, the production company started by Riz Ahmed. Some funding came from the BBC, which ensures that the film is seen on UK television. The film was first shown in the Panorama section of the 2020 International Berlin Film Festival, where Strand Releasing picked it up for US distribution and the BFI acquired distribution rights in the UK; it had a limited release in cinemas and was critically acclaimed, winning the Best Narrative Feature at the 2020 San Diego Asian Film Festival.

The film received a 15 classification from the BBFC for very strong language, emotional upset related to serious illness, references to racism, moderate threat from hallucinations and some moderate sexual references.

Social, political and cultural contexts

The film focuses on the issues around identity, specifically the experience of second-generation British-Asians and the South Asian diaspora. The casting of the Bollywood and Lollywood (the Pakistani equivalent) star Alyy Khan as Zahir's father Bashir brings an additional layer of authenticity to the narrative via his mainly Urdu dialogue.

Section 1 British film since 1995

The film is also deeply personal for both Tariq and Ahmed; Zed's home movies from his childhood, which feature at the beginning of the film, are Ahmed's personal ones of his own family. Tariq has talked in interviews about his Pakistani heritage and how this film links with his desire to piece together his identity growing up as a first-generation Muslim immigrant in the United States. This was intensified by the terrible feeling of being an outsider after 9/11, feeling that somehow, he carried a burden of responsibility although he remains unsure about his identity as a Muslim.

The journey of navigating Muslim identity is shown with humour when complex religious practices are manipulated or rejected by those from the second generation, demonstrated through them smoking outside of the mosque while prayers are heard in the background, for example. When a fan, who in a moment of **bathos** has mistaken Zed for rival rapper RPG, accuses him of being a 'coconut' (brown on the outside and white in the middle), the filmmakers are highlighting the theme of unity not rivalry. The ensuing fight seems to trigger the devastating illness in Zed, which forces him to piece together the strands of his identity.

The social and cultural contexts of the film are complex, the ways in which Zed's parents try to keep Pakistani culture alive at home through whispered prayers, food, references to the evil eye and cupping are rejected by Zed, his concerns are in opposition to his background: black rappers such as Dante Smith (Ahmed as Riz MC did support him as Mos Def early in his rap career) and life in New York far away from the UK. Zed's American girlfriend, Bina, points out the hypocrisy of Zed's lyrics, who raps about his roots in the UK while not having visited his parents in two years, signalling that there is complexity and confusion around being both British and Pakistani. Unravelling this and coming to terms with it forms the narrative arc of the film.

There is a distinct blurring of boundaries between Ahmed's own life and that of the protagonist Zed. Both are rappers with a version of their names made more convenient for western pronunciation, or perhaps borne of a desire to assimilate – Riz is a shortened version of Rizwan. On this subject, in an interview with *Vanity Fair*, Ahmed talked about the self-editing of his name that took place in order for him to fit in. He said that now, as an adult, he sees these two names as symbolic of the way that Asian people can feel the struggle to pull away from their original culture while still retaining a sense of a whole identity.

This comment epitomises the tension between the desire to assimilate and the ambivalence that the protagonist feels towards his roots. This sense of ownership of identity and dislocation is at the heart of *Mogul Mowgli*, and the autoimmune condition forces Zed to confront his inner struggle to reconcile the different and conflicting parts of his identity; in the words of Ahmed, 'the body is not recognising itself'. He has inherited the condition from his father, so it is used to explore the theme of intergenerational trauma and the legacy of Partition (see Independent activity box) passed on in the DNA. Ahmed acknowledged in interviews that he had read Bessel van der Kolk's influential book *The Body Keeps the Score* (2014), which argues that traumatic or overwhelming experiences can affect the body.

Ahmed wrote all of the music and lyrics for the film, and many of the lyrics in Zed's rap songs are taken from Ahmed's work with the Swet Shop Boys. Zed even wears Swet Shop Boys' merchandise in the opening when he performs on stage. This draws attention to Ahmed's rap career, directing the audience to the lyrics of his other songs, and also further blurs the boundaries between fact and fiction in a similar way to magic realism, where the hallucinations and memories provide additional insight into the events depicted on screen.

Proma Khoshler suggests in her review for *Mashable* online magazine, '"Mogul Mowgli" is Riz Ahmed's Soul Laid Bare' (2021), that the story combines the things most highly prized by Ahmed: rap music, fighting against the oppression of minorities and the theme of identity. Ahmed links the deep sense of authenticity in the film to Tariq's background in documentary filmmaking. In an interview for Slant magazine, he talked about Tariq demanding an authentic and natural performance.

Independent activity

Consider the rest of Ahmed's work as a rapper with the Swet Shop Boys (see image above) and as Riz MC. Make notes about his perosna as a rapper and the concerns he expresses in his lyrics.

Bathos: humour derived from the juxtaposition of something important with something trivial.

Independent activity

Read about the Partition of India in 1947 and watch the beginning of the film. Why do you think the film opens with Bashir's train journey from India to Pakistan as a child?

The film's title is inspired by Swet Shop Boys' 'Half Moghul, Half Mowgli', from their 2016 album *Cashmere*. In the song Moghul refers to the Moghul Empire in South Asia, a reminder of Ahmed's heritage extending back before colonialism and Partition, with a line of descent from great rulers. This heritage is spliced with the character of 'Mowgli', the protagonist in Rudyard Kipling's collection of stories *The Jungle Book*. The series, set in India, was first published in magazines in the late 1800s and then made popular by the animated Disney film, released in 1967. *The Jungle Book* stories explore the same feelings of dislocation: the man-cub (Mowgli) is removed from his village and forced to adapt to living in the jungle; in Ahmed's version, the jungle becomes the concrete jungle of London. The brother Mowgli meets in the first story, 'Mowgli's Brothers', is the black panther Bagheera, who teaches him about the jungle; in the film, Bagheera becomes the black rappers, who are Zed's mentors. The sense of dislocation is pronounced in both: Mowgli is neither part of the jungle nor the village. Zed is neither part of the British, Pakistani or rap community, and he doubts the validity of the means – rapping – he chooses to express his identity. His insecurities about his status in the rap world are played out in a hallucination at the height of his illness, via a rap battle against a group of black rappers.

As Zed tries to sleep on his final night in New York, he composes a song along similar lines; his constant need to examine his identity and status forms part of an existential crisis and anxiety over his value. Here, he references the rose and the poppy. The poppy is referred to elsewhere in the film as a weed, something unwanted that has taken root. But the poppy also links to artwork from the Moghul Empire, where it was painted extensively, even on the walls of the Taj Mahal, perhaps symbolising the rulers' love of opium. This image appears during a flashback to Zed's final performance in New York, after he has received the devastating news that the aggressive treatment for his disease will likely affect his fertility. Zed performs the track 'Where You From' (taken from the Riz MC album *The Long Goodbye* – see below), which refers to the brown bodies of Indian soldiers fertilising the ground where poppies grow, a reference to the soldiers in the British-Indian Army who fought for the British Empire in the First World War.

This image indicates the expansive definition of British-Pakistani identity, including the legacy of India's colonial past and the impact on personal identity, which forms part of the central ideology of the film. The poppy is also a symbol of peace, but those who contributed to that peace have been eliminated through British colonial amnesia. The political context of the Partition of India is at the heart of this narrative.

The film is very much intertwined with Riz MC's concept album *The Long Goodbye*, released in March 2020, shortly before the film's cinema release. It has at its heart the same central questions of identity and belonging. Track 2, 'Toba Tek Singh', forms part of the central motif in the film. Toba Tek Singh is a city and district in the Pakistani (formerly Indian) province of Punjab. It is also the title of a satirical short story written by Saadat Hasan Manto and published in 1955, and the hometown of Manto's protagonist in the story. Manto fiercely opposed Partition, and the story focuses on the protagonist's anxiety over where his home will be located after Partition. Zed shares this anxiety about home, family and his own identity, and the anxieties are personified in the film by the hallucinatory figure of a man wearing a flowered headdress (a sehra), traditionally worn by South Asian grooms at their wedding. The man absurdly announces that he is Toba Tek Singh and is a surreal manifestation of Partition itself, intergenerational trauma and Zed's increasingly fragmented identity and imagination.

> **Image search**
> **Zed's personas**
> Watch the opening 15 minutes of the film and compile a series of screengrabs that show Zed's persona as a performer, a son and a family member. How is a relationship established between the viewer and the different ways in which Zed's character is developed?

Film form

Cinematography

The film is shot in 4:3 ratio. Tariq told *Filmmaker Magazine* that he deliberately chose a female cinematographer, Annika Summerson, in order to 'soften the image' in a 'male-heavy' film. Summerson's cinematography is used in subtle, subjective and sometimes surprising ways. For example, when Zed is in a hospital bed or a wheelchair, the shot depicts him in the lower third of the frame. Consequently, the negative space symbolises his vulnerability and is in distinct contrast to his life pre-illness, which is centrally shot and features big close-ups of him, symbolising his feelings of apparent control. The 4:3 ratio results in a portrait-sized, intimate frame. Yet within it not all images are clear; the use of shadow, shallow focus and framing devices – doorways and a shower cubicle, for example – often mean that elements of the image are obscured. And as Zed struggles to find meaning in his own life when he confronts his family relationships and heritage, Zed and the viewer have only a partial understanding of events, creating a vicarious experience.

The image above is a medium close-up of Zed performing in New York, taken from the start of the film. The use of deep focus gives an insight into his success as a rapper on the brink of a European tour. In contrast, when Zed is performing in the imaginary rap battle, he is at the side of the frame, reflecting his deeply felt insecurities as a rapper. This is emphasised by the use of shallow focus, which has the image of his imaginary adversary, a black rapper, out of focus. The rapper represents Zed's guilt and shame about his perceived cultural appropriation; the words of the rapper draw attention to black ownership of hip hop and its links to black history.

The big close-ups often appear like enigmatic portraits. In the exchanges between Zed and Bina, and then Zed and his father, the viewer is left to interpret the feelings of each character and decipher the nature of the rift in the two relationships; this intimate cinematography suggests that there is little room for two people in the frame, emphasising how disconnected Zed is from others, and ultimately himself. The camera is tightly focused on Zed for much of the film, or we see events as he sees them through point-of-view shots, creating a subjective style of cinematography.

In the opening, the camera movement is often hand-held, following the action, creating a sense of immediacy, which takes the viewer along on the journey of self-discovery in the way that a documentary might. For example, in the scene near the beginning of the film where the younger members of the family debate names, a hand-held camera moves between them, following the fast-paced conversation and moving over to where the parents sit for reactions. This documentary-style cinematography invites the viewer into the family to learn some important information in a natural way: Zed's cousin suggests that acknowledging his real name will solve his problems and Bashir claims that he doesn't remember fleeing from India at the time of Partition.

4 Trainspotting (Boyle, 1996) & Mogul Mowgli (Tariq, 2020)

The brightly lit stage at the opening of the film contrasts starkly with the natural lighting of London. The muted colours and realism bring Zed's background to the fore of the narrative: this is the reality that he will be forced to acknowledge. More expressionist lighting is used for the hallucinations; there is a spotlight on the veiled man in the dark hospital ward as the past mocks the present and Zed is forced to confront the associated shame and guilt. The flashbacks/memories (or imagining) of the train journey Bashir took from India to Pakistan as a child is shot in partial darkness, with shafts of sunlight illuminating dust. The forcible transportation by train of displaced people who suffer horrifying violence is a reference to the Holocaust; the presence of dust highlighted by shafts of sunlight breaking into the darkened train full of terrified people, often wounded, is a stark reminder of mortality.

Mise-en-scène

The colours green and white dominate throughout; they are there at the outset with muted green trees at night, and the shots on the train have a green filter which, alongside the darkness, creates a sense of mystery and horror. This continues with the darkness onstage juxtaposed with the green and white stage lighting. Later, for his visit home, Zed wears a green sweatshirt and jogging bottoms. The greens and creams of the furnishings in his parents' house are softer and more comforting, a feeling that Zed is not willing to acknowledge. These colours suggest a deep psychological need for Zed to connect with his roots, signalled by the colours of the Pakistani flag (green represents the Muslim majority in Pakistan, white all other minority religions, while the colours further represent prosperity and peace). This colour palette links to his father and his heritage; the point-of-view shot as Zed wakes in the hospital is of out-of-focus green and white lighting, hinting that it is his DNA which has brought him here.

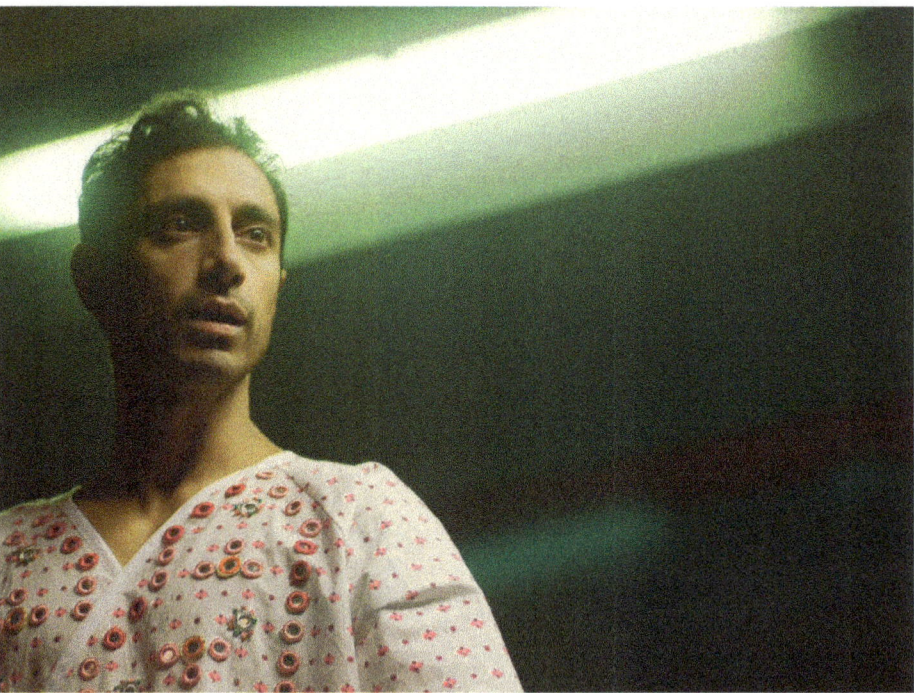

Legacy is a key theme and, for Zed, Bashir's legacy is one of past businesses failures, leaving Zed with a sense of shame and fear of failure. One particular object links the two men: with youthful disregard for the past and disrespect for his father, Zed has partially taped over one of Bashir's cassettes, *Partition: Songs of Trauma*, with his early raps, where he announces himself as 'Zeddy Boy '96'. When a song showing the trauma of Partition breaks through, Zed peels off the *Jungle Zed* sticker from the cracked front cover of the case to reveal a picture of a South Asian man wearing a sehra that covers his eyes. Typical of a magic realist aesthetic (when the magical world is present in the real world), this ordinary image becomes the hallucination which embodies Zed's fear of confronting his past and facing up to the shame he felt as a child over his father's failures. The magical version of this man comes to inform the narrative of real-world events and is vital for the viewer's understanding of Zed's psychology and character arc.

The hospital gown is another ordinary object which becomes transformed in the narrative in a magical way to depict Zed's journey back into his heritage. The transformation of the gown from an ordinary hospital gown to an embroidered kurta (see image on the previous page) occurs when Zed finds himself in a rap battle, reflecting the inescapability of his heritage and the beginnings of his subconscious mind starting to acknowledge that his heritage also brings power. The hallucination reveals Zed's guilt about his father's Nigerian hair salon, which links with his insecurity as a Pakistani rapper and the fear of cultural appropriation. His character arc moves from this to an empowering pride in his heritage when he wears the royal version of the gown later in the film.

Editing

The editing is fast paced, with conventional, seamless editing intercut with surreal images to form montages. This style of editing is crucial in creating the magic realist aesthetic where the dream sequences, memories and hallucinations are used to inform the more realistic moments. The editing constantly makes the connection between past and present and father and son, revealing to the viewer the parts needed to create a whole person. The climax of this idea occurs in the sequence where Zed is undergoing chemotherapy, during which he sees in a dream Bashir put on all of the clothes from his business ventures before falling to the floor with numb legs. Zed falls to the floor as he tries to get to him. When he reaches his father, the train noise starts and they both begin to shake, forming a surreal match on action placing both of them on the train. A cutaway reveals they are being watched by the frightened and partially concealed face of Bashir as a boy. Scenes of his father's frustration and breakdown in the restaurant are then intercut with wounds of the people on the train and Nasra calmly stacking shelves in Lyfields while the shelves are rattling. The sequence culminates in a shot where we follow Zed in the now fully transformed hospital gown, to see the man in the sehra on the floor, symbolising that Zed has finally acknowledged and assimilated his father's past. This chemotherapy-induced hallucination, edited in montage, is typical of the magic realism present throughout the film. When we cut back to Zed awake, his face is initially covered with the dust from the train.

The word *Bismillah* (which begins a Muslim prayer) is sometimes used in the film to mark the transition of one scene to another; for example, at the cut to the dream world while Zed is under anaesthetic, and the three cut-away shots into close-ups of dust particles followed by the terrified face of Bashir as a child. The cut-back to the present is to a big close-up of Bashir's concerned face, linking past and present and imbuing his character with a sympathetic depth. This word, spoken non-diegetically, possibly as a thought, perhaps suggests the beginning of Zed's openness to his religion, heritage and culture, or at the very least an acknowledgement.

Towards the end of the film, long takes in the toilet/bathroom, at first in hospital and then at home, reflect the real consequences of the illness and the need for his father's support. Similarly, the extended close-ups on Zed's feet, showing him re-learning to walk, suggest a long rebirth of his unified identity.

Sound

The film opens with a train whistle, and the sound of the tracks over the opening credits establishes the idea of a difficult and terrifying journey into the darkness: the terrible journey of Bashir from India to Pakistan, and the journey to healing on which Zed must embark. Sound is often used in a symbolic way, typical of magic realism, to reveal the concerns that haunt both father and son. As Zed struggles with his identity in the rap music that pervades the film, the sound of the traumatic journey from India to Pakistan also dominates the soundscape, constantly linking father and son. For example, the sound of the rattling train returns during the family scene early in the film, as the uncle suggests that the younger generation need to know about Partition. As the bloodshed and massacres of Partition are mentioned in the dialogue, vibrating objects can be seen out of focus in the foreground of the frame and, while the camera shows us Zed's slightly shocked reaction at the suggestion that his father has 'seen some crazy shit', but doesn't remember it, in contrast we hear the guilt and shame of Bahir in his dialogue; he didn't try to save people, he just hid.

A refugee special train at Ambala Station during thhe Partition of India

As Bashir is revealing the guilt and shame from his childhood, the intrusion of the sound of that terrifying journey is perhaps allowing Zed to have some newfound respect for his father. Later, Bashir's whispered prayers on the Tube home from the hospital become the whispered prayers of child Bashir hiding on the train.

Sound bridges are used to connect the fragmentary elements of the narrative; for example, as Zed reacts to the news of his potential infertility, as we see a big close-up of him looking off screen, we hear the sound of his track 'Where You From' (a slightly modified version of the Riz MC track). Cutting from the hospital to a flashback of Zed's New York gig, the sound bridge subtly suggests his train of thought – rather than dwell on the bloodline as his father does, Zed's concern is his legacy as a rapper and the upcoming European tour, although the lyrics of the song are concerned with the treatment he has received as a result of his heritage.

Performance (A level only)

Ahmed starts the film with Zed rapping with a fury and intensity, in contrast to the measured and detached way that Ahmed performs the same songs as Riz MC. At the start of the film, Zed's face is expressive and he is constantly moving, demonstrating the restless drive and ambition he has. In the portrait-style close-ups, his reactions are often easy to read through facial expression, for example the look of disgust on his face at the dismissive way his dad talks to his mum.

Ahmed has talked about his preparation for the role, during which he rapidly lost around 10 kg (22 lb) to demonstrate the progression of Zed's illness. Together with the framing, this indicates fragility, which creates a sense of child-like vulnerability and stasis, from which he can build a healthier body and sense of himself. In the middle section of the film, his body and his face become much more still and his reaction shots are much harder to decipher. However, his angry sarcasm about his rival rapper RPG is a glimpse of his earlier performance.

In the final third of the film, his gradual rebirth towards a new, unified identity shows a gradual return to facial and bodily mobility, but perhaps reflects the measured calm of Ahmed himself.

Aesthetics

The aesthetic is magic realism, a style that shows a surreal magical world intertwined with reality and social realism, where scenes are lit realistically in real settings and with natural performances and dialogue. The combination of these aesthetics allows Tariq to explore the familiar territory of the rejection of his parents' culture by their second-generation adult child, and the psychological impact of displacement for both generations. Social realism has a documentary aesthetic, but, as Zed's mind and body start to break down, the aesthetic becomes more surreal. This highlights how a surreal aesthetic is used to create the interconnected sense of past and present, real and imaginary, particularly through editing and sound. The film also has music documentary aspects, particularly at the opening.

Representations

Gender

Femininity

Women in the film are shown as powerful and pragmatic, in contrast to some rather foolish and self-absorbed men. While Zed's father struggles to establish himself as a successful businessman, his mum, Nasra, keeps the family going by working in Lyfields grocery store, and this is reinforced by her line about having to always clean up after the men.

A stereotypical representation of her maternal qualities is typical of the ways that South Asian mothers are represented. She is consistently caring and concerned, more interested in seeing her son than a new washing machine, only concerned for his welfare. Significantly, she is not hysterical or emotional; at the climax of the clash between approaches to his condition when Zed falls in the shower, Bashir continues to argue with Zed and his mum simply calls for a nurse. Crucially, she is the one at the beginning of the film who identifies the similarities between the two men, which neither will accept until the resolution, as they are equally stubborn.

The representation of women is positive throughout, even though the film is not concerned with exploring femininity in any depth. Just as Nasra has wisdom and holds the family together, Vaseem, Zed's manager, is tough, operating in the male-dominated music industry, assertively shutting down Zed's suggestion of doing the tour in a chair. She is also shown as pragmatic, filling the slot with rival rapper RPG and crucially seeing the bigger picture, that rather than the competition, RPG is telling the same story, and she appeals to Zed to see RPG as part of a bigger struggle.

Her line is juxtaposed for comic effect with RPG's silly viral video 'Pussy Fried Chicken', satirising egotistical, materialist, inane rap lyrics and videos objectifying women. Ironically, despite his disdain, it is Zed's ego that is preventing him from seeing that Vaseem is right.

The film is also populated with confident professional women: Bina, Dr Mayberry, his consultant neurologist, and other nurses and doctors.

Masculinity

Zed's insecurity about his masculinity, bound up with his idea of success and his legacy, is directly linked to his view of his father as a failure. The sequence where Zed is under anaesthetic and has an anxiety-fuelled dream that he is in the

> **Independent activity**
>
> Read about the ways in which Riz Ahmed prepared for the role of Zed. Find examples in the film where his impact created a strong response in you as a viewer.

> **Independent activity**
>
> Read about magic realism and the significance of the magical world for the real world. Identify where the hallucinations and flashbacks become significant for a deeper understanding of reality.

4 Trainspotting (Boyle, 1996) & Mogul Mowgli (Tariq, 2020)

schoolroom at the mosque, unable to read from the Quran, shows us Zed's insecurity about his identity. His vulnerability is shown by his hospital gown and then by a wrestling match with a much bigger opponent who, on the line 'I got you', becomes the man in the sehra, then RPG, and then the man again who says 'Welcome home'. Here his fear of the extensive history and culture of his past combines with his fear of comparison with RPG, who is a manifestation of the ridiculous inferior performer he fears himself to be. Both are derived from a rejection of his cultural heritage, which could be seen as a form of internalised racism against himself.

Zed is also terrified of being identified as his father, who he has perceived as a poor role model for masculinity; through a variety of techniques, particularly editing, the viewer is able to see the obvious similarities between them. Zed has grown up with a sense of shame over his perception of his father's weakness and failure in his business enterprises. The scene that follows the fight outside of the mosque is a flashback to Zed's father's restaurant; the leering close-ups and pleonastic diegetic sound (a diegetic sound that is noticeably louder than it would be in reality) create a feeling of horror, insinuating that the customers seem to have very little respect for Bashir. The scene becomes more than a straightforward flashback as the young Zed emerges from a storeroom as his present self, symbolising the legacy he carries from that time.

The representation of masculinity is complex. The viewer is shown the types of men that Zed does not want to be; this can be traced to the intergenerational emasculating effect of Partition, which affects the ways in which first- and second-generation South Asian men struggle to find a sense of their own worth, buried beneath layers of assumed identities that don't quite fit. The treatment prescribed for Zed's illness – the symbolic representation of the legacy of Partition – is to take away his potency as a man, but it also allows him to reconnect with his father and see that the only way to become a man is to embrace the similarities between them.

Ethnicity

The representation of the South Asian identity is inextricably linked with the representation of gender, and masculinity in particular. Commentators have suggested that the film has a raw and refreshingly authentic representation, derived from what may be considered a 'brown gaze'. Rather than Hollywood telling South Asian stories through a 'white gaze' for a white audience, which would be reliant on stereotypes and clichés, Tariq constructs a brown gaze. An important part of this is the way that references to aspects of South Asian culture, such as the burning of chilis to determine the presence of the evil eye, are not explained for the viewer; the film assumes a shared understanding and knowledge of the culture, history and religion of the South Asian diaspora.

The unexplained reference to Toba Tek Singh is a key example of this. This symbol functions on two levels – to the uninformed, as a mysterious figure who generates an emotional response, but also, for those with knowledge, a homage to Manto (as Tariq has said) and a potent symbol of the trauma of Partition.

The way immigrants are treated in Britain is signalled by the lyrics of 'Where You From', which refers to prejudice and violence. The struggle to survive as an immigrant in Britain is symbolised by the layers of clothing that Bashir puts on, poignantly demonstrating the number of ways he has tried to make a living before collapsing exhausted.

Narrative

The film creates a vicarious experience through the use of a shared point of view in the linear parts of the narrative. We experience many of the events as Zed does, particularly his illness and the impact on his rap career, and his subsequent intense anger and disappointment.

Independent activity

Working on your own or with another student, plot the narrative structure of two films you are studying for **Component 1 Section C: British film since 1995**. Consider how performance supports the character arc at key points in the narrative.

Use the following framework:

1 Exposition: the introduction of the main characters, genre and setting.
2 Inciting incident: the event that happens which changes everything and presents a problem that the protagonist must solve.
3 Rising action: action taken by the protagonist or others to rectify the problems caused the inciting incident.
4 Climax: the final decision made by the protagonist that will solve the problem; this is usually a dramatic scene involving some sort of conflict or confrontation.
5 Resolution: the way in which the problem is resolved, and a sense of learning and development in the protagonist.

This linear narrative is intertwined with non-linear elements – flashbacks, home movies, hallucinations – and this creates a privileged point of view where the magical aspects provide insight that Zed lacks. For example, he is haunted by young Bashir's suffering long before he realises it.

Critical approaches to narrative

The film's structure is built around a series of binary opposites. It would be useful to explore the ideas of the personal and the political, or the individual and the group, differences between first- and second-generation South Asians, father and son, success and failure.

Ideology

Ahmed has talked about his British identity in the widest sense, arguing that it should be much more inclusive, linking back to Britain's colonial past, and there are key messages in the film about this interconnectedness of people. These are explored in Zed's lyrics and extended through the examination of legacy through bloodlines, art and the idea of success, epitomised by Zed having to accept RPG as the next generation and a part of his legacy.

The character of RPG, although often comic, is crucial for delivering the message of collective success in opposition to individual drive and ambition. Zed's attitude to RPG is shown to be toxic, and while this is done through humour, for example his derogatory comment about RPG's face tattoos, it is undermined by a close-up of RPG, which reveals that one of those tattoos is 'Zed', showing the endearing adoration that RPG has for his hero. Furthermore, Nabhaan Rizwan's performance, with his child-like half smiles, encourages sympathy, which reinforces messages of collectivism and community. Giving the song to RPG is a turning point in Zed's character arc and represents a sharing of the burden of the trauma from the past; it is collective, not individual. RPG's version of Zed's song 'Toba Tek Singh' is extremely significant at the resolution of the film; the burden of the trauma is a shared one. The theme of interconnectedness is intensified as Zed and his father come together, no longer caring who is singing the song, as they are singing it together.

The film is also concerned with the legacy of trauma. Zed is disconnected from his past and the history of his ancestors, perhaps due to Bashir's refusal to talk about it, and this is symbolised by the autoimmune condition. The illness is, on the surface, a link to the past through DNA, but in more symbolic terms it is the result of self-loathing and internalised racism, especially when it comes to rap. There are important messages about the toxic way that immigrants from South Asia have been treated in Britain, and the negative impact that this has had on different generations' physical and mental health.

Taking a post-colonial ideological critical approach

The post-colonial critical approach is an established theoretical approach in which the legacy of imperialism is examined in a text. Some commentators have questioned the concept of 'post-colonial' as – in a similar way to 'post-feminism' – 'post' suggests that feminism is over, which is far from the case. Likewise, although the British Empire has ended, colonial attitudes are still pervasive and its legacy still causes trauma, as seen in *Mogul Mowgli*. Kritva Rana writes about (post) colonial issues in the film (see 'The (Post) Colonial Demasculinisation within *Mogul Mowgli*' (2020) in *British Asian Women's Magazine*). She particularly discusses the emasculating effect of colonisation, as the colonised man is perceived to be lacking the masculinity of the European male colonisers.

This article suggests that a post-colonial approach is combined with an ideological approach that considers gender, in this case masculinity, which could be considered

Stretch & challenge

Watch the *Mogul Mowgli* Q&A from the BFI London Film Festival 2020, which you can find on YouTube.

Stretch & challenge

Research post-colonial theory and think about why it might be a useful approach to take when understanding the themes of this film.

as an approach in itself. Rana argues that the two are very much linked through the emasculating effect of powerlessness.

This idea is portrayed through the horror aesthetic in the flashback to Bashir's restaurant, a specific immigrant space named after his home (Karachi Chilli). But even here Bashir is humiliated, and this shame is transferred to Zed. The way this sequence is constructed shows that years later in Britain, the chaos and trauma of India during Partition has an emasculating effect through financial insecurity and health implications due to displacement and repression. The shaking of the traumatic and terrifyingly violent train journey which continues to bleed into the present is linked to the numbness in Zed's legs caused by the illness, which symbolises inertia: the long-lasting emasculating effect of Partition.

The continual prejudice externally, and the guilt and shame internally, lead to a crisis in male identity; Bashir and the different ways in which he has tried to earn a living are reflected in the scene with multiple layers of clothing, and this links to young Bashir hiding under piles of clothing and his subsequent shame. The stubbornness, determination and drive that binds Bashir and Zed shows a need for control over the legacy of colonialism; Bashir has struggled and been humiliated in Britain. The motif of the train journey shows that the trauma of the colonial past cannot be repressed.

The other crucial motif is the man who represents this heritage, culture and colonisation through reference to Toba Tek Singh; the place and the story take us back to the suffering and death experienced during Partition. Zed's triumph at walking despite the mocking laughter from the man with the sehra represents the possibility that, despite the odds represented by the man, the trauma of the colonial past can indeed be healed.

Further guidance on ideological approaches from Guidance for Teaching on the Eduqas website

The specification recommends that centres study either political or feminist critical approach in relation to the films listed in the specifications, though centres may wish to choose their own. Through its particular content and context, the film being studied raises specific issues; these issues make clear how the film needs to be interrogated. In other words, the film does its own recommending in terms of which critical approach to choose.

For example, the themes within *This Is England* (Meadows, 2006) suggest that it lends itself to a political approach or one that considers toxic masculinity, whereas *Fish Tank* (Arnold, 2009) may lend itself to a feminist approach, given that it was written and directed by female filmmaker Andrea Arnold and focuses on the female experience, constructing the female gaze. Similarly, a feminist approach to *Saint Maud* (Glass, 2019) would seem the most likely, as it was written and directed by Rose Glass, and subverts some of the sexist elements usually found in the horror genre. It may be interesting to consider an ideological approach that addresses racial identity and Muslim representation in *Mogul Mowgli* alongside the representation of the lasting trauma faced by immigrants and the legacy of Partition. *Mangrove* (McQueen, 2020) and *This Is England* make an interesting pairing, as they both address the impact of black culture on young working-class people in late 1960s Britain, particularly the influence on the original skinhead movement.

It is important to note that past examination questions often ask for the evaluation of the usefulness of a particular ideological approach for understanding the film. When you are considering an ideological approach and applying it to a particular sequence from the film, don't forget to consider why this approach has been useful for identifying themes, but also acknowledge its limitations. It is useful when thinking about the limitations of a specific ideological approach to identify another approach which may illuminate other aspects of the scene, with some examples. Examiners are expecting to see a response to the question which constructs a debate where the usefulness of the approach is evaluated for around two-thirds of the answer, and another possibility suggested in the final third. Your conclusion should briefly summarise the debate, relating back to the key words from the question.

Conclusion

Trainspotting remains an era-defining film and is one of the most successful UK films of the 1990s. Aside from its ability to talk to a generation and capture the zeitgeist, it remains (despite the huge critical and financial success of 2009's *Slumdog Millionaire*) Danny Boyle's defining film. While its vibrant soundtrack, its aspirational new stars (Ewan McGregor most famously), its wit, its controversial representation of Scotland and its energetically edited, beautifully shot material led to some criticism for its perceived glamorisation of a drug-fuelled lifestyle, true or not, the marketing for the film certainly communicated to its audience a sense of cool, featuring iconic portrait mid-long shots of the main characters as well as trumpeting the arrival of a new wave of UK cinema.

In *Mogul Mowgli*, his debut narrative feature, along with co-writer and star Riz Ahmed, director Bassim Tariq tackles the complexities of identity in the British Asian community head on with humour and honesty. The film is an interesting example of an independent production which has achieved considerable critical and cultural success, raising issues of colonialism and post-colonialism referencing the partition of India, the role of the British Indian Army in World War 1 and the world of rap music. It is significant in its representation of South Asian identity in Britain, moving representations away from stereotypes and into something more recognisably authentic; something which some commentators have identified as a 'brown gaze'. The use of a magic realist aesthetic makes it visually stunning and memorable, adding a complex layer of symbolism to the film, which invites the viewer to understand the ways in which tensions within a person's identity can cause a breakdown and subsequent re-building of that person's identity, pertinent to people who are the second generation of South Asian families and also relating to universal themes of masculinity, father/son relationships, the relationship between mind and body and personal insecurities. The film also deals with artistic integrity and the legacy that an artist leaves behind from their creative output, creating a meta-layer of meaning to the film, it is a film about the relationship between a piece of art and the artist or artists themselves. There is much to read and watch online about this multi-layered film and both Ahmed and Tariq have given extensive interviews, keen to promote the film and discuss its many themes.

Study tip

Don't just watch the films on the specification. Watch and read about the other British films made around the same time.

Study tip

Practise exam technique by summarising and analysing a film still from a chosen film in less than five minutes. A good answer makes a point and backs it up with technical and theoretical terms.

4 Trainspotting (Boyle, 1996) & Mogul Mowgli (Tariq, 2020)

Section 2

AS: European film
A level: Global filmmaking perspectives

Group A European film

This chapter will help you prepare for **Component 2: Global filmmaking perspectives** on the A level course and **Component 2: European film (AS)**.

The focus is on the three core areas of study. This chapter will use the French/Turkish film *Mustang* (Ergüven, 2015) and *Portrait of a Lady on Fire* (Sciamma, 2019) as case studies.

For AS
You answer one question from a choice of two and must refer to both your chosen films. You should spend 50 minutes on your response.

For A level
You will answer one 40 mark question from a choice of two, requiring reference to two global films: one European and one produced outside Europe. You should allow 60 minutes for your answer.

The specification says
Global film extends the range and diversity of narrative film, requiring the study of two films, each representing a distinct geographical, social, cultural world and a particular expressive use of film form.

Mustang explores the lives of five orphaned girls in a remote Turkish village who are growing up in a strict environment with arranged marriages looming over them.

Portrait of a Lady on Fire is a poetic manifesto about the female gaze, about a love affair between two young women in Eighteenth-century France.

5 Mustang (Ergüven, 2015) & Portrait of a Lady on Fire (Sciamma, 2019)

Mustang (Ergüven, 2015)

Mustang is the debut feature film of Turkish-French director Deniz Gamze Ergüven, who co-wrote the screenplay with Alice Winocour. The screenplay draws on the experiences Ergüven and her cousins witnessed while growing up in Turkey and of young Turkish women more widely.

Portrait of a Lady on Fire (Sciamma, 2019) is a powerful lesbian love story set in the 1760s. It intimately portrays forbidden sensual desires between Héloïse, a noblewoman who rejects the husband selected for her by her mother and refuses to sit for a portrait that will be sent to him, and Marianne, a painter hired to complete her portrait who must pose as Héloïse's companion and paint her in secret.

This chapter will explore both films' credentials as a way of looking at European cinema, including examining contexts, film form, representation, ideology and critical approaches to narrative.

> **Independent activity**
>
> Select a film you are studying for Global filmmaking.
>
> - Identify at least three examples of its national cinema.
> - On the surface it is about (summarise plot in one sentence) …
> - But beneath the surface, this film is also about …
> - What genre do you think this film is?
> - What do you think are the film's key messages and values?
> - What function does the protagonist(s) have in the film?
> - Is there a character that can be seen in opposition to them? What's their function/purpose?
> - How do they contribute to the film's message and values?
> - Identify a key moment in the film, which sums up the film's message and values.

Mustang

Mustang (Ergüven, 2015) is set in Turkey and centres on five sisters, aged 12–16, who find their lives transformed one summer. Their parents have been dead for ten years and they live in a remote Turkish village with their uncle and grandmother. The film's exploration of gender, youth and identity met with mixed reactions, with international critics praising the film for its depiction of 'what it means to be young and female in Turkey' in 'Mustang Review – Teen Tension in Anatolia' (Ide, 2016). However, in Turkey the film met with criticism, as Ergüven reported,

> … I'd had some very aggressive, negative critiques there [in Turkey], the kind of thing I hadn't received anywhere else.

The criticism stemmed from Ergüven not being 'Turkish enough' (she was born in Turkey, moved to France when she was two, and spent her childhood between the two countries as dictated by her father's governmental work commitments) and by its brutal depiction of the young girls' forced marriages, sexual abuse and imprisonment. These issues will be discussed further in the social and political contexts, and the representation sections below.

Although filmed in Turkey, covertly to not anger local residents, the film is a French–German–Turkish co-production, with the majority of the $1.3 million budget coming from France. As will be outlined in more detail in the section on institutional context (pages 171–173), co-productions are common in European cinema and give filmmakers access to funding for the distribution of films across the continent. The French film industry was supportive of the film from the outset, and submitted it as their official entry to the Academy Awards, where it was nominated for the Oscar for Best Foreign Film. It also scooped up awards at the Cannes Film Festival, the Césars (France's 'Oscars') and, despite not being in French, it won four awards at the Lumières, which honours the best in French-speaking films. It also won awards in Poland, Canada, Sweden, the UK and the USA.

Mustang's representation of young women in Turkey speaks more widely about the plight of women in some parts of the world where women's rights are limited. The film brings to the fore issues regarding female education, employment opportunities, and the oppression and sexual abuse at the hands of older male family figures. Ergüven screened the film in a women's prison in France and said that there were women there from all over the world who had experienced the same treatment. Women from very different cultures and locations could relate to the story (Chung, 2016).

European cinema

There are 50 countries in Europe, with five of these sharing territory with Asia, including Turkey. Just as it is hard to define what Europe is, the same can be said for European cinema. Each country explores its own political, social, cultural past and present within its national cinema. Some may have a structured film industry producing both mainstream commercial fare, and independent art house films, while others may have little or no film industry. The films that are praised at film festivals and subsequently distributed internationally tend to be the countries' 'art house' output and not necessarily indicative of the films being watched domestically. The films' aesthetics are governed by the institutional and cultural context in which they are produced.

Independent activity

Search online for two different versions of the poster for a film you are studying.

- Make a note of the country of origin, and look at the use of images and text.
- What differences and similarities do you notice? How do the differences affect your response to the film?
- Do the images used suggest a particular mood?
- What additional information about the film's institutional and social/cultural/political contexts can you gain from the posters?
- Design your own poster, using both images and text.

The history of cinema in Europe is over 120 years old, with France considered the birthplace of 'the moving picture', when in December 1895 the Lumière Brothers gave their first paid, public screening in Paris. France has a robust film industry with national and regional governments supporting film production (both internationally, through co-productions, and nationally) and cinema exhibition. In 2016, the year *Mustang* was released in the UK, France enjoyed the highest cinema attendance in Europe, 212.7 million, followed by Russia (192.1 million) and the UK (168.3 million).

The BFI *Statistical Yearbook* 2017, which examines UK film production and cinema-going in 2016, reported that there were 165 European (excluding UK) films shown in UK cinemas. These accounted for 20.1% of all films released and grossed £40 million, a 3.2% share of the box office. In comparison there were 217 American films (26.4%), accounting for 58.9% of the box office, grossing £743.1 million and 176 (21.4%) UK films, grossing £452.9 million (35.9% share).

Country of origin of films released in the UK and Republic of Ireland, 2016 – the year *Mustang* was released in the UK

Country of origin	Number of released	% of all gross (£ million)	Box office gross (£ million)	Box office share (%)
USA	217	26.4	743.1	58.9
UK studio-backed*	20	2.4	359.2	28.5
UK independent	156	19.0	93.8	7.4
All UK	176	21.4	452.9	35.9
Other Europe	165	20.1	40.0	3.2
Indie	–	157	19.1	15.5
Rest of the world	106	12.9	10.4	0.8
Total	**821**	**100.0**	**1,262.0**	**100.0**

Notes: Box office gross – cumulative total up to 21 February 2016. Figures/percentages may not sum to totals/subtotals due to rounding. * 'Studio-backed' means backed by one of the major US film studios.

Source: comScore, BFI RSU analysis

Mustang was released in France in June 2015, but would not open in the UK until the following May, by which point it had been enthusiastically received internationally and had been among the nominees for Best Foreign Film at the Golden Globes and Oscars. It grossed just over £300,000 at the UK box office: the highest grossing Turkish film released in the UK, beating *Once Upon a Time in Anatolia* (Ceylan, 2012), which had grossed £277,447.

Contexts

Institutional contexts

Cinema-going and filmmaking in Turkey

Cinemas in Turkey attract significant audiences; in 2014 the European Audiovisual Observatory reported that cinema attendances in Turkey had risen by 14.8% to 50.4 million admissions. In the same year, UK admissions were 157 million (Iris, 2014).

Mustang was released in Turkey in 2015; in that year 420 films were screened in Turkey's cinemas: 134 were Turkish, 140 were from the USA and 126 were international, predominantly European.

Turkish cinema encompasses both mainstream commercial cinema (Ye-şil-çam) and independent art house cinema (New Turkish Cinema). In 2015 the biggest hit of the year was the comedy *Düğün Dernek 2: Sünnet*, selling 5.8 million tickets and grossing Turkish lire 67.2 million (£16.38 million) at the box office. *Mustang* may have been honoured internationally but domestic audiences were small in comparison: with a limited release its audience in Turkey was 17,500.

Although made predominantly with support from the French film industry, Ergüven's film is closely aligned with the aesthetics and subject matter of a new wave of Turkish films that emerged in the 1990s. These films have garnered praise and audiences internationally, offering a social commentary on contemporary Turkey. Common themes include national and ethnic identity and religion, and gender-based issues. Directors considered part of New Turkish Cinema are Nuri Bilge Ceylan, Zeki Demirkubuz, Semih Kaplanoğlu, Yeşim Ustaoğlu, Reha Erdem and Derviş Zaim.

> **Independent activity**
>
> Watch a film by one of the New Turkish Cinema directors mentioned on this page and compare it with *Mustang* to get a sense of New Turkish Cinema.

European co-productions and funding

Securing financing is crucial to European filmmaking; with that in mind, most European countries have film commissions, with many offering tax incentives, funding and production support.

Mustang is a CG Cinema production (France), co-produced with Bam Film (Turkey), Vistamar Filmproduktion (Germany), Uhlandfilm (Germany) and the Doha Film Institute (Qatar). The lead producers were CG Cinema, which was founded in 2013 by producer Charles Gillibert, with the aim of supporting films by auteur directors. The film's budget was $1.3 million, with funding received from the German–French mini-traité, Film-und Medienstiftung NRW, Eurimages and the Doha Film Institute, among others.

Mustang was awarded the Europa Cinema's Label Award at the 2015 Cannes Film Festival. The receipt of this award is pivotal in the distribution journey of a European film, as it helps support the promotion, circulation and exhibition of a film across Europe by providing financial incentives to cinemas within their network. Europa Cinemas, founded in 1988, is an integral element in the production, distribution and exhibition of European films. Via its MEDIA programme (Creative Europe), it provides operational and financial support to cinemas that commit to screening a significant number of European non-national films. In 2024, there were 3,121 cinemas in 783 cities in 39 countries in the network. *Mustang* received Eurimages funding. You can learn more about Europa Cinemas impact at their website

Women film directors

Mustang opened in the USA in November 2015, hot on the heels of significant activity, legally and socially, to investigate the lack of women working at the highest levels of filmmaking, and to raise the profile of those that were.

In 2012, film director Maria Giese, frustrated by the difficulty of getting work in Hollywood, met with the Equal Employment Opportunity Commission and the American Civil Liberties Union about sexual discrimination in the film industry. Her three-year research and campaigning reached its peak in October 2015, when it was reported that the Equal Employment Opportunity Commission had officially launched its investigation into discrimination against female film and television directors.

The same month, the Los Angeles branch of Women in Film and Television, launched the #52FilmsByWomen hashtag as part of their 'Trailblazing Women' initiative with Turner Classic Movies. They simply asked filmgoers to pledge to watch a film a week directed by a woman for a year. This campaign has helped to raise the profile of female directors, particularly global filmmakers. It has led to female-led curation at film festivals and streaming services, and the launch of the F-rating, which is awarded to films that are directed and/or written by a woman. If the film also features significant women on screen in their own right, it is TRIPLE F-rated. The rating is designed to support and promote women and redress the imbalance in the film industry. The F-rating can be seen as a complement to the Bechdel Test explored in the representation section of this book (page 50). *Mustang* is considered a triple F-rated film, and passes the Bechdel Test.

The October 2015 issue of the BFI's *Sight & Sound magazine* had a cover line 'The Female Gaze' and championed 100 female-directed hidden gems that had been forgotten or unfairly overlooked. This heightened awareness of gender inequality and representation would have helped to raise the profile of *Mustang*, which had a strong female creative presence both behind and in front of the camera.

Copyright BFI. Used with permission.

Further information

Women in film in 2015

An examination of the top 250 films at the box office in 2015 revealed that only 3.6% were directed by women, 4.4% written by women and 10.4% produced by women.

The Center for the Study of Women in Television & Film report that women took 22% of key on-screen roles in the top films of 2015, the most since study began in 2002. They also analysed the ethnicity of the key role and reported that 'the percentages of female characters of color were largely unchanged …' (Lang, 2016).

Read the full article from *Variety*: 'Study: Female Protagonists on the Rise in Hollywood – but the Majority Are White' (Lang, 2016). Do you think anything has changed since this article was written?

Social, cultural and political contexts

Child marriage in Turkey

At the heart of *Mustang* are the arranged marriages and importance placed on the virginity of the four eldest sisters. Critics of the film railed against the depiction of Turkey that was being disseminated internationally through the success of this film, stressing that this is not the experience of all Turkish young women. However, Turkey, particularly rural Turkey, remains a patriarchal society where women are seen as the property of their fathers and then their husbands. In the absence of the parents, the patriarchal figure here is the uncle. His behaviour and the experiences of the sisters is a narrative construct: this is a fiction film and will be the experience of some young women in Turkey but not all.

However, women's behaviour in public, virginity and marriage are all common topics of conversation in Turkey. According to the website Girls Not Brides (2017), a global partnership of more than 800 civil society organisations committed to ending child marriage and enabling girls to fulfil their potential, Turkey has one of the highest rates of child marriage in Europe, with an estimated 15% of girls married before the age of 18.

The legal marriageable age is 18, but parents can apply for exemptions for 16- and 17-year-olds, there are also reports of illegal 'marriages' with girls as young as ten. The influx of desperate Syrian refugees to Turkey has seen many Syrian parents effectively selling their daughters into marriage.

In addition, the website Girls Not Brides (2017) indicates that Turkey's patriarchal structure is a significant factor, reporting that:

★ Girls and women are expected to conform to traditional gender norms and expectations.
★ Violence against women and girls is common and tolerated.
★ School attendance remains low for girls, with little importance placed on their education.
★ Girls are often valued for their ability to be good wives and mothers.

5 Mustang (Ergüven, 2015) & Portrait of a Lady on Fire (Sciamma, 2019)

Independent activity

Has this information on child marriage and women in Turkish society aided your understanding of the issues in *Mustang*? Visit the Girls Not Brides website to find out more. List five ways in which the film depicts these issues visually and within narrative.

Independent activity

Although the young women playing the sisters have a more liberal upbringing than their on-screen counterparts, they too feel the pressures of Turkish gender oppression. Read the following two articles:

- *IndieWire* (Buder, 2015) 'Meet France's Oscar Entry, "*Mustang*", a Controversial 5-Headed Monster of Femininity'
- *Irish Examiner* (Barlow, 2016) '"*Mustang*" is a Stirring Tale of Girlhood'

What do the young stars of the film and the director say about life in Turkey?

Independent activity

Do you consider *Mustang* to be an example of realist cinema? Through an examination of its film form write a 400-word essay. This should be analysis, not an evaluation of the film.

They add that the figures for underage marriage could be much higher as:

★ Turkey has a poor birth registration system, which means that families can marry their daughters without fear of repercussion.
★ Most child marriages are unregistered and take place as unofficial religious marriages.

In addition to the explicit depiction of child marriage in the film, Ergüven also incorporates controversial comments by Turkish politicians on the appropriate chaste behaviour of young women, shown in background news footage.

Since the film's release, there has been some success in moderating legislation linked to child marriage. In November 2016, the Turkish government withdrew a bill that would allow perpetrators of sexual assault to be exonerated if they married their victims. MPs, human rights campaigners, the public and the international community feared that the bill would legitimise rape and encourage child marriage.

Domestic violence in Turkey

With the culture of child marriage comes one of domestic violence.

Domestic violence rates are high. In 2016 Turkey's Ministry of Family and Social Policies reported that 86% of women experienced physical or psychological violence from a partner or family member (Sheva, 2016). In 2015, 300 women died as a result of domestic violence (Hudgins, 2017), more than double the 2014 UK figure (McVeigh & Colley, 2015).

Further information

Italian Neorealist Cinema

Mustang uses a style that is inspired by Italian Neorealism. Italian Neorealism is a term used to describe the films produced in Italy after the Second World War. They were produced with very low budgets and the aesthetic was a creative reflection of what can be achieved with little money.

There is no fixed list of which films or directors contributed to the body of films known collectively as Italian Neorealist. It is generally considered that the movement began with *Rome Open City* (Rossellini, 1945) and ends with *Umberto D* (De Sica, 1952). Other key films were *The Bicycle Thieves* (De Sica, 1948) *and Germany Year Zero* (Rossellini, 1948).

What is Neorealism? Is it a genre? A style? A movement? No matter the label placed on this unique body of films, it is clear that at their heart is a group of people's personal response to the war, and the distinctive way they used film as a powerful tool to deal with their memories and relate their experiences to a larger world.

Rossellini and De Sica, the most significant post-war Italian directors, took to the streets to make their films. Using real locations, hand-held cameras, non-professional actors and relying on improvisation, they produced films that seem to be completely truthful. But in fact they are not telling the truth but only a version of it, as sieved through the collective memories of the directors and actors, infused with a strong ideological and political agenda. The films blurred the lines between documentary and fiction and were greatly admired outside Italy by 'intellectual' cineasts in Britain, American and Europe.

Because the filmmakers' technical equipment was sparse, there was a freedom of visual style as well as freedom of subject matter. Their films focused on the current state of the nation and the recent past under German occupation and local resistance. Their attitude was to show the everyday reality, the life of the working classes in post-war Italy.

Film form in European cinema and *Mustang*

As there are 50 countries within Europe, it is important not to make sweeping generalisations about a single European film aesthetic. The films that are, in the main, discussed within the academic study of European cinema are those of the national 'art house' cinema. The notion of an 'art house aesthetic' is one that David Bordwell addresses in his chapter 'The Art Cinema as a Mode of Practice' (2002), where he writes:

> ... art cinema defines itself as realistic cinema. It will show us real locations (Neorealism, the New wave) and real problems (contemporary 'alienation', 'lack of communication' etc.) ... Art cinema is classical in its reliance upon psychological causation; characters and their effects on one another remain central ...

Mustang certainly draws on the aesthetics of the Neorealism movement through its use of real locations, observational cinematography, non-professional actors, and its exploration of the social and political issues among the working class.

Cinematography

Mustang is shot naturistically, with the shooting style being fluid and hand-held. The camera appears almost incidental, merely capturing the lives of the five young women, in an observational 'fly-on-the-wall' documentary style. This authentic approach may obscure the intentionality of the cinematography. Cinematographers David Chizallet and Ersin Gok utilise the full range of cinematography techniques to visually portray the characters and plot arcs.

Mustang was shot in colour using an Arri Alexa Plus digital camera, which is considered to provide a 'superb overall image quality ... [and] efficient production workflow at low cost' (Stephen, 2015). It was used in conjunction with Zeiss Super Speed Lenses, which are praised for producing images that are 'much sharper and show a much higher contrast'.

The way the camera moves in the film mirrors the mood of the scenes. There is a freewheeling exuberance to the scene where the girls are playing in the sea and when they go to the football match. These moments of freedom are matched by the looseness of the camera. In the sea sequence, the camera is held back in a wide shot so we can see all the actors, and the interaction between them in the same way as the neighbour does. At the football match, the camera is much closer to the girls and the objective camera places us in the midst of the action. The switch to a high-angle shot looking down on them reinforces the close-knit relationship of the girls. Ergüven described the cinematographers as being, 'in orbit around the actors, like a cat, staying close' (Cooke, 2016).

In the home, the scenes are more measured, and more controlled to mirror their restrictiveness and lack of freedom. There are longer takes, and the camera is held back, to allow the action to unfurl. The five girls are often framed together, which reinforces Ergüven's view shared in the *Observer* (Cooke, 2016) that,

> They became one body with five heads: a single rebellious entity.

Increasingly, as the girls are married off and become separated from one another, they become isolated in single close-ups or two-shots.

Independent activity

The film focuses on the five sisters and their response to their imprisonment by their uncle and his plans to see them married.

Select at least two of the sisters and trace their journey through the film, highlighting their reactions at significant narrative points, and how this is shown through the film form.

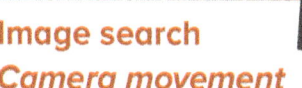

Image search
Camera movement
00:02:30–00:04:30
Watch the beach scene and observe how the camera mirrors their freedom.

Independent activity

Compare and contrast the opening sequence at school and in the sea from *Mustang* with another film you have studied, in terms of its narrative function, and the expectations they provoke in the viewer.

As Lale narrates the film, there are a number of close-ups of Lale looking at things: she is seen looking out of windows, through doorways, always looking for a way out, there are also shots from Lale's viewpoint.

The versatility of the camera can be seen in how it works in both the bright daylight scenes, and in the darker scenes in the family compound.

The lighting is naturalistic and makes great use of the daylight, with many of the interior shots back-lit to emphasise the girls' imprisonment, by drawing focus to the brightness from which they are separated. The lighting also reflects the change in seasons, which is aligned with the five girls' emotional journey from the optimistic bright sunlight of the start of the summer holiday; through to the dimming autumn light and the realisation that their childhood dreams have ended.

Mise-en-scène

The film is set in a rural, coastal town in northern Turkey, 1,000 km from the city of Istanbul. These two key locations – the rural, coastal town and Istanbul – are used within the film to reflect the tension between the past and the future, oppression and freedom. The rural setting is depicted as a place of conformity, rooted in tradition with strict patriarchal rules. Here, the girls are being watched and judged and their innocent play with the boys in the sea is observed and reported to their grandmother and uncle. The city is represented as a place of freedom, which Lale dreams of escaping to as their plight becomes increasingly desperate.

Within the rural community, the family home becomes their prison, as the uncle, determined to bring the young women into line, imprisons them. Throughout the film, we see their freedoms being stripped away as bars are added to the windows, the walls are built up higher and gates are added, and yet they still find ways to escape.

Props are used to indicate the girls' transformations as they reach an age deemed appropriate for marriage. The grandmother removes possessions that may corrupt them (computer, televisions, phones, make-up, items of clothing) and replaces them with those required to train them in the skills required to be good wives: props linked to cooking, cleaning and sewing.

Costume is an important element of the girls' identity that is gradually stripped away from them. To reinforce Ergüven's conceit that the five girls are one character with five heads, the girls share a striking similarity, you believe they are sisters, and this is in large part due to their very long brown hair, which, in contrast to the older women in the village, is uncovered. We first see them in their school uniform of white shirt, black skirts and ties; then in casual clothing of tight-fitting denim jeans and T-shirts. As their freedom is stripped away, they are forced to wear 'shapeless shit-coloured dresses' that have been made for them; and then, as they marry, in white wedding dresses.

Editing

Mustang opens with Lale's narrating.

This framing device ensures that Lale remains central to the edit, with the action largely being shown from her perspective as she narrates it from some safe place in the future. The film, although told in flashback, is in the most part linear and follows conventional narrative structure. There are two temporal ellipses, both from Lale's perspective:

★ As she sleeps after Ece's funeral, there is a brief memory/dream/flashback (it is not clear which) of Ece smiling.
★ As she sleeps in the bus to Istanbul, again she dreams, this time of her three elder sisters in the back of Yasin's truck on the way to the football match.

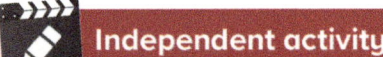

Independent activity

Film theorist Annette Kuhn writes that 'mise-en-scène can be the site of extraordinarily complex and subtle meanings' (Kuhn & Westwell, 2012). With reference to a particular sequence from *Mustang*, identify how mise-en-scène can be used to demonstrate this. Write a 400-word essay.

Independent activity

Read the *Guardian* article 'Interview: Deniz Gamze Erguven: "For Women in Turkey it's Like the Middle Ages"' (Cooke, 2016).

Both memories are depicted as golden-moments through their soft, diffused lighting; their brief, seemingly indiscriminate, inclusion marks them as important recollections for Lale.

The editing is paced to support the scenes' emotional content, and mirrors the girls' freedom or oppression. There is a preference for long takes, offering opportunities for the viewers to absorb the interactions between characters – the nuance of the performances. As the film is told from Lale's perspective there are very few sequences of parallel action; like the girls, we are trapped with them, experiencing what they experience. A key exception is the sequence when the girls escape the family home to go to the football match in a nearby town. The sequence of them at the match is fast paced, with quick-cuts of the girls having fun; this is cut between the shots of the uncle and his friends getting ready to watch the match on TV, and their aunts preparing food, with the TV on in the background. Tension is being built – will the girls be spotted? The aunts take decisive action and cut the power to the house, and then to the whole village. Although the village scenes are not witnessed by Lale, her narration reinforces her viewpoint by saying that she only found out later what the aunts had done.

Sound

Music plays an important role in setting the tone of a film and here Ergüven employs two styles of music.

Independent activity

Read the article 'Q&A with Warren Ellis – Composer of *Mustang*' by Milan Records (Chamboredon, 2015). Write a summary of Ellis' key ideas for the soundscape of *Mustang*.

The film's title, *Mustang*, alludes to the wild horses that roam free in North America. This is seen visually in the opening scenes where the girls run as a pack with their long hair flowing, and by their untamable nature, but it is also developed in the non-diegetic music score from Warren Ellis. Ergüven had originally considered using Turkish composers, but in the edit felt that that was not suitable. She tried a piece of Ellis' music from one of his westerns in the scene where the girls are being paraded in the village, which she felt was reminiscent of a scene from a western, and it worked, so she approached him.

Ellis has scored some of the contemporary cinema's significant contemporary westerns including *The Proposition* (Hillcoat, 2005), *The Assassination of Jesse James by the Coward Robert Ford* (Dominik, 2007) and the post-apocalyptic drama *The Road* (Hillcoat, 2009). Ellis had three weeks to score the music but Ergüven was clear about the music cues she needed and utilised some of Ellis' music from previous films with new compositions.

Independent activity

Watch the scene where the sisters are paraded in the village (approximately 31 minutes into the film) with the scene about Sonnay and Selma's wedding (approximately 41 minutes). Focus on the use of Ellis' score and the more traditional Turkish music. How do these affect the mood of the scene? Now try the scenes with different music. What do you notice?

Turkish music is also used, predominantly diegetically, in the wedding scenes, including music by Baba Zula, Selim Sesler and Ahmet (Dede) Yurt.

The diegetic sounds are naturalistic, adding authenticity to the film, Lale's non-diegetic voice-over is used intermittently to indicate significant moments, such as the last time all five sisters will be together.

Independent activity

Write a 500-word essay on the significance of the cinematography, editing and sound in the football match sequence.

A key sequence to examine is the sequence of the girls on the coach and at the football match approximately 28 minutes into the film. The heady mix of music, the girls' shouts, laughter and cheers combined with the editing and cinematography reinforce their freedom, which is juxtaposed with the quieter scenes back in the village.

Performance

This was the debut film for four of the young girls: Günes Sensoy (Lale), Ilayda Akdogan (Sonay), Doga Zeynep Doguslu (Nur) and Tugba Sunguroglu (Selma). Elit Iscan (Ece) had previously worked in film and television.

5 Mustang (Ergüven, 2015) & Portrait of a Lady on Fire (Sciamma, 2019)

> **Stretch & challenge**
>
> In an article on films starring mostly non-professional actors, Papadakis (2016) writes in 'The 30 Best Films Starring Mostly Non-Professional Actors':
>
> > The non-professionals' lack of training, together with their presumable real-life matching to a specific location, time period, or story, is often responsible for creating the delusion that they don't really act, which can be a perfect tool in a director's pursuance for a more realistic or documentary-like feel.
>
> The casting and performances of the five young women in *Mustang* was praised by critics. Read Papadakis' article on non-professional actors and watch at least one of the 30 films. Research how the films you are studying for Global filmmaking were cast and compare the acting performances of non-professional and experienced actors.
>
> Then write a 500-word essay answering this question:
>
> How important are casting and performance in establishing a sense of realism in the films you have studied for global filmmaking?

As a way to help shape their characters, Ergüven gave the girls film recommendations to watch. The films included Andrea Arnold's *Fish Tank* (2009), the Dardenne Brothers' *The Kid with a Bike* (2012), Ingmar Bergman's *Summer with Monika* (1953), David Lynch's *Wild at Heart* (2006), Stanley Kubrick's *Lolita* (1962) and Jean-Luc Godard's *Vivre sa vie* (1962).

Central to the performances is authenticity, which is an indicator of a film that draws on Neorealism film techniques. To support Ergüven's perception of the five girls as a five-headed monster, their performances have an ethereal nature to them. The proximity of the five girls – the jumble of arms and legs – at times supports this.

Independent activity

Watch Selma and Sonay's joint wedding (at approximately 39 minutes), and examine the performances of these two sisters, their grooms and Lale. Make notes on facial expression, body language and movements. What do you learn about the characters at this moment?

The reviews praised their performances:

> She [Ergüven] gets appealing and fiercely committed performances from the five young actresses at the story's center. (Brody, n.d.)

> A superbly acted study of suppression. (Parkinson, 2016)

> Ergüven's luckiest break was finding the five charismatic young women to portray these powerful and truly individual characters. (Means, 2016)

Section 2 Group A European film

> ### Further information
>
> **Art house and mainstream cinemas**
>
> There are broadly two types of cinemas in the UK: those that are considered 'art house' and those that programme mainstream films.
>
> In general, global films are usually found showing at an art house cinema. These cinemas are often independent or part of a small chain. The programming of these films may be published weeks or months in advance, and the cinema may have special film seasons and additional educational or community events. In general, these cinemas only have one or two screens, with three or four screenings a day.
>
> For cinemas catering to audiences seeking blockbuster and mainstream films, the opening weekend is crucial, and you may find that the new release is showing in multiple screens. It is usual for a mainstream cinema to wait until the Monday or Tuesday after the opening weekend to see what films they will programme the following week. Mainstream cinemas tend to have areas dedicated to the sale of popcorn, fizzy drinks and sweets (though this is increasingly common in art house cinemas now too).
>
> With advances in digital technology, distributors of art house films offer opportunities for audiences to stream their films at home, and the BFI, through its Film Audience Network, supports cinemas in programming films from outside the mainstream.
>
> All cinemas are struggling post-pandemic, with the rise of streaming services. Many are introducing screenings of sports events and concerts to try and attract audiences.

At the Lumières (French awards celebrating the best in French cinema), all five girls were jointly nominated in the Best Newcomer award, a prize which they won.

The cinematography and editing work to support the performances, by allowing time for the viewer to study the nuance of the performances, as each girl responds to their change in circumstances.

Aesthetics

The incremental stripping away of the girls' freedom is reflected aesthetically, reinforcing the narrative and character arcs. The hand-held camera draws us close to the action, and as the sisters find themselves trapped in the family home so too does the viewer.

Representations in *Mustang*

Mustang is told from the perspective of Lale reminiscing back over a period of a few months when the five girls' lives 'suddenly' changed. The characters in European art house films such as *Mustang* tend to be more than mere 'characters', and serve as a prism through which to gain greater understanding of a society's beliefs and cultures, through their representation of age, gender and ethnicity.

Age

The characters' age is at the heart of the narrative, as the film explores the tension between the elder characters (uncle, grandmother and extended relations/friends) and those of the younger generation (the five girls and the local boys).

In Turkey, a traditional family unit would be under the authority of the father or oldest male, who would demand respect and obedience. In a rural community, as depicted in *Mustang*, the family would live together until the daughters married and then they all would live with her husband and in-laws. Parents would expect to be looked after by their children in old age.

> ### Independent activity
>
> Read the review of *Mustang* in *Variety* (2015), by Jay Weissberg. What does he suggest about the contribution cinematography makes to the 'art house aesthetic' of *Mustang*?

Respect for elders is an expectation in Turkish culture, which is why Lale's behaviour seems so refreshing and exhilarating. As the youngest of the five sisters, she seems the most resistant to falling in line with the restrictions under which they are placed. When the neighbour, Mrs Patek, tells their grandmother about their activities in the sea, Lale yells, showing no respect for elders.

In punishment for their behaviour, the uncle imprisons them in the family home, and then proceeds to marry them off; at the end of the summer they do not return to school. The uncle and grandmother represent a generation of tradition where the supreme authority of the family rests with the father, but the household is mother-centred. In the absence of the children's parents, the grandmother has been raising the girls and running the household. When they are imprisoned in the home, Lale describes it as a 'wife factory', as their elder female relatives prepare them for married life.

When the girls are shown in smaller groupings, it is frequently paired with the eldest two, Sonay and Selma, and the younger Nur and Lale are often seen together. This leaves Ece, the middle sister, somewhat isolated. This separation from her siblings takes on a new meaning when the audience realise that Ece is the victim of abuse inflicted on her by Uncle Erol. Such exploitation often leads to people carrying a burden of secrets, which can ostracise them from others. The isolation Ece feels in this film may be a contributing factor to her sudden shocking suicide.

Gender

According to Gönül Dönmez-Colin in *Turkish Cinema: Identity, Distance and Belonging* (2008),

> Women have been the focus of Turkish cinema since its beginnings. (page 142)

She highlights that in

> ... the second half of the 2000s several courageous works have appeared exposing sexual taboos, particularly regarding violence against women, drawing attention to the reality that social maladies will not disappear through denial of their existence. (page 170)

She ends her chapter on gender, by saying,

> Turkish filmmakers' interest ... in the real issues of men and women alike, in a sincere, honest, analytical and non-judgmental way, is a feat for Turkish cinema. (page 179)

Although made a decade later and with French financing, Ergüven's *Mustang* can clearly be seen as part of New Turkish Cinema's desire to expose and challenge societal concerns, with regards to gender and sexuality.

Through the five sisters, Ergüven explores a wealth of issues regarding the transition from childhood to womanhood. The catalyst for their change in circumstances is their innocent play in the sea with the boys, considered sexual by an older female neighbour. Their grandmother chastises them for their 'disgusting' and 'obscene' behaviour.

Although they are all forced to take part in the 'wife factory', no adult is shown talking to them about sex. The repetition of the marriage proposals with their formal phrasing, followed by the grandmother's preparations and the wedding itself, are all indicative of a cycle from one generation to the next, reinforcing women's subservient place within Turkish society. As part of the marriage preparations, the grandmother is shown taking out a worn copy of 'All About Sex', and reminiscing about her own marriage at age 14 to a man she did not know but learned to love.

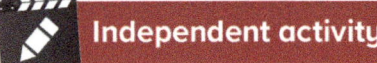
Independent activity

Read 'Oscar-Nominee "*Mustang*" Puts Turkey in Unwanted Spotlight', in Women's eNews (Hattam, 2016).

What does Hattam say about the role of female children in the family in Turkey?

Further information

On 22 January 2018, the *Hürriyet Daily News* (a Turkish news source) reported on a recent survey carried out by Associate Professor Selda Sivaslıoğlu of the Women's Research Center at Gazi University in Ankara, Turkey. The survey further highlighted the problem of child marriage in Turkey (pages 173–174), and revealed that the institutional isolation of young girls in Turkey played an important part in their subsequent forced marriage:

> Before getting married 25 percent of the girls said they had no friends. Twenty percent said they have friends but are not permitted to meet them. Fifty percent have never gone to a cinema or theater. Sixty percent do not have access to the internet. Eleven percent say they do not share their problems with their families. The situation gets even worse after their marriage, with 66 percent saying they are left with no friends at all ...

The survey was carried out among 600 girls, including 300 pregnant girls, who had been brought to hospitals. Of these girls, 25% were married to relatives.

Read more on the *Hürriyet Daily News* website, 'Survey Sheds Light on Severity of Turkey's Child Marriage Problem'.

Their authoritarian Uncle Erol, the patriarch, is shown as old-fashioned and judgemental. He is both fixated on ensuring their honour is upheld and secure by forcing the elder sisters to have virginity tests, but at the same time is sexually abusing at least one, if not two of them. The elder aunts and grandmother all train them for a life of marriage and servitude, but also protect them by cutting the electricity so Uncle Erol does not see them at the football match.

Ethnicity

Turkey is a transcontinental Eurasian nation located between Europe and Asia. Ninety-five per cent of the country is in Asia and 5% in Europe. *Mustang* is set in the Anatolia region, which is in the Asian region.

Turkey is a secular state, meaning there is no official state religion, although 99.8% of the population identify as Muslim, making it one of the most predominantly Muslim countries in the world, and the only one where religion has no place in the running of the state. Religion is strictly a private affair, as with other European countries; however, in rural communities there are still deeply held beliefs with regards to women's domestic destiny. Within rural communities it is much easier to carry out underage marriages and withdraw children from school before the legal leaving age.

Mustang is very much rooted in this rural location, with the more ethnic diverse and enlightened city of Istanbul seen as a place of refuge. At the time of *Mustang*'s release, Istanbul was Europe's largest city with a population of 14.8 million (2017), compared to London's 8.7 million (2016).

Independent activity

Read '*Mustang*: Five Girls and the Fate of Women' by Fabien Lemercier (2015). What was Ergüven's message?

Independent study questions

Q The aesthetics of a film define not only the look but also the meaning of the film. How far is this true of *Mustang* or other films you have studied as part of global filmmaking?

Q How does the film convey the key social or political issues in Turkey? How are these reinforced through its film form, rather than narrative?

Q How do representations (of age, gender, ethnicity) help us identify with the characters and their roles within the film?

Q How does the film use location to explore issues of freedom and oppression?

Q To what extent do you think *Mustang* presents either clear or ambiguous messages of life in Turkey for young women today?

Independent activity

Investigate Laura Mulvey's male gaze theory and the female gaze in cinema. Create a table to help you identify the ways of looking in *Portrait of a Lady on Fire* and the other films you have studied.

Portrait of a Lady on Fire

Portrait of a Lady on Fire (Sciamma, 2019) is a film about how we look or 'gaze' at a film and its subjects; the act of looking and the receiving of the look, all constructed through the eyes of a female director and writer, Céline Sciamma, who has called the film 'a manifesto about the female gaze'. It subverts the traditionally male way of looking.

Sciamma visualises and explores the women's desire for freedom, artistically, intellectually and sexually. The film is set against the backdrop of patriarchal 18th-century society that would reject the love these women have for each other.

Contexts

Institutional, social and political contexts

Portrait of a Lady on Fire was produced by Lilies Films, Arte France Cinéma and Hold Up Films. Sciamma had already directed a trio of female-led coming-of-age films, *Water Lilies* (2007), *Tomboy* (2011) and *Girlhood* (2014), where characters like those in *Portrait of a Lady on Fire* are seeking freedom and exploring new identities. Sciamma is an activist and founding member of the 50/50 by 2020 movement, which is fighting for equal pay in the French film industry. During the César Awards in 2020, the *Portrait of a Lady on Fire* team walked out of the ceremony after Roman Polanski was awarded Best Director. Polanski is a controversial filmmaker under an Interpol red notice for pleading guilty to unlawful sex with a minor in the USA in 1977 and other accusations of sexual assault. His César win proved a divisive topic among French filmmakers; *Portrait* lead actress Adèle Haenel led the walkout, shouting 'The shame!' as she exited, and later came forward to accuse director Christophe Ruggia of sexually harassing her as a teenager. The Polanski win validated Sciamma's view that the industry was systemically patriarchal, keeping its head in the sand and ignoring the #MeToo and 50/50 movements. *Portrait of a Lady on Fire* went on to win the Queer Palm and Best Screenplay at the Cannes Film Festival. In 2023, the César Awards announced that any nominee who has been accused of sexual misconduct would be banned from the ceremony 'out of respect for the victims' (Lockyer, 2023). Haenel and Sciamma are leading the underrepresented voices in French filmmaking, which many believe is currently dominated by white male bourgeoise perspectives, both on and off camera.

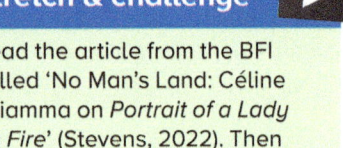

Stretch & challenge

Read the article from the BFI called 'No Man's Land: Céline Sciamma on *Portrait of a Lady on Fire*' (Stevens, 2022). Then respond to this question: How is this a film about 'the power of looking'?

Note: you will revisit this article in the Conclusion to this section.

Cultural context

Portrait of a Lady on Fire is a period film set in pre-revolutionary France: a male-dominated world.

Sciamma told *Sight & Sound Magazine* (2019) that:

> I found out there was an amazing moment in art history in the second part of the 18th century, just before the French Revolution, when there was a rise of a female artistic scene, because of the fashion for portraits. There were hundreds of women painters at that time. There's a hypothesis that women actually invented self-portrait.

France's national motto, 'Liberté, Egalité, Fraternité', was established during the French Revolution, and in the film's pre-revolutionary era these notions are explored as themes. We have examples of characters that cross three tiers of French society in the era. Héloïse is part of the nobility (the highest form of social class during this period, also known as the aristocracy), Marianne is part of the liberal bourgeoisie (the ruling class) and Sophie is a proletariat (working class); these women support each other in the spirit of equality.

Film form

Mise-en-scène

It is notable that the key locations selected are remote, seemingly apart from the world of men. The island is wild, beautiful and challenging to navigate. Similarly, the chateau is beautiful but empty, in need of care; the interiors are plain, stark, devoid of colour, a representation of Héloïse. She has been shut away in a convent, isolated from society, but beneath the severe exterior she is wild and passionate.

We associate costume dramas with a lush and vibrant colour palette. Sciamma opted for a stark and minimal approach with 'pops' of the tactile vibrancy we associate with opulent costume dramas. The most opulent colour is reserved for the 'costume' in this drama; Héloïse's deep green dress is a symbol of her family's wealth and expectation. The green portrait dress was selected by her mother to appeal to her male suitor and visualises the formal and restrictive expectations of her future role as 'wife'. Her costumes reflect her evolving identity, from her plain convent clothing which catches fire, to the simpler, freer white gown she wears in the portrait of her in later life, and of course the ghostly wedding dress that Marianne reproduces in her painting of Orpheus and Eurydice.

In the image on the previous page we see how Sciamma is using colour and costume to make a statement in a key scene: red for Marianne, blue for Héloïse and white for Sophie, a tricolour of patriotic colours to demonstrate this is the ideal society. In this scene they are equals – the noblewoman cooks, the artist serves and the maid is at her leisure (working on her own piece of artistic expression); they work together to support the individual most in need.

The paintings are an important prop. The portraits have power (the Contessa describes her portrait as 'she', as if it has its own sense of agency) and are used in symbolic moments. The first faceless portrait catches fire where the heart should be; this happens as the women's romantic feelings for each other are starting to catch alight. Marianne's first portrait observes the rules of portraiture, but it is lifeless; there is no soul in the painting. The second is a collaborative effort between painter and 'muse'; we see them mix paint together. It is through art that the women can discuss their feelings. Héloïse begins to experiment with her own artistic expression, moving from the object to an active agent. She directs Marianne to paint her recreation of the abortion and she asks for Marianne's self-portrait in her book; through art she finds her voice.

Independent activity

Investigate the work of Hélène Delmaire, the artist employed to create the paintings and sketches in the film. What is it about her work that resonates with the messages and values of the film?

Cinematography

The camera is the eyes of the audience. The camera's gaze evolves from observational, desiring, to loving, reflecting the way that Marianne and Héloïse look at and feel for each other.

First, as Héloïse is introduced, the camera adopts a more observational gaze. At this point, Marianne has to steal glances of Héloïse; it is shot in hand-held, cinéma vérité style (see Cinematography in *Taxi Tehran*, page 195) – chasing her down like prey, the shot has momentum and a sense of danger. This moment is shot through the point of view of Marianne. We are desperate to be able to look at Héloïse, but we are denied. It is 20 minutes into the film before we see her face – she is an enigma.

The camera's way of looking slowly moves into a more desiring gaze. These are point-of-view long takes that follow the movement of the characters; they are less urgent and fleeting than the previous observational style and reflect the characters' growing interest and desire.

Finally, the camera gives us a loving gaze. Here Marianne becomes the subject of the look and we increasingly see her through Héloïse's eyes, demonstrating that there is equality and mutual feelings of love.

Cinematographer Claire Mathon wanted the light to be similar to paintings of the era; soft with few shadows. In paintings of the era, the subject appears luminous as if light emanates from them rather than on them; in the portrait scenes in the film, the room is flooded with natural light to create this effect on both women. In the love scenes, natural light and zoned candlelight create a dream-like intimacy.

There is no male gaze in the film; the cinematic eye is female. The director, writer, star and cinematographer are all women. Sciamma's 'manifesto of the female gaze' is personified by a slow and intense style that lingers on beautiful, delicate details, but it is the intensity of the long take reaction shots that allow the audience to drink in the strength of feeling between the two, and through the point-of-view shots experience the vulnerability and power of being the object of the look and the observer.

Sound

Sciamma has constructed a soundscape that is entirely ambient; there is no musical score to anchor our emotional response. That does not mean that there is no music; when music is employed it is extremely impactful – it bursts through the scene.

First, there is the music made by the choir of women on the beach. This music is not pretty, refined or gentle; it demonstrates the power created by this group of women. It becomes overwhelming, alien, strong and dangerous, like the intensity of Marianne and Héloïse's desires.

The second key use of music is the use of Vivaldi; first by Marianne as the lovers start to bond with each other – she describes the music as 'the coming storm'. Then it is used poignantly in the final moments when we are observing Héloïse at a concert. Here, the music is powerful, beautiful; as we watch Héloïse's reaction, we experience with her the wave of sound, like waves of memory and emotion crashing through the film. The use of music throughout makes this moment more emotive.

The soundscape created with dialogue, silence and diegetic sounds of footsteps is rhythmic. All these layered tones are used to punctuate scenes, like a musical score.

Editing

Due to lack of a musical score, pace and emotion is created in the edit as well as performance; the takes are long, in particular when we experience a point-of-view shot with Héloïse or Marianne as the subject of the camera's 'gaze'. Brief glances are replaced by long, lingering close-ups, allowing the audience to experience the growing tension between the two women through the desiring gaze of the camera. And the growing length of the takes inform the audience that Héloïse is slowly becoming more at ease with her role, being the object of the look from Marianne and the camera, and Marianne becomes more confident with her role as observer and as object of the gaze. Eventually, as they become at ease with each other, the roles reverse and they are both the observer and the observed.

Performance

The performance style is naturalistic, still and contained. Their passion for each other must be hidden and internalised; they are living in a world in which their relationship would be punished. Their passion is one that was unseen in society, and, as previously discussed, there is no music to anchor or lead the audience's emotional response. Adèle Haenel (Héloïse) and Noémie Merlant (Marianne) were kept separate in the rehearsal process to create uncertainty and tension in their performances. The uncomfortable tone of the performances creates a discomfort in the audience and an awareness of the oppressive nature of the look. The film is constructed in a flashback; at the start Marianne is being looked upon by her pupils and appears at ease under their gaze.

This is a film all about 'looking'. At the start of the film, Héloïse is deeply uncomfortable with her place in the world. As an object to be dressed, her image captured and looked upon, she rejects Marianne's look with discomfort disguised as frosty distain. Only when she is part of the creative process, an equal partner, does the art come to life.

In the image above we see Haenel (Héloïse) using her look as a weapon. We are in the early stages of their love affair and we are stealing glances at her. Here she looks back; it is a shock. Her look is bold, it is an attack; she is turning the objectifying look back at Marianne and the audience. Her performance encapsulates the power of looking. Héloïse does not respond to being told to pose or 'smile'; Marianne has to give something of herself to the relationship to earn that intimacy. When Héloïse teaches Marianne that she is also subject to the look, both women share the vulnerability of being looked at; this shared bond ignites their love affair.

Aesthetics

The bittersweet love story is set against the backdrop of an oppressive society that objectified and punished their love. The powerful emotions played out on screen are juxtaposed by the simplicity of the aesthetic; the stripped-back set and costume designs, and seemingly natural light that illuminates the intensity of their desire.

Representations

Age

The different ways in which we see women react to the rules of society demonstrates a generation gap. La Comtesse (Valeria Golino) represents the older generation; she is the most powerful character on screen and masterminds the marriage between her daughter and an unseen Italian nobleman from Milan. Sciamma presents this woman as an Italian outsider trying to selfishly return to her home country, under the pretext of offering her daughter a better life.

Once La Comtesse leaves, Marianne, Héloïse and Sophie represent the younger generation, who, within the microcosm of this island of women, can rebel against convention, quietly in isolation, unseen by patriarchal control. In the bittersweet resolution of the film, the women have to submit to society's patriarchal expectations. Héloïse must marry, and their love can never be.

Gender

On the island away from the oppressive eye of men, our protagonists are free to live and love as they wish. The island is a utopia for Héloïse, a world like the off-screen convent that offered her an equality she describes as 'a pleasant feeling'.

The island setting is a 'no man's land'. The absence of men on screen does not mean that their presence is not felt in the film; the off-screen count is seen as a representation of Héloïse's fears, a masculine unknown. For Marianne, it is the reputation of her father that allows her to live as freely as she does. She is educated and well-travelled, and will inherit her father's studio. However, she has to submit her paintings to be viewed under her father's name.

The world of women in this film is a safe space of solidarity where the audience is required to look at areas of women's lives that are not explored on film very often; for instance, Marianne's period pain and the abortion scene. The audience is made to confront Sophie's pain with a lengthy take of her reaction, in the same way Héloïse makes Marianne watch the abortion and later paint it. Art is not without risk, and the world of women is seldom documented in history. The film is not exploitative in its scenes of nudity either; the lack of emotive music and the long take cinematography show the naked female form as a matter of fact; the eroticism in the film derives from the intimacy of their touch, not by gazing at their naked form. The scene where the lovers get high has a cinematic trick in it where the audience is momentarily led to believe that we are seeing a close-up of an intimate area. A pan reveals this to be an armpit; this leads the audience to think about their reactions to the image.

Ethnicity

French film is one of the leading lights of European cinema, from the invention of film to the French New Wave, to today. The film is set in the Brittany region of northern France, not the cultural centre, Paris. Sciamma has chosen a remote island battered by the ocean, away from the world of men.

The dynamics of the French class system are explored in *Portrait of a Lady on Fire*, with the roles of the noblewoman, the liberal bourgeoisie and the servant creating fleeting utopian equality within the crumbling system of nobility in pre-revolutionary France.

> **Independent activity**
>
> Look again at the article from the BFI called 'No Man's Land: Céline Sciamma on *Portrait of a Lady on Fire*' (Stevens, 2022). What does Sciamma suggest about the dynamic between co-creators?

Independent study questions

Q How does cinematography explore the protagonists' love for each other?

Q How does the location symbolise the social structure in France?

Q How are women represented in this film?

Conclusion

In *Mustang*, through the five sisters, Ergüven has offered a snapshot of the lives of young women in Turkey, at a crucial time in a woman's development from child to adult. Each girl reacts differently to their 'sudden' transition from freedom and hope to oppression and despair. Although set in a specific country, Ergüven was delighted to receive comments from women from other cultures who saw their story portrayed in *Mustang*, thereby demonstrating the universality of cinema and the importance of global filmmaking.

Portrait of a Lady on Fire director Céline Sciamma told *Sight and Sound Magazine* that:

> Cinema has a strong hierarchy. And that's the same even on my sets. I'm in charge; I get to create the world I want to live in for two months. You have power. The question is: what are you going to do with that power?
>
> (Stevens, 2022)

Section 2

A level: Global filmmaking perspectives

(Not studied at AS)

Group B Film produced outside Europe

This chapter will help you to prepare for **Component 2: Global filmmaking perspectives** on the A level course. The focus is on the three core areas of study only. This section will use the Iranian film *Taxi Tehran* (Panahi, 2015) and *Parasite* (Bong Joon-ho, 2019) as case studies.

For A level
You will answer one 40-mark question from a choice of two, requiring reference to two global films: one European and one produced outside Europe. You should allow 60 minutes for your answer.

The specification says
Global film extends the range and diversity of narrative film, requiring the study of two films, each representing a distinct geographical, social, cultural world and a particular expressive use of film form.

Taxi Tehran is ... concerned with repression, this time in Iran where filmmaker Jafar Panahi makes a film despite being banned – a film entirely shot from cameras installed in the dashboard of the taxi he drives.

Parasite is a biting satire on class hierarchy, through the story of the poor Kim family who ingratiate themselves into the lives of the wealthy, yet gullible and complacent Park family.

6 *Taxi Tehran* (Panahi, 2015) & *Parasite* (Bong Joon-ho, 2019)

Taxi Tehran (Panahi, 2015)

Taxi Tehran is presented as a found-footage documentary film, filmed entirely from a taxi being driven through the streets of Tehran by the director Jafar Panahi. From a camera on the dashboard and hidden cameras in the taxi, he films the conversations of the passengers he picks up. However, as themes emerge it becomes apparent that these are staged conversations using non-professional actors.

Parasite (Bong Joon-ho, 2019) is a darkly comic satire which becomes more and more horrific. In some ways the second half of the film could be described as gothic horror, although in this case, the 'ghost' turns out to be real and the threat posed by inequality more horrific than any supernatural threat.

This chapter will explore both films' credentials as a way of looking at Global filmmaking, including examining contexts, film form, representation, ideology and critical approaches to narrative.

Global filmmaking

Global filmmaking usually refers to films that are made outside of Hollywood but not, in your case, in the UK. You may see these films described as foreign films, foreign-language films, films not in the English language, world cinema or International films/cinema.

By exploring films from around the world, you will gain insights into different approaches to storytelling and filmmaking practices, thereby extending your knowledge of narrative film.

In the UK, we tend to see global films as those not in the English language; as a result they generally receive a more limited cinematic release and are often found in art house cinemas and on streaming services, rather than in multiplex cinemas. The films being distributed internationally may only represent a fraction of the country's filmic output, but those selected tend to be visually arresting and offer insights into the country's culture and political situation, past or present.

In reference to *Taxi Tehran*, director Jafar Panahi is seen as part of the New Iranian Cinema film movement (art house), whose films are in opposition to Iranian popular cinema (commercial). The films of the New Iranian Cinema and those of the Iranian New Wave, which came before it, have garnered much praise internationally. However, within Iran they have often courted controversy with their social and political messages, which are at odds with the government's edicts on what is allowable.

Taxi Tehran

Background

Censorship and legal issues

This film was made outside of the official Iranian commercial film industry. In 2010, the Iranian government issued Panahi with a 20-year ban on making films, after he was charged with making propaganda against the regime.

This was the third film he made and had distributed internationally after receiving the ban. The film premiered in competition at the 65th Berlin International Film Festival in 2015, where it won the Golden Bear (the Festival's highest prize) and the FIPRESCI Prize (the International Federation of Film Critics' prize). Panahi was unable to leave Iran so his niece, Hana Saied, who appears in the film, collected the award on his behalf.

Taxi Tehran's pared-down aesthetic, use of non-professional actors and focus on political and social issues is indicative of Panahi's work and global art house cinema more widely.

Further information

A filmmaker silenced

In 2003, Panahi was arrested and interrogated by the Information Ministry of Iran.

In 2009, there were reports that Panahi had again been arrested, but he was quickly released and a statement issued that he had been arrested by mistake. In February 2010 he requested permission to attend the 60th Berlin Film Festival to participate in a panel discussion on 'Iranian Cinema: Present and Future. Expectations Inside and Outside of Iran', but his request was denied. The following month he was arrested again. An international campaign led by leading filmmakers, critics, actors and institutions urged for Panahi's release. He had been named a member of the Cannes Film Festival jury in May, where his absence was made apparent by leaving his chair empty. The same month he was released on bail while he awaited trial.

In December 2010, Panahi was placed under house arrest, and the Iranian government issued him with a 20-year ban on writing scripts, directing films, giving interviews with Iranian or foreign media and leaving the country. In addition, he was sentenced to six years in jail, a sentence that could be activated at any time. Panahi has been in and out of jail in the interim years. He was last arrested on 11 July 2022, as at time of writing, but was released 48 hours later after going on hunger strike. In the article 'Jafar Panahi Goes Through Red Lights', published in *Le Monde* (Golshiri, 2015), Panahi's daughter, Solmaz, discusses her father's response to the ban and the very real threat of being sent to prison, saying that he would be willing to die for the sake of his films.

The 20-year ban has not stopped Panahi from making films. While under house arrest, in collaboration with Iranian filmmaker Mojtaba Mirtahmasb, he made the documentary *This Is Not a Film* (2001). It was shot over four days in a ten-day period in March 2011, using a digital camcorder and an iPhone. The film depicts Panahi like a caged animal, struggling to adjust to life in his home. He is filmed making phone calls to his lawyer, watching TV, talking about his past films and the one he was in the process of making when he'd been arrested the previous year. The film was smuggled out of Iran in a cake and screened at the Cannes Film Festival in May 2011. His wife and daughter attended.

Closed Curtain (2013) saw Panahi working in collaboration with director Kambozia Partovi. The film was screened at the Berlin Film Festival where it won the Silver Bear for Best Script. Partovi and cast members Maryam Moqadam and Hadi Saeedi were in attendance but, despite pleas to the Iranian government by the festival director, Panahi was not allowed to attend.

Taxi Tehran (which Panahi again defied the ban to make), in which he also stars, has the appearance of a found-footage film, with much of the film being captured via a camera on the car's dashboard, Omid's smartphone and his niece Hana's digital camera. There are further hidden cameras to provide coverage of Panahi and the back seat. This presentation brings into question whether he has actually 'made a film' or whether he is just offering a filmed record of him driving through the streets of Tehran, talking to his passengers.

Jafar Panahi's filmography

Panahi came of age during a period of huge political and social change in Iran. He was 19 in 1979, when Iran saw the collapse of the dynastic royal family, and the rise of the Islamic State under Ayatollah Khomeini.

He was already engaging with filmmaking through his attendance at the Kanoon Institute, where he met and was mentored by Abbas Kiarostami. In 1980, at the outbreak of the Iran–Iraq War, he was conscripted into the Iranian military where he served for two years, producing a war documentary for Iranian television. After completing his deployment, he enrolled in the Tehran College of Cinema and Television and graduated in 1988, the year the war ended. The end of the war, combined with Khomeini's death the following year, led to a renewed alternative filmmaking community, who were keen to explore contentious issues that had been previously impossible.

The Ministry of Culture and Islamic Guidance had been founded in 1984 with the remit of providing state funding for films that supported the strict Islamic beliefs and represented their approved view of Iran to the world. They also restricted films that did not support these views.

Emerging filmmakers, keen to reflect a view that was deviant from approved subjects, shifted the focus to films with children at their centre, as these were not as heavily scrutinised. Filmmakers used them as the vehicle for telling their stories from a child's perspective. Panahi's first two films had children in the central role. His feature film debut, *The White Balloon* (1995) based on a screenplay by Abbas Kiarostami, won four major international prizes including the Camera d'Or at the 1995 Cannes Film Festival. It was selected as Iran's entry for Best Foreign Language Film at the Academy Awards, and when the Iranian government tried to withdraw the film from consideration, the Academy refused. The government forbade Panahi from travelling to the USA to promote the film; neither was he allowed to hold any phone interviews. His follow-up film, *The Mirror* (1997), a blend of drama and documentary, won seven international awards.

> **2015** *Taxi Tehran* (Taxi)
> **2013** *Closed Curtain* (Pardé)
> **2011** *This Is Not a Film* (In Film Nist)
> **2006** *Offside*
> **2003** *Crimson Gold* (Talaye Sorkh)
> **2000** *The Circle* (Dayereh)
> **1997** *The Mirror* (Ayneh)
> **1995** *The White Balloon* (Badkonake Sefid)

The White Balloon (Panahi, 1995)

The Circle (2000) is critical about the treatment of women under Iran's Islamist regime; it was this shift away from films about children that led to Panahi coming up against greater government interference. He had to wait a year to get an official shooting permit. The film was shot in 35 days over a 53-day period. He submitted the film to international festivals without permission, and it won the Golden Lion at the Venice Film Festival, among a number of other major awards. The Ministry later banned the film in Iran. Fearing that the film might be confiscated, Panahi made copies and hid them around Iran.

Crimson Gold (2003) is based on real events and centres on a pizza delivery man who attempts to rob a jewellery store. Like *The Circle*, Panahi submitted it to overseas festivals where it won the Un Certain Regard at Cannes. The film was later banned in Iran.

> ### Stretch & challenge
>
> Watch a second film (where possible) from the same director as a film you are studying as part of Global filmmaking, then answer the following questions:
>
> 1 What was your favourite scene of the film and why?
> 2 What did the film tell you about the country in which it was set?
> 3 What would you consider to be the main messages of the film? How did you relate and respond to these messages?
> 4 Could you sense any signature characteristics within this film compared with any other films of theirs you have studied?

Contexts

Institutional contexts

The Iranian film industry

The Iranian film industry has risen and fallen in line with the country's political situation. The first films shot in Persia (renamed Iran in 1935) were filmed in 1900 by the Shah's (King of Persia) official photographer, Akkas Bashi. These early films were non-fiction newsreels capturing the Shah's social and religious ceremonies. The first full-length silent fiction film, *Abi and Rabi*, was not made until 1930, by Ovanes Ohanian. The first sound film was *Lor Girl* (Sepanta, 1933). Due to the Second World War, no Iranian films were made between 1937 and 1947, but foreign films were screened, dubbed into Farsi. After the Second World War a group of new filmmakers experimented with newsreel and documentary forms, and in 1949 the National Iran Film Society was established. The Iranian film industry saw a rapid growth between 1950 and 1965, with an increase in film production and cinemas.

Independent activity

Watch at least one other contemporary Iranian film and make a note of the social and political issues raised in it. Write a 400-word essay comparing the film to *Taxi Tehran*.

The 1960s was a significant turning point for Iranian cinema: in the first half of the decade approximately 25 commercial films were released a year; by the end of the decade this had increased to 65. As the 1960s progressed, alongside the state-endorsed commercial cinema there emerged a group of filmmakers who wanted to reflect the lives of ordinary Iranian people on film.

The first two films considered part of this Iranian New Wave were *Qeysar* (Kimiai, 1969) and *The Cow* (Mehrjui, 1969). The former led to a trend in gritty urban noirs, the latter to a strand of films focused on rural poverty. This tension between the rural and urban is at the heart of *Tranquility in the Presence of Others* (Taghvai, 1972), in which an Army colonel moves from the country to the city and finds it difficult to adjust. The film was banned in Iran for its political and social messages. Abbas Kiarostami, considered the greatest Iranian filmmaker, worked on *Qeysar*, and soon began tackling issues in films that had previously been taboo such as teenage conflict (*A Wedding Suit*, 1976) and government corruption (*The Report*, 1977). These films, made by socially conscious filmmakers, only represented a small fraction of the films being produced; the vast majority were still supporting the Shah, which, although waning, was still a powerful force.

This first wave of films ended in 1979 with the Iranian Revolution. With the Shah in exile and Iran now under the leadership of Ayatollah Khomeini, the founder of the

Islamic Republic of Iran, the film industry became centralised. Khomeini considered film a key propaganda tool for reinforcing the teachings of Islam and subsidised films that supported his views, while censoring and banning any views that were critical of the regime.

The Ministry of Culture and Islamic Guidance was founded in August 1984 and is still in existence today. With regard to film production, it oversees the entry and exit of audio-visual materials and the activities of film producing centers. It issues and can also revoke licenses and supervise the film-makers' activities.

This means that the Iranian government will support film activity that is aligned with its political and religious outlook, and look to marginalise and ban those that present a view of Iran that is unfavourable.

The end of the Iran–Iraq war in 1988 and the death of Khomeini in 1989 led to division and power struggles over the different visions of Islam. Out of this new political climate emerged the New Iranian Cinema film movement. Although the Ministry of Culture and Islamic Guidance was still firmly in place, changes in technology had loosened its grip over filmmakers, and these filmmakers, including Mohsen Makhmalbaf, Abbas Kiarostami and Jafar Panahi, began to enjoy critical and commercial success internationally. Female film directors also emerged, among them Rakhshan Bani-Etemad, Samira Makhmalbaf and Forugh Farrokhzad, whose films challenged women's place within society.

Conventions of New Iranian Cinema are:

★ experimentation with film form and style
★ ambiguity over whether what you are seeing is documentary or fiction
★ open endings, leaving audiences to interpret meaning
★ focus on ordinary people in contemporary Iran (rather than historical events)
★ women as central characters, offering insights and commentary on their role in society
★ philosophical and moral conversations on society.

Technological changes
Filming on 35mm celluloid is expensive: to shoot, process, edit and distribute. As a way of controlling filmmaking, the Ministry of Culture and Islamic Guidance would offer subsidies to filmmakers whose scripts endorsed their beliefs.

With the emergence of digital cameras in the late 1980s, it became possible for filmmakers to film more cheaply and swiftly. This cinéma vérité approach had been popular with the post-war Italian Neorealist filmmakers, and those of the French New Wave in the 1960s.

In Iran, this allowed filmmakers to film more covertly, flying under the radar of government officials. Which, coupled with the rise of domestic home entertainment systems (the VCR in the 1980s and DVDs from the late 1990s) made distribution far easier.

Panahi's banned film, *Offside* (2006), was widely seen in Iran via bootleg DVDs. The importance of the 'video pirate' is discussed in *Taxi Tehran*, as Omid argues that without him access to Western cinema would be impossible, and that his work is a 'cultural activity'.

The importance of film festivals
The films of the New Iranian Cinema are held in high regard in the West, where they challenge stereotypical notions of society, particularly when it comes to women, but also reinforce the oppressive regime under which they are made, through their lack of distribution and support in Iran.

It is not the quantity of New Iranian films that makes them a significant player on the world stage, but their quality, which is measured, in part, by their performance at international film festivals.

Jafar Panahi

The Cannes Film Festival has been particularly supportive of New Iranian Cinema: in 1991 it screened *In the Alleys of Love* (Sinai, 1991). The following year Abbas Kiarostami won the Palme d'Or with *Life and Nothing More* (1992); he would win again in 1997 with *Taste of Cherry*. Jafar Panahi won the Camera d'Or in 1995 for *The White Balloon* and the Prix Un Certain Regard in 2003 with *Crimson Gold*. Between 2000 and 2016, Iranian films have won 15 major awards at Cannes.

Among the dozens of other festivals that have supported Iranian filmmakers are Venice and Berlin, which have similarly awarded Iranian films on multiple occasions. These film festivals form an important part of the film's distribution and marketing, ensuring that New Iranian Cinema has stayed a central part of the global filmmaking community since its emergence in the early 1990s.

Social, cultural and political contexts

The Iranian Revolution of 1979 and its aftermath

In the 1960s, the Shah embarked on an extensive modernisation programme, drawing on extravagant Western ways. His party to celebrate 2,500 years of the Persian Empire in 1971, was a public relations (PR) disaster, and the next few years saw increasing unrest among the population, which led to a series of riots, strikes and demonstrations in the late 1970s.

The Shah's excessive consumption and alignment with America and the West led to the rise of anti-Shah campaigners, including Ruholla Khomeini, a Shi'ite Muslim, known as 'Ayatollah' (the term for a leading Shia scholar). In 1962, he had been arrested for his campaign against the pro-Western regime of the Shah. His arrest made him a national hero. In 1964 he was exiled, but while living abroad he continued to urge his supporters to overthrow the government. The Shah's government collapsed in January 1979. The following month Khomeini returned and, following a national referendum, he declared Iran an Islamic republic and appointed himself Iran's political and religious leader for life. Islamic law was introduced across the country and Western influences were forbidden.

Anti-government demonstrators in Tehran confronting soldiers over the government's decision to delay the arrival of Ayatollah Khomeini during the Iranian Revolution, 1979

In his first speech in Iran, Khomeini spoke of using films to spread the teachings of Islam, and began restructuring the film industry to ensure that all films supported his messages, and censoring any criticism of the new regime. Between 1979 and 1985 about 100 films were released.

In September 1980, Iraq (under Saddam Hussein) invaded Iran, and for the next eight years these neighbouring countries were at war. It is estimated that a million Iranian soldiers and civilians died, and 250,000–500,000 Iraqis.

The end of the Iran–Iraq war in 1988 and the death of Khomeini in 1989 led to division and power struggles over the different visions of Islam. Out of this new political climate emerged the New Iranian Cinema film movement.

Film form in New Iranian Cinema and *Taxi Tehran*

The New Iranian Cinema that emerged in the last decade of the 20th century has become a distinctive film movement very much rooted in the place and time in which it emerged. Filmmakers keen to express opinions that were in contrast to those of the post-1979 Revolutionary Islamic Republic, developed their own film form and style.

Working within budgetary constraints and utilising the developing digital technology, these filmmakers created a film form rooted in realism. Real locations, casts comprising non-professional and professional actors, long takes, limited settings/confined spaces, give these films a sense of authenticity and realism, which blurs the lines between documentary and narrative fiction filmmaking.

Cinematography

The visual style of New Iranian Cinema draws on previous cinematic film movements, most notably Italian Neorealism and cinéma vérité.

Italian Neorealism emerged in post-war Italy, where filmmakers took to the streets and, using minimal equipment, available lighting and a mix of professional and non-professional actors, told simple stories of life in Italy. Key figures in this film movement are Roberto Rossellini and Vittorio De Sica. Panahi credits *Bicycle Thieves* (De Sica, 1948) as being an influence on his work.

Cinéma vérité (sometimes called observational cinema) is a style of filmmaking that was initially used in documentary cinema, where the subject is filmed with as little interaction with the filmmakers as possible. There is limited directorial control and these films rarely use narration to guide the viewer. The filmmakers present their images and leave the audiences to interpret meaning. This naturalistic style of filmmaking was adopted by those working the French New Wave in late 1950s/early 1960s, who encompassed authentic dialogue, hand-held camera movement and filming on location to create films that looked realistic.

With the arrival of digital cameras, Iranian filmmakers were able to embody the spirit of these film movements to tell their stories. Given the low-budget, low-tech nature of New Iranian Cinema, there is a tendency for the camera to hold back and let the action unfold in relatively long static shots, or with minimal slow panning movements. There are few complex camera movements or angles, and the use of hand-held cameras brings an immediacy to the action. The shaky camera, or slight out-of-focus shots, align with the cinéma vérité observational style.

Although it may at first seem as though the cinematography in *Taxi Tehran* is limited to a single camera on the dashboard, it soon becomes clear that Panahi is introducing a number of cameras through which he can explore the nature and power of filmmaking.

The film opens with a fixed POV shot through the front windscreen, and the audience hears passengers speaking. A male passenger notices the camera on the dashboard and assumes it is an anti-theft device (the first of two references to hidden surveillance cameras, the second being the security camera footage Panahi watches on an iPad). Panahi turns the camera to face the front-seat passenger. This is the camera we see Panahi adjusting to film through the front windscreen or into the car. About nine minutes into the film, it cuts to a shot of the driver's seat, where it is revealed that Panahi is the driver. This shot is from a hidden camera.

The vast majority of the shots are medium close-ups of the front-seat passenger with cutaways to Panahi.

Mise-en-scène

New Iranian Cinema is rooted in realism, and this is reflected in the choice of settings where, for financial, aesthetic and socio-political reasons, real locations are prioritised over studio sets. Whether the setting is rural or urban, exterior or interior it supports the story, themes and characters.

The film's two locations are indicated in the film's title – *Taxi Tehran* – but once you have gained an understanding of the circumstances in which the film was made, and the narrative structure, this title offers alternate meanings.

The physical location is a taxi driving through the streets of Tehran, but, through the passengers that Panahi interacts with, we are shown a microcosm of life in the Iranian city. For instance, the juxtaposition of the poor boy collecting bottles and pocketing money that has been dropped is shown in parallel with a middle-class 'white' wedding, and Hana's insistence that he return the money so that her film does not depict 'sordid realism'. The first passengers depicted have polar-opposite political views on crime and capital punishment, while the dying man is desperate to dictate his will in order for his wife to inherit his house.

The taxi also alludes to the physical constraints placed on Panahi by the Iranian government. He is unable to leave Iran, and for some time had been placed under house arrest. The taxi offers him a certain degree of freedom and anonymity, while at the same time confinement.

There are very few props featured outside those that are used support the film's themes. Phones, Hana's camera, the iPad and the pirate DVDs are all used as

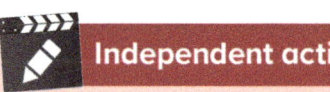

Independent activity

Create a storyboard of the sequence with the man who has been knocked down. This will give you an insight into where the cameras are, and how they are being used. Make a note of how long each shot is held and the transitions between them.

triggers for conversations about surveillance, films, cinema and filmmaking with the people who get into the taxi. Two other significant props are used:

★ **Goldfish:** two elderly women who get in with two fish that they want to take to Ali's Spring as part of their annual birthday tradition. In Iran, goldfish represent life and traditionally Iranians incorporate goldfish into their new year festival. This festival and a young girl's desire to buy a goldfish is the central premise of Panahi's first film *The White Balloon* (1995).
★ **Red roses:** human-rights lawyer Nasrin Sotoudeh gets into the taxi with a large bouquet of red roses. She addresses the dash-cam and places a rose beside it saying, 'This is for the people of cinema because the people of cinema can be relied upon. Just like you. I put it here.' This is an optimistic gesture, as a red rose is a symbol of love and beauty.

> **Independent activity**
>
> Find three examples of where a camera is being used within the context of the film, and write 100 words on its use as both a prop and as part of the film's cinematography.

Editing

There is a tendency in New Iranian Cinema to eschew conventional patterns of continuity editing, such as the shot/reverse shot, in favour of longer takes with minimal camera movements to draw focus.

Taxi Tehran appears to be edited conventionally, with no obvious shot transitions, or fragmentary editing through temporary or spatial ellipses. However, the very absence of these techniques is in itself a manipulation, as films rarely unfold in real-time.

In line with the simple cinematography, the editing appears naturalistic, and largely follows a pattern of cuts between the passenger and Panahi, or through the front windscreen. The pace of editing is leisurely, with shots held for up to three or four minutes with no edits. There are the occasional 'fade to blacks', which are used in conjunction with a POV shot through the front windscreen, and the use of non-diegetic music to mark the transition between one sequence and the next.

> **Independent activity**
>
> Select two films you are studying for Global filmmaking. In what ways does the closing sequence of your chosen films confirm messages and values working through the film as a whole? Write a 400-word essay.

Sound

The **sound design** for *Taxi Tehran* supports the cinematic conceit of filming within a taxi. The sound is largely diegetic, as captured through the dash-cam and hidden cameras' mics, and there is no additional sound recording in evidence. Consequently, there are some events that are seen but not heard, and others heard but not seen.

At times the audience witnesses activity outside the taxi, but does not hear it, such as the bride and groom, or we can hear activity in the car such as Omid taking calls in the back-passenger seat, but with the camera fixed on the front-seat passenger or filming out of the front windscreen. The audience does not always know who is speaking.

> **Sound design:** involves performing and recording new sounds and editing previously recorded audio, such as sound effects and dialogue. These are combined to create an overall soundtrack to a film.

6 Taxi Tehran (Panahi, 2015) & Parasite (Bong Joon-ho, 2019)

Independent activity

Watch ten minutes of the film with the subtitles turned off. This will allow you to better focus on the juxtaposition between sound and image.

Paying particular focus to the soundtrack, divide your page into two columns and in column 1 write notes on what you see, and in column 2 what you can hear.

- Can you always see what you are hearing?
- Can you always hear what you are seeing?
- How has the filmmaker used sound to guide your perception of the image and the action?
- Is the filmmaker's use of sound realistic?
- How has he used and/or integrated diegetic and non-diegetic sound?

Independent activity

What features of New Iranian Cinema can you identify in *Taxi Tehran*?

The film opens with a fixed POV shot out of the front windscreen, while the car is waiting at a street crossing, and is held for just over a minute. The audience sees modern Tehran pass before their eyes, as young men dressed in Western clothes and traditionally dressed Iranian women wearing hijabs walk back and forth. Motorbikes, cycles and cars are streaming from all directions. Approximately a minute and half of the car driving through the streets follows this. This shot is accompanied by non-diegetic music, which appears to be both traditional and Iranian although this is hard to verify in the absence of credits. The shot ends when a male passenger comments on the camera and the camera is turned to show a head and shoulder shot.

The film ends with an example of an action heard but not seen. Panahi and Hana have left the car as they look for the two women at Ali's Spring. Two young men on a motorcycle pass and double back. The camera is in its fixed position out of the front window, but you can hear the glass being broken, and what sounds like rummaging through the glove compartment. As one of the men pulls the camera out of the cradle the screen goes black; however, their voices are still being recorded via the other cameras. You can hear one saying, 'He's coming!', with the other responding that he is looking for the USB, followed by the sound of the motorbike driving away. This final crime ties in with the conversations about crime and poverty that have punctuated the film, but also alludes to Panahi's punishment by the government, of having his filmmaking ripped away from him.

Performance

Panahi cast non-professional actors in this film, as he has done on previous occasions. The film has no credits, and there are no credits on the DVD or on IMDb. In the film's closing slide, Panahi explains that this is because the Ministry of Islamic Guidance approves the credits of distributable films. Panahi says that he is indebted to everyone who helped him – the film wouldn't exist without their support.

Further information

Nasrin Sotoudeh

One of the passengers Panahi picks up in his taxi is Nasrin Sotoudeh, one of Iran's leading human rights lawyers. She and Panahi became friends after they both received the European Union's Sakharov Prize for freedom of thought.

Sotoudeh and Panahi spent two days together working out what to include in their taxi conversation. Given their shared interest in human rights, this would be central to this section of the film. Their conversation covers prison interrogations, hunger strikes and censorship.

How does social, cultural and political information such as this about your close study film affect your response to it?

Two of the actors are his niece, Hana Saeid, and the human rights lawyer Nasrin Sotoudeh, both of whom are essentially playing versions of themselves. The extent to which the others are playing themselves or versions of themselves is the subject of much debate both within the film and in its critical reception.

After the first couple – the mugger and teacher – exit the car, Omid the dealer of pirate DVDs recognises Panahi and is convinced that the couple were actors, as he recognised dialogue from a previous Panahi film. Panahi neither confirms nor denies they are actors or that he is making a film. Other than the mugger, Hana and Nasrin, no other passenger comments on the camera or appears to be aware that they are being filmed. Their performances are naturalistic, which is in keeping with the documentary style of the film.

Panahi's use of film form, combined with the absence of commentary through interviews, ensures that the extent of the film's documentary and narrative fiction parameters remain unclear. As we have mentioned, the film has no opening or closing credits, so no actors or technicians are credited. However, the themes that emerge through the conversations with the 11 people he encounters broadly fall into three key areas:

★ crime   ★ women in society   ★ filmmaking.

He explores his own problems of making an 'un-distributable film' via his conversation with his young niece, Hana, who is making a short film as a school project. In order to make a distributable film, students were told they had to respect the following rules:

1. Respect for the Islamic headscarf.
2. No contact between men and women.
3. Avoid sordid realism.
4. Avoid violence.
5. Avoid the use of a tie for good guys.
6. Avoid the use of Iranian names for good guys; instead use the sacred names of the Islamic saints.
7. Avoid discussing political or economic issues.
8. During the course of the film, Panahi breaks all of these rules.

Aesthetics in New Iranian Cinema and *Taxi Tehran*

The aesthetics of New Iranian Cinema are closely aligned with both the limits and freedoms of working in a system at odds with the state-funded and supported film industry.

Stylistically the films seem to lack drama and sensationalism, which aligns them to the Italian Neorealist movement. However, much is revealed through these simply-framed, unbroken long takes. The filmmakers allow the viewer to absorb the action on screen, which, by using non-professional actors, naturalist lighting and real locations, has an air of authenticity.

These filmmakers have developed a cinematic language which combined with their thematic concerns is closely aligned with the realist film movement. A number of films, such as *Taxi Tehran*, play with documentary film conventions within a narrative fiction context.

One of the reasons that Iranian films have become so popular in the West is the perceived contradiction between such aesthetically distinctive films and the repressive conditions under which they are produced.

Independent activity

Read 'My Interview with Jafar Panahi' by Doug Saunders (2007) online and write a short essay on how Panahi tackles issues of censorship in the film *Taxi Tehran*.

Independent activity

The casting of non-professional actors is a convention of New Iranian Cinema, and world cinema more widely. Select two world cinema films which feature children, and research how they were cast and what was the critical and audience response.

Independent activity

How do you think the film's aesthetics contribute to the social and political messages of the film?

Representations in New Iranian Cinema and *Taxi Tehran*

The filmmakers of the New Iranian Cinema are keen to reflect contemporary Iranian social and political concerns. The themes and characters they depict are at odds with the state-funded films and they therefore find themselves with limited, if any, distribution in Iran.

The characters in *Taxi Tehran* are clearly representing a cross-section of Iranian social and political perspectives: men and women; young and old; rich and poor; victim and perpetrator; filmmakers and film watchers; a human rights activist and a supporter of capital punishment; traditionalists and modernists.

Age

There are a number of ages represented *Taxi Tehran*; at one end of the spectrum are the two elderly women who are enacting their annual pilgrimage to Ali's Spring to release their current two goldfish and collect two new ones. If they do not do this by midday, they are convinced that they will die. These two women seem to represent the past, when myths and storytelling were central. At the opposite end is Hana, with her inquisitiveness and education she represents the future. However, her future is coloured by the education she is receiving under the current regime in Iran. Her future is shown in stark contrast to the young boy she chastises for not returning the money he found. Although approximately the same age, he is out working, collecting bottles for recycling rather than studying.

The present and future of filmmaking is represented in this film with Panahi as the established director passing advice and wisdom to a film student (stop reading about/watching films and make them) and to his niece.

Gender

In the style of a scripted reality TV show, the characters discuss or embody the film's three central themes: crime, filmmaking and women's place within Iranian society.

Iran is a male-dominated society, and there are written and unwritten rules about what women can and cannot do, with education being an area of discontent. However, there are many educated professional women in Iran including lawyers, doctors, teachers, engineers and filmmakers. This is reflected in *Taxi Tehran* by the inclusion of a teacher in the opening scene, and the lawyer/human rights campaigner in the closing scene, with a budding filmmaker reflected in his niece, Hana.

The teacher is shown as feisty and able to hold her own in an argument about crime and capital punishment with a man who claims to be a 'freelance mugger', clearly showing the benefits of a middle-class Iranian education. Hana is a confident and ambitious young girl, who is flourishing through education, but her education is clearly skewed towards the state's views of social and political matters, demonstrated through the list of rules she has to obey if she wants her film to be distributed.

However, the film also depicts women whose position is not as secure. The wife of the man knocked over by the car seems more agitated by the potential loss of her family home than she is her husband. Without a will, all their property will go to her husband's male relatives, leaving her penniless and homeless.

Hana also relates a story about a neighbour, a young woman, who was in love with a man from Afghanistan. When her father and brother found out, they beat him up and forbade her from seeing him again.

Human rights lawyer Nasrin Sotoudeh discusses a real case with which she was involved. British-Iranian female student Ghoncheh Ghavami was arrested in 2014 for protesting for equal access to sporting events in Iran. She was sentenced to one year in jail and had been held in solitary confinement in Evin Prison for 100 days when she went on hunger strike. She was released soon after.

The male characters also embody a cross-section of society, with perspectives from a criminal and then later a victim of crime. This latter character, Mr Arash, is the subject of Hana and Panahi's conversation about the depiction of a 'good guy' in a film. According to the rules Hana has been given, he should not be wearing a tie (a sign of Western business practices) and should not have an Iranian name.

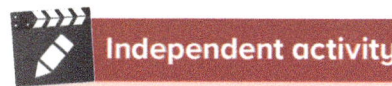

Independent activity

Read Mark Hallihan's 'The 10 Best Iranian Films About Women' (2016) on the Taste of Cinema website and 'Iran's Big Woman Problem: All of the Things Iranian Women aren't Allowed to Do' by David Blair (2015) on the *Daily Telegraph*'s website.

With these articles in mind, select one of the female characters in *Taxi Tehran* and examine how she is portrayed.

Ethnicity

The films of New Iranian Cinema are rooted in their national identity. These films are set in contemporary Iran, and for the most part are focused on the lives and concerns of Iranian people. Here, Panahi explores the diversity of political, religious and social views through the prism of education, class and age.

The anecdote about the Iranian father and brothers beating the Afghan boyfriend of their daughter/sister offers an insight into the strained relationship between these neighbouring countries.

Independent study questions

Q How does Panahi use film form to bring to the fore the film's social and political messages?

Q How does Panahi employ techniques of documentary filmmaking in this film and how does this affect your response to it?

Q In what ways does knowing about the circumstances in which Panahi made the film affect your reading of the film and its themes?

Q How does the film explore the relationship between men and women?

Q Given that the Iranian government states that films should 'avoid violence', how is 'violence' depicted in *Taxi Tehran*?

Parasite

Contexts

Parasite (Joon-ho, 2019)

Parasite is best known for being the first non-English language film to win the 2020 Academy Award for Best Picture, and Bong Joon-ho and his co-writer Han Jin-won are the first Asian writers to win the Academy Award for Best Original Screenplay. The film was successful in every way, making $262.7 million at the global box office with a relatively low production budget of $15.5 million, and appearing on many critics' best films lists. *Parasite: Black and White Edition* was released in 2020, elevating the film's status as a work of art; Bong stated that his aim was to make the film feel 'like a classic' and for the performances 'to come across more strongly'. *Parasite*'s narrative revolves around two identical families in terms of family members – mother, father daughter, son – from the opposite ends of the social divide. The film invites viewers to compare the two families, asking us to consider who the parasites are. On a superficial level it seems to be the Kim family who are parasitic, infiltrating the wealthy Park family through deception. However, on closer examination the Park family in their helplessness are also parasites.

Production contexts

The South Korean film industry

Although lesser known by global audiences than other Asian film industries, South Korea has a thriving film industry. Bong has said in interviews that he hopes that the success of *Parasite* will bring Korean cinema to the attention of a global audience.

Parasite is typical of South Korean cinema, which is known for its dark comedies and narratives about social class. These styles were developed during the golden age of South Korean cinema in the early 1960s, when censorship was relaxed and films that dealt with realistic issues could be made – South Korea's version of Italian Neorealism. This was followed by a regime that imposed heavy censorship, lasting until 1997 when the Korean New Wave began, during which the government encouraged makers of films, art and music to compete in the global market. Along with Kim Jee-woon and Park Chan-wook, Bong Joon-ho is one of the key directors of this movement. The South Korean New Wave incorporated the staples of Asian cinema, horror and violence, but linked to the country's history of conflict, invasion, social issues and the rapid growth of the economy due to technological innovation, including using the device of dark humour.

The black and white aesthetic of the re-release of the film links it to notable works of the golden age of South Korean cinema, such as *The Housemaid* (Kim Ki-young, 1960), which Bong has cited as an influence. This film is also concerned with class differences; the narrative involves the destruction and chaos brought into a middle-class family by the housemaid.

All of Bong's films have been commercially successful, and *Parasite* is currently the highest grossing South Korean film.

Independent activity

Watch *The Housemaid* (Kim Ki-young, 1960) and what Bong Joon-ho has to say about it (both are available on YouTube). Note the ways in which this film influenced Joon-ho's construction of *Parasite*.

Social, cultural and political contexts

An important political and social context of *Parasite* is South Korean economics. The film shows the aftermath of the 2008 global economic crisis and the 1997 Asian financial crisis which preceded it; both badly affected the economy of South Korea, widening the gulf between rich and poor. The reasons for South Korea's economic problems are complex and one of the issues explored in the film is population density. The cramped living spaces and competition for employment depicted at the opening of the film take the viewer in a very visceral way into life as a poor person in South Korea, in which the Kim family are being doused with insecticide and the environment is soaked with urine. Here, concerns about social inequality and the desperate struggle for survival align viewers with the Kims, creating sympathy. As Bong has suggested in an interview with Steve Rose for the *Guardian* (2020), Korea is known for its glamour and technological advances, but he aims for this film to depict the reality by highlighting the gap between rich and poor and the difficulties faced by young people.

Parasite suggests that poverty or wealth is determined by birth, with no possibility of change. This idea is also reflected in South Korean phrases: gold spoon for those born into wealth, such as the characters Park Da-hye and Park Da-song, and dirt spoon for those born into poverty, like Kim Ki-woo and Kim Ki-jung. The film supports the idea that it is impossible to transcend these barriers, other than temporarily through deception.

Linked with the political context of economics and the social context of wealth and poverty is the political context of capitalism. The film examines the effects of late capitalism on both the wealthy and the poor; it is possible to consider capitalism itself as the parasite, determining the aspirations of the hosts to continue to thrive. The film satirises the ways in which the wealthy are able to ignore their exploitation of those in poverty in a disturbingly comic way. For example, we see Geun-sae, the former housekeeper's husband, turn on the lights upstairs for Mr Park (Dong-ik) by banging his head on the light switches, shouting respect as he does so, a visceral portrayal of the way that those in poverty revere the wealthy and the unquestioning way that the wealthy accept their entitlement to a luxurious lifestyle, ignoring the existence of poverty. Dong-ik seems to believe that this is motion-sensor technology, but the viewer has a horrific, visceral awareness of the reality.

Dong-ik also demonstrates the ways in which class, wealth and status are maintained. His smooth passage through life is demonstrated by the classical and operatic non-diegetic music that accompanies him at the beginning of the film. He expects people to respect the Park family's place in the hierarchy, exemplified by the deferential behaviour of the former housekeeper Moon-gwang, and while the Kims may seem disrespectful, they are also in awe of the Park family. In the scene where they inhabit the Park's house while the family are away, they discuss what they admire about the Parks, despite the mess they make of the house in an incredibly short space of time.

Despite the implication that social mobility is impossible, the ending at first leads us to believe that it is a realistic possibility by showing a version of the ending before revealing that this is just a fantasy. Bong said in an interview for *GQ Magazine* (Paiella, 2019) that in reality it would take a member of the South Korean working class 564 years to save up enough money to buy the Park's mansion. This demonstrates the extent to which the fallacy of social mobility embodied in the American Dream – anything can be achieved by hard work – is still pervasive in contemporary capitalism. The starting point is not equal, and although the Kims' daughter (Ki-jung) seems to look like she fits in better – her brother describes how she looks the part watching television in the bath – she is the only member of the Kim family to be killed at the end, which also reveals in a brutal way that there is no fitting in; it was an illusion.

Capitalism as the parasite has inbuilt mechanisms to ensure its survival. As well as creating aspiration among the poor and a sense of entitlement among the rich, it manipulates the poor, keeping them stuck in poverty by fostering an admiration for the rich and a contempt for their own kind. This becomes increasingly clear during the film as the working-class characters view their peers as competitors rather than collaborators. This implies an internalised self-loathing and snobbery in the working-class psyche, which is a desired response for the continuation of capitalism and a two-tier society. The second half of the film becomes a battle between the two poor families rather than an attempt to overthrow the rich. Working for the Park family brings the Kims close to wealth, but the meagre pay does not allow them to acquire it, and even though we may admire their cleverness in securing the jobs, the jobs themselves are degrading. By showing the ways in which people admire the rich, even when seemingly exploiting them, Bong highlights the cruelty of capitalism. The Kims are taunted by their closeness to the Park's wealthy lifestyle, something they can never achieve, which is reinforced by the film's bleak ending.

This critique of capitalism, or perhaps the worst aspects of human nature and the idea of infiltration, is intertwined with political and historical contexts. As we see through South Korea's history, inequalities in wealth and opportunity are hallmarks of post-colonial societies. The way in which the Park family idolises the USA mimics the imperial past, during which many of the colonised looked up to their colonisers, and long after the USA left Korea, its legacy persists. For example, Da-song's new tent won't leak as it's 'from America', says Mrs Park confidently.

A marker of status in the film is the correct use of the English language. Proficiency in English is a requirement for Korea's college system as a legacy of the colonial past. Although, as Mr Kim points out, there are more graduates than graduate jobs when he says that even a security guard job attracts a large number of graduate applicants.

Korea has a long history of being invaded by both China and Japan. It was annexed by Japan and became a Japanese colony in the early 1900s, and then at the end of the Second World War when the Japanese surrendered the country became

Independent activity

Examine the ways in which the two families are presented in the poster for the film. Consider how a knowledge of context helps in your understanding of the poster.

divided, the North becoming communist under the influence of the Soviets and the south capitalist under the influence of the USA. The Korean War (1950–1953), during which the North was backed by Soviet and Chinese troops and the South by the USA and allied UN countries, led to the deaths of around three million people. There followed a period of hostility between North and South Korea, with occasional bouts of conflict. The resulting trauma of conflict is reflected in the film; Bong has commented in an interview with the *Guardian* (Rose, 2020) that conflict between North and South Korea has created divided families, and great suffering and anxiety. The article, entitled 'Korea seems glamorous but the young are in despair', provides his perspective on modern-day Korea.

To establish capitalism, South Korea was subject to a series of military dictators who were supported by the US military, and the wealth generated in the country during this period was intertwined with US financial interests. It is suggested in the film that the Park family's wealth is derived from business associations with the US. There are still 28,500 US soldiers stationed in South Korea today, reflecting that the threat of war is far from over.

Film form

Cinematography

Shots in the Kims' apartment are often framed to highlight how cramped, damp, dirty and cluttered it is, signalling extreme poverty. This is particularly true of the shots in the bathroom. For example, when Ki-woo and Ki-jung desperately search for Wi-Fi, as Ki-woo stretches out his arms to hold up his phone, the viewer can see that the room is incredibly narrow, allowing us to take in everything in the room in a single frame. Depth of field is often used to establish important information about living spaces as indicators of social class. For example, at the film's opening, as we see the grubby socks drying from the ceiling of the semi-basement apartment in the foreground, we can also see the street outside with people oblivious to the Kim family's living conditions in focus in the background, suggesting that they are a forgotten underclass. As the camera begins to tilt downwards, the framing emphasises the bags of rubbish piled up just outside the window by having them at eye level, suggesting that the inhabitants of the apartment are also discarded rubbish. Despite the indicators of slum conditions, the mood is not one of desperation, indicated by the moment of sunlight catching Ki-woo's hair and the closeness of the family unit, which is emphasised by the tight framing.

Shallow focus is often used to draw attention to the Kim family's use of deception. For example, when the chauffeur is driving Jessica/Ki-jung home and he is asking her where she lives, the camera is positioned in front of him, putting his honest question and identity into sharp focus while the shadowy figure of Jessica is out of focus in the back of the car. Pull focus is used to bring Jessica into focus as she tells the chauffeur to drop her off at the station, followed by a close-up shot to create alignment between her and the spectator, despite her deception, and encourage admiration for her confident intelligence.

Long shots are used to establish stark contrasts in locations to reflect class differences. Sweeping long shots of Ki-taek and his children escaping the Park's house in the torrential rain focus on the enormity of the stairs down to the slum area, showing the concrete walls surrounding them and highlighting the fortress-like structure around the wealthy neighbourhood, which is designed to keep the poor away and unacknowledged. The size of the wall, stairs and force of the rain serves to reinforce a sense of the utter hopelessness of poor people having aspirations; these shots make the size of the forces working against them very clear. This is further insinuated through high-angle shots of the people from the slums sleeping in the gym, squashed together and powerless; this invites sympathy and emphasises the resilience of the working class. It also invites the viewer to consider that if they are the parasites, they are impossible to exterminate.

Lighting is used to create a clear visual distinction between the two social classes represented by the two families. The Park family are associated with natural, brilliant sunlight, pathetic fallacy suggestive of their unquestioning sense of entitlement, whereas the Kim family's semi-basement apartment is often seen in darkness and rain, generating a vivid sense of the struggle of the poorest members of society. This is compounded by the artificial lighting in the Kims' apartment, generated by harsh strip lights emitting a slightly green hue, which casts a visceral and unforgiving view of grim reality, designed to generate an ambivalent response of sympathy mixed with repulsion. In direct opposition, the Park's house has aesthetically pleasing, symmetrically arranged lighting, shown in symmetrically composed shots. It emits a soft, warm glow and shields the wealthy Park family from any sense of grim reality. It symbolises the enticing nature of guilt-free materialism; the soft, warm lighting and bright sunlight suggest a sense of entitlement, free of social conscience. Through generating these responses, the spectator is being asked to examine how enticing capitalism is alongside the resultant misery for those excluded from the tiny elite.

Mise-en-scène

Constructed sets for the two houses allowed for a careful manipulation of mise-en-scène. The props inside the Park's mansion were very expensive: for example, the $2,500 bin in the kitchen and the enormous original artwork by Seung Mo Park on the living room wall. The Kims' house, by contrast, is full of everyday household objects cluttered together to signify extreme poverty.

A prop that becomes a motif is the Scholar's Stone (or Landscape Stone), which represents Ki-woo's aspiration to advance socially. He clings to the possibility of social mobility despite evidence to the contrary. This is symbolised by his need to save the Scholar's Stone from the flood; it seems to magically rise to the surface for him, another visual indicator of the compelling nature of his aspirations. Desperate to cling to the slight rise in wealth and status he has achieved working for the Parks, he decides to use the stone to kill Guen-sae, but instead he receives a near fatal blow to the head from it. His aspirations become a weapon to be used against him; those who wish to join the elite are made more miserable than those who just seek to exist. The stone is flimsier than it seems, symbolising the misleading nature of the wealth that it seemed to promise, signalling that his aspirations are ill thought through and insubstantial. The power of the stone as a symbol is humorously undermined by twinning it with urination. First, when Min is arriving and the Parks are celebrating the money gained from folding pizza boxes; then as the Kims celebrate their successful employment with the Parks (the stone clearly visible behind), a man urinating in the street is a comic reminder that in reality they have only made a very slight advancement. It takes Ki-woo much longer to acknowledge that the rock has no power to bring about his aspirations. At the end of the film he places it in a river, although he still retains his aspirations.

The forged degree certificate represents the wasted talents of the Kims. Ki-jung is shown to be determined, talented, confident and fiercely intelligent, yet there is no way for her to advance in South Korean society. It also suggests that a degree is worthless since there are so many of them in circulation. This, together with the rising unemployment rates for South Korean graduates, questions the value of a university education and the promise that it will aid social mobility. Is being a poorly paid private tutor the best a qualified psychologist and art therapist could achieve?

The Kims' poverty is signalled in a number of ways: the redundant mobile phones, which have no signal or Wi-Fi unless it's stolen, the mouldy bread being eaten by Ki-taek, and the stink bugs which also inhabit the apartment, suggesting that the Kims are only one rung higher in the food chain. In direct contrast, the extreme wealth of the Parks is signalled through spaciousness, and objects displayed for aesthetics rather than practical purposes. For example, the beautiful display of subtly lit pottery in a large cabinet in the Park's kitchen, which ostentatiously covers the entire wall, creates a beautiful entrance to the cellar storeroom, but is of little practical purpose.

As suggested by Bong in his analysis of *The Housemaid*, stairs are a significant indicator of wealth in South Korea, as well as symbolising an elevation in status. The Parks walk upstairs to enter their house and then again to enter their living quarters. There is a large flight of steps down to the slums where the Kims live; their basement flat is entirely set on one low level, indicating poverty and vulnerability to flooding. It appears that they live on the same level as the sewers.

Smell itself becomes a motif in the film and part of the mise-en-scène. The visceral smells of insanitary living conditions – urine-soaked streets, musty washing, sewerage-infested flood water, clouds of insecticide and cheap food – infest the poor people's homes. This invites the viewer to consider their response: Is it sympathy? Does it trigger a social conscience? Or does the response of the viewer match that of the Parks? Do we feel repulsed by the poor? Da-song observes that the Kims all have the same smell. This creates tension, as their deception could be uncovered, but on a deeper level it symbolises their admirable unity and strength as a family, as well as the way in which they can dress up as people from a slighter higher stratum of society, but their smell betrays them. The smell of the poor people symbolises slum living conditions. Smell is used as a way of structuring the narrative, as the increasing detection of smell creates mounting tension in the narrative.

The use of Indigenous American artefacts as children's toys reminds the viewer that South Koreans have little understanding of the complex history of the USA and surrounding contemporary issues of cultural appropriation. Just as the Park family fail to face up to the reasons why the poor people on the subway have a certain smell, they and others of their class are ignorant of oppressed people and, ironically, of American history, despite their reverence for the country.

Editing

Editing is used to juxtapose rich and poor to startling effect. For example, as Choi Yeon-gyo is being driven by her chauffeur, Kim Ki-taek, she explains on the phone to a friend that the flood was a blessing, suggesting that it has got rid of the pollution, perhaps unknowingly referring to the poor people who drowned in the flood.

A cut then reveals the extent of the devastation for the poor people. She is oblivious to their suffering, unaware of the slums and so self-absorbed that it doesn't occur to her that her driver has probably lost his home in the flood. Editing is used to parallel the members of the two families. For example, as Ki-woo contemplates the power of the Scholar's Stone, assessing its power to bring wealth to the family, there is a cut to Da-song in the garden as he surveys his luxury home from his American 'tent', which is actually a tepee, which serves to highlight that Ki-woo is doomed from birth to be poor whether he has the stone or not. In a late-capitalist society, both sons have the same materialist beliefs, one desperately aspiring to wealth and the other feeling entitled to it. When the Kims wake up in the cramped gym, there is a cut to the Park family home where we see them waking to the sun shining and the sounds of birds. The cut between Ki-jung amid hundreds of others in the gym, as he answers the phone call about Da-song's impromptu birthday party, and Yeon-gyo alone at her spacious dressing table, is a visual reminder of the extremes of wealth and poverty through juxtaposition.

Later in the film, as the Kims desperately try to maintain their position at the Parks' home against the threat of Moon-gwang and her husband, editing is used to link the suffering of the lowest in status. A shot shows Moon-gwang waking with a head injury in the bunker, from which there is a cut to the Kims going into the flooded apartment, emphasising that it is the poorest people who pay the price for the wealth of others. In an extremely visceral moment of continuity editing, a match-cut is used to connect semi-basement and bunker: Ki-jung is seen battling with the sewerage exploding from the toilet, and this is cut with Moon-gwang vomiting into the bunker toilet. This use of editing emphasises the idea that capitalism thrives where the poorest members in society are struggling to exist, rather than those poorest people being unified to fight against inequality. It is interesting to note the pragmatism of Ki-jung as she sits smoking on the exploding toilet; she has accepted the situation, which contrasts with her brother, who retains his aspirations.

Sound

Diegetic sound is used in a similar way to lighting in *Parasite* to reflect the different experiences of the rich and the poor. The Kims hear dogs barking (a cinema staple that signifies working-class life) and the noise of the street above, particularly the deafening sound of the stink bug fumigator. The Parks, on the other hand, hear birdsong and gentle breezes. The soundscape contributes to the idea that the wealthy are protected from the reality of life in South Korea; their experience is peaceful and exclusive.

The non-diegetic music used is often contrapuntal (a sound that doesn't seem to match the visual image). For example, the film opens with a melodic piano solo written and performed by Jung Jai-il; it is in a major key, setting a tone of harmony and hope, which initially seems at odds with the desperate, impoverished Kims. However, it establishes their resourcefulness, unity and optimism, exemplified by the way that Ki-woo is able to keep the pizza box work and then his reaction to the Scholar's Stone – 'this is so metaphorical' – assuming that it will bring wealth to the family.

Non-diegetic music is used in a straightforward way to signify the Parks' smooth journey through life. For example, the classical music heard as Don-ik arrives at work displays his easy passage through life, reflecting the ease with which the elite maintain their position in society through cultural capital. However, classical music is also used to create ironic humour. The track 'The Belt of Faith', composed by Jung, accompanies the montage which shows the scheme to replace the chauffeur and housekeeper with the Kim parents, reaching a crescendo and conclusion at their success. This music, with its rising tone of triumph, suggests that deception also has a smooth passage when the wealthy are so protected, entitled and naïve; their own signifiers of comfort and security allow a way in for the parasitic Kim family. Non-diegetic music is also used to undermine the Park family's arrogance and create comedy. For example, the sound of triumphant drums accompanies Don-ik's conclusions about the underwear in his car, and the diegetic sound of opera is played in the Parks' house to accompany the visual of Mrs Kim as the new housekeeper; here, the music ironically reflects her mood. The light and comic tone created by this music makes these sequences entertaining and extends the idea that signifiers suggestive of social mobility can be easily acquired. But the pace of the music also reflects the superficial nature of these wins – actual social mobility is beyond their reach.

Sound supervisor/re-recording mixer Ralph Tae-Young Choi, who has also worked with Bong on other films besides *Parasite*, has spoken about the pleonastic sound of doors in the film, which he used to emphasise the extensive barriers to wealth. This use of sound contributes to the overall aesthetic of wealth and poverty, matching both mise-en-scène and lighting. The sound in the bunker was also designed to reinforce the horror aesthetic; the sound of the water flowing through the pipes was enhanced and sounds were created that suggested that the air in the bunker is heavy. These sounds link the bunker with the semi-basement apartment and exemplify the irony of the lack of solidarity between the inhabitants of both locations. Sound also symbolises the desperation of these characters, for example ambient sound is used to emphasise Ki-woo's anxious state when he re-enters the bunker to kill Guen-sae. The air itself seems to emit a high-pitched sound, so that the way the bunker sounds (and looks) is horrific in its unfamiliarity, creating a feeling of it being an eerie and unnatural space, where anything could happen.

Performance

Initially it seems that Ki-woo may be the protagonist, but quickly it becomes apparent that we are equally invested in each character. Through the structure of the parallel families, the viewer is encouraged to compare performances and the impact they have on meaning and response. There seems to be a stark difference between them in some ways. In a comparison of the mothers, Chung-sook, played by Jang Hye-jin, is older and wiser than Yeon-gyo, played by Co Yeo-jeong; her face is often crumpled into a frown or expressing anger at her husband's passivity, or she sarcastically grins at someone's foolishness, expressing her cynical world-weariness. In contrast, Yeon-gyo has a more open facial expression with expressive eyes, and is shown to be more emotional. The two mothers' performances are indicators of wealth and privilege, or a lack thereof.

Independent activity

Observe the ways in which each family is introduced in the first third of the film. Then find three close-up images of the Kims, Parks, and the housekeeper and her husband. Analyse their facial expressions. How do they relate to the theme of social inequality? How and why are we as the audience aligned with each one?

When comparing the two daughters, Jung Ji-so plays Da-hye as the stereotypical lonely, uncommunicative teenage girl, and there are close-ups on her big, mournful eyes. The revelation of the depth of feeling she has for Ki-woo, as well as the physical strength and determination shown in her rescue of him at the climax, is a surprising revelation that it is not just the Kims who are playing a role. This contrasts with the self-assured and manipulative performance of Park So-dam as Ki-jung, whose often has a wry smile as she enjoys executing her clever schemes.

The Park family members are presented as kind-hearted and rather naïve people, which imbues them with a beguiling, sympathetic quality. So it feels shocking in the moments when it is brought to the viewers' attention that they choose to be oblivious to the suffering all around them. For example, recoiling from the smell of poor people, rather than examining why those people might smell, highlights to the viewer that it is a deliberate choice to exploit others to maintain their lifestyle. The Park parents are symbols of some of the worst aspects of capitalism. Oblivious to the poor and seeing their employees as dispensable, they could be seen as the antagonists, yet their likeability through some charming performances reminds the viewer of the beguiling nature of capitalism and its insidious nature.

Aesthetics

The aesthetic of colonialism is created through recurring motifs, one of which is the appropriation of the culture of Indigenous Americans, a reference to the colonial history of Korea's coloniser, the USA. On the surface this may be bathetic, seen, for example, through the two fathers reluctantly dressed in feathered headdresses and carrying toy tomahawks at a child's birthday party, but the colonial past is kept alive through the reverence that wealthy Koreans have for Americans – the Park family aspire to be as American as possible, sending Da-song to cub scouts. Another colonial motif is the English language itself, the language of the US colonisers and therefore the language of power, which keeps the colonisers in the country.

To gain status, characters adopt English names. Mr Park (Dong-ik) is Nathan; we are introduced to him through a headline from a magazine – 'Nathan Park Hits Central Park'. Nathan/Dong-ik is the head of a fictional tech company that has links with the USA; this suggests that Dong-ik's allegiance is to the USA rather than South Korea and its people, represented by the Kims. The Kims' daughter, Ki-jung, poses as Jessica, who has studied in the US state of Illinois; so impressed is Mrs Park (Yeon-gyo) that she doesn't ask for evidence of her studies. The Kim's son, Ki-woo, is introduced by Yeon-gyo to the housekeeper as Kevin. Kevin/Yeon-gyo attempts to speak English to impress Ki-woo, who has acquired status as an English teacher. The absurdity of such a notion is highlighted by the ease with which he can fake it by simply having an English name and easily forged documents. Yeo-gyo is desperate for her daughter to learn English. Ironically, Ki-woo himself is excluded from the college system by failing the entrance exam four times, mocking the difficulty of the English section. In the battle for power between the two families, the Kims use English to gain access to the Parks' world. Here, it is interesting to note that what the Parks may consider to be a marker of their wealth, power and status – the connection with the USA through their use of the English language – is used against them by the Kims.

As part of this aesthetic, the wealthy are seen to shun Korean culture; for example, all the food prepared at Da-song's party is foreign and the guests arrive in foreign makes of cars – status is acquired by looking like the *colonisers* rather than the colonised. The Parks' house has a Western aesthetic and contains household appliances that many South Koreans do not own, such as a dishwasher and a dryer. In fact, the house could easily be in America – there is nothing Korean about it. The Parks' only concession to being Korean is their guilty pleasure of cheap noodles, but eaten with sirloin steak to ensure that class distinctions are always upheld.

The aesthetic of economics, both in regard to wealth and poverty, is important throughout the film. The opening scenes – of characters hanging washing out, and damp socks that are partly responsible for poor people's musty smell – are associated with dampness, sewage and overcrowding, creating the aesthetic of poverty. South Korea is seen globally as the developer of high-speed wireless internet, yet the Kims, even though they need it to seek work, must steal it.

There is a horror aesthetic created by both the green lighting and concrete sparseness of the bunker, and by the graphically violent scenes that link to Bong's earlier works and notable works of South Korean cinema, as well as what has been called the 'extreme aesthetic' of Asian cinema. Here, the use of horror, with its concern for class, has a gothic quality. For example, the extent of the rain as the Kims descend into the slums is accompanied by an eerie sound in the air – they have transformed into their monstrous, murderous selves and are descending into raw and basic humanity.

Representations

Gender

Parasite's narrative is driven by female desire. Women are shown to be the driving force in marriage and family life and are represented in a positive way. Mrs Park (Yeon-gyo), even though in a more traditional role confined to the domestic sphere, does make important decisions that affect the family, while Mrs Kim (Chung-sook) is represented as the long-suffering wife of an ineffective patriarch. When we are first introduced to Mrs Kim, she is sitting knitting while her husband apparently sleeps. The desperate need for Wi-Fi, which they can't afford, is revealed: they need WhatsApp to get pizza box folding instructions to earn a meagre amount. Chung-sook appears to be the real head of the household when she sarcastically asks her husband: 'What's your plan?' A cutaway shot then shows a medal and a photo of her mid-throw, looking strong and powerful. The plaque under her medal reads National Classification, Athletics Championships, Korean Federation of Athletics in 1992 (translated), juxtaposing her former success with her current desperate situation with a comedic suggestion of violence towards her inert husband. The fact that the medal itself is silver, not gold, hints at the fiercely competitive nature of Korean society and late capitalism.

The husbands in each family are reliant on women. When rescuing items from the flood, Ki-taek chooses to save his wife's medal, perhaps as a reminder to himself that in every way he is the weaker character. It is women in each case who try to ensure that their loved ones survive and thrive. While Dong-ik may seem to be more of a traditional patriarch, providing for his family, commanding the rather disturbing respect of Geun-sae and the admiration of his wife, the film gently and often comically undermines his status as the head of the household and complacent member of the elite.

Age

The use of the two easily comparable families depicts the problems in both Korea and universally for parents, young adults and children. A dissatisfaction with the growing problem of wealth inequality is a very relatable concern, and this is pronounced in the portrayal of the younger generation of the Kim family, who are limited in their opportunities for advancement due to unemployment and poverty. Bong has talked in interviews about the importance of positioning the viewer with the Kims; we understand life in South Korea from the perspective of both middle-aged and young adults. The most striking distinction is between the two men and the ways in which the optimism of the son is in opposition to his apathetic and defeated father. The nihilistic outlook on life that Mr Kim espouses in the scene in the gymnasium invites viewer empathy for the endless cycle of suffering inflicted on the poor – everything that happens creates far more devastation for the poor. Despite hearing

> **Final Girl:** the last remaining character at the end of a horror film featuring a group of young people who have been killed one by one, the final girl who is usually the most intelligent of the female characters who displays the resourcefulness to survive and issue a warning to others.

his father's tone of defeat, Ki-woo's unrelenting optimism continually shifts the tone of the film, even in the darkest of moments. This suggests that it is a vital characteristic in the young, necessary for the survival of the human race. The ensuing tragedy is that the viewer helplessly watches Ki-woo retain hope of a better future despite all of the indicators that this future is an impossible dream.

The other tragic outcome for the younger Kims is that the impressively talented and resourceful Ki-jung becomes the pretty female victim of the transformed Geun-sae as a now monstrous killer. The tragedy of this knowing departure from conventional horror tropes where Ki-jung should have been the **final girl** underlines the key messages of the film about the myth of social mobility; she cannot warn future generations.

The other key representation of a working-class adult male in the film, Geun-sae, shows the consequences of pursuing aspirations from within literal entrapment. Some shots in the bunker reveal Geun-sae's aspirations to become a lawyer; we see books on law and an extensive book collection, suggesting that working class people, despite being well-read, are vulnerable to debt and the danger posed by loan-sharks. This acts as a warning to those with hopeful aspirations such as Ki-woo, further highlighting the terrible futility of those born without advantage aspiring to the lifestyle of families like the Parks.

The younger members of the Park family, despite their wealth and indulgences, are depicted as lacking parental affection and a close family bond: Da-hye is an introverted journal writer, seemingly filled with archetypal teenage angst, and Da-song, although considered difficult by his orderly, formal and naive parents, is shown to be a child desperate for attention. It is interesting to consider the scenes with Da-song and Jessica to see how readily Da-song responds to attention and affection, and in a similar way Da-hye responds with affection in the form of crushes on her young male English teachers.

In terms of representations of the family, we see the closeness of the Kims as a unit, depicted by the number of on-screen conversations they have, in opposition to the approach of the Park parents, who spend money on their children but are never seen talking to them. This representation of parents allows the viewer to see the flaws in a society which values money and status over the quality of relationships.

Ultimately, the representation of age is very closely linked to social class. Through it, the viewer is drawn to the theme of loyalty and the tragedy that rather than fighting against the rich, the poor choose to attack each other.

Ethnicity

When discussing the representation of ethnicity, as all of the characters in the film are from South Korea (commonly called Korea), the main representation for consideration is Koreans. However, as well as presenting a snapshot of life in Korea, Bong portrays and gently mocks some of the best and worst traits of human nature, making the representation also of humanity in general. The representation of life in Korea is ambivalent, drawing the viewer's attention to the intelligence and resourcefulness of all of the characters, but this is matched by their ruthless ambition, which fits in with Bong's overarching satire of capitalism. Korea is associated with the typical hallmarks of capitalism; for example, the film depicts enterprising business owners from the pizza delivery firm to Mr Park's internationally successful tech company. The name of this company, Another Brick, briefly seen on the wall behind him, is acknowledged by Bong in the DVD commentary to be a reference to the anti-establishment song by Pink Floyd; even Mr Park's company name in its undermining nature ridicules the complacency of wealthy Koreans.

A negative portrayal of life in Korea is suggested by the working-class struggle for survival, the terrible living conditions in the cramped semi-basement apartments (banjihas) and the desperate search for employment which eventually drives the working-class characters to become monstrous as they cling on to a slightly better life. This emphasises the life and death situation that the Kims, Moon-gwang and her husband are in. While the characters may be likeable, they show that they are willing to cross a moral line if put in a desperate situation, disregarding any notions of class loyalty.

The representation of the wealthy Koreans, as exemplified by the Park family, can also be seen as negative, as they too have no loyalty or empathy for others. For example, at the climax of the narrative, Mr Park (Dong-ik) behaves with shocking disregard for Mr Kim (Ki-taek) as a human being, seeing him only as a driver who can drive his son to hospital, rather than a father whose concern is for his daughter. It is interesting to consider how close to the truth of human behaviour this shocking, satirical moment is, moving the representation away from Koreans and into horror film territory: the dark side of human nature – the monster within, which will emerge in life and death situations, a theme which dominates the final act of the narrative.

The Park family represent wealthy Koreans: those who benefit from capitalism. They exist in their own version of the world with no awareness or interest in anything outside of it. This is a largely negative representation of Koreans and ultimately the individualistic ideology of capitalism. Rather than look at the place that they live and the gulf between rich and poor, their focus is on the US and ways to seek more gratification and status from it. The smell of the poor and reactions to it by the Parks is a clear motif of this selfish individualism, highlighting social inequality. Their disgust at the smell of the poor becomes more pronounced as the film progresses; a physical revulsion by those who benefit from capitalism to those they see as lesser than themselves.

As with the representation of poor Koreans, the portrayal of the Parks when considered as individuals, rather than what they represent, is mostly positive. They are likeable, sympathetic characters, in part created by some really engaging performances. This directs the viewer's attention to the film's messages about the ruthless, callous attitudes of both rich and poor encouraged by an individualist, competitive, capitalist society. The most negative representation is of capitalism; although the film satirises the worst aspects of life in Korea and seems to present a negative representation of Koreans, the political ideology and the colonial past are referenced as the cause. On an individual level, it is interesting to consider how viewers might feel towards Ki-taek when he stabs his employer. The bleak ending re-enforces the message that there is little possibility of change; one working-class man trapped in the bunker has been replaced by another and a new wealthy family will buy the house. The new family show that even the rich are replaceable, and, ultimately, there are no beneficiaries of late capitalism.

Through depicting the Park family's worship of all things American, satirised by the naive fascination with indigenous American history transferred to Da-song by his scout leader, Bong is also able to explore some stereotyped representations of indigenous Americans. This relates to the superficial commodification of indigenous culture linking to the crass commercialism of capitalism, and perhaps also references the ways that Koreans in their obsession with the US reduce the long and complicated history of oppression to fashionable objects such as tomahawks, teepees and headdresses. Bong uses the offensive stereotype of the violent, warmongering, savage indigenous Americans to expose the superficial attitudes to history and culture in Korean and capitalist societies.

Meaning and response

While the proficiency of *Parasite*'s filmmaking style has been universally praised, there is an interesting variety of responses to the film's themes and messages. *Parasite*'s portrayal of late capitalism has resonated with audiences globally; some commentators have even suggested that Bong is pandering to South Korea's colonisers by making the film so universal in its themes. The film has even been used by North Korea to praise their communist regime, although this of course does not mean that life in North Korea is being promoted as an alternative.

Other reviewers in the West have been impressed that a South Korean film can be so frank about the issues present in the country, finding it refreshing to see problems being aired rather than repressed. The implication is that there can be an openness about life in South Korea which is well known to be lacking in North Korea. This openness is celebrated by Bong himself, who said in an interview for *Vulture* that while the film isn't a documentary, it does reflect the reality of life in Korea.

And maybe the film has highlighted the terrible living conditions of some South Koreans to the authorities. As a result of global attention after the Oscar wins, the Korean government said that it will stop granting permits for landlords to rent out semi-basement apartments, or banjiha, showing that despite the film offering no solutions to the issues it raises, it has brought about some positive change in South Korea.

The film has also drawn attention to wealthy South Koreans building bunkers in their houses. This is a reference to the constant fear of invasion by North Korea or a crash in the economy, undermining the complacent sense of security exhibited by the Parks and suggesting that all can be lost in an instance through war or economic crisis. As Moon-gwang explains to the Kims, such bunkers are common in houses owned by the wealthy to protect them from being chased by creditors or an invasion. This is an example of bathetic comedy where communism and capitalism are linked, suggesting ultimately that parasitic humans are all the same regardless of political ideology. It also acts a symbol for the underclass; Geun-sae has been rejected by Korean society, yet is still in awe of the Parks. He is also the invisible victim of the Kims, as since they expelled his wife, their former housekeeper, Geun-sae is discovered living in the bunker, where he has starved for four days. Moon-gwang also makes reference to North Korea by suggesting that pushing the button to send the blackmail video is akin to pushing the button to instigate nuclear war. He further extends this analogy by mimicking a famous North Korean news presenter. So, the couple and the bunker come to represent the threat of both North Korea and capitalist economics to South Koreans, just as the Kims represent the threat of the reality of life in South Korea to the America-facing Parks.

Parasite satirises the ways in which people tend to look upwards in aspiration rather than downwards to show that there is little difference between themselves and those who they consider to be inferior in wealth and status. This is highlighted in a conversation between Mr Kim (Ki-taek) and Geun-sae; there is irony in the way that Ki-taek views life in the bunker with horror, failing to see that this is not much different to life in a semi-basement apartment. This links to the anti-capitalist messages of the film – those in power create the conditions that encourage conflict among the poorest and most disempowered people in society, escaping any blame for social inequality themselves.

The paralleling of the two families, as well as exposing the wealth divide, does ironically indicate that as human beings there is little difference between them. All eight characters are portrayed sympathetically, and the film suggests hidden depths in each one. For example, Ki-jung exhibits intelligence and resourcefulness in her scheming, and at the end Da-hye is physically strong and determined as she rescues the injured Ki-woo. This paralleling of characters emphasises the absurdity of judging people by their social class or wealth; the birthday party and its aftermath reveals that everyone is a parasite fighting for survival. In addition to the bleak message about the myth of social mobility, there is the typical horror message that the veneer of civilisation is very thin, that we all have a monstrous side when pushed to fight for survival, and that everyone is a parasite trying not to be exterminated.

Independent study questions

Q How does Bong Joon-ho use film form to bring to the fore the film's social and political messages?

Q In what ways does knowing about the history of Korea affect your reading of the film and its themes?

Q How does the film use a horror aesthetic in the second half?

Q How do you see the ending of the film? What do you think its overall message is about human nature and social mobility in South Korea?

Conclusion

For over 25 years, New Iranian Cinema has dominated the global filmmaking landscape, with Jafar Panahi being a leading figure within this film movement. He made *Taxi Tehran* five years into his 20-year ban from filmmaking, but when asked in 2014 if Iranian cinema had a future, he was optimistic, if somewhat despondent about his place within it.

The success of *Parasite* is both cultural and critical. Through this film Bong has raised his status as an important filmmaker and brought Korean cinema to global attention. The film has brought about significant change in Korea, according to NBC News (2022), which reported catastrophic flooding in Seoul in which three people died and thousands of people were left homeless. The Korean authorities have said that they will no longer grant licences for semi-basement apartments, or banjihas. This demonstrates the power of film to bring serious socio-economic issues to global attention and to produce important change.

Section 2

A level: Global filmmaking perspectives

(Not studied at AS)

Documentary film

This chapter will help you prepare for **Component 2: Global filmmaking perspectives** on the A level course. Alongside the core areas of study you will need to apply the specialist study areas of **Critical Debate 2: The significance of digital technology in film and Filmmakers' theories.** This section will use *Stories We Tell* (Polley, Canada, 2012) and *For Sama* (Al-Kateab & Watts, 2019) as case studies.

For A level

One question from a choice of two must be answered on the **Component 2** paper. The full question is worth 20 marks and should be allocated 30 minutes.

The specification says

The documentary film in its contemporary form has become a much freer form, utilising cinematic techniques in ever more creative ways to tell 'factual' stories while problematising the divide between fact and fiction.

In Stories We Tell the filmmaker engages in an investigation into her family, specifically seeking the identity of her genetic father.

In For Sama, Syrian filmmaker Waad al-Kateab combines performative and observational modes to document her experiences as a young mother during the Battle of Aleppo.

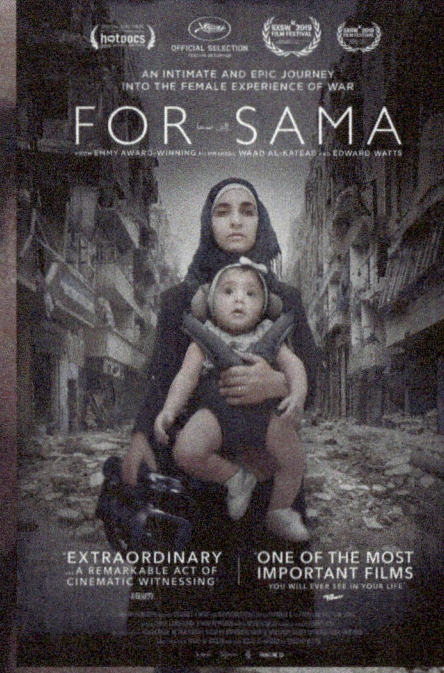

7 Stories We Tell (Polley, 2013) & For Sama (Al Kateab & Watts 2019)

Stories We Tell (Polley, 2013)

Stories We Tell is, on the surface, a fascinating exploration of Sarah Polley's family, including archive footage and insightful interviews with her relatives and family friends. The film initially paints a portrait of her enigmatic and charismatic late mother, actress and television personality Diane Polley, who died when Sarah was a child. The film goes on to examine Sarah's relationships with the writer and actor Michael Polley, the man who raised her as his own daughter, and film and theatre producer Harry Gulkin, who is revealed to be her biological father. The film is moving, revelatory, at times humorous and full of surprises.

This chapter will address the core areas of study in relation to Stories We Tell and For Sama by exploring the conventions of the documentary form and the different modes of documentary used in this film. The section will also examine the role digital technologies play in this genre and compare Polley's approach to those of other significant documentarians, and filmmakers' theories in relation to For Sama.

Documentary

Early silent films often simply recorded something real and showed it to an audience. Take as an example the famous 1895 Lumière Brothers' film *L'arrivée d'un train en gare de La Ciotat* or, as it is often referred to, *Train Pulling into a Station*. The film is entirely comprised of real-life footage of a train's arrival at a station, and therefore could be seen as an early example of the documentary genre.

The documentary genre has been defined in many different ways since its inception. John Grierson, who came up with the term, referred to documentary as,

> the creative treatment of actuality. (cited in Eitzen, 1995, page 82)

Grierson's definition allows that there is a creativity to documentary filmmaking that suggests the filmmaker has a role to play in shaping the film and telling the story in an imaginative and compelling way. The word 'actuality' can be understood as fact, which is reflected in Bordwell and Thompson's definition, in their textbook *Film Art* (1997). They say,

> a documentary film purports to present factual information about the world outside the film. (page 42)

The use of the word 'purports' is interesting as it questions the reliability of the form and raises the issue of whether documentaries can ever really present an objective truth. Singleton and Conrad are very specific, defining documentaries as,

> Film[s] of actual events; the events are documented with the real people involved, not with actors. (2000, page 94)

This is problematised when reconstructions, a staple of many films from this genre, are taken into account. Perhaps a broader definition is more helpful, like the one from James Monaco, who describes documentary as,

> [A] term with a wide latitude of meaning, basically used to refer to any film or program not wholly fictional in nature. (2000, page 94)

What these definitions demonstrate is that the term documentary has multiple contested meanings. However, the genre, in its many forms, continues to fascinate audiences and has as great an impact today as in the early days of cinema when audiences allegedly ran from screenings of *L'arrivée d'un train en gare de La Ciotat* in fear of being struck by the locomotive.

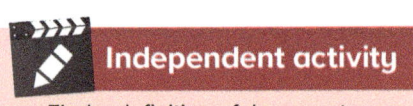

Independent activity

Find a definition of documentary that you feel best encapsulates the genre and write 100 words on why you like this definition and how it reflects *Stories We Tell*.

L'arrivée d'un train en gare de La Ciotat **(Lumière Brothers, 1895)**

Stories We Tell

Stories We Tell is an invitation to the audience to question the authenticity of the documentary form. Spectators are encouraged to assess the reliability of personal testimony and whether or not there is such a thing as objective truth. Are the stories we tell a true portrayal of the past and, if so, why do they differ from others' recollections of the same events? Can memory ever be really relied upon? The film also exposes the constructed nature of documentary film by interspersing reconstructions with archive footage without revealing this to the audience. The film arguably misleads the spectator for a large portion of the narrative while purporting to tell the truth and, in doing so, raises interesting considerations regarding the 'true' nature of the documentary form as a representation of fact. It is for this reason that *Stories We Tell* is a useful case study for analysing this genre.

Contexts

Production contexts

Documentary is often regarded as a somewhat niche genre, but a quick scroll through the titles currently available on Netflix and other streaming services confirm the popularity of this type of film. Most documentary films still tend to get limited theatrical releases and *Stories We Tell* is no exception. Even though Sarah Polley was an established name in the film industry, through both acting and directing, and the film won multiple awards, *Stories We Tell* initially opened on just two cinema screens and its widest release was 70 screens according to boxofficemojo.com (2017). However, despite this, according to the National Film Board blog, *Stories We Tell* is one of the most successful Canadian films of all time and made the TIFF All Time Top Ten List. The film certainly achieved critical acclaim with a metascore of 91 and a rating of 'universal acclaim' on metacritic.com (n.d.). *Stories We Tell* won the 2013 New York Film Critics Circle Award for Best Non-Fiction Film and the 2013 Los Angeles Film Critics Association Award for Best Documentary. The film was also awarded the Allan King Documentary award at the 2012 Toronto Film Critics Association Awards.

Patricia Aufderheide (2008) states that there are three main sources of funding for documentary filmmakers: corporate or governmental sponsors, advertisers and users. *Stories We Tell* was produced by the first of these, specifically the National Film Board (NFB) of Canada, an organisation hugely supportive of the documentary genre. The NFB in its various guises has championed the documentary form since John Grierson's involvement in 1938, through the Second World War propaganda and newsreels to 1980s televised vignettes of Canadian culture.

In 2009 the Board collaborated with the Canadian Film Centre on a theatrical documentary development programme, Creative Doc Lab, which led to the production of, among other films, *Stories We Tell*. Polley's decision to work on the project with these organisations was deliberate because she wanted the freedom to experiment.

Independent activity

Watch *Fahrenheit 9/11* (Moore, 2004) and note the reasons you feel it was such a box office success.

Social and political contexts

A 2012 BBC News article by Lorraine Mallinder (2012) asked 'What Does it Mean to Be Canadian?' One of the points made in this article is that Canada is a diverse nation made up of over 200 ethnic groups spread over six time zones.

Mallinder quotes John Ralston Saul, who said of Canadians, 'they accept that difference is actually quite interesting'. This embracing of diversity points to a culture that is non-judgemental and open-minded: traits we can certainly see in the Polley family depicted in *Stories We Tell*.

The Polley family certainly have enlightened and progressive views. This is evident in relation to gender roles, in particular Michael's attitude to his wife's work and choices. Canada as a whole fairs well in terms of gender equality, coming 20th in the World Economic Forum's 2013 Global Gender Gap Report in the year of release, but the film reveals the misogyny of the 1960s as the camera pans across judgemental tabloid news reporting Diane having lost custody of her children.

Cultural context

The prevalence of 'reality' television and mockumentaries in contemporary culture may impact upon audience response to this documentary. Spectators may be more cynical and less believing now, as they are increasingly exposed to scripted 'reality' television programmes where situations are constructed for entertainment purposes.

Approaches to storytelling and the way narratives are structured in film continue to change and become more complex in the quest to offer audiences something new

Independent activity

Listen to the Sarah Polley interview on the NPR website (2013) and note Polley's observations on her approach to making this film.

and surprising. Films with plot twists have a long history of popularity among filmmakers and audiences alike. *Stories We Tell* reflects the evolution of cinema, offering something new, not a plot twist but a construction twist.

Film form in documentary and *Stories We Tell*

Documentary films share many conventions with fiction films, such as the range of shot types used, the use of music to create mood and tone, and clever editing to construct compelling narratives. The far from exhaustive list of documentary conventions explored here arguably includes aspects of film form seen in a range of films of all genres. Fiction films in various genres, particularly social realist films, co-opt the conventions of documentary to convey a sense of realism.

★ **Hand-held camera:** it is often suggested that a hand-held camera conveys a sense of the real. It creates the sense of actually being there as it captures the camera operator's movements and changing perspectives: the image can be blurred at times through camera shake, and the frame is unfixed and often shifts erratically. Additionally, hand-held cameras can convey a sense of energy and emotion, as a result of rapid movement and/or the frame moving unevenly or fitfully. The archive footage and the reconstructions in *Stories We Tell* both use a hand-held camera with very unpredictable movements at times. The use of this technique for both these helps to contribute to the sense that all the footage is from the same source, and therefore authentic.

★ **Voice-over or narration:** occurs when a voice is heard on the soundtrack without a matching source in the image. In other words, we hear the voice speak but we cannot see the speaker utter the words. The voice often explains or comments on the visuals, presents a point of view and leads the audience towards a preferred reading. Michael Polley's voice is probably the dominant voice-over in *Stories We Tell*, but the film is unusual in the way that it includes footage of him recording it, making the filmmaking process seem transparent.

★ **Talking heads:** talking heads are interviews with experts or witnesses, often filmed in their home or workplace, offering their perspectives on the events being documented. These are often shot in medium close-up or medium shot and adhere to the rule of thirds. Captions are often used to identify the participant to the audience. *Stories We Tell* makes use of this convention and all participants are framed similarly, which contributes to the sense that they play equal roles in telling this story.

Stretch & challenge

Compile a more exhaustive list of documentary conventions through your own research. For each convention find an example from *Stories We Tell* to illustrate its use. If the film does not use the particular convention find an example from the films of the other directors you are considering, i.e. two from Peter Watkins, Nick Broomfield, Kim Longinotto or Michael Moore.

★ **Archive footage and photographs:** existing recordings or images that can be used to evidence that events took place. These can include stock footage, usually held by libraries or television companies, which can be used time and again for different purposes. *Stories We Tell* relies primarily on the Polley family's own archive of home movies but includes extracts from an existing documentary on Harry Gulkin too.

★ **Reconstructions or re-enactments:** performances of real events that have already happened but not been recorded. They often include actors playing the parts of the real subjects. How *Stories We Tell* differs from most other documentaries in this regard is that the re-enactments included here are presented as genuine footage for the bulk of the narrative.

★ Subjects are often **hyper-real** or **extraordinary**, as audiences are drawn to worlds outside of their own experiences or people different from those they know. The subjects of *Stories We Tell*, although arguably just Sarah's family members, are extraordinary in some ways. Outside of the complexity of their relationships they are renowned, accomplished, charismatic and entertaining people who are noteworthy in their own right.

Modes of documentary

Bill Nichols is an important documentary theoretician and in his seminal text, *Introduction to Documentary* (2010), he divides the documentary genre into six oft-cited 'sub-genres' or modes.

Exploring these further is a useful way in considering the approach or approaches Polley takes in *Stories We Tell*.

★ Coming to prominence in the 1920s, **poetic** documentaries are often non-linear with no clear narrative and rely instead on the juxtaposition of images and sound to create mood, tone and ultimately convey the filmmaker's message in a rather abstract way. An example is Reggio's 1982 film *Koyaanisqatsi*.

★ **Expository** documentaries came to prominence around the same time but often feature an authoritative voice-over and convey a clear point of view. Consider *March of the Penguins*, Jacquet's 2005 film.

★ A later development of the documentary genre, popularised in the 1960s, is the **participatory** documentary. These films include direct engagement between the filmmaker and the subject. The filmmaker is often seen on screen asking questions and expressing their perspective. An obvious example is Michael Moore who never shies away from expressing his point of view, as seen in *Bowling for Columbine* (2002).

Bowling for Columbine (Moore, 2002)

★ **Observational** documentaries, which started at a similar time, were a response to criticisms of earlier forms. Filmmakers used smaller cameras, available now due to advances in technology, and aimed to let their cameras record their subjects without intrusion. Philibert's 2003 film, *Être et avoir*, uses this technique to offer the audience access to a rural school in France.

★ **Reflexive** documentaries, which evolved in the 1980s, draw attention to their own construction, often showing the process of the film being made. The intention of this can be to be transparent about the process and perhaps sidestep any questions about the ethics of the filmmaker. Nick Broomfield regularly, but not always, highlights his own involvement and the technologies of filmmaking in his work. Take as an example his 1992 documentary, *Aileen Wuornos: The Selling of a Serial Killer*. This film is as much about Broomfield securing an interview as it is about Wuornos' life and crimes.

★ **Performative** documentaries tend to be very personal and often focus on subjective truths that are significant to the filmmaker themselves. An example of this is *Tongues Untied*, a 1989 film by Marlon Riggs, who tells his own life story as a way of exploring the life of gay black American men.

Stretch & challenge

Watch the six films used here, or extracts from them, as examples of Nichols' modes. For each film, analyse a sequence in detail, commenting on all aspects of film form.

Être et avoir (Philibert, 2003)

Stories We Tell has a number of aspects that place it within the reflexive mode of documentary, such as the shots of Polley at the mixing desk or behind the camera, but it shares traits with other sub-genres too, such as the voice-over from the expository mode. This is not unusual in documentaries, where overlap of modalities within a film is common practice.

A mode of documentary not included in Nichols' schema is that of the personal documentary, one that *Stories We Tell* possibly represents most coherently. These films are generally autobiographical and combine interviews and voice-overs with archive footage, photographs and artifacts to explore a person's life.

Polley herself has an ambivalent attitude to this mode of documentary, as she states on the NFB blogsite (2012). She says that personal documentaries have always made her 'a bit squeamish' and that, although she's seen some really good ones, they 'often push the boundaries of narcissism' and can feel 'more like a form of therapy than actual filmmaking'.

Maybe this accounts for the fact that for a film that explores her family, and indeed her very coming into being, she at times seems like quite a peripheral participant. She is seen throughout the film but only rarely as the focus of a scene and her voice is seldom heard. In particular, her opinions and emotions are rarely explored in any depth.

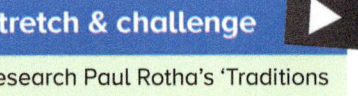

Stretch & challenge

Research Paul Rotha's 'Traditions of Documentary' in *Documentary Film* (1935), as an alternative way of categorising films in this genre. Summarise each 'tradition' in ten words.

Storytelling and construction of 'truth'

Documentary filmmakers usually wish to convince the audience of the authenticity of what they are representing. *Stories We Tell* challenges this, as one of the key themes of the film is how many different versions of events can be held within just one family.

As is made clear by the title and indeed the opening words, this film is about storytelling. The audience may glean from the opening quote from novelist Margaret Atwood and the first words of Michael Polley's narration that what follows will not be a straightforward story, the plot may not follow a traditional structure and at times **narrative devices** may not be what they seem.

The film feels like a personal journey of discovery. There is a sense that Polley did not always know what form the film would take or how the story would be told. However, what is clear is that Polley has a very democratic approach to storytelling and strongly believes that everyone's experience and perspective are equally valid. This is expressed within the film in an email to Harry, where she says that she's uncomfortable with her involvement in telling the story unless it includes their experience of it, as well as her family's. She admits to not really knowing how to tell the story but is keen to ensure that everyone's point of view is included.

Also in communication with Harry, Polley reveals a core belief that there is no such thing as **objective truth**, as everyone's version of events will differ.

This can be seen in Harry and Michael's conflicting memories of Diane's memorial service and in the participants' differing memories of whether Diane knew she was dying. The general consensus appears to be that she was aware of this fact, yet Michael disagrees. Perhaps it is too painful for him to imagine her confronting her imminent mortality.

Harry has a different perspective on whether accessing the truth is possible, stating that you have to limit this access to people who are directly involved and affected by an event. He believes that in terms of Diane's story, the truth was only his to tell. His recollections might be 'faulty at times' but he isn't going to lie.

So the participants in this film do not agree on how close to the facts the documentary can get or even on how best to approach seeking the truth.

Narrative devices: techniques used in order to tell a story.

Objective truth: one truth that is the same for all people.

Bias: a concentration on one particular area or viewpoint.

Balance: different elements are treated equally.

Polley can be heard in the film asking participants for the 'whole story' and specifies 'in your own words'. This is crucial as it suggests she is at once looking for the whole truth, not just edited highlights, but it also acknowledges that each account is an individual's perspective of the truth. She is expecting unique, probably somewhat conflicting, accounts. She also asks for their opinions on the documentary, which reflects just how self-reflexive this film is, as the audience is reminded they are watching a documentary and invited to question the form as well as the content.

Documentary films also raise issues of **bias** and **balance**, as the audience questions if the accounts are tainted by prejudice and whether an even-handed representation of events is being conveyed. *Stories We Tell* explores these notions in its examination of the truth.

Film form
Cinematography

Polley uses cinematography techniques from numerous different modes of documentary. The conventions of the talking heads in medium shot to medium close-up from the participatory interview are featured, moments of fly-on-the-wall filming reflect the observational documentary style and there are performed scenes, or reconstructions, as in drama documentaries. The overall effect of this range of filming techniques contributes to the reflexive documentary style: a film that does not simply explore the relationship between the director and the subject(s) but rather the director and the audience.

The film does feature real archive footage of the family, including a section made up primarily of close-ups of Diane through which the audience is at once invited to scrutinise her, although she is never fully revealed.

This arguably reflects the film as a whole, as Diane remains somewhat enigmatic; a portrait made complex by differing accounts of a woman the audience does not get to meet. These close-ups are possibly used to elicit an emotional response from the spectator as they precede Sarah asking Michael to recount his memories of the day Diane died. Polley may have intended the audience to connect with Diane at this moment and perhaps therefore feel her loss more keenly.

Another emotive extreme close-up is used during the reconstructed scene of Sarah revealing to Michael that he is not her biological father. To some spectators this may lose some of its intensity as it is a scripted and performed recreation of a real moment from the past.

Techniques are used to encourage the audience to believe, for most of the narrative, that all the footage of the family is real. An example of this is the reconstructed footage of the play rehearsals, which are out of focus, shot with a shaky camera and have a voyeuristic feel. The audience is placed at a distance, sometimes behind props or parts of the set, like somebody filming but not wishing to interrupt.

A contrasting example, but one that also creates verisimilitude, is the way that 'Diane' breaks the fourth wall and interacts with the camera operator in an extract from a 'home movie' eight minutes into the documentary. This informality feels authentic as it is likely to resemble the natural human behaviour spectators will be familiar with from their own home movies.

Perhaps to discourage the audience from doubting the authenticity of any of the footage, the voice-over explains the importance of home movies to the family and, in particular, Michael's preoccupation with recording his family's life.

Stretch & challenge

Research Michael Renov's four fundamental tendencies and note what you think the primary purpose of this film was according to his categorisations.

Image search
Diane's representation and its wider meaning

00:02:37–00:04:06

Compile a collage of the images of Diane in this scene, and annotate them with detail which shows how she is represented. Consider how they reveal the personal narrative of Sarah Polley and the wider misogynist narrative of the time.

Image search
How 'real' is the documentary?

00:06:16–00:07:53

Watch the compilation of home movies that illustrate the section on Diane. Compile a set of screengrabs which reflect the style of these home movies and give the viewer insight into the real Diane.

00:07:54–00:10:30

Then compare this with the way that Diane is shown in the reconstructed home movies that follow. Compile a set of screengrabs from this section and decide what you think the impact of juxtaposing the real with the reconstructed home movies is on the meaning of the film, and the issue of the authenticity of the documentary.

7 Stories We Tell (Polley, 2013) & For Sama (Al Kateab & Watts 2019)

Further evidence of this interest in home movies is seen in a photograph of Michael and Diane, which includes the Super 8 camera. These cameras and the associated film stock date back to 1965 and were most widely used for home movies. Super 8 footage has a nostalgic quality, a softness brought about by circular film grain and warmth of tone. The inclusion of this photo contributes to the spectator potentially reading all the film's Super 8 footage as real archive home movies.

The film makes use of much more contemporary digital cameras for the recent interviews, with the resulting footage being much sharper. This could be interpreted as more accurate and reliable, capturing the real without the cloudy nostalgia. To confuse matters further, Polley also uses 16mm footage for some of the more contemporary scenes, thus blurring the line between the past and the present, and contributing to the confusion. This may be instrumental in avoiding the audience spotting the deception.

Panning, alongside the aforementioned use of a hand-held camera, is an interesting example of how camera movement is used in this film. Panning is used effectively to provide insight for the spectator. An example is the pan around Michael's chaotic home, which could point to the fact that he may not be coping too well, thus revealing more to the audience than he knows.

Mise-en-scène

The mise-en-scène in this film is crucial in creating the sense that the reconstructions are real archive footage rather than re-enactments of events. Capturing the period accurately through location choices, set design, costume and styling to mislead the spectator is one central aspect of this.

Another technique is Polley's inclusion of artefacts, for example playbills and articles about Diane's roles in theatre. These are typical of documentary films and thus contribute to the sense of authenticity.

From the outset, Polley also includes the technology of filmmaking – cameras, lighting rigs and mixing desks – to create the impression of transparency in how the film is constructed. The audience may feel that, as she is being so open about the filmmaking techniques, she can be trusted.

Editing

The narrative structure of *Stories We Tell* is non-linear, as the audience are drip-fed new information throughout the film. The non-linear structure helps to create enigma by taking the audience step by step into the past. It is relatively late in the film, for example, that we learn of Diane's first marriage.

The focus of the film is not apparent from the outset either. Initially, this appears to be a film primarily about Diane, Sarah Polley's mother, but it is later revealed to be as much about her father, or fathers. The narrative has the twists and turns of a fictional film, creating suspense and intrigue but ultimately, at least partially, satisfying the audience's desire for **narrative closure**. The relationships will continue to evolve off camera but the audience has a sense that a new equilibrium has been reached, with Sarah Polley having a positive relationship with both Michael and Harry.

> **Narrative closure:** the feeling of finality generated when all the questions asked in a story are answered.

The complexity of the edit, mixing interviews, real archive footage and reconstructed scenes occurs from the beginning of the film, encouraging the spectators to passively accept the style and immerse themselves in the narrative. On first viewing the spectators are likely to be so caught up in the narrative that they don't pick up on hints that not all the footage they are seeing is real. Only on a second viewing, once the artifice has been revealed, is a spectator likely to fully appreciate the trickery at work. They may then question why they didn't at various moments ask themselves who was filming or indeed why a particular moment was being recorded at all. An example of this is the memorial for Diane; with hindsight clearly a reconstruction as funerals are rarely captured on film.

The editing in *Stories We Tell* is at times used to evoke emotion. An example of this is the use of archive footage of a solemn Sarah Polley as a child, which cuts to Michael discussing with her how close he and her mother came to aborting her.

Additionally, a juxtaposition of Sarah Polley and her mother, similar both in terms of framing and facial expression, is strangely emotive as it invites the audience to consider their connection and appreciate what Sarah has lost.

On the NFB website, Polley (2012) acknowledges the agonising process of editing and how crucial it is in constructing a coherent and engaging narrative. She states,

> I have spent five years deciding, frame by frame and word by word, how to tell this story in this film.

Sound

The music that bookends this film is contemporary and highly emotive. 'Skinny Love' by Bon Iver and 'Demon Host' by Timber Timbre are both melancholic and ghostly. The latter immediately follows Michael recounting his last words spoken to Diane, so the song's opening line 'Death, she must have been your will', is highly pertinent and designed to provoke an emotional response. To add to this, the song is momentarily contrapuntal, as it is played over archive footage of Michael and Diane having fun at the beach. After a brief fade-out to allow Michael to continue to speak it fades back in to accompany a series of shots of long duration of the film's main participants all looking pensive as if reflecting on Diane and her death.

Music is, however, also used to humorous effect at times. The archive footage sometimes appears more comical and light due to the choice of music. Instrumental music by Abraham Lass is used sporadically throughout the film. It is taken from *Play Me a Movie: Piano Music to Accompany Silent Movie Scenes* and this link to cinema contributes to the sense of stories being told – a 'truth' being constructed.

The language use in this film is at times sophisticated. The voice-over includes use of Latin, complex terminology and a rather poetic turn of phrase. Michael's cultural capital (see Key term definition, page 47) is clear and likely to appeal to a similarly educated audience.

7 Stories We Tell (Polley, 2013) & For Sama (Al Kateab & Watts 2019)

Use of a Super 8 camera for the archive footage and reconstructed scenes means no sound was recorded. This arguably helps Sarah Polley blend the footage, as there is no need for voices to be mimicked. It could be argued that this makes the performed scenes less of a deception, as at least no words were being put in anyone's mouths.

In some ways Sarah Polley's voice is heard least in this film and she addressed this in the NFB blog post she wrote (Polley, 2012):

> I declined to use a '**voice of God**' first person voice over narration because it felt false, self involved, and besides the point. But I found I could lose myself in the words of the people closest to me. I can feel and hear and see their histories, and I wanted to get lost, immerse myself in those words, and be a detective in my own life and family.

Voice of god: a narration technique in which the narration is given anonymously and authoritatively.

Performance

Performance may initially seem less relevant in documentary than other film genres, as what the audience is watching is expected to be real but, as already explored in this section, *Stories We Tell* is a little different. For the sections of the film that are reconstructions it is crucial that the performances be as naturalistic as possible so as to contribute to the sense of authenticity.

The film also includes interviews and voice-overs that are performances in themselves. Consider Michael's voice-over, which is scripted and rehearsed. Sections are performed and sometimes repeated until 'right'. Consider also Polley's siblings, readying themselves for their interviews at the beginning of the film, considering how to sit, how they will be framed and what they want to say. They ask, 'What's my frame?' and state, 'Showtime', drawing attention to their performance and the constructed nature of documentary.

As well as a crucial aspect of film form, performance is arguably one of the key themes of this film. Michael and Diane meet while in a play together and fall in love while pretending to be other people. Michael says they were, 'playing two roles, rather than Michael and Diane'.

Aesthetics

A home movie aesthetic is created through the use of Super 8, a format the film's producer Anita Lee said is loaded as,

> it already comes with this notion of nostalgia and the past. It's a medium of a certain time. We associate Super 8 with home movies lost in basements ...
> (Doucet, 2015)

This aesthetic is arguably quite romantic and there is a softness to the look of the film at times. This is not unusual for a Sarah Polley film.

This is Sarah Polley's seventh film and producer Anita Lee suggests common themes running through Polley's work:

> Her signature is to look at relationships deeply and honestly in a microscopic way, and the emotional waves these relationships have on the people around them. A deep exploration of intimate relationships at different stages was at the core of *I Shout Love*, *Away from Her* and *Take This Waltz*, and now *Stories We Tell* takes this territory to a new level.
>
> (CinemaReview.com, 2017)

Polley's work is clearly linked thematically through her focus on relationships and there is a recurring visual style too: a sense of nostalgia.

Representations

It could be argued that documentaries are less likely to rely on stereotypical or archetypal representations, as the people presented are real and therefore multifaceted, complex and changeable. However, documentary films are still constructed – still mediated – allowing the filmmaker to make decisions about what to show the audience of these people and, their lives and just as importantly, what not to show. As Krystin Arneson puts it in *Artifacts* journal (2012),

> No matter how objectively a filmmaker approaches a topic, they will always be filtering the topic through their personal lens not just the camera's.

Age

As the film explores families, a wide range of ages are represented. This includes Sarah and her siblings as both children and adults, Harry and Michael as middle-aged and elderly people, and the youngest generation of children and grandchildren at play. Although this array of ages is represented, the film makes few comments about age, perhaps another example of Polley's democratic approach to filmmaking. A person's account of events is given no more status just because they have the wisdom of age.

One notable exception is the way that Diane is depicted. One aspect of how youthful she appears is the sad fact that she died young, so the audience don't see her age; aside from this she has a vitality and energy captured in home movies and in comments by people who knew her. Her son John describes her as, 'a really young soul'. This facet of her character could link with the irresponsibility of some of her actions and may encourage the audience to be less critical of her.

Gender

If we consider Western societies' expectations of women and the representation of Diane in this context, the film offers a refreshing lack of judgement of her for her transgressions. Diane is a complex individual who, unsurprisingly, adheres to some stereotypes and challenges others. Women are often represented as the homemaker and mother, something we certainly see in *Stories We Tell*. Early in the film it is established, through an interview with Joanna Polley, that gender roles were very conventional in the family home. Speaking of Diane, she states that she had done all the cooking, cleaning and looking after the children.

This is backed up by Michael Polley, the father, who states that he was a good husband, in a 'providing way'.

The contribution of Mark Polley also confirms that Michael gave up acting for more secure employment to fulfil the role of the breadwinner. These comments are anchored through archive footage of Michael chopping wood and Diane with the children, to secure the contrasting representations in the spectators' minds. The representations are more complex though, as the audience also sees Michael being very attentive to a baby, which contradicts what we hear about him leaving all parenting duties to Diane, and his closeness to Sarah after Diane's death is detailed in his voice-over.

When it comes to sex, the representations of Michael and Diane challenge social expectations because she is portrayed as being freer and uninhibited and with a higher sex drive than Michael. He is certainly modest about his own sexual prowess, saying that spending the night with 'a dead wombat' may be more exciting than a night with him.

Diane's liberal attitude to sex is central to the film's narrative and her infidelity during her marriage to Michael is presented in a very matter of fact manner with refreshingly little judgement from most of the central contributors. A notable exception is Mark's comment that she was 'out of control' but he concludes his comments with a fond smile. When the film explores Diane's adultery during her first marriage, which resulted in her losing custody of her children, the inclusion of a newspaper clipping conveys that not all of the general public were as understanding about a woman transgressing society's rules. It is mentioned in the film that this was the first time a woman lost custody of her children due to infidelity.

The film also considers the role of the 'father' exploring the importance of genetics and nurture. Michael and Sarah are presented as particularly close, as they spent a lot of time together after Diane's death and this bond is unbroken by the revelations about her parentage.

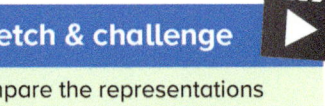

Stretch & challenge

Compare the representations of Michael and Diane. What language is used to describe them? What do we see them doing? Write 400 words including an exploration of the role gender plays in these differences.

Ethnicity

David Hulchanski of the University of Toronto has argued that in recent years, after a period of greater integration, Toronto has re-segregated along income and ethnic lines (see York University, n.d.). This film is predominantly populated by well-educated, economically comfortable, white Canadians, so there is a lack of any racial diversity represented but perhaps this reflects the society and social circles the Polley family is part of.

As ethnicity also incorporates religion, the representation of Jewish culture in this film can be explored. Harry is Jewish and Sarah joins his family for the Jewish Passover festival, and mentions the fact that this is novel for her.

This sense of difference is arguably reinforced through the juxtaposed images of Sarah dining with Michael and the Polleys and the cut to images of her at the Passover dinner. The shots of Passover include traditional Jewish foods and rituals.

Alternatively, the fact that these scenes are shot using the same type of camera and similar camera movements, could be read as a suggestion that the two meals have more similarities than differences. They are just families enjoying a meal in each other's company.

The significance of digital technology in film

Digital technologies have had a massive impact in the film world, from the accessibility of YouTube to the expensive effects of CGI. In the world of documentary more people have the means to tell their stories because cameras are more affordable and films can be distributed immediately online. This has led to a democratisation of the form. Smaller, lighter cameras also mean the camera operator is freer, more locations are within reach and the camera is less obtrusive, arguably making it less intimidating to the subject. Little of this is relevant, however, when we look at *Stories We Tell*, but this does not mean that the digital/film debate is irrelevant.

However, as this documentary uses digital and film cameras, and the sequences filmed on digital are actually the more static aspects of the film, it could be argued that in terms of flexibility and practicality the choice of digital or film had minimal impact.

Forty per cent of the film is from the family's old Super 8 movies, and Super 8 cameras (Canon 1014 AZ, Canon 1014XLS and Nikon R8) are used in the reconstructions to help create the illusion of archive footage. This technique was time-consuming as it took three days to process the film. This could be seen as a challenge of working in this format but the resulting footage is all the more convincing for having been produced authentically rather than just using a filter in post-production.

The digital camera used in *Stories We Tell*, the Sony CineAlta HDW-F900R, is used for the contemporary interviews, and the crispness of the image anchors those moments in the present. It helps create the sense of distance between the family now and the events of the past. This is complicated somewhat by Polley using 16mm footage for some of the contemporary moments. This could be seen as a further method for confusing the audience and helping to pull off the narrative's deceit. In this film at least, digital is the honest form accurately capturing the real while Super 8 is romantic, nostalgic and ultimately less reliable — like memory itself.

> **Independent activity**
>
> Read Charles Matthau's (2012) article about film versus digital, 'How Tech Has Shaped Film Making' on the *Wired* website, which was written at the time of the release of *Stories We Tell*. Summarise his arguments in less than 50 words.

Filmmakers' theories and *Stories We Tell*

In the exam you should be able to write about filmmakers' theories in relation to the film you are studying. You have to be able to write about two of the following filmmakers' approaches to the form:

★ Peter Watkins
★ Nick Broomfield
★ Kim Longinotto
★ Michael Moore.

This section will focus on Broomfield and Longinotto but there is further guidance about these filmmakers plus Watkins and Moore on the WJEC/Eduqas online resources page.

> **Stretch & challenge**
>
> Watch Kenneally's (2013) documentary *Side by Side* to gain a fuller understanding of the differences between film and digital. Summarise these in a table.

Nick Broomfield

Nick Broomfield has been making documentaries since the 1970s and is arguably one of the genre's most famous names, frequently featured in the pages of film magazines and a regular on the film festival circuit. The Film Studies specification argues that,

> Broomfield, like Michael Moore, has developed a participatory, performative mode of documentary filmmaking. Broomfield is an investigative documentarist with a distinctive interview technique which he uses to expose people's real views … he keeps the filmmaking presence to a minimum, normally with a crew of no more than three.

This is certainly true of the bulk of his work — films such as 1998's *Kurt and Courtney* and 2003's *Aileen: Life and Death of a Serial Killer* — and is the style of filmmaking he is most known for. Watching a Broomfield film, the audience expect to see him on camera, asking probing questions and trying to expose the truth about his subject. He has inspired numerous other documentary filmmakers such as Louis Theroux. This approach can be compared to aspects of *Stories We Tell*, as Polley is present on screen and the apparatus of the documentarian can be seen but the crew members are minimal and their presence unobtrusive.

Over time, Broomfield's approach to documentary has shifted and he is either completely absent from the screen, as in the dramatised documentary *Ghosts* (2006), or only occasionally heard posing a question, as in *Whitney: Can I Be Me* (2017).

Nick Broomfield

Again, these techniques can be seen in Polley's film, which includes reconstructions of real events and Polley's voice off-camera leading her interviewees through their recollections.

Ghosts (Broomfield, 2006)

 **Independent activity**

Listen to the podcast 'Nick Broomfield: The Interview Technique' (2008) and note any references Broomfield makes about his technique that link with Polley's approach to constructing *Stories We Tell*.

Kim Longinotto

Kim Longinotto

Kim Longinotto has had a long and successful career, encompassing films such as *Divorce Iranian Style* (1998) and *Sisters in Law* (2005). Her films often focus on women and she explained her reasons for this to Kira Cochrane at the *Guardian* (2010), stating that she empathises with:

> the outsiders, the people struggling. If women have no rights, if they are completely powerless, then they're the ones that you're going to want to make films about.

Her championing of those without power can be linked to what she describes as her 'problem with authority' (Lacey, 2010), which includes a distrust of documentaries that strongly push the spectator towards a specific reading.

To avoid aiming for a preferred reading, Longinotto's work largely fits within the category of observational films, also known as cinéma vérité, which was popularised in the 1960s. Documentarians working within this sub-genre tend to use light cameras, giving them greater freedom and access to places that may not have been seen before. They also shoot a lot of footage and construct the narrative in the editing room. These films are arguably more impartial than films featuring persuasive voice-overs and interviews. They aim to capture reality as honestly as possible and invite the spectator to interpret it however they want to. The decisions taken about what to film and how to edit the footage do, of course, mean reality is still mediated by the filmmaking process.

Longinotto has said,

> I don't think of films as documents or records of things. I try to make them as like the experience of watching a fiction film as possible, though, of course, nothing is ever set up.

(Quinn, 2012, page 145)

Longinotto differs from Broomfield as she is always absent from the screen and she forgoes a lot of the techniques conventionally associated with documentaries. Her use of voice-over is minimal and she avoids captions or formal interviews. In a 2006 interview with the *Guardian*'s Helen Pidd, entitled 'The Invisible Woman', Longinotto said,

> I love the way Nick [Broomfield] appears in his films, but I don't want you to be thinking about me, or the camera or the filming when you watch my films. I want you to feel that you're there, standing where I am and going through the emotional experience.

This contrasts well with Polley's approach, which often reminds the audience they are watching the film. Yet Polley's film still finds a way to convey the emotions of the director and the subjects. For example, the audience hears Polley's feelings through her emails to Harry, read out late in the film and second-hand through Michael, recounting her distress when she hears that the story about her parentage is out.

Longinotto likes to leave her documentaries open, avoiding narrative closure, as she wants her films to raise questions rather than provide answers, while Polley's film does provide some answers, such as the identity of her biological father. However, as it is documenting real people's experiences made complicated by the twists and turns of life, the spectator is left with some unanswered questions. This is made very apparent by the last-minute revelation that Geoff Bowes had lied about the nature of his relationship with Diane. The biggest enigma of them all is the question of who can we really trust?

Independent activity

1. Read the chapter on Kim Longinotto's approach to documentary from James Quinn's (2012) book *This Much is True: 14 Directors on Documentary Filmmaking*, and summarise her observations in under 100 words.
2. Read the section about Longinotto in Jason Wood's book *Talking Movies: Contemporary World Filmmakers in Interview* (2007).

Independent study questions

Q What questions remain at the end of *Stories We Tell*?

Q Do we hear any particular person's point of view more clearly than others?

Q What purpose does Sarah Polley's presence in the film serve?

Q What technologies were used in this film and what were their possibilities and limitations?

Q How does this film compare with the work of Nick Broomfield and Kim Longinotto?

For Sama

For Sama (Al-Kateab & Watts, 2019) is a multi-award-winning documentary. It is the most nominated documentary at the BAFTAs and winner of the Golden Eye Award for best documentary at the 72nd edition of the Cannes Film Festival. It brought the horrific reality of the situation in Syria and its devastating effects on the city of Aleppo to global audiences. It is both an accomplished piece of journalism and an intimate account of Al-Kateab's life in Syria. This is an interesting combination for the study of documentary, as the former is suggestive of objective truth-telling (giving the viewer a window onto the world) and the latter suggests a more subjective, personal approach to the telling of events.

In terms of documentary mode, *For Sama* is primarily observational, with over 500 hours of footage of real events as they happened to choose from in the edit, which took two years to complete. Al-Kateab's hand-held camera does not shy away from anything; we see mass burials, dead bodies and a copious amount of blood on the hospital floor, all of which, together with the sounds of bombers, gun fire and explosions, give the viewer a vicarious experience of living through a violent conflict. Typical of observational documentaries, the long takes and minimal use of non-diegetic music give the film an immediacy and visceral sense of objective truth.

However, the editing choices and the way that voice-over narration is used also make the documentary poetic and personal. In the edit, Al-Kateab and Watts used less than 10% of the available footage, which highlights the constructed nature of the documentary through a selection process. In fact, they originally edited a linear version, but decided that it was too bleak and opted for a more poetic and thematic style of editing, dedicating the film to Al-Kateab's daughter, Sama, and making it a letter to her.

The final lines of voice-over unite the documentary modes, combining the personal and the political. Al-Kateab speaks of the smell of Aleppo on her new baby, Taima's, skin and the importance of her footage to retain her sense of home.

By linking the birth and her extended Aleppo family with the footage, and following it with a montage of the happier, more hopeful times in the film, the footage itself, the 12 hard drives that she smuggled out of Syria, show the world the reality of the revolution and subsequent war, but also serve a purpose for Al-Kateab personally: she has carried her home with her.

Contexts

Production contexts

Al-Kateab has explained how the film came about in an interview on the website Seventh Row (Lazic, 2019), called 'Waad Al-Kateab and Edward Watts on their doc *For Sama*'. Al-Kateab was sending footage to Channel 4 for their TV series *Inside Aleppo*, and they introduced her to Ed Watts and suggested she worked with him to create a feature-length documentary using the extensive amount of footage she had.

Edward Watts is a well-known British documentary maker and he had been hoping to find a way to tell the story of those living through the war in Syria; he was interested in the idea of ordinary people rising up and challenging the regime, and fighting for their freedom. From Al-Kateab's point of view, she wanted the film to resonate with Syrian audiences and also connect with a much wider audience, so she valued Watts' input as an outsider, due to his knowledge of how audiences around the world might respond. Together they decided that the film would focus on ordinary Syrians and the impact of the attacks on their lives, rather than being an examination of the political factors. For example, towards the end of the second third of the film when we learn that the hospital has been bombed, with the loss of some of the Al-Kateab's friends and colleagues, she narrates the facts in terms of human cost when she speaks of constant bombardments and the lack of space to grieve.

Edward Watts

Al-Kateab felt strongly that everything should be recorded. There is a sense that she is compelled to keep filming, even in the darkest moments, a feeling shared by a woman in the film who has just lost her son. In her grief she is shouting at Waad (some critics have misinterpreted this moment to mean that the woman was objecting to the filming, but it is exactly the opposite), but it becomes clear that she too is angry; she wants her grief to be filmed for the world to see. Al-Kateab continues to film the woman's raw grief as she pleads for her son to wake up. Rather than seeing this as intrusive, because the woman has given permission, the viewer understands that Al-Kateab is not alone in wanting the world to bear witness to the suffering.

For Sama is an independent production produced by Channel 4 News, ITN Productions and Frontline, which is a US investigative documentary programme that focuses on socio-political issues. It is produced by the WGBH Educational Foundation and is distributed by the Public Broadcasting Service in the USA. The production companies involved clearly align the documentary with investigative journalism, which is in the public interest, and ensure that *For Sama* is readily available to view on television.

Waad Al-Kateab at the 72nd Cannes Film Festival

Al-Kateab first started working with Channel 4 at the end of 2015 as part of a team of five citizen journalists working together in Aleppo. Channel 4's involvement also played a part in Al-Kateab and her family's safety and survival; they expedited UK visas for them to escape from Syria when it finally became too dangerous to stay, due to the news that Hamza, her husband and one of the few doctors left in Aleppo, was being targeted personally by the regime.

The BBFC gave the film an 18 classification for disturbing scenes and images of real dead bodies. This classification is relatively rare in the mainstream film industry as it limits audiences and therefore revenue. But here, profit is much less significant than authenticity and Al-Kateab's need to show the atrocities as they really happened.

> **Independent activity**
>
> Look at the film's website, Action For Sama, and make notes about Al-Kateab's aims and messages to viewers of the film.

Social and political contexts

The political context surrounding the war in Syria is complex, but the documentary clarifies the situation for the viewer, who may be unaware of the details. As Al-Kateab says on the Action For Sama website, she wanted to capitalise on the 'incredible reaction' to the film and convert this into positive action to help people in Syria.

Al-Kateab filmed events over a period of five years, from 2011 until 2016, showing the uprising and indiscriminate mass bombardment that followed and focusing on the destruction of Aleppo. The final drone shot shows that the city has become uninhabitable during that time; the camera follows the lone figure of Waad as she walks along a street of rubble and destroyed buildings with baby Sama strapped to her front. This encapsulates the question at the heart of the film: was she brave or foolish to stay? In a very moving and intimate way, the narration explores the complex emotions surrounding this dilemma.

Producer Waad Al-Kateab, director Edward Watts and Hamza Al Kateab pose the 72nd Cannes Film Festival

The social context of the impact on women and children in particular is highlighted through editorial choices and the film's structure. The film features grieving children who have lost their relatives; the sequence showing two grieving young brothers is particularly distressing, but there is also grief for friends who have left and grief for their home. Part of the social context is how the conflict affects ordinary Syrians' rights to education and medical care; it is horrific to realise that the bombing is targeting schools and hospitals, and eventually Hamza himself, which makes the family's remaining in the city untenable.

Cultural context and digital technology debate

Al-Kateab started out as a **citizen journalist** when she was studying at the University of Aleppo from 2011. She began recording protests on her phone and sending her footage to Channel 4 for their TV series *Inside Aleppo*. Citizen journalism has emerged as a powerful force in recent years due to the rise of digital technology – in this case a smartphone, a digital camera, borrowed drones and the internet. Al-Kateab shot footage of the uprisings on her phone, allowing her to document events as they unfolded.

When asked by the Canadian documentary magazine *POV* (Mullen, 2019) about the importance of the link with Channel 4, Al-Kateab explained that their support gave her hope that she could reach a wide audience and that the regime would not be able to prevent Syrian voices from being heard.

Throughout the duration of the conflict Syrians feared that the mainstream media would ignore both the peaceful nature of the uprising, and the extent of the regime's brutality in crushing it and actively targeting ordinary Syrian people. Also, as highlighted by Al-Kateab, they worried that the media would misrepresent the role of the Free Syrian Army (FSA). The advantage that citizen journalists (and to some extent independent documentary filmmakers) have over mainstream media is that they can set their own news agenda, which was very important for Al-Kateab, as she had an inside understanding of the situation, capturing events as they happened. This means that in *For Sama* there is no need for reconstructions, a common feature of documentaries, which by recreating a version of reality can arguably manipulate the truth. This idea of manipulation is referenced by Watts in the same interview for *POV* magazine: he suggests that the documentary can counter the manipulation of events by the regime and present the true reality of the conflict.

However, there is an argument that digital technology can encourage the deceptive nature of documentary, making things seem 'more real' than they really are. Even though the footage captures events as they unfold, the editing process creates a narrative that reflects the filmmakers' agenda. Also, due to the existence of digital technologies, there is a wealth of available footage to select from in the final edit, which allows for extensive discarding of footage and therefore differing presentations of the events.

> **Citizen journalist:** an ordinary person who participates in the collection, reporting and dissemination of news, usually due to finding themselves on the scene before anyone else.

Stretch & challenge

Find videos online that discuss the concept of the citizen journalist. Make notes on the surrounding debates and how this links to the use of digital technologies in *For Sama*.

7 Stories We Tell (Polley, 2013) & For Sama (Al Kateab & Watts 2019)

Storytelling and construction of 'truth'

In some ways, *For Sama* is also a reflexive documentary. Al-Kateab is both the filmmaker and a character in the story; we see her filming as she shows herself in the mirror and we see the impact of events on her life with great intimacy – we witness the hospital scans of both of her babies. To distinguish between Al-Kateab's two roles, when discussing or writing about the film, it is useful to refer to the 'character' as Waad and the filmmaker as Al-Kateab. Neither are her real name, which in itself highlights the significant amount of danger she and Hamza are still in today.

At the end of the first third of the film, when the bombing is taking place just behind the family's house, in one emotional moment of sheer terror for her life, Waad breaks the fourth wall by occasionally looking straight into the lens, and talking to her static camera. Her desperate prayer connects the spectator to Waad, creating alignment through her words and proximity to the camera. The level of intimacy is all the more of a privilege when we realise that Al-Kateab as a filmmaker has chosen to include this moment in the film. By showing herself, it draws our attention to the constructed nature of the documentary. This is also highlighted by seeing her with her camera, for example the moment during her second scan where there is a cut-away shot to her filming. It is deliberately impossible for her to film her own scan, the choice to include this shot, therefore, reminds the audience that the film is a construction, and in a reflexive way draws attention to the artificiality of documentary itself as a genre. This is a moment that encourages a critical distance and is a reminder of the intertwined stories of creativity: a filmmaker making an important socio-political artefact, and a woman creating a child.

Film form

Cinematography

The cinematography is mostly chaotic, hand-held, creating a sense of immediacy, transporting the spectator straight into the midst of events as they happen with all of the ensuing confusion and terror that a sudden bombardment provokes. This is contrasted with frequent close-ups of Sama offering hope, and the continuation of normal life and the people of Aleppo and Syria itself. Then there are close-ups of children's suffering; for example, there is a close-up shot at the hospital of the side of a small boy's face, which is covered in blood. This acts as a reminder of the potential fate of Sama, her children and all the children of Syria. Even worse, there are close-up shots of the bound hands and feet of the dead body of a very young child. A boy with a dusty, blackened face talks about his dead family, another is shown crying in a close-up at the news of his brother's death. The filmmakers have included these distressing shots as part of their agenda to shock the viewer into action.

High-angle shots of various parts of the hospitals are used in a conventional way to emphasise the feeling of helplessness as Hamza and his team treat so many people;. They also show patients being treated on the floor in crowded corridors, highlighting the heroism of Hamza and his team. The voice-over tells us that in the second hospital there are 300 new patients each day. The extent of the devastation is also shown outside the hospital, using drone shots that capture the destruction of Aleppo's buildings in contrast to sunshine and blue skies.

The close-ups of everyday life punctuate the grief and violence, but rather than provide relief they often contribute to the sense of bleakness present in lives under siege. For example, we see Afraa Hashem (the Al-Kateab's best friend) looking at a bowl of contaminated rice, the only food left for her family; a close-up reveals weevils floating on the top, highlighting in a visceral way just how desperate the situation is. However, in the same sequence there are close-ups of Afraa's happy face as she receives the gift of the persimmon fruit. Perhaps the most joyful section of the film is the moment where we see the Al-Kateab family briefly together, with Sama as a toddler looming into shot as the camera sits on the floor. This type of shot connects the viewer to the family, increasing our emotional investment in them and conveying our common humanity.

Mise-en-scène

The hospital is a key location; it allows the filmmakers to portray the devastation and impact of the bombardments on families, and in particular on children. Seeing grief-stricken children and children's dead bodies is difficult viewing, but the mise-en-scène makes the deliberate choice to make the film as distressing as possible to counter the world's desensitisation to the events in Syria. The hospital, built up and run by Hamza and his colleagues, is destroyed part way through the film, but fortunately they discover an abandoned building that was originally designed as a hospital and are able to continue their work.

The city of Aleppo is also a vital component of mise-en-scène. The action takes place during the siege of Aleppo and the state of the city is established at regular intervals via drone shots, which show the increasing devastation, for example the collapsing buildings the sides of which have been blown off, and streets covered in rubble and dust. Scenes of dust are juxtaposed with scenes of snow, emphasising how the natural beauty of Aleppo has been superseded by the human-made devastation of war.

In terms of conflict, the protestors, with their green, white and black striped flags and Syrian Arab Republic banners, are important for communicating the idea that the people are rising up together against a corrupt and oppressive regime in peaceful protest. The shockingly violent reaction of the regime to the uprising is signalled by mise-en-scène: the guns, bombers in the sky, dead bodies, mass graves and copious amounts of blood. The voice-over tells us that the blood is on the clothes and bodies of those still living, but it cannot be cleaned because the water has been cut off; a poignant and visceral symbol of the horrific levels of senseless killing.

Editing

Rather than editing to create a linear narrative, Al-Kateab and Watts decided to edit the film in a non-linear way. Watts told *POV* magazine (Mullen, 2019) that the use of flashback enabled a more truthful representation of events and a variation in tone, allowing the filmmakers to mix humour and moments of love and warmth with violence, destruction and death.

Placing a baby at the centre of the narrative gives spectators hope for the future when they enter the story. For example, at the end of the second act there is a sequence where a newborn baby is seemingly dead, but against all the odds is revived. From a close-up of the baby's face as he cries, there is a cut to the mother on a trolley, and the voice-over tells us it's a miracle that they're both alive. As we cut back to the crying baby, we hear Al-Kateab say that babies and children give them the strength to carry on.

There is then a fade to black with the inter-title '8 months earlier'. We fade out to a shot of a fish tank and the camera pans round to the sleeping face of newborn baby Sama. It is both a mother's and filmmaker's editing choice. As a mother, Al Kateab is clearly reminded of her newborn Sama when she films the near tragedy in the hospital; as a filmmaker, she includes both babies to create hope – their existence is presented as a miracle amid the death and destruction of war.

The editing creates a stream-of-consciousness-style narrative, where Al-Kateab moves backwards and forwards in time, explaining things to Sama, which makes it clear to the viewer that this is not just a factual documentary. It is not just about *what* happened but *how it feels* to have such tragedy happen to you – that is the story that Al-Kateab feels compelled to tell. Through the focus on everyday life in a warzone Al-Kateab wants her viewer to understand the terrible tension that exists between the decision to flee for your own safety or staying to help others. When asked about the non-linear narrative structure, she told *POV* magazine (Mullen, 2019) that the use of flashback mirrors the natural thought process, helping to show how their thoughts kept returning to the central question of when to leave Aleppo.

Al-Kateab uses editing to emphasise her personal experience and understand the decisions she made, but it also enables the viewer to generalise from that and understand why there are refugees from Syria all over the world. Al-Kateab has said in interviews that another aim of *For Sama* is to increase compassion for Syrian refugees through increased understanding.

Sound

Diegetic sounds are vital for creating an authentic experience of the events taking place and are an important convention of observational documentaries. The sounds of gunfire, bombings, shouting, screaming and crying are all hard-hitting, and these moments of extreme violence often take the viewer by surprise, mimicking the way the people of Aleppo are constantly in danger of being killed, but meanwhile have to go about their everyday lives. At the opening of the film, after Sama has been located, diegetic sound is used to depict the camaraderie and relief of the hospital work; we hear Sama's excited laughing and babbling. Then then are instances where we see and hear Hamza experiencing sheer grief. Quite near the beginning, they are in a lift in the hospital after the death of a child. We see Al-Kateab filming in the mirror and the camera lingers on Hamza as he is crying; it is intensely moving to hear his raw grief. The diegetic sounds of the conflict are terrifying: the sound of sirens, the sudden loud explosion as the bombing starts, and the intensity of wailing and crying – these sounds are vital for conveying the reality of the experience.

After the voice-over where Al Kateab has introduced herself as a headstrong teenager, the word 'you' (Sama) is the moment where everything changes. As the still image becomes close-up footage of the baby, we hear Sama's gurgling mixed with the terrifying sounds of increasingly loud explosions and panicked voices of the adults around her. This juxtaposition of innocence and the horror of war creates tension and visceral reality; the sound is accompanied by smoke and the flash of the explosions.

The voice-over begins again, addressing Sama; this device allows Al-Kateab to both narrate events to the future, older Sama and the outside world, but also reveals her moments of doubt and confusion, which is vital for creating a relationship between filmmaker and spectator. Al-Kateab said in the interview for Seventh Row that they wanted the footage to speak for itself, with minimal need for a voice-over. This sparing use of voice-over makes the appearance of Waad's voice more poignant.

In one surprising and desperate moment, Waad confesses that she regrets coming to Aleppo and meeting Hamza. The impact of this revelation is stark and confusing; it is interesting to consider why Al-Kateab has chosen to include such a line, which shows her at one of her lowest points.

Subjective camerawork, POV shots and the voice-over together produce a personal and poetic tone, which creates an emotional connection between subject and spectator. This makes the constant scenes of death, injury, grief and destruction almost bearable. In line with observational documentaries, the use of non-diegetic music, in this case composed by Nainita Desai, is minimal and understated; the images and diegetic sounds are allowed to speak for themselves. When the score *is* played, then, it increases the sense of poignancy in particular moments. For example, in the section an inter-title identifies as 'January 2013', sad, low single notes accompany images of body bags following the massacre, then the dead bodies being taken out of the river, followed by shots of the mass grave. Here, the score underlines the tragedy and intense sadness, but also highlights the Syrian people's endurance – they are just getting on with dealing with the aftermath of the massacre.

Slow piano music is used to capture the ambivalent feelings of joy and fear at Sama's birth, accompanied by the sound of Waad crying. The voice-over addresses the new baby and speaks of hope, but this is immediately followed by the ominous and sad single notes as we are shown drone shots of Aleppo in ruins. The editing of both visuals and sound always takes the viewer back to the terrible reality of the conflict.

This is especially highlighted in the wedding section. The narration even draws the spectator's attention to this by comparing the sound of their singing with the sound of the bombs, suggesting that at some moments human warmth, compassion and love can drown out the death and destruction. However, the intimate moment where they dance to the diegetic song 'Crazy' by Julio Iglesias is quickly replaced by an establishing shot of the city and the familiar music of sadness and tragedy.

The sequence where the hospital is destroyed is a typical example of how the soundscape is used to capture both the physical and emotional reality of life under bombardment. It starts with Sama sleeping peacefully, but Waad's voice-over interjects, and she speaks of the transient nature of her happiness as she hears the Russian planes overhead. This is followed by drone shots of explosions and smoke over the city. The return to the hospital is accompanied by sinister electronic music, which represents the devastating impact of the Russian warplanes.

The central message of the film is communicated through sound, initially through the voice-over, particular those moments that include Sama directly. Waad feels that Sama understands the events around her; that she can see this in her eyes. This is followed by strings, which signal sadness and tragedy over the diegetic sound of children crying, with the direct and hard-hitting narration that directly asks for help. The suggestion is that if a baby can understand the situation, then surely the rest of the world can.

Performance

With the exception of the deliberate filming of herself, mostly in the mirror, the people in the film are in such terrible and desperate situations that they seem unaware of or unconcerned by the presence of the camera, allowing Al-Kateab to capture the events and raw reactions untampered by self-conscious performances.

Through the mirror shots, Al-Kateab reminds the viewer that this is a personal constructed account. Although she is living through an experience unimaginable for most viewers, she is relatable as a vulnerable human being and mother (she is

pregnant twice and caring for a baby for the entirety of the chosen footage). But she is also a committed journalist and activist who is compelled to keep filming, motivated by the desire to counter the regime's propaganda with her footage.

Hamza also shares her desire to capture the truth of the situation in Aleppo and Al-Kateab positions him as the hero of the narrative. At times he is aware of the camera, but he is mostly shown battling through terrible circumstances to treat patients, such as the water being cut off. In one sequence there is a high-angle shot of a hospital corridor crowded with injured people; the narration tells us that the hospital sees almost 300 patients a day. Hamza is shown treating a person, professionally and calmly who is asking for serums, and the narration details the importance of Hamza's work at the hospital.

The other exception is Afraa Hashem and her family. They are also activists and educators, and so are consciously aware of the purpose of the documentary. They speak directly to camera and contribute to the overall message of the documentary. But they also lift the tone; Afraa's constant joking and smiling is inspirational. In her testimony, which appears on the Action For Sama site, she explains that the film is a permanent record of the suffering of the people of Aleppo. This is exemplified in the sequence with the contaminated rice, showing the viewer they have no choice but to eat it; this bleak moment is followed by one of joy, the gift of the persimmon.

Sama herself, with her wide-eyed innocence, stands in for the perhaps rather naïve viewer, who has no understanding of the situation in Syria, so that the narration, while addressed to Sama, feels like it is being addressed to us.

Aesthetics

The film's aesthetic is closely tied to the modes of observational documentary: noticeable hand-held camera movements, long takes, mostly diegetic sound and chaotic action in real time. There is also a poetic and personal aesthetic, which becomes confessional at times through the use of the personal voice-over and fourth wall breaks.

Symbolic shots of beautiful flowers in Al-Kateab's garden, shown later to be destroyed by dust from the nearby bombing, signify that the garden is a microcosm of the entire country. In one particularly moving sequence, Hamza is shown watering a dust-covered dead plant, a powerful symbol for his work tending to the injured and dying.

At the start of the final third of the film, a red filter is used for a POV shot. As Waad looks up at Sama's baby mobile, Waad's voice-over explains the trauma of the violence, symbolised by visions of blood that stay with her. From here there is a cut to the hospital floor covered with blood; it is being mopped but is so copious and there is no water so it is just being smeared on the floor, a poignant reminder of the ongoing presence of injury and death and a symbol of both the determination to keep going and the futility of their endeavours. An intimate moment of trauma communicated through a visual metaphor juxtaposes with a scene of stark reality, which expertly combines the personal and the political, allowing a real connection to be made between Waad and the spectator through these vicarious and visceral experiences.

Representations

Age

In addition to Waad, Hamza and Sama as central figures in the documentary, the film features Afraa Hashem and her family. As a teacher, we see her struggle to continue educating children, as well as her struggle to feed her family. Al-Kateab takes care to name each member of the family and show them undertaking everyday activities in their apartment. Although there is the subtle detail that they are wearing coats inside, reminding us of their hardship – being both cold due to the heating being cut off and ready to flee at any time – Afraa brings warmth and hope to the film. Al-Kateab's voice-over celebrates their bravery and positions them as friends and allies.

Children are given space in the film to talk and give their views. We see a close-up of Afraa's son being interviewed on the balcony of their home about the decision to stay or leave; as he starts to cry, we hear exploding bombs in the distance, a distressing juxtaposition between a child's sadness over his friends moving away and the very real threat to their lives. It is interesting to note that children are given equal status to adults in the film and that everyone is treated with kindness and respect. The other side of this is that these children have lost their childhood; there is no covering up of the unpleasant reality for them.

The film also celebrates the children's resilience. In one scene we see them playing in a burnt-out bus at a party organised by Afraa's husband, Salem. They are painting the bus in bright colours amid the rubble, and we see Sama held by Al-Kateab, a paint brush in hand. It is simultaneously a moment of joy, an act of defiance and an incredibly moving scene amid such obvious devastation.

Afraa with her children

Gender

The central question at the heart of the film concerns the dilemma of a mother who is also a filmmaker: whether to stay and help others, make a stand against injustice, or flee to save herself and her family. The ensuing guilt of either choice is portrayed again and again, as Al-Kateab's, through voice-over, explains to Sama when she asks her child to forgive her.

The voice-over portrays the personal, female experience; it often includes Waad's thoughts which she cannot voice. For example, in a scene where we see that a very young boy has died and his older brother says that the parents have also died, the camera pans from the dead child to Sama, and Al-Kateab's voice comes in candidly to tell Sama and the viewer that sometimes the best that can be hoped for is the death of the parent before the child. The following panning shot shows the damaged building and black smoke, and we hear the call to prayer. Al-Kateab's narration continues to highlight the need to see people outside of the hospital who are still alive.

7 Stories We Tell (Polley, 2013) & For Sama (Al Kateab & Watts 2019)

Through this personal style of narration and direct footage of the events, the viewer gains both a factual and emotional experience of what it is to live in a warzone, and a human connection and empathy with Al-Kateab as a filmmaker and Waad as a mother.

The oppression of women by the patriarchal Assad regime is suggested by the changing clothing of the women we see as the regime enforces the Islamic dress code. This is highlighted in the scene where Al-Kateab is filming herself in the mirror, covering her ordinary way of dressing and hairstyle with a chador. The inclusion of this sequence and the construction of Waad's new identity in the mirror suggests that this is enforced compliance rather than a choice.

Ethnicity

The film is concerned with the representation and misrepresentations of the Syrian people. It aims to clarify that, as was the case during the Arab Spring protests, the uprising against the corrupt and brutal Assad regime was non-violent, but the response of the regime was horrifically violent; the Russian-backed regime targeted civilians and indiscriminately bombed the country.

In interviews, Hamza has been keen to stress that the Western media has often focused on more sensationalist stories of beheadings and terrorism, and has failed to report on the rebellion of the people. This documentary aims to bring the peaceful protest of Syrian people to global attention, to celebrate their resilience and bravery. Al-Kateab described her message for audiences in the interview with *POV* magazine, in which she highlights the need to show global audiences the truth of what is happening in Syria, countering the regime's propaganda.

Filmmaker's theories and *For Sama*

Debates about the possibility of the truthful nature of observational documentaries are complex. Typical of observational documentaries, there are noticeably long takes in *For Sama*, which add to the authenticity of the footage. It is untampered, showing the real-life unfolding of events, which gives the sense of objective truth. However, as the person with the camera, Al-Kateab chooses what to shoot, which dilutes this view of objective reality. So, while viewers are vicariously experiencing being in Aleppo during the rebellion and conflict, we are seeing one person's choices of what exactly is shown. For example, hand-held, chaotic long takes, shots of the floor, and shots of the hospital's walls as Al-Kateab runs from the explosions near the hospital are all included to create a sense of authenticity and immediacy, which often leaves the viewer with graphic images illustrating the awful reality of life in a warzone.

It may be useful to study Al-Kateab's approach to documentary making alongside that of Kim Longinotto. Longinotto also makes observational documentaries that often highlight the female experience. Through *For Sama*, Al-Kateab gives a female perspective on the stereotypically masculine domain of war. In an interview published in *Huck* magazine (Goh, 2019), she commented on how war has always been seen as a masculine concern, and she identifies her responsibility as a female journalist to report women's experience of the events. So in the way that *Sisters in Law* (2005) gives a voice to women whose experiences may never have been understood outside of Cameroon, Al-Kateab gives the women of Aleppo a voice by documenting their experiences and putting herself and Afraa Hashem at the centre of the narrative.

Stretch & challenge

Do you find the filming of the more distressing scenes in *For Sama* too intrusive? Justify their inclusion and decide whether or not you think they are respectful.

Longinotto is known for her respectful approach to her subjects, keeping the crew to a minimum and using observational techniques such as long takes to give her female subjects space to tell their stories. While Al-Kateab puts her own story at the centre of *For Sama*, and her film has more of a confessional intimacy, there is still a strong sense of respect and admiration for the people of Aleppo. It is interesting to consider whether some of the long takes are intrusive, showing too much of people's suffering, or if Al-Kateab and Watts are as respectful as Longinotto when it comes to their subjects.

Independent study questions

Q Which sections illustrate the idea of observational documentary and which are more poetic and reflexive?

Q What is the effect on the viewer of addressing the film to Sama?

Q How do the filmmakers create a sense of authenticity through the use of digital technology?

Q How does Al-Kateab and Watts' approach compare with Kim Longinotto's? Compare the two with one other filmmaker's theory you have studied.

Conclusion

Documentaries are inherently about truth and none more so than *Stories We Tell*. The film starts by lulling the spectator into a false sense of security through its apparent transparency with regards to its construction, but by the end the audience are left asking what is real and who can be trusted. The film doesn't answer those questions. Instead, it highlights themes of time and memory and the blurring of boundaries between what is real and what is reconstructed, with actors representing in visual terms the debate about the difference between subjective and objective truth. Ultimately, the idea of how people remember events, and, more importantly how they feel about the emotional truth, is the concern of this documentary.

For Sama is a fascinating example of how a documentary can simultaneously present both a personal account of events and a piece of high-quality journalism, documenting events as they unfold. The focus on the suffering of children makes the film difficult viewing; this raises some interesting questions about voyeurism and documentary, although the framing device of addressing the film to Sama goes some way to explain how the impact of war on the lives of children is more relevant to Al-Kateab. Ultimately, the focus on children makes the film much more effective in serving its political purpose of providing an account of the events in Syria that denounces the regime's propaganda, drawing the viewer's attention to the importance of documentary as an art form.

Section 2

A level: Global filmmaking perspectives

(Not studied at AS)

Film movements – silent cinema (1)

This chapter will support your work on Film movements: silent cinema in Component 2 of the A level course. Alongside the core areas, you should be prepared to tackle questions on the specialist area, Critical debate 1: The realist and the expressive. The textbook offers two case studies, *Sunrise* (Murnau, 1927) (in this chapter) and a collection of shorts by Buster Keaton (in Chapter 9). You only need to study one option.

For A level

You will answer one 20-mark question from a choice of two on the **Component 2** paper. You should allow 30 minutes for your answer.

The specification says

The silent period saw filmmakers working to develop film narrative and film form and to communicate ever more effectively through purely visual means. Film during this period is associated with the wider cultural and artistic movement of modernism. Film history identifies two key film movements: German Expressionism and Soviet Montage.

Sunrise is made by the most celebrated of German Expressionist directors, F.W. Murnau, but in Hollywood not Berlin.

Learners will be required to explore critical debates about realism and the expressive within this section.

8 *Sunrise* (Murnau, 1927)

Made in Hollywood for William Fox Studio, *Sunrise: A Song of Two Humans* was directed by celebrated German director F.W. Murnau, who had established his reputation working in the German Expressionism film movement.

Murnau is regarded as one of the most gifted and inventive film directors who has worked in silent cinema. He directed 21 films, but many have now been lost. His three significant German films are *Nosferatu* (1922), *The Last Laugh* (1924) and *Faust* (1926). *Sunrise* (1927), the first film he made in Hollywood, is considered one of the greatest silent films. He died in 1931, a week before the premiere of his documentary *Tabu: A Story of the South Seas* (1931).

Filmmakers working in the German Expressionism film movement sought to present the inner life of their characters. They achieved this through their creative use of film form. They are seen in opposition to the dominant American films that aimed to represent a real world in a conventional manner. *Sunrise* combines elements of both, and therefore offers an interesting combination of American narrative cinema and German Expressionist styling.

This section will explore the German Expressionism film movement, which emerged in Germany after the Second World War, and, through an examination of its film form, how *Sunrise* can be seen as part of this movement. The section will be concluded by addressing the key critical debate in film history, realist versus expressive filmmaking.

Further viewing – key German Expressionist films

The Cabinet of Dr Caligari (1920) Director Robert Wiene

The Golem (1920) Directors Paul Wegener and Carl Boese

Destiny (1921) Director Fritz Lang

Nosferatu (1922) Director F.W. Murnau

The Last Laugh (1924) Director F.W. Murnau

Faust (1926) Director F.W. Murnau

Metropolis (1927) Director Fritz Lang

Pandora's Box (1929) Director G.W. Pabst

German Expressionism films

The German Expressionism film movement features a number of highly regarded German films released between 1919 and 1929. For a film movement that flourished and declined within a decade, its impact is large in cinema history. While it never replaced the realist aesthetic that dominates cinema, modern cinema would not be the same without these groundbreaking films.

Both Orson Welles and Alfred Hitchcock drew on many of the visual motifs to develop the psychology of their characters.

Although made within the burgeoning Hollywood studio system, *Sunrise* displays many of the hallmarks of German Expressionism: a pervading sense of dread, off-kilter camera angles, and high- and low-key lighting. It also employs those from another popular German film genre of the 1920s: the Kammerspielfilm (or chamber drama). This type of film explored a crisis in a character's life in detail; the emphasis being on slow, evocative acting and telling details, rather than extremes. They had less international impact except for *The Last Laugh* (Murnau, 1924), which, as does *Sunrise*, integrates both expressionist and Kammerspielfilm aesthetics.

Further information

F.W. Murnau (1888–1931)

Friedrich Wilhelm Murnau, formerly Plumpe, was born in Germany in December 1888. As a young boy he staged short plays for his friends and family, and was an admirer of Ibsen and Shakespeare. He studied philology at the University of Berlin, and then art history and literature in Heidelberg. It was there that he was spotted by theatrical impresario Max Reinhardt who invited him to join his actor-school. During the First World War he served as a company commander at the eastern front and then with the Imperial German Flying Corps undertook a mission in Northern France. A crash landing in Switzerland led to his arrest and internment, where he became involved in the prison's theatre troupe and wrote a film script. After the war he teamed up with actor Conrad Veidt and established his own studio. Their first film, *The Boy in Blue*, was released in 1919 and like most German Expressionist films explores notions of duality. It was his adaptation of Bram Stoker's *Dracula*, *Nosferatu*, in 1922 that firmly established him as a leading filmmaker of the period. The international success of *The Last Laugh* (1924) led to an invitation to Hollywood, where he made *Sunrise*. The arrival of sound in 1927 saw a period of upheaval, which Murnau was still negotiating when he died in a car crash in 1931 just before the release of his documentary film *Tabu: A Story of the South Seas*.

Narrative themes and characters

The themes of expressionist cinema were often dark, drawing on the devastation that followed the Second World War.

The films were not confined to contemporary settings; they could be placed in historic or futuristic settings, thereby 'disguising' critiques on recent history and the contemporary social and political environment.

Recurring themes:

★ narrative oppositions/doubling/duality
★ the known and the unknown
★ temptation
★ fear of death, consequences of dying
★ alter-ego, other person within us, doppelgänger
★ sale of oneself for material advantage
★ the creation/existence of fantastical beings living within 'normal' existence
★ notion of being able to control other people

- ★ extreme situations/excessive responses
- ★ the emotional undercurrent of human existence
- ★ fascination with and fear of modern urban life and technology.

Characters were often:

- ★ obsessive
- ★ tortured
- ★ melancholic
- ★ anti-heroic
- ★ mad
- ★ paranoid
- ★ overwrought.

As is implied by the film's subtitle, *A Song of Two Humans*, *Sunrise* is a **dialectical** film, with doubling and oppositions central to its narrative and character arcs.

> **Dialectic:** two opposing or contradictory ideas or views are juxtaposed as a way of examining and discussing them.

- ★ **Narrative structure:** the film is set over one day and two nights, making significant use of day/night signalled by the iconography of the sun/moon. Key sequences such as the boat journey across the lake and the tram ride are shown as they travel to and from the city. This repetition allows for clear comparisons on how the characters' relationship changes.
- ★ **Characters:** this duality is further developed in the three central characters, where the characters are used to stand for good/bad. We see the man, from the first sunset to the second sunrise, move from bad (affair and murder attempt) to good (in love, reunited with his wife), from the path of sin (the subjective POV shot through the marshes to his mistress), to redemption (a new dawn rises). The good/bad woman is seen by the counterpoint between the angel/temptress, wife/mistress. This is discussed further in the Gender representation section later in this chapter (page 254).

These narrative and character dialectics are further developed in the film form:

- ★ **Sunrise/sunset:** the film is set over two days so we see two sunrises; note how different the couple are in the first (not speaking, no eye contact, the man planning the wife's murder) and the second (the mistress on her way back the city, the couple united and kissing).
- ★ **Day/night and sun/moon:** in the first moonlit night, the man lies with his mistress imagining life in the city, and plotting his wife's murder. In the second, he has been to the city with his wife, and they are now the couple embracing, with plans for the future.
- ★ **Country/city and rural/urban:** here the fascination with and fear of modern urban life and technology is explored as the two simple country folk find themselves in the vibrant city. The country is where the city dwellers rush to for their summer vacation in the film's opening sequence. The version of the country depicted in the narrative present is one of darkness and betrayal. The rural idyll is shown in the maid's memory of when the couple were happy. This image is further referenced in the painted backdrop at the photography studio and in the fantasy dissolve from the cityscape when they fall in love again.
- ★ **Blonde wife/dark-haired mistress:** the hair colouring signifies innocence and sultriness. The wife is costumed in matte whites, and the mistress in shining blacks.

> **Independent activity**
>
> Watch the two tram rides in the film and make notes on of the mise-en-scène, particularly the body codes of the man and the wife.

Further information

Key moments in US/European cinema (1895–1927)

1895: December, in Paris the Lumière Brothers held the first public exhibition of 'moving pictures'.

1900s: Significant filmmaking activity in the USA, UK, Germany, France and Denmark. As the films were silent there was no language barrier.

1914–1918: In 1914, 25% of films shown in the UK are British, by 1926 only 5%. Germany establishes a national filmmaking centre, and produces centrally endorsed films. The USA becomes the dominant filmmaking community, a situation that remains a hundred years later.

1915: William Fox founds Fox Films and opens his studio in Hollywood. Post-First World War Europe relies heavily on imported films.

1920s: German government-endorsed films continue, while independent production companies make films critical of the government. US cinema continues to grow, increasingly relying on film stars and 'star' directors.

Mid-1920s: German Expressionism becomes a significant film movement attracting considerable attention from audiences and filmmakers in Europe and the USA. Soviet filmmakers working in isolation develop their political and ideological cinema, utilising montage editing and typage (casting non-professional actors in lead roles).

1926: Experimentation of films with synchronised sound. Leading this sound revolution is Warner Brothers. *The Black Pirate*, starring Douglas Fairbanks, is the first feature film shot in two-colour Technicolor. Fox Studios hire Murnau to make a 'masterpiece'.

1927: Warner Brothers release *The Jazz Singer*, the first feature film with synchronised sound, music and dialogue. *Sunrise* opens in the USA in November, with synchronised music and sound.

Contexts in German Expressionism

Institutional context

The German film industry

The First World War decimated the film industry across Europe, except in Germany. In 1911, there were 11 film companies in Germany, by 1918 there were 131. The German government, seeing the propaganda potential of cinema, encouraged film activity that supported its ideology.

In January 1917 the German government, led by General Ludendorff (Commander in Chief, 1916–1918), formed BUfA (Bild und Filmamt), with the intention of bringing together all Germany's film activity. The film industry benefitted from state funding of studios, equipment and distribution at a time of great financial hardship.

In 1919, the German government BUfA was renamed UfA (Universum Film Aktiengesellschafat [German Film Studios]), and sought to further unify the film industry, gradually taking over many small companies. The Treasury plus industrial and private capital provided a third of its funding. The role of UfA was to make profitable full-length commercial and art house films. It soon embarked on international co-productions, which gave it considerable power in the worldwide film market.

A few independent film studios survived, including Decla-Bioscop, which made what is considered to be the first German Expressionist film, *The Cabinet of Dr Caligari* (Wiene, 1920), which hides its anti-government message within a crime melodrama. The studio did not have the funding to match UfA's big-budget costume dramas, so went the other way and made its world representational through its expressionist mise-en-scène. Soon other filmmakers borrowed its aesthetic, including many of UfA's most successful films.

A year later, in 1921, UfA took over Decla-Bioscop, acquiring the Berlin-Babelsberg studios (they soon became the best-equipped studios in Europe). That year 246 films were made in Germany, more than any other European country.

For the German film industry, 1924–1929 were relatively stable years, as the German currency was under control (after a great depression), wages for skilled workers had roughly doubled, as had its industrial production. In 1929, industrial film exports were 34% higher than in 1913.

The Cabinet of Dr Caligari (Wiene, 1920)

The Wall Street Crash of 1929 in the US brought about a world economic crisis. The withdrawal of American loans to Germany led to massive unemployment and poverty, which contributed to the rapid rise of fascism.

Transition from silent to sound

Sunrise was made and released on the cusp between silent and sound films.

William Fox wanted a prestige film, and looked to Germany and Murnau to make him a 'masterpiece'. Fox had been impressed by *The Last Laugh* (Murnau, 1924), which had been an international critical and commercial success.

Murnau arrived in Hollywood in July 1926. The following month Warner Brothers released *Don Juan* (Crosland), a romantic adventure starring John Barrymore. This was the first full-length film to be released with synchronised music and sound effects. In October 1926, Al Jolson had starred in a short film, *A Plantation Act* (Roscoe), in which he could be heard singing three of his theatrical hits. Buoyed by this success, Warner Brothers conceived a full-length film integrating songs, music and sound effects – *The Jazz Singer*.

A year later, in October 1927, *The Jazz Singer* (Fleischer & Furie), again starring Al Jolson, opened. Despite its uneasy blend of silent film (outdoor locations, fluid camera movement and inter-titles) and sound sequences (static studio shots), when Jolson ad-libbed the immortal line, 'You aint heard nothing yet', he changed movie history, as for the first time, audiences heard synchronised speech, song, music and sound effects in a full-length film.

The film became a major hit, even though many cinemas had to screen it as a silent film, as they did not have the sound equipment. It grossed $3.9 million at the US box office, and became one of the top three high-grossing films of the year.

Sunrise opened in the wake of *The Jazz Singer* phenomenon, in November 1927. It had synchronised music and sound effects, but most cinemas were still running films as silent, with live music. Reviews were generally favourable, but it failed at the box office and, given its high production costs, Fox lost money. It is now widely considered one of the greatest silent film achievements.

In 1929 it won the first Academy Awards for Best Cinematography and Actress, and with *The Jazz Singer* ineligible (the Academy thought its inclusion would be unfair for the silent films), it was named Best Unique and Artistic Picture, beating competition from *Chang: A Drama of the Wilderness* (Cooper & Schoedsack, 1927) and *The Crowd* (Vidor, 1927).

Soon audiences were demanding more 'talkies' and, although silent filmmaking continued for a few more years, the popularity of silent films declined. Many were hastily re-cut and released as B movies, or new dialogue scenes/music/sound effects were crudely added.

Cultural context: expressionist artistic movement

Expressionism as an artistic movement extended across all the arts: music, painting, sculpture, theatre, dance, literature and film. It emerged in Germany in the early 1900s, attracting a number of creative and innovative composers (Arnold Schoenberg, Alban Berg, Anton Webern) and artists (Wassily Kandinsky, Paul Klee, Edvard Munch).

They were concerned with a visual representation of the inner soul and psychology. Using colour and shapes, artists created bizarre and outlandish images that were intended to be shocking. Expressionist music rejected the 'traditional forms of beauty' and was discordant, with extremes of volume and texture.

Given the primitive nature of film at this time, the creative output for 'live action' expressionism came from the theatrical world, most notably Max Reinhardt. Many of the film directors who are associated with expressionism obtained their grounding in the theatre (Fritz Lang) or art (F.W. Murnau).

Stretch & challenge

Make notes for a film review of one of the silent films you have studied. Use the following list as a starting point, commenting fully on the different areas. Always ask yourself, 'How well does the film work?':

- Plot
- Themes
- Script
- Direction
- Cinematography
- Editing
- Sound
- Setting, costumes & make-up
- Performance

Comment on the following values for the film:

A Entertainment value
B Learning value
C Artistic value

How well did the film work overall for you?

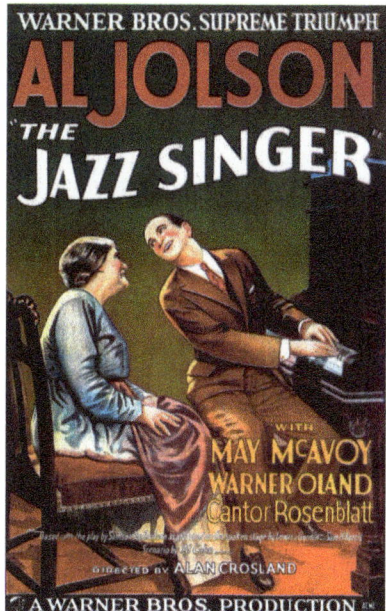

Stretch & challenge

Watch episode 1 of the documentary *Cinema Europe: The Other Hollywood, Where it All Began* (Brownlow, 1995) on YouTube. This will give you insights into the wider context of silent filmmaking across Europe.

8 Sunrise (Murnau, 1927)

Independent activity

Watch *The Cabinet of Dr Caligari* and make notes on its film form, i.e. cinematography, mise-en-scène, editing and performance. Then watch *Sunrise* and make notes on its film form. How do they compare?

A precursor to the German Expressionist film movement is *The Student from Prague* (Wegener, 1913); its story of a man selling his soul to the devil is one that expressionist film directors would return to, including Murnau's last German film, *Faust* (1926).

The first film that drew together the political, philosophical and visual elements of expressionism was *The Cabinet of Dr Caligari* (Wiene, 1920). With its two central characters, Dr Caligari and Cesare, representing the government and the 'common man', the film drew clear parallels between irrational authority (authority intent on compliance through fear and pressure) and blind obedience. It was well received critically, and soon other filmmakers were integrating its aesthetic and approach to storytelling.

Social and political context: the First World War and its aftermath

The First World War ended in November 1918: a war that left 8.5 million dead and 21 million wounded. It had devastated Europe; leaving nations determined that this could 'never happen again'. The German people had to come to terms with emotions of guilt, despair and revolution, while living in extreme poverty. It is estimated that 700,000 Germans died of starvation between November 1918 and June 1919.

The films that emerged at this time drew on Germany's recent past, its present situation, and have been read as a warning of what was to come.

There are no explicit war films, with the German Expressionist filmmakers using subtler ways to confront the devastating experience of the First World War and its aftermath. Exploring issues such as mass murders (*The Cabinet of Dr Caligari*, Wiene, 1920), sacrifice (*Nosferatu*, Murnau, 1922) and modernity (*Metropolis*, Lang, 1927).

Film form in German Expressionism and *Sunrise*

Further information

Inter-titles

There are far fewer inter-titles in *Sunrise* than in other American films of the period. German Expressionist filmmakers were keen to rely on the visuals, rather than words, and in *The Last Laugh* (1924), Murnau had no inter-titles.

The world presented in these films is one of darkness, disillusionment, paranoia and betrayal. They used film form to show visually the state of mind of the characters who were unable to express their thoughts into words – except in the inter-titles.

The turmoil of the characters can be seen in the lighting design, off-kilter camera angles, exaggerated performances, slanted sets and forced perspectives that combine to give the films a distorted view of the work that corresponded with the emotional complexities of the characters.

Cinematography

Murnau's command of lighting and composition, together with fluid camera style and editing, is evident in *Sunrise*, turning it from mere melodrama to cinematic poetry. Murnau worked with the cinematographers, Charles Rosher and Karl Struss, to achieve the film's startling visual style. Rosher and Struss were rewarded with the Best Cinematography award at the first Academy Awards held in 1929.

Image search

Inter-titles, performance and mise-en-scène in Sunrise 00:11:00–00:016:00

Watch the scene in *Sunrise* where 'the man' meets 'the woman from the city' (his mistress). Murnau experimented with special effects on a significant title card 'Couldn't she get drowned?', with the text sliding down the screen and disappearing. How does performance and mise-en-scène also make meaning in this scene?

German Expressionist filmmakers were concerned with making visual the characters' emotions and used the subjective point of view to good effect. An example of this can be seen when the man is walking to see his mistress in the marshes, approximately ten minutes into the film. This use of subjective camera is made even more striking by the way the camera moves. In Germany, Murnau had developed innovative overhead camera tracking movements, which created fluid and sophisticated moves through space, which he used in *Sunrise* to great effect in the moonlit marsh, funfair and city traffic sequences. This technique creates an unusual illusion of depth and vastness, and an apparent weightlessness. This was possible as Rosher and Struss were using an electric camera rather than hand-cranking.

Section 2 Film movements – silent cinema (1)

The way the camera frames the shot, how far we are from the action and how the camera moves all contribute to the emotion of the scene. Key uses are:

★ extreme/oblique camera angles, to create and add an off-kilter view of the world
★ titled angles to disorientate
★ camera angles to distort the size of the character
★ high camera angles to create the feeling of being looked down on
★ shifts of viewpoint
★ violent camera movement.

Stretch & challenge

Watch any two silent films. Write a 500-word essay on how the filmmaker has used either continuity/discontinuity editing or lighting to develop themes.

Independent activity

Read Pamela Hutchinson and Alex Barrett's '10 Great German Expressionist Films' (2017) on the BFI website. Annotate the ten images, noting what you can learn about the films and characters from the lighting and mise-en-scène.

Stretch & challenge

Watch the sequence of the man walking to meet his mistress again. Write a shot list comprising types of shot, camera movement and angles.

8 Sunrise (Murnau, 1927)

A striking use of camera and shot types in *Sunrise* can be seen on the couple's first boat journey to the city when the man tries to murder his wife. High-angle shots looking down on the wife make her seem smaller and more vulnerable as her husband towers over her. The use of subjective close-ups of the husband, from the wife's POV, are an exaggeration – too close for a real POV shot – and make visual the emotions of the character, in this case – fear.

The dramatic use of lighting is an important part of the expressionist film aesthetic. Key lighting uses are:

★ high contrasting blocks of light and shade (chiaroscuro)
★ low-key lighting to produce dark or semi-darkness. What is hiding in the shadow?
★ harsh lighting to produce unusual shadow effects, making faces distorted or partly hidden in shadow
★ back lighting to create long shadows in the foreground
★ on-screen practical light sources to draw attention to a particular character or object.

Expressionist filmmakers also employed a number of special effects to develop the mood and aesthetic. These effects were created in-camera and on set, many of which can also be seen in the films of Georges Méliès and Buster Keaton. Today, many of these would be achieved by CGI and/or digital editing.

★ **Split-screen masking/superimposing/double exposure:** achieved by partially masking the frame and rewinding the film and shooting the unexposed part again.
★ **Matte painting:** a hand-painted (usually) photorealistic image, combined with live-action footage.
★ **Forced perspective:** to create an impression of depth, a combination of **matte paintings**, **models** and **miniatures** and smaller people are placed in the background, in contrast to those of normal scale in the foreground.
★ **Slanted sets and props:** slanting ceilings, walls and floors means that through the camera they appear to be larger and deeper.
★ **Rear projection:** as the foreground action is being shot, a previously photographed background scene is projected onto a large translucent screen from behind, or front projection.

> **Further information**
>
> At the time *Sunrise* was made, the maximum length of a celluloid reel was 200 feet. They were shooting at 16 feet per second (fps), which meant that the longest take would have been three minutes.

A good example of a combination of in-camera, on-set and editing special effects is the scene following the couple's metaphorical wedding, approximately 43 minutes into the film. The vast cityscape was created using forced perspective, matte painting and models. So bound up in their new-found love, they step out into traffic as if in their own world, oblivious to the traffic (superimposed in the foreground, rear projection in the background). As they walk, the background magically changes to a country setting (a dissolve to a rear-projected image) a visual manifestation of their perfect happiness, reminiscent of the maid's memory from earlier. They are brought out of this fantasy world by the honking of horns and are now back in the city traffic.

Mise-en-scène

Fritz Lang, director of *Metropolis* (1927) and *Spione* (1928), was, like Murnau, a director renowned for his German Expressionist aesthetic.

As both directors developed their style in a period where there were no 'pages of dialogue', they developed a sophisticated use of mise-en-scène to bring to the fore the emotions of the characters.

The setting is used as an emotional landscape linked to the feelings of the characters. Therefore, filmmakers used setting/props to develop these through:

★ abstract sets with heavily stylised décor
★ angular/jagged sets to create a sense of unease and tension
★ distorted shapes created by objects, shadow or mass to signify a nightmarish world or an anxiety

- ★ unnaturally distorted images
- ★ extremes of composition (cluttered/bare)
- ★ characters merging with their setting or functioning as an extension of the set
- ★ distinctive/exaggerated hair and make-up
- ★ frequent use of mirrors, glass and reflective surfaces.

Murnau had an entire village set built by the side of Lake Arrowhead in the San Bernardino Mountains for the country sequences and huge highly stylised sets constructed on the Fox lot for the city and fairground sequences. The city street set alone is thought to have cost $200,000 (equal to almost $3 million today) to build. For the tram ride almost a mile of track was laid by the lake with further track on the studio city set.

Even if drawing on realist traditions in their design, as with the houses in the village, the expressionist techniques of manipulating scale, using over-/under-sized props and tilting the sets or furniture are used to create an uneasy, distorted feel.

The city sets recede slightly in the distance, producing deep focus shots. This, combined with manipulation of perspective (forced perspective), creates an overwhelming vastness to the cityscapes. As a result the couple seem small, vulnerable and out of place. Technology and the city are presented as threatening and amoral.

The film's dialectical narrative structure can be seen in the composition, where the repeating of key events shows how their relationships have shifted.

In the first half of the film, body proximity and lack of contact between man and wife are distant, either separated by space within the single frame, or framed in single shots. For the second half they are usually seen together in the centre of the frame, holding one another.

> **Image search**
> **Editing in *Sunrise***
> 00:44:00–00:47:00
> Watch this walking sequence and the following montage scene, and make a note of the transitions between shots and the pace of editing in the two. How is the editing used to portray their emotions?

> **Stretch & challenge**
> Watch at least two other German Expressionist films (not studied in class). Make notes on what elements of film form they share with *Sunrise*.

> **Independent activity**
> Construct a shot-by-shot analysis of one scene. Discuss in detail how the shots contribute to the continuity, pace and mood of the overall form of the film.

Editing

Although German Expressionist films are, in the main, presented in a linear form, filmmakers often employ more experimental editing techniques designed to obscure rather than express continuity.

8 Sunrise (Murnau, 1927)

Sunrise opens with a dissolve through the credits to a real train, and then to a model train. This is followed by a montage sequence of images of the bustling city in the summer time, and trains bringing the city folk to the peace of the coast and country. This frenetic opening sequence represents the city, and is followed by much more graceful shots of the city folk arriving at the lake. This opening highlights the different spaces through the camera movements, angles and editing. It also indicates to the audience that this is not going to be a classical Hollywood movie.

Using discontinuity of narrative to disrupt or confuse the narrative flow, such as quick cut-ins, flashbacks, flash-forwards, dreams and fantasies, offers insight into the characters' emotional and psychological states, or their histories. In *Sunrise*, discontinuity of narrative can be seen in fantasies (the man drowning his wife), cut-ins (shot of the bulrushes to show how they are playing on his mind) and flashbacks (the man selling a cow).

Although an in-camera technique at this time, double-exposure superimposing shots over one another also serves as an indirect form of narration, see image opposite.

Sound

Sunrise was released in 1927 with a synchronised music and sound effect track. For Murnau this was a new feature, and he uses it to great effect in key moments such as the lyrical rural idyll music juxtaposed with that of the bustling jazz of the city when the man and his mistress imagine life there.

In one of the film's most expressionistic sequences, sound in conjunction with cinematography and mise-en-scène plays a part in generating the chaotic atmosphere. When the couple first arrive at Luna Park, night has fallen and the park is illuminated by electric lights, very different from the candles and lanterns of their village. Crowds gather and stream into a tunnel, with shadows silhouetted on the wall and floor. The camera moves into the park, where miniature planes circle, huge roller-coasters thunder past, and there are water fountains and elephants.

The images are not edited as montage but as controlled extended shots, which, combined with the manipulation of scale, fuels an overwhelming sense of hedonism and confusion. This is further emphasised through the montage of diegetic and non-diegetic music and sounds; the tempo and volume increases with urgency and is interspersed with the crashing discordant bells, rings, people shouting and loud laughter.

A powerful use of a single sound can be heard when the man, fearing his wife has drowned, calls out across the lake. The score fades, and all we can hear is the plaintive sound of a French horn standing in for his calls into the darkness. A horn with an upwards inflection is used when the maid calls out that his wife has been found.

Performance

In the three lead roles, Murnau cast well-known American film stars.

Janet Gaynor (wife) had her screen debut as an extra in a 1924 comedy short; three years later, she was one of Hollywood's leading ladies. She had built her reputation playing warm-hearted, fresh-faced young women. She was awarded the first Best Actress Academy Award for her roles in *Sunrise*, *Seventh Heaven* (Borzage, 1927) and *Street Angel* (Borzage, 1928).

George O'Brien (man) came to Hollywood in the early 1920s, initially finding work as a cameraman before moving into acting. His star turn in John Ford's hit western *The Iron Horse* (1924) established him as a popular leading man.

Margaret Livingston's (woman from the city) screen debut was in 1916 and she made over 50 films in the silent era.

As emotions could not be portrayed through a vocal performance, attention had to be paid to all the non-verbal communication elements. Their body contact, proximity,

Independent activity

Watch the scene of the man the morning after he has been planning his wife's murder (approximately 20 minutes into the film). What techniques have been used to disrupt the narrative? What further meanings are being conveyed by these techniques?

Independent activity

Many silent films today are released or exhibited with new scores or live accompaniment, so be careful to check whether the version you are watching has the original or new soundtrack. If you have access to the Eureka reissue of *Sunrise*, once you have watched the film with the original score composed by Hugo Riesenfeld and Ernö Rapée, watch the film again with the alternate Timothy Brock score. How does the music affect the character and narrative?

Stretch & challenge

Watch PBS's 'Crash Course Film History #7 German Expressionism' on YouTube.

Hollywood film noirs were heavily influenced by German Expressionism cinema. Watch a film noir such as *The Lady from Shanghai* (Welles, 1947) and list the similarities between the two film movements.

orientation, movements, gestures, facial expressions, body posture, eye movements and general appearance all contribute to the development of character and story, the establishment of mood and to conveying emotions.

In the first half of the film, O'Brien is frequently shot from behind to emphasise his bulk, or with downcast eyes as though unable to face the world. He looms out of the darkness, or stays hidden in the shadows. His lumbering hunched-over, heavy-footed gait in the first half was created by wearing weighted shoes. In the second half, when he is happy, there are more brightly lit eye-line shots from the front, where we can see his eyes and smiling face. Only for him to return to his earlier monstrous images when his mistress comes to him after the storm.

Gaynor's performance demonstrates how much can be done with so little. Her transformation from sorrowful, downcast wife to one filled with joy is shown through small facial expressions, gestures and body posture. The camera frequently holds her in shot for some time, allowing us to take in her nuanced performance. Her entry back into the kitchen after her husband has left to meet his lover allows us to see through body posture and facial expression that this has become a regular occurrence.

In contrast, Livingston's body gestures are larger. She strides confidently through the village; she wiggles exotically for her lover. Her costume and styling – a slinky black satin dress and dark, bobbed hair – offer a darker sexuality and eroticism.

Further information

The first Academy Awards, now better known as the Oscars, were held at the Hollywood Roosevelt Hotel in Los Angeles, May 1929. They are presented by the Academy of Motion Pictures Arts and Sciences (AMPAS), which was established in 1927 by Louis B. Mayer head of Metro-Goldwyn-Mayer (MGM) as an organisation that would mediate labour disputes without going through the unions, and to improve the industry's image.

The Awards given in 1929 were for films released in 1927 and 1928. In this first year there were 12 categories including some which are no longer featured such as the Best Engineering Effects and Best Title Writer. Some of the awards were awarded for a specific film, such as the Cinematography category, which Rosher and Struss won for *Sunrise*. The Best Actor and Actress awards were given for a body of work, so Janet Gaynor's win for *Sunrise* also reflected her work on *Seventh Heaven* and *Street Angel*. The Best Actor award went to Emil Jannings who had been the star of Murnau's last three films in Germany: *The Last Laugh* (1924), *Tartuffe* (1925) and *Faust* (1926), and had now made a name for himself in the USA.

In this first year there were effectively two Best Picture awards: Outstanding Picture was won by the First World War epic *Wings* (Wellman, 1927) and Best Unique and Artistic Picture was awarded to *Sunrise*. This latter category was not included in any subsequent years.

Aesthetics

Lotte Eisner, who wrote the first critical assessment of Murnau's work, said in *The Haunted Screen* (1969):

> In Friedrich Wilhelm Murnau, the greatest film-director the Germans have ever known, cinematic composition was never a mere attempt at decorative stylisation. He created the most overwhelming and poignant images in the whole German cinema. (page 97)

Sunrise combines elements of Kammerspielfilm's realism, but exaggerates these by employing expressionistic elements to bring to the surface the emotions of the characters. With Fox's unlimited budget and vast resources available to Murnau in Hollywood, he was able to develop his strong aesthetic on a larger canvas. With *Sunrise*, he did indeed create the 'masterpiece' William Fox had sought.

Stretch & challenge

'Expressionism in the German cinema was more than a style; it was an atmosphere and an ethos.'

With this quote from 'Murnau's *Midnight* and *Sunrise*' (Wood, 1976) in mind, compare and contrast Murnau's approach to that of another German Expressionist filmmaker.

Independent activity

What added interest can be found in your chosen film by placing it within the context of other work by the director or film movement or other examples of its genre? Make a list of ten examples.

Representations

The film was made in 1926/1927, but the unnamed setting and characters allow them to stand for anywhere and anyone. The city represents the present (jazz bands, luxury fashion, electric lights and motor cars) and future (spectacular modernistic sets); the country, the past (horse-drawn carts, candles/lanterns and lack of decoration).

Within these spaces, we can explore issues of representations of age and gender and a lack of representation of any ethnicity other than white.

Age

The ages of the three central characters are not given, but the fragility and passiveness of the wife indicates that she is younger than her husband. The predatory woman from the city exudes confidence, but there is an element of 'desperation' in her pursuit of this married man, indicating that she may be a few years older than he is. The actors were 20 (Gaynor), 31 (Livingston) and 27 (O'Brien).

Gender

The central characters in *Sunrise* are so simple that they take on archetypal qualities. They are unnamed, referred to as only the man, the wife and the woman from the city. Two are defined by their gender (man and woman from the city), but the third by her role (wife).

The dialectical of the narrative is reinforced by the two female roles whose function is both archetypes (good wife/wicked mistress) and also personification of locations. The wife belongs to the day, the past and the country. The woman in contrast reflects the night, the present/future and the city.

The wife is shot in soft, bright but diffused light, which bounces off her blonde hair, giving her a halo effect. She radiates innocence, which is emphasised in her matte, light-coloured, cotton clothing and bonnet. Her glowing brightness is a signifier of purity. In the first third, she is shown in the domestic setting, cooking and caring for her baby and husband. We see her tenderly covering the husband with a blanket even though he has been out all night with his mistress. Her role is simply one of loving 'wife', regardless of her husband's treatment towards her.

In contrast, the woman from the city exudes sexuality. She can be seen as an example of the new woman, a frequent archetype in the German culture of the period. In 1919 women had been given right to equality of education, civil service appointments and professional pay.

This new freedom and employment opportunities among single women were seen as a threat to the traditional mother/wife role. The new woman was seen as a sign of modernity and sexual liberation, and became an enduring image throughout the period, especially the mid-to late 1920s.

By having the wife triumph over the woman from the city, suggests that being a mother and wife was the desired role for women at this time.

Considering Murnau's own homosexuality, it is interesting to note how he explores sexuality and what it means to be a man in his films. In many of his films, men are not portrayed as stereotypically virile, masculine types, but instead as emotionally confused.

Whereas the duality of good/bad woman is shown through the wife/woman from the city, the male equivalent is seen in the man, who is alternately monstrous and 'normal', depending on which of the two women he is being influenced by.

Further information

Representation of gender and sexuality in *Nosferatu*

Murnau's first success was *Nosferatu* (1922), the first film version of Bram Stoker's 1897 novel *Dracula*. The plot concerns *Nosferatu*'s lust for the blood of Harker and his concurrent undying love for Harker's wife, Mina. Unlike *Sunrise*, where the archetype of good wife/wicked mistress are shown in two characters, here they can be seen as two sides of one woman. Mina is both the innocent wife and temptress; at the end of the film she seduces *Nosferatu*, tricking him into stepping into the sunlight. Her character, although crucial to the film's plot, does not have a great deal of screen time. The film concentrates mainly on the male/male relationship between *Nosferatu* and Harker. It has been argued that Murnau's own homosexuality has some bearing on the dominance of male/male relationships, conflicting depictions of masculinity and the downfall of a man by a woman in his films.

Nosferatu (Murnau, 1922)

Ethnicity

For contemporary audiences watching silent films, the absence of non-white actors is striking. In most Hollywood films of the period, people from minority ethnic groups were usually depicted as racist stereotypes such as the noble savage stereotype of Indigenous Americans, savage Arabs, Mexican bandits, Asian-American waiters and black servants or simple buffoons. This was compounded by the frequent casting of white actors in these roles, whose make-up (known as blackface/yellowface) and costuming would allude to the characteristics of the minority ethnic group being depicted.

Sunrise's setting is expressionistic; although, offering the illusion of reality, its styling marks it as different. All the actors are white, including those that may traditionally have been ethnically cast such as waiters or jazz musicians.

Stretch & challenge

Compile an annotated bibliography

Research one of the films you are studying from a variety of sources: web, books, magazines, DVD extras, podcasts.

Compile an annotated bibliography of between six and ten of the most significant items. Each item should be appropriately referenced and be accompanied by a brief note (about four lines) explaining how each particular item is relevant/useful to your study. The bibliography should conclude with a short paragraph that identifies items which were not selected for inclusion in the bibliography, offering reasons why.

> **The specification says**
>
> In the 1940s, the French film critic André Bazin set in motion a major debate when he argued that both German Expressionist and Soviet Montage filmmaking went against what he saw as the 'realist' calling of cinema. This opposition between the realist and the expressive has informed thinking about film from the beginnings of cinema when the documentary realism of the Lumière Brothers was set in opposition to the fantasy films of Méliès.

Critical debates: realism versus expressionism

The first moving films were screened in Paris 1895, when the Lumière Brothers projected their 'actualities', short one-or two-minute films depicting the real events. Soon, slightly longer (two to three minutes) narrative films emerged, including those of stage magician turned filmmaker, Georges Méliès, who employed both physical magic and early in-camera special effects to create his fantastical worlds.

Within a decade, films became longer and the craft of film language and film form developed, allowing for more complex narratives and characters. A key figure in the transition from 'primitive' early cinema to the classical period was the American director D.W. Griffith. He joined Biograph films in 1908 and over the next five years made over 450 one- and two-reel films (a reel was approximately 10–12 minutes). With these he experimented with film form, exploring how cinematography, mise-en-scène, performance and editing could be used tell a story. In their documentary on Griffith called *D.W. Griffith: Father of Film* (1993), renowned film historian-archivists Kevin Brownlow and David Gill call him 'the father of film'.

His films laid the template for what has become known as 'classical Hollywood cinema', the term was coined by Bordwell and Thompson in *Film Art* (1997), and is used to define films that follow 'a chain of events in a cause–effect relationship occurring in time and space'. The term is also used when talking about narrative films made elsewhere. These films sought a sense of **verisimilitude** through their narrative, characters and film form.

> **Verisimilitude:** about giving the appearance of reality or truth. This does not mean that the world is presented as real, just believable within the context of the world in which the film is set. For example, we know that in the real world, people do not break into song when they fall in love. In a musical, we accept this convention, but if this happened in a gritty thriller, it would be out of place.

Alongside 'classical narrative cinema' emerged film movements, such as German Expressionism and Soviet Montage that utilised film form in striking ways which were anti-realist. These films defied the classical 'cause–effect' relationship through their use of montage editing and narrative discontinuity, as can be seen in *Sunrise*.

While *Sunrise* employs many techniques that support its inclusion as an example of German Expressionism through its desire to bring to the fore characters' emotions, it also employs a realist aesthetic. Its use of both special effects, montage, editing and disrupted narrative mark it as expressionist, whereas its long takes allow for greater appreciation of nuanced performance, a style more closely aligned with the realism of the Kammerspielfilm and classical Hollywood cinema.

Through his seamless blend of expressionism and realism, Murnau created a film that is an enduring legacy to the silent film, which by 1927 had developed into a sophisticated mode of storytelling.

Film director Peter Bogdanovich (2011) wrote that if he was:

> teaching a master class in filmmaking, among the first things I'd assign would be a look at the pictures released in 1927/28 … [these films] marks the end of the only dramatic art form ever presented to the masses without spoken words, a kind of universal language (needing translation only on the easily altered title-cards). For just 33 precious years, from December 1895 in Paris, to December 1928 in the entire world, publicly exhibited movies in pantomime had enthralled the planet, had the largest audience in the history of the earth, either before or after.

> **Independent activity**
>
> Watch 'How Silent Movie Special Effects Were Done', on YouTube. This is a short film showing how special effects were achieved during the silent film era.
>
> Identify and analyse three uses of special effects in *Sunrise*. How does their use support the characters/narrative and convey further meaning?

Conclusion

Although not a financial success for Fox on its release, *Sunrise*'s success at the first Academy Awards indicates that the American filmmaking community recognised its innovative cinematography and film form.

It is now considered one of the greatest films of all time.

We will leave the final word to the *New York American*'s prescient film critic, quoted in Eisner's *The Haunted Screen* (1969), who when reviewing the film in 1927 said:

> For years after most cinema successes of today are forgotten, Sunrise will be re-issued wherever movies are shown.

Independent study questions

- Q: How is film form used to support the dialectical oppositional of the wife and the woman from the city?
- Q: In what ways does *Sunrise* reflect the German Expressionist aesthetic, and in what ways does it differ?
- Q: How are special effects and editing used to disrupt the narrative, and what meanings are created by their use?

Section 2

A level: Global filmmaking perspectives
(Not studied at AS)

Film movements – silent cinema (2)

This chapter will support your work on **Film movements: silent cinema** in **Component 2** of the A level course. Alongside the core areas, you should be prepared to tackle questions on the specialist area, **Critical debate 1: The realist and the expressive**. The textbook offers two case studies here, a collection of shorts by Buster Keaton and *Sunrise* (Murnau, 1927). You only need to study one option.

For A level
In the **Component 2, Section D** examination there are 20 marks at stake and the expected writing time for an answer is 30 minutes.

The specification says
The silent period saw filmmakers working to develop film narrative and film form and to communicate ever more effectively through purely visual means. Film during this period is associated with the wider cultural and artistic movement of modernism.

A very different contribution to Modernism is represented by the work of Buster Keaton, the most surreal of the great innovative American silent comedians of the period. His work adapts vaudeville to confront the problem of living as the incongruous 'little man' in an age of accelerated change.

Learners will be required to explore critical debates about realism and the expressive within this section.

9 Buster Keaton

Buster Keaton was a true auteur of silent film comedy. Between 1920 and 1922, Keaton directed, co-wrote, edited and starred in 19 short comedy films, known as **two-reelers**. These films were beautifully crafted, funny and inventive. Their popularity helped cement Keaton's star persona and as a result Keaton rose to international stardom. This chapter explores four of the Buster Keaton short comedy films selected for the A level examination:

★ *One Week* (Keaton & Cline, 1920): Buster Keaton attempts to build himself and his wife a flat-pack house. This film was the first two-reeler released by Buster Keaton Productions on 1 September 1920. It was an instant success and featured some dazzling special effects, including a spinning house built on a turntable.
★ *The Scarecrow* (Keaton & Cline, 1920): a fast-paced comedy comprised of a number of chase sequences. The film is most famous for its ingenious set design, as objects in Keaton's house take on surreal and dual functions.
★ *The 'High Sign'* (Keaton & Cline, 1921): Keaton is hired by a gang to kill a wealthy businessman while also being hired by the businessman as a bodyguard. *The 'High Sign'* was filmed in 1920 and was Keaton's first solo two-reeler. However, Keaton wanted the film shelved as he was unhappy with it, resulting in a delayed release in 1921.
★ *Cops* (Keaton & Cline, 1922): Keaton unwittingly throws a bomb into the middle of a police parade, resulting in him being chased all over Los Angeles by the city's police force. This film is considered by critics to be Keaton's most accomplished short film.

This collection of Keaton short films showcases his most striking work and illustrates his trademark style and themes. These films are representative of the most sophisticated and artistic American silent film comedies of the early 1920s. Film historian Kevin Brownlow (1992), describes Keaton's style in the two-reelers as simple set-ups with flat comedy lighting and spare use of intertitles. Common themes that reoccur in these films are Keaton's relationship with machinery and modernity and heterosexual romance.

> **Two-reelers:** short silent films around 20 minutes long. During the 1920s, comedy two-reelers were screened in cinemas as supporting films for a feature-length film.

Buster Keaton

American silent film comedy

Comedy, particularly gag-based and slapstick comedy, was a popular genre and movement of the silent era. Visual comedy was the perfect genre for silent cinema, as gags could be shown without the need for dialogue and were understood by all audiences, including immigrant populations in the USA who may not have been fluent in English. Early film pioneers exploited film's potential to create gag-based comedy. The Lumière Brothers' early film, *Le Jardinier/The Gardener* (Auguste & Louis Lumière, 1895), is one of the very first examples of film comedy. The 45-second film depicts a simple practical joke involving a boy who pranks a gardener by stepping on his hose. The gardener chases the boy, catches him and spanks him.

The Gardener **(Lumière Brothers, 1895)**

Independent activity

Watch early examples of film comedy, including *The Gardener* (Lumière Brothers, 1895). Write 200 words on the following question:

How do Buster Keaton's two-reelers develop from early examples of film comedy?

Film comedy emerged in the USA as a staple genre in 1912 when entrepreneur Mack Sennett founded the Keystone Company and studios. Keystone quickly gained a reputation for short, gag-based and fast-paced physical **slapstick** comedies. Keystone was the biggest producer of American comedy films in the mid-1910s. Its most popular series of films was the Keystone Cops, featuring inept, comic policemen. The trend for mocking and outwitting policemen continued in American film comedy and is exemplified by Keaton's film *Cops*, where Keaton's character is chased by the Los Angeles police.

The 1920s was the golden age of American film comedy. Buster Keaton was one of many 'classic' silent clowns, including Roscoe 'Fatty' Arbuckle, Charlie Chaplin and Harold Lloyd, who all developed their craft at Keystone. Other popular comedians included Laurel and Hardy and Charlie Chase. Roscoe 'Fatty' Arbuckle often collaborated with Keaton and the two were a major influence on each other's comedy style. Keaton was influenced by Arbuckle's character-motivated gags. Arbuckle stated that,

> if anyone gets kicked or has a pie thrown in his face, there's going to be a reason for it.
>
> (Koszarski, 2005, page 157)

Slapstick: a farcical form of physical comedy, popular in early film comedy. It usually involves violent, physical action, such as pratfalls, chases and practical jokes.

Star system: the system used by Hollywood studios to create and exploit stars. Studios would publicise films using star personas as the main selling point. Publicity departments would create a public image of the star, sometimes changing their name and details about their personal life.

By the 1920s, American film studios had established the **star system**. The distinct personas and comedy style of the great silent comedians were developed by the studios in which the comedians honed their craft. Many of these silent comedians were given a great deal of control over their films. In 1919, film executive Joseph M. Schenck set up Buster Keaton Productions and gave Keaton complete creative freedom in writing, directing and acting. As a result of this creative freedom and star system, slapstick comedians of the early 1920s were more concerned with character development and star performances than in the early slapstick films.

Film scholar Charles Wolfe, in *Idols of Modernity* (2010), lists the following conventions and pleasures of American silent film:

- ★ falls and chases played for big laughs
- ★ stunts which thrill audiences
- ★ star comedians with intriguing personalities
- ★ implausible scenarios
- ★ stories told efficiently and clearly
- ★ evoking of dream-like states
- ★ critiques of American society.

Buster Keaton's physical comedy developed from vaudeville, a popular form of variety entertainment in the USA from the 1880s to the early 1930s. In vaudeville shows, a variety of performers, including acrobats, singers and comedians, would perform short 'skits'. Buster Keaton himself was born into a family of performers. He performed in vaudeville with his father Joe and mother Myra as one of the 'Three Keatons'. Keaton adapted his vaudeville performance of acrobatics and comedy gags to films.

> **Independent activity**
>
> Apply Wolfe's conventions and pleasures of American silent film to one Buster Keaton short film. Give specific examples of each convention from your chosen Keaton short film.

Film form

Cinematography

All four Buster Keaton shorts use flat lighting. Flat light has little shadow and creates an even and bright look. This type of lighting was common in silent comedy films as it enabled the audience to look around the frame and watch Keaton interact with his environment. Many of these two-reelers were shot mainly outdoors in daylight hours, therefore, Keaton could use the natural light. The entirety of *Cops* was shot outdoors, making use of outdoor studio lots and the local Los Angeles vicinity, rooting the surreal gags in real locations.

Deep focus gives a sense of perspective in *Cops*

Expressionist: expressionist films depict a widely distorted reality for emotional effect.

Stretch & challenge

Watch clips from early Keystone Cops films produced between 1912 and 1917. Compare representations of incompetent policemen in the Keystone Cops films to the policemen in Buster Keaton's *Cops* (1921).

Keaton employs deep focus to provide a sense of perspective and contribute to the humour, as we can see the gag developing in the background. In *One Week*, the audience clearly sees the train in the background hurtling towards the makeshift house. In *Cops*, Keaton takes a nap on the horse carriage while the city can be seen unfurling in the background. Keaton was adept at using cinematic space to build up a gag. The locomotive at the start of *The 'High Sign'* appears enormous in the frame, making Keaton look small and overpowered, then it speeds off into the background.

In these short films, Keaton's character is often placed at the centre of the frame. This gives each frame a clear symmetry and allows the audience to focus on how Keaton interacts with the world around him. The camera is straight-on at eye-level, with no **expressionist** angles used so as not to distract from what is happening in the scene.

A common convention at Keystone was to shoot chase sequences in long shot. Keystone's influence on Keaton is evident in the chase sequences in *Cops*. Notice how during chase sequences in *Cops* the camera stays static in long shot as the action takes place clearly within the frame. Camera movement is used only to emphasise a gag, as seen in *One Week*, where the movement of the camera mimics the high winds and adds to the absurdity of the gag as Keaton and his wife try not to get swept away by the winds.

Mise-en-scène

These short films display Keaton's fascination for engineering and gadgets. One of Keaton's trademarks was mechanical comedy, where mechanical objects are used and may take on a dual purpose. In *The 'High Sign'*, household furniture and parts of the house take on additional functions such as the floor having a trap door. In *The Scarecrow* all the mechanical objects in the house take on dual functions, exploited for comic effect, such as the gramophone player which functions as an oven. There is a symmetry in the use of mise-en-scène as exemplified in the final sequences of *The 'High Sign'*. Here the house resembles a dolls' house, with the screen split into four in perfect symmetry, enabling the audience to witness what is happening in each room of the house simultaneously.

The Scarecrow (Keaton and Cline, 1920)

Independent activity

Discuss how Keaton uses geometric shapes and symmetry to accentuate gags in his short films. Give specific examples from each of the four short films you are studying.

Objects and props in Keaton's films can function as characters and appear to take on a life of their own. This is evident in the use of the houses in *One Week*, *The 'High Sign'* and *The Scarecrow*, which all seem to come to life. The house in *One Week* seems to conspire against Keaton and his bride. The hurricane causes the house to revolve manically, a gag for which Keaton ingeniously used a giant turntable.

Objects in Keaton's short films are often imposing and appear larger than they may do in reality. Keaton utilised his small frame, appearing in front of or next to large objects. The merry-go-round and train in *The 'High Sign'* appear large and imposing. Likewise, the ever-expanding newspaper engulfs Keaton for absurd comic effect.

Editing

Editing and shots are structured around the development of the gag and edited for precise comic timing. Keaton was an intuitive editor; he described his approach to editing as,

> pacing – for fast action, you cut things closer than normal. For a dramatic scene, you lengthen them out a little bit more.
>
> (Brownlow, 1992, page 43)

Editing in *The 'High Sign'*, *Cops* and *One Week*

Find the scene in *The 'High Sign'* (which starts at around 5 minutes 30 seconds into the film) where the dog tries to catch and eat the steak that is revealed every time Keaton rings the bell. The editing is perfectly timed to enhance the comedy through

Section 2 Film movements – silent cinema (2)

cross-cutting, from Keaton stepping on the pedal to make the bell ring, to the dog outside lunging at the steak. The fast editing and cross-cutting build up the comedy as the poor dog tries repeatedly in vain to catch the steak.

In the opening of *Cops*, the framing and editing create the gag. At first, the mid-shot of Keaton clinging onto the bars makes us believe he is in prison. Then, the film cuts to a long shot, which reveals that Keaton is in fact behind the bars of a garden gate. This shot also demonstrates how Keaton is 'locked out' from the wealthy world his girlfriend inhabits.

In *One Week*, identify the **iris shot**. It is used in conjunction with the torn calendar to signal the end of a scene and the start of each new day, suggesting the passage of time from one shot to the next.

Sound

Although these are 'silent' films, early film audiences would always experience film with live musical accompaniment, usually a piano. There is no set synchronised score, therefore the musicians in the theatres would play along to the film to heighten the emotion and emphasise the comedy. Silent films compensate for the lack of audio cues through exaggerated performances and a focus on the purely visual elements of cinema. Film historian Gerald Mast (1979) argues that due to the lack of sound, silent films have a hypnotic quality. For Mast,

> lacking natural sound, the silent film works on the ear solely by means of the effects of cutting and motion on the eye … The movement of physical comedy … perfectly suits the silent visual hypnosis. (page 202)

Performance

Keaton's nickname was 'The Great Stone Face' due to his deadpan expression. Keaton learned this technique when performing in vaudeville with his family, as he noticed that when he did not emote at the end of a gag, the audience found the gag funnier. His deadpan persona differs from other silent comedians of the day such as Charlie Chaplin, who would often use a range of exaggerated facial expressions to heighten the gags.

Keaton uses his large eyes to emote. His face and eyes imply innocence, as he seems unperturbed by the hostile world around him. Keaton's more subtle style was typical of the new trend in silent cinema from 1912 for a 'verisimilar' acting style. Actors would mimic everyday human responses in a slightly more realistic fashion. This contrasted with the 'histrionic' style popular before 1912, where actors used broad and exaggerated movements that bore no relation to how people respond in real life. Keaton was a physical, agile actor, who incorporated his acrobatics into his films and performed all his own stunts. His body becomes an element of the mise-en-scène as he positions himself within the architecture and setting. A good example of this is where Keaton is being chased by the dog through a ruined building in *The Scarecrow*. Keaton leaps through the windows and across the ledges of the building with ease.

Representations

These short films foreground representational issues regarding gender, rather than age and ethnicity. Women tend to function in the narratives of these Buster Keaton shorts as devices for conflict and as Keaton's love interests. However, in *One Week* the female actress, Sybil Seely, who plays Keaton's wife, has a much stronger role. She is his equal, as the two characters pull together to build and retain their house. Seely, however, still reinforces traditional gender roles as she cooks breakfast while Keaton attempts to build the house. In *One Week*, Keaton acknowledges the voyeuristic role of the camera in the sequences where Seely takes a bath. When

Iris shot: the frame is partially masked in a circular frame, mimicking the iris of the eye. The iris shot may be used to begin or end a scene or draw our attention to something in the frame. Iris shots were a common convention in silent cinema.

Independent activity

Watch versions of one of the Buster Keaton shorts with different musical accompaniment (there are plenty of examples on YouTube). State in 200 words how your experience and response to the film changes when accompanied with a different musical soundtrack.

The Goat (Keaton and St Clair, 1921)

Independent activity

Watch two short Charlie Chaplin films: *Easy Street* (Chaplin, 1917) and *The Immigrant* (Chaplin, 1917). Note three ways in which Chaplin's style of comedy and persona are similar to Keaton's and three ways in which their style of comedy and persona differ.

Independent activity

Stories and gags in Buster Keaton's films are told visually. Title cards are only used when necessary. Write a short essay based on the following question: Explain how Keaton tells a story and/or gag visually. Focus on one sequence from a Keaton short film.

Independent activity

Consider the following:

Women function merely as love-interests in Buster Keaton's short films.

How far do you agree with this statement? Give examples from the four Keaton short films which support this statement and examples which oppose it.

Stretch & challenge

Search online for artist Thomas Hart Benton's 1930 mural *America Today*. Look at the 'Instruments of Power' panel of the mural. Write down the similarities between the panel and Buster Keaton's short films.

Independent activity

Choose one sequence from *The 'High Sign'* and one sequence from *One Week*. Write down how each sequence typifies Keaton's aesthetic style. Compare the aesthetic style of the two sequences in your analysis.

One Week (Keaton and Cline, 1920)

Seely drops her soap while bathing, a hand appears and covers the lens, as if to protect Seely's modesty. Seely breaks the fourth wall by smiling at the camera, aware she is being watched. Seely also plays Keaton's love interest in *The Scarecrow*. Here, Keaton states, 'I don't care how she votes. I'm going to marry her' – a reference to the success of women's suffrage, as most American states had granted women full voting rights by the end of 1919. Keaton's girlfriend in *Cops* is represented as snobbish and cruel, in contrast to his sweet young bride in *One Week*. She functions mainly as a plot device, as her rejection of Keaton leads him into a series of mishaps.

Silent film comedians often played childlike and naive characters which, to a certain extent, defy traditional masculine roles. In *One Week*, Keaton struggles to conform to traditional masculine roles as he is unable to build a home for his wife or cope with the most basic of tasks. In these shorts, Keaton is unable to control the environment around him and often only luck gets him through. However, Keaton does possess some typical masculine traits, as he uses his physical strength and performs all his own stunts. He also demonstrates ingenuity with building and using mechanical objects.

Aesthetics

All four of these Buster Keaton shorts share an aesthetic style that is typified by symmetry, frames, parallel lines and circular imagery. Consider the composition of the hanging salt and pepper pots in *The Scarecrow*. The characters sit at the table at each end of the frame in symmetry and the hanging pots create horizontal, vertical and diagonal patterns. Compare this to the symmetry created in *Cops* as Keaton creates a see-saw effect with a wooden plank. Film scholar Charles Wolfe in *Idols of Modernity* (Petro, 2010) places Keaton's aesthetic style within the wider cultural contexts of American art of the 1920s and 1930s, which, during a time of rising consumerism, emphasised the beauty and simplicity of everyday objects. Art in this period featured geometric shapes and reflected the flourishing industrial age and an interest in the movement of trains and ships. It was a period that celebrated the creativity of engineering and was also one of technological change, as the production line method of factory production was introduced by Ford in 1907.

Social, cultural and political contexts

Buster Keaton's fascination with the workings of mechanical objects bridges the end of the 19th century and beginning of the 20th century, with the rise of new industries and the expanding consumer culture. American society of the 1920s was one of increased consumerism, as advertisers began to link products to idealised lifestyles and saw the potential of film to sell products. Keaton developed the idea for *One Week* after viewing a Ford Motor Company documentary *Home Made* (1919). The documentary demonstrates how Ford workers can build their own affordable, pre-fabricated homes. In *One Week*, Keaton attempts to construct the ideal home for himself and his new bride and live an ideal married life. However, the film undercuts this notion of the idealised life, as Keaton is unable to construct a home for himself and his bride.

These shorts depict Keaton as both confused and fascinated by the mechanical world. The house in *The Scarecrow* was a reference to the comic illustrations of American illustrator Rube Goldberg, which were published in national newspapers. Goldberg drew characters surrounded by crazy contraptions as a comment on how devices can often confuse us and complicate our lives.

A Rube Goldberg illustration

Cubism was an influential artistic movement of the period. Artists such as Pablo Picasso and Georges Braque would break objects down into distinct areas or forms, creating abstract and fragmented images. Buster Keaton references cubism in *One Week* for comic effect, as the house takes on a cubist form, resembling an abstract, angular face. The roof takes on the appearance of a tiny hat, while the pickets on the front porch resemble large teeth.

Keaton was fascinated with modes of transport, reflecting a general fascination at the time with the locomotive, and the motor car, such as the Ford Model T, manufactured between 1908 and 1927, opened up the possibility of motor transport to middle-class Americans. *One Week* features gags with cars and motorcycles. The climactic gag is when a steam locomotive comes hurtling through the house, while *The 'High Sign'* begins with Keaton being kicked off a locomotive. Locomotives were associated with modernity, speed, romance and danger. The locomotive, or steam train, featured heavily in silent cinema. The earliest films, including the Lumière Brothers' *L'arrivée d'un train en gare de La Ciotat* (1895), featured moving locomotives.

Cultural contexts and critical debates: the realist and the expressive

Louis and Auguste Lumière and George Méliès were key pioneers of early cinema. The Lumière Brothers used the camera as an instrument to record the world as it was. Their films are the beginnings of a realist, documentary cinema, in contrast to the magician George Méliès, who used the camera as a tool to create magic and a fantasy world. Méliès demonstrated the possibilities of the camera to create tricks and defy the laws of the real world. His most famous short film, *A Trip to the Moon* (1902), is one of the first examples of science fiction cinema and how cinema could be used to create fantasy worlds. His use of special effects, colour and constructed sets contrasts with the documentary style films of the Lumière Brothers. Keaton, like Méliès, was interested in the magical possibilities of cinema. However, Keaton uses this for comical purposes. For instance, the surreal over-sized newspaper gag in *The 'High Sign'* defies the norms of the real world and appears to open like a magic trick.

Tom Gunning, in his 1986 essay 'The Cinema of Attractions', argues that early silent film, from 1895 to around 1907, was a visual spectacle rather than a narrative cinema. It is in this early period that trick films, 'chase' films and slapstick comedy films were popular. These genres were well-suited to the new medium and modes of exhibition, as early short films were often viewed at travelling shows and fairgrounds. Early films were usually very short, anything from 30 seconds to a few minutes long.

> **Independent activity**
>
> Search for cubist paintings by the artists Pablo Picasso and Georges Braque. Write down three similarities between these paintings and the house in Keaton's *One Week*.

> **Independent activity**
>
> For each Keaton short film, write two modes of transport used in it and state briefly how Keaton uses each one for comic effect.

> **The specification says**
>
> *In the 1940s, the French film critic André Bazin set in motion a major debate when he argued that both German Expressionist and Soviet Montage filmmaking went against what he saw as the 'realist' calling of cinema. This opposition between the realist and the expressive has informed thinking about film from the beginnings of cinema when the documentary realism of the Lumière Brothers was set in opposition to the fantasy films of Méliès.*

> **Independent activity**
>
> Watch three Lumière films and three Méliès films. Write a short essay of 300 words stating the differences between their films.

Surrealism: an international 20th-century movement of artists, writers and philosophers who valued the unconscious mind and dreams. They rejected conventional moral and artistic values. The surrealists were heavily influenced by the work of Sigmund Freud, particularly his book *The Interpretation of Dreams* (1899), which argued that our dreams reveal our unconscious motivations or desires.

Stretch & challenge

Watch Keaton's feature-length film *The General* and compare the narrative structure with the narratives of the four short films you have studied. Answer the following short-essay question:

To what extent are the gags in *The General* integrated into the narrative? How does this differ to the development and function of gags in his earlier short films?

Independent activity

Choose one of the Buster Keaton short films. Write down three examples of surrealism in the film.

However, as film developed from around 1905 onwards, films became longer and therefore it was possible to more fully develop characters and storylines.

Buster Keaton's comedy films combine the 'cinema of attractions' tricks, gags and chases with a narrative cinema. Keaton referred to his gags as 'cartoon gags', ones that are **surreal** and function almost as magic tricks. The use of outdoor locations and natural lighting are in the realist mode, while the surreal gags and elaborate sets are more expressionistic and surrealist.

Surrealists adored silent comedy with imagery that adored the logic of the real world and anarchic gags that mocked figures. The surrealist filmmaker Luis Buñuel praised the films of Buster Keaton and Charlie Chaplin as 'the finest poems that cinema has produced' (2002, page 123). Surrealism blends dream-like imagery and reality, placing otherworldly images in a realistic context. Buster Keaton's shorts feature surreal gags such as the image of a man carrying a piano over his shoulder in *One Week*. Keaton's surreal gags take place in recognisable, realistic locations, such as the streets of Los Angeles in *Cops* and the fairground in *The 'High Sign'*.

The 'High Sign' lacks a cohesive narrative structure in comparison with the other short films in this study. *One Week* has a clear narrative structure, with each day revealed on the paper calendar torn away.

In Keaton's later feature-length films, such as *The General* (Keaton & Bruckman, 1926), gags are more integrated into the plot and far less surreal than those in his earlier short films. Keaton himself explained how the mode changed in feature films:

> After we stopped making wild two-reelers and got into feature length pictures, our scenario boys had to be story-conscious. We couldn't tell any far-fetched stories, we couldn't do farce comedy, for instance ... Story construction became very important to us.
>
> (Sweeney, 2007)

Independent study questions

 How do Buster Keaton's short films reflect the style and conventions of American silent film comedy?

 Discuss how performance and mise-en-scène in Buster Keaton's short films contribute to the overall aesthetics of his films.

 Do Buster Keaton's short films reflect the realist or expressive modes of silent cinema?

 Discuss how far Buster Keaton's short films reflect cultural contexts associated with American silent film comedy.

Section 2

A level: Global filmmaking perspectives

Experimental film (1960–2000) (1)

This chapter will focus on the experimental film question from the Component 2 paper Global filmmaking perspectives. This area of study is exclusive to the A level and alongside the core areas of study you will need to apply the specialist study areas of **narrative** and **auteur**. This is a single film study and our initial focus will be on the paired example of two European avant-garde films from the 1960s: the experimental art house feature, *Daisies* (Chytilová, Czechoslovakia, 1966) and the short experimental film, *Saute ma ville* (Akerman, Belgium, 1968).

For A level

In the **Component 2, Section D** examination there are 20 marks at stake and the expected writing time for an answer is 30 minutes.

The specification says

Alternatives to mainstream narrative film have been present throughout cinema history. The choice here is of films from 1960 to 2000. Over this period New Waves have often challenged the mainstream.

Two 1960s feminist films are linked: Chytilová's *Daisies* from the Czech New Wave offers a surrealist exploration of feminist issues in a politically repressive society while Akerman's short film *Saute ma ville* offers a view of isolation within the domestic space.

Note: Chapters 10 and 11 offer two choices of case study for this module – only one should be studied.

10 *Daisies* (Chytilová, 1966) & *Saute ma ville* (Akerman, 1989)

***Daisies* (Chytilova, 1966)**

Film is an international business and even Hollywood has now woken up to the need to appeal to an international market. With US box office figures in decline, the importance of having a product that can cross borders and continents is increasingly important. However, this unit goes beyond the merely international flavour of film and looks more closely at the specifics of the film world that exist beyond mainstream Hollywood.

This unit allows the student to explore filmmaking from beyond the mainstream confines of Hollywood and Britain's fiction filmmaking. The material will challenge aesthetic and narrative expectations as well as offer philosophically charged material to disentangle and explore. The films studied here are not necessary to learn in tandem but are rather only offered to provide choice.

The analysis of *Daisies* and *Saute ma ville* will first look at their position in the 1960s European avant-garde, and, second, critique their formal and ideological experimentation.

The avant-garde

Stretch & challenge

Research some of the avant-garde art movements referenced on this page such as Dada, surrealism and expressionism Consider how they may have impacted on filmmaking.

An 'avant-garde' is a military term applied to an advanced unit that literally led the way. It was used in terms of cultural analysis in the mid-1800s in France and is now synonymous with any art movement that pushes the boundaries of the form into areas that are at the very least controversial if not taboo. Avant-garde art, be it literature or music, painting or film, has the power to outrage audiences and critics, and can often lead to prohibition, censorship or even imprisonment. Since its dawn in the 1890s, film has allied itself to a number of avant-garde artistic movements such as those of Dada, surrealism and expressionism. In revolutionary Russia the constructivist art movement influenced the likes of Eisenstein and Vertov.

Even today, many postmodern artists have turned to filmmaking to express their artistic visions. The avant-garde is ever present but it undoubtedly reached a high water mark in the 1960s in Europe.

The mid-to-late 1950s and the 1960s was a period of enormous social, political and cultural upheaval. As a new generation of children born during or just after the calamity of the Second World War came of age, their interests and value systems failed to coincide with the generation that preceded them, the generation of their parents: the veterans. This new generation, the baby boomers (so called because they also represented a birth rate rise), were characterised by their attempts to reconfigure old ideologies and their distrust of mainstream authority.

It is no surprise, then, that the 1960s saw the development of a 'generation gap'. Into this gap numerous youth-oriented counter-ideologies and counter-movements developed. For example, there was the Campaign for Nuclear Disarmament's (CND's) response to the Cold War and later the anti-Vietnam War movement (the average age of USA conscripts was 19). There was a sexual revolution fuelled in part by the contraceptive pill and the legalisation of abortion, as well as more open attitudes to sex before marriage. Then there was the rise of global pop stars such as The Beatles and the Rolling Stones, and the first rock music festivals such as Woodstock. Additionally, the rise of counter-culture ideologies led to an increased use of recreational drugs and a rejection of societal norms; something encapsulated by the mantra of LSD (lysergic acid diethylamide) guru Timothy Leary, 'Turn on! Tune in! And drop out!' These largely youth-focused movements also coincided with significant advances in technology, leading to such events as the space race (man first walked on the moon in 1969), the dawn of computers, the growth of TV as a mass medium, and increased ownership of highly aspirational mass-produced objects such as cars and household electrical goods.

Stretch & challenge

Research this period in more depth. YouTube is awash with resources on the phenomena of civil rights, gay rights, alternative lifestyles and movements in the 1960s, and so on. Indeed, it is highly likely that what you discover will impact or consolidate what you have learned in other areas of the specification. For example, the films you may have studied in **Component 1, New Hollywood**, such as Francis Ford Coppola's *Apocalypse Now* (1979) and Miloš Forman's *One Flew Over the Cuckoo's Nest* (1975), are mainly defined by their counter-culture stance.

Finally, there were the politically focused movements of the disenfranchised, such as the civil rights movement, gay rights activism, second wave feminism, ecological 'green' movements and the increased popularity of neo-Marxism. Even on a spiritual level there was a rejection of the old theocratic viewpoints enshrined in Christian dogma, and a discovery of Eastern philosophies and religions such as Buddhism and Hinduism, with their focus on such practices as yoga and meditation. Indeed, such was the tsunami of new ideologies that it was and is legitimate to talk of the era involving a 'counter-culture'.

The 1960s was a decade where the world took a dramatic U-turn, when youth-focused rebellion and the quest for personal and political freedom became paramount. The art world also responded to, if not led, this new era of freedom and non-conformity, so in filmmaking the world witnessed a number of 'new waves'.

Independent activity

Research other films that arose from the radicalism of the 1960s and 1970s. Consider controversial classics such as *A Clockwork Orange* (1972) or *2001: A Space Odyssey* (1968), both directed by key auteur Stanley Kubrick.

The most famous new wave is the French New Wave, the Nouvelle Vague, which certainly pioneered a number of key theories and styles that have become common features of both the contemporary academic and practical film worlds. Without the contribution of the Nouvelle Vague to film history and theory, we would not have theoretical terms such as 'auteur' or be familiar with techniques such as location shooting, improvised acting and jump-cuts. At the heart of the French New Wave lay an informality of style and a willingness to experiment with form and subject matter. Initially realist in their focus, new wave filmmakers swiftly got swept up in the maelstrom of counter-culture debate and discourse, so their sense of freedom and adventure was applied in other countries under different socio-political conditions leading to more ideologically radical work. It is against this backdrop that we must place *Daisies* and *Saute ma ville*.

10 Daisies (Chytilová, 1966) & Saute ma ville (Akerman, 1989)

Daisies

Context

Daisies (Chytilová, 1966) is an unashamedly avant-garde film with a strong feminist ideology. It is experimental at virtually every level: in film form, narrative and characterisations. In brief, this is not a realist text but rather, arguably, a surrealist one. We approach this film not, then, in terms of social realism and a depiction of late 1960s Czechoslovakia but rather in terms of absurdist cinema and an oblique counter-culture critique of political authoritarianism and patriarchy. However, the film absolutely emerges from a specific socio-political context, as explored below.

Social, cultural, political contexts

The Prague Spring and the Czech New Wave

Czechoslovakia no longer exists. It fell apart as a nation and split into two countries, the Czech Republic and Slovakia, in 1993 after the collapse of the Berlin Wall and the end of the Soviet bloc. The ideology of communism led by the USSR or Soviet Union came to a relatively peaceful end in 1989. The iron curtain came down and the countries of eastern Europe, such as Poland, Hungary and Czechoslovakia, were able to dismantle their one-party communist states and set up open democracies on a western European model.

However, *Daisies* has its origins within the communist system. Overt criticism of the state was forbidden and films were banned if they were deemed anti-communist. Under such political conditions the role of the avant-garde becomes much more important than in more tolerant liberal societies, so the aesthetic experimentation of artists can have powerful effects and consequences for the spectator.

Everything came to a head in 1968 (a year also famous for student protests in Paris) in a brief period of official state relaxation of Soviet policy, called the Prague Spring. A power struggle in a time of economic crisis had led Alexander Dubček to take control of the communist party in Czechoslovakia. Dubček was a reformer who wanted to loosen the control of the communist party while still retaining one-party control. He also was keen to relax censorship laws and encourage greater press freedoms. Perhaps unsurprisingly, on 20 August 1968 Moscow used troops and tanks from the Warsaw Pact and the Soviet Union to invade Czechoslovakia and reassert Moscow's authority. The invasion led to Dubček's arrest and proved to the West that democracy was not viable for those people still living under the control of the USSR. The Prague Spring was over almost as soon as it began and the Czech New Wave ground to a halt. Chytilová found working increasingly hard and her film *Daisies* was banned.

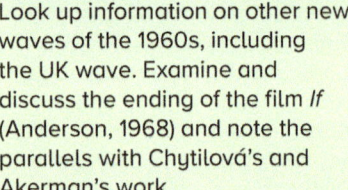

Stretch & challenge

Look up information on other new waves of the 1960s, including the UK wave. Examine and discuss the ending of the film *If* (Anderson, 1968) and note the parallels with Chytilová's and Akerman's work.

Institutional contexts

The Czech film industry, like many non-English speaking countries, has a long history and its most famous film studio, Barrandov, which opened in 1933, remains one of Europe's major filmmaking facilities. The industry's most productive and creative era was during the period of increasingly relaxed attitudes in the mid-1960s, when the state funding of film became more tolerant of films that weren't part of the prescribed Soviet model called social realism. This in turn led to critical acclaim overseas, not least in the Oscars, where two films, *The Shop on Main Street* (Kadár & Klos, 1965) and *Closely Watched Trains* (Menzel, 1967), won the award for Best Foreign Language Film. The rise of, now internationally acclaimed, auteurs in the then Eastern bloc, such as Roman Polanski from Poland and Miloš Forman from Czechoslovakia, also encouraged interest in the region. Indeed, Forman, the foremost of the Czech directors, eventually fled the repressive communist regime and ended up in Hollywood, making such great films as *One Flew Over the Cuckoo's Nest* (1975) and *Amadeus* (1985). However, in the mid-1960s it seemed legitimate to start talking about a new wave of Czech filmmakers.

Independent activity

Read about George Orwell and take a look at the most famous film adaptations of his most popular novels: *Animal Farm* and *1984*. Consider the aspects of these texts that critique communism.

Many of these filmmakers, like Chytilová and Forman, attended the state-run film school FAMU in Prague's Film and TV Academy of Performing Arts. With the state funding their films and access to the nearby Barrandov film studio, the Czech New Wave filmmakers produced more upscale versions of film compared to the more financially threadbare films of the French Nouvelle Vague. There was equally a greater ideological resistance to the communist regime among this artistic Czech community than was found in the more liberal nation of France. With the collapse of the Prague Spring in 1968, the communist hierarchy re-established its ideological control over cinema and artistic culture as a whole and the bright bloom of freedom, artists such as Chytilová had briefly experienced, withered and died.

Věra Chytilová as auteur

Věra Chytilová (1928–2014), 'the first lady of Czech cinema', made her debut feature in 1963, with the experimental *Something Different*, but she remains most famous for her work on *Daisies*. Despite falling foul of communist party censorship, she continued making feature films, shorts and documentaries until her last directorial work in 2006. Born into a Catholic family and originally a student of philosophy and architecture, she worked as a clapper girl at Barrandov Studios before applying to study at FAMU. Her graduation piece, *Ceiling* (1962), was widely distributed among British film societies in the 1960s and *Something Different* was shown at the first International Festival of Women's Films in New York in 1972. Peter Hames, in his excellent and recommended accompanying booklet to the Second Run DVD 2009 rerelease of *Daisies*, notes that 'while she was one of the few women directors to make a major impact in the early 1960s, her work also functioned as a harbinger of developments in feminist film theory in the 1970s'.

The DVD also includes an excellent hour-long documentary of Chytilová.

In a *Guardian* interview with Kate Connolly (2000) following her award for an Outstanding Contribution to World Cinema at the 35th Karlovy Vary Film Festival, it was noted that Chytilová doesn't identify herself as a feminist, but more as an individualist who sees herself as a rule-breaker. This is reflected in the way that the Czech media described her, after she collected her prize, as aggressive and inflexible. Like many of the filmmakers working in Czechoslovakia under a totalitarian regime at that time, Chytilová had to be tough to survive.

Chytilová's acerbic and tough qualities have also garnered her the nickname 'the Margaret Thatcher of Czech film'. Certainly, in *Daisies* this does not come over, as her actresses are clearly having a great time and the film as a whole has a playful, whimsical lightness and charm. Chytilová was a philosophically and artistically minded woman with an interest in stories about women. Her films were also adventures in formal and aesthetic experimentation.

Daisies is, then, the film that from an auteur standpoint defines her oeuvre: feminist, philosophical, experimental and aesthetically charged.

In terms of her specific authorial signature, Carmen Gray (2016) said that Chytilová had a 'taste for visual symbolism and multi-layered associations'. She also worked regularly with her husband, the cinematographer Jaroslav Kučera. Her frequently surreal, often incisively parodic and blackly comic films drew on nature for their striking images and abstraction, and some of her opening sequences are really memorable, not least in *Daisies*. Chytilová's auteur signature is, then, a stylistically strong one, but perhaps her strongest attribute is the thematic treatment of material with her focus on anti-patriarchal feminism, as well as more broadly her interest in artistic and aesthetic freedom. It would be a mistake to pigeonhole her as a feminist but rather she is a freedom fighter, an artist less concerned with labelling and more focused on unfettered expression.

Miloš Forman

Stretch & challenge

Watch one of Miloš Forman's Hollywood films, such as *Amadeus* (1985) or *One Flew Over the Cuckoo's Nest* (1975) and consider how they can be read as critiques of an oppressive and bureaucratic communism.

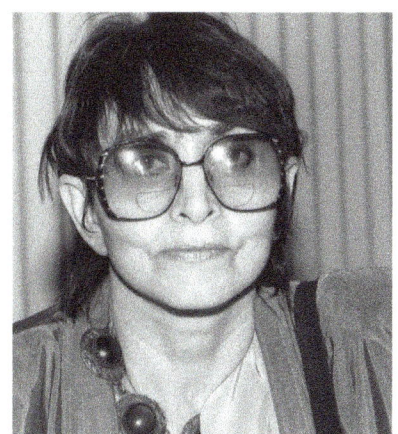

Věra Chytilová

10 Daisies (Chytilová, 1966) & Saute ma ville (Akerman, 1989)

Narrative

Narrative construction relates to the whole film and as such *Daisies* needs to be first considered holistically before we engage more carefully in the themes and particular formal film aspects of the text. The film's experimentalism thus limits the utility of such notions as three-act structures and character arcs. The plotting of the film is chaotic and as such there are many ellipses, and temporal duration is significantly fractured. There are no helpful framing devices to aid exposition such as voice-overs or flashbacks, although some on-screen text is included but its meaning is often oblique. The dialogue is not naturalistic and there is a significant ambiguity affecting our experience of cause and effect as well as character identification (the protagonists are Marie 1 and Marie 2). However, whatever ambiguities are developed in the film's experimental approach to narrative there is little doubt that the film positions us to revel in and enjoy the antics of the two Maries. The film focuses on two teenage women: Marie 1 and Marie 2. They are not individuals (although Marie 1 is brunette and Marie 2 is blonde) but are rather interchangeable archetypes representative of modern female youth. They too describe themselves as dolls and in one early scene act like mechanical puppets with the accompanying sound design of creaking wood and joints. The narrative, as referenced above, is highly unconventional and very loosely plotted. Chytilová refers to the films as 'a philosophical documentary in the form of a farce' (Horton, 1991, page 98), so clearly, generically, there is a nod to the comedic but equally, underscoring the absurdity of the film, there is a philosophical message about alienation and estrangement, something key to the movement of **existentialism** that was then in vogue.

The film is open in terms of its meanings, as the cast were encouraged to improvise from the script.

That said, the film starts with images of aerial warfare and ends with explosions, suggestive of a critique of militarism. The girls are often vacuous, silly and wilfully destructive, perhaps suggesting that they are examples of a vapid, depoliticised and disengaged youth. Conversely, Chytilová's husband, who was also the film's cinematographer, the highly respected Jaroslav Kučera, felt that audience identification with the girls might occur precisely because they are so wild and anarchic. Questions of their empowerment, or their coded critique of patriarchy, must then be contrasted with the idea that unfettered aesthetic experimentation can become a redundant and unhelpful exercise, and that for the world to truly change (for the bombs not to go off) something more considered is needed. The film, interestingly, was banned on its release for its wasteful attitude to food in a time of food shortages rather than its philosophical and social critique. Another criticism came from the leader of the Czech surrealists, who dismissed the films as 'decorative cynicism'. Some, too, have argued that male viewers may find the film less engaging then females, as the film resists simplistic and cosy female representations and men are the butt of many of the jokes.

Existentialism: a philosophy that emphasises the existence of the individual person as a free and responsible agent.

Stretch & challenge

Research films that have been banned in the UK. What are the common issues that lead to their being banned? A visit to the BBFC's website will explain everything. Consider too how important it is that the BBFC is not politically aligned.

Independent activity

Consider these issues:

1. What is the distinction between censorship and classification?
2. Why might censorship be a problem for an artist or thinker?
3. Where in the world does heavily politically motivated censorship exist?

Film form

The students of this film need to remember, however, that the aesthetic choices made by Chytilová are many and varied precisely because she does not want to be constrained by any artistic conventions, such as the need to present realism through naturalistic settings or acting styles or continuity editing. If a dominant aesthetic is present then it is a surreal and experimental one: an aesthetic that rejects cinematic norms.

Cinematography

Many shots are tableaux, representing a controlled camera style in contrast to a freer use of hand-held camerawork. There is a painterly eye in much of the shot construction. A full variety of shot types are utilised and the colour palette is widely varied, ranging from garish colour to sepia and single-colour filters. The use of colour is often surreal and embedded in the construction of the mise-en-scène.

The film begins with images of stock military aerial footage from the Second World War, colourised with filters to create a striking contrast with a recurring imagery of the metallic grey cogs and pulleys of a moving machine. The music is sinister and powerful, largely drums and trumpet, which further adds to the militaristic and mechanistic connotations. Clearly, the world of the two Maries is violent and alienating – a machine age.

The opening credits and title sequence then cuts to the two Maries, shot in long shot, in bikinis. They are half asleep and move like dolls, discussing the fact that no one understands them and that the world is bad and so they too should be bad. This is a depiction of disaffected youth and objectified women. A further symbolic binary is developed through the juxtaposition of warfare and machines, with two young women sunbathing: the active infliction of pain and death is therefore contrasted with passive and sensual pleasure.

Also of note here is the film's playful nod to early film experimentalism and the contemporaneous use of LSD. The surrealism of psychedelia is thus referenced with a fairly lengthy 'phantom train ride'.

Mise-en-scène

The settings, despite their evident realism, are richly symbolic, such as the disused factory and the banquet – both towards the end of the film. The latter setting, which provides the locus for the film's dénouement, is one of many scenes involving food and eating. A recurring plot device and symbolic motif involves Marie 1 and Marie 2 meeting middle-aged men at expensive restaurants, playing coquettes and conning the men out of food. Each man is presented as bemused and ridiculous but nevertheless a symbol of predatory patriarchy. Later in the film the women note that they have pulled this trick on these doting elderly men five times already. However, what is perhaps understated here is that the girls are, at the very least, offering or pretending to offer their sexual favours to elderly men in order to eat. Perhaps as a reaction to having to debase themselves, the food the women order is often excessive in quantity and quality, and Marie 2 in particular is shown in close-up, deliriously gorging herself on cake. This is significant, as students of French history may know, in reference to another young, foolish and independent, Marie: Marie Antoinette.

These scenes are counterpointed with two set-piece moments of anarchy where Marie 1 and Marie 2 destroy, first, the bourgeoisie formality of a dated and farcical cabaret, and, second, an equally outmoded formal banquet, which is symbolically unattended but splendidly laid out with extravagant dishes and delicacies.

The cabaret scene is purely comedic and shows them getting joyously drunk, taunting the stuffy clientele and eventually getting flung out of the venue. The banquet scene, however, demands more attention, not least because it continues the themes of food and excess.

Another scene worth identifying in terms of its mise-en-scène is one of the many surreal and heavily symbolic sequences which involves Marie 2's young lover, a lepidopterist (butterfly collector). The phrase is a sexual reference in Czechoslovakia to promiscuous men who seek out beautiful women. In this scene we see the film's only explicitly sexual scene involving Marie 2's nudity, something she conceals with beautiful but dead butterflies.

Later, back in the girls' apartment, the butterfly lover phones Marie 2. The two girls listen dismissively to his absurdly romantic love talk where he asserts that Marie 2 'does not belong to this century'. Like an exhibit in a display case he wants to preserve her beauty and effervescent sexuality. By containing her he hopes to control her. He is a man who clearly idealises women for what they represent, rather than what they are. As he twitters away on the phone the girls devour yet more food, but this time food that is phallic in shape such as small bread rolls, gherkins and sausages. They then chop up an egg and then a banana: two more symbolic foods.

> ### Image search
> ### The opening of Daisies 00:00:00–00:01:54
>
> Watch the first scene from the beginning of the film and compile a series of images which represent the destruction of war and show industrial machinery. Comment on how the two together set the context of the history of Czechoslovakia until 1966.
>
> Then watch from the end of the titles to 00:03:59 and compile a series of images which represent the Maries as young women. What ideas about women and feminine archetypes are suggested by these images?

> ### Stretch & challenge
>
> Explore the phantom train rides of early cinema. Also look at the experimental colour shorts made for the General Post Office in the UK in the 1930s by experimental artist and filmmaker Len Lye.

> ### Image search
> ### The butterfly collector
> 02:00:26–02:28:00
>
> Watch the sequence with the butterfly collector and Marie 2. Compile a series of screengrabs that show how the filmmakers encourage the viewer to make a connection between the butterflies and Marie 2. How could this scene be used to argue a feminist interpretation of the film?

> ### Independent activity
>
> Explore the UK art house film *The Duke of Burgundy* (Strickland, 2015), which is concerned with, among other things, the idea of butterfly collecting and sexuality.

10 Daisies (Chytilová, 1966) & Saute ma ville (Akerman, 1989)

Finally, they chop up and eat pictures of food and hang up the phone. The man, a symbol of men in general, is not nourishing, like the copious amounts of food that Marie 1 and Marie 2 eat, and doesn't sate their sexual or digestive appetites.

Editing

A riot of techniques are used with little interest in continuity, hence the frequent use of jump-cuts, match-cuts, staccato editing and so on. Discontinuity in editing is Chytilová's favoured device. This of course impacts on the spectator's narrative involvement and certainly helps develop the notion that Marie 1 and Marie 2 are interchangeable archetypes rather than separate identities.

One such use of a match-cut occurs early in the film when Marie 1 strikes Marie 2 and, as she falls, she transitions from a black and white sun deck into a vibrantly coloured meadow, swapping her bikini for a white summer dress and a garland. The meadow is dominated by daisies and is symbolic of Eden. This is anchored when both women find a tree with apples (knowledge) and a peach (pleasure). Marie 2 (the blonde) eats the peach. A further trick eye-line match occurs when Marie 1 looks off frame and asks Marie 2 a question, only for the subsequent cut to be in another location but the conversation to continue unabated. Such experimentation in terms of continuity editing quickly alerts the spectator that this film will not play by any rules, least of all those concerning editing. The film has established its playfulness with time and space, and any sense of realism has been jettisoned early on.

Sound

As with all the other aspects of film form there are realist scenes and conventionally scored scenes, but occasionally the use of non-realist juxtapositions occurs for comic effect: the ticking of clocks, the movement of puppets and so on. The mechanised and militaristic opening sequence referred to above is also particularly atmospheric in its use of non-diegetic music to unsettle and disturb the spectator.

Performance

Performances in the film are melodramatic, stylised and at times improvised. There is little focus on characterisation, back-story and arcs. Marie 1 and Marie 2 are types of people not actual people. Their intimated death at the end of the film is symbolic rather than real. The two actresses sustain non-naturalistic performances and dialogue throughout the film, never breaking character to become real characters.

Aesthetics

Chytilová is driven by the desire to experiment with film form and *Daisies* is therefore a riot of visual and audial play: play with bite but often just sheer, playful, exuberant fun. Thus, Marie 1 and Marie 2 in many ways seem the embodiment of Chytilová the artist, gorging herself on the medium, as in the scene above where Marie 2 consumes cake.

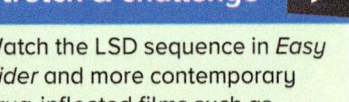

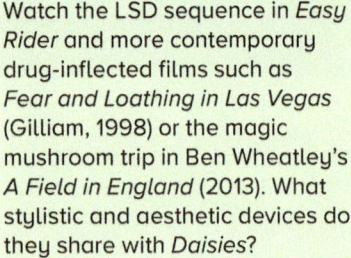

Watch the LSD sequence in *Easy Rider* and more contemporary drug-inflected films such as *Fear and Loathing in Las Vegas* (Gilliam, 1998) or the magic mushroom trip in Ben Wheatley's *A Field in England* (2013). What stylistic and aesthetic devices do they share with *Daisies*?

All aspects of film form are distorted as detailed in the section on auteur signatures (page 271), but one key element that stands out is her aesthetic choices of colour. The film has a specific psychedelic quality at times and one can't help but postulate on Chytilová's first- or second-hand experiences of LSD (arguably the definitive drug of the 1960s counter-culture). Chytilová also uses numerous light filters to colourise the entire frame. These striking colour juxtapositions are in contrast to the more conventional cinematic lighting used in shots like the one with the butterfly collector. The final shot of the two girls lying on the dinner table is tonally sepia, suggesting the colour and purpose has literally been washed out of their lives. Chytilová thus uses colour and its absence to make broader points about her culture and her protagonists, and it is this, in part, that indicates she is making aesthetic decisions.

Representations

Ethnicity

Ethnicity is not diversely presented in *Daisies*. The common ethnicity represented is white European and all the performers appear to be indigenous Czechoslovaks. Whether the omission of other racial identities is ideological is arguable but certainly European film was beginning to open up to the notion of representing other minority ethnic groups. This film's white European cast, then, is largely in line with other works of the period. Stereotypes of white Europeans are of course hugely broad but the ones presented in this film are largely of middle-class and educated dilettanti, collectors and body builders, aesthetes and gourmands and, in the case of the two Maries, free to have fun and seemingly unshackled by responsibility.

Gender and age

In *Daisies*, gender and age are undoubtedly parodied. Marie 1 and Marie 2 are presented to us as two attractive and energetic young women who need nourishment (intellectual and physical) but seem to only find the latter in terms of their ravenous dinner dates with elderly and pathetically represented men. These guardians of patriarchy are ruthlessly parodied as foolishly lecherous and absurdly romantic, and even the younger of the men they befriend, the lepidopterist, merely wants to preserve Marie 2 as an exhibit, not as a real woman. Marie 1 and Marie 2 are embodiments of a newly liberated youth, revelling in the dynamism and wonder of the world. However, the old world order re-establishes itself at the end of the film. Marie 1 and Marie 2, 'youth', pay the price for their freedom as the film ends with their supposed death beneath a falling chandelier and then the bombs start going off.

Men are clearly ridiculous in these young girls' eyes and the absence of men their age suggests the desire to present men in this film as patriarchs. Even men who may be nearer their age are presented as silly poseurs who are only interested in the girls as objects of desire.

In another scene in their apartment towards the end of the film, the girls start cutting up magazines, extracting photographs of faces and bodies, which the audience glimpse in very fast montages. They then cut each other up in a playful scissor fight that employs some clever trick photography and editing, becoming, in the process, literally disembodied representations of women.

They eventually end up 'looking for nourishment' in a disused non-specific facility or factory, where we glimpse the machine that we first saw in the opening shot of the film. They then stumble on the banquet room, which is laid out with a sumptuous feast but is otherwise symbolically deserted. Initially shot in black and white, when Marie 1 breaks a glass, the film switches to colour. A long take follows, showing the girls moving from seat to seat and trying various dishes. Their messy and anarchic table manners soon descend into a food fight. They then dance on the dining table and swing on a beautiful crystal chandelier that hangs above it. Appearing to fall from the chandelier they literally end up in deep water. Calling for help they state they don't want to be bad. On-screen text notes that, 'Even if they had a chance, it would probably look like this.' There is a sense, then, that the film is reprimanding them and that they too are contrite.

Returning to the banqueting hall with brooms, now dressed in newspapers and whispering, they proceed to tidy up their mess. 'We'll be happy if we work hard', they note. Having tidied up (not at all convincingly), they recline together (like corpses or dolls) on the dining table. A clock ticks, an audial refrain at various times that has been used throughout the film. Perhaps connoting urgency or timeliness. Their last words are: 'We're really happy. But it doesn't matter.' Their vacillation and confusion is profound.

The chandelier falls on the girls, who are lying on a table, and there follows military archive footage of bombs going off. Finally, the film finishes with an aerial tracking shot over a bombed-out city, presumably from the Second World War.

10 Daisies (Chytilová, 1966) & Saute ma ville (Akerman, 1989)

Independent activity

Try to find other films that mix up colour palettes. In the golden age of silent cinema this was a common practice but try to find examples from more contemporary films.

As the destruction and desolation unfurls, the sound of a machine gun shoots the words of the dedication onto the screen:

> This film is dedicated to those whose sole source of indignation is trampled-on-trifle.

The final sequence, like the film as a whole, is oblique, but clearly the work ethic beloved of communists has not given the girls happiness, as one grins like a mask while the other looks blank. The pleasures of a promiscuous sex life or the trappings of a wealthy bourgeoisie lifestyle have similarly left them unfulfilled. The film is bookended with scenes and sounds of warfare, and certainly the prognosis for youth and young women in this film is not positive. That said, what remains is the effervescent comic hilarity of Marie 1 and Marie 2, and the sheer exuberance of the cinematic experimentation.

In conclusion, *Daisies* is absolutely a film of its time. Spearheading, as any avant-garde work should do, an attack on the dehumanising of the bourgeois and their political values, the film is a triumph. Gender and freedom are foregrounded as issues (something important to Chytilová) but equally the work transcends mere polemic. Yes, the targets are an outmoded patriarchy and a violent war machine that keeps on turning, but equally what is attacked is the aesthetic notion of what a film should be. By playing so drastically with the form of film, the very idea of film is undermined and challenged. The narrative is symbolic and oblique. The characters are at best stereotypes of a certain kind of man and, in terms of Marie 1 and Marie 2, interchangeable. The acting styles (particularly of Marie 1 and Marie 2) are stilted and anarchic. The use of jump-cuts, coloured filters, sped-up and slowed-down footage, staccato edits, time lapse, montage and non-sequential edits in terms of location all serve to disorientate the spectator and the art form. In *Daisies*, Marie 1 and Marie 2 are embroiled in an existential battle for their identities and so is the actual film.

Saute ma ville

Chantal Akerman

Saute ma ville (*Blow Up My Town*, 1968) is a short film produced by Belgian, Chantal Akerman (1950–2015) when she was only 18, having just left the Belgian film school Institut National Supérieur des Arts du Spectacle et des Techniques de Diffusion after one term. The film was successfully screened at the Oberhausen Short Film festival in 1971 and launched Akerman on her long film career, where she became an established figure in feminist discourse and an artist known for using long takes and filming with a minimalist, slow and impassive camera style. The year 1968 was politically turbulent in France, and the film's radicalism extends out of this social context and the aesthetic context of the French New Wave. Despite this being Akerman's first film, it sets up interests pursued in her other films (most notably *Jeanne Dielman, 23, Quai du Commerce, 1080 Bruxelles* (Akerman, 1976)) with their focus on isolated women.

In this surreal and experimental short, Akerman directs and acts as the main protagonist. We ostensibly see her returning to her apartment, cooking, cleaning and then eating, before she finally commits suicide by blowing herself up. Akerman would years later take her own life, so this final scene is now infused with a tragic and unintended irony.

The film's technical formal experimentalism and radical ideology are developed in a number of ways, as we will now explore.

Narrative

The narrative expressed in this film is very experimental. On a simple level, a young woman returns to her flat to cook. However, she finds firstly the lift does not respond to her call and then, subsequently, when in her flat, her actions descend into farce. For example, the act of cleaning her shoes and dancing become chaotic and messy.

As an experimental work the film unsurprisingly eschews conventional narrative structuring, so we don't really have anything like a three-act structure and even the character arc is oblique, with action and plot largely focused on domestic activity. There is no on-screen text to guide exposition and only illegible vocalisations to further our comprehension of the character and scene. Neither is time clearly expressed, with evident ellipsis between action and no concrete guide to the hours that have passed. Only the spatial treatment is dominant throughout: a recurring motif of entrapment within the domestic sphere. We are clearly aligned with this character but her eventual death is symbolic rather than emotive for the spectator. Thus, Akerman's spare poetics create an impactful scene, heavy on realism in the dreary domestic space and emphasised with a minimalist approach to camera work and editing.

Film form

Cinematography

The film is dominated by the use of hand-held cameras and a seemingly improvised cinematographic style. Akerman resists the more mainstream approach to filming a human subject by cutting in from long shot to close-up; thus much of her film is shot in long shot. This device serves to alienate the audience from the film's protagonist and is developed through the use of a long shot in a mirror. In a number of reflections in mirrors, Akerman returns her own gaze, reclaiming her identity at the same time as she paradoxically objectifies herself. Her disappointment at her reflection arguably leads to her suicide.

Mise-en-scène

The film is shot in a cramped kitchen, devoid of even a view, and throughout the film Akerman's conventionally dressed young woman seems hemmed in by her domestic surroundings. Three posters on the kitchen door: a black man in close-up, a cartoon smurf saying 'Go home!' and a close-up shot of Akerman with the words 'It's me' could all be read as symbols of her infantile alienation and segregation within the home. Women are not 'at home in the home' is one ironic interpretation.

Editing

Jump-cuts and a lack of continuity are noticeable, unhinging Akerman's work from time. The space of the kitchen is, however, treated in the opposite fashion and it is the very lack of editing that enables Akerman to develop the idea of the heart of the home and domesticity as redundant, absurd and claustrophobic space. By holding shots she bears witness to the modern-day drudgery of women.

Sound

There is no synchronised diegetic sound. Most sound effects are produced as Foley but they are not slickly made and actually jar with the audience, destroying any sense of realism. The overall effect is vaguely comedic until the grim dénouement. Indeed, the central portion of the film is muted and the main protagonist does not speak. Instead, we are privy to what appears to be an inner monologue of discordant humming and garbled muttering. The explosion that presumably kills the protagonist is communicated only through sound and a black screen but is then followed by the protagonist humming again and Akerman herself reading the credits. The patriarchal ideology of female domestication is clearly challenged aurally. Woman have no voice.

Performance

The performance style is absurdist with little attention to characterisation, back-story or narrative arcs. The acting style is exuberant and unnatural, again a break with realism. The protagonist clumsily cleans her kitchen floor, hurriedly eats her supper, comically cleans her shoes, daubing polish all over her legs and socks, and, finally, messily applies beauty cream to her face. Much like in *Daisies*, Akerman's characterisation is that of an archetype (oppressed woman) rather than a study of an individual's psychic collapse. Her death in the film is then a symbolic death of an outmoded form of femininity and the explosion at the very end of the film presages the revolutionary end of patriarchy.

In summary, this film sits very well with *Daisies*. It is the product of another female auteur, arising out of a politicised femininity in the broad context of 1960s European avant-garde filmmaking. Both films adopt a surreal and absurdist approach (there is humour in both films) and so disdain conventional narrative. As a consequence, both films have unnamed and largely symbolic performers acting in non-realist styles. The films conclude with the female protagonists symbolically dying as they fail to make sense of the world or the world fails to make sense of them.

What distinguishes the films is their production contexts: the psychedelic and hugely ambitious feature-length *Daisies* emerging from a state-funded communist film industry with access to studio facilities and a professional crew; *Saute ma ville* emerging from an amateur background, shot in black and white on a micro-budget with a very small crew in virtually one location. Nevertheless, both films are clear examples of a broad 1960s counter-culture working together with an avant-garde aesthetic to push forwards feminist discourse. The films produced are then philosophical and ideological challenges to the status quo of patriarchy (then and now) and as such are examples of very personal films from two remarkable female auteurs.

Aesthetics

Akerman is largely known for her single-camerawork and realism, which involves long takes. Her aesthetics are in some sense constrained by budget (hence black and white film stock and a single-camera shoot) and scale but also by her desire to depict real lives. The surrealism of at least this short film derives partly from her absurdist sound design, disorientating jump-cuts and a refusal to conform to conventional film mechanics such as using cross-dissolves to show time passing.

Representations

> **Stretch & challenge**
>
> Watch another one of Akerman's more polished features, such as *Jeanne Dielman, 23 Quai du Commerce, 1080 Bruxelles*.

The key representations in *Saute ma ville* are, not unlike *Daisies*, the two social identities of age and gender, and like *Daisies* the experience presented from an ethnic point of view remains white, liberal and educated. Akerman's housebound protagonist is a counterpoint to the liberated young women of *Daisies*. Indeed, even their eventual fates are similar, although Akerman's is at her own hand. Some commentators have argued that the final scene in the film is an oblique reference to Akerman's Jewish descent and thus a reference to the Holocaust and its horrific use of gas ovens to execute millions. Whatever the meaning, it is clear that the domestic space represented here is alienating. Where the girls in *Daisies* play and explore, Akerman's tragic figure has only kitchen utensils and cleaning products as toys. In *Daisies*, society forces Marie 1 and Marie 2 back to conform. In *Saute ma ville* society hasn't even opened up, so the prison of Akerman's domestic space can only be defeated by the most solemn form of self-expression – suicide.

Summary of the auteur debate

In terms of the auteur debate, Chytilová can be seen as the primary creative force behind *Daisies*. Her three previous films were also concerned with the position of women in various spheres of society: fashion in *Ceiling*, 1961, the workplace (a factory) in *A Bagful of Fleas*, 1962, and both professional sport (gymnastics) and marriage in *Something Different*, 1963. This focus on the female experience and challenges to patriarchal society suggests a consistency of thematic concerns in Chytilová's work, and a case could be made for her status as an auteur, as her films also have a recognisably experimental style, using juxtapositions and a playful approach to film as an art form.

However, the concept of auteur can be challenged here and elsewhere in the course, as films are not the result of a single person's vision. It is important to challenge the concept of the auteur, seeing film as essentially collaborative. *Daisies* is a good example of film as a collaborative art form. It can be argued that the film has three 'authors', who were all key figures in the Czech New Wave: Chytilová as director and co-writer; Ester Krumbachová, co-writer and designer; and Chytilová's husband, cinematographer Jaroslav Kučera. He was known for abrupt colour shifts, jump cuts and rapid-edit photo montages, all of which are pervasive in *Daisies*. This suggests that in terms of a signature visual style, it is possible to argue that Kučera's style dominates, highlighting the flaws within the concept of the auteur.

The use of subversive surrealism was typical of the Czech New Wave, which unlike other European New Waves, could not use realism as an aesthetic to reveal the reality of everyday life in those societies. Instead, Czech filmmakers used a more playful approach to their art to ridicule the authorities in a way which was hard to detect. Rather than taking an auteur approach, a more fruitful way of looking at *Daisies* is to see it as a typical film of the Czech New Wave; this allows for a greater understanding of both style and meaning.

As *Saute ma ville* is Akerman's first film, it is difficult to analyse it within an established body of work which reflects a clear and consistent visual style and set of themes and messages

This knowledge of the film as her first piece of work immediately makes the concept of auteur somewhat redundant as there is no established body of work to judge it against; however it could be argued that this film reflects the beginning of an auteur approach. *Saute ma ville* does establish a visual style that Akerman would continue to use, both realist and experimental, and the consistent concerns with rebellion against gendered views of domestic labour would continue in her work.

As with *Daisies*, it is more useful for understanding the key themes of the film to consider the political, social and cultural contexts rather than the concept of Akerman as an auteur. The film is clearly linked to the experimental style of the French New Wave and the protests in France in 1968, which combined the twin movements of rights for women and for workers. A knowledge of these contexts allows the viewer to see that restricting women to the futile and absurd domestic sphere will have disastrous consequences for them and for society.

The key thematic that links both women as filmmakers is a broadly feminist, experimental and liberal approach, with an emphasis on issues of personal, political and artistic freedom. Where they may differ is in their specific signatures: Chytilová was a maverick and collaborative artist whose radical experimentation allowed for a huge variety of stylistic and technical features, whereas Akerman champions a more minimalist approach, evoking a higher degree of realism. As discussed, the context in which they worked may account for these features more than an auteur approach, and in the case of Chytilová, a position within a particular film movement and a collaboration with other filmmakers within it.

Section 2

A level: Global filmmaking perspectives

Experimental film (1960–2000) (2)

This chapter will focus on the experimental film question from the Component 2 paper Global filmmaking perspectives. This area of study is exclusive to the A level and alongside the core areas of study you will need to apply the specialist study areas of narrative and auteur. This is a single film study and the cult postmodern experimentation of *Mulholland Drive* (Lynch, 2001) will be explored here.

For A level

In the **Component 2, Section D** examination there are 20 marks at stake and the expected writing time for an answer is 30 minutes.

The specification says

Alternatives to mainstream narrative film have been present throughout cinema history. The choice here is of films from 1960 to 2000. Over this period new waves have often challenged the mainstream.

In *Mulholland Drive*, Lynch combines surrealism with a neo-noir aesthetic to explore the dark underbelly of Los Angeles.

Note: Chapters 10 and 11 offer two choices of case study for this module – only one should be studied.

11 Mulholland Drive (Lynch, 2001)

Mulholland Drive is an enigmatic, surrealist film that has fascinated audiences and critics since its release in 2001. The film tells the story of aspiring actress Betty Elms, who has just arrived in Los Angeles to pursue her dreams, when she meets and befriends an amnesiac (Rita) hiding in her aunt's apartment. Several other seemingly unrelated stories are eventually revealed to connect in a number of ways.

Like all of Lynch's works, *Mulholland Drive* has achieved cult status, and is considered by many commentators to be a masterpiece and the pinnacle of the director's artistic output. A major part of its appeal is that it can be enjoyably rewatched endless times in the search for a coherent interpretation and understanding of its symbolism.

In the *Guardian* article 'Mulholland Drive: David Lynch's Masterpiece is a Wide-Open Work of Art' (2017), John Patterson compares *Mulholland Drive* to the surrealist filmmaker Luis Buñuel's film *The Discreet Charm of the Bourgeoisie*, released in 1972. He suggests that, in terms of meaning, Lynch's work is much more open to interpretation.

Mulholland Drive (Lynch, 2001)

Mulholland Drive can be researched extensively to find a variety of interpretations, which contribute to its status as a cult film. The most accepted interpretation is that the first two-thirds of the film are the dream or fantasy of depressed actress Diane, possibly because she is dying, and that the final third of the film is present-day reality, albeit slightly more complex than a straightforward portrayal of reality, as it includes both hallucinations and flashbacks. Even with this interpretation there are still quite a few moments that are difficult to tie up neatly. For example, it seems quite excessive for Diane to imagine the scene with Adam (a struggling Hollywood director) and the pool guy, or the cowboy, despite her desire to see Adam humiliated. Also, darkly comedic scenes showing the incompetence of a bungling hitman (who Diane had hired to murder the actor Camilla Rhodes who is Diane's former lover) seem to go beyond Diane's possible hope that the hit failed, and that Camilla is still alive. The abrupt changes of tone are hard to place within a coherent narrative; scenes of dark comedy reminiscent of the Coen brothers don't entirely fit with the idea of Diane's heartbroken rewriting of events. So although this would seem to be the most plausible explanation of the narrative, even this interpretation does not provide a coherently constructed narrative into which all events can be neatly slotted.

The cowboy appears throughout the film, which suggests that maybe the 'reality' third is not actually real. There are also moments where Diane seems to be struggling to maintain the dream, and especially on second viewing it seems that reality is breaking through: the dog faeces in the courtyard at Aunt Ruth's apartment and Betty seeing (what is probably) Diane's decomposing corpse; these and other examples suggest that what we are seeing is the battle between Diane's conscious and unconscious mind, or perhaps the twin agendas of Lynch to show the underbelly of Hollywood and his character Diane's story of her disappointments there.

To study the film or enjoy it as a spectator, it is necessary to discard notions of conventional neatly tied-up Hollywood narratives and accept that this is a film by a surrealist filmmaker who rejects the mainstream. When the film was due to air at the Cannes Film Festival, Lynch asked the cast not to discuss the story with the press, feeling that it would ruin the experience.

As Naomi Watts has said in an interview about the film, there has to be a notion of truth and authenticity in Lynch's work beyond a neatly constructed narrative. This suggests that the truth being revealed is less about coherent narrative and more about emotional truths; how it feels to be broken-hearted, constantly disappointed, powerless and perhaps, most of all, guilty. Ultimately, it is a film about acting and the power of film; something that the spectator knows is fake yet it still has an enormous influence on their thoughts and emotions. If it is interpreted on a meta level (a film about film itself) then concerns about it fitting together neatly become less relevant. Many people, critics and fans, have formulated absurd interpretations of the film's narrative, but despite this, key themes are obviously apparent: the corrupt reality of LA and Hollywood and the disturbing nature of love and desire.

An interesting interpretation of the film is proposed in the documentary *Lynch/Oz* (Philippe, 2022). In the section titled 'Multitudes', filmmaker Karyn Kiyoko Kusama recounts that after a screening of *Mulholland Drive* at the 2001 New York Film Festival, during a Q&A, Lynch referred to *The Wizard of Oz* as something constantly on his mind. Kusama sees the first two-thirds of *Mulholland Drive* as a 'dreamscape given life', with Diane's reality as 'the failed version of Betty's life'. She also believes that Lynch was inspired by *The Wizard of Oz* and the life of Judy Garland as epitomising the fate of young women in Hollywood. *Mulholland Drive* certainly seems to be concerned with tragic stories of Hollywood: a director who loses control of his film and female actors who either can't get cast or are reliant on powerful men to select them.

Diane's story of a young, blonde woman aspiring to Hollywood stardom who dies too young is an archetypal one. The film therefore has an emotional impact on many viewers; it is bleak and shocking to see a young woman so full of hope be destroyed by her dreams. It brings to our attention the terrible insecurity and lack of control of those who aspire to act or direct in Hollywood. This is highlighted in the auditions for Adam's new film, *The Sylvia North Story*. The film is taken over by apparent mobsters, the Castigliane brothers, who insist he cast the unknown actress Camilla Rhodes as the lead. The quality of the other singer's performance at the audition is irrelevant; the looming presence of the studio executives, emphasised by the line 'this is the girl', reveals that the director is just a puppet of the studio. While this sequence can be seen as an indication of Diane's bitterness at not being cast in a leading role, it leaves a lasting impression of the sinister machinations of Hollywood.

Contexts

Cultural context of surrealism

The film must be seen within the cultural context of surrealism, which started as an avant-garde (outside of and in opposition to the mainstream) art movement originating in the early part of the 20th century. Surrealism aims to explore and portray the unconscious mind in art, revealing truths of unconscious fears and desires. For film this may seem a contradictory notion, as filmmaking itself involves making deliberate choices. However, influenced by Sigmund Freud and his work *The Interpretation of Dreams* published in 1899, this was in part overcome by incorporating dreams, both the dreams of the filmmaker and of characters within the narrative, and this allows access to truths about the human psyche. In most surrealist films, and *Mulholland Drive* opens with this, there are multiple references to falling asleep.

Dreams were also a vital component of one of the earliest surrealist films, *Un Chien Andalou*, made in 1929, a collaboration between filmmaker Luis Buñuel and artist Salvador Dali based on the dreams of both men. Buñuel dreamt of the moon with a cloud passing over it and this led to one of the most shocking graphic matches ever constructed: a razor blade slices a woman's eye (possibly symbolising the need for viewers to open their eyes to the more creative possibilities of film) and Dali's dream of ants emerging from his hand (possibly dark unconscious desires arising from within).

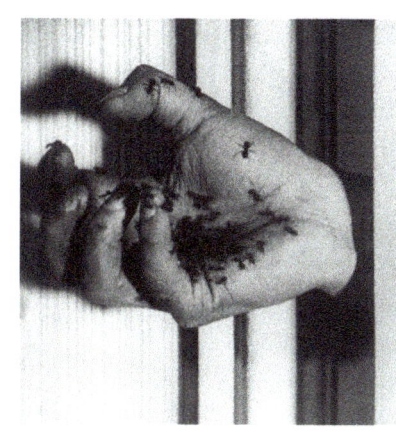

Similarly, Lynch relies on dream states to generate ideas. He has said that beyond the idea of a femme fatale in Hollywood, he had no further ideas. This suggests that Lynch constructed the film based on ideas accessed through meditation from his unconscious mind. Watching the film, it is possible to surmise that the processes of making films within the narrow confines of the Hollywood film industry was on Lynch's mind. Of course it is impossible to definitely attribute ideas to Lynch, as all of the depictions of Hollywood are potentially products of the embittered imagination of Diane as a failed, once hopeful young starlet. The empty blue box is possibly a reference to the empty box in *Un Chien Andalou*; the symbolic significance of the box in each film is deliberately unclear.

Bunuel and Dali both claimed that their short film had no meaning. They expected their first audience of French artists and intellectuals to violently object to the lack of a discernible narrative, and Buñuel has claimed that they carried rocks in their pockets expecting to be attacked. With fabulous irony, the audience loved it and film commentators have repeatedly offered rational explanations of the meaning of the film ever since. We can conclude that the short film reveals to spectators their great need, perhaps instinctive or perhaps nurtured by the mainstream film industry, to construct a narrative, even where there seems to be none overtly present. The film also has a meta level as a vehicle for demonstrating the creative possibilities of film as a medium, as an art form, not explored within mainstream filmmaking.

The need to find a story, believe in the characters and make emotional connections with them works on two complex levels in *Mulholland Drive*. First, there is Diane's need to construct a different narrative of her life in Los Angeles, which reaches a climax in Club Silencio, even though Betty and Rita are told that their experiences are fake by the mysterious and menacing club host, cut-away shots reveal the emotional intensity of the experience. This is the moment where Diane, and the viewer, must leave the constructed story of Betty and Rita behind, the illusion and perhaps comfort of a predictable neo-noir genre film.

Just as Diane must confront the terrible reality of her life, the second level is for the spectator, who is asked to consider the way that films affect their emotions and imagination. Are our imaginations able to go beyond the limits of conventional genre tropes, the film asks, and understand emotional truths free from concerns about piecing events together?

Surrealism originally informed by Sigmund's Freud's approaches to psychoanalysis is psychological in nature, drawing the attention away from ideas of coherent genre and narrative to the idea of subjective reality and how it is constructed. Surrealist films tend to use realist mise-en-scène but have bizarre and often unexplainable actions within them, suggesting the emotional truth of how things feel. And while many surrealistic techniques, for example non-linear narratives, have entered the mainstream, these can be easily pieced together as chronological, which is not the case with *Mulholland Drive*. The disruptions to continuity editing in the final third, of the film for example, the neighbour comes to take the ashtray but it is still on the table in the next shot of the film, imply that this is a flashback governed by a stream-of-consciousness-style narrative.

Social and political contexts

The social context of the callous treatment of young women in Hollywood is a familiar one since the beginnings of the industry. The film acknowledges that Hollywood is a place of glamour and excitement where dreams can become reality. It celebrates the golden age of Hollywood of the 1940s and 1950s by referencing iconic films of the era: *Sunset Boulevard* (Wilder, 1950), *All About Eve* (Mankiewicz, 1950) and *Gilda* (Vidor, 1946).

Independent activity

Watch *Un Chien Andalou* (Buñuel, Dali, 1929) and consider how the unconscious mind is revealed by filmmaking techniques. Can you see any of these surrealist techniques in *Mulholland Drive*?

Stretch & challenge

Watch *Sunset Boulevard* (Wilder, 1950), *All About Eve* (Mankiewicz, 1950) and *Gilda* (Vidor, 1946). How does *Mulholland Drive* reference these films?

These films all feature complex female protagonists. 'Rita' sees the poster for *Gilda* on the bathroom wall and adopts the name; those viewers familiar with the film and Rita Hayworth's career will be able to make the connection between Rita and the sexually alluring femme fatale Gilda. Rita Hayworth famously said that the role ruined her real relationships, as men were too captivated by the fantasy version of her to appreciate her as a real person. *Mulholland Drive* references this through the danger inherent in constructing a fantasy version of a person and a comment on the power of films to blur the boundaries between actors and reality, so that people expect real life to be as it appears in films. This both celebrates the power of film as a medium to seep into the collective consciousness, but is also a reminder of Hollywood's murky past where women are concerned, as illustrated by Rita Hayworth's story. Hayworth was of Spanish descent on her father's side (reality and the film are blurred here, too, as Camilla seems to be of Spanish origin, occasionally and inexplicably speaking in Spanish). In the early part of her career on contract with Fox Studios, Hayworth retained her original surname of Cansino, shortening Margarita to Rita, and was cast in 'exotic' roles. When her contract with Fox ended, she was signed to Columbia, who felt that her surname sounded too Spanish, so she adopted her mother's maiden name of Hayworth, which made her sound more American. This is a typical story in the star system; the way Hollywood studios in the Golden Era manufactured personas for their stars that defined and controlled their lives, robbing them of their identity. This often resulted in extreme transformations, especially for the female stars, who were forced to change their hair and lose weight (studios often handed out diet pills). In Hayworth's case, the studio encouraged her to emphasise her Irish/American side (inherited from her mother) by dying her hair from black to red, and to have electrolysis to change her hairline, so that she had a larger forehead, making her 'look less Spanish'.

Sunset Boulevard and *All About Eve* are both concerned with the precarious position of women in acting careers, particularly as they age; they both depict the fetishisation of youth and beauty within the creative industries. *Mulholland Drive* suggests that female actors have little agency in their careers and that the studio still has the power to be destroyer of dreams rather than a maker of them. The transformation of Rita in the film to look more like the all-American Betty mimics the way that Hollywood studios have robbed women of their identities.

The political context of capitalism is epitomised by the film industry, according to *Mulholland Drive*. Los Angeles is the location of a corrupt and sinister Hollywood; the city is not portrayed as a glamorous location, despite the glittering view of the city's lights from the road itself. The film offers a critique of capitalism and emphasises the fallacy of the American Dream by showing that there is no genuine opportunity to achieve your dreams through mere hard work and determination. Los Angeles is populated with hitmen, gangsters and sex workers, seen at hot dog stands and cheap burger restaurants, suggesting that the closest many hopeful young women may get to Sunset Boulevard is a waitressing job at Winkies. The Hollywood dream is closely allied to the American Dream, through which people are encouraged to aspire to the gated apartments and mansions on Mulholland Drive populated by the film industry elite. However, the film suggests that these places are full of danger and misery.

Attention is also drawn to Hollywood as a place of misery for directors, as well as actors. In addition to Diane's bitter disappointment, perhaps the reality that also breaks through in the dream sequence is Lynch's jaded view of the industry. At the end of the scene at Ryan's Entertainment, where director Adam smashes the windscreen of the car owned by the Castigliane brothers and drives away triumphantly, the spectator is positioned with Adam. This is starkly at odds with Diane's agenda to strip away Adam's smug superiority; instead, the length of the sequence showing the satisfaction of his revenge aligns the spectator with Adam. The non-diegetic sounds of quickening drum beats create a sense of urgency and tension, which positions the viewer with Adam – we too having been terrified by the Castigliane brothers – and then the pleonastic sounds from the impact of the golf club on the car are very satisfying, emphasising spectator alignment with Adam, particularly as the sequence is so entertaining.

Production contexts

The idea for the film was originally conceived as a spin-off television series of Lynch's cult TV series *Twin Peaks* for the character of Audrey. A pilot was shot but not picked up by the intended network, so Lynch moved on to make his next film, *Lost Highway*, which was released in 1997. Eventually, Studio Canal approved production of *Mulholland Drive*.

The production was financed independently, which allowed Lynch to retain creative control, and picked up for distribution by Universal. It was critically acclaimed upon its release, and Lynch shared the prize for Best Director at the 2001 Cannes Film Festival with Joel Coen (who won for *The Man Who Wasn't There*). However, box office performance was disappointing; *Mulholland Drive* is not the type of film that Hollywood can easily market. Ease of marketing is the antithesis of a surrealist such as Lynch, who as an artist has little regard for box office success.

The DVD version of the film was released in 2002 and Lynch insisted on releasing it without chapters to encourage an immersive experience in a single, continuous viewing, as one would experience watching the film in a cinema. Again, it's like a continuous dream that doesn't quite make sense. (Like many artists, Lynch is known to have a real disdain for explanations, preferring to leave the text to speak for itself.) Universal, however, insisted that Lynch produce ten clues to be included in the DVD box, a compromise perhaps in light of industry demands to recoup their losses at the box office through DVD sales by aiding the viewer's understanding of the plot.

Independent activity

Find the article 'David Lynch's DVD Clues to "Unlocking" *Mulholland Drive*', published on the SCREENRANT website (Tomerlin, 2021). Read the ten clues and decide how useful you think they are, if at all. What do they tell you about Lynch's approach to filmmaking? Research how other people have used these clues to interpret the film.

Experimental narrative

Surrealist films follow dream logic and are often episodic in nature, leaving the spectators to use their imagination to both interpret the segments and make connections between them. Experimental narratives demand a creative input from the viewer, which accounts for the enormous variety of interpretation of *Mulholland Drive*. The film opens with the car crash, detectives and the missing, very sleepy woman; 11 minutes later there is a seemingly unrelated scene of a man and his psychiatrist in Winkies. All that links these scenes is the use of iconic Hollywood locations: here Sunset Boulevard. On second viewing, the man's phrase about his terrible feeling has enormous narrative significance. The re-enactment of a dream is pertinent to Diane's narrative and of course for cinema itself, cleansing them of terrible feelings and desires.

It is only after a montage of mysterious phone calls about the missing girl, made by and answered by men, that the arrival of Betty seems to present the viewer with a protagonist. Close-ups and high-key lighting make her happiness infectious and the viewer aligns with her immediately. The music 'Mr Roque/Betty's Theme' establishes a hopeful atmosphere, but the juxtaposition in tone is jarring; this world now seems to be too good to be true – helpful strangers in the form of the old couple and the taxi driver make it feel like a fantasy placed alongside a nightmare. Perhaps we, like Diane, are so desperate for this reality to be true, and as consumers of Hollywood narratives we are quite used to suspending our disbelief and accepting the fantasy. The postmodern hyper-realism here alerts the viewer to how easy it is to want to accept a simplistic fantasy version of life, of how this need is met by movies.

It is not just a case of *Mulholland Drive* having a non-linear narrative. While the final third of the film, especially the dinner party sequence, does help the viewer construct a sense of a linear narrative, there is no definite timeline of events. A process of constructing and then reconstructing a narrative once everything changes reveals to the viewer that rather than be preoccupied with concerns of a neatly tied-up narrative, the focus should be on ideas, thoughts, feelings and awareness of film as an art form.

Rather like *The Wizard of Oz*, the reality section of the film is populated with people that we have already seen in versions of in the dream. However, unlike that film, reality is much more nightmarish than the dream. This nightmarish quality of the real Los Angeles is highlighted by minor characters becoming much more dislikeable in reality. Adam's mother Coco, for example, is peevish, impatient and dismissive of Diane, in direct opposition to the warmth Coco shows to Diane on arrival at Aunt Ruth's apartment. The most extreme example of this occurs when Betty becomes the barely recognisable Diane; it is interesting to consider whether the spectator can still maintain their allegiance to Diane as the protagonist, when everything about her Betty self is so disrupted.

On first viewing there seems to be no narrative connection between episodes. For example, the sequence featuring the sinister figure of Mr Roque, who has the power to have the director replaced and the film shut down, is followed by the hitman, in a moment of very dark comedy, accidentally shooting a woman through a wall. The shift in tone is abrupt and while an exterior panning shot between the two scenes implies that the connection is simultaneous action elsewhere in LA, the only discernible connection is the negative portrayal of Los Angeles – there seems to be no connection between Mr Roque and the hitman in narrative terms. It is only on second viewing that the possibility that events are being filtered through Diane's perception allows the viewer to make connections: her wish to see Adam humiliated provides an explanation for her failure to secure decent roles and perhaps her hope that the hitman didn't really kill Camilla, although some commentators believe that, despite the appearance of the key in the second part of the film, Camilla is still alive.

The appearance of the key as a motif in the dream section of the narrative is a moment of intense mystery. The key looks like something from a magical world; however, the blue key as seen in the ordinary world of sleazy Los Angeles is a battered, old, hand-painted key representing grim reality. The blue box, which it opens in the final part of the dream, seems to signal reality, as in a surreally impossible shot; the camera zooms into the darkness of the blue box, and it is time for Diane to wake up. The involvement of a blue key in both sections of the narrative encourages the spectator to use their imagination to find meaning and develop their own version of the narrative.

Typical of an experimental, surrealist narrative, the tone of the narrative and viewer response to characters is constantly shifting. For example, some scenes align the spectator with Adam as the underdog: the scene at Ryan Entertainment, the scene with the cowboy and at the cheap hotel; in these scenes, film language positions the viewer to sympathise with Adam. However, the narrative of *Mulholland Drive* doesn't fully allow the spectator to build a consistent response to his character; it is almost like the agenda of both dream-makers (Diane's need to humiliate Adam and Lynch's portrayal of the abused director) are clashing. The charismatic presence of Billy Ray Cyrus puts the film into darkly comic territory, through which the viewer is reminded of the real-life wealth and success of Adam; we see his luxurious Mulholland Drive mansion, and the smooth jazz music radiates the smugness of the real Adam. Here the entertainment is provided by the emasculation of Adam, who leaves the scene humiliated and covered in bright pink paint.

Rather than just scenes being out of chronological order, the narrative offers a much more complex view of a story. The reality sections of the film don't help the viewer construct a timeline, as the scenes are happening on different levels of reality. For example, as the now awake Diane is standing in the kitchen, it seems that Camilla has come back, we cut to a smiling, immobile Camilla and then back to a very emotional version of Diane. The next cut to Diane disrupts the 180° rule and places Diane on the other side of the frame, with Diane's expression of self-loathing making it clear that this was just a fantasy. A tracking shot then follows closely behind Diane's dressing gown as she approaches the couch; on it is a naked Camilla, and Diane is now wearing denim shorts, while the piano ashtray on the coffee table shows that this is a flashback. On the line 'it's him isn't it', there is another flashback to the set of *The Sylvia North Story*. This seems to lead into a continuation of the previous flashback, as Diane asks Camilla to leave. The complexity of the narrative here creates a highly subjective view of reality, arguably just as much as the dream section.

Lynch as auteur

It is possible to talk about a Lynchian aesthetic, use Lynchian as an adjective, and easily cite typical trademarks such as disjointed narratives, symbolism, blending genres and sub-genres, use of doubles, mixing dreams and reality, often confusing the viewer; these things seem to point in the direction of Lynch being an indisputable auteur.

To create a debate, the concept of auteur itself can be challenged. First, it is possible to see the film as a collaboration, as Lynch has worked with the same team across multiple films: cinematographer Peter Deming, editor Mary Sweeney and the composer Angelo Badalamenti. When we examine the role each collaborator plays in creating the whole, these features could be considered to be present across the work of the entire team.

Often the discussion of an auteur can be a reductive one with too much focus on listing and identifying features, it may be more useful to see the film as primarily typical of particular film movements – surrealism as considered earlier, and also postmodernism.

The film has three important features of postmodernism: fragmentation, hyper-realism and inter-textual refencing. There are references to classic Hollywood films and another example would be the enigmatic *Persona* (Bergman, 1966), a surrealist horror that invites extensive discussion and multiple interpretations reflecting the same themes of duality and identity. Viewers may find pleasure from identifying many other references. Postmodern films are often more rewarding for the viewer, with cultural capital and the references giving the viewer a more intellectual experience of the film. Lynch also rewards viewers who have prior knowledge of his other films. For example, having prior knowledge of *Blue Velvet* (1986) would help the spectator to understand that Lynch's films are about the horror lurking beneath the surface of American life and identity.

A lack of tangible meaning and messages has led some commentators to argue that although Lynch's films do have a visual style and technical competence he cannot be considered an auteur. A typical argument would be the one posed by

Stretch & challenge

Read about Lynch's auteur signature features and find examples of how they are used in *Mulholland Drive*. Do you find auteur a useful concept?

David Lynch on the set of *Mulholland Drive*

Amy Glynn, writing in her article 'David Lynch is Not an Auteur: On the Enduring Brilliance of *Twin Peaks*', published in May 2017 in the online magazine *Paste*, where she acknowledges that although there is a clearly recognisable Lynchian aesthetic and a reoccurrence of the surrealist preoccupation with dreams and the unconscious mind as thematic concerns, the lack of definite meanings or conclusions regarding these themes makes his work much more nebulous and open-ended. Therefore, she concludes the multiplicity of meanings constructed by individual viewers defy the definition of an auteur in terms of a consistency of messages and values across a body of work.

This compelling argument suggests a fundamental flaw in applying the definition to filmmakers who are also artists, suggesting that it creates a narrowness of interpretation that doesn't credit the intelligence and imagination individual spectators bring to the film.

Film form

Cinematography

When watching *Mulholland Drive*, the viewer is often aware of the presence of the camera through hand-held camera movements, which are noticeable. For example, it is smooth and dream-like in the scene in Winkies where the man is recounting his dream to his psychiatrist. A pan right reveals the empty space by the till where the psychiatrist was in the dream; after the psychiatrist has concluded that the man wants to re-enact the dream, the camera repeats the same movement, showing that the dream has begun, as the psychiatrist is now filling the negative space at the till. This transports the man into his dream so easily, suggesting a very thin line between dreams and reality. Within the scope of the narrative, it is another warning to Diane that reality and the dream coexist.

At other times, shaky camera movements are used to disrupt any realist notions of narrative. For example, when Betty and Rita go to Diane's apartment, they travel by taxi; as the taxi starts to move there is a shaky shot of the palm tree-lined Sunset Boulevard, perhaps a POV shot from the taxi itself. The shakiness signifies the instability of the Betty/Rita fantasy, which is about to be challenged by what they find there. Shots looking up at the palm trees lining what is probably Sunset Boulevard are iconic; here the shakiness also reflects the intangible nature of the Hollywood dream, so difficult to achieve and hold on to.

> **Image search**
> ***The dream – or nightmare – of LA and Hollywood*** 00:17:03–00:21:50
>
> Watch the scene where Betty arrives in LA and goes to Aunt Ruth's apartment. Compile a set of screengrabs which show the dream of LA and Hollywood – how does Lynch make this enticing for the viewer? Do any of the screengrabs suggest that this is also a place of nightmares?

POV tracking shots are used to create a sense of both characters and the viewer being compelled towards danger. The most extreme example of this is when approaching Club Silencio; a worm's-eye tracking shot propels the viewer to what seems to be a place of extreme danger. This shot is combined with the sound of wind, which is Hollywood shorthand for mystery and change. The host has a devilish look, and the club is dark and dingy. The grim reality of Diane's life in Hollywood must be confronted – both her failure to make it and her impending death. Betty just fades away. In the sequence at Ryan Entertainment where Adam must choose Camilla Rhodes, the horror of Hollywood is depicted through big close-ups full of the menace and intensity of Vincenzo Castigliane, as he gives a low scream of frustration and authority, accompanied by drums for emphasis. There is a cut to a mid-shot of his brother, who says the line which becomes a motif: 'this is the girl'. There is a cut back to the big close-up of Vincenzo, who responds 'this is no longer your film', followed by a cut to a slighter higher angle of Kesher, making the power dynamic clear. This invites sympathy for directors working within Hollywood studios, separate from Diane's possible fantasy of revenge. As Kesher repeats the same words, the shot invites sympathy for the moment of his defeat and highlights the brutality of the Hollywood money-making machine for everyone.

Mise-en-scène

This is a film about Hollywood and Los Angeles itself. Locations are significant in establishing the simultaneous glamour and misery of the place where people go to realise their dreams of working in the movies.

The 1950s clothing and hairstyles in the jitterbug contest scene suggest that the narrative is set during this time, and fans of Lynch will recognise the familiar theme of the dark side of life in 1950s America. However, the contest is portrayed using contemporary technology to overlay images of the same three couples dancing, immediately challenging any notions of realism and establishing the idea of young people in Hollywood being interchangeable and replaceable. Once the film starts, the clothing becomes more in line with the time the film was made, although Rita retains the look of the 1940s femme fatale with her tight dress and red lipstick, initially suggesting that Diane's view of the world is stuck in the past. When we see the real Camilla, this look is maintained, possibly suggesting that roles for women have not progressed.

There is a stark contrast between Diane in her grimy-looking grey bathrobe (she wore a pristine pink version in the dream section) and the fantasy version of Camilla, still shown as a femme fatale in bright red lipstick and dress, with the line 'you came back'. The next shot is the empty space, which shows that we have just seen another version of Diane's fantasy mise-en-scène, perhaps signalling here that discovering a sense of objective reality will be denied to the viewer. Diane's reality has a much darker mise-en-scène. This, together with Naomi Watt's performance, as she twists her face into a grimace of disappointment, shows her reluctance to return to this reality.

Although in line with its setting – the iconic palm-tree-lined boulevards, Hollywood studios, sound stages, glamorous apartments and a mansion with a pool – much of the film takes place in two apartments, Aunt Ruth's and Diane's. Despite Betty declaring that Aunt Ruth's apartment is 'unbelievable', POV shots reveal that it is quite ordinary, with dingy brown walls and dark wood, and soon the music and POV tracking shots signal that it is a place of danger; a horror aesthetic points to a harsher reality than the one Betty appears to be perceiving. Later on, when we see Diane's apartment, it is interesting to note that there are some similarities between the two – the kitchen units are the same, although they are a hopeful yellow in Aunt Ruth's and have a sickly green hue of jealousy and insanity in Diane's. It is probable that Aunt Ruth has died before Diane moved to Hollywood; she says at the dinner party that she was able to come with the money left to her by Aunt Ruth, which would then mean that Diane has entirely conjured up the apartment in her imagination, so it is not that different from where she actually lives. Her real apartment reflects the lack of care she gives to herself in her state of utter misery; the windows are dirty and the place is dingy.

As in classical Hollywood melodramas, mirrors are used to signal constructed identity, the hiding of secrets. The sequence in the bathroom where 'Rita' adopts her name is shot in the mirror, with the poster showing Rita Hayworth in another mirror. In a later sequence shot in the same mirror, where Rita becomes blonde, the camera pans across wigs as if Betty and Rita are in a theatrical dressing room rather than Aunt Ruth's bathroom, to reveal the two women in the bathroom mirror. The blonde wig makes Rita look more like Betty; in terms of the Diane narrative, this perhaps suggests that, like a Hollywood studio, she wants to possess and control her star. The dream has taken away her name and her natural hair colour, which mimics how studios treated their stars in the golden age of Hollywood. Diane says admiringly that Rita has a familiar look, which implies both her narcissism and refers to the homogenisation of young women in Hollywood. Lynch, therefore, uses the artifices of the Hollywood star system to show how endemic and enduring these ideals are.

Editing

The use of superimpositions reinforces the shadowy dream world, which is hard to decipher; for example, the overexposed transparent images of the old couple towards the end of the jitterbug contest combined with the overexposed smiling image of Betty, full of hope. A version of this image appears at the end of the film, but this time the image of Diane is more translucent and provides a jaded version of the young woman who arrived in Hollywood. This editing creates a circular narrative, suggesting the endless cycle of misery caused by dreams of working in the industry. The city lights in the background reinforce the idea that LA is the 'city of dreams', which in most cases seems to destroy those who come to live out their dreams. However, it is possible to see some hope in the smiling image of Diane and Camilla, the translucence of the image perhaps indicating that their love exists in some form of reality.

Conventional continuity features are used in a much more creative and symbolic way in surrealist films, often to disrupt continuity rather than create it, and, rather than being seamless, the editing here often draws attention to itself. For example, at the height of the quest for Rita's real identity and the realisation that she may be Diane Selwyn, there is a slow dissolve between a tracking shot of the palm-tree-lined Sunset Boulevard. Another example is when Betty is pondering the money and the key; a shot of Adam driving and being told his film is in disarray is followed by a tracking shot of palm trees, which then dissolves in a graphic match to a close-up of Betty, in which her arms are at similar angles. This is a more symbolic use of continuity features; here, the matching through dissolves reveals Betty's hopes and dreams. Graphic matching is also used again in a more prophetic way: the decomposing body on the bed, Diane asleep, and then Diane waking up are all shown in exactly the same position seeming to suggest Diane's death, but the ease of interpretations is prevented by disruptions in continuity. The first body has longer hair than Diane and is wearing black, the sleeper the cowboy talks to is also wearing black, but when we see Diane actually wake up, she is wearing grey.

The logic that links scenes is personal to Diane, so that the sequencing of shots often confuses the spectator. For example, just after the scene where Betty and Rita find the money and the key in Rita's bag, there is a cut from the close-up of the key to the Pink's Hot Dogs sign. The editing has followed Diane's train of thought from those items to the area of Los Angeles where she imagines the hitman may be operating, and then back to the scene with Betty and Rita. The cutaway to the hitman follows the connections that only Diane's brain could make, giving the viewer an intimate connection with Diane. There is also a cut from the wide-eyed Betty looking at Rita covering her face with her hands as she tries to remember their significance, to a close-up of Adam driving. This links the shot directly to Camilla's relationship with Adam – at this moment Diane holds them both responsible.

In some shots, the idea of long takes is taken to extremes. The camera remains for a short moment in the same position even though the actor has left the shot, creating a sense of the camera struggling to keep pace with the action. This mirrors the experience of the viewer, who is probably struggling to keep up with events too. For example, when Aunt Ruth returns as the dream sequence is coming to an end, a POV shot shows her looking at her bedroom. She then leaves the room, but the camera does not follow. The illogicality of Rita remaining after Betty has left the dream and then Aunt Ruth returning suggests that Diane is desperately clinging on to the dream, even though she can no longer maintain the persona of Betty – the lingering of the camera at this moment signifies her reluctance to leave the dream. Just as the cinematography is subjective, here the editing choices can only be explained in a subjective way. In both sections of the film, the viewer is inside the mind of Diane Selwyn.

Sound

The film's score was composed by Angelo Badalamenti, who also plays Luigi Castigliane, the terrifying studio executive/gangster who bullies people over inadequate espresso. Badalamenti has collaborated with Lynch as a composer on his other work.

The big band sound of trombones and drums at the jitterbug context captures the optimism of 1950s America, but its repetitive nature matches the visuals in creating a surreal tone. Badalamenti's compositions, too, are vital for setting the mood and possible symbolic meaning of particular scenes. For example, there is a low and menacing synth version of the love theme when Betty and Rita find the decomposing corpse, which signifies the close connection between love and death.

The diegetic sound used in the film's dream section does not always suggest realism; there are actions or objects in shot that should emit sounds, but they don't. For example, when Betty first arrives in Aunt Ruth's apartment and walks around, we hear her footsteps, but as she goes into the bedroom and sees Rita's bag and clothes on the floor, the footsteps disappear and instead non-diegetic, low synth music takes over to signal that she is in danger and that emotions have overtaken reality. The lack of ordinary environmental sounds intensifies the hypnotic, dream-like quality of the film.

At other times, ordinary sounds are intensified and made pleonastic. Knocking, for example, becomes a motif signalling unwelcome interruption – the intrusion of an unpalatable reality. It is likely that there is intermittent knocking on Diane's door as she sleeps, which is probably her neighbour and the detectives. The first time this happens is the knocking of Coco with Louise Bonner, followed by Betty and Rita knocking on what they think is Diane's apartment, and the knocking as Diane wakes from the dream.

Performance

This is a film that celebrates the power of performance; it marvels at the idea that, even though the spectator is aware the actor is pretending, their performance still has incredible power to move us. In discussing performance, the focus must be on Naomi Watts in this her breakthrough role. During an interview with Lynch, Watts (Betty/Diane Selwyn), Justin Theroux (Adam Kesher) and Laura Harring (Rita/Camilla Rhodes) for the Criterion DVD release, Watts discusses the blurry boundaries between her own and Diane's search for stardom in Hollywood. She had struggled in Hollywood for ten years before she secured the role in *Mulholland Drive*, and she talks about auditions where the director showed little interest in her. She says of the meeting with Lynch that he was able to see her true ability as an actor, and see her for herself.

Naomi Watts as the aspiring actor Betty Elms

Her performance as Betty – all wide eyes and constant smiles – depicts the character of Diane at her best, arguably the true Diane before Hollywood destroys her. The stark contrast between her performance as Betty and then as Diane has led some commentators to see them as two separate characters rather than two versions of the same character; the transformation is so stark, Watts' face is contorted in misery, her jaw is clenched, eyes brimming with tears.

Perhaps more pertinent is the way in which brilliant performances contrast with mediocre ones, suggesting that true talent is irrelevant in Hollywood. When Betty and Rita are rehearsing, it's clear that Rita lacks talent – she simply reads the lines. This serves to reveal Diane's belief that Camilla was cast due to her sexual allure rather than her acting ability. Betty's wooden reading is transformed into a stunning reinterpretation of the scene in the actual audition, which, when Betty is not immediately cast, highlights the idea that great acting is not always a key component in the making of films.

Watts' performance as Betty could be seen as a meta performance, so deliberately false in a way that perhaps creates an emotional distance between the character and the spectator, or draws the viewer in emotionally, as we want to believe in the fairy tale. It is ironic, then, that during the audition Betty's acting style feels more believable at the moment when we know that she is acting. This mimics the experience of spectators and the power of the human imagination to suspend disbelief – they become detectives in the film but we, the viewers, enjoy being detectives unravelling the narrative of the film. This draws our attention to how far we as audiences desire to imitate what we see on the cinema screen.

The film celebrates the power of performance and the skill of the actor coupled with the imagination of the viewer to suspend their disbelief; while knowing it's just acting, the viewer can believe in the reality of the character and the story for the duration of the film. This idea is really put to the test at the narrative turning point when Watts and Harring are shown to be playing another version of their characters.

Representations

Ethnicity

In the film, Hollywood seems a place where almost everyone is white, though there are several black backing singers in the audition scenes for *The Sylvia North Story*. This could be partly due to the 1950s setting, as suggested by the mise-en-scène.

The singer at Club Silencio is possibly Spanish, but ethnicity is not the issue here. It is likely that the club itself should be interpreted on a meta level as symbolic of the power itself to affect spectators and communicate the reality of emotion that transcends language. Even though the well-known song 'Crying' is sung in Spanish, Betty and Rita are visibly moved. Both are crying; it doesn't even matter that the song isn't live, as film isn't – it still has an incredible power.

Lynch signals that the sinister figures who control Hollywood, the Castigliane brothers, are Italian and potentially part of the mafia. Although if we apply a meta reading, it is more likely that the film is pointing out that Diane's (and the spectator's) imagination is dominated by Hollywood films, and therefore as a spectator, we become aware of how easily we read films according to simplistic mainstream film genres and character stereotypes.

Age and gender

The film delves into the murky, patriarchal world of Hollywood corruption and the impact this has on women's lives in a way that invites empathy for every hopeful, smiling woman who arrives in the bright sunlight and palm-tree-lined roads of Los Angeles, as Betty does. It is difficult to separate the representation of women from the representation of Hollywood, a place where auditions are never fair and even those with incredible talent are overlooked, although this can be seen as a product of Diane's unconscious mind justifying her failure to be cast in a significant role. The ease with which viewers can recognise female character archetypes for both Betty as an ingénue (young, naïve and hopeful) and Rita as a femme fatale (dangerous and desirable), offers a critique of typical mainstream restrictive one-dimensional roles for women. These roles lead to the destruction of the young hopefuls, but also the male hero, whose lust is incited by the femme fatale. Betty/Diane was doomed from the start.

Talent also seems irrelevant, the closest these young hopefuls get to working in Hollywood is waitressing at the Winkies on Sunset Boulevard, or worse a sex worker on the side street next to it, or destitute behind it (the homeless person is played by a woman). These pretty young blonde women are therefore shown as interchangeable. Betty, who serves Diane as she meets the hitman, looks very similar to Watts, and in the 'dream' section, the waitress's name badge reads Diane, suggesting that in the production line of Hollywood, young women are easily interchangeable and replaceable. This references a key theme in *All About Eve* and *Sunset Boulevard*, both of which deal with the terrible misogyny and insecurity faced by female actors. The final mirror shot of Phoebe in *All About Eve* shows a distorting mirror, suggesting an infinite supply of identical versions of hopeful young women; Eve has already been replaced. This theme is also explored in Chazelle's *La La Land*, another film that features rigged, soul-destroying Hollywood auditions and rooms of young women who all look and behave identically. *La La Land* also celebrates the power of film and the illusion to move us, while offering a biting satire of Hollywood and LA. As with *Mulholland Drive*, the dream is contrasted with the grim reality, and both films have a climatic sequence at a club where the female protagonist must face up to the reality of the choices she has made.

Winkies on Sunset Boulevard becomes a key location in both sections of the film's narrative, as it is prominent in Diane's mind as the location where she meets the hitman. Diane seems to conform to the misogynist trope of the scorned woman with out-of-control emotions, which is derived from Victorian notions of 'unhinged' and 'hysterical' women. If we accept that the first two-thirds of the film are Diane's dream or fantasy version of events, then the stark reality of Diane's life allows the viewer to understand the extent of her jealousy and bitterness. It is debatable whether this extremity of emotion turned to thoughts of murder is a backwards look at the femme fatale from an earlier era, an ambivalent representation of powerful women in a time when women lacked it, or a cinematic blaming of women for the evil actions of men. In the *Guardian* article 'Deviant Obsessions: How David Lynch Predicted our Fragmented Times' (2023), Phil Hoad argues that, as a male filmmaker, Lynch has an unusual ability to defy misogyny and the male gaze in his representations of women.

The meta layer of meaning – this is a film about a film – allows for any potential criticism of representation to be aimed at the industry rather than Lynch; this is because Diane's imagination is possibly limited by her obsession with Hollywood. The apparently real section of the film also draws attention to the failure of Hollywood and mainstream narratives to positively represent women, and the imagined audition from the dream sequence highlights this to an absurd degree as Betty and Rita mock the badly written screenplay that Betty is rehearsing. Diane's unconscious mind creates one-dimensional character types for women, and the dream shows the reliance of her imagination on Hollywood to conjure up a more acceptable version of reality.

Diane constructs her ideal lover as an amnesiac version of herself; via the familiar Hollywood amnesia trope (the character's memory, or parts of their memory, are wiped), she has the chance to build her ideal version of Camilla as Rita. It is debatable whether this is reducing homosexual desire to the idea of sameness, a familiar homophobic trope, or whether it is a more general comment on the narcissistic nature of desire. However, when the real Camilla is revealed, she looks like a femme fatale but lacks the charm. Instead, she is cruel and sadistic, and the sympathy created here for Diane highlights Diane's humanity in wishing for a nicer version of her girlfriend.

In the *Sylvia North* audition scene, it is suggested, through the romantic cliché of extreme close-ups in shot/reverse shot between Adam and Diane, that there is a potential romance or recognition of talent there. It is therefore heartbreaking to see that in Diane's best version of herself on the set of *The Sylvia North Story*, where she has seemingly mesmerised Adam and could potentially be cast, she chooses love and Camilla, referring to a promise she made.

Some commentators have seen the representation of lesbianism as negative. The writer of 'Queer Uncanny#1: *Mulholland Drive* "Have You Done This Before?"' (2012), which can be found on the Global Queer Cinema website, suggests that here is a representation of lesbians that refers to the trope of the tragic lesbian, through which lesbian characters in a film are often killed (Diane) or returned to their true heterosexuality (Rita). However, in the context of a film about the nightmarish world of Hollywood, it is possible to see Camilla's 'straightening' as her choice to pursue roles rather than prioritise her romantic relationship. Perhaps it is because the heterosexual casting couch is still the only way for women to get parts that Camilla is attracted to Adam to further her career; some commentators have even detected a career-orientated attraction between Camilla and Luigi Castigliane. Lynch's use of doubling, not just of characters, but also of narrative moments, highlights the sadness that when Diane is confronted with the same choice (as Betty), she chose differently. This is also reminiscent of *La La Land*, with its bittersweet ending showing Mia's own sacrifice.

Aesthetics

Despite Diane's desperate desire to create a fantasy version of Camilla, and even more desperately, a version of events where the hit has failed due to the incompetence of the hitman, the horror aesthetic portrays the reality of her life in Hollywood. As her mind tries desperately to cling on to romantic Hollywood amnesia storylines (maybe Diane has a memory of MGM's film *Random Harvest* (LeRoy, 1942) stored in her unconscious), the dominant horror aesthetic – created through menacing diegetic music, darkness in the interior shots and terrifying point of view tracking shots – is at odds with her version of events. Although on first viewing the spectator has no awareness of Diane, alignment with her is building from the outset.

Following Betty's arrival at the LA airport, which conveys a hyper-real aesthetic of happiness and wide-eyed wonder, there is a cutaway shot to elderly people, their faces now twisted into menacing grins, accompanied by low, sinister music. Diane, and possibly the viewer, ignores a series of warnings that are a staple of the horror genre. Despite Betty's response of delight, Aunt Ruth's apartment is dark and dingy, and as Betty explores the apartment we see it through horror cinematography – POV tracking shots accompanied by tense electronic notes that signal danger. This is followed by a warning from a mysterious witch-like woman, Louise Bonner. This aesthetic is perhaps indicative of the battle occurring in Diane's unconscious mind as she struggles to maintain the dream; indications of reality keep breaking through.

Lynch's breakdown of the narrative into three parts (discussions on which can easily be found online) may be useful in understanding the use of aesthetics. In the perfect fantasy section of the film, the dominant aesthetic is still horror, highlighting the disconnect between Betty's perception of events and that of the spectator. Despite Betty and Rita's clear excitement as they become detectives and follow clues in an attempt to find Rita's true identity, sinister music plays as detectives watch them. The hellish location of Club Silencio signals are all suggestive of horror.

Throughout the film, danger and then death are signalled, initially, it is suggested that Camilla is the threat, then the sinister controllers of Hollywood and finally Diane's own demons, which result in her suicide. The horror aesthetic acts as a warning to the viewer that all is not what it seems; through its use from the outset, Lynch uses film language to direct the viewer to look beneath the surface and see that the Hollywood dream is never far away from the nightmare. The scene near the beginning where the man re-enacts his dream, which points to the surrealist nature of the film, is shot in a terrifying way through hand-held POV tracking shots, a familiar staple of the horror aesthetic. Although the function of the scene is perhaps to suggest that Diane is trying to distract herself from the real significance of Winkies, it reinforces the idea that homelessness and death are likely outcomes for those who believe in the Hollywood dream.

Dreams are used to create a hyper-realistic aesthetic, where reality is exaggerated to such an extent that it becomes unstable. The dream-like, episodic narrative structure contributes to this aesthetic, as well as the abrupt tonal changes. The lighting, performance and mise-en-scène used to depict Betty create a softness and brightness to the world that is enticing. Misled by the Hollywood dream, Diane's version of her arrival in Hollywood, breathily excited and so hopeful, goes beyond Diane as a character; it is the product of Hollywood and the American Dream. This is indicated by the noticeable presence of the colour pink twinned with blonde hair – this extends beyond Betty's hair, clothing and lipstick to Camilla Rhodes in the audition and Adam's wife Lorraine. This hyper-real aesthetic suggests that the Hollywood dream of idealised femininity is all around us; it allows the viewer a way in to see how Diane and other young women have been mis-sold a view of this world.

Conclusion

There is much to debate about the experimental nature of *Mulholland Drive*'s narrative and much that can be researched in terms of interpretations, as suggested in this chapter. Understanding the film as surrealist narrative is a fruitful way to analyse the narrative elements and deconstruct the ways that Lynch deliberately draws our attention to familiar Hollywood tropes.

In terms of the auteur debate, this is a film which maybe challenges the concept of auteur in relation to surrealist works, as films without a definite meaning, perhaps Lynch's films cannot be linked to a consistent body of thematic concerns. However, an absurd and nightmarish world might be considered to be utterly Lynchian.

PART 3 PRODUCTION
Production skills

This part will help you to prepare for Component 3: Production on the A level and AS Film Studies courses. It should be noted that for AS the film production is an **extract of 2½ to 3 minutes*** in length but the AL is a **short film of 4 to 5 minutes*** in length. Written work takes a similar approach, with AS writing a screenplay extract of 1,200 to 1,400 words* and AL a full-length, short film screenplay of 1,600 to 1,800 words. The essence of your practical coursework (30% of the qualification) is to put into practice what you have learned. It is marked internally by centres and will probably be timetabled once the course is well under way.

To further focus you there is the requirement to produce an Evaluative Analysis of your creative work, which for A level must feature some narrative analysis of at least three short films featured in an anthology of texts provided by the exam board (Teaching from 2017 For Award from 2019, Version 5 August 2023). This initial study of the short film form is intended to guide your creativity, so we'll start with it, by focusing on how to analyse short film. If taking the AS you do not need to study the short films.

* **Note:** these limits set by the exam board will be enforced rigorously and marks will be deducted if they are not adhered to.

Focus for AS level
Option 1: Film extract (2½–3 minutes) **or**

Option 2: Screenplay for an extract (1,200–1,400 words) and photographic storyboard (approximately 20 shots), **and**

Evaluative analysis (1,000–1,250 words) with no required focus on the set short films.

Focus for A level
Option 1: Short film (4–5 minutes) **or**

Option 2: Screenplay for a short film (1,600–1,800 words) and photographic storyboard (approximately 20 shots), **and**

Evaluative analysis (1,600–1,800 words) with reference to 80+ minutes of short film study.

The specification says
Production is a crucial and synoptic part of the specification, giving learners the opportunity to put into practice the filmmaking ideas they develop throughout their course of study.

The Silent Child (Overton, 2017)

How to analyse short film (A level only)

Short film is a term that lacks a precise definition other than the idea of 'length', but it is a very definite error to assume that a short film is merely a slimmed-down long film. Historically, of course, the form has been around since the dawn of film history with the work of pioneers such as the Lumière Brothers. They were absolutely short filmmakers, although due to necessity rather than aesthetics: they filmed for about a minute or so until their film ran out and they hadn't at that time developed notions of editing. However, today filmmakers make 'shorts' for a whole raft of reasons but most obviously as a means of creative entry into the industry, starting at the ground floor to build a portfolio of work, develop ideas and experiment with technique before hopefully embarking on feature film-length material.

So what types of short film are there? The Academy (AMPAS) in the USA, which bestows Oscars, define it as 'a film under 40 minutes in length' and it has been awarding live action shorts since the 1930s. Currently, AMPAS awards Oscars for three short film formats:

★ documentary (short subject)
★ short film (live action)
★ short film (animated).

All three genres are relevant for AS or A level study. Animated films must be filmmaking projects rather than screenplay and storyboard, and documentaries also tend to be made as films, whereas short fictional films lend themselves to both filmed projects or screenplays and storyboards.

> **Short film:** according to the Academy of Motion Picture and Sciences (AMPAS), a film under 40 minutes in length.

 Independent activity

Take a look at some of the recent winners of short film awards to gain a greater understanding of the conventions of short films.

On a practical level, short films tend to be small scale and low budget. This means that the cast, sets and plot lines, for example, tend to be discrete and limited, very often revolving around one or two characters and their reaction to a specific event in a specific location. Low-resolution endings in short films are common, as well as a more experimental treatment of non-mainstream subject matter.

A level students only must study **at least three short films** totalling **a minimum of 80 minutes in length for this unit**. One example selection would be five films:

★ *La Jetèe* (Marker, France, 1962) 28 minutes
★ *The Wrong Trousers* (Park, UK, 1993) 30 minutes
★ *About a Girl* (Percival, UK, 2001) 9 minutes
★ *The Gunfighter* (Kissack, US, 2014) 9 minutes
★ *High Maintenance* (Van, Germany, 2006) 9 minutes.

All totalling 85 minutes.

The reasoning for these choices is that these films have varied production contexts, in most cases strong generic features, and both experimental and mainstream narrative structures. They therefore have a good spread of formal qualities and aesthetic choices to study. The films chosen also fall into the following categories:

★ two fairly long-form shorts: the very experimental art house science fiction classic, *La Jetèe*, and the mainstream animation, *The Wrong Trousers*
★ a social realist film, *About a Girl*
★ a high-concept postmodern comedy-western, *The Gunfighter*
★ a near-future science fiction film, *High Maintenance*.

Detailed guidance on the Evaluative Analysis will follow, but these short films must be linked to the analysis of narrative structure and key elements in your own work, showing how they have had an influence on the construction of it. However, an ability to analyse film in terms of the three core areas covered earlier in this book is also essential and you would be best advised to revisit these relevant sections in this book before starting your short film study and subsequent practical work.

The **three core areas** are:

1 **The key elements of film form:** cinematography and lighting, mise-en-scène, editing, sound and performance
2 **Meaning and response:** representations and aesthetics
3 **The contexts of film:** social, cultural, political, historical and institutional

Of equal importance is your ability to revisit the knowledge and insights gained in your study of some of the **specialist study areas:**

★ spectatorship
★ narrative
★ ideology.

As we will see, 'narrative' is a major focus for the short film, but a sense of spectatorship and a discussion of ideology are vital for an analysis of the meaning and response that your work has created, influenced by the 80 minutes of short films (just A level) and approximately two other films which could be considered to be cinematic influences.

A superb analysis of *any film*, let alone a short film, would aim to include some insights into the following fundamental questions:

1 What aspects of **film form** are used and why?
2 How does the film encourage the **spectator** to feel?
3 What **aesthetic** decisions have been made and why?
4 How and why is the **narrative** shaped?
5 What **genre features** are present?

6 What **institutional**, **social**, **political**, **historical** and **cultural contexts** have influenced the film's production and reception?
7 Has this film contributed to **critical debate**?
8 What kind of **representations** and **ideologies** are present?
9 Is there evidence of an **auteur** at work?

The exam board suggests a particular focus on these three areas for the Evaluative Analysis:

1 Narrative structure
2 Cinematic influences: linking the key elements of film form such as sound design, mise-en-scène and cinematography, along with narrative devices to the work you have produced
3 Creating meaning and effect through the use of the key elements of film form such as sound design, mise-en-scène and cinematography

Consequently, this section will refer to each of these areas in the following very short film analyses of three focus films: whether you are analysing your own films, or the films that have influenced you or the films in the anthology, you will need the same skills.

It is also worth remembering that all practical work follows a 'brief' supplied by the exam board. These will be changed every three years, so please check on the exam board website or speak to your teacher to gain a clear understanding of the expectations for your production work.

Narrative plays a fundamental part in the practical unit, not only in terms of the product's construction but also in terms of its evaluation. You should then constantly revisit the narrative sections in this book before starting to draft a screenplay or plan a film shoot and then, of course, again when constructing your Evaluative Analysis.

Narrative theory is complex but it can be neatly summarised, as explored earlier, in terms of the formalist distinction between **plot** and **story**. This may sound odd so think of it like this:

★ **Who** is the film about?
★ **When** does it take place?
★ **Where** does it take place?
★ **What** happens?
★ **Why**?
★ **How** does it happen?

And then most crucially …

★ **How have I been shown** it happening?

If still struggling with the concept of narrative, try answering the following questions:

★ Is the plot linear or non-linear?
★ Are there flashbacks or flashforwards?
★ Is the plot episodic?
★ Is it circular?
★ Where and when does the film start?
★ Where and when does it end?
★ Do various storylines interweave at critical plot points?
★ Do characters move in an 'arc'?
★ Does the film follow the traditional three-act structure?
★ Are there ellipses?
★ How do mise-en-scène, cinematography, editing and sound contribute to the development of the narrative?
★ Is there repetition or a framing sequence, perhaps with an actual narrator?
★ Are there very clear lines of conflict built into the film?
★ Is the film ideological in terms of its narrative construction?

- ★ Is there a twist?
- ★ Is there an enigma in the set-up – a problem to be resolved?
- ★ Are characters in conflict?

Questions such as these will help you navigate the theory and support your analyses, but equally they will help with your planning for the production.

We can now briefly explore three of the five selected short film texts:

La Jetèe (Marker, France, 1962) 28 minutes

Contexts

This French short film by the avant-garde artist and filmmaker Chris Marker was released in 1962 and remains a favourite on film courses around the world, as its experimentation with film form and narration is strikingly original. An ultra-low budget deconstruction of the moving image, the film is also a product of the French Nouvelle Vague, the film movement of the late 1950s to mid-1960s that challenged conventional filmmaking tropes and techniques. Marker's film is very much in the experimental tradition of this movement. In essence, the film is almost wholly constructed from male voice of God narration and still photographs. Marker himself referred to the film as a photo novel (*un photo-roman*). It is shot in black and white using naturalistic settings despite its science fiction dystopian vision of a post-apocalyptic future where scientists are using prisoners to experiment with time travel. The film title refers to an airport jetty, observation deck or viewing platform, a location significant in terms of the narrative, as it features both at the start and the end of the film.

1 Narrative structure

The main feature of this film's narrative structure is its concern with 'time' and the effect of time travel on the nameless protagonist, a prisoner known as 'The Man'. He is compelled by scientists to go back and forth in time as well as into the future. The Man is obsessed by images from his past, in particular the killing of a strange man that he witnessed as a child on a viewing platform at Orly Airport, in Paris. The central section of the film concerns the man's romantic relationship with a woman who he also vividly remembers from the observation platform when he was a child. Returning to that moment, he discovers that the man he saw being killed, a death also witnessed by the woman he now loves, was himself from the future. Thus, the film concludes with a surprising twist.

2 Key elements of film form

Marker uses grainy black and white film and a number of strikingly shot close-ups, especially in the subterranean scenes involving medical experimentation. The Man's doctors are often shot in low angle, creating unease and a clear sense that he is a hapless pawn in their machinations. The mise-en-scène, fittingly for a low-budget film, is spartan in the subterranean settings and, when The Man is sent back in time, contemporaneous images of Paris are used. The futuristic scenes are largely created through make-up and clothing. Marker's creation of a near future and far future is therefore sparse but utterly compelling and convincing. The rather morose narration is intended to convince the audience of the realism of the desperate times screened and the subdued mise-en-scène complements rather than derails the imagination.

A lesser director or even a director with a slightly bigger budget may well have produced an unbelievable vision of the two futuristic settings. By downplaying the future in both its forms (near and far) the past becomes the fantasy world, the playground of time. In other words, it is our past and our memory of the past that shape the present and the future. Our fascination with the past is also about our realisation that in some ways we can never escape its effect. We are therefore trapped in the past.

Study tip

Creativity is not like a tap. You can't just turn it on and off. Creativity needs nurturing and judgement can often get in the way, so practise just brainstorming ideas. Avoid critiquing until much later. Use the world around you for inspiration. Start with what you know. But start. Do something. Use pictures or words jumbled together or news stories or real-life events to start your creative journey. Or go back to what you know about genre conventions or representational tropes and try to subvert them. Finally, you can even pay homage to existing filmmakers or adapt plays or poems or novels that you have read. But in the end being creative involves hard work and engagement – it's not a magical process of inspiration but a little like mining for gold dust.

> **Stretch & challenge**
>
> Research the French New Wave in more depth. YouTube has numerous video essays on the subject and many with a specific reference to auteurism. Look also at other famous experimental short films such as the surrealist masterpiece by Dali and Buñuel, *Un Chien Andalou* (France, 1929).

> **Stop-motion animation:** where the camera is repeatedly stopped and the subject is moved incrementally to produce, once a number of separate shots have been made, the illusion of continuous movement. Claymation uses clay models and stop-motion animation, as in the work of Nick Park and Aardman. This type of animation is distinct from the other main forms of animation such as hand drawings, CGI, rotoscoping, animatronics and motion capture.

3 Creating meaning and effect

The film is infused with a bleak Cold War sensibility. Man has destroyed his world. Everything is broken and survivors have moved underground to conduct their fiendish experiments. Perhaps significantly, The Man's tormentors, who send him back and forth in time, whisper in a sinister way in German: a reflection on the cruel experimentation that the Germans undertook in the Second World War. Sound is also powerfully used to create an elegiac mood with a non-diegetic choir scoring the scenes of nuclear destruction at the start of the film as well as the final heartrending climax on the observation platform at Orly. Heartbeats too are used to raise tension and highlight the extreme medical experimentation taking place. A core idea of the film is that time cannot be escaped. Thus, the mind-melting climax where not even love saves the day.

The Wrong Trousers (Park, UK, 1993) 30 minutes

Contexts

The maker of this animated film, Aardman Studios, has produced some of the most popular and idiosyncratic animated work to come out of the UK in the last 50 years. The mainstream success of Wallace and Gromit (the films' two protagonists) has led to a mini-franchise of three other shorts and a successful feature-length film, *The Curse of the Were Rabbit* (2005, UK). Aardman specialises in **stop-motion animation** and has been critically lauded on a global level, not least at the 1994 Oscars where *The Wrong Trousers* won an award for the best animated short. Wallace and Gromit remain a fixture at the BBC, and the TV Christmas viewing figures for some of their comic outings have been very high, reflecting their family-friendly mainstream appeal and quintessentially British character. This mainstream prowess and critical acclaim is not achieved on the cheap, however, and *The Wrong Trousers* was budgeted at £650,000.

1 Narrative structure

The Wrong Trousers is not experimental, as *La Jetèe* clearly is. *The Wrong Trousers* is primarily about the homely relationship of two characters: a middle-aged cheese enthusiast and inventor, Wallace, and his very smart, brave and capable pet dog, Gromit. The two live in a terraced Victorian house somewhere in the north of England and the majority of their adventures stem from Wallace's inventions. These are 'Heath-Robinson' styled contraptions, which run throughout the house. For example, in the opening sequence of the film we see Wallace being woken in the morning by a mechanical hand and tipped into his trousers, before disappearing through a trap door to land at the breakfast table.

In *The Wrong Trousers*, however, Wallace has appropriated some ex-NASA hardware, robotic legs called Techno-Trousers, which he reprogrammes to provide Gromit with 'walkies'. These robo-legs have suction pads on their feet, enabling the person wearing them to walk up walls and on to ceilings. It is this ability which impresses their new lodger at the house, a mysterious Penguin, who, it transpires, is the arch-criminal Feathers McGraw, who is set on stealing a huge, famous diamond from a nearby museum. Trapping Wallace in these robo-trousers (the wrong trousers, of course), the Penguin uses him to steal the jewel but is then caught by Gromit back at the house.

The narrative thus detailed is delivered in a linear way with clear exposition given to us in dialogue and through cunningly positioned pieces of mise-en-scène such as newspaper front pages.

The Penguin is silent like Gromit and all their character identity is largely communicated through expression and performance. Wallace, a bald, middle-aged man, talks with a northern accent and has conventional tastes such as tea and cardigans, string vests and slippers. He is a gentle and rather hapless eccentric who often needs to be rescued by his resourceful and loyal canine friend, Gromit. *The Wrong Trousers* concludes, therefore, with the Penguin's arrest and Wallace and Gromit settling down to some tea and Wensleydale cheese. The desired impact of this characterisation on the audience is one of nostalgic whimsy. Wallace is an asexual eccentric: lovable and dopey, a child-man with an all-consuming hobby of invention. His world is pre-digital, a fondly romanticised view of 1960s England with its gentle and homely references to teapots, biscuits, tank top jumpers, slippers and antimacassars.

2 Key elements of film form
The film is replete with cinematic influence from a history of film viewing. The climatic sequence, with the chase on a toy train track through the house, is evocative of westerns or action movies such as *James Bond*, which have all used the train as a narrative device upon which to stage action. There is also something of the kitchen-sink drama too in Wallace and Gromit: their world is a vaguely nostalgic one, a recreation of a dimly recognisable 1960s UK town. Wallace's inventions are not at all high tech and his van is clearly a dated model: if truly social, realist Wallace would be a white van man, always on his mobile phone, and Gromit would be a fierce Staffordshire terrier rather than the cuddly loyal hound that he is. Chimney pots, garden gates, cars with starter motors, false teeth, cloth caps, and hair nets, etc. all clearly locate the film in the memories (cinematic or real) of Nick Park, who was born in 1958 in Lancashire. The humour, too, is largely physical and clearly derives from the era of comedy shorts produced by Hollywood throughout the silent era and into the age of sound: shorts produced by such comic legends as Laurel and Hardy and Charlie Chaplin, for example.

3 Creating meaning and effect
The effect of this film is largely comic and wistfully nostalgic. The eccentric characterisations, in particular of scatty Wallace and the icy, calculating Penguin, operate brilliantly against the resourceful and resilient Gromit. Crime is shown not to pay and friendship triumphs over adversity. Even the Techno-Trousers escape from the bin that Wallace put them in, to flee into the sunset and freedom, a trope that is also focused on in the first Wallace and Gromit short film, *A Grand Day Out* (1989). Equally, England is depicted as a functional but rather odd place: a harmless and rather quirky country stuck in the past.

Eric Kissack

The Gunfighter (Kissack, 2014) 9 minutes

Contexts

This short film is a postmodern whimsy, playing with the genre conventions of the western and the comical conceit of a narrator who not only can be heard by the performers but who also instigates action rather than merely commenting upon it – basically, a voice of God whose honesty causes more problems than it resolves. Eric Kissack is a film editor and emerging filmmaker, and his varied and largely comedic work, including *The Gunfighter*, can be seen on his website. The film was shot over a weekend at a small film studio on a low budget of $25,000, with most of the money going on production design and costume. One set is used and the voice of God is performed by established comedic actor, Nick Offerman; the cast otherwise are unknown actors.

1 Narrative structure

The structuring of *The Gunfighter* begins with the eponymous gunfighter's classic entrance into a Wild West saloon. There are literally a few seconds of establishment with a dusty street scene before he enters the saloon, eyes hidden by the brim of his Stetson. Over the course of nine minutes, we learn from the narrator a whole raft of private information about all the people present in the bar. These revelations eventually lead to a violent and fatal shootout for all present, despite an attempt by the gunfighter to ignore the voice and plea for peace and tolerance. Of the stock characters present, alongside the stereotypically manly gunfighter, we meet a saloon sex worker, a number of cowboys and a tough-talking barman. The sex worker is the last woman standing but the voice of God punctures her self-satisfaction with the news that she'll be killed the following day by a rabid wolf. Structurally the film has a linear delivery with a high sense of resolution and strongly delineated characterisations bordering on the stereotypical. The film's climax ('the ballet of death' referred to by the Voice) is indeed a full-blown cinematic shootout playing to the most generic of resolutions associated with the western.

2 Key elements of film form

The film is absolutely inflected by the western. The mise-en-scène, music, colour and lighting codes all pay homage to the classic western iconography: grizzled, dusty gunfighters; card-playing townsfolk; trigger-happy cowboys; bounty hunters; feisty saloon girls; and tough-talking barmen. The shootout acts as a satisfying and inevitable end to the narrative and again is a homage to the many westerns of the past and present, which are concluded in a blaze of gunsmoke and bullets.

3 Creating meaning and effect

The main effect of this film is comedic. By playing with the convention of a voice-over that can be heard by the entire cast, a number of intriguing opportunities arise, not least the idea that the 'voice of God' can reveal aspects of people's behaviour and thinking, and so humiliate and/or enrage all present. One message, then, may be that brutal honesty is not always so smart and may indeed lead to disaster. Much of the humour is crude and sexual in content, and many of the men present have secret sex lives exposed to the gathering. The gunfighter himself has homoerotic thoughts about a cowboy present, who is himself revealed to enjoy dressing up dollies. Thus, the film plays with the conventional representations of stock characters in a stock situation through the cinematic device of a mischievous narrator or 'voice of God'. Even genre conventions are mocked when sex worker Sally comments on the usually non-diegetic ominous music score, which is now heard by everyone, suggesting that something bad is about to happen, something the narrator (much to the chagrin and disdain of those present) refers to as 'a ballet of death'. Despite its postmodern irony and genre-revisionism, the film does contain some problematic representations, such as characters feeling and

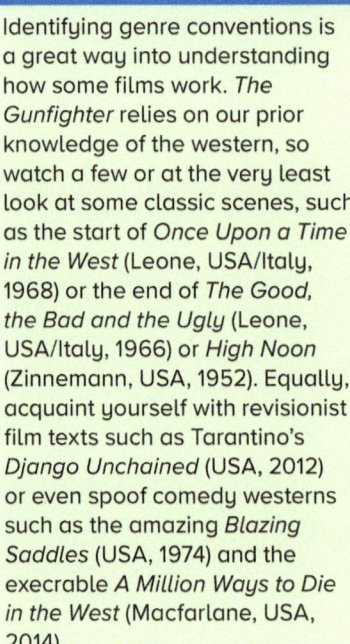

Stretch & challenge

Identifying genre conventions is a great way into understanding how some films work. *The Gunfighter* relies on our prior knowledge of the western, so watch a few or at the very least look at some classic scenes, such as the start of *Once Upon a Time in the West* (Leone, USA/Italy, 1968) or the end of *The Good, the Bad and the Ugly* (Leone, USA/Italy, 1966) or *High Noon* (Zinnemann, USA, 1952). Equally, acquaint yourself with revisionist film texts such as Tarantino's *Django Unchained* (USA, 2012) or even spoof comedy westerns such as the amazing *Blazing Saddles* (USA, 1974) and the execrable *A Million Ways to Die in the West* (Macfarlane, USA, 2014).

being shamed for their same-sex attraction in defiance of the normative gender roles expected of them. Racial representation is dealt with in a more progressive way through the device of the black barman, but even his role becomes defined through a perceived aberrant sexuality, as it is revealed he sleeps with white women.

How to write a short film screenplay

A screenplay forms the written basis for most films. Without a screenplay it is very hard to raise finance or generate interest from potential cast and crew. The purpose of the screenplay is to present character and story information in an accessible and hopefully atmospheric way. It also enables producers and key cast and crew to see what elements they need to work on in terms of their contribution to the project. Like any form of specialist writing, a screenplay has a very specific format that the exam board want all candidates to replicate.

The format favoured is called a 'master scene script' and its conventions are as follows:

- ★ single column with wide margins
- ★ sequential page numbering (top right)
- ★ mf (more follows – bottom right)
- ★ dialogue centred, with speaker's name in upper case
- ★ slugline (see below) and sound in upper case
- ★ character name in upper case on first appearance only
- ★ font – courier 12 point.

Each scene must be numbered and accompanied by a 'slugline', which consists of the following:

- ★ an indication of where the action takes place – interior or exterior (INT or EXT or INT/EXT)
- ★ location descriptor
- ★ lighting descriptor – DAY or NIGHT or TIME
- ★ scene/action descriptor (with succinct description of character on her/his/its first appearance)
- ★ essential camera or edit instructions in exceptional circumstances* – in upper case – such as SLO-MO or TIME-LAPSE)
- ★ action written in present tense.

A good 'short film' screenplay will contain some of the following elements:

- ★ A small cast of rounded characters introduced with sharp psychological detail.
- ★ Evocative and relevant references to atmospheres and environments.
- ★ Convincing dialogue (beware writing in a vernacular you are unfamiliar with) and avoid lengthy monologues unless the work demands it, like in the short film *About a Girl*.
- ★ Sensitive exposition – clunky exposition announces itself, a feature spoofed in the Austin Powers films by the character Basil Exposition.

Screenplays must also be accompanied by a photographic storyboard, which will be discussed below.

The best way to explore screenplays is to read some. There are many free sites online that have scripts of feature films and short films available. Often the final visualisation in film is very different from the actual screenplay as read, and discovering this is a useful thing to do. A film I have used in the past that is excellent for this task and is also on the specification is the closing sequence of *Casablanca*. This film had a number of writers and the script was being written sometimes as cameras were rolling, but it still reads beautifully and translates seamlessly to the big screen. Indeed, budding screenwriters still revere the clarity and brevity of this screenplay, regarding it as a classic of its kind.

* Screenplays do not include camera direction. A well-written screenplay will visualise the scene in the reader's mind but will not tread heavily on the toes of the technical teams who realise the screenplay on film: people such as directors, editors and cinematographers.

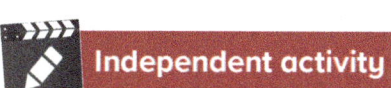

Independent activity

Convert the first page of a novel into a screenplay.

Stretch & challenge

Watch 'Masterclass – Robert McKee Dialogue Analysis for *Casablanca*' on YouTube, which analyses a scene from *Casablanca* in terms of Robert McKee's idea of subtext. Then produce your own video analysis of a scene from the film.

Casablanca aside, what makes a great short film script? The question is in some sense the same for any kind of creative activity involving narrative and character. Answer the following questions about your work and the work of existing filmmakers and you will come some way to at least being able to assess what a good screenplay is:

★ **Are the characters sympathetic?** If not sympathetic, then are they at least people the spectator will root for, an anti-hero for example? Consider *Pitch Black Heist* (Maclean, 2011) where an interesting contrast is created between the two characters through the use of binary oppositions: youth and age, or professional and unprofessional, for example. Both of the main characters are sympathetic; consider how information about them is gradually revealed and the significance of humour as the action becomes more absurd. Characterisation is created in this short film by well-written and often witty dialogue, but also think about how mise-en-scène and action contribute to how we feel about the characters. For example, the scene where Michael dances allows the viewer to see the character as a relatable figure with emotional depth, hinting at a family dynamic.

★ **Is the plot simple?** The plot seems to be a straightforward planning and execution of a heist, but the surreal opening crane shot of the mock-up of the heist using boxes and the black and white aesthetic suggest something more complex and art house than just suspense and action. As the two protagonists are waiting an unusually long time for the heist to start, it becomes clear that this is a character-driven narrative rather than an action-driven one, and towards the middle of the film there are sequences such as miming to the same song during the game of pool and arm wrestling. Such sequences begin to suggest a similarity between the two characters which wasn't apparent in the opening. Liam was very much the joker, arranging the biscuits in a phallic shape on the plate, and Michael seemed eager to take the heist seriously; all of this of course leading to the twist that the heist served a very different purpose for Michael from the assumed initial goal. A secondary goal is clear at the end: revenge on his father.

★ **Is the dialogue essential?** It is possible to write a successful screenplay with minimal use of dialogue, and the marking criteria refers to the purposeful use of dialogue. It is advisable to use action and visual clues to tell the story alongside the dialogue. It's the character that matters. Gromit the dog is silent in *The Wrong Trousers* but he has bags of character, as evidenced by his actions and mannerisms. This hints at a classic piece of filmmaking advice, 'Don't tell – show!' Don't have a character say: 'Quentin is so nervous!' Show us Quentin being nervous, pacing a room, chewing a nail, etc. Don't tell the spectator something that could be as easily shown on screen.

★ **Is there an atmosphere?** The timing and setting of a scene has its own in-built atmosphere. For example, external shots of the so-called 'golden hours' of dawn and dusk are brilliant for evoking a slightly plaintive and wistful mood. Mist, rain, snow, thunder and lightning all create dramatic atmospheres. Then there are settings and sounds. What could be more evocative of natural rhythms and passing time than the sight and sound of waves crashing onto shingle? What about a ticking clock? These images will be brought to life via a filmed cutaway of a clock's second hand ticking in extreme close-up (ECU) or an extreme long shot (ELS) of waves crashing into a shoreline, but in the screenplay they need description.

★ **Have you written about the mise-en-scène?** Of equal importance to establishing an atmosphere is an effective description of mise-en-scène. In *The Silent Child* (Overton, 2017) the locations of an ordinary childhood – the living room, the park, the landing at the top of the stairs and the swimming pool, for example – are used to emphasise that the protagonist Libby is able to have fun and communicate with the social worker Joanne, as opposed to the scenes with her own family where she is largely ignored. The use of a middle-class house is significant in challenging stereotypes about privileged and underprivileged childhoods; this may work well with an analysis of *About a Girl* if childhood is the

theme of your production work, or with *Stutterer* (Cleary, 2015) if your theme is communication or isolation.
- ★ **Will the spectator know when and where the film is taking place?** Using on-screen text or an establishing shot of a sign can help to situate the action in an easy and relatively simple way.
- ★ **What resolution is on offer?** Short films have the luxury of not having to tie up loose ends. In other words, they can end on enigmas or merely the resolution of one simple plot line. The rest is left up to the spectator. Ever since the French New Wave, feature films have at times dared to end on an inconclusive freeze-frame (think of the end of *Vivre sa Vie* (Godard, 1962) or *This Is England* (Meadows, 2006)) or a cut just on the realisation of an important narrative point (think of the final shot of *Memento* (Nolan, 2000)). Short films have this luxury in abundance and are often open-ended, leaving the spectator thinking about the ending and the possibilities suggested; *Pitch Black Heist* is an interesting example of this. *High Maintenance* also has a twist ending which leaves the viewer wondering about the seemingly never-ending cycle of the differing expectations of a romantic relationship according to gender. The ending makes a humorous reference to gender stereotypes, but leaves the viewer pondering the overall messages about the problems caused by these long after the film has ended.

A final point worth making is that screenplays should be heavily drafted. (Remember that the exam board only allows one draft with teacher involvement.) Just like an editor will often fuss and worry over film footage for weeks until it resembles a final product, so too must the screenplay writer expect to make many revisions to the work. Thus, a scene may be rewritten at the last moment or another scene removed. A character may be written out and dialogue freshened up to sound more realistic. A good writer knows when to stop fiddling with their work but they equally know that an excessive fondness for the first draft will probably result in something bloated and unfocused.

How to write the AS Production film extract

Many screenwriters (and the exam board) employ a rule of thumb stating that one page of the screenplay equates to one minute of screen time.

Given that the screenplay requirement asks for between 1,200 and 1,400 words for AS and 1,600 and 1,800 words for AL, and that the storyboard should approximate one-and-a-half minutes of screen time for AS and two minutes of screen time for AL (or roughly two pages of the screenplay), then the script itself should not be far in excess of between five to ten pages long.

Extracts are, as the word implies, extracts from significantly longer imagined works. Likewise, a short film will probably have some narrative conclusion, albeit an enigmatic one.

Students often like to tell stories and those stories usually have some resolution. Even in an extract there can be a satisfying sense of conclusion.

However, if you do decide to make an extract for AS then the exam board's briefs seem in part designed to guide you to either the start or the end of the project. The initial set-up and exposition of a film can be neatly contained in the first few minutes of a project, just as the last few minutes usually give us the conclusion of character arcs and plotlines, the resolution of enigmas or conflicts, and of course the swerve-ball of a 'twist ending'.

Storyboard guidance and layout

A storyboard is a visual illustration of a scene or two (it is not the entire short film!) and it must accompany the screenplay option. It would, however, be useful if it

> **Independent activity**
>
> There are numerous script sites online. Read through a few opening scenes and then watch the final result. The script for *Curfew* (Christensen, 2012) is available online and will help you analyse the construction of a screenplay for a short film, as required by the third bullet point of the marking criteria.

> **Independent activity**
>
> Look back at the short films you have studied. How could you continue them beyond their current endings? Write a further scene.

accompanied, at least informally, any film production work. So, even though the focus of this section of the textbook is the screenplay option, the principles expressed here can absolutely be applied more generally to the planning of a film shoot.

As suggested earlier, the storyboard must consist of about two minutes of screen time or two pages from the actual screenplay. This will mean the generation of approximately 20 storyboarded shots. The submitted storyboard must be digitally photographed and the generally accepted conventions of the form must be used as follows:

★ Shot number and shot description such as: 'Shot 1. Close-up of protagonist's face.'
★ Reference to framing such as: 'Shot 1. Close-up of protagonist's face ranged right.'
★ Duration of shot. Note: even five seconds of screen time is a long time!
★ Reference to detail in the mise-en-scène.
★ Reference to camera movement.
★ References to editing techniques such as 'CUT' or 'DISSOLVE TO'.
★ References to sound design such as 'diegetic' or 'non-diegetic'.

Other requirements are as follows:

★ Images are 'indicative', which allows for creative location and genre choices: science fiction or war film, for example. However, the mise-en-scène should be constructed to match the screenplay as far as possible.
★ Five found shots (shots impossible to film such as an ELS of the Earth in space or an explosion) can be submitted but they must be credited.

A storyboard template is available on the Eduqas website.

Limiting the size of the shots often reduces their impact while showing the image flow on screen is encouraged by the inclusion of more than one picture – hence, this author's preference for two (or more) images. Unless black and white for aesthetic reasons, the images must be printed in colour and the industry aspect ratio should be consistently followed. That means don't shoot portrait shots on your phones. Landscape all the way.

Supporting text should be in a note form only and follow a consistent pattern of expression. No extended prose and certainly no dialogue.

It is also possible to illustrate a complex camera move by linking two shots with an arrow or even showing on-screen movement with arrows.

The biggest mistake students make when constructing storyboards is trying to cover the entire length of the film in too few shots: the exam board requirement is for a continuous sequence and it is a good idea to write the scene number from the screenplay at the top of your storyboard. Flow, shot variety and appropriate technical detail are the key to a well-conceived storyboard.

Mark scheme for the screenplay option

A little under two-thirds (max. 25) of the 40 marks available in the practical aspect of the screenplay option are given for the following Structural Elements:

★ Excellent knowledge and understanding of elements of film.
★ Excellent ability to construct a product appropriate to the brief.
★ Excellent, appropriate, meaningful and sophisticated sense of mise-en-scène through sluglines and scene descriptions.

The final third (max. 15 marks) relates specifically to Key Elements:

★ Excellent knowledge and understanding of screenwriting.
★ Excellent and consistent use of the 'master scene script' layout.

Stretch & challenge

Listen to a radio play. Storyboard the opening few minutes of sound design.

Independent activity

Visit the StoryboardThat website and storyboard a favourite scene from one of the films on this course.

- ★ Purposeful and convincing dialogue.
- ★ Excellent variety of shot types, camera angles and (if appropriate) camera movements, editing and sound design in the storyboard.
- ★ Excellent narrative sequencing in both the screenplay and storyboard, skilfully establishing meaning in a sophisticated way.

It is clear from this rubric that for this practical option to achieve a top grade it must be cinematically sophisticated in its execution and that an effective use of film form is required along with a formal, skilful and consistent presentation of the narrative brief chosen.

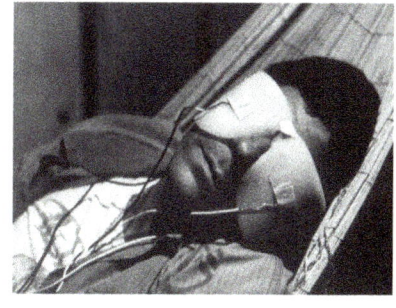

La Jetèe (Marker, 1962)

Evaluative Analysis – guidance for the screenplay/storyboard option

The Evaluative Analysis has a maximum word limit of 1,800 words for AL and 1,250 for AS. Staying in word limits is important and failure to do so is penalised as part of the mark scheme.

With a focus on AL, where the short film compilation needs referencing, the actual analysis of the 80 minutes' worth of short films studied should be throughout the piece, with links made to your own work.

The mark scheme is also clear on what kind of written work is expected for the band 5 criteria for the Evaluative Analysis for the screenplay/storyboard option:

> Excellent application of knowledge and understanding of how narrative features and dramatic qualities of short film are constructed, including through dialogue.
>
> An excellent consideration of the cinematic influences on the production, including short films.
>
> An excellent and perceptive evaluative analysis of how visual/audio and narrative elements are used to create meaning for spectators in relation to other professionally-produced films, including short films.
> (Source: WJEC A Level Film Specification 2017, Version 5 August 2023)

Screenplay extracts are essential for a good Evaluative Analysis.

Page numbers should be in the top right-hand corner and a threefold footer is favoured such as:

| Student name | Screenplay title | Smithtown College 2024 |

Font sizes should not exceed 12 points, should not be anything other than a simple font such as Arial, and film titles should always be in italics with brackets in normal case featuring (director, country of origin, if not UK or USA, and year of release) on first mention; for example, *The Wrong Trousers* (Park, 1993).

The filmmaking option

As previously discussed in the section giving an overview of the Practical work, a brief must be followed and an attention to narrative must form the core of the project. So too must you plan and prepare in terms of a study of the short film form and the production of a (non-assessed) storyboard and screenplay. But, unlike the storyboard and screenplay, which are relatively simple products to produce in terms of technology used, now there is a requirement to engage fully with filming and editing technologies.

It is also worth remembering that this project will be assessed as solo work and that all students must be in charge of the camerawork, editing and the direction of any non-assessed assistants such as sound recordists. It is also worth noting that all practical work will be authenticated and monitored by teachers through five stages before the final stage of the work being handed in:

1 Submission of initial ideas – these could be test shoots.
2 First drafts of storyboards and/or screenplays focusing maybe on just one scene.
3 Mid-project overview – perhaps at the formal complete first draft stage of the screenplay or the 'rough cut' of the film.
4 Student confirms the work is theirs.
5 Directing instructions for non-assessed assistants are submitted.
6 Final work handed in.

Clearly, then, planning and authentication are key. Without either, the production will be a failure.

A final note: performances aren't marked but a canny director will cast well and try to elicit a strong performance. This may be in part down to something very simple such as not accepting the first take of a scene and allowing performers to rehearse. So even though performance isn't assessed, a committed performance at least can make the project as a whole seem satisfying.

Making a film: things to do and not do

Most student filmmakers at A level have fairly generic tastes and the exam board seems happy to encourage this: 'it is recommended that learners … plan genre-based extracts which do not rely on shots impossible to film …' (WJEC/Eduqas Specification 2017, Version 5 August 2023).

There is good sense in this advice, as different genres beat to varied narrative rhythms. For example, the climax of a generic vampire film is usually a bloody one involving the death of the antagonist vampire; another stylised death is demanded in the generic rise and fall saga of a gangster who usually dies in a swarm of hot lead. The generic conventions of a film include its narrative plot points and typical characterisations. That's what makes the short western film referenced above, *The Gunfighter*, so funny. It plays with the often-seen trope of a lone gunman entering a bar and causing trouble for the various stock characters in the bar: saloon girls, a bartender, cowboys playing cards and tough locals. Thus, on one level the visual iconography is largely generic. Genre revisionism occurs most obviously when the narrator's voice is overheard by everyone in the scene, a device that triggers all the action to come. An informed knowledge of the western genre has absolutely informed the production of this film. So, using a genre you know well is a brilliant way to show you can both conform to and perhaps even challenge genre expectations. One easy way to do the latter is by playing with gender and racial stereotypes. *The Gunfighter*, for example, has a black barman and makes a comedic note of the fact in the screenplay.

However, some genres come with health warnings and a degree of caution is encouraged. Real stunts can go wrong and real weapons may kill. No guns or knives is good advice. The key is to be smart about what you use. Accidents happen and there are often ways to imply violence rather than depict it: thus, a spinning car tyre and the Foley addition of screeching rubber evokes a chase just as effectively as depicting it.

So, genre should be your friend but so too should the following top ten filmmaking tips:

1. **Write a short script.** Without scripted dialogue, editing conversations will not work well unless shooting the whole scene in a single take, otherwise you will create awful jump-cuts. The whole crew should then read through the script before further planning takes place and your performers will obviously need time to practise their lines. As the last thing they will probably have available to them is lots of time, keep dialogue simple.
2. **Make a brief storyboard.** Planning shots will help everyone know what they're doing and aid creativity. Today, there is no need to draw a storyboard unless you have the necessary speed and skills to do so. Instead, photograph on your phone the rough 'look' of the film and use this in your first cast and crew meeting.
3. **Shot variety.** Including a varied diet of shots will showcase your talent as a cinematographer and make the viewing experience more satisfying, certainly for a generic film where fast-paced editing is an expectation, such as a chase or a fight. Shot variety is therefore key: aim to mix up your framing and angles and camera moves. Also aim to record the same action from as many angles as possible. If you do this you will need to pay attention to continuity in the mise-en-scène as well as dialogue and framing. A famous rule to pay attention to is the 180°/30° rule which aims to maintain convincing continuity between shots and avoid jump-cuts. It is most famously explained in terms of shot/reverse shot conversations where failure to adhere to the rule can result in an error called 'crossing-the-line'. This would result in characters jumping from one side of the screen to the other and screen direction being lost, thus leaving the audience both confused and aware of the filmmaking techniques being used. Indeed, many of the best edits are invisible.
4. **Five seconds lead in and out.** This aids editing as it means you know the equipment is recording and each scene has a natural stop and start. Professional crews would use a clapperboard and identify the scene number and the take. This verbal format can be adapted and used as follows:
    - Director: 'QUIET ON SET! ROLL CAMERA!'
    - Camera person: Press record button. 'Camera rolling. 5, 4, 3, 2, 1 …'
    - Director: 'Scene 1, Take 1 (pause 2 seconds), ACTION!'
    - Director: 'CUT!'
5. **Rehearse.** 'Practice makes perfect' is a terrible cliché precisely because it's terribly true. The kind of people who are reading this textbook are probably not the kind of people who will rush a film shoot at the very last minute but those that do inevitably produce poor work. Filmmaking is both a technical and creative art form and it involves a number of people both in front of and behind the camera. As such it is something that by definition cannot be left to the last minute. **Plan. Rehearse. Plan again. Rehearse once more. Now shoot.** An ideal situation but the stress-free way to do the job.
6. **Shoot cutaways.** Cutaways are really useful shots to cut to and create interest. They are great for establishing mood and atmosphere, a creepy doll just sitting there, a portrait, a flower or butterfly, a drop of water, some litter, you name it! If cutting from a scene to a cutaway and then back to the scene adds something to the spectator experience or the narration then it's time well spent.
7. **Ensure all cast/props are available for re-shoots.** Even professionals need to re-shoot but without the cast/props it is very difficult. Re-shoots are almost inevitable as there is often a scene you wish you had shot or an aspect of the narrative that seems unclear once filmed and needs focusing through the addition of another scene. A classic error is for a mate to help with your filming and then get a haircut or go on holiday and come back with a deep tan. Also make sure clothes and props used for the shoot are kept safe and accessible until the film is complete.

8. **Mise-en-scène.** This really matters, so take the time to get it right. Dress your characters and have them operating in a world that you have at least tried to make your own through the addition of posters, cutaways, props and lighting. The films of Wallace and Gromit feature a wonderful mise-en-scène such as photographs, newspapers and so on, all of which give insights into the characters and the world they live in.
9. **Sound.** Recording sound on location is very difficult and many beautifully shot films are let down by shoddy sound recording. Avoid, if you can, windy conditions and get your performers to deliver lines with gusto and vim. Try to shoot with your sound levels visible on the camera monitor and re-shoot anything with the metre tipping into the red. Aim to shoot plenty of location Foley and be prepared to add even more in post-production. Sound too needs to be mixed carefully in the final edit, making sure your sound isn't swinging about wildly and uncomfortably in terms of volume. If it is, your audience will hate you and each sound spike will act like a visual jump-cut and remind us all we are watching a film. **Record a wild track.** Shoot a minute or two of ambient sound in whatever location you are in; this really helps smooth over sound glitches caused by switching shots in a noisy location like a station platform. If this doesn't happen, the sound could be different in each take, and sound continuity is broken.
10. **Maintenance and housekeeping.** There is a basic error that students make in terms of kit and that's not maintaining it. Batteries die. So charge them overnight. Light bulbs pop or break. Get replacements. Memory cards corrupt. Have spares. Try not to shoot everything on one card for just this reason. Make back-ups always. Don't leave cameras outside or in car boots: they can get wet or damp or stolen, all of which are disastrous. If looking back at footage shot before actually coming to the edit, try to make a log of shots that are good and shots that are not. That way editing will become a slicker affair, as many students waste reams of time looking at every scene shot and laughing at the outtakes, thus wasting valuable edit time. Finally, let people know where you are and ask permission if filming in public spaces. It would be a courtesy to the public and the local constabulary that you tell them you're shooting a horror film in the nearby woods. Fail to do so and, as the sounds of your actor's faux screams are drowned out by a police helicopter and the red dots of a SWAT team's infra-red gun sights dance on your foreheads, you may wish you'd told someone you were making a film.

Independent activity

A Band 5, the top award for a piece of screenplay writing, should include all of the elements listed below. Copy the script from the following pages and use marker pens to colour code when you think the writer is using or evidencing the following:

- Applies an excellent knowledge and understanding of elements of film.
- Demonstrates an excellent ability to construct a screenplay.
- Incorporates an excellent sense of mise-en-scène through sluglines and scene descriptions.
- Excellent use of appropriate and meaningful location(s).
- Excellent application of knowledge and understanding of screenwriting.
- Purposeful and convincing dialogue.
- Narrative skilfully sequenced.

Mark scheme for the film option

A little under two-thirds (max. 25) of the maximum 40 marks available in the practical aspect of the Filmmaking option are given for the following Structural Elements:

★ Excellent knowledge and understanding of elements of film.
★ Excellent ability to construct a product appropriate to the brief.
★ Excellent, appropriate, meaningful and sophisticated sense of mise-en-scène.

The final third (max. 15 marks) relates specifically to Key Elements:

★ Excellent knowledge and understanding of cinematography, editing and sound.
★ Excellent variety of shot types and camera angles.
★ Resourceful, purposeful and controlled camera movement (if appropriate).
★ Editing meaningful and clear, and showing a range of continuity features.
★ Excellent use of effective sound to establish mood and appropriate audience response.

It is clear from this edited rubric that for practical work to achieve a top grade it must be cinematically sophisticated in its execution, and that an effective use of film form is required along with a skilful narrative focus on the chosen brief.

Summary

★ Practical work 30% of total mark: Project 20%; Evaluative Analysis 10%.
★ Two practical options: Short film (for A level) or extract (for AS); Screenplay and Storyboard.
★ For AL a compilation of short films must be studied and referenced (80 minutes in total from a list of text provided) in the Evaluative Analysis; part of this focus will be on cinematic influences, so reference other films too.
★ One of the four briefs must be chosen.
★ Evidence of planning is vital in terms of assessment and professionalism.
★ The storyboard must be photographed (about 20 frames).
★ The screenplay must use the format suggested.
★ Filmmakers are responsible for their own cinematography/editing/directing.
★ Performance isn't assessed.

Exemplar student film script

Here is the opening extract from an inventive and well-written screenplay by a former student of A level Film Studies for you to consider. The script's title page reads: *The Deep End*.

1   INT. THERAPIST'S OFFICE- MIDDAY

It is a gaudy, gargantuan room with no windows or natural light, fairly bare of furniture, except from two standing lamps and two plastic chairs in the centre of the room and a collection of patronising, 'self-help', posters. On one side sits HENRY PLANTER, 14, who is dressed in a lurid yellow diving suit, complete with snorkel and goggles. Sitting opposite Henry is ELLA GARCIA, a therapist in her mid-20s. Ella wears chapped lipstick and a dishevelled bun in her hair. She sits fumbling awkwardly with the monstrous book that is strewn across her lap. The book is titled 'HOW TO - A BEGINNERS GUIDE TO THERAPY'.

Ella is clearly overwhelmed by the book, skimming through before landing on a page and running her delicate finger down the bind. She then smiles to herself with admiration. Raising her head, ELLA'S gaze lands on HENRY.

                ELLA

        How much sugar do you
        intake on a daily basis?
        Shall I put a 1-2 or 3-4?

Raising her glasses, she waits for a response. Henry sits still, giving her nothing but the sound of heavy breathing through his snorkel. Ella leans slowly forward, closing in on Henry.

                ELLA

        ... Have there been any
        disconcerting influences on
        your life? ... I hear you've
        been causing your mother a
        lot of stress.

Ella leans back, stumped by the lack of response. She is becoming increasingly flustered.

                    ELLA

    It can be a confusing time,
    being a teenager.

    (beat)

    So many emotions, puberty is
    such a hard time ... and drugs!

Ella purses her lips, aggressively scanning through the book for the next thing to say, her eyes darting between HENRY and the book.

                    ELLA

    Well ... I can't see any
    apparent cause for concern.
    (beat)

    How are you handling the sexual
    frustration? It can be hard as a
    teenager to control your ... (beat)
    ... 'urges'.

Ella pauses, blushing deeply. She slams the book shut, trying her best to avoid eye contact with Henry.

                    ELLA

    Well Henry, that seems to have
    covered all our scheduled
    sessions.

Ella gets up and walks past Henry, who is still deadpan and unresponsive. Before exiting, Ella awkwardly pats Henry on the shoulder.

2   EXT. RESIDENTIAL STREET. DAY

LEXI PLANTER, early 40s, Henry's mother, is waiting for him outside the therapist's building. Lexi has bleach blonde hair and wears a fitted T-shirt with her own face on. Henry exits the building, crossing towards Lexi. He walks slowly, stumbling over his diving flippers as he steps down off the pavement, looking searchingly down the street.

                    LEXI PLANTER

    Hennie! Hennie, baby!
    Mummy's here darlin'!

Henry grimaces through his snorkel, embarrassed at his mother's garishness.

                    LEXI PLANTER

    Well Henry, I'm glad we're
    finished with all that therapy
    bollocks. What you need is a
    good friend. Then everything
    can go back to normal.

Lexi pats Henry harshly on the back, causing him to flinch and stumble. The two of them then walk towards their car as Lexi is glued to her phone taking selfies of herself and Henry.

> LEXI PLANTER
>
> My fans are gonna love these Henry. I'm gonna caption it "My baby's normal again", hashtag no more therapy!
> (beat)
>
> You are gonna be normal, aren't you Hen. Take off that silly diving suit. Yeah?

Henry rolls his eyes at his mother's ignorance and sighs deeply through his snorkel. He then slides into the family car, bashing his snorkel on the top of the door as he gets in.

3   INT. HENRY'S BEDROOM. DAY

The bedroom is cramped and claustrophobic. Clearly, it hasn't been renovated since Henry was a child, with remnants of the peeling cerulean blue wallpaper, plastered with cartoon fish and other ocean life.

Henry sits alone at the desk inside his room, still dressed in the diving suit but his goggles are raised to his forehead and his snorkel hangs next to him, no longer in his mouth. He opens the notebook, slowly picking up the pen and chewing it, contemplating his thoughts. He then takes a weighty breath and writes 'HOW TO BE NORMAL' on the opening page.

Henry sighs again, turning the page and writing "SECTION 1: FRIENDS". He then pauses, taking a moment to think, whilst tapping his pen against the table. In the distance, Henry hears faint laughter of children playing in the room next door. He then smiles and shrugs, writing "1a.Sarah and Katie" down on the page.

FLASHBACK

4   INT. PINK. PRINCESS THEMED BEDROOM. DAY

Henry enters the room in which SARAH PLANTER, 7, and KATIE PLANTER, 9, sit playing with their dolls, giggling giddily. The girls look up to and notice HENRY standing, watching them.

> KATIE PLANTER
>
> Wanna play?

Henry looks down at the girls, nodding with reluctance. In response to Henry's nod, the girls turn to each other and grin cheekily.

The girls begin to dress Henry in ridiculous tutus and feather boas, making him play with their dolls and tea sets.

It becomes increasingly apparent that Henry is not enjoying playing with his sisters. Henry's breathing picks up, as the games escalate and, in his eyes, the girls transform into twisted, demented, demonic creatures with fangs and nightmarish clown-faces. The demonic girls then grab and claw at him, forcing Henry to play with them. The room becomes augmented through Henry's eyes, the girls' laughter turning into cackling squeals. The room is plastered with their lurid shadows, surrounding and consuming Henry.

5   INT. HALLWAY. PLANTER HOUSE. DAY

Henry runs out into the hallway, leaving the pink nightmare behind. As he runs, Henry pulls off the fancy dress clothing, looking emotionally scarred.

END FLASHBACK

6   INT. HENRY'S BEDROOM. DAY

Henry is still sitting at his desk, as he crosses out "1a. Sarah and Katie", shivering at the memory. Henry begins to look around the room for inspiration, until his gaze lands on a humungous and tremendously out of place photo of his mother, singing at the opera (the photo is also signed by Lexi). Henry sighs and writes "1b. MUM" onto his page.

FLASHBACK

7   INT. SMALL FAMILY KITCHEN. DAY

Lexi is sitting on the kitchen stool. In one hand she holds a kitschy red phone, the other she uses to twiddle with the phone cord. Henry is sitting on the stairs, eavesdropping on his mother's conversation.

    LEXI PLANTER

    Oh Shazza, I'm just so
    worried, why can't he be
    like a normal son? (beat)
    He's ruining my image!

Lexi listens to her friend on the other side of the line. She nods.

    LEXI PLANTER

    So, are you recording Bake
    Off?

Henry rolls his eyes and goes back to his room.

END FLASHBACK

8   INT. HENRY'S BEDROOM. DAY

Henry still sitting at his desk, quickly crosses out "1b. MUM" from his list and glances out the window staring at his neighbour watering his garden. Henry then writes "1c. MR. Lucas @ NO. 25".

Glossary of key definitions

Aesthetic: the style adopted by an artist (in a film's case the filmmaker) or a film movement. For example, despite the different settings of *Trainspotting* (Boyle, 1996) and *Slumdog Millionaire* (Boyle, 2009), both films share a visual look and feel, created by the director's high-energy visual style, by way of his choice of camerawork, editing and music. German Expressionism was an artistic movement that encompassed theatre, dance, architecture, painting, sculpture and film. The aesthetic shared between expressionist films included exaggeration in performance, setting, lighting and disorientating camera angles.

Aspect ratio: the shape of the image; this affects the composition of the shots. The first aspect ratio used was 4:3: the first number refers to the width of the screen and the second to the height. Therefore, for every 4 inches in width, there will be 3 inches height.

Asynchronous sounds: sound effects that are not matched with a visible source of the sound on screen.

Auteur: certain directors have a strong aesthetic, and you will begin to see recurring visual styles and motifs in their films. These directors have become known as auteurs.

Background (BG): in contrast to the FG, the depth of field is altered by the cinematographer, which can add further meaning.

Balance: different elements are treated equally.

Bathos: humour derived from the juxtaposition of something important with something trivial.

Bias: a concentration on one particular area or viewpoint.

Binary opposition: when two characters or ideologies are set up against one another. It is an important concept of structuralism and can be used to structure representations and help create meaning.

Canted angle: when the frame is deliberately slanted to one side. This is often to portray an intoxicated or unbalanced character or to help convey a sense of unease or disorientation.

Chiaroscuro lighting: this term is borrowed from painting, and refers to the bold use of dark and light. It was a favourite for filmmakers whose work falls into film movements or styles that were filming in black and white, particularly German Expressionism, horror and film noir. It is a kind of painting with light and shadow that makes dramatic moments impactful. It tends to lose its dramatic impact in colour.

Cinematographer: responsible for the look of the film; in charge of the camera technique and translates the director's vision onto the screen, advising the director on camera angles, lighting and special effects.

Citizen journalist: an ordinary person who participates in the collection, reporting and dissemination of news, usually due to finding themselves on the scene before anyone else.

Conglomerate: a company that owns and controls a diverse range of other businesses.

Cultural capital: the knowledge culture, for example literature, films, art and theatre, that a spectator brings to their viewing of a film, which adds extra meaning to that film as a result of associations.

Demographic: sector of the population.

Depth of field: the distance between the nearest and furthest objects in a scene that are in sharp focus in a shot.

Dialect: a form of language that is peculiar to a region or social group.

Dialectic: two opposing or contradictory ideas or views are juxtaposed as a way of examining and discussing them.

Emotional contagion: the creation of empathy; we tend to align our emotions with those we see on screen.

Existentialism: a philosophy that emphasises the existence of the individual person as a free and responsible agent.

Existing property: an existing form of art, such as a film, play, song, book or comic book, that already has a fan base, thus bringing a guaranteed audience to any new film based on the property.

Expressionist: expressionist films depict a widely distorted reality for emotional effect.

Film stock: the type of film used to shoot the film on.

Foreground (FG): people, objects or action closest to the camera.

Frames per second (fps): the frame rate, or the speed that individual frames are projected to give the allusion of movement.

French New Wave: a movement in French cinema of the late 1950s and early 1960s. Directors, such as Jacques Demy, Agnes Varda, Alain Resnais, Claude Chabrol, Jean-Luc Godard and Francois Truffaut, created stylish, energetic and self-conscious films. French New Wave films were typified by on-location shooting, naturalistic acting and ambiguous or unresolved endings. While New Wave directors were inspired by Hollywood auteurs such as Hitchcock, they often broke the rules of Classical Hollywood films. For instance, in *Breathless* (Godard, 1959) the opening scene lacks an establishing shot and a conversation scene breaks the 180° rule.

Grading: colour film always needed to be graded to make sure that colours remain consistent. Like lighting, grading affects the mood and feel of a film. Documentaries are often 'ungraded' and appear flat and lifeless. By grading, filmmakers draw emphasis to colour themes, such as red in *Shaun of the Dead*, or visually emphasise the mood of a scene by taking out the red, to leave a scene looking blue and chilly. With digital technology it is possible to manipulate the colour palette of a scene or even a whole film.

High concept: films centred on a relatively simple scenario that can be easily pitched with a succinctly stated premise.

Intertextual: the practice of one media text paying homage to or referencing another. An example would be Sebastian in *La La Land* swinging around a lamppost like Gene Kelly's character Don in *Singin' in the Rain*.

Iris shot: the frame is partially masked in a circular frame, mimicking the iris of the eye. The iris shot may be used to begin or end a scene or draw our attention to something in the frame. Iris shots were a common convention in silent cinema.

Juxtaposition: the positioning of two shots, characters or scenes in a sequence to encourage the audience to compare and contrast them.

Leitmotif: a reoccurring piece of music that represents characters, actions or themes.

Meta: a deliberate reference to another text and the meaning that brings, often with a sense of irony.

Motif: a recurring element that has symbolic significance in a narrative.

Narrative closure: the feeling of finality generated when all the questions asked in a story are answered.

Narrative devices: techniques used in order to tell a story.

Non-linear editing (NLE): a digital form of editing and the standard for filmmakers today. Because it is digital, you never lose files, you can edit in any order, you can edit audio and video at the same time, and you can revert to previous versions. This means that you can be more experimental in the editing suite and return to an older version if needed.

Post-production: the work that is required to complete the film, after shooting, including the edit, sound mix, music composition, colour grading and computer-generated imagery (CGI) special effects.

Pre-production: the period prior to filming, where key decisions are made, including securing funding, selecting actors and creative personnel, choosing locations, building sets, designing costumes and determining the film's aesthetic, and planning the production schedule.

Production: the period of actual shooting. As this is the most costly part of the project, much planning is done in the pre-production process, with daily shooting schedules prepared to ensure that the material required in each location or with a group of actors is secured. Most films are shot out of sequence.

Proxemics: the positioning of characters in relation to each other, props and location.

Rite of passage: a ceremony marking an important stage in someone's life.

Scene: may consist of one shot or a series of shots depicting a continuous event.

Second wave feminism: a period of feminist activity that began in the USA in the early 1960s and continued to the early 1980s.

Sequence: a series of scenes of shots complete in itself. A sequence may occur in a single setting or several settings, i.e. a car chase. Action should match in sequence, where it continues across several consecutive shots with straight cuts – so that it depicts the event in a continuous manner.

Short film: according to the Academy of Motion Picture and Sciences (AMPAS), a film under 40 minutes in length.

Shot: used to mean different aspects of the filmmaking process.
- For the cinematographer a shot is from the moment the camera starts rolling (action) to the end (cut).
- For the editor a shot is a continuous scene or sequences between two cuts or edits.
- Refers to the process of shooting a film, e.g. 'we shot four minutes of screen time today'.
- There are different types of shot, which refer to the distance between the camera and the subject.

Slapstick: a farcical form of physical comedy, popular in early film comedy. It usually involves violent, physical action, such as pratfalls, chases and practical jokes.

Socio-economic status: an individual or group's social position in relation to others, based on education, occupation and income.

Sound design: involves performing and recording new sounds and editing previously recorded audio, such as sound effects and dialogue. These are combined to create an overall soundtrack to a film.

Star system: the system used by Hollywood studios to create and exploit stars. Studios would publicise films using star personas as the main selling point. Publicity departments would create a public image of the star, sometimes changing their name and details about their personal life.

Star vehicle: films that are sold on the popularity and persona of the leading star. A role may have been written or produced for this particular star.

Stop-motion animation: where the camera is repeatedly stopped and the subject is moved incrementally to produce, once a number of separate shots have been made, the illusion of continuous movement. Claymation uses clay models and stop-motion animation, as in the work of Nick Park and Aardman. This type of animation is distinct from the other main forms of animation such as hand drawings, CGI, rotoscoping, animatronics and motion capture.

Structuralism: the idea that films can best be understood through an examination of their underlying structure, including exploring how meaning is produced through binary oppositions.

Surrealism: an international 20th-century movement of artists, writers and philosophers who valued the unconscious mind and dreams. They rejected conventional moral and artistic values. The surrealists were heavily influenced by the work of Sigmund Freud, particularly his book *The Interpretation of Dreams* (1899), which argued that our dreams reveal our unconscious motivations or desires.

Synchronous sounds: contribute to the realism of film as the sounds heard match the actions on screen.

Tentpole: a movie with a massive budget deemed by the studio to carry less financial risk. It is marketed heavily and given an extended saturation release. Its revenue is intended to help financially support the other films released by the studio.

Trope: a recurring or significant theme.

Two-reelers: short silent films around 20 minutes long. During the 1920s, comedy two-reelers were screened in cinemas as supporting films for a feature-length film.

Verisimilitude: about giving the appearance of reality or truth. This does not mean that the world is presented as real, just believable within the context of the world in which the film is set. For example, we know that in the real world, people do not break into song when they fall in love. In a musical, we accept this convention, but if this happened in a gritty thriller, it would be out of place.

Vertical integration: when a company controls the different stages of a product's process or construction. During the studio era, the Big Five Hollywood studios were vertically integrated, as they controlled production, distribution and exhibition.

Voice of god: a narration technique in which the narration is given anonymously and authoritatively.

References

Allen, K. (2015) 'How Long are those Oscar Coattails for Box Office Indie Films?', CNBC, www.cnbc.com/2015/03/06/how-long-are-thoseoscar-coattails-for-box-office-indie-films.html?view=story&%24DEVICE%24=native-android-tablet.

Alvarado, M. & Gutch, R. (1987) *Learning the Media: Introduction to Media Teaching*, Palgrave.

Anderson, A. (2013) '10 Lessons on Filmmaking *from Beasts of the Southern Wild*'s Benh Zeitlin', *Filmmaker Magazine*, http://filmmakermagazine.com/65614-10-lessons-on-filmmaking-from-beastsof-the-southern-wilds-benh-zeitlin/#.Wh-p07p2tTA/.

Anthony, A. (2017) 'Jordan Peele on Making a Hit Comedy Horror Movie Out of America's Racial Tensions', *The Guardian*, https://www.theguardian.com/film/2017/mar/04/jordan-peele-interview-get-out-its-about-purging-our-fears-horror-film-daniel-kaluuya.

Arneson, K. (2012) 'Representation through Documentary: A Postmodern assessment', *Artifacts*, https://artifactsjournal.missouri.edu/2012/03/representation-through-documentary-apost-modern-assessment/.

ARRI News (2017) '*Beasts of the Southern Wild*', www.arri.com/news/news/beastsof-the-southern-wild.

Aufderheide, P. (2008) *Documentary Film: A Very Short Introduction*, Oxford University Press.

Baker, S. (2011) *Media Studies Key Concepts: Representation*, www.slideshare.net/tinkertaylor1981/representation-revision-booklet.

Barlow, H. (2016, 1 March) '*Mustang* is a Stirring Tale of Girlhood', *Irish Examiner*, www.irishexaminer.com/lifestyle/artsfilmtv/mustang-is-a-stirring-tale-ofgirlhood-384801.html.

Barson, M. *Douglas Sirk*, Britannica, https://www.britannica.com/topic/University-of-Munich.

Beck, J. (2016) *Designing Sound: Audiovisual Aesthetics in 1970s American Cinema*, Rutgers University Press.

Biancolli, A. (2012) '*Beasts of the Southern Wild Review*: Wet and Wild', SFGate, www.sfgate.com/movies/article/Beasts-of-the-Southern-Wild-review-Wet-and-wild-3686131.php.

Blair, D. (2017) 'Iran's Big Woman Problem: All of the Things Iranian Women aren't Allowed to Do', *The Telegraph*, www.telegraph.co.uk/women/womens-life/11875128/Iranswomen-problem-All-of-the-things-Iranian-women-arent-allowed.html.

Bogdanovich, P. (2011) '1928: The Last and Greatest Year of the Original Motion Picture Arat, B.S. (Before Sound)', IndieWire, www.indiewire.com/2011/01/1928-the-last-andgreatest-year-of-the-original-motionpicture-art-b-s-before-sound-131788/.

Bordwell, D. & Thompson, D. (2012) *Film Art: An Introduction*, McGraw.

Bordwell, D., Staiger, J. & Thompson, K. (1988) *The Classical Hollywood Cinema: Film Style and Mode of Production to 1960*, Routledge.

Bouie, J. (2015) 'Where Black Lives Matter Began', slate.com, www.slate.com/articles/news_and_politics/politics/2015/08/hurricane_katrina_10th_anniversary_how_the_black_lives_matter_movement_was.html.

Boxofficemojo.com (2016a) 2016 Domestic Grosses, www.boxofficemojo.com/yearly/chart/?yr=2016&p=.htm.

Boxofficemojo.com (2016b) Studio Market Share, www.boxofficemojo.com/studio/?view=company&view2=yearly&yr=2016&p=.htm.

Boxofficemojo.com (2017b) Stories We Tell, www.boxofficemojo.com/movies/?id=storieswetell.htm.

Bradshaw, P. (2012) '*Beasts of the Southern Wild Review* – Superbly Energetic Vision of Climate Catastrophe', *The Guardian*, https://www.theguardian.com/film/2012/oct/18/beast-southern-wild-review.

British Film Institute (BFI) (2017) Statistical Yearbook, www.bfi.org.uk/education-research/film-industrystatistics-research/statistical-yearbook.

Brody, R. (n.d.) '*Mustang*', *The New Yorker*, www.newyorker.com/goings-onabouttown/movies/mustang.

Brownlow, K. (1992) *The Parade's Gone By...*, University of California Press.

Buder, E. (2015) 'Meet France's Oscar Entry, '*Mustang*,' a Controversial 5-Headed Monster of Feminity', IndieWire, www.indiewire.com/2015/11/meet-frances-oscar-entrymustang-a-controversial-5-headedmonster-of-femininity-50271/.

Bunuel, L. (2002) *An Unspeakable Betrayal: Selected Writings of Luis Buñuel*, University of California Press.

Calhoun, D. (2016) '*La La Land*', *Time Out*, www.timeout.com/sydney/film/la-la-land.

Chamboredon, J.C. (2015) 'Q&A with Warren Ellis – Composer of *Mustang*', Milan Records, https://milanrecords.com/qa-with-warren-elliscomposer-of-mustang/.

Chivers, S. (2011) *The Silvering Screen: Old Age and Disability in Cinema*, University of Toronto Press.

Chung, N. (2016) 'Toast Points for the Week of January 15th', The Toast, http://the-toast.net/2016/01/15/toastpoints-week-of-jan-15th/.

CinemaReview.com (2017) Stories We Tell, www.cinemareview.com/production.asp?prodid=13494#.

Cleary, S. (2021) 'Where to begin with Douglas Sirk', BFI, https://www.bfi.org.uk/features/where-begin-with-douglas-sirk.

Cochrane, K. (2010) 'Kim Longinotto: "Film-making Saved My Life",' *The Guardian*, www.theguardian.com/lifeandstyle/2010/feb/12/longinotto-film-making-saved-life.

Cooke, R. (2016) 'Deniz Gamze Ergüven: "For Women in Turkey it's Like the Middle Ages"', *The Observer*, www.theguardian.com/film/2016/may/15/.

Coplan, A. (2006) 'Catching Characters' Emotions: Emotional Contagion Responses to Narrative Fiction Film', *Film Studies*, 8, www.academia.edu/6434449/Catching_Characters_Emotions_Emotional_Contagion_Responses_to_Narrative_Fiction_Film.

Cox, D. (2012) Why Do Films Do Such a Bad Job of Portraying Old People?', *The Guardian*, www.theguardian.com/film/filmblog/2012/feb/28/films-bad-job-portraying-oldpeople.

Davis, D.K. & Baron, S.J. (1981) *A History of Our Understanding of Mass Communication*, Wadsworth Publishing.

Deguzman, K. (2024). 'What are the Major Film Studios – Hollywood's Big Five', StudioBinder, https://www.studiobinder.com/blog/what-are-the-major-film-studios/.

Desta, Y. (2019) 'The Joker Didn't Inspire the Aurora Shooter, But the Rumor Won't Go Away', *Vanity Fair*, https://www.vanityfair.com/hollywood/2019/10/joker-aurora-shooting-rumor.

Dodds, F. (2020) 'Joker' Proves the Power of Empathy, *Variety*, https://feature.variety.com/joker/joker-proves-the-power-of-empathy.

Dönmez-Colin, G. (2008) *Turkish Cinema: Identity, Distance and Belonging*, Reaktion Books.

Doucet, A. (2015) 'Ontological Narrativity and the Performativity of the Stories We Tell Stories We Tell', *Visual Studies*, 30 (1): 98–117, www.tandfonline.com/doi/abs/10.1080/1472586X.2015.996415?src=recsys&journalCode=rvst20.

Driscoll, C. (n.d.) Modernism, Cinema Adolescence: Another History for Teen Film, screeningthepast.com, www.screeningthepast.com/2011/11/modernism-cinema-adolescenceanother-history-for-teen-film/

Dyer, R. (1997) *White: Essays on Race and Culture*, Routledge.

Dyer, R. (1998) *Stars*, BFI Publishing.

Earle, S. (2017) 'The Politics of Nostalgia', *Jacobin*, www.jacobinmag.com/2017/01/donald-trumpinauguration-nationalism/.

Ebert, R. (1969) '*The Night of the Living Dead*', *Reader's Digest*.

Ebert, R. (1991) 'It's High Tide for Black New Wave', *Roger Ebert's Journal*, www.rogerebert.com/rogers-journal/itshigh-tide-for-black-new-wave.

Edwards, G. (2014) 'Fight the Power: Spike Lee on "Do the Right Thing"', *Rolling Stone*, www.rollingstone.com/movies/news/fight-the-power-spikelee-on-do-the-right-thing-20140620.

Eggert, B. (2008) '*Night of the Living Dead*', *Deep Focus Review*, https://www.deepfocusreview.com/definitives/night-of-the-living-dead/.

Eisner, L.H. (1969) *The Haunted Screen: Expressionism in the German Cinema and the Influence of Max Reinhardt*, University of California Press.

Fiske, J. (2010) *Introduction to Communication Studies*, 3rd edn, Taylor & Francis.

Freud, S. (1899) *The Interpretation of Dreams*.

Friedman, L.D. (2000) *Bonnie and Clyde*, BFI Publishing.

Gallagher, Tag. (2005) 'White Melodrama: Douglas Sirk', *Senses of Cinema*, https://www.sensesofcinema.com/2005/feature-articles/sirk-2/.

Geiger, J. & Rutsky, R.L. (2013) '*Casablanca*', in *Film Analysis: A Norton Reader*, W.W. Norton.

Girls Not Brides (2017) 'Turkey', www.girlsnotbrides.org/child-marriage/turkey/.

Global Queer Cinema. (2012) 'Queer Uncanny#1: Mulholland Drive "Have You Done This Before?"', https://reframe.sussex.ac.uk/gqc/2012/06/26/queer-uncanny1-mulholland-drive-have-you-done-this-before/.

Glynn, A. (2017) 'David Lynch Is Not an Auteur: On the Enduring Brilliance of Twin Peaks', pastemagazine.com, https://www.pastemagazine.com/tv/twin-peaks/david-lynch-is-not-an-auteur-on-the-enduring-brill.

Goldstein, J.H. (1998) *Why We Watch: The Attractions of Violent Entertainment*, Oxford University Press.

Golshiri, G. (2015) 'Jafar Panahi Goes Through Red Lights', *Le Monde*, www.newwavefilms.co.uk/assets/1143/Jafar_Panahi_goes_through_red_lights.pdf.

Gomery, D. (1998) 'Hollywood as Industry', in The Oxford Guide to Film Studies, ed. J. Hill & P. Gibson (eds), Oxford University Press.

Google Arts & Culture. '1968: The Year that Changed America', https://artsandculture.google.com/story/1968-the-year-that-changed-america/ggUBmE4X0VXGIA?hl=en.

Gray, C. (2016) 'Vera Chytilova for Beginners', BFI Film Forever, www.bfi.org.uk/news-opinion/news-bfi/features/vera-chytilova-beginners.

Grobar, M. (2017) 'From "Boogie Nights" to "Mean Streets": *La La Land* Sound Editors on Damien Chazelle's Sonic Inspirations', *Deadline*, http://deadline.com/2017/02/la-la-land-oscarsai-ling-lee-mildred-iatrou-sound-editinginterview-news-1201899086/.

Gross (2020) '"The System's Broken"' and "Joker" director aimed to explore that on screen', NPR.org, https://www.npr.org/2020/01/06/793336776/the-system-s-broken-and-joker-director-aimed-to-explore-that-on-screen.

Guerrasio, J. (2017) 'Allison Williams breaks down the infamous Froot Loops scene in "*Get Out*"', Business Insider, https://www.businessinsider.com/allison-williams-get-out-froot-loops-scene-2017-5.

Gunning, T. (1986) 'The Cinema of Attractions: Early Film, its Spectator and the Avant-Garde', *Wide Angle*, 8 (3&4).

Hall, S. (1973) *Encoding and Decoding in the Television Discourse*, Centre for Contemporary Cultural Studies.

Hallihan, M. (2016) 'The 10 Best Iranian Films About Women', Taste of Cinema, www.tasteofcinema.com/2016/the-10-best-iranian-films-about-women/.

Hardy, R. (2015) 'Easyrig Mini is a Budget Version of One of the Most Interesting Camera Stabilizers Out There', No Film School, https://nofilmschool.com/2015/03/easyrig-ministory-heart-video.

Harris, A. (2016) '*La La Land*'s Many References to Classic Movies: A Guide', *Slate*, www.slate.com/blogs/browbeat/2016/12/13/la_la_land_s_many_references_to_classic_movies_from_singin_in_the_rain_to.html.

Hattam, J. (2016) 'Oscar-Nominee "*Mustang*" Puts Turkey in Unwanted Spotlight', We.News, http://womensenews.org/2016/02/133986/.

Hauke, C. (2013) *Visible Minds: Movies, Modernity and the Unconscious*, Routledge.

Hoad, P. (2023) 'Deviant obsessions: how David Lynch predicted our fragmented times', *The Guardian*, https://www.theguardian.com/film/2023/jan/09/david-lynch-twin-peaks-director-predicted-our-times.

hooks, b. (2012) 'No Love in the World', www.newblackmaninexile.net/2012/09/bell-hooks-no-love-in-wild.html.

Horton, A. (ed.) (1991) *Comedy/Cinema/Theory*, University of California Press.

Hudgins, S. (2017) 'A Chronic Problem: Violence Against Women in Turkey', Huffington Post, www.huffingtonpost.com/sarabrynn-hudgins/a-chronicproblem-violenc_b_13649898.html.

Hurriyet Daily News (2018) 'Survey Sheds Light on Severity of Turkey's Child Marriage Problem', www.hurriyetdailynews.com/survey-shedslight-on-severity-of-turkeys-childmarriage-problem-126103.

Hutchinson, P. & Barrett, A. (2017) 10 Great German Expressionist Films, BFI, www.bfi.org.uk/news-opinion/news-bfi/lists/10-great-german-expressionist-films.

Ide, W. (2016) '*Mustang* Review – Teen Tension in Anatolia', *The Guardian*, www.theguardian.com/film/2016/may/15/mustang-review-women-ruralturkey-oscar-nominated.

Independent Film & Television Alliance (2013) IFTA FAQs, www.ifta-online.org/sites/default/files/FAQs_updated+Sep2013.pdf.

Independent Film & Television Alliance (n.d.) 'What is an Independent?', www.ifta-online.org/what-independent.

Iris (2014) 'The New Cinema Communication', www.obs.coe.int/documents/205595/264635/IRIS%2B_2014-1_ENcomplet.pdf/bbc3325b-379b-46ec-9664-e879e0b6b452.

Isenberg, N. (2017) *We'll Always Have Casablanca: The Life, Legend, and Afterlife of Hollywood's Most Beloved Movie*, Faber & Faber.

Kael, P. (1967) '*Bonnie and Clyde*', *The New Yorker*, www.newyorker.com/magazine/1967/10/21/bonnie-andclyde.

Kenigsberg, B. (2012) '*Beasts of the Southern Wild*: A Republican Fantasy?', *Time Out Chicago*, www.timeout.com/chicago/film/beasts-of-the-southernwild-a-republican-fantasy.

Klawans, S. (2018) '*Night of the Living Dead*: Mere Anarchy Is Loosed', Criterion Collection, https://www.criterion.com/current/posts/5390-night-of-the-living-dead-mere-anarchy-is-loosed.

Koszarski, R. (2005) *Fort Lee: The Film Town*, Indiana University Press.

Kuhn, A. & Westwell, G. (2012) *A Dictionary of Film Studies*, Oxford University Press.

Lacey, L. (2010) Kim Longinotto: Capturing Women in Critical Transitions, www.theglobeandmail.com/arts/film/kim-longinotto-capturing-women-incritical-transitions/article1211066/.

Lang, B. (2016) 'Study: Female Protagonists on the Rise in Hollywood – but the Majority Are White', Variety, https://variety.com/2016/film/news/study-female-protagonists-on-the-rise-in-hollywood-but-the-majority-are-white-1201701004/.

Lemercier, F. (2015) 'Deniz Gamze Ergüven: Director', Cineuropa, www.cineuropa.org/it.aspx?t=interview&l=en&did=293768.

Leszkiewicz, A. (2017) 'In Defence of *La La Land*', *New Statesman*, www.newstatesman.com/culture/film/2017/02/defence-la-la-land.

Lévi-Strauss, C. (1995) *Myth and Meaning: Cracking the Code of Culture*, Schocken Books.

Lidz, F. (2012) 'How Benh Zeitlin Made Beasts of the Southern Wild', Smithsonian Magazine, www.smithsonianmag.com/arts-culture/how-benh-zeitlinmade-beasts-of-the-southern-wild-135132724/?device=iphone&noist=&page=4.

Mallinder, L. (2012) 'What Does it Mean to be Canadian?', BBC News, www.bbc.co.uk/news/world-radio-andtv-18086952.

Mast, G. (1979) *The Comic Mind: Comedy and the Movies*, University of Chicago Press.

McNary, D. (2017) '*La La Land* Director Damien Chazelle Explains His Approach to Casting the Original Musical', *Variety*, http://variety.com/2017/film/news/damien-chazelle-lala-land-casting-1201978332/.

McVeigh, T. & Colley, C. (2015) 'We Record All the Killing of Women by Men. You See a Pattern', *The Guardian*, www.theguardian.com/society/2015/feb/08/killing-of-womenby-men-record-database-femicide.

Means, S.P. (2016) 'Movie Review: Spirited Girls Face Religious Restrictions in Powerful *Mustang*', *Salt Lake Tribune*, http://archive.sltrib.com/article.php?id=3410725&itype=CMSID.

Metacritic (n.d.) 'Stories We Tell: Movie Details & Credits', www.metacritic.com/movie/stories-we-tell.

Miller, J. (2017a) 'Emma Stone and Ryan Gosling's *La La Land* Costumes Were Inspired by These Old Hollywood Stars', *Vanity Fair*, www.vanityfair.com/hollywood/2017/02/emma-stone-ryan-gosling-la-la-landcostumes.

Miller, J. (2017b) 'The Clever Tricks that Made *La La Land* Look Technicolor and Timeless', *Vanity Fair*, www.vanityfair.com/hollywood/2017/02/la-la-land-production-design.

Millman, Z. (2017) 'Never Shined So Brightly: The Use of Color in *La La Land*', Film School Rejects, https://filmschoolrejects.com/color-in-la-la-land-26939a11accd/.

Ministry of Culture & Islamic Guidance (2017) Introduction of Ministry, www.farhang.gov.ir/en/profileofministry/responsibilities.

Mohdin, A. (2020) 'Racism's still around': Notting Hill 50 years on from *Mangrove*, *The Guardian*, https://www.theguardian.com/uk-news/2020/nov/27/racisms-still-around-notting-hill-50-years-on-from-mangrove.

Monaco, J. (2000) *The Dictionary of New Media: The New Digital World*, Harbor Electronic Publishing.

Most, M. (2013) 'Conversation with Cinematographer Ben Richardson about his Work on *Beasts of the Southern Wild*, by Benh Zeitlin, *AFC*, www.afcinema.com/Conversation-withcinematographer-Ben-Richardsonabout-his-work-on-Beasts-of-the-Southern-Wild-by-Benh-Zeitlin.html?lang=en.

Mudde, C. (2016) 'Can We Stop the Politics of Nostalgia that Have Dominated 2016?', Newsweek, www.newsweek.com/1950s-1930s-racism-useurope-nostalgia-cas-mudde-531546.

Mueller, M. (2016) 'How Damien Chazelle Made *La La Land* for Just $30m', ScreenDaily, www.screendaily.com/features/how-damienchazelle-made-la-la-land-for-just-30m/5112184.article.

Mulvey, L. (1999) 'Visual Pleasure and Narrative Cinema', in L. Braudy & M. Cohen (eds) *Film Theory and Criticism: Introductory Readings*.

Mulvey, L. (2009) *Visual and Other Pleasures*, Palgrave Macmillan.

Murphy, M. (2016) 'LA Transcendental: How *La La Land* Chases the Sublime', *New York Times*, www.nytimes.com/2016/11/06/movies/la-laland-stars-ryan-gosling-emma-stoneand-los-angeles.html.

Nelson, G. (2017) 'The Unbearable Whiteness of *La La Land*', *Paste Magazine*, www.pastemagazine.com/articles/2017/01/the-unbearablewhiteness-of-la-la-land.html.

Newby, R. (2018) 'The Lingering Horror of "*Night of the Living Dead*"', *The Hollywood Reporter*, https://www.hollywoodreporter.com/movies/movie-news/why-night-living-dead-is-more-relevant-ever-1145708/.

Nichols, B. (2010) *Introduction to Documentary*, Indiana University Press.

O'Falt, C. (2017a) 'How *La La Land* Cinematographer Linus Sandgren Taught His Cameras to Dance', *IndieWire*, www.indiewire.com/2017/02/la-la-land-cinematographydirector-of-photography-linussandgren-1201776704/.

O'Falt, C. (2017b) 'Why *La La Land* Was So Much Harder to Edit than *Whiplash*', *IndieWire*, www.indiewire.com/2017/02/la-laland-damien-chazelle-tom-crossediting-filmmaker-toolkit-podcastepisode-21-1201785368/.

Ordona, M. (2017) 'Lights, Camera, Colors Give La La Land its Lavish Look', *Los Angeles Times*, www.latimes.com/entertainment/envelope/laen-mn-0216-craft-la-la-look-20170216-story.html.

Ortner, S.B. (2012) 'Against Hollywood: American Independent Film as a Critical Cultural Movement', *Journal of Ethnographic Theory*, 2(2), www.haujournal.org/index.php/hau/article/view/hau2.2.002/1004.

Papadakis, P. (2016) The 30 Best Films Starring Mostly Non- Professional Actors, Taste of Cinema, www.tasteofcinema.com/2016/the-30-best-films-starring-mostly-nonprofessional-actors/#ixzz55TZqXXdl.

Parkinson, D. (2016) '*Mustang* Review', *Empire*, www.empireonline.com/movies/mustang/review/.

Patterson, J. (2017) '*La La Land*: Why this Magical Musical Will Transport you From Trump-World', *The Guardian*, www.theguardian.com/film/2017/jan/09/why-musical-la-la-land-will-transportyou-from-trump-world.

Patterson, J. (2017) '*Mulholland Drive*: David Lynch's masterpiece is a wide-open work of art', *The Guardian*, https://www.theguardian.com/film/2017/apr/10/mulholland-drive-david-lynch-rerelease.

Polley, S. (2012) 'Stories We Tell: A Post by Sarah Polley', *NFB*, http://blog.nfb.ca/blog/2012/08/29/storieswe-tell-a-post-by-sarah-polley/.

Pidd, H. (2006) 'The Invisible Woman', *The Guardian*, www.theguardian.com/film/2006/mar/14/television.

Quinn, J. (2012) *This Much is True: 14 Directors on Documentary Filmmaking*, A&C Black.

Rana, K. (2002) 'The (Post) Colonial Demasculinisation within *Mogul Mowgli*', *British Asian Women's Magazine*, https://www.britishasianwomensmagazine.com/website/the-post-colonial-demasculinisation-within-mogul-mowgli-2020.

Rea, S. (2012) '*Beasts of the Southern Wild*: A Magical Trip to Bayou Country', *The Inquirer*, https://www.inquirer.com/philly/entertainment/movies/20120713__Beasts_of_the_Southern_Wild___A_magical_trip_to_bayou_country.html.

Renee, V. (2013) 'Roger Ebert on the Nature of Film: A Movie is Not a Logical Art Form', *Nofilmschool*, https://nofilmschool.com/2013/07/roger-ebert-movie-not-a-logical-art-form.

Rotha, P. (1935) 'Traditions of Documentary Film', www.scribd.com/document/267134051/Paul-Rotha-Documentary-Film.

Sarris, A. (1962) Notes on the Auteur Theory. *Film Culture*, (Winter 1962-3).

Saunders, D. (2007, 23 May) 'My Interview with Jafar Panahi', http://dougsaunders.net/2007/05/interview-jafar-panahiiran/.

Schatz, T. (1998) *The Genius of the System: Hollywood Film-making in the Studio Era*, University of Texas Press.

Severson, K. (2020) 'Is "*Joker*" Dangerous? The Joker Movie Controversy Explained', *StudioBinder*, https://www.studiobinder.com/blog/joker-movie-controversy.

Shadoian, J. (2003) *Dreams and Dead Ends: The American Gangster Film*, Oxford University Press.

Sheva. A. (2016) '86% of Turkish Women Suffer Domestic Abuse', Arutz Sheva, www.israelnationalnews.com/News/News.aspx/210182

Singer, M. (2012) Read '"*Beasts of the Southern Wild*", Pros and Cons: Weighing the arguments around the most divisive movie of the year', *IndieWire*, https://

www.indiewire.com/news/general-news/beasts-of-the-southern-wild-pro-and-con-weighing-the-arguments-around-the-most-divisive-movie-of-the-year-129578/.

Singleton, R.S. & Conrad, J.A. (2000) *Filmmaker's Dictionary*, 2nd edn, Lone Eagle.

Siskel, G. & Ebert, R. (1989) Siskel & Ebert 1989 – Best of 1989, www.youtube.com/watch?v=XjYS8EUakgs.

Smit, D. (2012) *Ingrid Bergman: The Life, Career and Public Image*, McFarland.

Stephen (2015) A Review of the ARRI Alexa XT Professional Production Camera, http://4k.com/camera/a-reviewof-the-arri-alexa-xt-4k-productioncamera/.

Stevens, I. (2015) 'Rebel Charm: Benh Zeitlin on *Beasts of the Southern Wild*', Sight & Sound, www.bfi.org.uk/news-opinion/sight-soundmagazine/interviews/lff-blog-rebelcharm-benh-zeitlin-beasts-southernwild.

Stevens, I. (2022) 'No man's land: Céline Sciamma on *Portrait of a Lady on Fire*', BFI, https://www.bfi.org.uk/sight-and-sound/features/no-mans-land-celine-sciamma-portrait-lady-fire.

Stevenson, B. (2017) From Los Angeles to *La La Land*: Mapping Whiteness in the Wake of Cinema, Senses of Cinema, http://sensesofcinema.com/2017/feature-articles/from-losangeles-to-la-la-land/.

Summit Entertainment (2016) *La La Land* Production Notes, www.lionsgatepublicity.com/uploads/assets/LA%20LA%20LAND%20NOTES%20FINAL%209.7.16.pdf.

Sweeney, K.W. (2007) *Buster Keaton: Interviews*, University Press of Mississippi.

The Numbers, '*Night of the Living Dead* (1968)', https://www.the-numbers.com/movie/Night-of-the-Living-Dead-(1968)#tab=summary.

Tomberlin, J. (2021) 'David Lynch's DVD Clues to 'Unlocking' *Mulholland Drive*', Screenrant, https://screenrant.com/mulholland-drive-movie-david-lynch-clues/.

Tookey, C. (2009) *Casablanca*, Movie Film Review, www.movie-film-review.com/devFilm.asp?ID=2637.

USC (2017) Hollywood Sticks to the Script: Diversity, On Screen and Behind the Camera, Remains Elusive, https://news.usc.edu/125565/hollywood-sticksto-the-script-films-arent-more-inclusivedespite-a-decade-of-advocacy.

Weisssberg, J. (2015) 'Film Review: *Mustang*', Variety, http://variety.com/2015/film/festivals/mustangreview-cannes-1201500486/.

Welsh, I. (1994) *Trainspotting*, Vitage.

WJEC (2017a) Film Studies AS/A Level (From 2017), http://wjec.co.uk/qualifications/film-studies/eduqas-filmstudies-as-level-from-2017/.

Wolfe, C and Petro, P (ed). (2010). *Idols of Modernity: Movie Stars of the 1920s*, Rutgers University Press.

Wood, R. (1976) 'Murnau's Midnight and Sunrise', *Film Comment*, May–June.

York University (n.d.) *Ethnicity & Neighbourhood*, www.yorku.ca/anderson/geog2060su15/ethnicity%20and%20neighbourhood.pdf.

Zacharek, S. (2019) 'The Strange Story of "*Joker*", a Modern Moral Panic', *Forbes*, https://www.forbes.com/sites/danidiplacido/2019/10/07/the-strange-story-of-joker-a-modern-moral-panic/.

Index

A

Aardman Studios 302
abstract forms 21
Academy Awards 253
Academy of Motion Pictures Arts and Sciences (AMPAS) 253
A Clockwork Orange (1971) 37
active spectatorship theory 117
additional dialogue recording (ADR) 34
ad-libbing 41
adolescence 55
aerial shot 11
aesthetics 5–6, 57–65, 90–1, 114, 132, 151, 163, 179, 210–11, 226–7, 238, 253, 264, 274, 295–6
age, representations of 54–7, 92, 101, 115, 133, 141, 151, 179–80, 186, 200, 211–12, 227, 238–9, 254, 275–6, 293–5
Akerman, Chantal 276, 279
Alien (1979) 11, 17, 75–7
Al-Kateab, Waad 231–41
All About Eve (1950) 73–5
All That Heaven Allows (1955) 64
ambient sounds 34
    see also diegetic sound
Another Round (2020) 16
archive footage 220, 226
Arrival (2016) 30
art house cinema 179
artificial light 15
aspect ratio 7
asymmetrical composition 20
asynchronous sound 37
audience response 116–18
aural link 6
auteurs 6, 82, 97–100, 105, 278–9, 287
avant-garde 268
awards 127

B

baby boomers 95
background 9
background artists 34
back light 15, 17
Baker, Steve 44
bathos 157
Battleship Potemkin (1925) 32
Beasts of the Southern Wild (2012) 125–36, 143
Beatty, Warren 100
Beau Travail (1999) 62
Bechdel Test 50
Beck, Jay 89
Belfast (2021) 17, 77–9
Berger, John 46
bias 223

binary opposition 45
black and white 18
Black Lives Matter 71–2, 129
body codes 38–9
Bogdanovich, Peter 256
Bong Joon-ho 202–15
Bonnie and Clyde (1967) 81, 99
    aesthetics 91
    cinematography 87
    cultural, political and social contexts 93–7
    editing 88
    film form 84–5
    mise-en-scène 87–8
    performance 90
    representations 92–3
    sound 88–9
Bordwell, David 175
Bowling for Columbine (2002) 221
Boyle, Danny 146
Boyz n the Hood (1991) 53
Branagh, Kenneth 78–9
Brand, Neil 36
breaking the fourth wall 27, 34
Breathless (1959) 84–5
British Board of Film Classification (BBFC) 72, 77
British film 77–9, 145–6
    see also *Mogul Mowgli* (2020); *Trainspotting* (1996)
Broomfield, Nick 229–30
Burton, Tim 98

C

camera angles 11–12, 28, 32, 84, 88
camera movements 13
cameras 14, 229
capitalism 203–5, 213–14, 284
Captain Fantastic (2016) 36, 43, 54–7
Carol (2015) 57, 63–5
Casablanca (1942) 18, 81, 98
    aesthetics 90–1
    cinematography 86–7
    cultural, political and social contexts 93–7
    editing 88
    film form 83–4
    mise-en-scène 87
    performance 90
    representations 92–3
    sound 88–9
casting 42, 48, 113, 132
censorship 67–8, 74–5, 190–2
Chazelle, Damien 107–9
chiaroscuro lighting 15
child marriage 173, 181
children 54–5, 133, 239
Chungking Express (1994) 62

Chytilová, Věra 271, 274
cinema attendance 82
cinema industry 179
cinematographer 7
cinematography
    colour 17–18, 21
    composition 19–21
    definition 7
    in documentary 223–4, 234–5
    lighting 15–17, 85–6
    shots and camera angles 7–14
    silent cinema 261–2
    see also mise-en-scène
cinéma vérité 14
Circle, The (2000) 191–2
citizen journalists 233
City of God (2002) 12, 18, 30, 32
city symphonies 33
classicism 41
close-up shot 9, 84
Cold War era 103, 269
colour 17–18, 21, 24–5, 183
    psychology of 21
coming of age narratives 55
communication
    body codes 38–9
    non-verbal 37–9
    verbal 39–40
composition 19–21
contextual comparisons 81
continuity editing 28, 83, 88
continuous take 33
contrapuntal sound 35, 37
costume 23–5, 88, 176
costume designer 24
crane shot 13–14
crash zoom 13
creativity 301
Crimson Gold (2003) 192
cross-cutting 28–9, 32, 88
crossing the line 28
cubism 265
cultural capital 47
cultural contexts 68–9, 96, 147, 156–8, 173–4, 182, 264–6, 282–3
Curtiz, Michael 98–9
cut 28
cutaways 6
Czech New Wave 270, 279

D

Daisies (1966) 268–76, 279
Davis, Bette 74
Dee, Sandra 101
deep focus 10
demographics 118

depth of field 9, 10
dialect 132
dialectical film 245
dialogue 89
    see also verbal communication
diegetic sound 6, 34, 36, 37, 89, 139–40, 208, 236
directors 6
dissolve 29, 32, 88
distribution 72, 82, 127–8
documentary 217–41
    aesthetics 226–7, 238
    cinematography 223–4, 234–5
    construction of truth 222–3, 234
    editing 225, 235–6
    mise-en-scène 224, 235
    modes of 221–2
    representation in 227–8, 238–40
    sound 225–6, 236–7
dolly shot 13
Do the Right Thing (1989) 12, 50–4, 82
dramatic irony 140
Dyer, Richard 45

E

Edeson, Arthur 99
editing
    continuity 28, 83, 88
    in documentary 225, 235–6
    experimental techniques 32–3, 112, 274
    montage 32–3, 68–9, 88
    non-linear 31
    shot length 31–2
    silent cinema 262–3
    superimpositions 290
    time and space 30, 140–1
    transitions 28–9
Eisenstein, Sergei 32, 68–9, 135
emotional contagion 135
equality 45, 92–3, 119
Ergüven, Deniz Gamze 169, 178, 187
establishing shot 7, 11, 28, 83–4
ethnicity representation 50–4, 70–2, 93, 102, 116, 134, 141–2, 152, 164, 181, 186, 201, 212–13, 228, 240, 255, 275
European cinema 170–87
Evans, Walker 86
existentialism 272
existing properties 73–4
experimental film 268–96
explicit meaning 5
expressionism 247, 256
    see also German Expressionism film movement
extreme close-up shot 10, 84
extreme long shot 7

eye-level shot 11
eye-line match 28

F

fade 29
Far from Heaven (2002) 64
femininity 49
feminist ideology 119–21, 279
Fennell, Emerald 47
fill light 15
film festivals 127, 193–4
film form 5–6, 83–5, 301–4
filmmaking tips 310–12
film noir 16
film stock 7
final girl trope 103, 212
First World War 248
flashbacks 30, 88, 131
flashforwards 30
foley artist 34
foreground 9
formalism 41
Forman, Milos 271
For Sama (2019) 217, 231–41
fourth wall 27, 34
frames per second (fps) 7, 31
framing 6
    definitions 7
freeze-frame 29
French New Wave 14, 84–5, 91, 96–7, 269

G

gender inequality 50
gender representation 45–50, 66–7, 92–3, 115–16, 133–4, 142, 151–2, 163–4, 180–1, 186, 201, 211, 227–8, 239–40, 254–5, 275–6, 293–5
German Expressionism film movement 243–57
Get Out (2017) 125, 137–43
Glazer, Jonathan 58–9
Goodfellas (1990) 37
grading 17
Graduate, The (1967) 83
Grierson, John 217
grouping objects 20–1
Gun Crazy (1950) 85
Gunfighter, The (2014) 304

H

hair 24–5
Hall, Stuart 118–19
hand-held cameras 14, 174, 220, 277
Hayes, Todd 63–4
Hays Code 74–5, 77
hidden meanings 5
high-angle shot 12

Hitchcock, Alfred 6, 33, 45–6, 97, 244
Hollywood
    Classical period 14, 31, 64, 68, 72–3, 81–5, 91
    contemporary 107–8
    New Hollywood 75–7, 82–3, 85
    star system 260–1
    studio system 73–5, 82, 98, 104
House of Flying Daggers (2004) 22
Hulk (2003) 29
hypodermic needle model 117

I

ideology 119–21, 135, 143, 154–6, 165
Imitation of Life (1959) 100–3, 105
implicit meaning 5
improvisation 41–2
independent films 72, 82, 104, 125–43
inequality 45, 50
intertextuality 117
Irréversible (2002) 30
Italian Neorealist cinema 174

J

Jenkins, Barry 60–2
Joker (2019) 8, 107
    spectatorship reading 121–3
Jones, Duane 103
jump-cuts 28, 149
juxtapositioning 23, 32, 37, 55, 207–8, 286

K

Keaton, Buster 259–66
key light 15
King, Martin Luther 50, 103, 143
Kissack, Eric 304
Kohner, Susan 102
Kubrick, Stanley 58
Kuleshov effect 32

L

La Jetèe (1962) 301
La La Land (2016) 17, 36, 42, 96
    aesthetics 114
    cinematography 110
    cultural, political and social contexts 109–10
    editing 112
    ideology 119–21
    mise-en-scène 111–12
    performance 113–14
    representations 115
    sound 112–13
    spectatorship reading 119
Lee, Spike 50–1
leitmotifs 35

Index

Leszkiewitz, Anna 120–1
Levi-Strauss, Claude 45, 57
lighting
    direction of 16–17
    intensity 17
    low-key 85
    source 15
    three-point lighting 15, 85
Little Women (2019) 11
Loach, Ken 58
locations 23
Longinotto, Kim 230–1, 240
long shot 8
low-angle shot 12, 14
low-key lighting 85
Lumière Brothers 171, 245, 256, 259, 265, 298
Lynch, David 281–96

M

Mad Max: Fury Road (2015) 31
magic bullet theory 117
magic realism 126
mainstream cinema 179
make-up 24–5
Malcolm X 50, 103
male gaze 46, 67
Mangrove (2020) 70–2
Mankiewicz, Joseph 73–4
Man Who Fell to Earth, The (1976) 58
Man with a Movie Camera (1929) 33
Marker, Chris 301
Marxism 135–6
masculinity 48, 115–16
match-cut 29, 32
match-dissolve 29
McQueen, Steve 70–2
meaning 5, 213–14, 302–5
medium close-up shot 9
medium-long shot 8, 84
medium shot 6, 8
Memento (2000) 30
method acting 41–2
midshot *see* medium shots
mise-en-scène 21–5, 86–8, 111–12, 130–1, 138–9, 160–2, 176, 183, 196–7, 206–7, 224, 235, 250–1, 262, 273–4, 277, 289–90
Mogul Mowgli (2020) 145, 156–67
Monroe, Marilyn 67
montage editing 32–3, 68–9, 88
Moonlight (2016) 14, 60–2
Moore, Juanita 101–2
motif 69, 99, 206
Motion Picture Association of America (MPAA) 72

Mueller, Matt 108
Mulholland Drive (2001) 9, 281–96
    aesthetics 295–6
    cinematography 288
    editing 290–1
    mise-en-scène 289–90
    performance 292–3
    representations 293–5
    sound 291–2
Mulvey, Laura 46
Murnau, F.W. 243–4
music 6, 33, 35–6, 88–9, 108, 110–11, 131, 140, 149, 177, 209, 225, 237
music supervisor 33
Mustang (2015) 169–73, 175–81, 187

N

narration 34, 220
    see also voice over
narrative closure 225
narrative devices 222
narrative structure 30, 83, 117, 152–4, 164–5, 245, 272, 276–7, 300–4
natural light 15
New Hollywood 75–7, 82–3, 85
New Iranian Cinema 195–201
Nichols, Bill 221
Night of the Living Dead (1968) 11, 17, 103–5
nihilism 155–6
Nomadland (2020) 7, 20
non-diegetic sound 6, 34–6, 88–9, 209, 237
non-linear editing 31
non-verbal communication 37–9
Nosferatu (1922) 255
Nouvelle Vague 269

O

O'Bannon, Dan 76
objectification 45, 48–50
Odessa Steps sequence 32
off-screen spaces 27
Oscars *see* Academy Awards
overhead shot 11
over-the-shoulder shot 11, 28

P

pacing 31, 140
pan 13
Panahi, Jafar 189–201, 215
Pan's Labyrinth (2006) 24
parallel sounds 35, 36
Parasite (2019) 23, 189, 202–15
Parks, Rosa 102
Peele, Jordan 125, 137–43
Penn, Arthur 86, 88, 94, 99–100
performance

communication 37–40
improvisation 41–2
method acting 41–2
style 40
see also films by name
Performance (1970) 58
Phillips, Todd 121–2
Play It Again Sam (1972) 96
pleonastic sound 34
Point Blank (1967) 83
point-of-view (POV) shot 6, 12
    see also eye-level shot
Polanski, Roman 182
political contexts 70–2, 93, 102–3, 128–9, 137–8, 146–7, 156–7, 192–5, 203–5, 233, 269, 283–4
political propaganda 68–9
Polley, Sarah 217–29
Portrait of a Lady on Fire (2019) 12, 169, 182–7
post-colonial critical approach 165–6
Postman Always Rings Twice, The (1946) 100
post-production 17
Prague Spring 270
pre-production 7
production 6
Production Code 67
Promising Young Woman (2020) 25, 47–50
props 23
prosthetics 24
Psycho (1960) 29, 68
Pulp Fiction (1994) 68

R

racism 70–2, 101–3, 137
    see also ethnicity representation
ratings 72–3, 77
reaction shot 6
realism 40–1, 130, 160
reconstructions 220
re-enactments 220
representation 43
    of age 54–7, 92, 101, 115, 133, 141, 151, 179–80, 186, 200, 211–12, 227, 238–9, 254, 275–6, 293–5
    in documentary 227–8, 238–40
    of ethnicity 50–4, 70–2, 93, 102, 116, 134, 141–2, 152, 164, 181, 186, 201, 212–13, 228, 240, 255, 275
    of gender 45–50, 66–7, 92–3, 115–16, 133–4, 142, 151–2, 163–4, 180–1, 186, 201, 211, 227–8, 239–40, 254–5, 275–6, 293–5
    in silent cinema 263–4
    underrepresentation 44
rites of passage 55

Rocky III (1982) 36
Roeg, Nicholas 58
Rogue One: A Star Wars Story (2016) 108
Romero, George A. 105
Rope (1948) 33
Rosen, Bob 126
rule of thirds 19

S

Saint Maud (2019) 19–20
Sandgren, Linus 110–11
Sarris, Andrew 97
Saute ma ville (1989) 268, 276–9
scenes 31–2, 83
Sciamma, Celine 182–7
Scott, Ridley 76–7
screenplay writing 305–7
second wave feminism 92
Second World War 16, 82, 94, 96
sequences 31–2, 83
setting 23
shallow focus 10
Shaun of the Dead (2004) 8, 17, 26, 32
She's Gotta Have It (1986) 51
Shining, The (1980) 58
shooting sequence 6
shot
    definitions 7
    length 31–2
    transitions 28–9
    types of 7–13, 28
shot/reverse shot 28, 31, 84
silence 36, 140
silent cinema 259–66
Sirk, Douglas 104–5
slapstick comedies 260
slow-motion 32
Small Axe (2020) 70
social contexts 66, 95, 102–3, 128–9, 137–8, 146–7, 156–7, 203–5, 269, 283–4
Some Like It Hot (1959) 66–8
Sotoudeh, Nasrin 198–9
sound
    asynchronous 37
    bridges 162
    contrapuntal 35
    diegetic 6, 34, 36, 37, 89, 139–40, 208, 236
    music 6, 33, 35–6, 88–9, 108, 110–11, 131, 140, 149, 177, 209, 225, 237
    non-diegetic 6, 34–6, 88–9, 209, 237
    parallel 35, 36
    pleonastic 34
    silence 36, 140

    silent cinema 263
    synchronous 37
    voice-over 132, 149–50, 220, 225–6, 236–7
sound design 197
sound recordist 33–4
South Korean film industry 203
Soviet Montage 68–9
special effects make-up 24
spectatorship 116–19, 121–3, 134–5, 142–3, 218
Spione (1928) 15, 17
staging 26
Stanislavski method 41
star system 260
star vehicles 81
Steadicam 14
Steiner, Max 89, 99
stereotyping 45, 52–4, 102, 134
stop-motion animation 302
Stories We Tell (2013) 217–29, 241
storyboard 307–8
Strike (1925) 68–9
structuralism 45
Sunrise (1927) 243–57
Super 8 cameras 224, 226, 229
superimpositions 290
surrealism 151, 161, 163, 265–6, 282–3, 285–7
Sweet Sixteen (2002) 58
Swimmer, The (1968) 83
symmetry 19
synchronous sound 37

T

talking heads 220
Tarantino, Quentin 14, 68, 98
Taxi Tehran (2015) 189–90, 195–201, 215
teenagers 101
    see also adolescence; children
television, rise of 82
thirds, rule of 19
This Is England (2006) 6, 28, 166
three-point lighting 15, 85
tilt 13
Tookey, Chris 98
Touch of Evil (1958) 33
tracking shot 13
Trainspotting (1996) 21, 27, 145–56, 167
    aesthetics 151
    cinematography 148
    cultural, political and social contexts 146–7
    editing 149

    film form 147–8
    ideology 154–6
    mise-en-scène 148–9
    narrative structure 152–4
    performance 150–1
    representations 151–2
    sound 149–50
transitions 28–9
tropes 102–3
    see also typage
Turner, Lana 100–1
two-shot 9
2001: A Space Odyssey (1968) 29, 58
typage 69

U

under lighting 17
underrepresentation 44
Under the Skin (2013) 58–9

V

verbal communication 39–40
vertical integration 82
Vertigo (1958) 16, 19, 25, 31, 45–7, 121
Vertov, Dziga 32–3, 68
Vietnam War 94–5
visual style 5–6
Vivre sa vie (1962) 29
voice-over 132, 149–50, 220, 225–6, 236–7

W

Wallis, Hal B. 95, 98
Warner, Jack 94, 97, 98
Watts, Edward 231–41
Welles, Orson 244
We Need to Talk About Kevin (2011) 22, 31
whip pan 13
White Balloon, The (1995) 191
Wilder, Billy 66–7
wipe transition 29
Wolfe, Charles 261
women
    film directors 172–3
    male gaze 46, 67
    objectification 45–50
Worst Person in the World, The (2021) 10
writing a screenplay 305–8
Wrong Trousers, The (1993) 302

Z

Zanuck, Darryl 73–4
Zeitlin, Benh 126–36, 143
zoom 13

Index **331**

Acknowledgements

Photos reproduced by permission of: **p.7** © Searchlight Pictures/Everett Collection Inc/Alamy Stock Photo; **p.8** *t* © Warner Bros/Moviestore Collection Ltd/Alamy Stock Photo, *b* © Universal Pictures/Pictorial Press Ltd/Alamy Stock Photo; **p.9** © Universal Pictures/LANDMARK MEDIA/Alamy Stock Photo; **p.10** © Arte France Cinéma B/Reel Films/Album/Alamy Stock Photo; **p.11** *tr* © GRANGER, NYC - Historical Picture Archive/Alamy Stock Photo, *c* © Ron Harvey/Everett Collection Inc/Alamy Stock Photo, *br* © Columbia Pictures/LANDMARK MEDIA/Alamy Stock Photo; **p.12** *t* © Universal Pictures /LANDMARK MEDIA/Alamy Stock Photo, *l* © Moviestore Collection Ltd/Alamy Stock Photo, *b* © Curzon Artificial Eye// Hulu/Moviestore Collection Ltd/Alamy Stock Photo; **p.15** © Everett Collection Inc/Alamy Stock Photo; **p.16** *b* © Nordisk Film/LANDMARK MEDIA/Alamy Stock Photo, *br* © Paramount Pictures/LANDMARK MEDIA/Alamy Stock Photo; **p.17** *c* © Moviestore Collection Ltd/Alamy Stock Photo, *tr* © Photo12/7e Art/ Rob Youngson/Focus Features/Alamy Stock Photo, *r* © Everett Collection Inc/Alamy Stock Photo; *t* © Moviestore Collection Ltd/Alamy Stock Photo, *b* © GRANGER - Historical Picture Archive/Alamy Stock Photo; **p.19** *c* © Paramount Pictures/LANDMARK MEDIA / Alamy Stock Photo, *b* © A24/LANDMARK MEDIA/Alamy Stock Photo; **p.20** *t* © A24/LANDMARK MEDIA/Alamy Stock Photo, *c* © Lifestyle pictures/ Alamy Stock Photo; **p.21** © Miramax/LANDMARK MEDIA/Alamy Stock Photo; **p.22** *c* © Code Red/ LANDMARK MEDIA/Alamy Stock Photo, *b* © Sony Pictures Classics/courtesy Everett Collection/Alamy Stock Photo; **p.23** *l* © Photo12/7e ART/CJ Entertainment/Alamy Stock Photo, *r* © CJ Entertainment/Photo 12/Alamy Stock Photo; **p.24** © Moviestore Collection Ltd/Alamy Stock Photo; **p.25** *t* © Focus Features/ Pictorial Press Ltd/Alamy Stock Photo, *b* © Paramount Pictures/LANDMARK MEDIA/Alamy Stock Photo; **p.26** *c* © UNIVERSAL/Maximum Film/Alamy Stock Photo, *b* © A7A collection/Photo 12/Alamy Stock Photo; **p.27** © Miramax/LANDMARK MEDIA/Alamy Stock Photo; **p.28** © Warp Films/Pictorial Press Ltd/ Alamy Stock Photo; **p.31** *r* © Paramount Pictures/LANDMARK MEDIA/Alamy Stock Photo, *b* © Code Red/ LANDMARK MEDIA/Alamy Stock Photo; **p.32** © VideoFilmes/TCD/Prod.DB/Alamy Stock Photo; **p.33** © Moviestore Collection Ltd/Alamy Stock Photo; **p.38** (1) © Columbia Pictures/LANDMARK MEDI/Alamy Stock Photo (2) © WARNER BROS/Moviestore Collection Ltd/Alamy Stock Photo (3) © WARNER BROS/ LANDMARK MEDIA/Alamy Stock Photo (4) © BFA/CJ Entertainment/Alamy Stock Photo (5) © Warner Bros/LANDMARK MEDIA/Alamy Stock Photo (6) © BBC/Amazon Studios/LANDMARK MEDIA/Alamy Stock Photo (7) © Warner Bros/LANDMARK MEDIA/Alamy Stock Photo (8) © Warner Bros/LANDMARK MEDIA/Alamy Stock Photo; **p.39** (1) © FOCUS FEATURES/Moviestore Collection Ltd/Alamy Stock Photo (2) © 40 Acres & A Mule Filmworks/Photo 12/Alamy Stock Photo; **p.42** © United Artists/LANDMARK MEDIA/Alamy Stock Photo; **p.43** © Pictorial Press Ltd/Alamy Stock Photo; **p.46** *t* © Moviestore Collection Ltd/Alamy Stock Photo, *c* © Collection Christophel/Alamy Stock Photo; **p.48** © Focus Features/ Entertainment Pictures/Alamy Stock Photo; **p.49** © Focus Features/Pictorial Press Ltd/Alamy Stock Photo; **p.50** © GRANGER - Historical Picture Archive/Alamy Stock Photo; **p.51** *tr* © Associated Press/Alamy Stock Photo, *br* © 40 Acres & a Mule Filmworks/Entertainment Pictures/ Alamy Stock Photo; **p.52** © 40 Acres & A Mule Filmworks/Photo 12/Alamy Stock Photo; **p.53** © Universal Pictures/LANDMARK MEDIA/ Alamy Stock Photo; **p.54** *t* © Universal Pictures/LANDMARK MEDIA/Alamy Stock Photo, *l* © Universal Pictures/LANDMARK MEDIA/Alamy Stock Photo; **p.55** © Bleecker Street Media/Everett Collection Inc/ Alamy Stock Photo; **p.56** *tl* © WARNER BROS/Allstar Picture Library Ltd/Alamy Stock Photo, *b* © Cathy Kanavy/Bleecker Street Media/Courtesy Everett Collection Inc/Alamy Stock Photo; **p.57** © Weinstein Company Pictorial Press Ltd/Alamy Stock Photo; **p.59** © StudioCanal/LANDMARK MEDIA/Alamy Stock Photo; **p.61** © David Bornfriend/PLAN *B* ENTERTAINMENT/Photo 12/Alamy Stock Photo; **p.62** © David Bornfriend/PLAN *B* ENTERTAINMENT/Photo 12/Alamy Stock Photo; **p.63** © Pictorial Press Ltd/Alamy Stock Photo; **p.64** © Universal International Pictures/Photo 12/Alamy Stock Photo; **p.65** © Moviestore Collection Ltd/Alamy Stock Photo; **p.66** © kpa Publicity Stills/United Archives GmbH/Alamy Stock Photo; **p.67** © Allstar Picture Library Limited./Alamy Stock Photo; **p.69** © Pictorial Press Ltd/Alamy Stock Photo;

p.70 l © Trinity Mirror/Mirrorpix/Alamy Stock Photo, b © BBC/Amazon Studios/LANDMARK MEDIA/Alamy Stock Photo; **p.71** © BBC/Amazon Studios/LANDMARK MEDIA/Alamy Stock Photo; **p.72** © Joel C Ryan/Invision/Associated Press/Alamy Stock Photo; **p.73** © World History Archive/Alamy Stock Photo; **p.74** © ARCHIVIO GBB/Alamy Stock Photo; **p.75** © Moviestore Collection Ltd/Alamy Stock Photo; **p.77** © Universal Pictures/Pictorial Press Ltd/Alamy Stock Photo; **p.78** © Focus Features/LANDMARK MEDIA/Alamy Stock Photo; **p.80** © Ann Ronan Picture Library/Heritage-Images/The Print Collector/Alamy Stock Photo; **p.81** l © GRANGER - Historical Picture Archive/Alamy Stock Photo, r and **p.85** l © Everett Collection Inc/Alamy Stock Photo; **p.83** © Dom Slike/Alamy Stock Photo; **p.85** r © Pictorial Press Ltd/Alamy Stock Photo; **p.86** © Everett Collection Historical/Alamy Stock Photo; **p.87** © ScreenProd/Photononstop/Alamy Stock Photo; **p.91** t © GRANGER - Historical Picture Archive/Alamy Stock Photo, b © ScreenProd/Photononstop/Alamy Stock Photo; **p.93** © GRANGER - Historical Picture Archive/Alamy Stock Photo; **p.95** b © CSU Archives/Everett Collection Historical/Alamy Stock Photo, r © Keystone Press/Alamy Stock Photo; **p.96** © Moviestore Collection Ltd/Alamy Stock Photo; **p.97** © Pictorial Press Ltd/Alamy Stock Photo; **p.98** l © Archive PL/Alamy Stock Photo, r © Everett Collection Inc/Alamy Stock Photo; **p.99** (1) © AA Film Archive/Allstar Picture Library Ltd/Alamy Stock Photo (2) © Everett Collection Inc/Alamy Stock Photo (3) © Everett Collection Inc/Alamy Stock Photo (4) © Everett Collection Inc/Alamy Stock Photo; **p.101** c © UNIVERSAL PICTURES/Album/Alamy Stock Photo, tr © Album/Alamy Stock Photo, r © UNIVERSAL PICTURES/Album/Alamy Stock Photo, br © UNIVERSAL PICTURES/Album/Alamy Stock Photo; **p.102** © Don Ornitz/Globe Photos/ZUMA Press, Inc./Alamy Stock Photo; **p.103** © Everett Collection Inc/Alamy Stock Photo; **p.104** © Collection Christophel/Image Ten/Alamy Stock Photo; **p.106** © Pictorial Press Ltd/Lionsgate Files/Alamy Stock Photo; **p.107** © Summit Entertainment/Everett Collection Inc/Alamy Stock Photo; **p.108** © Pictorial Press Ltd/Alamy Stock Photo; **p.111** © Summit Entertainment/Everett Collection Inc/Alamy Stock Photo; **p.113** l © Photo12/7e Art/Ben Glass/Carousel Productions/Alamy Stock Photo, r © GRANGER - Historical Picture Archive/Alamy Stock Photo; **p.114** © Art Institute of Chicago/Giorgio Morara/Alamy Stock Photo; **p.116** © Dale Robinette/Summit Releasing/courtesy Everett Collection; **p.122** © LANDMARK MEDIA/Alamy Stock Photo; **p.123** © BFA/Warner Bros/Alamy Stock Photo; **p.124** © Moviestore Collection Ltd/Alamy Stock Photo; **p.125** © Fox Searchlight Pictures/Pictorial Press Ltd/Alamy Stock Photo; **p.128** tl © Cinereach/Photo 12/Alamy Stock Photo, c © Nathan Holland/Shutterstock.com; **p.130** © JOURNEYMAN FILMS/Album/Alamy Stock Photo; **p.134** © Moviestore Collection Ltd/Alamy Stock Photo; **p.135** © GRANGER - Historical Picture Archive/Alamy Stock Photo; **p.136** © Fox Searchlight Pictures/Entertainment Pictures/Alamy Stock Photo; **p.139** © Universal Pictures/Pictorial Press Ltd/Alamy Stock Photo; **p.144** © Miramax Films/Entertainment Pictures/Alamy Stock Photo; **p.145** l © Moviestore Collection Ltd/Alamy Stock Photo, r © Strand Releasing/Everett Collection Inc/Alamy Stock Photo; **p.148** © Miramax Films/LANDMARK MEDIA/Alamy Stock Photo; **p.149** © Moviestore Collection Ltd/Alamy Stock Photo; **p.150** l © Miramax Films/Entertainment Pictures/Alamy Stock Photo, r © Miramax Films/Entertainment Pictures/Alamy Stock Photo; **p.152** © Landmark Media/Alamy Stock Photo; **p.155** © Polygram/Pictorial Press Ltd/Alamy Stock Photo; **p.156** l © Gregor Fischer/dpa picture alliance/Alamy Stock Photo, bl © Christian Bertrand/Alamy Stock Photo; **p.159** © Moviestore Collection Ltd/Alamy Stock Photo; **p.160** © Strand Releasing/Everett Collection Inc/Alamy Stock Photo; **p.162** © Historic Collection/Alamy Stock Photo; **p.168** © Curzon Artificial Eye/Hulu/LANDMARK MEDIA/Alamy Stock Photo; **p.169** © GC CINEMA/VISTAMAR/UHLANDFILM/BAM FILM/KINOLOGY/CANAL+/CINE+/Album/Alamy Stock Photo; **p.173** With thanks to Sight and Sound; **p.178** © GC CINEMA/VISTAMAR/UHLANDFILM/BAM FILM/KINOLOGY/CANAL+/CINE+/Album/Alamy Stock Photo; **p.183** © 40 Acres & a Mule Filmworks/LANDMARK MEDIA/Alamy Stock Photo; **p.185** © Curzon Artificial Eye//Hulu/LANDMARK MEDIA/Alamy Stock Photo; **p.188** © Kino Lorber/Everett Collection Inc/Alamy Stock Photo;

p.189 © Kino Lorber/Everett Collection Inc/Alamy Stock Photo; **p.191** © October Films/Everett Collection Inc/Alamy Stock Photo; **p.194** *tl* © dpa picture alliance archive/Alamy Stock Photo, *b* © GRANGER - Historical Picture Archive/Alamy Stock Photo; **pp.196, 197, 198, 200, 201** © Kino Lorber/Everett Collection Inc/Alamy Stock Photo; **p.202** © Pictorial Press Ltd/Alamy Stock Photo; **p.204** © CJ ENTERTAINMENT/Album/Alamy Stock Photo; **p.205** © Neon new movie/LANDMARK MEDIA/Alamy Stock Photo; **p.208** © BFA/CJ Entertainment/Alamy Stock Photo; **p.216** © PBS Distribution/Everett Collection Inc/Alamy Stock Photo; **p.217** © Roadside Attractions/Everett Collection Inc/Alamy Stock Photo; **p.218** © Shim Harno/Alamy Stock Photo; **p.220** © Roadside Attractions/Everett Collection Inc/Alamy Stock Photo; **p.221** *c* © Entertainment Pictures/Alamy Stock Photo, *r* © New Yorker Films/New Yorker Films/Alamy Stock Photo; **p.224** © Roadside Attractions/Everett Collection Inc/Alamy Stock Photo; **p.226** © Roadside Attractions/Everett Collection Inc/Alamy Stock Photo; **p.229** © Roger Bamber/Alamy Stock Photo; **p.230** *t* © Moviestore Collection Ltd/Alamy Stock Photo, *l* © Channel Four Television Corporation/Everett Collection Inc/Alamy Stock Photo; **p.231** © Channel 4 News/Channel 4/Frontline/ITN Productions/PBS Distribution/WGBH/Album /Alamy Stock Photo; **p.232** *l* © Julie Edwards/JEP Celebrity Photos/Alamy Stock Photo, *bl* © Doreen Kennedy/Alamy Stock Photo; **p.233** © Frederick InjimbertZUMA Wire/ZUMA Press, Inc./Alamy Stock Photo; **pp.234, 235, 238** © Channel 4 News/Channel 4/Frontline/ITN Productions/PBS Distribution/WGBH/Album/Alamy Stock Photo; **p.239** © Afraa Hashem/Associated Press/Alamy Stock Photo; **p.242** © Pictorial Press Ltd/Alamy Stock Photo; **p.243** © 20th Century-Fox Film Corp/Everett Collection Inc/Alamy Stock Photo; **p.246** © Ann Ronan Picture Library/Heritage-Images/Alamy Stock Photo; **p.247** © Everett Collection, Inc./Alamy Stock Photo; **p.249** *t* © Scherl/Sueddeutsche Zeitung Photo/Alamy Stock Photo, *b* © GRANGER - Historical Picture Archive/Alamy Stock Photo; **p.251** © FOX FILMS/Album/Alamy Stock Photo; **p.252** © IFTN/United Archives GmbH/Alamy Stock Photo; **p.253** *tr* © Cinematic Collection/Cinematic/Alamy Stock Photo, *r* © Fox Film Corporation/Photo 12/Alamy Stock Photo; **p.255** © World History Archive/Alamy Stock Photo; **p.257** 20th Century Fox/Everett Collection, Inc./Alamy Stock Photo; **p.258** © Everett Collection Inc/Alamy Stock Photo; **p.259** *t* © Pictorial Press Ltd/Alamy Stock Photo, *r* © WolfTracerArchive/Photo 12/Alamy Stock Photo; **p.260** © GAUMONT/Album/Alamy Stock Photo; **p.261** © Jerry Tavin/Everett Collection Inc/Alamy Stock Photo; **pp.262, 263, 264** © Everett Collection Inc/Alamy Stock Photo; **p.265** © Archive PL/Alamy Stock Photo; **p.267** © kpa Publicity Stills/United Archives GmbH/Alamy Stock Photo; **p.268** © Filmové studio Barrandov/Photo 12/Alamy Stock Photo; **p.271** *tr* © Michal Kalasek/Shutterstock.com, *br* © Hans Kaulertz/Sueddeutsche Zeitung Photo/Alamy Stock Photo; **p.276** © WENN Rights Ltd/Alamy Stock Photo; **p.280** © Moviestore Collection Ltd/Alamy Stock Photo; **p.281** © THE PICTURE FACTORY ASYMMETRICAL PRODUCTIONS/IMAGINE TELEVIS/Album/Alamy Stock Photo; **p.283** © Moviestore Collection Ltd/Alamy Stock Photo; **p.285** © LANDMARK MEDIA/Alamy Stock Photo; **pp.288, 290** © Moviestore Collection Ltd/Alamy Stock Photo; **p.292** © Pictorial Press Ltd/Alamy Stock Photo; **p.297** © Pictorial Press Ltd/Alamy Stock Photo; **p.298** © Ron Harvey/ShortsTV/Everett Collection Inc/Alamy Stock Photo; **p.302** © TBM/United Archives GmbH/Alamy Stock Photo; **p.304** © WENN Rights Ltd/Alamy Stock Photo; **p.309** © Moviestore Collection Ltd/Alamy Stock Photo.